RETAILING
principles and practices
Seventh Edition

Warren G. Meyer
Professor Emeritus
Department of Vocational
and Technical Education

University of Minnesota
Minneapolis, Minnesota

Peter G. Haines
Professor of
Business, Distributive
and General
Vocational Education

Michigan State University
East Lansing, Michigan

E. Edward Harris
Professor of
Marketing and
Distributive Education
Chairperson
Department of Business
Education and
Administrative Services

Northern Illinois University
DeKalb, Illinois

Gregg Division   McGraw-Hill Book Company

New York   Atlanta   Dallas   St. Louis   San Francisco   Auckland   Bogotá
Guatemala   Hamburg   Johannesburg   Lisbon   London   Madrid
Mexico   Montreal   New Delhi   Panama   Paris   San Juan   São Paulo
Singapore   Sydney   Tokyo   Toronto

Sponsoring Editor: Mary Alice McGarry
Editing Supervisor: Sharon E. Kaufman
Design Supervisor: Karen Tureck Mino
Production Supervisor: Laurence Charnow
Photo Editor: Mary Ann Drury

Cover Photographer: Karen Leeds
Illustrator: Anne Gayler

Library of Congress Cataloging in Publication Data
Meyer, Warren G.
    Retailing, principles and practices.

    Sixth ed. by G. H. Richert and others, entered under
title.
    Includes index.
    1. Retail trade.   I. Haines, Peter George, joint
author.   II. Harris, Earl Edward, date, joint
author.   III. Title.
HF5429.R52 1981   658.8'7   80-24885
ISBN 0-07-041693-1

**RETAILING: Principles and Practices; Seventh
Edition**

    3 4 5 6 7 8 9 0 DODO 8 9 8 7 6 5 4 3 2

ISBN 0-07-041693-1

Preface

The Seventh Edition of *Retailing: Principles and Practices* is designed to prepare students for employment in retail stores and service businesses in the 1980s. Whether the individual is aiming for a job in selling, merchandising, store operations, finance and credit, personnel, or sales promotion, he or she will receive from this text a solid foundation on which to pursue a career in retailing goods and services. The text focuses successively on the competencies needed for easy entry, rapid adjustment, and planned advancement in retailing. The final unit, "Becoming an Entrepreneur," enables the student to integrate the many facets of retailing into a meaningful economic function, to assess the benefits and problems associated with retailing, and to consider the possibility of becoming an entrepreneur.

The Seventh Edition has been extensively revised and updated to reflect current technology and retail practices, including computerized inventory control, electronic cash registers, UPC and UVM systems, and electronic funds transfer. New techniques of visual merchandising, the new emphasis on retailing of services, and consumer protection legislation are also discussed in detail.

The information is presented in a lively and involving way. This edition "talks" to the student in simple, interesting language. It presents the material from the student's perspective at four stages of vocational development: (1) looking for a career in retailing, (2) getting started, (3) becoming a master employee, and (4) moving toward management and ownership. Competencies are approached in the approximate sequence that they are encountered on the job. To ensure transfer of learning, the authors not only show the student how a task is performed but also explain why it is done and, in many instances, why it is done differently in various job settings. In this way, the text prepares the student to cope with a variety of situations that may arise on the job.

Organization

Retailing: Principles and Practices, Seventh Edition, is organized so that it can be used equally well in schools with traditional class schedules and in those with modular, flexible schedules. The book fits any teaching system, whether it be cooperative, project, simulation, or traditional, because it is competency-based and carefully sequenced.

The text is divided into sections, units, and chapters. The first section of the book, "Looking for a Career in Retailing," has been reorganized to deal with vocational planning and guidance (see the Contents on pages vi and vii). This section provides essential background information on retailing and careers, which forms the foundation for Sections 2, 3, and 4.

The organization of Sections 2, 3, and 4 may be visualized as a grid with six competency areas on the vertical axis and three vocational development areas on the horizontal axis. The units are sequenced on both axes so that the instructor may structure the course to stress either the competency areas or the vocational development areas.

The six retail competency areas covered are (1) "Communications & Human Relations," (2) "Economics & Marketing," (3) "Merchandising," (4) "Selling & Technology," (5) "Advertising & Display," and (6) "Operations & Management." Teachers who wish to concentrate on one competency area at a time can—after completion of Section 1—follow any of the six areas, such as "Selling & Technology," through the book, proceeding from entry-level skills to the desired level of skill development. Although the book is not paginated in this way, the table of contents (pages vi and vii) makes it easy to organize the course in this manner.

Teachers who prefer the cyclical approach can follow the text in numerical order. This approach to the material serves to reinforce and interrelate important concepts. Using the cyclic approach, the teacher plans the course in four sections corresponding to semesters, quarters, or any part thereof.

In either approach, a student whose occupational goal does not require mastery of a given competency could omit the corresponding chapter or unit, thereby shortening the time needed to reach the goal.

Teaching and Learning Aids

The activities provided both at the end of each chapter and at the end of each unit serve to implement and to supplement what is learned from reading the text. There are three end-of-chapter activities.

♦ *Trade Talk:* To understand retailing, the student must understand the language of retailing. Vital retailing terms used in this exercise appear in boldface type where they are defined in the text.

♦ *Can You Answer These?:* The questions in this section are based on the facts presented in the chapter. Thus, the questions serve a twofold purpose: students find them a valuable study guide, and teachers find them a valuable measure of how well students can recall the information in each chapter.

♦ *Problems:* These questions ask the student to solve practical problems and to complete various business forms that are commonly used in retailing.

In addition to the three activities at the end of each chapter, there are also three end-of-unit activities.

♦ *Retailing Case:* This section presents a retailing case that provides opportunities for students to analyze what they have learned and apply it to new situations. In solving these cases, students must make judgments by inferring from the facts and concepts presented.

♦ *Working with People:* The human relations problems in this section have no absolute answers. Instead, these problems challenge students to think creatively while using a standardized problem-solving technique.

♦ *Project:* Each project is designed to take students out of the classroom and into the world of retailing, where they can apply what they learn in class to what is happening on the job.

Supporting Materials

The authors recognize that a good retailing course requires students to review and apply what they have learned. They also know that teachers need materials that support the textbook and help them use it most effectively. Consequently, they have developed several supporting supplementary materials.

Problems and Projects for Retailing. Two correlated student activity manuals accompany the textbook. The first manual contains students activities for Units 1 through 10 and the second manual for Units 11 through 22. Each unit is divided into six parts designed to supplement and enrich the learning experiences provided in the textbook. The first section deals with vocabulary and the second reviews the key points of the unit. The third section contains the working forms for all the problems in the textbook, as well as supplementary problems. The fourth section presents a retailing case and the fifth section presents a human relations problem. The sixth, and final, section provides work space for the unit project.

Objective Tests.   A set of objective tests is also available. It includes a test for each of the 22 units as well as midterm and final examinations. Each test contains four types of objective questions and is equipped with easy-to-score answer columns.

Teacher's Manual and Key.   The teacher's manual and key contains answers to all questions in the textbook, student activity manuals, and objective tests. It also offers detailed guidelines for organizing the course and suggestions for teaching it most effectively. Specific, detailed teaching suggestions are provided for each unit as are additional learning activities. A list of trade associations and publications is also included.

Acknowledgments

The authors of this edition acknowledge the many contributions of the late G. Henry Richert, who first conceived the idea for this text and who worked on the first six editions, beginning in 1938.

Many other people also contributed to the development of this book. Retailing teachers and marketing and distributive education specialists shared their time and knowledge with the authors, advising them of their needs and preferences for this revision. The authors are particularly grateful to four instructors who reviewed the manuscript for this edition: Dr. Ralph Wray, Illinois State University, Normal, Illinois; Dr. Mary Anderton, Memphis State University, Memphis, Tennessee; Ms. Gina Pickens, Central High School, Memphis, Tennessee; and Ms. Barbara Anderson, Thomas Jefferson High School, Tampa, Florida.

The authors are also appreciative of the help of the many retailers who supplied valuable ideas, background information, and photographs of their businesses. The authors would especially like to thank Ms. Patricia Mink Rath, of Carson, Pirie, Scott, & Co., Chicago, Illinois, and Mr. Richard Ploetz, of Dayton's, Minneapolis, Minnesota, for their valuable reviews of portions of the manuscript.

The authors are also indebted to Dr. Richard D. Ashmun and Dr. Donald P. Kohns, who reviewed the text and developed the student activity manuals.

Warren G. Meyer
Peter G. Haines
E. Edward Harris

CONTENTS

LOOKING FOR A CAREER IN RETAILING

It was a dull summer. I was bored with mowing lawns and worried too. Sure, I had money in my pocket now, but what about winter? And next year when I graduated? What kind of job was I going to get? I didn't have a clue.

Then one day I noticed a "Sales Help Needed" sign in the Tennis Ace store in the mall. I wasn't that keen on spending a lot of time in a store. You know, long hours, work on Saturdays, average pay. But to be honest, it was important to prove to myself that I could get a real job. So, I walked in.

I didn't know what to say when they asked me how long I would stay . . . if I wanted a career in sales . . . what I knew about the business world. But I *did* know sports. And I must have said something right, because I got the job.

It was rough at first, and at times I was pretty nervous. For openers, you have to know something about customers and about using a cash register. Then you have to know the right prices to charge and where to find everything in the store. I didn't do much real selling, but people would often ask me questions about which equipment was best.

I wasn't doing too badly, but I needed to know more. And *wanted* to know more—because retailing is much more interesting than I thought it would be. Every day is different. Lots of different people come in, and there are always new things to learn.

Looking at Retailing

What Is a Career?

CHAPTER

1

Communications & Human Relations

Economics & Marketing

Merchandising

Selling & Technology

Advertising & Display

Operations & Management

Felicia Dawkins had never taken a course in retailing or any other business subject. When she graduated from high school, Felicia didn't know what kind of work she wanted to do and had difficulty finding a job. Finally, with the help of her aunt, she managed to get a job as a stock clerk at the discount department store where her aunt worked. After 6 months, she became dissatisfied with the job and decided to look for one that she would like better and that would pay more.

She found a job as a salesperson at a retail clothing store. Even though the basic pay was the same as at the discount store, she thought that through commissions she might be able to earn more money. After holding this job for 6 months, Felicia realized that she wanted to manage or own a store one day. She wanted more responsibility, a higher income, and an opportunity for career advancement.

Felicia decided to enroll in the retailing management program at her local community college, which had a marketing and distributive education on-the-job-training program. During the next 2 years, she worked part-time at a clothing store learning the business and completed her 2-year degree program in retail management. Now, after 10 years, she is a partner in the store where she received her on-the-job training. Felicia hopes to buy out her partner when he retires within the next few years.

Yes, Felicia was smart to realize she'd need special training to get a job in the clothing business that would satisfy her and provide the advancement she wanted. If she hadn't seen this, she might have continued moving from job to job without getting satisfaction from any of them. Or she might even have become unemployed, as were many of her friends. But you are even more fortunate than Felicia, because you are studying retailing now.

You Have a Head Start

You have an advantage over Felicia and the 30 million young people who will join the labor force during the next 10 years because you're learning about jobs and careers while you are still in school. You still have time to learn about yourself, decide what you want from a career, try out different jobs, see how you like them, and investigate various careers.

Careers versus Jobs

When Felicia realized she wanted to manage or own a clothing store, she was deciding on a career goal. It took her more time to choose and prepare for her career than to select the jobs that she'd held previously. Felicia recognized the difference between holding a job and pursuing a career. A **job** is a collection of tasks, duties, and responsibilities. A **career** is the series of jobs held and the specialized occupational education received by a person during a person's lifetime.

Career Ladders and Lattices

In the course of a career, you will have several different jobs. If you plan each wisely, each job can be satisfying in itself. These jobs can also provide the experience necessary for getting ahead, or climbing up the career ladder. A **career ladder** is made up of a series of jobs at different occupational levels that lead to an occupational goal. The first rung on the career ladder consists of an entry-level job, the base on which to build a career in a particular field. On higher rungs of the ladder are career-level jobs. These jobs require more skill, knowledge, and responsibility than the entry-level jobs. Some people find self-fulfillment in career-level jobs. Others use them as rungs on the way to management-level positions.

You may move upwards or sideways on the career ladder until you find a spot that's right for you.

CAREER LADDER AND LATTICES FOR RETAIL WORKERS

| BUYER | STORE MANAGER | MANAGE-MENT LEVEL | STORE OWNER |

| DEPART-MENT MANAGER | SALES-PERSON | CAREER LEVEL | ASSIST. BUYER |

| SALES-CLERK | ENTRY LEVEL | WRAPPER | STOCK CLERK |

In a career, not every step is a step up. Sometimes people have to move sideways in order to achieve their career goals. For example, if you wanted to be a store manager, you would probably need experience in many jobs at the same level. You might begin with an entry-level job in receiving and then move to a job at the same level in sales. This type of sideways move is known as a **career lattice.**

It takes certain competencies and personal qualities to achieve success at each point on the ladder or lattice. In this book, **competency** means knowledge, attitudes, and skills needed on the job in order to be a satisfactory and satisfied worker. Some people learn too late in life that they either are not willing to follow the steps required in pursuing a certain career goal or that they don't have the competencies necessary to achieve that goal. But you have an advantage: You can form your career goal now while you're still in school.

Forming a Career Goal

Achievement of a career goal requires even more than careful planning, because hidden factors are involved. For example, when you get out of school, employers may limit the hiring of people in your career field. Or, for financial or other reasons, you may be unable to get the additional education you need to achieve your goal. As you can see, selecting and achieving a career goal is not a simple task. It is probable that you will change your mind about your career a number of times. You will be most successful if you (1) identify your own interests, aptitudes, and goals and (2) obtain information about the world of work by talking to people, reading about careers, and perhaps obtaining special training in school. By doing these things, you'll be more likely to pick the right career goal early in life.

Begin by Knowing Yourself

Not many people can look at themselves objectively and honestly assess their own strengths and weaknesses. Can you? Do you have a clear idea of the values by which you want to live your life? Do you really know what your interests, aptitudes, and goals are? Can you predict what you would do in a given job situation? In short, do you know yourself?

Your Interests. There are a number of ways in which you can explore your interest. Perhaps your school will be able to help you take an interest inventory. An "interest inventory" groups interests by categories, such as clerical, social, or mechanical. By answering questions about what you like to do, you reveal which categories interest you most.

Another way to learn about your interests is to ask yourself these questions: Which school subjects do I like best? Which do I like least? Why? What hobbies and leisure-time activities do I enjoy? Do I prefer to work on things by myself or with someone else? What did I enjoy about the jobs I've held? What did I dislike?

One difficulty in trying to determine your interests is that you may not have had an opportunity to develop them fully. You cannot be truly interested in something you know very little about. You may think you're interested in something only to find out, once you've started working at it, that it doesn't hold your attention.

Interest is a key factor in selecting a career, but it isn't the only one. There is no career in which you'll always be totally interested; every job has its boring or dissatisfying moments. And your interests may not always be helpful in forming a career goal. You may be interested in professional baseball or dramatics. Job opportunities in these areas are limited, however, to people who are very talented, highly trained, and highly motivated.

Your school counselor, state job service office counselor, or marketing and distributive education coordinator may be able to give you valuable information about matching your interests with career opportunities. But no matter how inter-

By taking an inventory of your interests, you can learn more about yourself.

ested you are in a career, you'll be able to succeed in it only if you have the necessary skill, talent, and motivation.

Your Aptitudes. An **aptitude** is an ability, capacity, or talent. Aptitude is different from knowledge; you may have an aptitude for mathematics even if you don't know algebra. Having an aptitude means that you find it easy to learn a particular subject.

Jobs consist of certain functions to be performed by workers. In order to perform these functions, an individual must possess certain aptitudes, such as reasoning ability, verbal ability, numerical ability, and manual dexterity. In the *Dictionary of Occupational Titles* (DOT), the Department of Labor divides jobs into three broad categories of functions based on their relationship to data, people, and things. Here is what the three categories mean:

♦ *Data*. Jobs that require a worker to use numbers, words, and symbols
♦ *People*. Jobs that require a worker to deal with human beings
♦ *Things*. Jobs that require a worker to work with inanimate objects, substances, or materials—in other words, to work with equipment or products

To find out your special aptitudes, it's a good idea to take tests administered by your school guidance counselor or your local state job service office. The scores you earn on aptitude tests are one indication of your potential—if you work up to your fullest capacity while taking the tests. Your school grades are another way to judge your ability in certain areas. These, too, are good measures only if you've been working up to your potential.

Your Work Needs. Obtaining satisfaction from work is important to a growing number of people. **Satisfaction** is a feeling of being pleased and fulfilled. You may get satisfaction from the realization that you've done a good job, from the knowledge that you've done something important, or from the certainty that you've helped or pleased someone. Different people obtain different satisfactions from their jobs; but it's almost impossible to be happy with your work unless you get some kind of satisfaction from it.

Your concern is to pursue a career in which the jobs you hold offer you what you want. But do you really know what you want? Finding out about your goals may require as much time and effort as learning about your interests and aptitudes. The more actual work experience and self-knowledge you acquire, the better chance you have of making accurate career-goal choices. Here are some common satisfactions and rewards provided by jobs. As you read them over, think about which ones are important to you.

Income.   The amount of money you earn means much more than the amount of material goods you can buy. Your income also plays a large part in determining your **lifestyle**, the way you live and things you like to do. But time is also important; to many people time is too precious to be wasted on a job that provides few satisfactions other than a big paycheck. Some of the most rewarding careers pay low salaries. Other careers offer low pay to beginners but are eventually very rewarding financially.

Prestige.   People tend to view certain careers and work activities as more important than others. Do you like the idea of having a job that impresses other people? Then you might find that a career in a field having high prestige meets your needs. But remember that in many instances the prestige connected with a job is superficial; a job that seems glamorous

Obtaining satisfaction by helping people is important to many workers in retailing.   Courtesy of Sears, Roebuck and Co.

Most people want recognition for their work and ideas. Courtesy of American Management Institute

to other people may not appeal to you. Be sure that you enjoy other aspects of the work besides its reputation.

Security. Do you want a career in which you have a good chance of steady employment and earnings throughout your working years? Then you should select a field that is growing in importance and in the number of people it employs. In the *Occupational Outlook Handbook*, the U.S. Department of Labor provides projections of employment statistics well into the future. Consult this handbook to find out which career fields are expanding. But don't overemphasize security. Nobody can be certain about what will happen in the future. A job considered secure now may not prove to be so later on.

Recognition. Like most people, are you pleased when others recognize your abilities or congratulate you on your accomplishments? Or doesn't this kind of attention concern you very much? **Personal recognition** is, essentially, other people's appraisal of you and your qualities. If

such approval is especially important to you, consider a career in a field where personal recognition can be achieved. Careers in which you work with other people are more likely to offer this type of satisfaction than careers in which you work alone.

Do you feel disappointed if you're not praised for the job assignments you've completed? Basically, **work recognition** is other people's appreciation of your work and effort. Do you need to receive credit for the work you do? Does praise for a job well done spur you on to even bigger achievements? Your desire for work recognition can be a strong motivating force in your career.

Your Lifestyle

Your job will form a major part of your lifestyle. So selecting a career to fit your lifestyle is an important step. Like everyone else, you live according to a set of values, goals, traditions, and emotional and physical needs. Your hopes for the future, your friends, and your family ties influence your lifestyle too. But where you will live and what you will do for a living are two of the most important considerations of all. The income and benefits that you'll get from a job are among the occupational factors that will determine your lifestyle. Your interests, hobbies, and beliefs are also affected by your job. Consider, then, how you plan to live, and choose a career that will be in keeping with your lifestyle.

Developing a Career Plan

As you begin to select potential career-field areas that match your abilities, you'll probably want to discuss your plans with your family, friends, and someone engaged in the career you wish to pursue. However, remember that careers which appeal to you may not appeal to them. Be careful not to choose an occupation simply because you admire someone who has chosen it or because someone else told you it was a good field to get into.

It's becoming more and more difficult to decide which career field to pursue because there are so many to choose from and the demand for workers keeps changing. You'll need to make your decisions carefully so that you're choosing a career field in which there is likely to be an active demand for workers when you're ready to go to work.

Your school counselor, state job service office personnel, and people working in the field of your choice can give you helpful advice. If they can't answer your questions themselves, they'll be able to refer you to other people, books, or articles that have the necessary information.

When you've tentatively chosen one or more career fields, that's the time to prepare a career plan. Decide how and when you will learn your career. Will you earn while you learn by working during the summer, over weekends, or during school vacations? If your career choice is in retailing, will you enroll in a marketing and distributive education program? Or will

you study business courses in school and work part-time?

As you develop your career plan, continue to examine your interests, aptitudes, and goals to see if what you have chosen is really the career for you. Career development is a continuous process during which you can learn about yourself as well as the world of work. A career plan should help you achieve the goals best suited to you.

The next three chapters in this unit give you an overview of the retailing field. You'll get an idea of the many different career opportunities that are available in retailing. As you read these chapters, think about the information you're being given in terms of developing your career plans.

Trade Talk

Define each term and use it in a sentence.

Aptitude	Job
Career	Lifestyle
Career ladder	Personal recognition
Career lattice	Satisfaction
Competency	Work recognition

Can You Answer These?

1. What is the difference between a job and a career?
2. What is the difference between a career ladder and a career lattice?
3. List several of the most common satisfactions and rewards provided by jobs.
4. What is one of the best sources of information on employment opportunities and projections?
5. How does a job affect a person's lifestyle?

Problems

1. Part of a career development is honest self-appraisal. Rule a form similar to the following. In the left column, write in the following: school subjects, hobbies, clubs and organizations, and social activities.

Write in the appropriate activities under each area. In the right column, tell what you like or dislike about the activities in each.

Area	What I Like	What I Dislike
Example: School subjects		
English	Reading poetry	Term papers

2. Rule a form similar to the following. In the left column, write the letter of each of the following tasks: (0) operating a cash register, (a) explaining store policy to customers, (b) filling out a sales check, (c) arranging a display, (d) handling a customer complaint by refunding a pur-chase price, (e) completing a payroll sheet, (f) operating a machine that prints price tickets, (g) demonstrating products to customers, (h) using the telephone to take merchandise orders, (i) teaching a new employee how to stock shelves, (j) maintaining customer goodwill, (k) doing housekeeping chores in the store, (l) attending a sales training session, and (m) describing a shoplifter to security per-sonnel. Place a check mark (√) in the appropriate column on the right to classify the task as requiring an aptitude for data, people, or things.

Task	Aptitude for:		
	Data	People	Things
Example: (0)	√		

What Is Retailing?

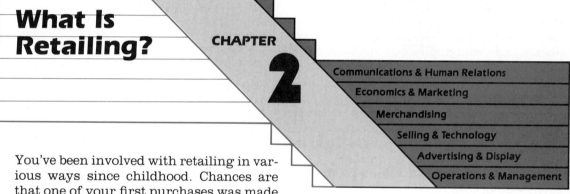

CHAPTER 2

Communications & Human Relations

Economics & Marketing

Merchandising

Selling & Technology

Advertising & Display

Operations & Management

You've been involved with retailing in various ways since childhood. Chances are that one of your first purchases was made in a retail store near your home, where you bought some candy or gum. Your first soft drink may have been purchased from a vending machine. Perhaps you remember waiting anxiously at the curb, with your money in hand, for the chimes of the ice-cream wagon. You may even recall your first trip to the barber or beauty shop to get your hair cut. All those experiences involved some form of retailing.

Retailing means different things to people. To some people retailing involves a place to shop for goods and services. To others, it means a job or a career, as discussed in Chapter 1. Let's look at retailing briefly from both viewpoints, since you'll always be a customer and may pursue retailing as a career field.

Retailing Activities

Retailing includes all activities involved in the sale of products and services to the final consumer. **Products** are goods grown or manufactured and available for sale. **Services** are benefits or satisfactions that improve the appearance, health, comfort, or peace of mind of their users. Retailing is the last link in the chain of marketing between those who produce or provide products and services at the one end and the consumer or user at the other. Its purpose is to serve the needs and wants of consumers.

Range of Activities and Outlets

Retailers perform activities such as buying and pricing, transporting and storing, advertising and selling, servicing, financing and risk bearing. These activities, which are discussed in this chapter, are carried on in stores or service businesses. They are also carried on through a wide range of non-store outlets such as door-to-door and telephone sales, mail order catalogs, and vending machines.

The Retailing Function

The **retailing function**—distributing to consumers—is performed not only by retailers but also by producers, manufacturers, and wholesalers. Here are some examples of how they carry out the retail function: producers can sell vegetables at a roadside stand; manufacturers can sell cosmetics through direct-to-the-home sales representatives; and wholesalers can sell candy through vending machines. Likewise, producers, manufacturers, and wholesalers may sell services such as repair services to final consumers. However, the vast majority of retailing is done by retailers who specialize in the field.

The **wholesaling function** is performed by dealers who buy goods, generally in large quantities, and sell them, usually in smaller quantities, to retailers for resale or to businesses and industrial users.

How Retailing Serves Consumers

Have you ever wondered how retailers decide what type and variety of products and services they should sell or offer? It is the consumer, the retailer's real boss, who helps make this decision. If consumers approve what is done, they reward the retailer with their continued business. A retailer can't survive very long without such votes of confidence from consumers.

Therefore, retailers are forced to change their ways of serving their customers; if they don't, a competitor will replace them. Retailing is what it is today because of this competition to gain the consumer's favor.

In our ever-changing society, the needs and wants of consumers don't remain the same. Technology, lifestyles, fashion, and many other factors affect consumer needs and wants. Think about the changes in retailing that have taken place since you were a child. What does all this mean? Just this: retailing is dynamic—exciting to progressive merchants. There's hardly a dull moment. The key to success is flexibility and willingness to change. In fact, progressive retailers often start changes.

Although the consumer is the retailer's real boss, retailing provides three major kinds of contributions to consumers: economic, social, and civic contributions.

Economic Contributions

Retailing serves the economic needs of consumers in four ways:

1. By supplying the right goods and services when and where they are needed with little or no delay.
2. By making it easy to select and compare the features, quality, and prices of the goods and services consumers want.
3. By fair pricing of goods and services—keeping prices low.
4. By helping to raise the American standard of living. (**Standard of living** is a term that refers to how well people live. It is measured by the amount and quality of goods and services that people have or use.)

Supplying Consumer Needs. One of the most important consumer needs that retailing fulfills is making products and services available *where* and *when* they are needed. Imagine for a minute that you need a new pair of shoes and there are no retailers nearby where you could compare styles and prices and get the proper fit. Think of how long it would take and how much it would cost to find and deal with

Retailers continue to expand their services to better serve their customers.
Kip Peticolas/Fundamental Photographs

shoe manufacturers in far-away places who might be able to satisfy your needs.

Retailers are purchasing agents for their customers. Retailers assemble the required products and provide the services needed when and where consumers want them. Thus, retailers are nearly everywhere today. Most people can buy just about anything they want within a short distance of their homes.

Helping Consumers Buy. Consumers may demand more than the mere availability of goods at convenient locations. They nearly always want to shop in stores where it is easy to select and compare the features, quality, and prices of the products and services they are interested in. Therefore, retailers compete to win the favor of potential customers by making easy shopping possible. Retailing will continue to be a vital service as long as consumers want to compare the features, qualities,

and prices of the products and services they buy.

Fair Pricing. A third way in which retailing serves consumers' economic needs is by keeping prices low. Studies have shown that distribution through retailers is generally less costly than direct distribution by manufacturers to consumers. Manufacturers sell relatively few products, such as cosmetics and cookware, directly to consumers. In our economic system, retailers compete vigorously with each other for consumer dollars by keeping prices low for products and services of similar quality. Many of the techniques that retailers use to compete successfully are discussed throughout this book.

Improving Our Standard of Living. As the final link in the chain of distribution between producers and consumers, retailers strongly influence what people buy and

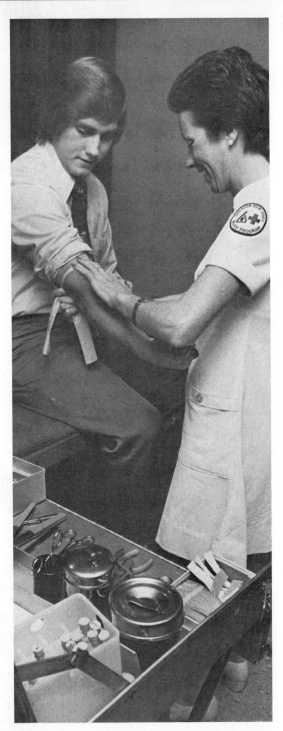

Retailers become involved in community projects like blood donor drives. *Courtesy of Irving Trust.*

consume. So retailers help to improve America's standard of living. Were it not for all the sales promotion efforts of retailers, (together with those of producers, manufacturers, and wholesalers) Americans wouldn't enjoy one of the world's highest standards of living. These efforts not only inform potential customers of the availability of new and improved products and services but motivate customers to buy. The end results are increased sales and a higher standard of living.

Another way in which retailing contributes to maintaining our high standard of living is by making mass production possible. (**Mass production** is the efficient, high-volume manufacture of large amounts of goods.) Mass production wouldn't work without an effective retailing system to distribute the mass-produced products to consumers. For example, the ability of our factories to produce millions of television sets would be of little value if there weren't an efficient way of getting those TV sets to consumers.

Social and Civic Contributions

In less visible ways, retailing also contributes to our social life and welfare as well as to our economic well-being. Here are two examples of this retailing function.

Throughout the ages, the marketplace has been a social gathering spot as well as a place to bargain and buy goods. Retailers today encourage people to meet at shopping centers and individual places of business. They do this by providing a variety of opportunities for customers to relax. Also, retailers support worthy civic and cultural enterprises such as the United Fund and other community projects. They work hard at becoming an integral part of the community. They know that a better community is a good investment.

Challenges and Opportunities in Retailing

Now that you have some knowledge about the purpose and roles of retailing in our social and economic system, you'll want to get answers to the following career-related questions about retailing:

1. What does retailing offer as a source of employment?
2. What are the benefits and limitations of careers in retailing?
3. What retail occupations have the potential for satisfying my work needs?

Ample Employment Opportunities

Retailing is one of the largest industries in the United States in terms of workers. There are more than 1.7 million retail firms with sales of over $700 billion. The field is made up of a large number of small businesses, a relatively small number of medium-size firms, and a small number of giant distributors. So, as a source of employment, retailing has many possibilities.

Also, retailing is a field in which you can work almost anywhere you like, because every community has some retail businesses. In a large city or small town, there will generally be a retail job for a qualified person. About one out of ten (14 million) workers in the United States is employed in retailing; nearly half of them are women. And the age range of people employed in retailing is extremely wide.

Employment opportunities in retailing are excellent for young people of either sex. Advancement is usually rapid if you're qualified and willing to learn, accept responsibility, and work hard. The percentage of supervisory and managerial positions is very high compared to other occupational areas. You'll find that the work environment is nearly always pleasant.

On the other hand, any field with all these advantages and as easy to enter as retailing attracts many people. Therefore, as a beginner, your wages may be relatively low and there may be strong competition from other employees. Your hours and days of employment will depend on the type of job you hold in retailing. If you

decide on a job in selling, your hours may be irregular.

Is retailing the right area of employment for you? It all depends on your abilities and what you want from your work. Retailing is such a broad occupational area and the jobs are so diverse that there are positions that fit almost any combination of work needs. Your selection of a career goal in retailing will be a matter of identifying the particular broad area that matches your interests and needs best. (Also bear in mind that most of the competencies required in retailing can also be used in many other types of businesses.)

Broad Areas of Retailing

Retail occupations can be grouped into five broad areas, or divisions, corresponding to the operating divisions of many retail businesses.

These are as follows:

1. Merchandising
2. Sales promotion
3. Store operations
4. Finance and control
5. Personnel

Here, each area is introduced briefly from the standpoint of career opportunities. They are described in detail in Chapter 8.

Merchandising. The **merchandising area** deals with the buying and selling of goods and services. Throughout this book you will hear about providing the customer with the right goods and services at the right place, at the right time, at the right price, and in the right quantities. Merchandising is a highly people-oriented area that includes occupations such as those of the salesperson, buyer, fashion coordinator, interior decorator, and merchandise manager. Do you enjoy working with people? Do you think any of these occupations seem right for you?

Sales Promotion. Any activity that helps build sales is a form of **sales promotion.** Advertising, display, special promotions,

There are five broad areas of retailing. In which area would you like to work?

and publicity all fit into this area. People in the sales promotion area are creative. Are you inclined to be creative? Do you like to draw, write, take photographs, and think up ideas? If you do, then sales promotion could be the area in retailing that matches your aptitudes.

Store Operations. The **store operations area** involves activities related to operation of the physical plant and the physical handling of merchandise (for example, receiving and marking). It also involves responsibility for such services as delivery, adjustments, alterations, store security, maintenance, supplies, fixtures, and equipment. Store operations personnel set the stage for the sale. How do you feel about working behind the scenes in a store? Are you good at working with equipment? If your answer's "yes," then store operations might be the retailing area that you'd like to investigate further.

Finance and Control. The **finance and control area** relates to the management of income and expenditures. Finance and control could be your opportunity in retailing if you enjoy working with figures. Workers in this area deal with activities such as financing the business, accounting, budgeting, cashiering, customer credit and collections, cost control, expense control, office management, and other operations that involve money.

Personnel. Workers in the **personnel area** are responsible for the selection, training, placement, advancement, and welfare of all employees. They are also responsible for the administration of all personnel policies. The area includes employee relations, counseling, health and welfare benefits, and executive development. If you like to work with people, this area would be a good place for you to begin your career in retailing.

Preparing for
a Career in Retailing

Retailing has other attractive features apart from the variety of jobs that it can offer you. It is easy to gain entrance into the retail field. You may not have to pass required entrance examinations, spend years studying, or get college degrees. However, to advance to management positions in large firms, it may be necessary to obtain a professional degree. There are many ways for you to prepare for a career in retailing.

You can apply for any entry job without any formal preparation and depend only on the training provided by your employer. That has been the common practice in the past and it is still common today. The advantage of this approach is immediate employment. But the disadvantage is beginning your working life with a very narrow idea of what retailing is all about, little knowledge of the meaningfulness of your work activities, and, perhaps, having no career goal in mind. This approach could lead to job dissatisfaction and greater difficulty in experiencing success. Do you remember how Felicia, in Chapter 1, became dissatisfied with her jobs before she decided on a career goal?

A better way to launch your retailing career is to build a sound foundation through formal retail instruction in school. During such training you can test your interests and abilities as well as gain an insight into the satisfactions and way of life associated with the areas of retailing. In this way, you can develop and evaluate a more realistic career plan. This career plan can serve to guide you and perhaps motivate you to study further if you decide that a career in retailing will satisfy your interests, aptitudes, and work needs.

You can start your retail training by enrolling in your high school's marketing and distributive education program. Courtesy of Distributive Education Clubs of America

To start your retail training in high school, you can participate in the marketing and distributive education program. When you graduate, you can either enter full-time employment or prepare for post–high school marketing and distributive education.

At the post–high school level, many communities offer programs in marketing and distributive education through community colleges and technical institutes. These institutions stress preparation for middle-level management and usually specialize in fields such as food marketing, fashion merchandising, wholesaling, real estate, insurance, and hotel-motel management. Many local school districts, colleges, and universities offer adult education courses through day and/or evening classes to update and upgrade the skills of people who are already employed.

Your success in retailing will depend a great deal on your willingness to prepare for a career. As you study this book, try to picture yourself in the occupations associated with the aspect of retailing being discussed. Think about each occupation, what it involves, what it requires from you, and how it matches your interests, aptitudes, and lifestyle needs.

Trade Talk

Define each term and use it in a sentence.

Finance and control area
Mass production
Merchandising area

Personnel area
Products
Retailing
Retailing function

Sales promotion area
Services
Standard of living
Store operations area
Wholesaling function

Can You Answer These?

1. What are the two types of contributions that retailers make to consumers?
2. What are the four ways in which retailing serves the consumer's economic needs?
3. What are the five broad areas corresponding to the operating divisions of a retail business?
4. What is the best way to launch a career in retailing?

Problems

1. Rule a form similar to the one below. In the left column, write the letter of each of the following products or services: (0) fruits and vegetables sold at a roadside stand, (a) hand cream bought in a drugstore, (b) candy sold in a vending machine, (c) house siding sold over the telephone, (d) shoe repair, (e) records sold by advertisement in a magazine, (f) meat sold at a grocery store, (g) eggs sold door to door in an apartment building, (h) jewelry bought at a craft show, and (i) a pair of shoes bought in a shoe store. Place a check mark (√) in the appropriate column at the right to indicate who performed the retailing function: retailer, wholesaler, producer, or manufacturer.

Product or Service	Retailer	Wholesaler	Manufacturer	Producer
Example: (0)				√

Kinds of Retail Businesses

CHAPTER 3

Communications & Human Relations

Economics & Marketing

Merchandising

Selling & Technology

Advertising & Display

Operations & Management

When you hear the word "retailing," do you picture a department store with a large variety of merchandise, a discount store with goods stacked on tables at bargain prices, or a supermarket with rows of packages lining the aisles? Almost everyone seems to picture the products that retailers sell. Most people forget that retailing also includes selling a wide variety of services, everything from dry cleaning to the rental of cars.

Retail firms can be classified in the following ways:

1. By type of managerial and ownership structure of the business—including independent, chain, leased dealership, or franchise
2. By where sales take place—in the store or shop or away from it
3. By what is offered for sale—a product or a service

In this chapter, the first two classifications are discussed. In the next chapter, you'll learn about the third.

Managerial and Ownership Structure

Almost all retail businesses can be classified as independents or corporate chains. This is true whether the firms sell products or services. Various types of managerial structures have emerged to serve the specific needs of consumer groups.

Independent Retailers

An **independent retail** firm is a retail outlet owned, operated, and merchandised independently and without affiliation with a merchandising association. Many independent retailers, however, want some of the advantages that chain stores enjoy. For example, they want discounts for buying in quantity, assistance in developing effective advertising and sales promotion plans, and help in designing sound accounting and records-control systems. In order to obtain these advantages, independent retailers are willing to give up some of their independence.

They can gain these advantages by joining a voluntary chain, by renting a business that is owned by a supplier (known as a leased dealership), or by entering into an agreement that makes them a part of a franchise chain. Although independent retailers remain independent under these plans, they do sacrifice some of their freedom. The three choices that an independent retailer has are described in detail in Chapter 37.

Corporate Chains

A **corporate chain** is a group of two or more stores linked together under one management and owned by a group of stockholders. For example, Sears, Roebuck and Co. is owned by a group of stockholders who select officers. The officers make decisions as to where new stores will be located. The stores in the chain are centrally owned and managed and usually sell more or less the same products and services.

When retailers buy in volume, they can pass on their savings to their customers.

The advantages of the corporate chain stem largely from its high sales volume, capacity to buy in huge quantities, and ability to employ workers with specialized talents to develop sales promotional materials. Because chains order large quantities of goods, they receive discounts from their suppliers. The size of the corporation also permits the hiring of a central staff of specialists who plan the advertising and sales promotion and control the inventory of the outlets. In addition, the central management staff coordinates the overall operation and lends assistance to local store managers.

Types of In-Store Retailers

Approximately 80 percent of all retailing takes place in retail stores. The remaining 20 percent is done in various kinds of nonstore retailing, ranging from vending machines and mail order to telephone selling. In-store retailers are usually classified by what they sell and how they sell it.

There are stores that sell enormous varieties of products and others that sell only one type of product, stores that offer many customer services and others that offer only a few, stores that sell at discount prices and others that sell only at list prices, and so on. As you read about all these different types of in-store retailers, think about whether you'd like to work in any of them and in what area. Merchandising, sales promotion, store operations, finance and control, or personnel?

General Merchandise Stores

A retail store that offers a wide variety of products for sale is called a **general merchandise store.** Its goal is to provide one-stop shopping. The mixture of products and services these stores offer ranges from that of the huge department store through the more limited stocks of the junior department store, the discount department store, the variety store, and the general store.

Department Stores. Not every general merchandise store is a department store. The U.S. Department of Commerce defines a **department store** as a retail establishment that employs at least 25 people and has sales of apparel and household linens amounting to 20 percent or more of total sales. A department store, the Department of Commerce also states, must sell items in each of the following lines of merchandise: (1) furniture, home furnishings, and appliances; (2) general apparel for the family; and (3) household linens and fabrics.

The modern department store also sells services such as appliance repair and gift wrapping; some stores even sell insurance. Large department stores are organized into main divisions and departments. Each division combines a number of departments selling related lines of merchandise. For example, the home products division has departments such as furniture, appliances, lamps, and housewares.

Many department stores have prospered and opened additional stores, often in the suburbs and usually in the form of a branch and twig stores. A **branch store** is a smaller version of the main store. It's also organized by departments. Usually it does not stock all the merchandise or offer all the services found in the main store. A **twig store** is a relatively small store that carries only one line of merchandise or a few related lines. Twigs are classified as department stores only because they are owned by parent department stores.

Junior Department Stores. Not quite a full department store, the **junior department store** carries a wide variety of merchandise and has a departmentalized organization. Many junior department stores began by specializing in moderately priced family wearing apparel and then added lines such as linens, yard goods, and draperies. Most F. W. Woolworth stores, for example, are classified as junior department stores.

Discount Department Stores. A departmentalized retail store that makes it a policy to sell limited assortments of merchandise at reduced prices is known as a **discount department store.**

Early discount retailers were able to reduce prices because their operating costs were low. Later, in response to customer requests, many discounters increased their range of merchandise, expanded facilities, and organized their stores by departments. Thus, discount stores became discount department stores.

Some well-known discount department stores are K-Mart, Zayre, Venture, Woolco, and Target. Many discount department stores have added credit and delivery services and have also increased personal selling service. Some have moved to high-traffic locations with high rents. To meet these expenses, they have increasingly turned to marketing private brands, on which they can realize a higher profit margin.

Variety Stores. A **variety store** is a retail firm that handles a varied assortment of goods in a relatively low price range. Variety stores are designed so that the customer can purchase products quickly with little or no assistance from store personnel. Housewares, cosmetics, sewing supplies, toys, and similar items sell well under these circumstances. Some variety stores are experimenting with merchandise, services, and price lines that are normally carried only by department and discount stores.

General Stores. The old-time general store was more than a retail outlet; it was

Specialty stores specialize in a limited merchandise line but offer a wide assortment of products within the line. Jane Hamilton-Merritt

also a post office, tavern, inn, and the center of community social life. Today, the **general store** supplies groceries, hardware, and some other inexpensive items such as grooming aids to consumers in rural and resort communities. Because the building is usually small, it cannot carry a large quantity of goods. The general store is decreasing in importance because of the declining populations in certain rural areas and the ease with which people who live in the country can drive to large shopping centers.

Limited-Line, or Specialty, Stores

A **limited-line, or specialty, store** is a retail firm that sells only one classification of merchandise. These stores may specialize in apparel and accessories, automotive supplies, food, hardware, building material, flowers, farm and garden supplies, antiques, home furnishings, or any other type of merchandise. Progressive retailers who specialize in a limited merchandise line offer a wide assortment of the products they carry, stay up to the minute with regard to new trends and fashions, supply sound product information, and provide efficient service.

Many specialized retail businesses have become so large that they have departmentalized in order to serve their customers better. Supermarkets provide a good example of the trend toward departmentalization. A **supermarket** is a self-service food store with at least four basic departments: grocery, meat, produce, and dairy. Many may sell non-food products as well.

A **convenience store** is a retail firm like 7-11 or Magic Marts that is located in consumer neighborhoods because it appeals to consumers who want to shop while other stores are closed. Such consumers want to purchase quickly a limited number of products—such as a loaf of bread, a quart of milk, or a newspaper—close to home. Many food retailers such as Red Owl, Dominicks, and Jewel are opening their own convenience or discount type stores in an effort to meet this type of competition.

Now let's take a look at the way retailers may be classified by how they sell their products and services.

Types of Non-Store Retailers

Not all retailers depend on customers to come to their places of business. A **non-store retailer** sells products and services by other means. Some of the main non-store retailing methods are direct selling, machine vending, mail-order retailing, and catalog showroom retailing.

Flea markets, garage sales, farmers' markets, and other non-store retailing outlets are also quite common in many communities. Some products and services are also sold through telephone soliciting.

Direct Selling

Marketing goods directly to the consumer in the home or place of business is known as **direct selling**. Products commonly sold by this method include cosmetics, encyclopedias, and cookware. Sales representatives in this field are often paid according to the sales volume of the products they sell. Other sales representatives are independent business people who buy the merchandise they sell. These sales representatives may make their sales by telephone, by home visits that have been arranged by telephone or mail, or by going direct to the home without any previous contact with the customer.

Another direct-selling method is street selling. Street salespeople range from the driver of the Good Humor ice cream truck to the vendors who set up booths on busy street corners to sell flowers, toys, and novelty items.

Vending Machines

Automatic vending machines can be found in many locations, including hotels, schools, service stations, airports, offices, theaters, and apartment buildings. Gum,

Vending-machine retailing is increasing in popularity. Kip Peticolas/Fundamental Photographs

candy, cold and hot drinks, and cigarettes are the most common items sold, but you can buy everything from books to clothing from some machines. Vending-machine retailing continues to grow because consumers are willing to pay extra for the convenience of having supplies readily available when and where they want them.

Mail-Order Retailers

A mail-order house sells through the use of an illustrated catalog or brochure that describes its goods in detail. Nearly everyone is familiar with the two largest mail-order houses—Sears and Montgomery Ward. Mail-order retailing has been growing because many department stores now have mail-order departments. Mail-order houses have also established catalog centers. These centers contain only catalogs from which the customer chooses merchandise. Still another type of mail-order retailing is done by "specialty houses," which deal in one line of merchandise,

such as novelties, garden supplies, or toys.

Catalog Showroom Retailers

A recent innovation in mail-order retailing that includes both in-store and non-store selling is the catalog showroom. A **catalog showroom** is a place where samples of merchandise are displayed, usually in a warehouse type building. Customers can examine items, locate them in the catalog, place an order, and pick it up or have it delivered. Customers can also order from a catalog at home.

What do you picture when you hear the word "retailing" now? The next time you go shopping, identify the type of managerial and ownership structure followed by the business you shopped. Is the business an independent or corporate chain retail establishment? And what about the business where you made your last purchase? Did you make it from an in-store retailer or a non-store retailer?

In the next chapter, you'll learn about another way of identifying retail businesses—by the services they offer or sell.

Trade Talk

Define each term and use it in a sentence.

Branch store
Catalog showroom
Convenience store
Corporate chain
Department store
Direct selling
Discount department store
General merchandise store
General store
Independent retail firm
Junior department store
Limited-line, or specialty, store
Non-store retailer
Supermarket
Twig store
Variety store

Can You Answer These?

1. What are the three ways in which retail firms can be classified?
2. What do retailers sell besides merchandise?
3. In what fields do corporate chains particularly flourish?
4. How does a twig store differ from a branch store?
5. List several types of non-store retailing.

Problems

1. Rule a form similar to the following. In the left column, list five new stores that have been opened in your area or neighborhood during the last 3 years. In the center column, list these new stores according to location. In the right column, classify these stores according to the six types of stores, such as department store, variety store, limited-line store, and so on.

Name of Store	Location of Store	Type of Store
Example: Sav-all	Brockton Shopping Center	Discount

2. Rule a form similar to the following. In the left column, list the names of ten kinds of different retail businesses from which you or your family have bought products recently. (If you're not sure of the business name, leave this column blank.) In the center column, list the product the retail business sells. In the appropriate column at the right, place a check mark (√) to classify the business as either an in-store retailer or a non-store retailer.

Name of Business	Product Store	In-Store Retailer	Non-Store Retailer
Example: Venture Vending Company	Candy		√

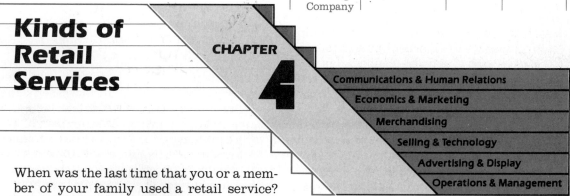

Kinds of Retail Services

CHAPTER 4

Communications & Human Relations
Economics & Marketing
Merchandising
Selling & Technology
Advertising & Display
Operations & Management

When was the last time that you or a member of your family used a retail service? If you're not quite sure what a retail service is, you might answer, "Oh, we don't use retail services." But when was the last time that you:

♦ Ate at a fast-food restaurant?
♦ Bowled at your local bowling alley?

♦ Rode a bus or a train?
♦ Had your hair cut or styled?

If you did any one of these things, then you used a retail service. In this chapter, you'll learn about all the different types of **service businesses,** which are retail outlets that offer mainly services. You'll also get an idea of the range of job opportunities in this area that will be available to you when you've finished your marketing and distributive education training.

Over the past 20 years, consumer spending for services of all types has tripled, while consumer spending for products has only doubled. Services have become so important that they now account for more than 40 cents out of every dollar spent by consumers.

This increase in the demand for services is directly related to the amount of money that people have available to spend. When the economy prospers and people have money to spend beyond satisfying their basic needs, they become more interested in the services they can buy. For example, they are more likely to ask for the services that accompany a purchase, such as gift wrapping, delivery, and installation.

There are two kinds of retail services—profit-centered services and sales-supporting services. **Profit-centered services** are those activities, benefits, or satisfactions that are sold to consumers to produce a source of income, or profit. In some cases, an entire business revolves around selling a service. In other cases, the service, although a source of income, is not the main business of the firm. For example, travel agencies get most of their income from providing travel services. However, many chain stores now also provide travel services for a fee, but this is not their major source of income.

Sales-supporting services are those activities, benefits, or satisfactions that are offered to support the sale of another product or service. Free parking provided by a store is an example of a sales-supporting service. Such services increase sales of the firm's other products by building customer goodwill, bringing customers into the place of business, making shopping easier, or making a product more attractive. Some sales-supporting services produce a modest profit; most do not.

Profit-Centered Services

There are many types of profit-centered services. They range from dry cleaning and hairdressing, to insurance and recreation. General merchandise retailers are increasingly moving into profit-centered service areas that were once considered the realm of specialized service businesses. Besides travel services, one large retailer offers mutual investment funds, automobile financing, and the fitting of eyeglasses. Other general merchandise retailers offer life insurance; many also rent equipment used in making home improvements.

To satisfy consumers, retailers of services must be as enterprising as retailers of products. Successful service retailers are willing to tailor their services to fit their customers' wishes. For example, because of customer demand, a dry-cleaning business might offer clothes-repair and alteration services.

Food Service

Today, the food service industry is growing. It is estimated that restaurants serve over 750 million meals weekly. This demand has been met by an increase in the number of restaurants, cafeterias, and drive-ins. In addition, the number of caterers providing food and service for small or large parties has grown. Because of the rapid expansion of the food service industry, the number of jobs in the industry is rising. This could be the retailing area where you'd like to begin your career. If it is, find out more about the food service industry.

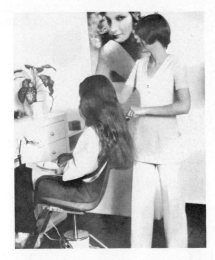

Services like haircuts—for you or your dog—are profit-centered. Courtesy of
(left) Simplicity Pattern Co., Inc. and (right) The New York School of Dog Grooming

Lodging Services

Americans travel extensively for both business and pleasure, and the lodging industry has grown to meet their need for places to stay. The industry must provide dining and recreation facilities as well as sleeping rooms. In fact, only half the income of a large hotel or motel comes from the sale of lodging space. The rest comes from providing food, beverages, and recreation. And it also comes from supplying services such as laundry and dry cleaning and from the shops that rent space on the premises. All these services will provide job opportunities for you when you have completed your training.

Not all travelers sleep indoors. Millions of people each year go on camping trips. Another retailing market is flourishing among travelers with trailers who rent space in state and private parks.

Financial Services

Consumers are demanding more and more financial services from banks, savings and loan associations, insurance companies, stockbrokers, small loan companies, credit unions, and finance firms. Finan-cial service businesses are responding to this demand by increasing both the types of services they provide to the public and the number of retailing functions they perform. Because they must engage in sales promotion to make consumers aware of the benefits that they can provide, these businesses can offer you many job opportunities if you're interested in the selling of financial services.

Recreation and Tourism Services

Some of the most popular types of recreation and tourism businesses are bowling lanes, boating marinas, golf courses, country clubs, theaters, hobby shops, amusement parks, and travel agencies. These firms continually engage in sales promotion campaigns. Customer reaction is what matters most in recreation and tourism retailing. Your study of retailing can also prepare you for careers in the recreation and tourism services industry.

Transportation Services

One of the main functions of airlines, railroads, bus companies, and car rental firms is to transport the customer from one

As people in the United States travel more for both business and pleasure, the lodging industry has grown to accommodate the increased need for places to stay. This field offers many interesting careers. *Courtesy of Sheraton Hotels and Inns.*

place to another. These firms, however, also recommend accommodations, arrange seating space, sell tickets, and make adjustments in travel arrangements. All these are retailing functions. The career opportunities for you in transportation services are extensive and previous retail experiences can be directly related to this career field.

But service businesses that transport travelers are only part of the overall transportation picture. A transportation network made up of various freight carriers stretches across this country. Part of the freight carrier's business is the retail marketing of transportation services. There are millions of jobs in thousands of companies that are involved in such diverse activities as transporting goods by air, rail, truck, and water. These include dis-patchers, route planners, and sales representatives.

Personal Services

Personal retail service businesses are concerned with individual care. Laundries, nursery schools, barber shops, health spas and gyms, photography studios, shoe repair shops, and dance studios are all examples of personal service businesses. Personal service businesses combine retailing and service production functions. For example, on the service production end, dry cleaners employ spotters and pressers. On the selling end, they employ salespeople at their counters to meet the customer and sell their service. Does the area of personal services retailing appeal to you?

Repair and Maintenance Services

The more customers buy mechanical products, the more they need repair services. They need people to fix cars, watches, and television sets. Many retail stores have established repair departments in answer to this consumer need. Many other businesses involve themselves only in the sale of repair services.

Most repair service workers are skilled; they have had mechanical or technical training. When they meet customers, they are also selling their firm's services. Also, repair service workers have an important role to play in building and maintaining customer goodwill because they are often in direct contact with customers. So customers view them not only as repair workers but as the firm itself. During the past few years, there has also been a significant increase in maintenance-type service firms such as car washes and cleaning services. If you'd like a career that combines working with things and with people, it

Many retail stores have established departments to meet their customers' need for repair services. Courtesy of B. Altman & Co.

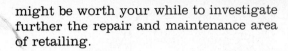

WATCH & JEWELRY REPAIR

Watches: complete servicing, replacement of necessary parts, new batteries for electronic and electric watches. Plus, a fine collection of leather straps. **Jewelry:** we re-string pearls and beads, remodel and repair jewelry, replace prongs, supply missing gemstones. We also repair and refinish silver and bronze baby shoes. Watch & Jewelry Repair, main floor, Fifth Avenue (212) MU9-7000.

B. Altman & Co

might be worth your while to investigate further the repair and maintenance area of retailing.

Rental Services

Not very many years ago, a consumer could rent only a house or apartment. Today there are service businesses that specialize in renting almost anything: cars, trucks, 10-ton cranes—or paintings to hang on the living room wall.

Retail rental services must carry the products and equipment local customers want, or they will soon be out of business. They advertise continually so that the potential customers—who often decide that they need something on the spur of the moment—will remember the name of the firm and where to obtain the desired rental products and services.

Sales-Supporting Services

Demand for sales-supporting services varies with the type of product sold and the customer served. Sales-supporting services will continue to be offered in retail stores whose customers have relatively high incomes. These customers are willing to pay higher prices or separate fees for product maintenance or service contracts. Retail businesses selling pleasure boats, automobiles, electric and gas appliances, television sets, and other mechanical items must be able to assure their customers that these products will be well serviced when necessary.

The average consumer, however, is price-conscious. So retailers who sell products through retail food chains, variety store chains, drugstore chains, and discount stores often have to deal with strong price competition. And in these retailing areas, many consumers are not always willing to pay for services. But because of increased costs, retailers are now forced to charge a modest fee for many sales-supporting services that they once offered free, such as delivery and credit. This charge is intended to cover costs; it is known as a **cost-recovery fee.** Cost-recovery fees make it possible to offer a service on a nonprofit basis and at no cost to the retailer.

The sales-supporting services that retailers now offer can be divided into five main categories:

1. Customer accommodation services
2. Credit services
3. Informational and advisory services
4. Merchandise handling services
5. Customer shopping conveniences

Customer Accommodation Services

The purpose of accommodation services is to maintain customer goodwill and to help ensure continued patronage. These services include:

- Adjustments, refunds, and exchanges: No profit is made by retailers.
- Guarantees or warranties: No profit is earned unless a fee is charged for an extended period.
- Cash on delivery: No profit is made by retailers.
- Approval sales: A profit is made by retailers if a fee is charged.
- Installations: A profit is made by retailers if a fee is charged.
- Repairs and alterations: A profit is made by retailers if a fee is charged.
- Special orders and customer services: A profit is made by retailers if a fee is charged.

Credit Services

Credit services give customers the power to purchase and use products and services at once while paying for them at a later, agreed-upon time. Credit has become a readily acceptable substitute for cash. The use of credit is expected to grow to the point where cash will seldom, if ever, be used. This situation is known as a "cashless society."

Today, customers expect retailers to provide the following credit services:

- Installment account: A profit may be made by retailers from interest charges if they provide financing.
- Revolving account: A profit is usually made if retailers finance.
- Ninety-day account: A profit may be made if retailers finance.
- Regular or 30-day charge account: No profit is made by retailers.

These credit plans are discussed further in Chapter 49.

Informational and Advisory Services

Informational and advisory services help customers make intelligent buying decisions. Some of these services are listed below:

- Fashion consultation: No profit is made by retailers.
- Wedding arrangements (bridal consultant and bridal register): No profit is made unless the retailer gets a percentage from the supplier.
- Educational services (classes in cooking, sewing, knitting, makeup, sports, and hobbies): No profit is made by retailers.
- Sales assisting and technical merchandise information: No profit is made by the retailers.

Merchandise Handling Services

Merchandise handling services make buying more convenient for customers. They include the following:

- Sales catalog: No profit is made by retailers.
- Drive-up windows: No profit is made by retailers.
- Layaway: No profit is made by retailers.
- Mail and telephone orders: No profit is made by retailers.
- Gift wrapping and packing: Sometimes covered by a cost-recovery fee.
- Storage: A profit is made by retailers if a fee is charged.
- Delivery and shipping: Sometimes covered by a cost-recovery fee.

Retailers offer cooking demonstrations to assist customers in making intelligent buying decisions. Ken Karp

Customer Shopping Conveniences

Customer shopping conveniences build customer goodwill. Some conveniences in this area are given in the list that follows:

♦ Parking: Often no profit is made by retailers; sometimes covered by a cost-recovery fee.
♦ Community services (charity festivals, scholarships, free concerts, and art shows): No profit is made by retailers.
♦ Store atmosphere and arrangement (layout, fixtures, noise and temperature control): No profit is made by retailers.
♦ Extended store hours: No profit is made by retailers.
♦ Customer services (information, check cashing, telephones, lockers, baby-sit-

ting, gift certificates, theater-ticket sales, and rest rooms): No profit is made by retailers.

In addition to their other benefits, many of these sales-supporting services, while yielding "no profit" as such, do help the sale of related products. For example, some retailers may make no profit by offering a bridal consultant service and a bridal register. However, because they make these services are available, the retailers may sell a wide range of products to the bride, her family, and her friends.

It is up to retailers to decide which of their services should produce a profit, which should "break even" (recover costs), and which must be offered as an expense of doing business in hopes that the service will attract customers.

Retailing of Products and Services Compared

The basic difference between the merchandising programs of those who sell products and those who sell services is that the former buy an inventory of goods for resale while the latter concentrate on the materials and labor needed to produce and sell their services. The retail store emphasizes the functions of buying, stocking, displaying, and selling merchandise, while the service business emphasizes the actual performance of the service.

Now that you've read Chapters 3 and 4 and completed this unit, your understanding of the retailing field should be more complete. But remember, these chapters are only an introduction to the many types of retailing businesses, some of the activities that take place in them, and the wide variety of jobs and careers available to you in retailing.

Throughout the rest of this book, you'll learn not only about the different retailing activities in detail but also how to take your first steps on the career ladder of retailing.

Trade Talk

Define each term and use it in a sentence.

Cost-recovery fee
Credit services
Profit-centered services

Sales-supporting services
Service businesses

Can You Answer These?

1. How has consumer spending for services changed in the last 20 years?
2. Name three examples of a profit-centered service and three examples of a sales-supporting service.
3. Why do many retailers charge a fee for certain sales-supporting services?
4. What five major categories of services do retailers offer to gain a competitive advantage?
5. What does the term "a cashless society" mean?

Problems

1. Rule a form similar to the following. In the left column, write the letter of each of the following items: (*a*) stereo equipment, (*b*) golf clubs, (*c*) refrigerators, (*d*) airline tickets, (*e*) hotel and motel rooms, (*f*) men's suits, and (*g*) cameras. In the right column, suggest two or more services that a retailer might offer to increase the sales of each item listed. Be specific in the reasons you give.

Product	Services That May Increase Sales

2. Rule a form similar to the following. In the left column, write the letter of each of the following types of businesses: (*a*) hardware stores, (*b*) department stores, (*c*) supermarkets, (*d*) gas stations, (*e*) restaurants, (*f*) laundries, and (*g*) dry cleaners. In the middle column, indicate the services you believe each of these types of businesses should offer. In the right column, give your reasons for your choice.

Type of Business	Services	Reasons

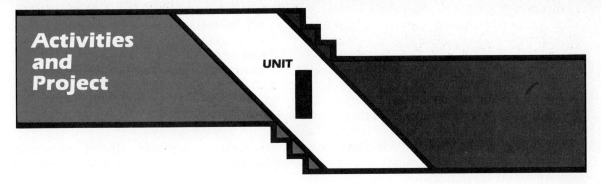

Retailing Case

"Could you please gift-wrap just the salad set?" asked the customer as Judy Rivera, a co-owner of the recently opened housewares store, was about to put the customer's purchases in a regular bag.

"I'm sorry," replied Judy, "but we don't provide gift-wrapping service." The customer appeared annoyed and said something to Judy about not shopping at the store again.

When the customer had left, Judy called Herman Rivera, her husband and co-owner in the store, from the back where he was working. "I really think we should reconsider our gift-wrapping policy," Judy told Herman. "Another new customer has just left angry and probably won't return because we don't gift wrap."

"But we've already been through the costs of providing gift wrapping," replied Herman. "You know we can't afford to give that service just yet. Perhaps we'll be able to offer it when we've got the store well established."

1. Of the six types of retail stores, what type do you think the Riveras are operating? Explain your answer.
2. Are Judy and Herman in disagreement over a profit-centered service or a sales-supporting service?
3. What could the Riveras do that would enable them to provide a gift-wrapping service and at the same time meet the costs of providing that service? Explain your answer.

Working with People

Sal Lombardo and Dick Stevens, both juniors in high school, have been discussing their career plans. Sal told Dick that after talking with his teachers and the school counselor, he had decided to enroll in the school's marketing and distributive education program. Dick didn't think that it was such a great idea. He said to Sal, "Why do you want to enroll in that program? That's all about retailing or something, isn't it? So, all you'll learn is how to be a salesperson. You ought to enroll in program that'll give you more career opportunities than that."

1. Identify the true problem.
2. What are the important facts to be considered in this problem?
3. List several solutions to this problem.
4. Evaluate the possible results of each solution.
5. Which solution do you recommend? Why?

Project 1: Planning Your Career

Your Project Goal

Given the desire to learn more about yourself, prepare an inventory of your interests, prepare an analysis of your aptitudes, identify your goals, and list and describe five possible careers in retailing that might help you fulfill your personal goals.

Procedure

1. On a separate sheet of paper, list the following questions under the major heading "Interests." Leave 3 inches of space after each question; you will need space, for your interests may change and you will want to record these changes.
   a. Which school subjects do you like best? Why do you prefer them?
   b. Which school subjects do you like least? Why do you dislike them?
   c. What hobbies and leisure-time activities do you enjoy?
   d. Which extracurricular school activities do you especially like to take part in? Why do you enjoy them?
   e. Are there any extracurricular activities in which you are not taking part and in which you would like to participate? Why?

2. Arrange an appointment with your guidance counselor to achieve the following purposes:
   a. To obtain from your counselor information about your interests or aptitudes that may assist you in learning more about yourself.
   b. To discuss with your counselor what you can do to learn about your interests and aptitudes.
   c. To make plans for carrying out the recommendations of your guidance counselor in order to learn more about yourself and your possible career choices.

3. On an additional sheet of paper headed "Aptitudes," list the following questions, leaving about 4 inches of space after each question.
   a. What is aptitude for data? People? Things?
   b. What did your guidance counselor tell you about your aptitude for data, people, and things while interpreting your school records and the results of aptitude tests that you took in school?

   c. What have you learned about your aptitudes from the subjects you have taken in school, from your hobbies, from extracurricular activities, from work experience, and from other activities?

4. On an additional sheet of paper headed "Goals," leave approximately 3 inches of space for each of the following:
   a. List five or six goals that you want to achieve in a career. Unit 1 discusses some goals that you may want to consider.
   b. Arrange these goals in order of importance to you.
   c. Explain why you feel that each of the goals is important to you and why some are more important than others.

5. On an additional sheet of paper, write the heading "Potential Careers."
   a. List five career goals toward which you might like to work. At least one of these should be in the field of retailing. (Note: The *Dictionary of Occupational Titles*, career literature, and discussions with retailers, the marketing and distributive education teacher-coordinator, your teachers, and personnel at the state employment service may be of help to you in selecting these goals.)
   b. Prepare a list of advantages and disadvantages and an explanation of the future opportunities of each of the career positions that you selected.

6. This project is related to Chapter 8 of this book, which you may want to look at now. Be sure to save this project for use with the project in Unit 3.

Evaluation

Your plan will be evaluated on neatness and the completeness of the information that you are able to gather and record about your interests, aptitudes, goals, and potential career.

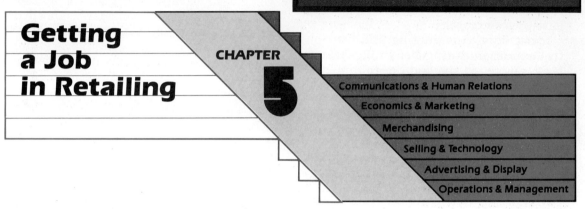

**Getting
a Job
in Retailing**

CHAPTER

5

Communications & Human Relations

Economics & Marketing

Merchandising

Selling & Technology

Advertising & Display

Operations & Management

Maria Martinez was now less than 200 feet away from Boylan's Department Store in the Park Central Shopping Center. As she walked in the shadows of the buildings, perspiration spread over the palms of her hands. She went over her appointment for what seemed like the hundredth time . . . personnel department . . . third floor . . . Mrs. Jackson . . . 2:30 p.m. . . . .

For nearly all job applicants, the first try is a fuzzy blend of faces, forms, pens, rooms, and butterflies. And Maria's experience was no exception. "I can remember looking at my application," she said, "and thinking nobody could be more scared than Martinez, Maria Catherine." Yet she was confident because she had prepared carefully for this day.

Maria was interviewed and tested, and now she has the job she wanted. What did Maria Martinez do to help ensure that she would be successful in getting that job?

Choosing the Type
of Retail Business

First, Maria studied the various types of retail businesses that would give her the satisfaction she wanted. She asked herself questions such as, "Which kind of retail business will help me advance toward my career goal?" When answering this question, Maria kept in mind the types of products and services sold, the experiences offered, and the level of customer service required; these would determine to some extent the type of people with whom she would be working. How did Maria go about finding out which type of retail business was best for her? Factors such as the following are important in helping you choose the type of retail business that's right for you.

Past Work Experience

Retail experience—part-time or full-time—will help you identify the kind of work you like best. For example, if you've worked part-time as a salesperson during the Christmas season, that can be a valuable experience.

If you're looking for part-time jobs in retailing, naturally you want to work in the kind of retail businesses that interests you most. But some businesses have more part-time jobs than others. In general, department stores, supermarkets, and restaurants hire the largest number of part-time employees.

Maria studied marketing and distributive education during her junior year in high school, so she had opportunities to learn about careers in marketing and to work part-time in the school store. In the school store, she learned to order, stock, display, and sell various types of merchandise to her classmates.

Interests, Hobbies, and Education

You can use your interests, hobbies, and education as a guide to the kind of job that will give you the greatest rewards and satisfactions. A hobby often gives you special knowledge and skills that you can put to good use in retailing. An interest in fashion may lead to a position in a dress shop. An interest in flowers or gardening can lead to a job in a florist's shop. And an interest in mechanics may open the door to a job in an auto-accessories store.

In what courses in school have you been successful? You might be able to use them successfully in some jobs. For example, did you develop an understanding of the principles of color and design in art courses? If so, you can use these skills in interesting positions in merchandise display, advertising, and selling. Accounting and mathematics courses may bring out an aptitude for figures that can be used in retail stores and service businesses.

Maria had learned from her marketing and distributive education experience that she wanted to work in a department store as a salesperson. She hoped someday to become either a store manager or owner. But first, Maria knew she had to learn how to be a good salesperson.

Benefits Offered by Retailing

When you are choosing a place to work, you should become familiar with the wages, working conditions, and various other benefits (vacations, retirement, hospitalization, and life insurance) offered by many retailers. The opportunity to advance on the job, to learn, and to gain valuable experience should be considered ahead of other benefits. But the benefits offered may be a deciding influence if everything else is nearly equal. Some firms offer excellent training courses and employee development and promotion programs. Accepting few benefits and a small salary in the beginning can be justified if you gain good experience that may be used later to obtain a better position or eventually begin your own business.

Making the Employment Contact

Once you have narrowed the list of possible jobs to the ones that interest you most, consider ways to contact prospective employers. There are many ways to go about locating the job you would like to have.

A recent survey of employees showed that the five leading job sources were:

1. Hearing about the job from friends, relatives of employees, and teachers
2. Applying for a job without knowing if the opening was available
3. Reading newspaper advertisements
4. Visiting a state employment job service agency
5. Visiting a private employment agency

Let Friends Help You

Is it unreasonable to ask friends or relatives to let you know about job openings?

Many courses in school relate to work in retailing. Karen Zebulon

Some people think so, feeling that they don't need help or that using "pull" is wrong. Letting friends help you is not necessarily using pull—most jobs are obtained only if the applicants really merit them. An introduction or recommendation from a friend is simply one way of meeting the employer. It is, therefore, wise to let friends assist you when they have contacts that you don't have.

Among those friends is your marketing and distributive education teacher-coordinator. Maria, now a senior, knew her marketing and distributive education teacher-coordinator from being in his classes during her junior year. She knew that Mr. Spano was well acquainted with many of the business leaders in the community, as these leaders had visited the marketing and distributive education class as guest speakers.

Prepare a Letter of Application

A **letter of application** is a written request applying for a job. A properly prepared letter of application is one of the best methods of finding out if a particular firm has a current or an anticipated job opening. Employers may receive hundreds of letters of application. But they select only a few of the best candidates for interviews, basing their selection on the candidates' letters of application.

First, employers look for letters that are attractive. The importance of this first impression cannot be stressed too much. Second, employers look for attention to the following points when reading the letter:

♦ Is it free from errors in grammar and punctuation?
♦ Is it free from typing errors?

This letter may serve as a model as you develop your own letter of application.

62-64 Almeria Road
Phoenix, Arizona 85008
January 2, 198-

Mr. Robert J. Jones
Personnel Director
Boylan's Department Store
404 West Main Street
Phoenix, Arizona 85008

Dear Mr. Jones:

I am interested in obtaining a sales position with your firm. I've had special training in the high school marketing and distributive education program and experience in the school store, so I believe I have the ability to fill the position of salesperson, which you advertised in today's Phoenix Sun.

You will see from my personal data sheet, enclosed, that I have enrolled in such high school courses as general business, marketing, retailing, and the Marketing and Distributive Education Project Laboratory to help me prepare to pursue my career goal. I have also kept a training plan to show what I have learned that would help me to become an excellent salesperson; I would like to show it to you.

Mr. José Spano, my marketing and distributive education teacher-coordinator, and others whose names I have included on my personal data sheet will be glad to help you, if you wish to contact them, in judging my knowledge, attitudes, and skills as they relate to my potential success as a salesperson in your firm.

I would appreciate an interview with you, at your convenience, to discuss my qualifications personally.

Sincerely yours,

Maria C. Martinez

Maria C. Martinez

Enclosure

◆ Is it a fair presentation of the applicant's strengths and what he or she has to offer?

Maria had prepared the first copy of her letter of application for Mr. Spano, her marketing and distributive education teacher-coordinator. You can also ask business or English teachers or business people to examine your letters of application and offer suggestions for improvement. An example of a properly prepared letter of application is shown on page 36.

Check the Help-Wanted Advertisements

The help-wanted advertisements in the local newspapers are very good sources of information about retailing jobs. The help-wanted columns contain many **blind ads**, which are ads that give only a post office box number and do not identify the employer. Such advertisements protect the employer from having to interview many unqualified people.

Following the directions in the advertisement is considered very important by the employer. For example, don't telephone in response to an advertisement unless the ad directs you to do so.

Check with Employment Agencies

There are several types of employment agencies that will help you find a job. The largest public agencies are the employment services operated by state governments in cooperation with the federal government. They are well informed of the employment picture both locally and statewide.

Most cities have one or more private employment agencies that are good sources

Check your local newspaper regularly to find out what job opportunities are available.

Operations Management

We are seeking an aggressive, growth-oriented person for the operations area of our rapidly expanding retail chain.

This individual must have a minimum of two years experience in at least one of the following capacities: assistant buyer, department manager, non-selling department manager, sales manager.

Salary commensurate with qualifications; full benefits provided. To apply, send confidential resume with salary requirements to: Director of Executive Placement Lord & Taylor, 424 Fifth Avenue, New York, N.Y. 10018

Lord & Taylor

An equal opportunity employer

---

of jobs. Private employment agencies operate to make a profit. The job hunter pays the agency a fee, usually a percentage of the first year's salary. In some cases, the employer pays the fee. When dealing with a private agency, be very sure that you understand who is to pay the fee and how much is being charged.

Handling the Interview

To convince an employer that it will be to the advantage of the company to hire you, you must demonstrate your interest in the job and make the interviewer aware of your talents and capabilities. The interviewer will begin to form an impression of you from the moment you meet. Here are a few tips to help you make that impression a favorable one.

Apply in Person

Never apply for a job by telephone unless you are instructed by the employer to do so. While you can sometimes make an appointment by telephone, it's better to show up in person. You will usually be told whom to see. If you're not, ask for the employment or personnel office. When going for the interview, always go alone—never take a friend or relative with you. If you brought someone along, an interviewer would get the impression that you lacked self-confidence and independence. And that's not a good first impression.

Make a Good First Impression

No matter what kind of job you are applying for, dress appropriately for the type of business. Avoid outfits that are too casual, too formal, or that call attention to themselves. Clean, freshly pressed clothes are a must. Of course, all interviewees should be immaculately clean. One way to determine whether or not you look right is to go to a place where you would like to work. Notice how the workers there look.

If you look right and know it and if you feel good, the chances are that you will also act right. Acting right means many things. It means walking with a firm, sure step—not shambling along with stooped shoulders. It means sitting straight—not slouching. And it means being able to read or sit quietly until your turn for an interview comes—not whistling or talking. It may mean just being patient and not looking bored if you have to wait.

Additional ways to make a good first impression include arriving 5 to 10 minutes early and being respectful to the receptionist and interviewer. Study company brochures, promotional materials, or catalogs if they are available in the reception room. You may be able to comment on these materials during the job interview.

Prepare a Personal Data Sheet

One of the best ways to present your talents and interests is by using a **personal data sheet,** or résumé. This is an outline of information about you as a potential employee. It presents such facts as your name, address, and telephone number. And it describes your career goal, education, work experience, and personal interests. It may also provide the names and addresses of several references—such as teachers, former employers, or club advisers—who are willing to discuss your work. An example of a well-planned personal data sheet is shown on page 39. Be sure to have this data sheet neatly typed. Ask someone to proofread the data sheet to eliminate any errors.

Bring a copy of your personal data sheet to the interview. If you are asked to fill out an application, you will find it convenient to have the facts already written out. The personal data sheet may also provide the employer with information that he or she could not obtain from the application form alone. It is wise to have a copy of your personal data sheet with you even if you have previously submitted one to the employer. In a large company, the interviewer may not have seen your personal data sheet before the interview.

Your personal data sheet should contain facts about your education and work experience and should present them in a clear, well-organized manner.

MARIA CATHERINE MARTINEZ

62-64 Almeria Road
Phoenix, Arizona 85008
(602) 555-9362

CAREER GOAL

Retail store manager or owner

EDUCATION

Will be graduated from Monterey High School, June 6, 198-,
with a major in marketing and distributive education
Student in Marketing and Distributive Education
Cooperative Program
Business subjects studied: general business, marketing, re-
tailing, Marketing and Distributive Education Project
Laboratory, typewriting (typing rate: 53 words a minute)

EXPERIENCE

Salesperson: Marketing and Distributive Education School
Store, Monterey High School, 19 Columbine Boulevard,
Phoenix, Arizona 85006, September 198- to June 198-

ACTIVITIES AND INTERESTS

Distributive Education Clubs of America—vice president of
local chapter
Monterey High School swimming team, comanager
Play lead guitar in small rock group
Hobbies include swimming and collecting records

REFERENCES

Mr. Harold O'Shea (neighbor), owner, Lincoln Drugstore,
1094 Hazelwood Drive, Phoenix, Arizona 85016
Mr. Harlowe Davis (principal), Monterey High School,
19 Columbine Boulevard, Phoenix, Arizona 85006
Mr. José Spano (marketing and distributive education
teacher-coordinator), Monterey High School, 19 Columbine
Boulevard, Phoenix, Arizona 85006

Fill in the application form neatly and accurately. It represents you to pro-spective employers. Courtesy of Gino's, Inc.

EMPLOYMENT APPLICATION
FOR GENERAL RESTAURANT WORK

SOCIAL SECURITY NO.

| 0 0 0 | 1 0 | 1 0 0 |

NAME __MICHAEL__ __B.__ __O'TOOLE__ ADDRESS __116 OAK ROAD__
First Name   Middle Initial   Last Name

APT. NO. __—__ CITY __PHOENIX__ STATE __AZ__ ZIP __85008__ AREA CODE __602__ TEL.# __555-9379__

EVER WORK FOR GINO'S OR RUSTLER BEFORE? __—__

IF YES, DATES AND LOCATION _____

AVAILABILITY:

ARE YOU LEGALLY ABLE TO BE EMPLOYED IN THE U.S.? ☒YES ☐NO   PART TIME ☒HOURS   FULL TIME ☐AVAILABLE:

	M	T	W	T	F	S	S
From	5	5	5	5	5	9	—
To	9	9	9	9	9	9	—

HOW FAR DO YOU LIVE FROM STORE? __1½ MILES__   HOW WILL YOU GET TO WORK? __BUS OR WALK__

SCHOOL MOST RECENTLY ATTENDED:

NAME __MONTEREY HIGH SCHOOL__ ADDRESS __19 COLUMBINE BLVD.__

TEACHER OR COUNSELOR __JOSÉ SPANO__ LAST GRADE COMPLETED __10__ GRADE POINT AVERAGE __3.1__

GRADUATED? ☐YES ☒NO   NOW ENROLLED? ☒YES ☐NO   SPORTS OR ACTIVITIES __SWIMMING__

MOST RECENT EMPLOYMENT

COMPANY __BURGER PIT__ ADDRESS __2606 EAST MAIN__ PHONE # __555-4566__

POSITION __DISHWASHER__ SUPERVISOR __E.A. DI ANGELO__ DATES WORKED: FROM __7/7/8-__ TO __PRESENT__

WAGE __$3.10 per hour__ REASON FOR LEAVING __WANT MORE RESPONSIBILITY__

COMPANY _____ ADDRESS _____ PHONE # _____

POSITION _____ SUPERVISOR _____ DATES WORKED: FROM _____ TO _____

WAGE _____ REASON FOR LEAVING _____

U.S. MILITARY:

SERVED? ☐YES ☒NO   ARE YOU A MEMBER OF AN ACTIVE RESERVE OR NATIONAL GUARD UNIT? ☐YES ☒NO

PHYSICAL:

ANY HEALTH OR PHYSICAL LIMITATIONS WHICH COULD AFFECT YOUR EMPLOYMENT? ☐YES ☒NO

IF ANY SUCH HEALTH OR PHYSICAL LIMITATIONS EXIST, PLEASE EXPLAIN __—__

DURING THE PAST 7 YEARS, HAVE YOU EVER BEEN CONVICTED OF A FELONY? ☐YES ☒NO   IF YES, DESCRIBE IN FULL _____

BONDING INFORMATION

1. Have you ever been short in your accounts in your present or past employment? . . ☐Yes ☒No
2. Has any company ever refused to issue or carry a Bond for you? . . . . ☐Yes ☒No
3. Have you ever been discharged from any employment? . . . . ☐Yes ☒No

I HEREBY BIND MYSELF, my heirs, executors and administrators to indemnify and keep indemnified and/or reimburse THE INSURANCE COMPANY for any and all loss, costs, and expenses incurred or sustained by it or for which, by reason of any act of mine, it may become liable under this bond or any other bond issued by it.

UNDER STATE LAW an employer may not require or demand any applicant for employment or prospective employment or any employee to submit to or take a polygraph, lie detector or similar test or examination as a condition of employment or continued employment. Any employer who violates this provision is guilty of a misdemeanor and subject to a fine not to exceed $100.

I CERTIFY THAT THIS INFORMATION IS ACCURATE AND COMPLETE. Giving incomplete or false information in an application for employment is a serious matter and is grounds for dismissal and forfeiture of related benefits. I hereby acknowledge notification, in compliance with the Fair Credit Reporting Act, that Gino's Inc. may request to procure information regarding my character, general reputation, personal characteristics or mode of living. Further information on the nature and scope of such inquiry, if one is made, will be made available upon request.

DATE __4/15/8-__ SIGNATURE __Michael B. O'Toole__

Please be sure to see the Manager when you've completed the application.

This application expires in 30 days.

In case of emergency phone __555-9379__

Interviewer or Reference Comments _____

We at Gino's offer Equal Employment Opportunities

Handle the Application Form with Care

As a job applicant, you will nearly always be asked to fill out the official application form of the firm. An **application form** asks the job applicant for information similar to that provided in a personal data sheet. Take this form seriously. Your qualifications may be judged by the care with which you complete it. Failure to follow directions or carelessness in completing the form has cost many applicants a chance at a job.

Interviewers use the completed form as a source of information from which to ask pertinent questions concerning education, experience, and personal data. So, information on the form should be complete and accurate. Your application form remains a permanent record in the files of the firm, and falsifying it, purposely or through carelessness, is a dangerous practice that can leave a bad mark on your record.

As a job applicant, you'll usually be asked to provide names of people to act as references. Courtesy demands that you ask such people in advance for permission to use their names. Double check the correct spelling of their names. Although a friend can be listed as a character reference, it is better to list people who know and will say honestly what you can do. The reference who can only say, "Well, he's a really nice guy" or "She's a pleasant girl" does the applicant little good. Above all, don't list a relative as a reference.

Examples of references include teachers, school principals, neighbors, members of the clergy, counselors, and employers. If you leave one job and go to another to better yourself, ask your former employer to serve as a reference for you. This is a good way to keep your reference list current.

Here are some tips to keep in mind as you prepare an application form:

♦ Carefully read everything on the application before starting to fill in the blanks.

You will avoid making mistakes and give the impression of being a careful worker. For names, dates, and correct spelling, refer to your personal data sheet.

♦ Neatly print on the form with a pen unless directions tell you otherwise.

♦ Answer every question that applies to you. For those that do not apply, write the word "none" or draw a line in the blank to show you didn't overlook it.

♦ Ask the person who gave you the application form any questions you may have, as, for example, whether you may use abbreviations.

♦ List all types of education, on-the-job training, or hobbies that have given you skills for any type of work for which you are applying.

♦ Accurately and completely describe your previous work experience, because employers prefer to hire applicants with skill, ability, and experience.

Be Sharp for the Interview

When you are called into the interviewer's office, move in with poise and confidence. If you receive an offer for a handshake, make it a firm one, but don't take the lead. Don't sit down until you are asked. When seated, try to sit up straight with both hands in front of you. When you speak, try to speak clearly and enunciate carefully. Take time to explain your statements so that your interviewer understands you fully. You may be expected to respond to a wide variety of questions about the business, yourself, and your future plans. So try to be prepared for questions such as the following:

♦ Why do you want to work for this company?

♦ Why do you think you would like working with us?

♦ Why do you think you will like retailing?

♦ What kind of work do you want?

♦ Would you rather sell or be in a nonselling position?

♦ Why do you think you are qualified for the job for which you are applying?

- What job would you like to have 5 years from today?
- What can you do for us?
- What salary do you expect?
- What leadership positions did you have in school?
- Have you belonged to school and community youth organizations or church groups?
- Do you have any health problems?

The personal qualities that most employers look for are sincerity and earnestness. They also look for a degree of confidence. But remember, too much confidence may seem like pride to many people. You may find the following suggestions helpful: Be pleasant and friendly during the interview. Show that you are interested in learning and in a future in retailing. Stress your strong points but do not hide your weaknesses. Emphasize your reliability and dependability. Last, recognize when the interview is at an end, thank the interviewer, and leave promptly.

A survey of employers showed that the ten leading reasons given for rejecting job applicants after the job interview were:

1. Little interest or poor reason for wanting a job
2. Applicant has a past history of job hopping
3. Inability of applicant to communicate during job interview
4. Poor health record
5. Immaturity (other than chronological age)
6. Sloppy personal appearance
7. Poor manners and irritating mannerisms
8. Unpleasant personality
9. Lack of job-related skills
10. Job application form poorly filled out

Be Prepared for Tests

Some large firms give tests in addition to interviews. Often, tests of basic arithmetic are used to eliminate those who are weak in this skill. Tests of clerical ability, such as number matching, may be given to applicants for nonselling positions. Tests of "manual dexterity" (the ability to use one's hands skillfully) are sometimes used in selecting people for positions such as checkers, packers, and markers. A few firms use tests to determine aptitude for leadership.

Do the best you can on such tests because they are another way in which the employer is evaluating you. Remember that your interview, personal data sheet, job application form, and test results are the ways you have of presenting yourself to the employer.

A Good Last Impression

Once the interview and testing procedure have been completed, you have an opportunity to make a good last impression. When the interview is over, rise and shake hands with the interviewer and express your appreciation for this opportunity. On your way out of the office, also thank the receptionist.

Within a day or two of your interview, write a short, sincere thank-you letter or note to your prospective employer to express your appreciation.

Trade Talk

Define each term and use it in a sentence.

Application form	Letter of application
Blind ads	Personal data sheet

Can You Answer These?

1. Why is it particularly wise to use a letter of application?
2. What are the six tips for preparing an application form?
3. Is it wise to have friends help you find a job in retailing? Why?
4. What kinds of questions may be asked of you during a job interview?
5. List several kinds of unsuitable job-interview behaviors.

6. What are the most common reasons that employers reject job applicants?

Problems

1. Rule a form similar to the following. Check the help-wanted advertisements in your local newspaper to locate job opportunities in retailing. Then list the current full- and part-time openings for a person like yourself and the wages currently being offered for beginners of your age and experience. If wages are not listed, indicate this with an (**X**) symbol. Many job listings may not include wage information.

Job Opening	Beginning Wage

2. Select one job in Problem 1 that would be consistent with your career goals and prepare a personal data sheet that you could use to apply for the job. Be sure to include the following information:

Name	Education
Address	Experience
Telephone number	Activities and
Career goal	interests
	References

Getting Paid

CHAPTER

6

Communications & Human Relations

Economics & Marketing

Merchandising

Selling & Technology

Advertising & Display

Operations & Management

Maria Martinez was looking forward to Friday because it was payday. This was indeed a special day for Maria because for the first time she would receive a paycheck.

As Maria slowly opened the envelope, her mind wandered for a second and focused on the new sweater and stereo record that she wanted to buy. As she finally got the envelope open, she noticed that she had both a check and a paycheck stub. "Hmmm," she said to herself, "Is this complicated—what do all these numbers mean? Why doesn't my check include all the money I thought I had earned? It's more than $25 short!" Maria then began to recall some of the things that she had learned in school, and again when she was hired, about federal and state taxes, social security, the various wage plans, and how pay is computed.

This chapter focuses on these and similar items related to getting paid.

How Retail Employees Are Paid

Several methods are used to pay retail employees. These methods vary according to the type of business, the kind of work done, quantity and quality of work, and the amount of responsibility carried. For example, the amount of money earned by those engaged in sales work usually depends on how much they sell. In merchandising businesses, employees who don't sell directly to customers are usually paid an hourly, weekly, or monthly wage. Some retail employees, such as waiters or waitresses, receive a salary plus tips.

Straight Salary

A beginner like Maria is likely to be paid a straight salary, which is usually re-

Maria Martinez was happy to receive her first paycheck but wondered what all the deductions were. Kip Peticolas/Fundamental Photographs

ceived in the form of a check every week or every other week. A **straight salary** means being paid a fixed number of dollars an hour for a fixed number of hours a week—for example, $3.50 per hour for a 40-hour week. So, if Maria works 40 hours a week at $3.50 per hour, her earnings amount to $140. If she works more than 40 hours, she may earn 1½ times her regular rate for each hour over 40 hours. Suppose she worked 48 hours one week. The example below shows how her wages would be figured:

40 hours at $3.50 an hour	$140
8 hours at $5.25 an hour (1½ x $3.50)	42
Total week's earnings	$182

Most nonselling employees—and many salespeople— are paid by the straight-sal-

ary method. Similarly, Maria and many beginning employees in retailing start out by receiving the federal minimum wage. The **federal minimum wage,** which is covered by the Federal Labor Standards Act, is the lowest amount that businesses are allowed to pay their employees. This federal law also established 40 hours per week as the maximum number of hours that people can work at their basic wage rates. For any additional time worked, a worker must be paid time and a half. Most states also have minimum wage laws. These laws apply to firms who do business within a state (mostly small firms) that do not come under the federal law.

Straight Commission

Some salespeople are not paid a salary at all. They are paid entirely on commission. In retailing, a **commission** is a percentage of the total amount of sales that the employee makes during the employee's pay period. If, for example, your commission is 5 percent of sales and you sell $8,000 worth of merchandise or services in a week, your total income for the week is $400. Commission rates vary, but a rate of between 5 and 8 percent is common when that is the only pay you receive. This is known as **straight commission**. Straight commission selling occurs most often in furniture stores, appliance stores, automobile dealerships, and other establishments that carry high-priced merchandise. Insurance agents and real estate salespeople are examples of those in service businesses who usually sell on straight commission.

Salary Plus Commission

As an incentive to increase sales, many salespeople are paid a straight salary plus a commission. Although commission rates vary, 1 percent is most common for merchandising employees who also receive a straight salary.

Assume that a salesperson's regular salary is $150 a week plus 1 percent commission and that the salesperson sells merchandise or services amounting to $1,500 during the week. The example below shows how the salary is figured:

Regular salary	$150
Commission (1 percent of $1,500 total sales)	15
Total week's earnings	$165

Commission and Drawing Account

Some employees prefer a straight commission because the more productive they are, the higher their income (and some straight-commission salespeople earn very high salaries). Others, however, don't like the "feast or famine" uncertainty of a straight commission. They prefer a variation known as the **commission and drawing account**. Since sales—and therefore commissions—vary, salespeople cannot always plan on a certain income each pay period. To overcome this uncertainty, the firm allows salespeople to draw a certain amount each pay period—for example, $150 a week. This amount is then deducted from their commissions.

For example, suppose a salesperson draws $150 each week for one month and sales are $8,000 at 8 percent commission. The example below shows what the calculations would be at the end of the month:

Commission (8 percent of $8,000 sales for 4 weeks)	$640
Drawings ($150 per week for 4 weeks)	600
Firm owes salesperson	$ 40

If, on the other hand, sales were only $4,000, the calculations would be somewhat different, as follows:

Drawings ($150 per week for 4 weeks)	$600
Commission (8 percent of $4,000 sales for 4 weeks)	320
Salesperson owes firm	$280

The $280 the salesperson owes the company will be carried over to the next month and deducted from commission.

Quota

Under the **quota**, salespeople are paid a straight salary but are also given a bonus for sales exceeding a predetermined quota. The quota is set by the store management. Salespeople get a percentage of all sales above that quota. Suppose a salesperson's quota is $4,000 and the bonus is 2 percent. If the salesperson sells $4,800 worth of merchandise, he or she draws a bonus on the $800 above the quota, or $16 (2 percent of $800). Of course, the salesperson gets a regular salary, too.

Premium Money

Sometimes salespeople are paid an extra amount for selling a particular item that is hard to sell. This extra amount is sometimes called **premium money** (PM) and is paid in addition to other compensation. (PMs are also called "spiffs" or pin money.)

HOSPITAL AND SURGICAL EXPENSE BENEFITS

A day for Semi — Private room and board for up to   **70**   days, for each period of disability

$500.00   Maximum for other covered hospital services plus   **75%** of the excess

$500.00   Maximum for emergency care as an out patient plus   **75%** of the excess

$300.00   Maximum for diagnostic x-ray and laboratory

Maximum surgical benefit according to the schedule of operations. **reasonable & customary charges for your area.**

MATERNITY BENEFITS

Maximum for hospital expenses plus for normal delivery. **Treated as any other illness**

See Item A on reverse side.

MAJOR MEDICAL BENEFITS

Semi — Private room and board of medical expenses in excess of the $100 deductible up to $250,000.00 maximum.

BENEFITS IF YOU ARE DISABLED

You will be eligible for a monthly income of   from Social Security.

Your Group Life Insurance, up to $7500.00   , may be used to provide a monthly income if you become permanently and totally disabled before age 60. A number of optional income plans are available. For example, your insurance would provide approximately $125.00 per month for   5   years. The remainder of your insurance, if any, would be continued as paid up insurance.

The vested portion of your Profit Sharing account will be paid to you in a lump sum or you may choose one of several other methods of payment. Any unvested portion will be paid to you at the rate of 10% annually until paid in full as long as you remain disabled.

The value of your Pension accrued to date will be held for you until your Normal Retirement Date.

See Item B on reverse side.

BENEFITS IF YOU DIE BEFORE RETIREMENT

$2500	Basic Life Insurance		Additional Accidental	
$5000	Supplemental Life insurance		Death Insurance	
–0–	Pension plan death benefit		Basic	$2500
$7898.43	Profit Sharing account		Supplemental	$5000
$ 255	Social Security lump sum benefit			
$1563.43	Total		Total	$7500

BENEFITS IF YOU LIVE TO RETIREMENT

Your Normal Retirement Date   **12-31-97**

Based on your **1979**   rate of compensation your monthly benefit at retirement is estimated to be

$200.00   From your Pension Plan.

$200.00   From your Profit Sharing account.

$300.00   From Social Security.

$700.00   Total estimated monthly income.

See Item C on reverse side.

In addition monthly benefits of up to may be payable to your spouse from Social Security.

YOUR PROFIT SHARING ACCOUNT

Profit Sharing

New participants are taken into the Employees' Trust as of December 31 of each year. If you have been in continuous employment for one full year on a December 31, you beome a participant as of that date.

Employed   **6-10-72**   You became a participant on December 31, 19 **73**

To December 31, 19 **78**

Accumulated share of Company Profit Sharing contributions	$3,979.15
Accumulated gain or loss from investments, earnings and forfeitures	1,298.04
	$5,277.19

For the year 19**79**

Your share of Company Profit Sharing contributions	$1,495.92
Gain or loss from investments, earnings and forfeitures	1,125.32
	$7,898.43

Your vested interest is   **70**   %

The amount of the premium for each sale varies—from as little as 10 cents to $200 or more. Premium money gives salespeople an incentive to sell slow-moving merchandise or merchandise that may take an extra effort on the part of the salesperson, such as initialed jewelry that the salesperson must take time to engrave. Sometimes this plan is discouraged by retailers to avoid the risk that customers might be sold something they don't really want, leading to loss of the customer's goodwill.

Fringe Benefits

In addition to wages paid to the employee, retailers also offer several benefits called **fringe benefits.** These are advantages that the company provides for its employees in addition to financial compensation for work. The number of benefits retailers offer varies from one retail establishment to another. Generally speaking, the larger the firm, the more benefits offered. Benefits should be counted as a part of your total income. These benefits may include the following:

◆ Employee discounts of from 10 to 20 percent on merchandise and services
◆ Medical, dental, and hospitalization insurance
◆ Paid vacations (usually 1 week's vacation after 1 year of employment and up to 4 weeks' vacation after several years of employment)
◆ Group insurance plans whereby life insurance can be purchased by employees at a lower cost than they could obtain elsewhere
◆ Retirement plans whereby the firm and the employee contribute to a fund that will provide a monthly income upon retirement
◆ Worker's compensation and unemployment insurance as required by law
◆ Employee cafeterias where food can be obtained at reasonable prices
◆ Social, recreational, and educational activities of various kinds
◆ Uniforms and work clothes

How Pay Is Computed

The amount of money you earn on your job is called **gross pay.** This is the amount earned before anything is subtracted from your check. There are always some deductions from your pay, however. Once all these deductions have been subtracted from your gross pay, you realize your take-home pay, or net pay.

Income Tax Deduction

There is a federal law that requires employers to hold back some of each employee's wages for payment of income tax. This is called **withholding tax.** When Maria started to work, she filled out a W-4 form—an Employee's Withholding Allowance Certificate. This form let her employer know how much of her pay must be withheld for federal income taxes. The amount of federal income tax withheld depends upon the amount of money earned and the number of tax exemptions claimed. **Tax exemptions** are allowances for people who rely on the wage earner for food, clothing, and shelter. Every wage earner can claim one exemption for himself or herself. Maria could claim only herself as an exemption.

Anyone who has an income of more than $2,050 a year must file a federal income tax return. This return must be filed by April 15 of the year following that in which the income was earned. Shortly after January 1, wage earners receive from their employers a W-2 form which tells how much they earned and how much tax was withheld. Taxpayers with incomes lower than $2,050 a year receive a refund for the taxes that were withheld from their pay. However, to get these taxes refunded, the wage earner must file a federal income tax return. The money is not refunded automatically. Because Maria started her new job in October, her income for the year was less than $2,050. So, Maria should file a federal income tax return to receive a refund for the taxes that were withheld from her October, No-

REGULAR PAY	SALARY CONTINUATION	OVERTIME	OTHER PAY	AMOUNT	GROSS PAY
140.00					140.00

HRS. PAID	HRS. NOT PD.	HRS. PAID	HRS. NOT PD.	HRS. PAID	HRS. WORKED					FOR PERIOD ENDING
40.0										09 12

FED. WITHHOLDING	SOC. SECURITY	STATE	WITHHOLDING	STATE	DISAB./UNEMP.	CITY	WITHHOLDING	TAXES
15.30	8.58	AZ	1.53					

MEDICAL	GROUP LIFE INS.	LONG TERM DISAB.	PENSION	CREDIT UNION	STOCK PURCHASE	BENEFIT PLANS
3.00	FREE					

				OTHER DEDUCT	111.59 NET PAY

DESCRIPTION	AMOUNT	DESCRIPTION	AMOUNT		
012-34-5678 SOCIAL SECURITY NO.	140.00 GROSS EARNINGS	15.30 FEDERAL WITHHOLDING TAX	BOND BALANCE	YEAR-TO-DATE	
612920 CHECK NUMBER	8.58 SOC. SECURITY	1.53 STATE WITH. TAX	CITY WITH. TAX	PENSION SINCE 12-1	

This is the stub from Maria Martinez's first paycheck. A paycheck stub shows all the deductions that affect the amount of a person's take-home pay.

vember, and December paychecks. Many cities and states also have an income tax, and employers are required to withhold income for these taxes also.

Social Security Tax Deduction

In addition to income tax, Maria and all other people employed in retailing have to pay social security tax, which is also referred to as **FICA** (Federal Insurance Contributions Act). **Social security** is a federal program that provides cash payments to workers who retire or become disabled or to the families of deceased workers. Both employees and employers contribute to the fund. The sum of money that is taken out of each employee's paycheck is matched by the employer and sent to the federal government.

Other Deductions

The number of other deductions from your paycheck will usually depend on your wishes. If you decide to participate in the company's retirement plan when you become eligible, a certain amount may be taken from your paycheck for your retirement fund. Whether or not you take out medical or life insurance is usually up to you. Most employees think that it is a bargain and choose to have the cost of the insurance deducted from their pay by their employer. If you belong to a union, you may ask your employer to deduct your union dues from your check. Many companies also offer automatic savings by deducting a specified amount to purchase U.S. Savings Bonds or by depositing money directly into the employee's personal savings account. Some employees have the contributions that they make to various community groups, such as the United Fund, deducted regularly from their paychecks.

Once you've got a job and received a few paychecks, you might find yourself catching your breath and wondering, "Where do I go from here?" That's a good question to ask yourself. But on a new job, your most important concern should be to get a good start and to build on your career plan. Some ideas to help you do this are given in the next chapter. If you use them, you'll probably find that you have answered the question, "Where do I go from here?"

Trade Talk

Define each term and use it in a sentence.

Commission
Commission and
  drawing account
FICA
Fringe benefits
Federal minimum
  wage
Gross pay
Premium money
  (PM)

Quota
Social security
Straight commission
Straight salary
Take-home pay
Tax exemptions
Withholding tax

Can You Answer These?

1. Why do some employees prefer the straight-commission method of compensation?
2. What commission rate is most common for employees compensated by the salary-plus-commission method?
3. What items may be included in the fringe benefits a company offers to its employees?
4. What federal taxes are required to be subtracted from your paycheck?
5. List five examples of possible deductions that can be made from a paycheck and that would therefore decrease take-home pay.

Problems

1. Rule a form similar to the following. In the left column, write the letter of each of the following types of businesses: (0) supermarket, (a) department store, (b) women's wear or menswear, (c) service business, (d) life insurance agency, and (e) furniture store. In the remaining columns, give the most common method of paying employees in each type of business, the reasons for your answers, and your source of information.

Type of Store	Methods of Compensation	Reasons	Sources of Information
Example: (0)	Straight salary	Emphasis on self-service	Manager of Atlantic Super-market

2. Pete Hilzen, a salesman for a local car dealer, is paid on a salary-plus-commission basis, with an agreement that he can draw against future commissions. His salary is $225 per week plus a commission of 1.5 percent on sales. Last week, Pete sold cars worth $26,298 and drew $250 against his commission. On a separate sheet of paper, make the computations necessary to answer the following questions: (a) How much was Pete's gross pay? (b) How much did he actually earn in commissions? (c) Did his draw exceed the commission he actually earned? (d) Will any adjustment be necessary in his pay next week? If so, what is it?

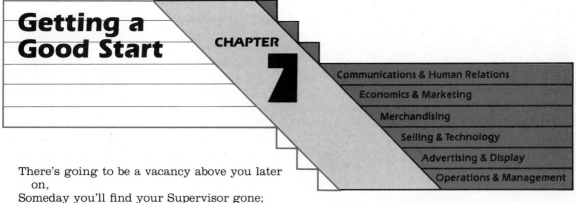

Getting a Good Start

CHAPTER 7

Communications & Human Relations
Economics & Marketing
Merchandising
Selling & Technology
Advertising & Display
Operations & Management

There's going to be a vacancy above you later
  on,
Someday you'll find your Supervisor gone;
Are you growing big enough, when this shall
  be the case,

To quit the job you're doing now and step into place?
Tomorrow's not so far away, nor is the goal you seek;
Today you should be training for the work you'll do next week.
The bigger job is just ahead, each day new changes brings,
Suppose that job were vacant now, could you take charge of things?
It's not enough to know enough to hold your place today;
It's not enough to do enough to scarcely earn your pay;
Someday there'll be a vacancy with greater tasks to do.
Will you be ready for the place if it is offered you?

—Anonymous

Setting the stage for a possible promotion begins with the first day on the job. Use the suggestions in this chapter as guides to help you get a good start and help build your career plan.

Starting Out

Start out by being sure you arrive at the job on time. If you work for a large company, check to see which door you should enter, and—if necessary—sign in. When you arrive at work, check that you are dressed in the same way as your coworkers. Unless you have been told something different, go directly to the person who hired you, being certain to arrive a few minutes ahead of time.

Handling Mistakes

During the first few weeks on a job, almost everything will be new to you. And you are bound to make mistakes because there are so many things to learn. However, to make as few mistakes as possible, try to listen carefully to instructions from your supervisor. Ask questions if you don't understand what is expected of you. If you do make a mistake, report it to your supervisor. Try to learn from your mistakes so that you don't make them a second time. But most of all, don't get discouraged. Smile, you'll catch on in a while!

Keeping Busy

Often, a supervisor can't tell exactly how long it will take to do a job. Sometimes, as a new employee, you'll complete jobs before your supervisor returns. When this happens, observe the work that experienced employees perform, and as you "learn the ropes," keep your eyes open for work that needs to be done. As you find time, learn to accomplish this work without being told. A supervisor will learn how much work you can do and will assign it as she or he gets to know you better.

Employers do expect a full day's work for a full day's pay. A supervisor will expect you to think for yourself and show an interest in your work by keeping busy.

Getting Acquainted with Coworkers and Learning Company Rules

Your supervisor may be too busy to introduce you to every worker, so don't hesitate to introduce yourself. However, while you'll want to be friendly with coworkers, it's important that you don't waste time visiting on the job.

If you haven't already done so, you'll need to learn about company rules so that you perform as you are expected to by your employer. Chapter 32 contains a discussion of company rules and policies that you should learn about.

Accepting Responsibility

You are usually hired to work a predetermined number of hours each week. Sometimes, though, there are a number of small jobs remaining at the end of your work period that you can do without taking much time or effort. If you leave without doing them, your supervisor probably won't complain. But if you stay just a few minutes, finish the job, and leave a clean work area, you can be sure your efforts will be noticed. Your supervisor will know that you're really interested in your work and will be glad you were hired. Even after

Getting to know your coworkers can be fun—and informative. *J. Schweiker/ Photo Researchers, Inc.*

the first day, your supervisor may realize that you're a good worker and may be somebody to look at for possible promotion!

Developing Good Work Habits

It's a good idea to ask yourself each day during your first few weeks on the job what new things you learned to do, what tasks you learned to do better, and which ones still need improvement. (A "task" is something you are assigned to do as a part of your job.) Asking for an opinion or for help will show that you are interested in doing your job well and that you are anxious to please. It will also encourage some supervisors to help you advance to a better job.

Remember that for the first few days, or even for the first few weeks on a new job, you are investing your time and your employer's time, money, and effort in training you. You may have to learn a great deal before you can turn out a full day's work that's equal to the work of most experienced employees. Also, as you do your job, keep in mind that you're building your reputation as a worker.

Building on Your Career Plan

In Unit 1, you completed a career-plan project. You learned more about yourself, your interests, your aptitudes, your goals, and some of the careers in retailing that might help you to fulfill your goals.

At the end of Unit 3, you'll be asked to continue building on this career-plan project by taking a more in-depth look at one of the careers in retailing. And the information in Unit 3 will help you accomplish this. But before you're ready to do that, you'll first want to examine some of the employment and promotional opportunities available in the total field of retailing.

It's an employee's responsibility to keep merchandise fresh and appealing. Jane Hamilton-Merritt

The information in the remainder of this chapter enables you to do that.

Learn about Employment Opportunities

Approximately 17 percent of all businesses in the United States are retailing firms. With 14 million employees retailing is the third largest industry in the nation.

The latest Department of Labor figures show that the field of retailing is growing in the number of people employed at a rate of about 4 percent each year. This trend is expected to continue in retailing as well as in the rapidly growing related service businesses which include firms that sell services such as travel, hotel and lodging, and other personal services.

Employment by Selected Types of Retailing Firms. In comparing retail employment in earlier years with that in recent years (see following table), government statistics show that the largest growth has taken place in food (65 percent). The increase of convenience food stores accounted for much of the growth in the food store area. Employment in variety stores has decreased by 17.4 percent. Other areas showing rapid growth in employment are women's apparel stores, furniture stores, and department stores.

Much of the growth in the food service career area is a result of the increasing popularity of franchising. Think of the number of Burger King, Wendy's, Arby's, and Long John Silver restaurants that you have seen spring up in the past several years.

Employment by Large Companies. The number of retail establishments has not increased a great deal during the past 50 years. In part, this is because firms have increased in size. On page 53 are the names of the 20 largest retailers in rank

RETAIL TRADE EMPLOYMENT: 1967–1980

	1967	1980	Percentage Change
Total retail trade	10,081,000	15,005,000	48.8
Department stores	1,324,000	1,730,700	30.7
Variety stores	313,000	266,500	−17.4
Food stores	1,405,000	2,318,700	65.0
Men's and boys' apparel stores	114,000	137,800	20.9
Women's ready-to-wear stores	252,000	352,900	40.0
Furniture stores	271,000	365,100	34.7
Household appliances	84,000	86,700	3.2
Eating and drinking places	2,191,000	4,749,000	16.8
Drugstores	426,000	518,300	21.7

Sources: U.S. Department of Commerce, *U.S. Industrial Outlook, 1977 with Projections to 1985* (Washington, D.C.: U.S. Government Printing Office, 1977), p. 212, and U.S. Department of Labor, *Employment and Earnings* (Washington, D.C.: U.S. Government Printing Office, June 1980), p. 56.

order by sales together with the number of employers and dollars in sales.

Employment In Small Firms. Approximately 85 percent of all retail firms in the United States are independently owned. These stores account for more than 60 percent of the total retail sales. A little less

THE 20 LARGEST RETAILERS

Rank	Company	Sales	Number of Employees
1	Sears, Roebuck and Co. (Chicago)	$17,514,252,000	424,000
2	Safeway Stores (Oakland, Calif.)	13,717,861,000	148,876
3	K-mart (Troy, Mich.)	12,858,585,000	242,983
4	J.C. Penney Company, Inc. (New York)	11,274,000,000	206,000
5	Kroger (Cincinnati)	9,029,315,000	69,038
6	Great Atlantic & Pacific Tea Company (Montvale, N.J.)	7,469,659,000	72,000
7	F.W. Woolworth (New York)	6,785,000,000	142,800
8	Lucky Stores (Dublin, Calif.)	5,815,927,000	63,000
9	Federated Department Store (Cincinnati)	5,806,442,000	112,500
10	Montgomery Ward (Chicago)	5,251,085,000	135,400
11	Winn-Dixie Stores (Jacksonville, Fla.)	4,930,538,000	58,700
12	City Products (Des Plaines, Ill.)	3,918,800,000	55,600
13	Southland (Dallas)	3,856,222,000	44,300
14	American Stores (Wilmington, Del.)	3,786,332,000	62,660
15	Jewel Companies (Chicago)	3,764,266,000	33,400
16	Dayton Hudson (Minneapolis)	3,384,849,000	39,000
17	May Department Stores (St. Louis)	2,977,190,000	71,000
18	Albertson's (Boise)	2,673,848,000	25,323
19	Carter Hawley Hale Stores (Los Angeles)	2,408,028,000	54,000
20	Grand Union (Elmwood Park, N.J.)	2,398,944,000	32,976

Source: *Fortune*, July 14, 1980, pp. 154–155. The cities shown in parentheses are where the headquarters of the companies are located.

than 95 percent of these stores employ fewer than 20 people. About two-thirds of the almost 2 million retail firms have fewer than four employees. Some people prefer to work in a small firm in hopes that someday they might own their own businesses. They feel a special pride in "being their own boss." Others choose to start their retailing careers with small firms because they want the opportunity to learn about all aspects of the business almost immediately.

Retailing offers more opportunities for ownership than do other lines of business. However, it should also be noted that the failure rate in retailing is high.

If your career goal is to go into business for yourself, study the field and get good practical experience to help cut down the chances of failure.

Equal Employment Opportunities. Retailing continues to be one of the career fields with the greatest number of opportunities for women—nearly 48 percent of all retail employees are women. The percentage of women employed in different types of retail firms varies from 16 percent among automotive dealers and service stations to 68 percent in apparel and accessory and general retail merchandise firms. In addition, there is a higher proportion of executives to employees in retailing than in many other fields, therefore there are more opportunities for promotion.

Learn about Opportunities for Promotion

Opportunities for promotion are available for both men and women. Approximately 10 percent of all retail employees serve in a supervisory capacity. As retailing continues to expand, the number of management positions will continue to grow. So whether you wish to own your own business or to become a supervisor, buyer, manager, or salesperson, there are plenty of opportunities in the field of retailing. There are also many different career paths

you can follow as you pursue your career goal.

In this unit, you've read about most of the things you need to know for entering employment in the retail field—getting the job, getting paid, and getting a good start on the job. In the next unit, you'll be given some general suggestions on how you can get promoted in your chosen retailing career. And you'll learn more about the retail sales area and the different types of occupations in those areas.

Can You Answer These?

1. Why shouldn't new workers be discouraged if they make some mistakes?
2. List several other items that are important to remember when starting a new job.
3. What is the annual growth rate for retailing?
4. What is the main reason that 90 percent of businesses fail?

Problems

1. Rule a form similar to the following. Then, visit supervisors in a retail business and ask them to decide what they feel are the important recommendations in getting a good start in a job. Record your answers on your form.

Business Name and Supervisor	Criteria Cited

2. Rule a form similar to the following. Then obtain a copy of *Survey of Current Business* or *Occupational Outlook Handbook*. Select five occupations in the field of retailing and, using either of the books, try to find the number of people currently employed in the occupations and expected employment growth. Record your answers on your form.

Occupation	Number of Employees	Expected Growth

Retailing Case

During the summer you are selling moderate-priced shoes in a shoe store located in a busy shopping center. On the average, you work a 40-hour week. You have been working at the store for 2 months on a straight salary of $150 per week and have sold about $1,000 worth of merchandise per week for the past 2 weeks. There is every reason to believe that you will maintain or perhaps increase that amount of sales. The manager asks you to choose between a straight commission of 8 percent of sales and a salary of $150 per week with an extra 1 percent commission on your sales.

1. What choice would you make? Explain the reasons for your decision in a paragraph.
2. List some additional information you may want to ask your employer.

Working with People

Before Brenda Slater was interviewed for the job of salesclerk, the receptionist asked her to complete an application form. While she was completing the form, Brenda realized that she didn't have all the information she needed. She couldn't remember the dates of the part-time jobs she'd held or the telephone numbers and correct addresses of the people she planned to use as references. So Brenda decided to leave those questions unanswered. When she was interviewed, the job interviewer, Rita Sanchez, asked Brenda for a copy of her résumé, or personal data sheet. Brenda told Miss Sanchez that she didn't have a résumé.

1. Identify the true problem.
2. What are the important facts to be considered in this problem?
3. List several solutions to this problem.
4. Evaluate the possible results of each solution.
5. Which solution do you recommend? Why?

Project 2: Determining the Difference between Gross and Net Pay

Your Project Goal

Given the opportunity to interview an employee in the accounting department of any retail business, determine the monthly deductions of three levels of employees to find the difference between gross and net income.

Procedure

1. Contact a person employed in the accounting department of any retail business. Request permission and make an appointment to interview this person.
2. Before you conduct the interview, on separate sheets of paper, rule three forms like the one on page 56.
3. Take these three forms with you when you conduct your interview. Cross out any deduction categories that don't apply and add any others that do.
4. When you return from your interview, add all the deductions to find the total. Then subtract the total deductions from the gross income, which will give you the net income per month. Do this for each form.

| Job Title: _____ |
| Gross income per month (a) $_____ |

Deductions:

Federal income tax	$_____
State income tax	_____
Local income tax	_____
FICA (social security tax)	_____
Union dues	_____
Medical insurance	_____
Life insurance	_____
Total (b)	_____

Net income
(subtract b from a) $_____

5. Was the figure for total deductions for each job title different or the same? If it was different, how do you explain this? Did the total amount deducted vary according to the gross income for each job title? If so, explain.

6. Write a short report summarizing your results and attach your forms to the report.

Evaluation

You will be rated on the completeness of your three forms and the reasons you gave to explain the differences among the total deductions for each job title.

Advancing in Retailing

Getting Promoted

CHAPTER

8

Communications & Human Relations

Economics & Marketing

Merchandising

Selling & Technology

Advertising & Display

Operations & Management

After about 6 months of working in the catalog department for Boylan's, Maria was assigned to the apparel and accessories department. Louise, her friend who had encouraged her to apply for a job, was also employed in that department. Recently, Louise has been coming to work late. Her store manager doesn't seem to notice it, but Maria and her coworkers do. Louise spends time explaining to them why she is late. Several times during the week, Louise also tells them about her personal problems with her mother's illness, her boyfriend, and her finances. Maria and her coworkers are becoming upset with Louise's problems and the way she is avoiding responsibility.

Upon her graduation in June, Maria was promoted to assistant department manager. One of the employees who reported to Maria was Louise. Louise asked the store manager why she didn't get promoted. What do you think the store manager told Louise? What do you think Maria learned about getting promoted that Louise

didn't learn? To what positions might Maria be promoted next?

In this chapter, we'll look at avenues of promotion and the competencies that you must develop for promotions to higher-level positions in retailing. We'll also look at the scope of retail employment and at some of the jobs in retailing that you might want to consider.

Avenues of Promotion

Maria's new position as an assistant apparel and accessories department manager was her third position at Boylan's. Being transferred out of the catalog department to a merchandising division job was the first step in her career ladder. The catalog department job was an entry-level position used by the management of Boylan's to identify potential candidates for promotion.

In general, jobs may be labeled as entry-level positions, career sustaining positions, specialization positions, and entrepreneurial positions. But a job that is an entry-level position for one employee may be a career sustaining position (lifetime job) for another, depending on the individual's career goal.

Avenues of promotion vary widely among industries and among stores and service establishments within an industry. For example, in the food marketing industry a national supermarket chain lists six steps in a career ladder ranging from first level positions as general grocery clerks, front-end cashier, and so on up to district manager. On the other hand, an authority on the finance and credit industry reports five levels beginning with various kinds of clerks, through two levels of tellers and several types of managers to senior management positions. Thus there seems to be no agreement on position levels among the retail industries. And, of course, there is little, if any, agreement among the firms within any segment of the retail industry.

In Maria's case, when she plans the course of her career, it will be her responsibility to identify the possible lines of promotion within Boylan's and other firms in which she may be interested. In addition she needs to know the answers to other questions such as, "Does the firm promote from within or does it employ outsiders when filling higher level positions?"

Competencies Needed for Promotion

If Maria was like most workers who get promoted from entry-level jobs, she could have been promoted for a number of reasons. Research has shown that the most common reason people get promoted is because of their ability to perform their entry-level jobs in an efficient and effective manner.

Entry-Level Positions

To succeed in an entry-level position, you must have the following important competencies as well as those described in Chapter 7.

♦ Ability to see a task through to completion (that is, to get the job done!)
♦ Ability to work with people
♦ Ability to listen and follow directions
♦ Ability to follow company policies
♦ Ability to stay with a problem and solve it
♦ Ability to work rapidly and accurately
♦ Devotion to job, enthusiasm, initiative, and a positive outlook on life
♦ Adaptability, honesty, loyalty to employer
♦ Willingness to stay in the field of retailing
♦ Knowledge of product or service features and how to present related selling points to customers
♦ Ability to assume responsibility

How you can acquire these and other vital competencies is discussed throughout this book.

Higher-Level Positions

If you want to be promoted higher up the retail career ladder, there are additional competencies that you'll need. These are:

♦ Ability to work (produce) at a consistently high level
♦ Adaptability to change and ability to work in difficult situations
♦ Supervisory skills, including ability to manage time and organize work so that things get done
♦ Skill in using various problem-solving techniques
♦ Skill in using oral and written communications
♦ Ability to get along and work with personnel employed in top management
♦ Potential for assuming additional responsibility
♦ Personal integrity

Career Opportunities in the Divisions of Retailing

In the field of retailing, jobs are often classified according to the functions that are performed in the various divisions of general merchandising retail firms. The most common classifications by function are:

♦ Merchandising
♦ Sales promotion
♦ Store operations
♦ Finance and control
♦ Personnel

Merchandising

The person responsible for all activities related to the buying and selling of goods is the **general merchandise manager.** Buyers and department managers, who are also key merchandising personnel, report to the merchandise manager. In addition to buying merchandise for sale, the **buyer** is in charge of generating sales, establishing prices, and estimating sales and profits. An important part of the buyer's job is stock control—seeing that merchandise is available in the right style, quality, and quantity. Helping the buyer are stock supervisors, salespeople, and stock clerks. Merchandising people primarily work with people, data, and ideas.

Sales Promotion

Good sales promotion attracts consumers to the business, helps salespeople overcome sales resistance, and builds goodwill. Sales promotion people—copywriters, artists, decorators, and display managers, among others—create and supervise advertising, plan the promotion of special events, and build window and in-

The buyer is responsible for ensuring that merchandise is available in the right style, quality, and quantity. Rhoda Galyn

terior displays. They work mostly with data, ideas, and different kinds of sales promotion materials and equipment.

Store Operations

The operations division maintains the business's buildings and equipment and obtains and distributes supplies. This division also operates such facilities as the warehouse, stockroom, restaurants, lounges, gift-wrapping stations, delivery services, adjustment desks, and parking lots. Receiving clerks, packers, stock clerks, assistant stockroom managers, and delivery clerks work for the operations division, which is headed by the **store superintendent**. Store operations people work mostly with data and equipment.

Finance and Control

The finance and control division employs bookkeepers, accountants, cashiers, billing clerks, file clerks, credit interviewers, office-machine operators, and other clerical personnel. Their work can be grouped into the following three major activities:

♦ *Credit and collections,* including the granting of credit to customers, billing, charging customers, and collecting delinquent accounts
♦ *Accounting,* including recording past performance, maintaining the payroll, and keeping track of the firm's liabilities (amounts owed by the firm)
♦ *Control,* including preparing budgets, maintaining inventory records, receiving and paying out money, and preparing financial reports

This division is headed by a **controller** (also known as a comptroller) who is in charge of all fiscal and accounting operations. People in this division must have a high aptitude for working with data.

Personnel

People in the personnel division work with the company's employees. They recruit and interview job applicants and develop training programs. They establish pay scales, administer pension and welfare plans, and maintain employee records. The jobs in this division include those of personnel clerk, recruiter, and personnel manager. People in the personnel division work mostly with people and data.

The Scope of Retail Employment

There is an incredibly wide variety of employment opportunities in retailing, a fact that few people, even those employed in retailing, realize. Here are some of the categories of retailing employment opportunities:

♦ Advertising and Display Services
♦ Apparel and Accessories
♦ Automobiles, Recreational, and Agricultural Vehicles and Accessories
♦ Finance and Credit Services
♦ Floristry, Farm, and Garden Supplies
♦ Food Marketing
♦ Food Service
♦ General Merchandise Retailing
♦ Hardware and Building Materials
♦ Home Furnishing
♦ Hotel, Motel, and Lodging Services
♦ Insurance
♦ Personal and Business Services
♦ Petroleum
♦ Real Estate
♦ Recreation
♦ Transportation and Travel

Career Opportunities in Five Retailing Areas

The five areas of retailing that employ the largest number of people are:

1. general merchandise
2. apparel and accessories
3. automotive and petroleum products
4. food marketing
5. food service

So it makes sense to learn more about the types of jobs at the various employment levels and which jobs offer the greatest promotional opportunities. Note that experience in one field of retailing is usually helpful in other fields. For example, what you've learned as a salesperson in a general merchandise firm would be valuable in a furniture store.

General Merchandise

Today more than 2.6 million people are employed in many types of general merchandise stores including department stores, discount stores, mail-order houses, and variety stores. Almost 70 percent of these employees are women. The fastest-growing area of general merchandise is in the mail-order category.

As a salesperson in a department store, you'll usually begin in housewares, notions, or other departments where a customer needs little assistance. As you gain experience, you'll move to positions of greater responsibility, selling high-priced items such as large appliances and furniture.

There are many career ladders in the merchandise retailing area. If you demonstrate that you're a good salesperson, you'll have the opportunity to advance in the field.

Apparel and Accessories

You can find career opportunities in seven kinds of apparel and accessory businesses. These are men's and boys' clothing and furnishings, women's ready-to-wear, women's accessories and cosmetics, children's and infant's wear, family clothing, furriers and fur, and miscellaneous apparel and accessory businesses.

If you're a successful salesperson, chances are that you'll be promoted to

There are many opportunities for successful salespeople in the apparel and accessory businesses. Ken Karp

higher-level positions in retailing. In the apparel and accessory field, if you've mastered all the competencies required of a good salesperson, you'll probably be on your way to success. The outlook for women is particularly bright, as over 65 percent of all employees in the industry are women.

Automotive and Petroleum Products

There are almost 2 million employees in the retailing area of the automotive and petroleum industry. Approximately 800,000 are involved in the sale of new or used cars, over 300,000 work in the automobile accessory business, and some 600,000 are employed in gasoline service stations. Only about 15 percent of these employees are women.

Gasoline Service Stations. Most gasoline service stations have one owner or lessee and two or three employees. Service stations are small businesses, but they offer diversified opportunities for beginning retailers. Approximately 39 percent of those who work at gasoline service stations are owners.

On the management level, there are opportunities for you to own or manage a service station. Other opportunities include becoming a buyer, sales manager, or district manager for one of the major oil companies. As an oil company representative, you'd call on service station owners and managers and help them run more efficient and more profitable businesses.

Tire, Battery, and Accessory Stores. You might prefer to enter automotive retailing as a salesperson for a tire, battery, and accessory (TBA) store. Some of these outlets are departments or branches of de-

If you're interested in a career in food marketing, you might consider an entry-level job such as a cashier. Michael Weisbrot

partment stores. Others are independent stores.

If you have the ability and desire to continue a career in the tire, battery, and accessory field, you may be able to move to a management-level position. Other higher-level jobs include those of parts buyer or store manager or owner.

Automobile Dealership. The position of automobile salesperson is one of the most common entry-level jobs in automotive retailing.

If you succeed in automobile selling, you'll be financially rewarded. And if you want to step up to management, you may become a sales manager or, in a large agency, a general manager. If you can raise the necessary capital, you could purchase your own dealership.

Food Marketing

Food marketing is the nation's largest business, with annual sales reaching an all-time peak each year. The typical American family spends approximately 25 percent of its income on food. Today, the average consumer enjoys better food and service than at any other time. And the increasing number of convenience food products continue to make living easier.

But food marketing is not all that is going on in supermarkets today. Major supermarket chains throughout the country have expanded and diversified their product lines to include general merchandise items. Supermarket shoppers are filling up their shopping carts with hardware, cosmetics, greeting cards, and toys as well as food. This trend toward one-stop convenience shopping continues to provide additional career opportunities for you as the industry grows at a rapid pace.

Food Service

It is estimated that Americans eat one out of every three meals away from home. This means that the food service industry provides over 750 million meals a week (about one out of every three eaten). There

As a waiter or waitress, you'll learn to provide customer services. Courtesy of Holiday Inns, Inc.

are self-service, buffet service, table service, and counter service establishments as well as drive-ins and fast-food outlets. Menus may be limited to a single item of food, offer a full range of American cuisine, or specialize in ethnic dishes. Almost 80 percent of the 490,000 food service establishments are located in urban areas.

In this chapter, you've learned about the many different areas in retailing. You've also learned about the career opportunities that are available to you in each area and how you can best prepare yourself for promotion. In the next chapter, you can take a closer look at some career opportunities in the merchandising division of retailing—that is, in sales occupations.

Trade Talk

Define each term and use it in a sentence.

Buyer
Controller

General merchandise
   manager
Store superintendent

Can You Answer These?

1. List several important criteria that a person should meet in order to win promotion.
2. What are the five areas of retailing that employ the largest number of people?
3. What is the fastest-growing phase of general merchandise retailing?
4. What career ladder do you want to climb? Why?
5. List some of the management-level roles that are available in the apparel and accessory businesses.

Problems

1. Rule a form similar to the following. In each column, list three duties of the job named in the column head.

Merchandise Manager	Personnel Manager	Store Superintendent	Controller

Exploring Retail Selling

CHAPTER 9

Communications & Human Relations
Economics & Marketing
Merchandising
Selling & Technology
Advertising & Display
Operations & Management

"I heard there's a sale on leather gloves here," Joan White said to her friend Nancy Marlon, as the two women entered Waters' discount store.

Following a salesclerk's directions, the two women found their way to the right place and were soon busy sorting through large countertop bins of leather gloves. "The prices certainly are reasonable, but the selection of sizes and colors isn't very wide," said Joan. "I think you take a 6½, don't you? Would that be a medium, do you suppose?"

"Right," answered Nancy. "But I like this light shade, and I can't seem to find it in a medium." She asked a clerk for help, but the clerk turned out to be a cashier who did not handle merchandise. After another search, the two women regretfully decided the store did not have Nancy's size in the color she wanted and left.

They went a few blocks to a women's specialty shop where Nancy had often shopped. "Why, good afternoon, Mrs. Marlon," said a salesperson as they entered. After hearing what Nancy wanted, the salesperson selected a half-dozen pairs of gloves and spread them out on the counter.

"Now these are pigskin, Mrs. Marlon: tan, fawn, and oyster white," she said, pointing at three of the pairs. "They are a classic style and an excellent grade of leather. If you intend to use the gloves just for driving, you might want to consider these," she continued, picking up another pair of gloves. "These have pigskin palms and string backs. They let you grip the wheel but have the coolness of a string glove. I've brought out a size 6 because this style seems to run a little large."

By the time Nancy was ready to leave the shop, she had purchased two pairs of gloves and a blouse. Joan had also bought gloves and was already planning to come back to the store to do some more shopping.

Why did Nancy and Joan buy their

gloves at the specialty shop rather than the discount store?

Some firms hire highly skilled selling personnel while others choose to depend more on advertisements and displays to sell their products and services. Customers often need and want someone to help them make buying decisions, and a skillful salesperson can lend the necessary personal touch. Courteous and efficient service does much to satisfy customers and build the reputation of a business.

Sales work offers career opportunities for high school and college graduates, for people who want to travel and those who do not, for salaried workers, and for those who want to own a business. As a salesperson, you can work for producers, manufacturers, wholesalers, or retailers. Almost 5.5 million people, or about 7 percent of all workers, are employed in sales occupations; more than 25 percent work part-time. Opportunities for women are excellent and continue to grow. Employment in sales occupations is expected to rise as fast as the average of all occupations through the mid-1980s at least.

Selling Occupations

The U.S. Department of Labor categorizes the most common selling jobs according to the amount of sales and sales-supporting work involved in a particular job. The categories are salesclerk, salesperson, and sales representative. Many people use the terms interchangeably, but actually each of them has a different meaning.

Salesclerk

In general, a **salesclerk** has little to do personally with helping customers make buying decisions. Depending on the size and type of firm, a salesclerk may obtain or receive merchandise, total sales of items, wrap or bag merchandise, and make change for customers. Salesclerks frequently clean and stock counters or tables with merchandise and set up displays or arrange merchandise on counters or tables. They are usually expected to price merchandise with stamps, tags, or marking pens. Occasionally, they will be asked to calculate a sales discount and keep records of sales, prepare inventories of stock, or reorder merchandise. Salesclerks may direct customers to the proper area of the store and help them find a particular size, color, or style.

Salesclerks are most commonly employed in food markets, discount stores, and similar retail firms that emphasize self-service.

Salesperson

The *Dictionary of Occupational Titles* contains the following partial definition of a salesperson's job. A **salesperson** "sells merchandise to individuals in a store or showroom, utilizing knowledge of products sold. Salespeople greet customers on the sales floor and ascertain make, type, and quality of merchandise desired. They display merchandise, suggest selections that meet customer's needs, and emphasize selling points of articles such as quality and usefulness."

The full definition of the job of salesperson emphasizes that in addition to suggestion selling, the salesperson may be expected to prepare a sales slip or sales contract and either receive payment or obtain credit authorization. A salesperson is usually expected to restock the displays, keep merchandise in order, ensure that stock levels are maintained, help in taking inventory, and order merchandise from the stockroom.

The effectiveness of salespeople can best be determined by their ability to help customers make buying decisions. The degree of selling skill required depends on the type of product or service sold and the kind of company. For example, as a salesperson selling expensive fur coats for an exclusive furrier, you'd have to be more skillful than a salesperson selling sweaters in a middle-priced department store.

Sales Representative

A **sales representative** sells products or services to consumers or businesses at a sales office, store, showroom, or customer's place of business or residence, using knowledge of the product or service sold. A sales representative may compile—from newspapers, businesses, telephone directories, and other sources— lists of prospective customers for use as sales leads. Sales representatives may travel to call on regular or prospective customers to solicit orders or talk with customers on the sales floor or by phone. They also build displays or demonstrate, using samples or catalogs to emphasize salable features. A sales representative is sometimes called a "sales agent" or "sales associate" and normally sells expensive

Three common categories of selling jobs are salesclerk (upper left), salesperson (right), and sales representative (lower left). Jane Hamilton-Merritt (upper left), Norris McNamara/Nancy Palmer Photo Agency (right), Russ Kinnel/Photo Researchers, Inc. (lower left)

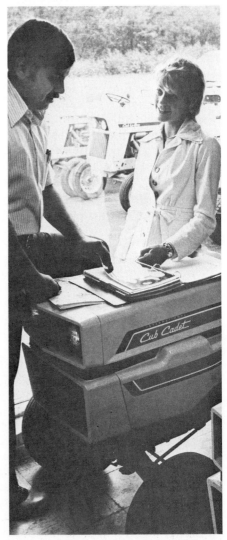

items such as automobiles, major home appliances, insurance, real estate, furniture, air conditioners, heating equipment, and similar products or services. Sales representatives spend a major percentage of their time using their selling skills, so they should be more effective than either a salesclerk or a salesperson.

Special Types of Retail Selling

Increasingly, retailers are using selected types of selling to increase their sales. These types of selling complement the common in-store selling methods. Direct selling, telephone selling, mail-order selling, and automatic vending are four of the most common methods used by in-store retailers as well as other retailers who do a good business by specializing in one or more of these special types of selling.

Direct Selling

When a sales representative calls on customers in their homes or places of business, that representative is engaged in direct selling. It is one of the oldest ways of selling consumer goods. In colonial days, the Yankee peddlers brought their wares to their customers by wagon and traveled to widely separated settlements where there were no other merchants. Today's competition is more intense.

One advantage of direct selling is that a company does not have the overhead expenses of a store building, equipment, display space, or retail stock space. Another advantage of direct selling is that sales representatives can demonstrate and show their particular products in the user's environment without having to compete with similar products on display in a retail store.

On the other hand, there is a relatively high turnover of direct-selling personnel due to the demands of travel, the hours required, and the challenges of selling different products to customers. This situation creates a problem in maintaining a well-trained sales force. To management, the cost of a sale in direct selling is higher than a comparable sale made in a store becase of the high commissions paid to the direct-sales representatives. Finally, many customers dislike dealing with a direct-to-the-home sales representative because they or their friends have had unpleasant experiences with other sales representatives. However, there are enough satisfied customers to make direct selling a profitable form of retailing. And you may want to consider this as an area of retailing in which to begin your career.

There are three basic types of direct selling: route selling, direct-to-the-home selling, and direct selling by retail stores.

Route Selling. **Route selling** combines delivery of a product with personal selling. Milk and bakery products are examples of food sold by route sales representatives. Usually, the company provides these salespeople with trucks. Some, however, are independent distributors who own their trucks and merchandise. They have regular routes and deliver to the same customers on a fixed schedule. Route sales representatives satisfy their customers with special services and convenience, as, of course, their customers don't have to leave their homes. Route sales representatives are constantly seeking new customers. You may find them welcoming the new families in their territory with a week's free delivery of their products in an effort to stimulate new business.

Direct-to-the-Home Selling. **Direct-to-the-home selling** of household goods, cosmetics, books, and services such as rug cleaning and home improvement has become more common in recent years. Some of the sales representatives involved in this kind of selling work from lists of prospective customers provided by their companies. Others are assigned territories and cover every house in the area. In many cities and towns, sales representatives are required to obtain a special permit before engaging in direct-to-the-home solicitations. Sales representatives display their samples or show their catalogs and arrange for later delivery of the goods the customer orders. Fuller Brush products, the *World Book Encyclopedia,* and Avon cosmetics are three well-known products sold in the home.

Other companies arrange for one customer, usually a homemaker, to invite other people to the home so that the sales representative can show merchandise to a number of customers. The person who holds this kind of buying "party" usually receives a discount on merchandise or a gift.

Direct Selling by Retail Stores. Some retail stores, in an effort to reach more customers and increase sales, send their salespeople to call on customers in their homes. Such salespeople may sell household appliances, home improvements, storm windows, and other high-priced items. For example, some stores send interior decorators to advise customers on the use of color in their homes. The decorators may suggest additional furniture or accessories that result in added sales for the store. Retail salespeople follow leads furnished by their stores. They have an advantage over the direct-to-the-home salesworkers because they can invite customers to come into their stores to see the merchandise.

Telephone Selling

Only a few retailers without stores concentrate on telephone selling, but those with stores have found telephone selling a valuable addition to their regular selling methods. They use the telephone to notify customers about special merchandise, renew old accounts, take orders, and get new customers. Customers generally accept calls from stores they know. They

Telephone selling is a valuable addition to a retailer's other sales techniques. Elizabeth Richter

find the telephone a useful shopping aid because it saves the time and effort required to go to a store and look for merchandise.

Notifying Customers about Special Merchandise. Some salespeople keep a list of their regular customers and their needs and wants. They then make a point of calling certain customers whenever the store receives a new shipment of merchandise that would be of interest to them. They may also call when a special sale is going to take place. In some cases, a salesperson may call a customer who was unable to find the wanted item when visiting the store. The salesperson tells the customer that the store has received the wanted item and asks the customer for permission to have it put aside.

Renewing Old Accounts. Some stores use the telephone to find out why customers have not been making any purchases. Sometimes the salesperson who calls inactive accounts finds that customers have not returned because something annoyed them. When customers reveal their reason for not buying, the salesperson can help to correct the situation.

Taking Orders. Many retail stores rely on telephone orders for a number of their sales. Some customers like to call their favorite store or their favorite salesperson to shop by telephone. Some large retail stores have telephone boards that are staffed by people trained to take orders for merchandise that has been advertised or shown in catalogs. These operators may also suggest merchandise to fill customer needs. Small stores may also offer telephone order service.

Mail-Order Selling

Some of today's largest retail businesses started out as mail-order houses. Even though they have added retail stores to their operations, they continue to do much of their business through the mail. Mail-order houses like Sears, J. C. Penney, Spiegel, and Montgomery Ward regularly send catalogs to hundreds of thousands of customers. Some of these catalogs may show over 150,000 items. There are more than 2,500 essentially mail-order companies. They sell products such as novelties, home furnishings, and wearing apparel. Increasingly, special promotion mailers are being used by department and specialty stores, gasoline companies, credit card companies, and encyclopedia companies.

Catalog selling has expanded tremendously in the past few years (see your mailbox). It will probably continue to grow—particularly with the gasoline shortage. This might be a career area you'll want to look over again.

Advantages for Customers. There are numerous customers who prefer to shop by catalog. They would rather fill in one order form at home than travel to a store, where they would have to wander from department to department to select their purchases. Customers find that the illustrations and detailed descriptions given in mail-order catalogs provide them with valuable product information that aids them in making sound buying decisions. They can shop at leisure in their homes and discuss their intended purchases with their families. If they make a mistake in ordering, they know that mail-order houses have liberal return and adjustment policies. But they must often plan their purchases well in advance to allow time for delivery.

Advantages for Retailers. Although the printing and distribution of large, colorful catalogs or the running of advertisements is costly, mail-order selling is profitable. This is because it eliminates the expenses of display and sales personnel.

Mail-order advertisements in magazines and newspapers are another way of obtaining business by mail. Like the catalogs, the advertisements usually picture and describe the merchandise, give the price, and either include a tear-out coupon or tell where the order is to be sent. Such advertisements not only attract immediate sales but also provide good prospects for future mailing lists.

Small manufacturers and producers of specialty goods find that they can reach many potential customers by advertising in magazines whose subscribers are interested in a particular line of goods. For example, nurseries advertise heavily in the spring editions of magazines read by homeowners and gardeners. In their ads, they may guarantee delivery of healthy plants within 1,000 miles of the nursery; by doing so, they open up a far greater retail market area than they would have if they relied only on customers within easy driving distance.

Mail-order houses regularly sell a wide variety of products to many thousands of customers.

Catalog Sales Unit. In addition to promoting sales by mailing out catalogs, some retailers also have catalog sales departments in their stores or actually have a separate catalog sales store. A **catalog sales department** is a service department within a retail store where customers can look at catalogs and place their orders. If they need assistance, they can get help from salespeople who are familiar with the organization of the catalog. These salespeople help the customers to place their orders and give them an approximate delivery date. All services offered by catalog sales units are available in these departments. In a catalog sales store or showroom, a customer can usually inspect samples of merchandise as well as obtain help from salespeople before placing an order. Sometimes a catalog sales store will handle limited stocks of small, popular items so that it can fill the customer's order for these items immediately. Other merchandise may be delivered from the company's warehouse to the store, where the customer can pick it up. If the item is large or bulky, such as a stove or a washer, it may be delivered directly to the customer's home.

Catalog sales stores may also have special catalogs on items like power tools and cameras. They may also have samples of materials that would be used for drapery and carpeting. The catalog sales store will send sales representatives to the customer's home to sell home improvements such as carpeting, a heating system, or kitchen modernization. The store offers free planning help, including measuring and the drawing of plans, and it will recommend the best types of materials for the job. It will also estimate the overall cost of the job, without charge, and take care of the complete installation.

Automatic Vending

Like mail-order retailing, another form of nonstore retailing is use of automatic vending machines. Customers insert their money into the machine and receive the chosen merchandise, along with any change that may be due. Sometimes a separate change-making machine is located near the vending machines. A change-making machine can "read" the face of a dollar bill that is inserted by the customer and return a dollar's worth of coins, which will be accepted by other vending machines.

Vending machines dispense such food items as soft drinks, coffee, milk, candy, cookies, ice cream, sandwiches, and fresh fruit. Some supermarkets have installed them outside the store to sell merchandise when the store is closed. Some factory cafeterias have installed vending machines that provide complete meals for their employees.

Some machines are used for selling non-food items, such as combs, hosiery, cosmetics, and fishing worms. Services are also sold by vending machines. A familiar example is the laundromat, with its coin-operated washers, dryers, and dry-cleaning machines. Vending machines that sell short-term insurance policies to travelers are used at airports.

The location of vending machines is important. Machines must be placed in areas where there is sufficient customer traffic and where the items being dispensed will be acceptable. Vending machines are found in airline, bus, and railroad terminals; in restaurants; in college dormitories; in offices; and in factories. Space is rented to the companies that operate the vending machines. These companies supply and service the machines and, as the owners, profit from their operation.

Now that you've finished this unit, you should have a good idea of the special types of retail selling jobs and careers, what it takes to succeed in retailing as well as how you can prepare yourself for getting promoted. Put what you've learned to use by reviewing your career plan now.

Trade Talk

Define each term and use it in a sentence.

Catalog sales
  department
Direct-to-the-home
  selling
Route selling

Salesclerk
Salesperson
Sales representative

Can You Answer These?

1. How do the duties of a salesperson differ from those of a salesclerk?
2. List some of the advantages and disadvantages for a company involved in direct selling.
3. What are several uses of the telephone for selling products and services?
4. What are some of the tips mentioned in this chapter on using the telephone successfully?
5. What are some of the items that vending machines dispense?

Problems

1. Rule a form similar to the following. In the left column, write the letter of each of the following selling tasks: (0) accepting money, making change, and giving cash-register receipts, (a) demonstrating a food blender, (b) showing customer on which shelf to find dog food, (c) helping customer match drapes with carpeting, (d) assisting checker in a grocery store to take a customer's order to the car, (e) showing customers how to operate mechanical toys, (f) giving customer a reduced price on breakfast food when a coupon is presented, (g) helping customer compare features of several fur coats, (h) giving samples and showing customer how to use a new line of cosmetics, (i) gift wrapping merchandise at a gift wrapping counter, and (j) helping customer select stereo components. In the column to the right, tell whether the employee who performs the selling task is a salesclerk, salesperson, or sales representative.

Selling Task	Type of Personnel
Example: (0)	Cashier (salesclerk)

2. Visit a retail store and discuss with a supervisor the different types of retail selling that the store engages in. Make a list of these types of retail selling.

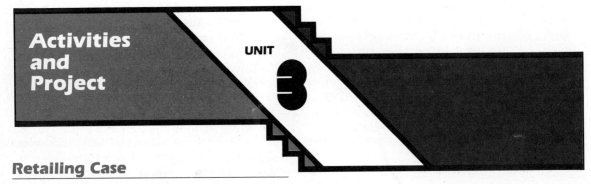

Activities and Project

UNIT 3

Retailing Case

Sam Geranian has been working at his entry-level position as a waiter in a full-service restaurant for over 2 years. Sam enjoys being a waiter; he likes the daily contact he has with people and wants to build a career in the food service industry. Judging from the tips the customers leave Sam, he's successful at his job. Some customers even ask to be seated at "one of Sam's tables" because they want Sam to wait on them. But Sam is beginning to wonder why he hasn't been promoted to a higher-level position, such as a dining room supervisor or shift supervisor.

The restaurant in which Sam has been working is one of a chain. And the company policy requires that all waiters/waitresses follow particular dress codes, such as wearing a white shirt or blouse every day, black pants or skirt, and regular shoes. The company knows that it's important for their employees who deal directly with the public to have a neat and uniform appearance. Every once in a while, though, Sam disregards this policy and waits on tables in blue jeans, a T-shirt, and sneakers. The assistant manager, Bill Wong, reminded Sam of the dress requirement the first few times Sam showed up dressed incorrectly. But when the assistant manager saw how effective Sam was as a waiter, he figured he'd just let Sam get on with doing a good job. He wouldn't bother him about dress anymore. Also, the assistant manager assumed that Sam couldn't be too interested in taking on the extra responsibility that would be required of him in a higher-level position.

1. Why do you think Sam isn't getting the promotion that he seems to deserve?
2. If you were the assistant manager at the restaurant, would you deal with Sam in the same way that Bill Wong did or differently? Explain your answer.
3. In Sam's situation, with a feeling that you're doing a good job and deserve promotion, what would you do?
4. Do you think the assistant manager of the restaurant will ever be promoted to a higher position, such as a manager? Explain your answer.

Working with People

"There goes the telephone again," said Carla Markova, a salesperson at The Bookworm bookstore. "Would you mind getting it?" she asked Linda Contini, a new part-time salesclerk.

"Hello? This is The Bookworm, Miss Contini speaking," Linda spoke into the phone.

"I'd like to place an order for a book," said the caller, "I know the name of the author and the publisher, but I can't remember the exact title. It's something like *Starting a Retail Business*."

"Well, I'm sorry," said Linda, "but if you don't know the correct title, I can't help you."

"But surely," replied the caller, "you can find out the title if I tell you the author and publisher?"

"No, I don't think so. Call back again when you've remembered the title," Linda told the caller. Linda added, "I'm sorry I can't help you," and hung up.

"What was that all about?" asked Carla when Linda was off the phone. Linda told Carla what had happened.

"Well, I'm afraid the customer was right," Carla told Linda. "Here on the counter is a reference book all booksellers use called *Books in Print*. It has listings by author, so that if we have the author's name and that of the publisher, we can nearly always find the correct title of a book."

1. Identify the true problem.
2. What are the important facts to be considered in this problem?
3. List several possible solutions to this problem.
4. Evaluate the possible results of each solution.
5. Which solution do you recommend? Why?

Project 3: Planning Your Career Ladder

Your Project Goal

Using the Unit 1 Project, "Planning Your Career," select the most desirable retailing career for yourself, outline the steps for preparing a career ladder, and prepare a career ladder and time schedule that you intend to follow as you pursue your career.

Procedure

Before starting this project, you will need the project for Unit 1 entitled "Planning Your Career," which you completed and had evaluated by your instructor.

1. Review the career planning project that you completed for Unit 1 and select a career that you, your teacher, and your counselor feel you can realistically pursue successfully.
2. Identify the jobs and the number of different positions you may have to hold during your career.
3. Prepare a brief description of each of the jobs identified in Step 2. You may find the *Dictionary of Occupational Titles* helpful in completing this step, both in terms of job information and of how to prepare such a description.
4. Draw a ladder and place each of the jobs identified in Step 2 on it. Attach a tentative timetable and an explanation of the plan you intend to follow as you pursue your career.
5. Hand in this completed project to your instructor together with the project for Unit 1.

Evaluation

Your career ladder will be evaluated on the completeness of the information that you compiled in Steps 2, 3, and 4 and on its neatness.

Looking at the Future of Retailing

Retailing Responds to Change

CHAPTER

10

Communications & Human Relations

Economics & Marketing

Merchandising

Selling & Technology

Advertising & Display

Operations & Management

Why do you react favorably to some new products, some new store services, and some new store practices while you accept others reluctantly? Chances are that those you like are the ones you understand and believe will help you personally. On the other hand, the new ideas and innovations that most people react to slowly or negatively are the ones that they don't understand or feel will not benefit them. Retailers too usually react much like the customers they serve—welcoming what they understand and believe to be personally beneficial and resisting the complex and impersonal things.

Now, look at the following two words—"computers" and "metrics." What is your reaction? In this chapter, you'll see that retailers are reacting much in the same way that you probably are. Retailers view computers as exciting and useful tools in processing the data needed in their businesses. And most retailers see metrics as something they have to accept because of

new laws and regulations. First, let's examine computers as they relate to data processing.

Data Processing in Retailing

Have you ever looked carefully at the punched tickets on merchandise? They are a part of one kind of data processing. **Data processing** is a procedure or a combination of procedures used to record information about a business transaction. This information is valuable in determining how many items have been sold and how many should be reordered. It also arranges this information into a meaningful report. When keypunched cards are used in data processing, it is called **automatic data processing**.

Automatic Data Processing

Automatic data processing consists of four major steps:

1. Information about such things as sales transactions, merchandise inventory, and credit is given to an operator, who keypunches the data onto computer cards using a card-punch machine.
2. After the cards are punched, they are put in a special machine called a verifier, which checks the accuracy of the cards.
3. The cards are then sorted into predetermined groups by a machine called a sorter.
4. Finally, the information contained on the cards is calculated and tabulated by putting the cards in the computer, which reads the cards and performs the mathematical calculations.

This process is time-consuming and may result in errors because of a keypunch mistake that isn't caught or a merchandise ticket that is lost and not tabulated. Although automatic data processing has advantages for some retailers, many retailers have now changed to more efficient ways of processing data, such as electronic data processing.

Electronic Data Processing

Electronic data processing (EDP) is a method by which information about a business is fed directly into a computer through terminals. Because this method eliminates the use of keypunched cards, it is much faster than automatic data processing. Electronic data processing simplifies the thousands of repetitive tasks that have to do with recordkeeping and stockkeeping.

Information that identifies the manufacturer, style, colors, price, brand name, units bought and sold, cost, and retail price is entered directly into a computer through **terminals** that are hooked up to the computer system. Some terminals resemble an electric typewriter. Other terminals are electronic cash registers located on the sales floor and are directly hooked up to the computer by a cable or indirectly through the use of telephones. The latter type of terminal is referred to as a "remote" terminal. There are different styles of remote terminals. Some are specially adapted to electric typewriters and others have a video screen connected to a keyboard.

How EDP Works. Electronic data processing uses a digital computer, which consists of five major components:

1. Input unit
2. Memory or data storage unit
3. Arithmetic or computing unit
4. Output or communications unit
5. Control unit

The input unit feeds information into the computer in the form of electronic (magnetic) impulses. The information can be fed into the computer in many forms—for example, it may be in the form of a merchandise price ticket that is coded with computer information. The small holes in a merchandise ticket or the "scraggly" lines on the package contain coded information about the product. This information is stored in the memory (data storage) unit of the computer.

The memory unit of the computer is similar to a brain; it saves the information until it is instructed to recall it and send it to the arithmetic (computing) unit. When instructed, the arithmetic unit of the computer will calculate the information from the merchandise ticket stored in the memory unit. The computing unit performs the operations of addition, subtraction, multiplication, division, and other operations, such as comparing two numbers. The computing unit produces information needed for sales records, merchandise inventories, and purchase records. The results are then stored until the information is needed.

When the information is needed, the output (communications) unit recalls it on either an "on-line printer" (which is similar to an electronic typewriter and prints automatically when instructed by the computer) or on a television-type monitor screen. The monitor screen offers buyers up-to-date information on sales and inventory very rapidly.

The last component of the computer is the control unit. This unit instructs the computer regarding which program is to be used. A **program** is a set of instructions arranged in a sequence that tells the computer what mathematical procedure should be performed and what types of reports are needed. The program is fed into the computer either by keypunched computer cards or by a terminal directly hooked up to the computer. The control unit also informs the computer what data should be stored. The control unit is programmed. A person called a "programmer" not only programs the control unit but also gives it instructions for operation.

Computers have widespread acceptance in retailing. And with increased sales volume, the price of computers is going down. But today, there are still small retailers who cannot afford to purchase a computer. Many of these retailers pay for the services of data processing centers to process their information. Small retailers deliver the essential information to the center by mail or telephone. The center then processes the information and generates the report. This gives even small companies immediate access to information.

How Retailers Use Electronic Data Processing

Some of the major reasons for using electronic data processing in retailing include:

♦ *Inventory Control*—reducing costs by minimizing markdowns and preventing out-of-stock merchandise because there will always be an accurate count of stock on hand. As sales information is fed into the computer, the output produces information telling the retailer how many items remain in stock. When items are shoplifted, the information will differ from the actual number in stock.

♦ *Buying and Pricing*—determining when to have sales promotions, how much to mark down the goods, when to purchase merchandise, and when to reorder.

♦ *Customer Credit*—determining who should be granted credit, keeping track of accounts, and analyzing buying and paying habits.

♦ *Financial Control*—determining what orders are outstanding, to whom the retailer owes money and who owes the retailer money.

♦ *Communications*—sending messages that can result in improved communications.

When instructed, the computer will also do the following:

♦ Generate information concerning sales
♦ Print unit-of-stock-item reports to determine what to buy and when to buy
♦ List merchandise that has been transferred to another location
♦ Release credit authorization
♦ Make sales forecasts

The computer is constantly being fed information about the business, either by a remote terminal or through the electronic cash register. Computers provide retailers using electronic cash registers or on-line terminals with instant sales data, credit checking, and other consumer-oriented functions. Electronic cash registers are designed to record sales information on either a paper tape or a magnetic tape. The tape is then fed into the computer, which processes the information for the retailer's use.

Point-of-Sale Systems

Increasingly, electronic cash registers are being used as part of a complete point-of-sale system. The **point-of-sale (POS) system** is a process of collecting data at the location where the sale is made and where the merchandise or service is transferred to the customer. When the point-of-sale system is used, the information on the sale is immediately fed into a minicomputer. This is done with an optical scanner that can read magnetic writing on merchandise tickets.

Optical Scanning

Optical scanning is a process of passing a coded ticket over a reading device or having a wand pass over a ticket. In 1973, the food industry adopted a specialized coding system called the **Universal Product Code (UPC)**. The UPC is a numbering system that assigns a unique number to every product. When the product passes through the checkout stand and is placed before an optical scanner, the price is automatically recorded into the register by a computer. Some retail stores have also adopted the UPC system. By moving an electronic wand over the ticket, the salesperson enables the cash register to record price and product information. Some of the benefits of this system are as follows:

♦ The universal product code identifies the manufacturer, item, style, and price. This aids the salesperson because the sales information is entered faster and more accurately than if the salesperson were to enter the information manually. (See Chapter 28.)
♦ Employee productivity is increased because the sales transaction takes less time, which allows the salesperson to assist other customers, especially during peak sales periods.
♦ Retailers are given an effective way to keep track of individual sales data if sales personnel are on commission.
♦ Retailers have available the number of items in stock at all times.

Point-of-Sale System Advantages

The point-of-sale system takes the salesperson through the steps of finalizing a sales transaction, reducing the time it takes to process a sale. The salescheck produced for customers fully describes (in English) the type of merchandise pur-

Fixed slot scanners are most often used in supermarkets. Cash registers with special keys and display terminals are widely used in fast food shops, while optical scanners with wands are widely used in general merchandise stores. Courtesy of NCR Corp.

chased. The computer system has helped to clarify many areas of confusion for both the salesperson and the customer. An example of this is in the area of credit and check authorization. Credit and check authorization can—typically in 2 seconds or less—be obtained from nearly 3,000 miles away. Also, the point-of-sale system provides a tighter control on credit-card usage and check cashing; it has greatly reduced the illegal use of credit cards and checks.

Some of the other advantages of point-of-sale systems are that it:

- Increases employee productivity because essential sales data are automatically recorded; the salesperson does not have to punch any keys.
- Eliminates employees' mathematical errors because all calculations are computed by the machine.
- Helps to avoid losses because of bad checks or poor credit status.
- Makes the accounting task simpler because figures are kept by the computer.
- Aids in inventory control.
- Helps management because it enables managers to watch employee productivity, keep track of slow and fast sales items, and give daily sales records.

The Future of the Computer in Retailing

The computer is becoming a part of everyday life, and it's here to stay. The systems for the future will become more complex technically but also easier to operate.

Increased Business Use

In business, computers will be used more. They will be easier to communicate with, easier to program, and easier to install and maintain. Computers in retailing could eliminate most manual processing of cash-register tapes and allow greater flexibility. In addition, errors may be virtually eliminated. Even small retailers of the future will find computers a powerful and affordable tool.

Increased Consumer Use

In the future, consumers may not have to leave their homes to do their shopping. Currently retailers are experimenting with electronic ordering. With electronic ordering, consumers call in their orders, giving their name and account number along with the style number, color, and quantity of the item wanted. Their call is answered either by a recorded message explaining to them how to place the order or by an operator. There are experimental computers that answer calls directly, but they are not yet perfected; the computer voice is still hard to understand. Home computers may be used in the future to communicate with business computers. Once the consumer has given the necessary information, the data are fed to a central computer system that sends the message to the retailer. The order is filled within just a few minutes and sent out.

Development of Metrics in Retailing

Are you ready for metrics? If not, it's time to start. On December 23, 1975, the Metric Bill S-100 was signed by President Gerald Ford. This bill declared that the United States would convert to the metric system over a period of years. So it's time to learn the metric system now.

Why Metrics?

You're probably wondering why the United States wants to spend time and money to convert to metrics. One reason is that the metric system is rapidly being adopted throughout the world, and the United States will be one of the last major trading nations to adopt it officially. Converting to metrics will give the United States many advantages. First, by converting to metrics, the United States will be able to maintain and improve efficiency of operation on an international basis and thus stay competitive. That is, at present, the United States is at a disadvantage in trading on an international basis because it has not fully converted to metrics. And this makes it difficult to exchange parts and components of goods, as the sizes we use are not the same as those of nations using metric measurements.

The advantages of converting to the metric system include the following:

- Calculations will be easier to perform because the system is based on units of 10, fewer units are required for measurement, and fractions aren't involved.
- Worldwide uniformity of measurement will be achieved and communications with other countries will be easier.
- Americans working in foreign countries won't have to be specially trained to use the metric system.
- We will more easily be able to exchange raw materials, manufactured products, and technological ideas with other countries.

Industries That Have Converted to Metrics

The wine and liquor industry has converted to metric packaging and other industries are following its lead. Many United States manufacturers are now putting both metric and nonmetric sizing on their merchandise. A good example of this is the Levi Strauss Company. Other compa-

nies, such as Sears, Montgomery Ward, and J. C. Penney have established consumer and manufacturer metric information centers to aid in the conversion to the metric system. Many food-processing companies are also developing recipes that have both the metric scale and the nonmetric scale. It is estimated that the conversion to metric will be complete between 1985 and 1990.

What Is Metrics?

The **metric system** is a system of weights and measures based on units of 10. This system was developed in the eighteenth century. Then, it was believed that metrics was a natural system which would be easy to use. The original metric system has been changed several times since its creation. The present metric system is called the International System of Units, or SI for short. The International System of Units consists of eight base units.

1. Meter: unit of length
2. Kilogram: unit of mass that is used for weight
3. Kelvin: unit of temperature
4. Second: unit of time
5. Ampere: quantity of electric current
6. Candela: measure of light intensity
7. Mole: amount of substance
8. Liter: unit of liquid weight

Many businesses are helping customers convert to the metric system. Courtesy of McDonald's System, Inc.

The following two charts show conversions from the metric system to the American National Standards Institute System.

METRIC TO AMERICAN

When You Know	You Can Find	If You Multiply by
Centimeters	Inches	0.4
Meters	Feet	3.3
Meters	Yards	1.09
Grams	Ounces	0.035
Liters	Quarts	1.06
Liters	Gallons	0.26

AMERICAN TO METRIC

When You Know	You Can Find	If You Multiply by
Inches	Centimeters	2.54
Feet	Meters	0.3
Yards	Meters	0.91
Miles	Kilometers	1.61
Ounces	Grams	28.4
Pounds	Kilograms	0.45

In this chapter, you've learned how retailers have to respond to change in order to remain competitive. The two major changes that retailers must deal with today are the use of electronic computers for data processing and conversion to the metric system of measurement.

In the next chapter, you'll find out about the major trends that are taking place in retailing now and being developed for the future. Many of these trends involve the use of electronic computers, so you'll also learn more about the importance of computers in retailing.

Trade Talk

Define each term and use it in a sentence.

Automatic data
  processing
Data processing
Electronic data
  processing (EDP)

Optical scanning
Point-of-sale system
  (POS)
Program
Terminals

Universal Product
  Code (UPC)

Can You Answer These?

1. How will the United States benefit from converting to metrics?
2. How has the computer affected retail companies?
3. What are the advantages of the electronic cash register?
4. What is the future of the computer in retailing?
5. What is the International System of Units?

Problems

1. Rule a form similar to the following, and complete the left column as shown. Then, using the metric conversion table provided in this chapter, complete the right column.

Products	Metric Equivalent
a. 1.1 yards of fabric	
b. 2 quarts of soda	
c. 5 inches of ribbon	
d. Rug measuring 9 × 12 feet	
e. 15 gallons of gas	
f. 8 ounces of milk	

2. Rule a form similar to the following. In the left column, write the letter of each of these uses of electronic data processing: (a) inventory control, (b) buying and pricing, (c) customer credit, (d) financial control, and (e) communication. In the right columns, note the advantages to the retailer and to the customer of each use.

The Uses of EDP	Advantages to Retailer	Advantages to Customer

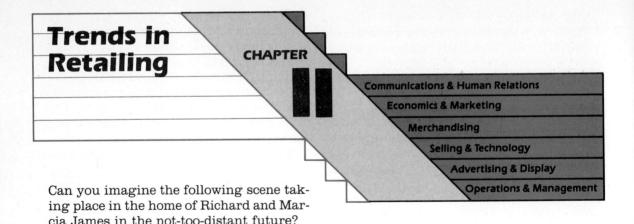

Trends in Retailing

CHAPTER

11

Communications & Human Relations

Economics & Marketing

Merchandising

Selling & Technology

Advertising & Display

Operations & Management

Can you imagine the following scene taking place in the home of Richard and Marcia James in the not-too-distant future?

Richard: I think I'll put on a videotape of the new movie. Do you want to watch it?

Marcia: Yes, just as soon as I do a little more shopping.

Richard: Please order me a small tube of toothpaste and some deodorant for my travel kit.

To do her shopping, Marcia goes to their tiny computer terminal with a televisionlike screen. To operate the terminal, all she does is press the button that connects her directly with the order departments of her favorite stores. She views the merchandise on the screen as the teleshopper scans the shelves. Finally she pushes the tally button on the console to recap and total her order. Marcia examines the recap and pushes another button on the terminal, which authorizes payment from her checkless bank account.

Using Automated Shopping Techniques

The technology is now available to make the scene just described a reality. Products in which sight, smell, touch, or personal service are not important to consumers are the most logical products to be sold and purchased through automated shopping techniques. Examples of these goods are soap, toothpaste, paper prod-

ucts, housewares, hosiery, food products, and some types of clothing.

Automated shopping techniques are most suitable for these goods because, increasingly, when consumers have to purchase them, ease in shopping, saving time, and economy are major considerations. The increasing cost of energy and the importance that consumers place on their time are making it even more desirable for them to shop from home. And in the decade ahead, computer technology will make such shopping economically possible.

Making Shopping Easier and Quicker

Many of the trends in retailing are based on appeals to the unique purchasing needs of consumers. The development of automated shopping techniques has grown out of retailers' attempts to satisfy consumers' needs more easily and quickly. Some of the automated shopping techniques that retailers are now using or will be using in the future are described in the text below.

Electronic Point-of-Sale Systems

Electronic point-of-sale (POS) systems used in conjunction with in-store computers are becoming more widespread in retailing. (You'll recall that these systems were discussed in Chapter 10.) In supermarkets, an increasing number of retailers are using scanners at checkout stations. Scanners can be used more and more in food stores because manufacturers are willing to mark their product with the universal product code (UPC), which can be read by the scanner. Scanners improve employee productivity and reduce employee errors; as a result, they save consumers time and money. Scanners also cut the retailers' bookkeeping and office expenses, and they can be adapted to accommodate the expected explosion in retailers' use of data communications during the 1980s.

Data Communication

Retailers' increasing use of computers has affected the way in which both spoken and written information is transmitted. The leading general merchandise stores and specialty stores are installing more sophisticated data communications networks. These are built around technology that transmits various forms of information—such as point-of-sale information, credit authorizations, and inventory levels—along high-speed transmission lines.

Electronic Funds Transfer (EFT)

To retailers, **electronic funds transfer (EFT)** refers to the transfer of money to the store's bank account from a customer's bank account. There is a growing interest in making EFT more operational because it's a time-saving device for both consumers and retailers. From the consumer's point of view, EFT saves time and makes shopping easier because it eliminates the need for writing out checks to pay for orders. From the retailers point of view, EFT represents a fast and safe method of making sales.

Teleshopping

Some kind of electronic system that will let consumers place orders from their homes will be possible in the not-too-dis-

tant future. We have already seen, at the beginning of this chapter, how Richard and Marcia made use of such a system. Consumers will be able to order their food and many other basic household necessities through the use of in-home television computer systems. For example, consumers will be able to use an in-home shopper to select merchandise displayed on the television screen, and they will also be able to use the computer system to order goods automatically on a schedule programmed to their needs.

Credit Plans

An increasing number of retailers are shifting their private charge-card programs to outside financial specialists such as MasterCard and Visa. The specialists generally can run the retailer's credit programs more effectively and economically. This trend is the result of several factors, among the chief of which are the higher costs of operating credit programs and soaring interest rates, which result in small returns on money invested in operating credit programs.

Paying Bills by Telephone

A consumer device available through a number of financial institutions throughout the country allows customers to pay credit-card bills by phone, using money from their savings accounts. This, of course, eliminates the writing of checks to pay those bills.

By using a code number, customers instruct a bank clerk which bills they want paid. Or they can send this billing information directly to the bank computer. Customers can use either rotary-dialed or push-button telephones to pay their bills. Retailers get their bank accounts credited each day. They also receive a report summarizing transactions by customers who used the system the previous day. The system's main advantage for the merchant is that it reduces the number of checks handled through the mail each day.

Today customers can make withdrawals from their bank accounts at any hour. Jane Hamilton-Merritt

Catalog Shopping

Catalog shopping used to be done primarily by rural residents, but today 25 percent of our population purchases goods through catalog order. Urban shoppers, too, are using catalogs, placing mail orders not only for household staples but also for expensive items such as sable coats and diamond bracelets. To bolster catalog sales, some retailers are producing catalogs of magazine quality. The catalogs now feature elegant, full-color photographs on high-quality paper.

Catalog shopping is becoming more widespread because consumers like the convenience of shopping by mail. And established merchants view catalogs as another way of satisfying their customers' needs and wants.

Superstores

Some supermarket chains are committed to or experimenting with "superstores." **Superstores** are defined as having 25,000 square feet or more of space with a good variety of food and non-food items—usually 70 percent of space for food and 30 percent for non-foods. They are service-oriented stores, often including a deli, pharmacy, florist, liquor department, and other scrambled merchandise lines. **Scrambled merchandising** refers to the addition of profitable new merchandise lines and services traditionally handled by other types of retailers and not basic to the main lines of the business.

Superstores satisfy the consumer's need for convenience by offering one-stop shopping. Supermarket chains are experimenting with superstores because such stores can carry a greater variety of merchandise and thus provide for most customers' needs.

Making Shopping More Economical

Retailers continually search for techniques that will result in lower costs to the consumer. Some stores may even eliminate or reduce customer services in an attempt to cut costs. Some of the most ev-

ident trends in this direction include limited-line groceries, "outlet" stores, home centers, and subregional malls.

Limited-Line Groceries

Grocery chains are moving increasingly toward limited lines, which is a new low-cost concept of retailing. **Limited-line groceries** fall somewhere between supermarkets and convenience stores. Limited-line groceries sell nonperishable staples at discount prices. They generally don't carry frozen foods, meats, produce, or milk. They do little advertising and provide no services such as bagging or check cashing. Typical of the limited-line stores are Kroger Company's Bi-Lo, A&P's Lo-Lo, and Aldi's Discount Market. These limited-line groceries do not accept credit cards or money-off coupons. In these stores, customers have limited choices of brands because few brands are carried.

In the not-too-distant future, consumers will be able to use in-home television computer systems to purchase merchandise. Courtesy of Viewdata Corp. of America

"Outlet" Stores

Another indication of the emphasis on cutting prices in retailing is the opening of more "outlet" stores. **Outlet stores** sell merchandise that various manufacturers want to dispose of at reduced prices for various reasons. Many of the items have labels removed. In the apparel field, the number of such stores is growing. In addition to women's and men's outlet stores, there are outlet groups emerging in the children's wear field. These outlet stores often advertise their goods at 30 percent below the regular retail prices.

Home Centers

In recent years, discount chains have added home improvement centers to their units. They have done this to meet the need of consumers who are do-it-yourselfers and home remodelers. These home centers carry such merchandise as wallpaper, plumbing materials, precut lumber, paneling, decorative shelving, and roofing materials. Some discounters have already made such home centers profitable. Home centers' dollar sales represent one of retailing's fastest-growing sectors.

Subregional Centers

Recently, shopping centers are being developed in established suburban consumer markets. These are areas where the population is stable and where competition is relatively weak. These areas are mostly made up of multifamily dwellings instead of single-family households. In these shopping centers, called **subregional centers,** space is more efficiently used by the tenants. The new standard-size shop is 10 to 15 percent smaller than it was 10 years ago. Subregional malls are

The limited-line grocery is a low-cost retailing concept that is increasingly popular. Courtesy of *Chain Store Age Supermarkets*, Lebhar-Friedman, Inc.

more efficient because they have reduced the number of square feet needed to serve a given market.

Making Shopping a Pleasant Experience

Shopping centers in all different sizes, shapes, and forms are emerging to serve the different needs of consumers who like to make shopping a pleasant experience. Shopping centers are increasingly being built in new and renovated downtown areas, in suburban areas, in small and large communities, and in historic and other tourist areas. The range of products and services sold continues to change rapidly.

Shopping centers in the United States are still expanding and most are prospering. Approximately 40 percent of all retail sales made in this country now take place in shopping centers. By the year 2000, it is estimated that more than 50 percent of retail sales will take place in shopping centers.

One of the trends in retailing today is to convert an existing building into many specialty shops. These are self-contained shops that specialize in items ranging from stationery to gourmet food. Also, the types of retail establishments located in shopping centers are changing drastically. Among the trends that are surfacing are a greater variety of eating places, more businesses offering services, more entertainment facilities, and more shops showing up-to-date fashions. Eating places and entertainment facilities are discussed below.

Eating Places

Nationally, as more meals are being eaten out, the number of eating places in shopping centers continues to increase. In some instances, these firms are becoming major traffic builders for their centers. Today, approximately 15 percent of the

Why do attractions such as the ice-skating rink make a shopping center location popular with many retailers? Courtesy of The Galleria, Houston, Texas

total space in shopping malls is devoted to food; 10 years ago, it amounted to only 10 percent.

Restaurants. There is a growing number of sit-down restaurants in shopping malls, and the number of gourmet food shops is also increasing. Even the higher-priced restaurants are more plentiful in the shopping malls. For example, the Strawberry Square Mall in Harrisburg, Pennsylvania, has 12 restaurants ranging from pizza places to luxury gourmet restaurants.

Fast-Food Outlets. An increasing number of fast-food tenants are opening facilities in major shopping centers around the nation. For example, McDonald's has an outlet at Water Tower Place in Chicago, Illinois. Sales in the fast-food outlets are increasing at a faster rate than sales in the full-service restaurants.

Entertainment Facilities

Entertainment facilities—including theaters, electronic games, and ice rinks—are also important to the success of shopping centers. Some developers of centers see entertainment facilities as a way to bolster revenues. The ice arena located in San Diego's University Town Center generated $1 million in revenues during its first year of operation. Also, some centers are experimenting with art galleries, cabarets, and electronic game centers.

Realizing Career Opportunities

In Units 1 and 2 you read about careers in the field of retailing and learned how to get a job. In Unit 3 you learned how to get promoted in the field. In this unit you have had an opportunity to learn about some of the new developments and trends in retailing. Whether you prefer to work in a large or a small firm, in a full-service or self-service firm, for somebody else or for yourself, all these career opportunities in retailing are open to you. In the chapters that follow, you will have an opportunity to learn how to get started, how to become a master employee, and how to move towards management and ownership careers in the field of retailing.

Trade Talk

Define each term and use it in a sentence.

Electronic funds
    transfer (EFT)

Scrambled
    merchandising

Limited-line
    groceries
Outlet stores

Subregional centers
Superstores

Can You Answer These?

1. What are limited-line groceries and why are they economical?
2. What types of things are shopping centers doing to make shopping more pleasurable?
3. What are some career opportunities in retailing for the future?
4. Name some recent trends that have developed in retailing.

Problems

1. Rule a form similar to the following. In the left column, write the letter of each of the following goods: (*a*) a soft drink, (*b*) sheets, (*c*) milk, (*d*) soup, (*e*) a sofa, (*f*) a sweater, and (*g*) a leather jacket. In the middle columns, indicate with a check mark (√) whether each is suitable or unsuitable to be sold by means of automated shopping techniques. In the left column, explain your decision.

Product	Suitable for Automated Shopping	Unsuitable for Automated Shopping	Explanation

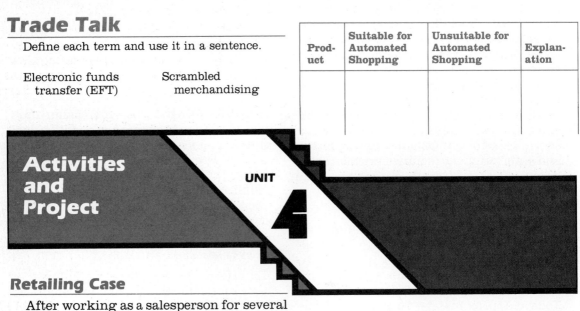

Activities and Project

UNIT 4

Retailing Case

After working as a salesperson for several years, you have been promoted to merchandise manager. The store is very concerned with the conversion to the metrics. As the merchandise manager, you have been asked to design a program to make the conversion to the metric system easy for both employees and customers.

1. Describe the methods and steps you would use to help the employees understand and use metrics.
2. Describe how you would assist the customers in understanding the conversion. Remember, all merchandise will be marked in metric measurements.

Working with People

You are an employee in a small, well-established retail clothing store that has operated in the same manner for the last 20 years. On Monday morning, Mr. Rivera, the owner, announced to his six employees that the store was going to change several procedures. He had decided it was time to get into the swing of things. The changes to be made include the installation of a new electronic computer, which will keep the inventory, do credit checking on customers, and eliminate the Rivera's charge cards. All accounting including payroll will also be computerized. Mr. Rivera explained that these changes were needed because the store was not keeping up with other stores in the mall and therefore losing profits.

Mr. Rivera's announcement caused a lot of gossip among the sales staff. Several of the employees said that the company would not be improving its business but would become impersonal, like all the other stores. Several of the employees began to think about quitting; they believed the computer would be replacing them.

1. Identify the true problem.

2. What are the important facts to be considered in this case?
3. List several possible solutions to this problem.
4. Evaluate the possible results of each solution.
5. Which solution do you recommend? Why?

Project 4: Examining the Trends in Retailing

Your Project Goal
Compare the advantages and disadvantages of each of the following trends in retailing for retailers and for their customers.

- Electronic point-of-sale systems
- Electronic funds transfer
- Data communication
- Teleshopping
- Credit plans
- Paying bills by telephone
- Catalog shopping
- Superstores

Procedure
1. Select several different stores that are using one or more of the items listed as trends.
2. Write a brief report describing each innovation the store is using. Include in the report the benefits to the customers and to the store and the possible disadvantages to both.

Evaluation
You will be evaluated on how carefully and completely you have described the trends as well as the advantages and disadvantages to the store and the customers.

2

GETTING STARTED

had been in the store for a couple of months, doing things like keeping the stock straight, cleaning up after closing, and inventory work. I also waited on customers, but since I didn't know much, I mostly rang up sales and wrapped the merchandise.

After a while, when I proved I could do some things right, the manager told me he wanted me to learn more. More money—that sounded great! And you know, I realized that I could go places in retailing. And to top it off, I could earn more money.

So, I began my new training. The manager said I was being "upgraded," which meant being trained to do more things and to do them better.

When school started, I asked for a transfer to a class to study retailing and marketing. I had to admit I needed to learn a lot. I especially needed some help in selling. Then I could handle it when people came in and asked for my recommendation on what brand of tennis balls to buy. I also needed to learn more about sales promotion, since the manager had asked me to help plan the fall sports promotion. I needed to learn more about consumers, and how to analyze a product. This business turned out to be more involved than I thought it was. There's a lot more to it than just carrying boxes!

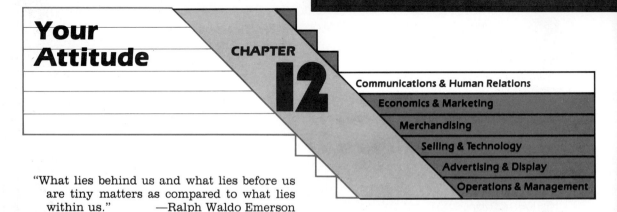

UNIT 5

Getting Along with Your Coworkers

Your Attitude

CHAPTER 12

Communications & Human Relations

Economics & Marketing

Merchandising

Selling & Technology

Advertising & Display

Operations & Management

"What lies behind us and what lies before us are tiny matters as compared to what lies within us."　　—Ralph Waldo Emerson

"Good, better, best, never let it rest until you do your best." This is the attitude that all retail workers must develop to perform well on the job and to be successful. In retailing more than in most other occupational fields, the ability to do your best is essential. Good retailing businesses are built by people who do their best in dealing with both customers and employees.

In this chapter of Unit 5, you'll be given some suggestions on how you can develop the type of attitude that you'll need for your retailing career. The suggestions are about planning for excellence, getting motivated, and learning to be successful.

Planning for Excellence

The first thing to keep in mind is that, just like everyone else, you're not perfect! But, also like everyone else, you can learn to do your very best. It's also a good idea not to demand perfection at every moment—of yourself or of anyone else. By developing the attitude that you expect only the best, not perfection, of yourself and of others, you'll not only achieve more but also be appreciated more. People usually give their best effort and develop the attitude of "good, better, best" if they don't feel that they'll be threatened if they fail to perform perfectly.

You may be wondering, "How can I plan to be excellent in a job if I don't know what excellence really is or when I will have achieved it?" One way to start is by setting goals for yourself. In Units 1, 2, and 3, you learned the why and how of planning a career in retailing. So plan your goals so that excellence, as you see it, is the ultimate end. It's up to you!

The following quote appeared on a menu in a restaurant—it illustrates the importance of goal setting: "As you wander on through life, no matter what your goal, keep your eye upon the donut and not upon the hole." Try to make sure that you will be able to achieve the retailing career goals you set for yourself. Figure out how and work hard to reach them. Then, when you've achieved those goals, set your sights higher, on bigger and better goals. Setting goals and achieving them is dependent upon your motivation, and motivation is the key to achieving excellence.

Getting Motivated

Motivation is really a two-part process. First, you must know something about yourself and have the feeling that you want to achieve success in your retailing career. Next, you must have enthusiasm and a positive attitude.

Know Yourself

How you see yourself as a retail employee will affect your success on the job. There may be a difference, however, between the way you see yourself and the way other people see you. In retailing, how you are seen by your customers, coworkers, and employers is very important. So it's a good idea to find out whether the way you see yourself agrees with the way others see you. In doing this, try to keep in mind that many of the behaviors you developed at home and in school will often be carried over into your retailing job. By comparing these behaviors with behaviors needed for success in retailing, you can find out something about yourself. Then you'll be in a position to get yourself motivated.

It's important to see yourself as others see you.

A list of some of the personal qualities that customers, employers, and coworkers find most desirable are listed below. To learn more about yourself, think about whether you have any of these qualities.

This list by no means covers all the qualities you may have. You'll probably be able to list some additional ones that are unique to you, your life goals, and your career in retailing.

Affectionate: having warm regard

Attractive: arousing interest or pleasure, charming

Cheerful: being full of good spirits, glad

Compassionate: having or showing sympathy

Dependable: being reliable, capable of being depended on

Enthusiastic: filled with zest, zeal, optimism, and a strong positive attitude

Expressive: being able to communicate real feelings

Flexible: being willing to change your mind and adjust to new situations

Forgiving: being willing or able to forgive or pardon

Helpful: being of service or assistance

Humble: being deeply or courteously respectful

Independent: making up your own mind, not being unduly influenced by others

Intelligent: being mentally keen or quick, rational

Kind: showing or having a considerate nature, gentle

Open-minded: being aware of what's going on and willing to learn from others and not be defensive

Outgoing: being friendly, responsive

Patient: enduring calmly without complaining or losing control

Persistent: having intense motivation to accomplish objectives even in face of heavy obstacles

Realistic: being aware of the complexities of situations but not overwhelmed by them

Self-accepting: believing in yourself and striving to achieve your true potential

Sense of humor: perceiving the fun of things

Sensitive: being aware of other people's thoughts and feelings

Thoughtful: being considerate, attentive

Tolerant: respecting the rights and opinions of others

How did you rate? What sort of picture are you getting of yourself? Ask yourself questions such as the following:

♦ What five of the listed qualities do I have?
♦ How can I improve these qualities?
♦ What qualities should I add to these five?
♦ What five things do I want most out of my life?

You may even want to ask yourself, "Who do I think I am?"

Understand Motivation

To be motivated, you must not only know something about yourself but also become enthusiastic about being motivated.

The following seven suggestions are designed to help you increase your motivation. The suggestion begins with you—it's up to you to want to be motivated. If you don't, all the aids in the world can't help you. But if you have the dedication, desire, determination, and discipline, you'll find the following suggestions helpful:

1. Care enough about yourself to want to improve.
2. Listen actively to discover your needs, wants, and problems.
3. Learn more of your own strengths and weaknesses and learn to like yourself.

4. Involve others and obtain their ideas and suggestions.
5. Give encouragement to and build on the strengths of others.
6. Make sure you acknowledge other people's performance according to the effort they have put into a job or task.
7. Do not demand perfection, but expect excellence.

Develop Optimism

Attitude is most easily observed when you ask someone a very simple question. That question is "Are you happy?" Just as a doctor can measure your degrees of body temperature by using a thermometer, you can measure the degree of optimism or pessimism in people around you by asking them if they are happy. What's the difference between an optimist and a pessimist?

♦ Optimists go out and secure sales; pessimists talk about how bad business is.

♦ Optimists see a person and think of a sale; pessimists see a person and think of work.
♦ Optimists feed on faith and enrich their opportunities; pessimists nibble on negatives and weaken their courage.
♦ Optimists see that many things in the world are improving; pessimists see that many things in the world are getting worse.
♦ Optimists enjoy the present; pessimists fear the future.

Retailing requires a certain amount of optimism because it's a people business and people tend to like people who are optimists. Based on whether they have a positive or negative attitude toward life, people basically can be classified into one of three categories. Into which of the following three categories would you place an optimistic and successful retailer?

1. People who *make things happen*

Most successful retailers are optimists.

2. People who *watch things happen*
3. People who *wonder what happened*

An optimistic retailer is, of course, a person who *makes things happen*. For example, at the beginning of winter, a sporting-goods retailer may offer a free cross-country ski clinic to customers who buy or rent skis rather than wait for cold weather to bring customers into the store.

Learning to Be Successful

If you're the type of person who reaches out to learn, then you're already on your way to being successful in retailing. By setting goals and eventually achieving them, you'll begin to develop your capabilities and gain confidence. But remember that no one is successful all the time. You must be willing to learn and to risk failure in order to experience success. Confidence is the feeling that it can happen. Failure is only temporary—never permanent—unless you let it be. The key is to keep on learning from successes and failures.

You can learn to be successful in your retailing career by understanding the circle of learning: adjusting to change, building a sound foundation, and realizing that success is a caring process.

The Circle of Learning

Learning can be described as a circular process that begins and ends with the learner. It's an activity that never ends. In retailing, because of rapid technological advancements, an understanding of this idea is especially important. Listed below are the four parts in the circle of learning:

1. Cultivate a desire to learn something new.
2. Begin to learn and possibly make mistakes or even fail.
3. Gain confidence with practice and experience.
4. Become secure with this newly acquired knowledge or skill.

The four D's of successful learning are:

♦ Discipline—a trained condition of order and obedience
♦ Dedication—a complete concentration of energy to a purpose
♦ Desire—a strong hope
♦ Determination—a firm commitment

If you try to follow the four D's, you'll make your career in retailing not only more interesting but also probably more successful. Why? Because learning to learn is just as important as what is learned. When you want to learn and succeed, you're on your way to succeeding. Remember, it is *attitude* plus *aptitude* that determines *success*.

Adjusting to Change

Because nothing stays the same for long in the field of retailing, it is essential for retailers to be able to adjust to change. And their attitudes toward change affect their ability to deal with it effectively. Retailers who ask themselves the question, "How could this change help me and others?" are off to a good start. In the same way, retailers who view a change as a challenge tend to accept and welcome it. On the other hand, retailers who view change as a bother tend to resist it and be irritated by it. As a famous writer once said, "An adventure is an inconvenience rightly considered; an inconvenience is an adventure wrongly considered."

You'll have an easier time adjusting to change and succeeding in retailing if you keep yourself in good health by eating properly and getting adequate rest and exercise. You'll tend to be more alert and have a positive outlook on life. It can be said that a person who accepts change is likely to adjust to it; a person who resists change may have difficulty adjusting. A person who can accept change also has the ability to be flexible and is therefore able to keep options open and to capitalize on change.

A Sound Foundation

Just as a contractor knows that a strong foundation is the key to a firmly erected building, so a foundation of positive attitudes will support your future career in retailing and allow it to withstand the tests of time. Such attitudes will help you not only to get off on the right foot in your

If you are physically fit, you will not find it difficult to adjust to change. Courtesy of Virginia State Travel Service

retailing career but also to advance as far as you want to go.

Success Is a Caring Process

A positive attitude to life may be summarized by the statement, "You win a few, you lose a few, some will get rained out; but dress for all of them." Or, to put it another way, don't give up before you've even tried. Success is a matter of caring not only about yourself but also about the kind of world you live in, your family, your job, and your friends.

The lifelong process of developing a strong, positive attitude can best be evaluated by answering one question: "If everybody in the world lived as you do now, worked as you do on your job, accomplished what you do each day, would our country be better off or worse off?" You *can* develop an attitude that you care enough to give your family, your job, your friends, and your life, the very best.

In this chapter, you've been given some suggestions on how you can develop the type of attitude that's essential for retail workers. In the next two chapters in this unit, you'll gain an understanding of why such an attitude is essential. Chapter 13 deals with communications and Chapter 14 with human relations. To be an effective retail worker, you'll need skills in both these areas. And you'll find that these skills will be a lot easier to acquire if you've developed a positive attitude first.

Can You Answer These?

1. What is the key to achieving excellence?
2. What are the five questions you can ask to improve your understanding of yourself?
3. What are the seven suggestions for motivation?
4. What are the four D's of successful learning?
5. What kind of people have the easiest time adjusting to change?

Problems

1. Rule a form similar to the following. In the left column, write the letter of each of the following personal qualities desired by customers, coworkers, and employers: (0) forgivingness, (a) humility, (b) helpfulness, (c) tolerance, (d) thoughtfulness, and (e) sincerity. In the two columns to the right, describe what you could do in school and on the job that would demonstrate the personal quality in action.

Personal Quality	Behavior in School	Behavior on the Job
Example: (0)	Forgive friends who may have said something untrue about me.	Forgive the supervisor who may have falsely accused me of making a mistake.

2. Rule a form similar to the following. In the left column, list your personality strengths (positive qualities). In the middle column, list your personality weaknesses (traits that should be changed). Be honest with yourself. Do you have more strengths than weaknesses? In the right column, list one or more steps you might take to correct your weaknesses.

Strengths	Weaknesses	How to Correct My Weaknesses

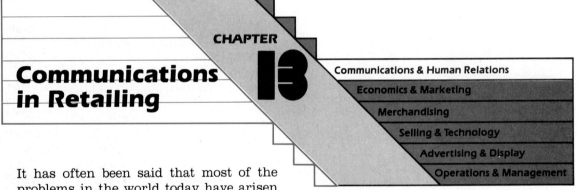

CHAPTER 13

Communications in Retailing

Communications & Human Relations

Economics & Marketing

Merchandising

Selling & Technology

Advertising & Display

Operations & Management

It has often been said that most of the problems in the world today have arisen because of poor communications. Why don't people communicate effectively with each other? In this chapter, you'll be given some answers to that question as well as some tips on how it is possible to become an effective communicator.

Just what is communications? **Communications** can be simply defined as the sending and receiving of messages. Communication takes place between two or more people, and good communication involves listening or reading the other person's thoughts as well as expressing or writing your own. To be effective, communication must provide for a two-way exchange of ideas, opinions, facts, or emotions.

In retailing, executives consistently emphasize the importance of communications. The reason they do so is because poor communications is one of the major problem areas in the day-to-day operation of their businesses. All too often, they have to spend a great deal of time and effort in trying to solve communication problems between their supervisors and employees and between their employees and customers. They know of too many businesses that have failed because of poor communications, so they continually guard against this happening in their own firms.

As retail firms grow in size, personal contact between employer and employee, salesperson and customer, and even supervisor and management becomes more difficult to maintain. It is management's responsibility to work continually to improve communications as a business grows. In fact, in most businesses, it's almost impossible to succeed in a supervisor's position without having developed effective communication skills. While face-to-face communication is usually more effective than any other type, problems of size and distance often make such personal contact impossible. For example, sometimes customer contacts have to be made through advertising, and employees and suppliers have to be reached through memos or letters or by telephone.

Verbal and Non-Verbal Communication

When you think of the ways in which you communicate with others, what comes to mind first? Writing? Or speaking or **verbal communication?** But have you ever thought of how you also let others know what you think and feel by **non-verbal communication,** such as smiling, laughing, touching, coughing, frowning, shaking hands, kissing, or even hitting? Non-verbal communication plays an important role in both the receiving and the sending of messages. For example, if your shoulders droop, your head hangs, and you shuffle along, you're telling people that you don't think much of yourself or that you are sad. However, when you hold your head and shoulders high and greet your customers or coworkers with a pleasant smile and cheerful "Good morning," you're demonstrating your friendliness, enthusiasm, and self-confidence. If you yawn

and act bored as you listen to your supervisor, you'll give the impression that you don't care. But if you watch everything that is done, listen attentively, and ask questions, you'll show that you're an interested and concerned worker.

Frequently, verbal and non-verbal communications are used at the same time. Your face and your body as well as your words tell others that you are angry, afraid, bored, sad, or happy.

Communication Sending Skills

The abilities in speaking and writing that enable people to express themselves effectively to others are called communication sending skills. To brush up your sending skills and to help you become an effective communicator, follow the suggestions in the next few pages.

Before actually sending a message, form a clear idea of what you want to say or write. Begin by thinking through the answers to questions such as these:

Who?   To whom are you talking or writing? What kind of people are they? Do they know enough about the subject to act upon your message? If they can't act upon your message, who can?

What?   What is the purpose of your message? What are you trying to say? What background information should you give? What should you leave out? In what form should you send your message? By way of a letter? The telephone? An ad? A speech?

Why?   Why is it important? Why should you tell your ideas to the person you're addressing? Why are you sending the message?

When?   When should you send the message?

How?   How should your message be communicated—in speaking or in writing? How can you be sure the receiver will lis-

A good retailer like this newspaper vendor uses both verbal and nonverbal communication. Jan Halaska/Photo Researchers, Inc.

ten to or read the message? How can you address your customers, coworkers, and supervisors in the most businesslike manner?

Speaking

The most important thing to remember when you are communicating through speaking is simply this: Think before you speak. Think about your intended listeners, who they are, the extent of their knowledge of the subject, and what it will take to capture their interest. This planning will help you to prepare a logically organized, clear, and brief message.

If you have to deal with customers, remember that poor or awkward grammar and poor enunciation or pronunciation may give them a bad opinion of everything about your firm.

No matter whom you're talking to, try to get your meaning across clearly. It will help if, without talking down to others, you use simple words and short sentences. If you speak too quickly, you will confuse your listeners. If you speak too slowly, you will bore them; and if you talk too much, you will frighten them away. Talk at a moderate speed and use voice inflections for emphasis. Your tone of voice can go a long way toward conveying your welcome and eagerness to be of service.

Remember that communication is a two-way process. So allow your listeners to express their own ideas. For example, listen to customers when they are expressing their needs and seek out the merchandise that answers these needs. Don't get upset if their opinions differ from yours. Avoid showing anger or bluntly contradicting your listeners. Instead, clarify the points you wish to make and end your message with a summary. If your communication has been well thought out and carefully presented, your views won't go unnoticed. By talking clearly and pleasantly and yet conveying spirit and enthusiasm, you'll be most effective in gaining the confidence of listeners.

Writing

The ability to write clearly is one of the most valuable of the communication sending skills. Written ideas need to be especially easy to understand because the receiver cannot always ask the writer questions. So don't assume that your reader will guess your meaning; make your ideas clear. You can do this by avoiding big words, long sentences, and too many ad-

jectives. Remember that when ideas are impersonal, they are more difficult to understand.

The main purpose of a written communication is to send a specific message. At the same time, however, the communication may reveal much about the writer's personality. Make sure your communication shows you at your best.

The following checklist can help you communicate effectively in writing.

1. Check your writing plan. Ask yourself:
   a. What is the purpose of writing?
   b. What is the expected result of writing?
   c. Who will the readers be?
   d. What action is wanted from the readers?
2. Check your outline. Ask yourself:
   a. What material or facts are to be communicated?
   b. Which of these are suited to the purpose of writing?

Remember that customers can hear the smile in your voice. Courtesy of Delta Air Lines

c. Is the outline arranged in a logical order?

d. Is the outline complete?

e. What illustrations or support materials are needed?

3. Check your written copy for clarity. Ask yourself:

a. Is the purpose clear?

b. Is it written in terms the reader knows?

c. Are unfamiliar words and abbreviations avoided?

d. Are important ideas emphasized?

e. Will the information be of interest to the reader?

f. Are your recommendations, conclusions, or ideas logical and clearly stated?

4. Check your copy for conciseness. Ask yourself:

a. Is the writing as brief as possible?

b. Does it get to the point quickly?

c. Are the sentences short and simple?

5. Check your copy for correctness. Ask yourself:

a. Is the grammar correct?

b. Are all the words spelled correctly?

c. Is the punctuation used properly?

d. Are facts and figures accurate?

6. Check your copy for completeness. Ask yourself:

a. Is it dated and signed?

b. Is it clear to whom it is to be sent?

c. Is it clear whether a reply is expected?

Communication Receiving Skills

In retailing, as in many other fields, most employees have to be skillful in the receiving skills of listening and reading because they are given many spoken and written directions, instructions, and suggestions.

Listening

Listening has been called the most important link in business communications because it is used the most. It's also the weakest link because many people don't know how to listen. The causes of poor listening are:

◆ *Lack of Attention*. People have short listening spans.

◆ *Lack of Understanding*. In a 10-minute conversation, a listener hears between 500 and 1,000 words. Some of these words are likely to have different meanings for the receiver and the sender, so they may be misinterpreted.

◆ *Difference in Speed*. People think much faster than they speak. Because the listener's thoughts travel faster than the speaker's words, the listener's mind tends to wander.

◆ *Poor Environment*. Physical factors such as noise can make listening difficult.

◆ *Bias*. Biased listeners interpret a communication in terms of their own prejudices, moods, and attitudes toward the topic or the sender. They don't view the topic or the sender objectively.

With all these obstacles to surmount, is it impossible to be a good listener? Not really—once you know about these obstacles, you can overcome them. Here is how you can become a better listener:

1. *Give immediate feedback*. One way to ensure real understanding is to make an immediate restatement of the communication. Even the best listeners will occasionally misinterpret the spoken word; therefore it's important to repeat the message to the sender. Simple feedback such as, "What you are saying, Mr. Jones, is . . ." or, "In other words, you want me to. . . ." Make certain that both sender and receiver are speaking the same language.

2. *Empathize*. Look at things from the other person's point of view. Use your imagination to enter fully into the speaker's feelings and motives.

3. *Be aware of your emotions*. When you hear something that makes you anxious, excited, or angry, don't let your feelings block out the message to which you are listening. If you're aware of your emotions, you'll be able to control them and thus increase your listening efficiency.

4. *Use your eyes as well as your ears*. A speaker's

Physical factors can be a cause of poor listening, as in this noisy boutique.

gestures and facial expressions will often tell you things that words cannot convey.

5. *Become involved.* In your own mind, add what you know to what the speakers say, fill in the gaps in their speech, and maintain a running summary of the message.

6. *Listen for ideas.* Effective listeners try to sort out general ideas. For example, in a talk that involves facts, figures, or statistics, good listeners concentrate on the main points and highlights of the statement.

7. *Watch for "smokescreens."* Listen to how the words are spoken. People may tell you one thing but really mean something quite different. With practice, good listeners can determine the reasons for the smokescreen and uncover hidden meanings.

8. *Take time to listen.* No matter how busy you are, it's important for you to listen to your customers, your coworkers, your supervisors, and your subordinates.

Reading

Like listening, reading is an important communications skill. Many retail workers find that they receive so many written communications that they have to enroll in a speed-reading course just to get through them.

You'll be able to do your business reading more quickly if you sort the material you receive according to its importance. In this way you will be able to decide which things you don't have to read at all, which you can read quickly, and which you must read thoroughly. A few minutes of sorting may save you a lot of reading time.

When you read important material, give it your full and critical attention. Decide what the writer's purpose in sending the message was and what the message means. When the writer states an opinion, look for evidence to support it. Ask yourself if the sender has left anything out of the communication. These reading techniques will help you respond appropriately to written communications.

In this chapter, you've learned how both verbal and non-verbal communications are used in sending and receiving messages. You've also been given some suggestions that will help you to improve the communications you send and the messages you get from the communications you receive.

In your retailing career, you'll find that to get along with others, you'll need more than good communication skills—you'll also need good human relations skills. Read the next chapter to learn about these skills.

Trade Talk

Define each term and use it in a sentence.

Communications
Non-verbal
   communications
Verbal
   communications

Can You Answer These?

1. Does non-verbal communication play an important role in both the receiving and sending of messages? Explain.
2. Why is communication a two-way process?
3. Is it easier to communicate in a large or a small business? Why?
4. What are the two most important ways of communicating?
5. What are some of the barriers to clear writing?

Problems

1. Rule a form similar to the following. In the left column, write the letter of each of the following statements: (*0*) "Don't get shook. You'll get your money back." (*a*) "Can I help you?" (*b*) "You oughta like it."

(*c*) "We don't have any red shoes." (*d*) "There ain't no cheap ones left." (*e*) "Look in that aisle over there." (*f*) "You'll have to wait your turn." (*g*) "Mrs. Nicos is busy right now, but she'll be with you in a few minutes." (*h*) "You'll have to pay cash; we don't allow any charges." (*i*) "You're wrong. We never carried those tools." (*j*) "You won't get a better deal anywhere in town." If the statement is appropriate, place a check mark (√) in the column in the center; if the statement is poor, write a better one in the right column.

Statement	Appropriate Statement	Better Statement
Example: (0)		If you have your sales check, your money will be refunded immediately.

2. In the three following memos, ideas or requests are communicated in writing. On a separate sheet of paper, write the letter of each memo and after it tell what, if anything, is wrong with the memo.

a. To: John Hennessy, Department Head
September 10, 19—
From: Gabriel Stanos, Store Manager
Subject: Vacation Schedules
I have not received your employee vacation schedule as of this date. You are the only department head who has not turned it in. It was due last Friday. I want it on my desk this afternoon.

b. To: Harry Schoen, Controller
September 11, 19—
From: Gabriel Stanos, Store Manager
Subject: Budget Cuts
It has been forcefully and justly brought to my attention that our anticipated sales volume is lagging by a percentage reduction of 4 percent. Please revise our

programmed expenses to coincide with this data.

c. To: Sally McCullough, Salesperson
September 13, 19—
From: Gabriel Stanos, Store Manager

Subject: Selling Habits
I have just received your latest shopping report from our shopping service. I would suggest that you improve on your ability to increase sales. It is important that you meet your monthly sales quotas. You seem to have had trouble in the past and we want to get that volume up.

Human Relations in Retailing

CHAPTER 14

Communications & Human Relations
Economics & Marketing
Merchandising
Selling & Technology
Advertising & Display
Operations & Management

"A man without a smiling face must not open a shop." This ancient Chinese proverb has been passed on for many years, along with many other sayings such as, "Always treat other people as you want to be treated," "Courtesy is contagious," "If you live in a glass house, don't throw stones," and "Don't pass the buck." These sayings and many others that you've learned from your friends and parents are really guides for effective human relations. **Human relations** is the process of getting along with people.

In retailing more than in most other career fields, human relations skills are essential because retailing is a people business. Retailing employees have to learn how to get along with customers as well as with coworkers and employers. Employers will accept a lack of some retailing skills and knowledge in a beginner who is still learning the retailing field, but they will not overlook an inability to get along with others. In fact, most people lose their jobs because they can't get along with others, not because they lack technical job skills.

People learn how to get along with others by solving human relations problems. Some people react to the problems of getting along with parents, family, and teachers by running away from home or by dropping out of school. When relations with others become unpleasant, they just want to walk out on the situation. But walking out seldom solves a problem, so it's best not to make a habit of it. In the long run, problems will be solved by handling difficult situations.

Employers don't like to hire people who run away from difficult situations. For example, many employers avoid hiring people who have quit school. They feel that someone who has quit in one situation may be in the habit of walking out on problems rather than trying to cope with them. When people begin a job, it's not unusual for them to find that they have to make many adjustments to achieve good human relations—perhaps as many as they had to make at home and in school. These adjustments cannot be evaded; they have to be faced and dealt with.

Human Relations Start With "You"

If you get the chance some time, try tape recording your conversations. You might be amazed to hear how often the word "I" is used. In order to make and keep friends, try using the word "I" less frequently and to use "we" or "you" more often. Your choice and use of words is a good starting place for improving human relations. So keep the following list in mind to help you do just that.

♦ The six most important words: "I admit I made a mistake."
♦ The five most important words: "You did a good job."
♦ The four most important words: "What is your opinion?"
♦ The three most important words: "If you please."
♦ The two most important words: "Thank you."
♦ The one most important word: "We."
♦ The least important word: "I."

Here is another way you become aware of or sensitive to others. Get into the habit of making the other person instead of yourself a center of conversation. To assess your sensitivity to others, ask yourself the following 14 questions and see if you are pleased with your honest answers.

1. Do I show an interest in my customers, friends, coworkers, and employers?
2. Do I have respect for the feelings of others?
3. Do I have an understanding attitude toward people?
4. Do I praise work that is well done, regardless of who did it?
5. Do I find it easy to talk with people?
6. Do I make promises sparingly and keep them faithfully?
7. Do I try to make new friends?
8. Do I keep an open mind on debatable questions and discuss but not argue?
9. Am I willing to listen to ideas and suggestions?
10. Am I dependable and loyal?
11. Do I avoid repeating unkind remarks I have heard about others?
12. Do I avoid criticizing just for the sake of being critical?
13. Do I avoid making exaggerated statements just to gain attention?
14. Do I avoid judging people merely by their appearance?

If you're really concerned and thoughtful regarding other people, you'll probably find your dealings with others to be generally pleasant. However, if you find yourself trying to cope with an unpleasant person, remember that "telling that person off" won't improve matters. People who are moody, cranky, or troublesome cannot be changed overnight.

Throughout your retailing career, you'll probably have to deal with customers who seem almost impossible to get along with. Their thoughts, actions, and emotions may sometimes leave you baffled, especially when their behavior is very different from your own. In such situations, don't be too quick to judge. No two people are alike in their thoughts and emotions because no two people are molded by exactly the same experiences. This fact causes difficulties that can lead to many misunderstandings. When you find yourself at odds with your supervisors or coworkers, try to understand them and learn as much as possible about their points of view.

Personal Qualities Desired by Employers

Most employers know from experience that the personal qualities of each employee have a lot to do with how the employee gets along with coworkers, supervisors, and customers. In a research study, over 1,000 employers selected from a list of 10,000 were asked to indicate what personal qualities they felt were most desirable in employees. The employers indicated that they believed honesty and dependability to be most important. They

If you are genuinely concerned about other people, you will probably find your dealings with others to be pleasant. Jane Hamilton-Merritt

believed that the following were also important personal qualities: loyalty, cooperation, initiative, industriousness, tact, enthusiasm, self-confidence, pleasant personality, neat appearance, punctuality, desire to learn, and mental maturity. Possessing these qualities will not only commend you to an employer but also will very likely help you to make and keep friends.

These personal qualities are so important that they are sometimes labeled "occupational survival skills." In other words, if you want to survive on the job, do all you can to develop and exhibit these qualities.

Loyalty and Honesty

Loyalty is expressed in many ways. One important aspect of **loyalty** is being really concerned about your firm and protecting its interests. As a loyal employee, don't destructively criticize the firm, its poli-

cies, its personnel, or its merchandise, especially to outsiders. Also, be very careful not to disclose details of business operations; some competitors are eager for such information.

Don't constantly complain or gripe to fellow workers, gossip, spread rumors, or undercut the supervisory staff. Griping and gossiping can be very destructive, especially when they cause other employees to become unhappy or dissatisfied with their jobs.

Honesty means being truthful, trustworthy, sincere, fair, and straightforward in one's relationship with an employer. It includes refraining from lying, cheating, stealing, deceiving, and taking advantage of the company. There are many situations in which honesty and loyalty overlap. Where money and merchandise are involved, honesty becomes a part of loyalty. Constant care in handling money and credit transactions demonstrates loyalty. When you are handling the firm's money and merchandise, there is only one kind of honesty—complete honesty. For example, workers should never take unfair advantage of their discount privileges by helping their friends obtain merchandise at less than the required price.

Giving 100 percent effort is another form of loyalty. Wasting time on the job results in loss of profit to the business. Those who are loyal to themselves and their firm don't take advantage of leniency in supervision by overstaying lunch hours, overextending coffee breaks, or loafing on the job. The really loyal employees give no less than their best effort at all times.

Loyalty also means being completely fair with coworkers and customers. To be fair, don't gossip about customers and coworkers, steal sales, fail to keep your word, betray confidences, or shirk responsibilities. As a loyal employee, also be very careful always to represent the firm in the best possible manner.

Cooperation

Cooperation means acting or working together with another or others for mutual profit. The following story is a good example of cooperation. During a hike, a group of boys came across an abandoned section of railroad track. Each, in turn, tried walking the rails but eventually lost his balance and tumbled off. Suddenly two of the boys, after considerable whispering, offered to bet that they could both walk the entire length of the track without falling off. Having been challenged to make good their boast, the two boys jumped up on opposite rails, each extending a hand to balance each other, and walked the entire section of track with no difficulty whatever. This in a nutshell is the principle of cooperation. It is doing more things more effectively and more pleasantly by cooperating with others.

The difference between a good retail firm and a poor one, an efficient depart-

Cooperation can make the difference between a department that functions smoothly and one that does not. Jane Hamilton-Merritt

ment and an inefficient one, is often reflected in the cooperation or lack of it among the people who work there. When people help each other freely and voluntarily, a spirit of teamwork comes into play that makes a department or company function smoothly. When there is no cooperation—no spirit of the helping hand freely given—what might have been pleasant jobs become grudging chores. Cooperative employees observe business rules and policies and gratefully accept advice from employers.

Initiative

Those who have the ability to see a job that needs to be done and the determination to go ahead and do it without being told are said to possess **initiative.** Personnel directors frequently point out that initiative is a prime requirement in the selection of people for supervisory and management training. Retailing is a field in which initiative is extremely important. It is especially important in smaller firms, where duties are usually less well defined and there is frequently less supervision than in large firms.

After you've been on a job for a while and have learned about the business and the job, the next step is to demonstrate initiative. You will do this by finding additional jobs that need to be done, learning how to handle emergency situations, and handling new duties without help from others. Another way in which you'll show initiative is by using your idle or leisure time to learn more about the field of retailing. For example, you could ask for product information to study. In doing so, you will probably impress your supervisor as a person with initiative.

Industriousness

Industriousness is steady, earnest, diligent effort. Besides willingness to put in a full day's work for a full day's pay, industriousness means keeping constructively occupied or busy. It is the opposite of watching the clock, stalling, or taking other actions to avoid working. Industrious workers attend strictly to business and are not distracted by noise or other disturbances. They work as hard when they are alone—for example, arranging stock or building a display—as when someone is observing them, and their work will be so well done that no one will have to check on them.

People who are industrious like their jobs, know their jobs, and are anxious to get ahead. They are well on their way to a good career in retailing.

Tact

The ability to say and do the right thing at the right time is called **tact.** Tact is particularly needed when you are dealing with people who have strong likes and dislikes, who have grievances, and who have opinions that are in sharp disagreement with your own. Customers, coworkers, supervisors, or employers don't like to be contradicted in other than a pleasant, tactful manner. But it can be particularly difficult to remain pleasant in situations such as handling customer complaints or being blamed by a supervisor for something you didn't do.

If you have **empathy,** or the ability to feel the way another person does, you'll have no problem in handling a delicate subject or an oversensitive customer with tact. You'll think seriously about what to say to avoid hurting or embarrassing others, which also means that you have good control of your emotions and actions.

Tact is developed through study, practice, and experience in dealing with people. In retailing, there are many times when tact is important. For example, in selling jewelry to a tall woman, a salesperson could say, "This long pearl necklace calls for someone of your height," rather than "You're too tall for the short strand."

Enthusiasm

Enthusiasm is an intense and eager interest in a subject. People show enthusiasm in many ways. On-the-job enthusiasm is most easily shown by looking alert and alive. Having a ready smile for customers, coworkers, and supervisory personnel also reflects enthusiasm. For example, by showing pride in your department and place of employment and by willingly doing more work than others, you'll demonstrate enthusiasm.

Enthusiasm is especially important to salespeople in convincing customers to buy because it has a positive and contagious effect. Comments such as "I'm excited about our new line of jackets, Mr. Zaltman," assures the customer of your belief in the product or service being sold. Also, if you demonstrate a positive attitude and are optimistic, others will be pleased to deal with you and you'll be a better overall employee and coworker.

Keys to Good Coworker Relations

Carefully considering how to be more thoughtful toward others can help you achieve friendly relations with coworkers. It has already been mentioned that demonstrating a concern for the feelings of other people can help assure pleasant relationships. And here are four additional keys for good relations with coworkers: (1) treat people as individuals, (2) never pass the buck, (3) stand up for yourself, and (4) stay on the team.

Treat Coworkers as Individuals

As a wise employee, you'll recognize that there are great differences in individuals and try to understand and accept them. No two coworkers are exactly alike. Some behave unpleasantly at work because they have problems at home, while others may have financial difficulties that make them grouchy or tense. Still others have personality problems that make them uncommunicative and even belligerent. Try to understand your coworkers' actions by putting yourself in their positions. For example, suppose a coworker, Larry, lost his temper quickly and shouted at you. Try to think why he behaved like this. Was it because Larry was feeling ill? Many peo-

If a coworker loses his temper, try to understand why he behaves like this.

ple get tired and irritable when they don't feel well. So, instead of becoming angry, stay calm and help Larry regain his composure.

People should be treated as individuals all the time, not only when problems are being solved. Learn the names of your coworkers, help them when they ask for advice, and listen carefully and respectfully to any suggestions they may offer.

Never Pass the Buck

Blaming coworkers for errors or shifting responsibility for a job to others is called **passing the buck.** Passing the buck is a sure way to become unpopular with coworkers. Those who can stand on their own two feet, do their job to the best of their ability, do their share of the work, and admit to their mistakes are normally well liked by their coworkers. Everybody makes mistakes, so by admitting mistakes and errors you show confidence—not lack of it.

Stand Up for Yourself

Some people believe they can get ahead by taking credit for someone else's work or by blaming someone else for their mistakes. If you find that a coworker is taking advantage of you or others, tell that person quietly but firmly that this practice can't continue. If this doesn't work, take the matter up with a supervisor or another appropriate individual. Supervisors and employers want to know what is happening. They want and need to know who is doing what so they can give the appropriate credit.

Stay on the Team

Workers' attitudes and performance can help establish smooth operations in a department and in the firm. Good retail teams, like good athletic teams, are built on a spirit of teamwork. Employees who are willing to pitch in, accept change, learn new procedures and techniques, and help others when help is needed are valuable members of a retailing team.

When you've been on the job for some time, be particularly aware of the needs of new employees. They may have special needs that require special attention. If you work with a cooperative spirit, you'll be liked and respected by your coworkers and you'll show that you've been successful in your on-the-job human relationships.

Now that you've completed this unit, you should have a better understanding of why the personal qualities that make up attitude and determine the ability to become an effective communicator and get along with others are so important in retailing. You should also have a clearer idea of the qualities you already possess and those that you lack or could improve.

Trade Talk

Define each term and use it in a sentence.

Cooperation	Industriousness
Empathy	Initiative
Enthusiasm	Loyalty
Honesty	Passing the buck
Human relations	Tact

Can You Answer These?

1. What is the first step toward good human relations?
2. How can you demonstrate to your employer that you are loyal?
3. How can empathy help you to be tactful?
4. What are the four keys to good coworker relations?
5. What should you do if someone tries to "pass the buck" to you?

Problems

1. Rule a form similar to the following. In the left column, write the letter of each of the following personal qualities: (0) loyalty and honesty, (a) dependability, (b) cooperation, (c) initiative, (d) industriousness, (e) tact, and (f) enthusiasm. In the

two columns to the right, describe what you could do in school and on the job that would demonstrate each personal quality in action.

Personal Quality	Behavior in School	Behavior on the Job
Example: (0)	Don't cheat on an exam.	Don't steal merchandise.

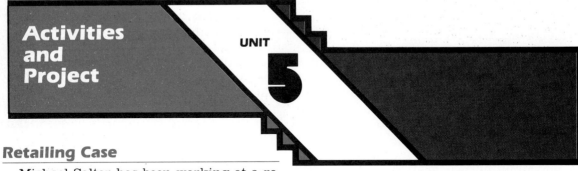

Activities and Project

Retailing Case

Michael Salter has been working at a record store for one week. On his first day, the store manager, Faith Smith, explained in detail the procedures to follow when customers wanted to use a credit card to pay for purchases. Michael was nervous that first day and didn't concentrate on everything Mrs. Smith told him, nor did he fully understand all the instructions. Because Michael didn't raise any questions, Mrs. Smith assumed that Michael understood the procedures. However, when Mrs. Smith checked on Michael the next day, she found that he was making errors that could cost the store money.

1. What communications skill did Michael neglect the first day on the job?
2. What do you think caused Michael's communications problem? Explain your reasons.
3. What communications skill did Mrs. Smith neglect when she was giving Michael instructions?
4. In what way do you think Mrs. Smith could have realized that Michael was experiencing a communications problem?

Working with People

In order to reduce costs and improve customer services, the supermarket in which Ted Singer has been working for a year has decided to install computerized checkout systems. The supermarket manager, Tom Washington, thinks that Ted is a hard worker and that his chances for promotion are good. Explaining this to Ted, Mr. Washington asked Ted to take a course in computer technology at the local community college, and told him that the company would pay the tuition. Mr. Washington explained to Ted that the course would help him gain an understanding of computerized checkout systems that would be useful for his future career with the supermarket. Ted, however, decided to turn down Mr. Washington's offer because he didn't like the idea of switching to computerized systems when he already knew the present system inside out. Ted figured he'd do something in the supermarket that didn't involve computers. Because Ted refused this offer, Mr. Washington no longer thinks of Ted as a suitable candidate for promotion.

1. Identify the true problem.
2. What are the important facts to be considered in this problem?
3. List several solutions to this problem.

4. Evaluate the possible results of each solution.
5. Which solution do you recommend? Why?

Project 5: Determining the Importance of Human Relations

Your Project Goal
Given the opportunity to interview a supervisor in any retailing field, determine the importance of human-relations skills on the job.

Procedure
1. With your teacher's permission, contact a person with supervisory responsibility in any area of retailing. Make an appointment to interview this person.
2. Before you conduct the interview, do the following:
   a. On a separate sheet of paper, prepare a questionnaire like the following:

Personal Qualities Desired by Employers	Rating (1–5)
In employees, what importance do you give to:	

   In the left column, list the seven personal qualities discussed in Chapter 14. In the right column, you will record the interviewee's responses. Record a rating of 1 if the interviewee thinks the quality is most desired; record 5 if it is least desired.
   b. On another sheet of paper, prepare a questionnaire like the following:

   The rating system is the same as in Procedure 2a.

Keys to Good Coworker Relations	Rating (1–5)
How important is it that:	
1. Coworkers treat each other as individuals?	
2. Employees never pass the buck?	
3. Employees stand up for themselves?	
4. Employees work as a team?	

3. Take these two sheets of paper with you when you go on your interview. Record the interviewee's responses carefully.
4. When you return from your interview, study the ratings for each question on both questionnaires. What do these results tell you about the importance of human relations in retailing? Think about it for a while, and then write a short report summarizing the results and explaining why some questions got higher or lower ratings than others. (You may want to re-read Chapter 14 to help you do this.)
5. Compare your result with those of other students in your class. What differences or similarities do you find? Did it make a difference in the results if the people interviewed were in different fields of retailing?

Evaluation
You will be evaluated on the reasons by which you justified the different ratings among the personal qualities and keys to good coworker relations.

The Changing Consumer Market

CHAPTER

15

Communications & Human Relations

Economics & Marketing

Merchandising

Selling & Technology

Advertising & Display

Operations & Management

It is Wednesday, 6:15 p.m. Jason Hamalian has stopped at a supermarket on his way home from work. He pauses a moment to scan his shopping list before checking out. A quick look in the cart shows that there are frozen TV dinners, doughnuts, breakfast rolls, potato salad, barbecued chicken, cole slaw, camera film, toothpaste, cough syrup, a pair of scissors and two spools of thread, a plant, plant food, potting soil, bread, milk, and meat. Really not a very unusual scene nowadays, is it? Yet how very different it is than it would have been 25 years ago!

Research reveals that many people today think of most shopping as something to be done as quickly as possible. A few years ago it was considered a pleasant way of spending time. What will shopping be like in 25 years? How many of the items in Jason Hamalian's cart would have been purchased by his grandmother in a grocery store 25 years ago? How many of them will still be purchased in a supermarket 25 years from now? These questions can't be answered with complete accuracy because retail merchandising is constantly changing to serve the changing needs and wants of consumers.

Consumers are all people who buy and use products and services. So the consumer market is made up of people with needs to satisfy and money to spend. Everyone is part of the consumer market because everyone spends money. But people differ in the amount of money they have to spend and in the things they are willing to purchase. Retailers who know what their customers want to buy have a head start in planning, buying, promotion, and the future of their businesses.

In short, retailers study the makeup of their consumer markets and try to determine what their customers will buy and how much they are likely to spend for different products or services.

Population Changes

According to U.S. government population projections, it's likely that over 260 million people will be living in this country by the year 2000. Their buying patterns will be important to retailers everywhere. Some of the things that influence buying patterns in this country have to do with age, metropolitan-suburban growth patterns, changes in number and size of households, and mobility of the population in general. All these things are discussed in the following sections.

Changes in Proportion of Age Groups

Retailers watch national, regional, state, and district changes in the proportion of age groups in their trading areas. By the year 2000, the percentage of teenagers and young adults (aged 15 to 29) will drop from almost 50 percent of the total population to 43 percent. So then retailers selling products and services such as sportswear, pizzas, and stereo records to consumers in this age group will be strongly affected.

The number of people in the older adult (aged 30 to 64) age group is increasing as a percentage of America's total population and is expected to have grown by 6.4 percent by the year 2000. A growth from 39.1 percent to 45.5 percent of the population in this age group will mean increased sales for retailers of travel and leisure services, restaurant services, home products, health services, furniture, and appliances.

Shift of Population to Suburban Areas

Local shifts in population are especially important in retail merchandising. For example, the average earnings of suburban families are one-fifth higher than earnings of city families. So, of course, suburban families usually spend more money than city families.

In general, the increase of the number of people living in outer-ring suburban areas is expected to continue as the number of people living in big cities declines. In many large cities, however, the population migration to the suburbs shows signs of leveling off and in some cases reversing itself. As a result, retailers are helping to rebuild downtown areas in cities such as Detroit, Kansas City, Philadelphia, Atlanta, Minneapolis, and Washington, D.C.

Standard Metropolitan Statistical Areas. To describe larger central cities and surrounding suburbs, the federal government uses the term *Standard Metropolitan Statistical Area* (SMSA). An **SMSA** consists of a county or a group of adjoining counties with a total population of at least 100,000 plus a central city with a minimum population of 50,000 (or two nearby cities with a combined population of 50,000). An SMSA must form a socially and economically integrated unit, and it must have almost no agricultural areas. An SMSA may span several states. For example, the New York City SMSA includes the states of New York, Connecticut, New Jersey, and Pennsylvania.

There are 221 SMSAs in the United States today, and 70 percent of the population lives in them. These areas have proved to be good consumer markets for retailers. The continued general growth of SMSAs means that more and more retailers will have to locate in suburban areas. And it also means that retailers will have to satisfy an increased consumer demand for items such as home- and lawn-care products, home furnishings, snow blowers, home freezers, do-it-yourself products, and home-entertainment and recreational items.

Inner City. As middle-income families move to the suburbs, the economic makeup of the inner city changes a great deal. Retailers in many central cities have to adapt their businesses to an entirely different consumer group. Retailers who are familiar with one set of buying patterns have to learn about and cater to an entirely

CORPUS CHRISTI
Sparkling City by the Sea

Sunshine...sandy beaches...gentle breezes.
Corpus Christi has a lot to offer.

Our SMSA is the market place of South Texas.
The Caller-Times reaches almost
8 out of 10 households in the metro market.

We are ranked 18th in per household retail sales,
98th in food sales and 91st in apparel sales.

When you buy Texas, make sure you've
got South Texas covered.

We'll put the wind in your sales!

Corpus Christi Caller-Times

Represented nationally by BRANHAM NEWSPAPER SALES

Sources: ABC Publisher's Statement 9/30/79
1979 S&MM Survey of Buying Power®

Standard Metropolitan Statistical Areas have proved to be good consumer markets for retailers. Courtesy of the *Corpus Christi Caller Times*

different set. This is because families that remain in the city often have less money to spend.

Changes in Number and Size of Households

Every time a person or a family sets up a new household, retailers of real estate, furniture, and household appliances and equipment have another potential customer. The number of new households is expected to increase a great deal and the size of the households to decrease. This is expected because of three major trends: (1) the tendency of young single people to live apart from parents, (2) the larger number of senior citizens who live apart from their adult children, and (3) the rising divorce rate.

For retailers, the number of households dealt with is often more important than the size of each household. For example, even if three households consist of only one person each, a salesperson may sell one blender to each of them, or three blenders in all. However, it is highly unlikely that the salesperson will sell three

blenders to one household that consists of three or more people. Retailers of furniture, housewares, and similar products and services essential for setting up a household can profit from this trend.

Mobility of Population

Americans are a mobile people. No longer is it taken for granted that people will stay in the town where they were born. In fact, approximately 20 percent of Americans change their addresses each year. In about 60 percent of these cases, the move is a local one. But in 40 percent of the instances, the move is to another state or county. So in a short period of time, the nation's population will be redistributed, with some regions growing more rapidly than others. The population of the Pacific, Sun Belt, and Mountain states is expected to increase faster than the population in other states.

Impact on Retailing. The mobility of the population may cause some retailers to be faced with the prospect of losing 20 percent of their customers every year. However, they do have the opportunity of gaining some new customers. To attract the new group, though, they must be alert to what goods and services are wanted. If they find that the new consumers in their community are very different from the old and if the retailers do not wish to make major changes in the nature of their businesses, they, too, should consider moving to new areas.

New Opportunities for Retailers.   In areas where the population is growing, retailers who have the greatest opportunity to take advantage of the mobility factor include:

♦ Retailers who sell well-known brands and those who operate easily recognized franchise chains.

♦ Retailers of rental services. Many newcomers prefer to rent big-ticket items rather than purchase them. They are reluctant to purchase when they think that they might have to move again soon.

♦ Retailers of clothing and home products. Newcomers purchase these types of items to make the adjustments required by climate and type of living.

♦ Retailers who advertise extensively and are a part of a nationwide credit plan. Newcomers often have to locate products and services they need quickly but cannot pay for them until a later date, when they have recovered financially from the cost of moving.

Income and Spending Patterns

When retailers want to increase their share of the consumer market, they must study not only population factors but also consumer income and how it is used. There are many kinds of income. **Personal income** is the amount of money a person receives from any source. Salary or professional fees, dividends, interest, and social security are some sources of personal income. **Disposable income** is personal income minus all federal, state, and local taxes. **Discretionary income** is the amount of money left after essential expenses have been met. Essential expenses include such items as clothing, rent, house mortgages, household utilities, local trans-

Retailers like Montgomery Ward are finding new opportunities to offer more services, like this "Legal Shop," to meet the needs of their customers. Courtesy of Montgomery Ward & Co.

portation, insurance, debt payments, and health care.

To retailers, discretionary income indicates the consumer's financial ability to purchase nonessential products and services. The amount of discretionary income consumers have is not necessarily the amount of money they will spend—they might save it, for example. However, it is the amount they could spend if they wished to do so. Discretionary income is also affected by the number of working members in a family. For example, a family that includes more than one working person will often have greater discretionary income.

American families spend about 10 percent of their income for clothing and accessories, 9 percent on medical and personal care, 5 percent on house furnishings and equipment, and 24 percent on housing. This does not mean that all families spend the same amount of money. Although a family with an income of $20,000 and one with an income of $10,000 may both spend 4 percent of their income on recreation, the dollar amount in one case would be $800 and $400 in the other.

Four major factors are increasingly having a major impact on the total amount of money that consumers spend for various products and services. These factors are inflation, the changing role of women, and changing family income patterns.

Inflation

During periods of inflation, or sharp increases in the costs of products and services, consumers can't spend as much simply because the purchasing power of their dollars has decreased. For example, consumers who, before inflation, could afford to eat out at least once or twice a week may have to cut out this expense

As their incomes increase, many consumers tend to spend larger amounts of money on nonessential, but desired, items. Richard Megna/Fundamental Photographs

during inflation because they have to spend more of their income on more costly essential items. So inflation reduces consumers' discretionary income and has a major effect on retailers who sell nonessential products and services.

Changing Role of Women

More women are working outside the home. In 1960, less than half of the work force consisted of women. By 1985, 58 percent of the work force is expected to be made up of women, with the largest gain in the 25 to 44 age group.

The average working woman today is married, 36 years old, and has one or more children under the age of 18 at home. This is in contrast to the more traditional average working woman of 1960, who was either young and unmarried or married and working to supplement the family income.

Less Time to Shop. Growth in the number of women who are workers, wives, and mothers all at the same time is more and more important to retailers. These women have less time to shop and are therefore less likely to go from store to store looking for bargains during the regular store hours. Especially when purchasing convenience goods, people who work—both men and women—are more likely to go to stores that are nearby, easy to get to, or open during the evening hours. Or they will buy through the mail or over the telephone. They usually prefer one-stop shopping even if it means paying higher prices.

Spending Patterns. Working people who can afford to do so spend larger amounts of money for time-saving products, services, and leisure products. Such products and services include major appliances, household equipment, repair service and rentals, sporting goods, travel, ready-made clothing, prepared and convenience foods, and restaurant meals. One implication of this for retailers is that when they advertise, they will now need to appeal to working women as well as to men.

Changing Family Income Patterns

Retailers need to study how income is distributed throughout various regions of the country and various segments of the population. The information from such studies can be extremely valuable to retailers in long-range planning. For example, in 1985, the average family income in the United States is expected to almost double the 1968 figure. In 1965, more than 40 percent of all families earned less than $15,000 and only 22 percent earned over $25,000. By 1985, almost 85 percent of all families are expected to be earning over $15,000.

However, this gain in income is not as large as it appears. Because of inflation, $15,000 can buy much less now than it could in 1965. Moreover, American consumers are now used to a higher standard of living. Many goods and services that consumers would have considered luxuries in 1965 they now consider almost necessities. So many families find their higher incomes inadequate to satisfy all their wants, and retailers must compete for every consumer dollar. Will this trend continue? The alert retailer must study the relevant data and make plans to take advantage of any possible changes.

In this chapter, you have been given an overall view of the changing consumer market, how this affects retailers, and what they can do to keep ahead and take advantage of such changes to better serve their customers.

In the next chapter, you'll learn in detail the information that retailers must obtain about consumers in order to offer the goods and services that potential buyers need and want.

Trade Talk

Define each term and use it in a sentence.

Consumers
Discretionary income
Disposable income
Personal income

SMSA (Standard
Metropolitan
Statistical Area)

Can You Answer These?

1. What does the shift in metropolitan-suburban population mean to inner-city and suburban retailers?
2. Why is an increase in the number and a decrease in the size of households important to retailers?
3. What does an increase in the disposable income of customers mean to a retailer?
4. How may family spending patterns be affected when the wife in the family works outside the home?
5. When discretionary income increases, which products and services are purchased in increased amounts?

Problems

1. Rule a form similar to the following. In the left column, write the letter of each of the following items: (0) birthstone rings, (a) bread, (b) coats, (c) TV sets, (d) gasoline, (e) oranges, (f) shirts, (g) shoes, (h) books, and (i) motorbikes. Place a check mark in one of the columns at the right to indicate whether the purchase of the item involved discretionary or nondiscretionary buying power.

Item	Discretionary Buying Power	Nondiscretionary Buying Power
Example: (0)	√	

Information about Consumers

CHAPTER 16

Communications & Human Relations
Economics & Marketing
Merchandising
Selling & Technology
Advertising & Display
Operations & Management

Why do you shop at one place of business in preference to another? Why do you avoid buying from some retailers in your community? Did you hear something bad about them or about their personnel? Did you have an unpleasant experience yourself? If so, do you think retailers are aware of how you and other people feel about their companies? By finding the answers to these questions, retailers can shed light on some of the major problems that they experience today.

The most critical problem that retailers experience, perhaps, is how best to identify and satisfy the ever-changing needs and wants of customers. To solve this problem and to succeed in business, retailers must have the attitude that the customer is king. They must make their business exist for the customer, not the customer for the business. This means that retailers must be able to provide the products that their customers want at prices they are willing to pay and at places where it is convenient for them to shop. The advertising and sales promotion techniques that a retailer uses must make the customers aware of the business as the place where their needs and wants can be fulfilled.

The Retailing Mix

Every retail firm caters to its own **clientele**. These regular customers of a retail

Retailers must develop the right combination of product, price, place and promotion for each item that they sell.

firm are changing constantly. Therefore, retailers must keep up-to-date information about their customers' needs and wants. To provide what their customers desire, retailers develop a **retailing mix**. This is a combination of a product or service sold at the right price, in a particular place, and with the support of desired services. This combination must be promoted to attract customers. The four P's of the retailing mix—product, price, place, and promotion—must be combined in such a way that they work together to serve customers and earn a profit for the business.

Combining the Ingredients

Yvonne Caldon sells a particular brand of badminton set in her two sporting goods stores. She knows that the set is a quality product and that badminton is a popular game. But these two facts won't assure her of selling the sets profitably. The product

is only one ingredient of the retailing mix. Yvonne must also think about the best place to sell it. At her downtown store, customers may buy a badminton set once in a while. So Yvonne keeps only a few sets in stock at that store. The bulk of the supply Yvonne keeps at her suburban branch store because she reasons that the demand will be greater there. She realizes that most people who live in the suburbs have lawns on which to play badminton, and also that they're more likely to shop for badminton sets in her suburban store rather than her downtown store. Yvonne must also think about "place" within her suburban store. She must locate the sets where the customers can find them easily—near the tennis equipment, for example.

To let her customers know that the product is available, Yvonne must also include promotion in the retailing mix. She can, for example, display a badminton set in the store so that customers can examine the equipment. And Yvonne can attract people to the store by advertising the set in her spring catalog and in the local newspaper.

When Yvonne considered price, she found that the badminton set sold very well at $19.95. However, she would have to sell the set at $25 or more to allow for sufficient profit. But when she priced it at $25, it sold poorly.

As you can see, even though three of the four P's work well together, the mix is unsatisfactory. In this instance, the product, promotion, service, and place are attractive to customers. But the high price has discouraged them from buying badminton sets in Yvonne's store. To solve this problem, Yvonne must adjust the combination of her retailing mix.

Adjusting the Combination

What can Yvonne Caldon do to achieve a satisfactory retailing mix? Should she sell a different, less expensive brand of badminton set? If she increases promotional effort, might she convince customers to buy the present brand at the higher price? Can she afford to accept a loss on badminton sets if the lower price attracts customers to the store and they buy other products as well? There are many ways Yvonne can adjust the four P's of her retailing mix to achieve a profit. However, whichever choice she makes, all four P's must work well together in satisfying her customers.

Making a wise decision requires information. Yvonne must know how her customers act in order to determine which changes in her retailing mix are likely to bring the most profitable results. For this necessary information, retailers rely on marketing research.

Sources of Information

The gathering, recording, and analyzing of all the facts relating to the sale of prod-

ucts and services from producer to consumer is called **marketing research**. This information must be organized logically and presented clearly so that it's useful to management in making decisions. Chapter 57 contains a detailed discussion of marketing research procedures.

Retailers need information to help them answer the following types of questions:

1. Who are the **target group** of customers, or the people retailers want as their clientele?
2. Where should the new business be located?
3. What hours should the business be open?
4. What should be done to improve sales of various products or services?
5. What price lines should be carried in stock?
6. Where should a new product or service be offered?
7. What services do the customers expect?
8. Where can expenses be reduced without losing sales?

It's almost impossible for any retailer to gather this information without some help. Wise retailers gather their information from as many different sources as they possibly can. And they consider many alternatives before making a decision. For example, they use trained market researchers, credit managers, buyers, department heads, and salespeople to help them gather data. And often, retailers will also, from time to time, call on any one of their employees for the information they need. But they must always be sure that the information employees provide is objective and accurate.

The sources of information that retailers use to help them in learning about their customers can be divided into two main groups: primary sources and secondary sources.

Primary Sources

Many stories have been told about owners of small businesses who stand at the entrances of their stores and talk with customers as they enter and leave. And many

Reviewing store records is one way of gathering primary data on customer reaction. Then the manager has to look for the specific problem.

of these owners have become heads of large businesses. Realizing the importance of information from customers, retail firms are increasingly making efforts to learn all they can about their customers' likes and dislikes regarding the business policies, merchandise, services, and personnel. The common primary sources that retail companies use to obtain this information are store records, customer complaints, interviews, and questionnaires.

Store Records. Customers react by either buying or not buying. What they buy or don't buy tells a great deal about their needs and wants. By keeping track of sales through detailed records, retailers get an idea of customers' likes and dislikes. As retailers study their records, for example, they may discover that a good number of people in the area hardly ever come to their place of business. Why? Often only one or two unsatisfactory prac-

tices are enough to drive some people away. A disagreeable cashier, for example, may cause customers to think unkindly of the entire business.

Customer Complaints. Complaints from regular customers can help retailers identify specific needs and wants. Even the customers who say they shop for only one or two things that they can't get elsewhere provide excellent information. Such comments make the retailer aware of bad experiences the customers may have had or something unfavorable they may have heard about the business. Unfortunately, many customers don't complain, no matter what kind of service they get. Instead of complaining, they simply never come back.

Interviews and Questionnaires. Many retailers obtain opinions about their stores by interviewing their customers infor-

Retailers obtain information from as many sources as possible, including their own employees. Jane Hamilton-Merritt

mally about the business's strong and weak points. They also ask their customers to suggest ways in which the business can be improved. Retailers can also acquire such information by using questionnaires or formal personal interviews. These sources of information may provide tips as to what products to buy and promote and which services to offer.

Other Primary Sources. Getting information from people who don't patronize a business is difficult. Tips about such people may often be obtained from associates in civic clubs and other community organizations. Asking neighbors and friends is another way of getting valuable information.

More and more retailers are conducting research studies to help them obtain other types of consumer information. For example, many retailers do comparison shopping to make sure that their prices are not out of line and to find out about the strategies their competitors use to attract customers.

Secondary Sources

In addition to their own observations, retailers can use the research of others. These secondary sources are useful and convenient because the information involved has already been gathered and prepared. This means that retailers can learn results without spending their own time gathering and organizing the data. When consulting secondary sources, however, retailers must sift out the information that applies to their own circumstances and that is useful for their own decision making. The common secondary sources that retailers use are trade associations, chambers of commerce, other retailers, and research reports.

Trade Associations. A trade association is a group of people in the same business who join together to pool their knowledge and search for solutions to common problems. Many associations have been formed on local, state, and national levels by retailers who sell similar products or services. Others have been formed to represent all the retailers in a certain area of a community. Many trade associations provide excellent sources of information about consumers, such as what types and prices of products or services they are buying or intend to buy in the months ahead.

Other Retailers. Another way retailers obtain information is by visiting retailers who operate similar types of stores in other parts of town or in nearby communities. Each retailer sees the other's weaknesses more easily than his or her own because people are more objective about others' problems. Similarly, retailers recognize other retailers' successes very rapidly and adopt them where they can.

Research Reports and Periodicals. Retailers also learn a great deal about consumers' needs and wants by studying research reports. Manufacturers, wholesalers, and advertising agencies spend huge sums of money on research to find better ways of distributing the product and services they sell. Also, other information about customer preferences can be obtained from articles in trade magazines, reports of government studies, articles in the business and financial sections of metropolitan newspapers, and consumer magazines. Listed below are some of the more commonly read periodicals that help retailers in staying up to date about the changing needs and wants of their consumers:

1. *Advertising Age.* Weekly magazine of advertising, with applications to retailing.
2. *Business Week.* Weekly magazine, with articles on all phases of business.
3. *Chain Store Age.* Monthly magazine, which specializes in information about chain stores.
4. *Fortune.* Fortnightly magazine, with articles on all phases of business.
5. *Harvard Business Review.* Bimonthly magazine, with articles on all aspects of business.
6. *Journal of Advertising Research.* Bimonthly magazine, includes articles on advertising in retailing.
7. *Journal of Marketing.* Quarterly magazine, with developments in all areas of marketing.
8. *Journal of Retailing.* Quarterly magazine, with developments in all aspects of retailing.
9. *Journal of Small Business Management.* Quarterly magazine, of interest to retailers and all other kinds of small business managers.
10. *Sales and Marketing Management.* Monthly magazine, of interest to retailers: annual survey of buyer power by county (based upon income, retail sales, and population in each county).
11. *Stores.* Monthly magazine, for members of the National Retail Merchant's Association, with emphasis on store management.

They also read other regular publications for retailers in specialized areas such as hardware, supermarket, franchise, furniture, department stores, apparel and accessory stores.

In this chapter, you learned that to remain competitive, retailers have to continually make sure that their way of combining the four P's of the retailing mix satisfies the needs and wants of their customers. And you found that retailers use many types of primary and secondary sources of information to help them put together a winning combination.

In the next chapter, you'll discover why retailers also have to provide consumers with many different types of information about their products and services.

Trade Talk

Define each term and use it in a sentence.

Clientele
Marketing research
Retailing mix

Target group
Trade association

Can You Answer These?

1. What are the four elements that make up the retailing mix?
2. Is one of the four P's of the retailing mix more important than the other three? Why or why not?
3. Name some of the ways in which a retailer can obtain primary source information.
4. What are some sources of secondary information that can help a retailer learn about consumers?
5. What are some of the benefits to a retailer of belonging to a trade association?

Problems

1. Rule a form similar to the following. In the left column, write the letter of each of the following activities that retailers might use in developing a retail mix: (0) a supermarket manager stocks three national brands of frozen orange juice, (a) a discount druggist sells toothpaste in the family-size tube for 69 cents, (b) the owner of a sandwich shop keeps a rack of candy and chewing gum on the cashier's counter, (c) the junior sportswear department is featured in the window display of a department store, (d) a car wash is built near an industrial park, (e) a diner sells books of discount tickets for meals, (f) a bank places an ad in the local newspaper, and (g) a bookstore manager sets up a stationery and greeting card counter. In the right column, write the part of the retailing mix that is affected or determined by the activity.

Activity	Part of Retailing Mix
Example: (0)	Product

2. Rule a form similar to the following. In the left column, write the letter of each of the following questions that might concern a retailer: (a) Should I expand my parking lot? (b) Which record albums should I order? (c) Should I offer charge accounts? In the center column, list several primary sources that could be of help to the retailer; in the right column, list several secondary sources that the retailer might consult.

Problem	Primary Sources	Secondary Sources

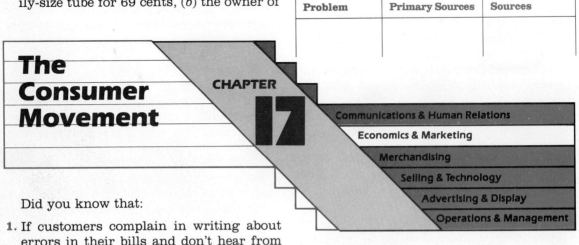

The Consumer Movement

CHAPTER 17

Communications & Human Relations
Economics & Marketing
Merchandising
Selling & Technology
Advertising & Display
Operations & Management

Did you know that:

1. If customers complain in writing about errors in their bills and don't hear from their creditors for 90 days, they may keep the disputed amount?

2. If consumers are turned down for credit, insurance, or a job, they have the right to

be told the name and address of the credit reporting agency that prepared the report which resulted in the rejection?

3. Mail-order retailers must generally fill orders within 30 days or offer customers their money back?

4. Labels on food products must list the product's ingredients in order of quantity?

5. If a credit card is lost, the customer is liable for only $50?

6. All wearing apparel selling for more than $3 is required to carry permanent care labels?

7. In some communities, retailers are required to mark all grocery items with their individual prices, regardless of whether the store has a computer checkout system?

8. In some states, retailers are not allowed to state that an item has been "marked down" when it has normally been priced at its current level?

Consumerism is the response of people and organizations to consumer problems and dissatisfactions. Consumers have both rights and responsibilities. And consumer rights are protected by laws and regulations. To avoid violating consumer laws and regulations, retailers must know and understand as much about them as they can. And as a retail worker, you should know about them too. Some guidelines that help retailers to respond to the consumer movement are given in Chapter 55.

Consumer Rights

In 1962, the late President John F. Kennedy, in an address to Congress, proclaimed that consumers have four basic rights:

1. *The right to safety.* We live in an affluent nation, where mass production and complicated distribution systems have increased the possibility of dangerous products being manufactured and sold. The right to safety means that the consumers have a right to be protected against dan-

ger from inferior products and deceptive industry practices.

2. *The right to be informed.* Consumers are entitled to the complete and accurate product information needed to make an informed choice among available products.

The right to safety is a basic consumer right. Jane Hamilton-Merritt

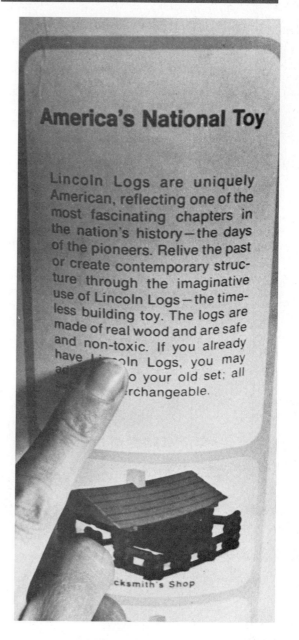

America's National Toy

Lincoln Logs are uniquely American, reflecting one of the most fascinating chapters in the nation's history—the days of the pioneers. Relive the past or create contemporary structure through the imaginative use of Lincoln Logs—the timeless building toy. The logs are made of real wood and are safe and non-toxic. If you already have Lincoln Logs, you may add to your old set; all interchangeable.

cksmith's Shop

They must be protected against fraudulent, deceitful, or misleading information, advertising, or labeling.

3. *The right to choose.* Consumers have a right to spend their money on any legal product or service they choose. They are further entitled to choose from a variety of products and services of satisfactory quality that are competitively priced.

4. *The right to be heard.* Consumers' views should be given consideration by retailers, manufacturers, and government alike. Consumers' interests are entitled to receive sympathetic consideration by government bodies in the formation and administration of policy on consumer issues.

Newspaper and magazine articles, books, and radio and television programs express public demand for new consumer legislation and clearly indicate that consumers are generally unhappy with certain business practices and with many products and services. For example, in a recent session of Congress, some 668 bills with some tie-in to the consumer movement were introduced.

Many consumers feel that their rights are sometimes violated. When dealing with certain retailers, consumers may find it difficult to get satisfaction for their complaints. They resent the impersonal treatment resulting from automation and computerized procedures. They dislike labels that provide only a skimpy amount of information and packages that make it difficult to determine the cost-per-unit price. And they blame "business," both manufacturers and retailers, for not providing them with the information they need to make wise purchasing decisions. Both retailers and manufacturers need to be alert and to accept a share of the responsibility for any shortcomings of the goods they sell.

Consumer Responsibilities

Since consumers have rights, they also have responsibilities. They cannot expect fairness in the marketplace unless they

Customers have a responsibility to bring complaints about merchandise to the retailer's attention. Jane Hamilton-Merritt

Retailers and consumers work together to distribute information to aid customers to become wise shoppers. *Courtesy of Chain Store Age Supermarkets,* Lebhar-Friedman, Inc.

too are fair. Informed consumers understand the American economic system and their role in it, particularly as it relates to making intelligent choices. They have a responsibility to learn essential information about products and services, the laws and agencies that protect them, and where to go when they have a problem. In dealing with retailers consumers should:

1. Treat cashiers and other store personnel courteously and respectfully.
2. Respect business operations—and the law—by not stealing, damaging property, or otherwise taking advantage of the store's commitment to please the customer.
3. Bring complaints about service, personnel, or merchandise to the attention of the store manager or assistant manager.
4. Not expect a refund or an exchange unless it is the store policy. There is no law dictating that a store must give refunds or exchanges except in cases where the product does not perform as it should.

Forces in the Consumer Movement

Over the past few years, the consumer movement has matured and become organized. Issues such as consumer grievances, credit privileges, product information and safety, food and drugs, and warranty protection have been successfully dealt with by three organized forces. These three forces are (1) voluntary consumer organizations, (2) federal government controls, and (3) state and local controls.

Voluntary Consumer Organizations

All voluntary consumer organizations coordinate the activities of groups and individuals interested in consumer protection and education; they also gather and supply information of value to consumers.

Voluntary organizations of consumers have increased rapidly. There are more than 400 voluntary consumer groups throughout the country with a combined membership estimated at 50 million.

In many cities, consumers have formed voluntary organizations. These groups work with a local retail merchants' organization to develop programs and distribute printed materials that help consumers to become wiser buyers. For example, a voluntary organization and local retailers may hold meetings in places such as a community building, a retail store, or in someone's home. There may also be informal courses at a local school or community college. These courses are usually available to all consumers who wish to attend. Meetings are built around consumers' questions, such as how to buy a used car, how to get a loan, how to deal with a collection agency, how to determine the quality of various products and services, and how to buy products in the right amount and the quality needed.

Some of the voluntary consumer organizations that have been particularly useful to consumers are better business bureaus; the Consumer Federation of America; Consumer Research, Inc.; Consumers Union; the National Safety Council; and the Underwriters' Laboratories. These organizations assist and protect the consumer by promoting good consumer legislation and ensuring that consumer laws are effectively enforced. They represent consumers before the government agencies that regulate or affect the sale of consumer products and services. These organizations also educate consumers to become wise buyers.

Federal Government Controls

Today, there are 1,000 federal government consumer programs administered by 33 different agencies and departments.

Enforcing consumer laws, however, is a major government problem. For example, four different government agencies share the responsibility of enforcing consumer laws involving interstate commerce, but they lack the financial and personnel resources to do so adequately. Today's consumer movement is mainly concerned with improving the effectiveness of existing federal laws and agencies.

State and Local Controls

In each state, there are state agencies responsible for regulating and supervising the conduct of local retail and service firms. Independent professionals, such as physicians and lawyers, and corporations operating only within the state are also regulated by various state agencies. Agencies in the various states are organized differently and have different names.

However, most have the same functions.

State departments of insurance supervise the activity of insurance firms operating in the state. The departments can give consumers assistance on such problems as unexplained cancellations of auto insurance, difficulties in obtaining a settlement with a company, or questions concerning rates. The state department of banking handles questions concerning the conduct and operations of banks.

State bureaus of weights and measures deal with questions about the accuracy of grocery scales, gasoline pumps, and other weighing and measuring devices. In many states, this bureau is part of the state department of agriculture.

Consumers have had many problems in getting honest and competent appliance and auto repair service. These problems have led several states and cities to require that repair workers and repair shops become licensed. Many other types of retailers of products and services are licensed by the state.

However, most state efforts to protect consumers have been held back by inadequate laws. A Federal Trade Commission survey showed that less than half the states could be said to have "good" laws banning deceptive selling practices. Also, the survey showed that less than half the states outlawed bait-and-switch advertising. Bait-and-switch advertising is offering a product at a low price to get customers into a store when the store actually has no intention of selling the product. Instead, the store's salespeople try to persuade customers to "switch" to a more expensive version of the product.

During the past few years, more and more states have enacted legislation to protect the consumer from unfair and deceptive advertising, selling, credit, and lending practices. States have also increased measures to enforce the laws that are already on the books. Almost all states now have an official in the state attorney general's office who is responsible for consumer affairs.

Consumers should be able to see warranties before they make purchases. Courtesy of Montgomery Ward & Co.

Some of these state agencies have been very effective in helping consumers. And in more and more states, consumers are getting representation at the executive level of state government. Many cities have also appointed consumer representatives on the local level and have enacted consumer legislation.

Laws Protecting Consumer Purchasing

As a result of federal consumer protective legislation, retailers have to be aware of and follow many rules and regulations that deal with consumer purchasing. The federal laws—as well as their purposes and functions—that retailers should know about are given in summary form in the table on pages 132–133. These laws, of course, do not affect every retailer.

Two laws that are of major importance to retailers are the Fair Packaging and Labeling Act and the Magnuson-Moss Warranty Act.

Packaging and Labeling

The Fair Packaging and Labeling Act has many implications for retailers. This act requires that packaged consumer products used in interstate commerce be honestly and informatively labeled. Some of the major provisions are that labels must:

♦ Identify the commodity and give the name and place of business of the manufacturer, packer, or distributor
♦ Give the common name of the product and list the ingredients in order of their importance
♦ Contain a statement of net contents in units appropriate for the product in a uniform location on the principal display panel
♦ Be free of such misleading terms as "jumbo pound" and "giant quart"
♦ Give the net quantity per serving if the number of servings is stated

This law also prohibits packaging the product with an unnecessary amount of packing material or air space.

Product Warranties

The Magnuson-Moss Warranty Act of 1975 gave the Federal Trade Commission the power to require clearly understandable and accurate wording in warranties. A **warranty** is an agreement that the manufacturer will be responsible for any defects in a product and will replace or repair a product that is faulty. Warranties on consumer products costing more than $10 must be available for consumers to look at before they buy. Consumers can also force manufacturers to keep their warranty promises. The Magnuson-Moss

Warranty Act specifically requires that all warranties must be easy to read and understand.

In this chapter, and in Chapters 15 and 16 in this unit, you've been given a lot of information about people you'll be dealing with all the time (directly or indirectly) in your future retailing career—the customers.

In Chapter 15, you learned how the consumer market is constantly changing and how retailers keep up and ahead of those changes by finding out about changes in population and income and spending patterns. In Chapter 16, you learned how retailers obtain and use this information in satisfying consumer needs and wants. And in this chapter, you've been given some idea of how consumers' demand for value in return for dollars they spend has created an enormous amount of legislation to see that they get just that. You also learned how retailers have to stay on their toes to obey the many consumer laws.

IMPORTANT CONSUMER PROTECTION LEGISLATION

Year	Name of Law	Purpose and Function
Product Safety		
1962	Food and Drug Amendments	Requires pretesting of drugs for safety and effectiveness and labeling of drugs by generic name.
1966	Child Protection Act	Bans sale of hazardous toys and articles.
1967	Flammable Fabrics Act	Broadens federal authority to set safety standards for inflammable fabrics, including clothing and household products.
1968	Federal Hazardous Substances Act	Requires retailer to prominently display a sign informing consumers of the fact that certain hazardous products are sold in that store.
	Toy Safety Act	Requires retailers to give consumers a refund if a toy is found to be dangerous.
1970	Public Health Smoking Act	Extends warning about the hazards of cigarette smoking.
	Poison Prevention Packing Act	Authorizes standards for child-resistant packaging of hazardous substances.
1972	Consumer Product Safety Act	Establishes a commission to set safety standards for consumer products and bans products presenting undue risk of injury.
1975	Auto Recall Repair Law	Requires tire, auto, and replacement-part makers to offer refund, replacement, or refund options on defective products.
Marketing Credibility		
1939	Wool Products Labeling Act	Requires that information about the textiles fiber content be included on a tag or label together with care instructions.

Are consumers important to retailers? By now, of course, you know the answer to that question. But to keep you on your toes as a future retail worker, it's a question you'll be reminded of again and again throughout this book. Don't forget the answer!

Trade Talk

Define each term and use it in a sentence.
Consumerism
Warranty

Can You Answer These?

1. What are the four basic consumer rights?
2. What are two responsibilities that consumers have when dealing with retailers?
3. What do voluntary consumer organizations do?
4. What consumer problems have led several states and cities to require that repair workers and repair shops become licensed?
5. Of the federal laws protecting consumers, what two are important to retailers?

IMPORTANT CONSUMER PROTECTION LEGISLATION (Continued)

Year	Name of Law	Purpose and Function
Marketing Credibility		
1958	Textile Fiber Products Identification Act	Requires that information about the textiles fiber content be included on a tag or label together with care instructions.
1966	Fair Packaging and Labeling Act	Requires producers to state what a package contains, how much it contains, and who made the product.
1975	Magnuson-Moss Warranty Act	Requires clearly understandable and accurate wording in ordinary language with every term and condition spelled out in writing for all warranties.
Fair Payment Arrangements*		
1968	Consumer Credit Protection Act (Truth-in-Lending)	Requires full disclosure of terms and conditions of finance charges in credit transactions.
1970	Fair Credit Reporting Act	Protects consumers from inaccurate or obsolete information. Guarantees the consumer's right to know what personal data are being reported.
1975	Equal Credit Opportunity Act	Makes it illegal for banks, retailers, and other lenders to deny or terminate credit on the basis of age, color, marital status, national origin, sex, or because one is on welfare.
	Fair Credit Billing Act	Sets up billing dispute settlement procedures and requires prompt correction of billing mistakes.
1978	Fair Debt Collection Practices Act	Protects consumers from being threatened, harassed, or otherwise abused by debt collectors.
	Electronic Funds Transfer Act	Provides protection for consumers if EFT transaction card is lost or stolen.

*See discussion in Unit 16.

Problems

1. Rule a form similar to the following. In the left column, write the letter of each of the following: (a) a can of soup that lists the ingredients in order of importance on its label, (b) a packet of crackers that doesn't give the name and address of the manufacturer, packer, or distributor, (c) a jar of pickles that doesn't give the number of servings, (d) 24 ounces of detergent packed in a container that could hold 48 ounces, (e) a bottle of ketchup whose label gives the net contents under the name of the product, (f) a bottle of soda with a label that says "The Big Fizz" but doesn't state that it's a carbonated beverage. Place a check mark (√) in the middle column if the product violates any provision of the Fair Packaging and Labeling Act. Explain why or why not in the right column.

Product	Violates Fair Packaging and Labeling Act	Reason

2. Rule a form with two columns. In the left column, write the letter of each of the following items: (a) warranty for a washing machine, (b) woolen pants, (c) department store credit-card bill, (d) tricycle, (e) credit application form, and (f) tires. In the right column, name the law that protects the consumer against deceptive practices on the part of the manufacturer or seller connected with each item.

Activities and Project

UNIT 6

Retailing Case

Summer's, an independent department store in a downtown area, has decided to update its men's department. The department store will now have to be more competitive with three new stores located in the shopping center on the edge of town: a large chain, a men's specialty store, and a discount store.

Summer's chiefly handles work clothes. Research carried out by some of its staff revealed that its competitors stock not only work clothes but also an assortment of sport clothes and other items. The large chain store turned out to be Summer's largest competitor because of the work clothes that it carries in its men's department. The men's specialty store carries a complete line of fashion clothes for men, but it does not carry any work clothes. The discount store carries a large variety of clothing, but it carries its stock in small quantities only. Its prices are lower than those of the other two stores.

The research staff at Summer's drew up the following chart, which analyzes the merchandise lines and prices involved. With the information they have obtained, they are now ready to consider such measures as adding or dropping lines, adjusting prices, and developing a new image for the store.

1. Is the research conducted by the staff at Summer's as complete as it should be? Why or why not? If not, what additional research should have been done?
2. Is it always advisable to do what competitors do? Why or why not?
3. What changes do you think should be made at Summer's? Why?

Product Line and Price Comparison

Item	Summer's	Chain Store	Discount Store	Specialty Store
Belts		$4 to $7	$2 to $6	$6 to $10
Cufflinks		$5 to $10	$3 to $7	$5 to $15
Dress slacks		$12 to $18	$6 to $14	$15 to $45
Gloves	$.55 to $5	$5 to $6	$2 to $6	$8 to $20
Jeans		$9 to $12	$7 to $10	$15 to $45
Shop aprons	$1.50		$1	
Socks	$.95 to $1.95	$.65 to $1	$.49 to $1	$1.25
Sport coats		$25 to $40	$20	$35 and up
Sport shirts	$4 to $7	$4 to $9	$3 to $7	$6 to $17
Suits		$40 and up		$55 and up
Sweaters		$8 to $15	$5 to $12	$14 to $60
Ties		$2 to $5	$1 to $3	$4 to $12
Underwear	$2.98	$2.98	$2 to $3	$4
Work pants	$5 to $12	$6 to $9	$4 to $6	
Work shirts	$3 to $8	$4 to $7	$3 to $5	
Work socks	$1 to $2			

Working with People

Ron is instructed by his employer, Mr. Clemenza, to go to the library and obtain some information for him. Mr. Clemenza would like to find out how their community compares with similar communities in the state with regard to such factors as population, age groups, education, occupations, and income. He also instructs Ron to obtain the same information about a neighboring community in which he is planning to open a new store. When Ron arrives at the library, he finds out that the new *Statistical Abstract of the United States* is not available, but that the library has on hand recent *Census of Population* and *Census of Retail Trade* reports. What should Ron do?

1. Identify the true problem.
2. What are the important facts to be considered in this problem?
3. List several possible solutions to this problem.
4. Evaluate the possible results of each solution.
5. Which solution do you recommend? Why?

Project 6: Finding Out Facts about Income and Spending Patterns

Your Project Goal

Given the opportunity to interview three retailers and three consumers, make a generalization about consumer income and spending patterns and how this affects retailers.

Procedure

Interview three consumers and three retailers and ask them, "What would you do with the money you gained if the government cut your taxes by 50 percent?" Record your answers, and compare the responses of the consumers with the responses of the retailers. Write up your findings and be prepared to discuss them in class.

Evaluation

You will be evaluated on the validity of the reasons you give for the customers' and retailers' answers and how you connect these reasons with consumer income and spending patterns.

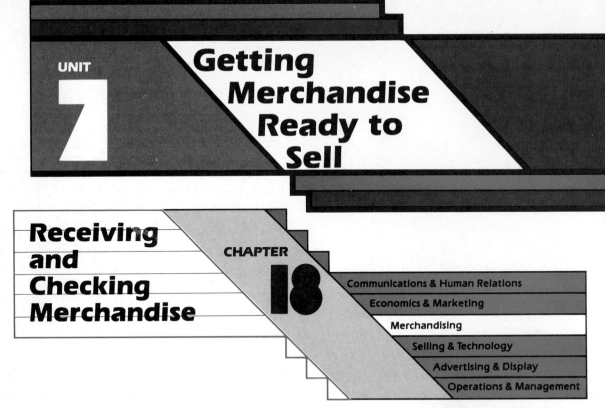

Receiving and Checking Merchandise

CHAPTER

18

Communications & Human Relations

Economics & Marketing

Merchandising

Selling & Technology

Advertising & Display

Operations & Management

Greg Bach's phone rang. It was Mrs. Koerner, personnel manager at the Martin Department Store. "Congratulations. You're hired. Report tomorrow at 3 p.m. to Mr. Moskowitz in the receiving and checking department." Greg was both pleased and somewhat anxious about this good news. He had originally applied for a part-time sales position at the Martin Department Store. Mrs. Koerner informed him at the time that all the sales positions were filled. Would he consider a position in receiving and checking instead?

Mrs. Koerner explained that experience in this department provides excellent training and an understanding of stock handling and records administration. She also mentioned that all management trainees spend a part of their initial training assignment in the receiving and checking department. This assignment helps them to understand the necessary

behind-the-scenes merchandise handling procedures.

Recognizing the Importance of Receiving and Checking

After completing the necessary forms at the personnel office, Greg reported to Mr. Moskowitz in the receiving and checking department. Mr. Moskowitz explained that retail merchandise flows from the supplier into the store, then from the receiving area onto the selling floor, and finally into the customer's hands. Ideally, that flow should be such that the store is never out of merchandise. The minimum inventory needed to produce maximum sales should be on hand at all times.

Understanding the Merchandise Flow—From Source to Sales Floor

The merchandise flow begins when a store buyer orders goods from a supplier, who may be a manufacturer or wholesaler. Merchandise is ordered by using a written **purchase order.** This is a form on which complete information about the kind and quantity of goods wanted and the terms of the purchase are recorded. When the supplier is ready to ship goods either to the store or to the warehouse (depending upon which location the buyer has specified), an invoice is prepared and mailed to the store. An **invoice** is a bill for the goods that specifies the description, quantity of items, how and when the shipment was made, and the terms of payment.

To get the incoming merchandise from the receiving area to the sales floor, retailers must develop a system. And it should be a system that will (1) receive the goods properly, (2) check the goods, (3) mark the goods for sale, and (4) distribute the goods to the proper selling area in the store. Depending on the size of the store, the steps in the system may be very simple or very detailed.

Where Receiving Takes Place

Goods are usually delivered to the receiving area of the store or to the appropriate warehouse of a chain. In large stores, the receiving area consists of a dock or platform where trucks are unloaded and a receiving room. The receiving area is usually at the side or back of the store, but sometimes it's in the basement.

Receiving-platform workers help unload the shipments as they arrive and move them into the receiving room. Forklift trucks may be used to move heavy loads placed on wooden platforms called **pallets.** Some stores have automatic con-

Receiving clerks move merchandise from the receiving dock into the receiving room. Jane Hamilton-Merritt

veyor systems consisting of moving belts or overhead railways built right out into the receiving dock.

Some goods may be received through the front door. In supermarkets, for instance, the supplier's sales representative sometimes brings dairy and bakery products in through the front door and stacks them on the shelves. Non-food items such as housewares and toiletries are also delivered to the stores by suppliers' sales representatives, who are called rack jobbers. **Rack jobbers** are wholesale suppliers who deliver the goods, set up the racks, and keep them filled through periodic visits to retailers.

The Consolidator Functions

Mr. Moskowitz explained to Greg that in this store the services of a consolidator are being used more and more. A **consolidator** is a person or group of people, either employed within or outside the company, who put together merchandise orders from many suppliers. The orders are then shipped to the store at one time by one carrier. A **carrier** is any form of transportation, such as a train, truck, or airplane.

To explain to Greg how consolidators do their job, Mr. Moskowitz discussed the ready-to-wear coat department. "The coat buyers," Mr. Moskowitz told Greg, "place orders through the consolidator to several different coat manufacturers. The consolidator then fills the orders from these manufacturers and sends one large coat shipment in a single truck. So this consolidated order means that we save the time we would otherwise spend in receiving and checking several smaller shipments from different suppliers."

Mr. Moskowitz also explained that to further speed the flow of the merchandise to the sales floor, the consolidator carefully unpacks the coats from the suppliers and hangs them on racks installed in the carrier's trucks. Suppliers' invoices are forwarded to the computer center by the consolidator. Magnetic price tickets are then prepared from these invoices by computerized equipment. A **magnetic price ticket** is a ticket that is printed in magnetized ink. The magnetic particles within the ink are arranged in such a way that a variety of merchandise information can be read by a computer. (See Chapter 19 for examples of such tickets.)

"When the coats arrive in the receiving area," Mr. Moskowitz continued, "they are moved off the truck racks directly onto racks suspended from the ceiling of our receiving area. After the magnetic tickets are attached to the coats, the coats are moved on overhead racks to our store shuttle trucks, which are equipped with similar overhead racks.

"This computerized and automated system allows the consolidator and our store receiving personnel to move goods from the manufacturer to the selling floor in a shorter period of time. So—as you see—the consolidator provides a valuable service to retailers by reducing the need to handle, unpack, receive, and check small orders from many different suppliers," he said.

The Receiving Functions

Mr. Moskowitz introduced Greg to Mary Nova. "Mary, I'd like you to meet Greg Bach. Mary Nova is an experienced receiver in our department. She's responsible for inspecting each shipment, noting how it was shipped, recording the freight costs, assembling packages of various shipments, and inspecting the physical condition of the shipment."

Maintaining Receiving Records. Mary explained that for all merchandise accepted, a record of the receipt of the shipment is made. She stressed that accuracy is very important because these records:

1. Show what merchandise has come in and will soon be ready to go on sale.
2. Tell the accounting department that payment is now owed to the supplier.

3. Inform the buyer or department head when the merchandise has been shipped and received.
4. Show whether it is necessary to make claims for damaged merchandise or incomplete shipments.

Some stores log or enter the details about a shipment in a **receiving book,** which is the record of all shipments received. The information entered includes the number of parcels, the time and date of the delivery, the name of the vendor, the weight of the goods, the shipping charges, and the name of the delivery firm. Since the invoice is usually mailed to the store by the vendor on the same day the merchandise is shipped, the invoice number and the price of the merchandise are entered in the receiving book. Smaller stores don't usually use a receiving book, but they do put receipts into a file folder.

Noting the Shipping Date. It is especially important that information regarding the **shipping date** is noted in the receiving book. This is the date when the vendor ships the goods to the retailer. This date is often used to determine when payment is due or when discounts may be taken. Many times a store will receive the vendor's invoice ahead of the merchandise. If the vendor ships the merchandise too early, the accounting department may record the order in the wrong selling month. This causes the merchandise department to be credited with either too much or too little inventory on hand within a selling period. So early shipment can distort turnover and profit records for a department's selling period.

In some cases, if merchandise isn't received by a certain date, the store has the right to automatically cancel or return the order to the vendor. These things are agreed to by the buyer and the vendor prior to the writing of the invoice. It is the receiving department's responsibility to alert merchandise buyers and managers

to possible violations or variances in the purchasing contract conditions.

Using Apron Records. Many stores use a type of receiving record called an **apron.** This record has spaces for all important information about the shipment from the time it was ordered until the time it is paid for. The information entered on the apron includes the department number, the order number, the terms on the order and on the invoice, the routing, and the date the shipment was checked. This statement is checked against the original purchase order to see that the quantity and description of the items are the same as ordered, that the price is correct, that the proper cash discount has been given, and that the shipping instructions were followed.

An important use of an apron is to prevent internal theft within the store. This record accompanies the merchandise from the receiving area to the selling floor. On the selling floor, the content of the shipment can again be checked by sales personnel to make sure that no goods have been lost, misdelivered, or stolen.

An advantage of the apron system is that it guards against paying duplicate invoices because the apron is made out only when the shipment is received. It is also used when the goods are marked and stored. The apron serves as a permanent record after the goods have been processed, because copies of the delivery receipt, the store's original order, and the vendor's invoice are usually attached to it.

Signing for the Merchandise. "Let's talk to John Kovacs, another receiving clerk," Mr. Moskowitz said to Greg. "He has just finished checking the number of packages in the shipment against the number indicated on the invoice."

"Yes, Greg," said John, "we must check the total number of packages received from either the invoice, the delivery receipt from the carrier (transportation company), or the **bill of lading,** which is the contract document between a shipper

REC CLK	SHIPPER OR VENDOR	SHIPPED FROM	REC VIA (CARRIER)	CARRIER'S NO.	PCS	WT	CHGS	DEPT	KEY-REC No.	DATE REC
RC	MORRIS UNIFORM CO.	N	E	18330	2	20	95	5	1001	1/7

SHORT 01 DAMAGE 01

CORRECT DEPT	TERMS	DUE DATE	TOTAL RETAIL	TOTAL COST	DISCOUNT	DEDUCT TRANSP	MDSE CKD BY	DAY
5	8 10 EOM / 10 / 30	2/10	363.75	250.00	20.00	☒ WE PAY ☐ THEY PAY No CHARGE BACK AMOUNT	CR	7

VEND INVOICE REF 75164 — INV CKD BY R 7

APPROVED FOR PAYMENT BY	DAY	KEY-SHEET CHECK OUT	EXTENSIONS	CHARGED TO DEPT AND PAID	MFGR. OR HOUSE CODE
Howard Smith	8				F 10

PURCHASE ORDER Nos 4537

RETAILED BY / DAY — ORDER CKD BY / DAY

INVOICE APRON

MFGR'S STYLE OR LOT NUMBER	5 16½ 24 A 6	7 18½ 26 B 6½	9 20½ 28 C 7	11 22½ 30 D 7½	13 24½ 32 E 8	15 33½ 34 14 8½	10 35½ 36 15 9	12 37½ 38 14½ 9½	14 39½ 40 15 10	16 41½ 42 15½ 10½	18 43½ 44 16 11	20 45½ 46 16½ 11½	COLOR	UNIT COST	TOTAL QUANTITY RECEIVED	UNIT DZ PCS EA YDS	ADDITIONAL SIZES→
1408				2	2	2	1	1	1	1			BLK		10		
					2	3	2						BR		7		
						2	2	2	1				GRY		7		

CLASS — UNIT RETAIL

ORIGINAL

KEY-REC No.

⬆ ATTACH INVOICE BELOW THIS LINE ⬆
OTHER PATENTS PENDING
DO NOT DESTROY! ACCOUNTING MADE FOR EACH KEY-REC

This receiving record is also called an apron. It provides important information about the goods received. Courtesy of Moss Key-Rec Systems, Inc.

and a carrier. We usually don't begin the process of receiving and checking merchandise until we've received the total number of packages shipped. Sometimes we have had to contact the supplier or carrier to locate missing or split-order packages. Occasionally, the missing package will arrive in a later shipment.

"Once we have assembled the correct number of packages in a shipment," John continued, "we check to make sure that the proper freight rates and charges for shipment weights have been made. If the shipment has arrived in good condition and everything is satisfactory, I, as the receiving clerk, sign for the shipment. But if containers are damaged and the shipment is short—or there are any other discrepancies—claims are made to the shipper or carrier. In most cases, I make a note on the bill of lading as to the damage or the shortage before the carrier leaves the premises. Because stores lose money if they can't prove claims for damages or shortages, receiving department personnel must count and check shipments carefully. Receiving personnel either pay the shipping charges to the delivery person or approve the delivery receipt and send it to the office for payment."

The Checking Functions

Greg assisted receiving clerk John Kovacs for several weeks. Then Mr. Moskowitz approached Greg about working with Lucille Anderson in the checking department. This department adjoins the receiving area so that packages do not have to be moved very far. (In some small stores, goods are checked on the sales floor, but most stores do not allow merchandise to go to the selling floor until it has been checked.) Sometimes, checking on the sales floor may be a safety hazard or an inconvenience to customers. Moreover, receiving records made out on the floor may not be accurate. Most stores use stationary tables in the checking area. Some use portable tables, bins, or conveyor-belt systems. Sometimes a combination of equipment is used.

When stationary tables are used, the merchandise is unpacked, checked for quantity and quality, and price-marked by one person in an area from which the goods move directly onto the selling floor. A disadvantage of this system is that salespeople or buyers usually have access to this area. Sometimes, they take needed merchandise off the tables without notifying the appropriate people. When portable tables are used, the merchandise is checked and then rolled to a separate marking room. From the marking room, the tables are moved to the stockroom or sales floor.

The bin system divides the receiving room into a receiving section and a marking section. Merchandise is placed in the bins on the marking side. This method prevents removal of merchandise until it has been checked and marked, but it involves further handling of the merchandise.

Still other stores use a conveyor-belt system, which moves goods from the receiving section to the checking section, then to marking, and finally to the stock areas.

How Merchandise Is Checked. Lucille told Greg that merchandise is checked for both quantity and quality. The **quantity check** is a count of the merchandise, and it is usually done by the checker who opens the cartons and removes the merchandise. This check is the most important in the receiving operation. The **quality check** determines whether the merchandise is of the quality ordered by the store. It may or may not be done immediately after the goods are received. In small stores this

may be done by a salesperson who has a knowledge of quality and values or by the owner or manager. In large stores, the buyer usually purchases a sample in the vendor's showroom. When the merchandise is received, it is checked against the sample. Some merchandise is checked by quality inspectors who may use standards and specifications that are established by the government, the manufacturer, or the retailer. Quality checks are usually made for big-ticket items such as appliances, furniture, electrical equipment, etc. Stores keep records of defective or damaged merchandise to identify those vendors who supply inferior or poorly packaged merchandise. A few large department stores, chain stores, and mail-order houses maintain their own testing laboratories where samples of incoming merchandise are tested for quality.

If the vendor is a regular and reputable supplier of the store, the quantity check is often more important than the quality check. The two common methods of checking quantity are the **direct check** and the **indirect, or blind, check.** (These methods are described in the table on pages 142-143.)

Returning Goods to the Vendor

Next, Greg was assigned to work in the returned-goods section of the receiving department. Greg's main responsibilities during this assignment were to pack return shipments, schedule returned goods' transportation, and notify the vendor of the return.

In some cases, when shipments were lost or damaged, Greg would file a claim, which means that a bill will be presented to the carrier for the loss or damage. Greg kept report forms that were filled out in the receiving room as soon as damaged goods or discrepancies in a shipment were found. These forms contain information such as the date of the report, the name

SUMMARY OF CHECKING METHODS

Checking Method	Procedures Followed	Advantages	Disadvantages
Direct check	Markings, notations, and numbers on packages are compared directly to the invoice information.	Fast and economical system because manufacturer's invoice is used.	Checker may not count or may be careless as amount is already known according to supplier's invoice.
	Packages are opened and inspected for quantity and quality as identified by the invoice.	Merchandise can be rechecked because it is still in the receiving area.	Manufacturer's invoices may not be available causing delay in checking.
Dummy invoice check	A list of contents is made on a blank invoice (dummy) form by counting the shipment.	Merchandise can be immediately moved to the sales floor without waiting for the vendor's invoice.	There is no comparison available between the vendor's invoice and receiver's count on the dummy invoice.
		Sales are not lost by delays in checking in merchandise.	Shortages are more difficult to identify.
Bulk check	Packages are checked, but not their contents. Sometimes used when shipments contain dozens, pounds, or other bulk units.	Faster, more economical method of checking bulk items.	May result in errors if contents of packages do not match outside package markings.
	Quantities marked on outside of the packages are used when checking.	Time and expense of checking individual boxes and packages are reduced.	Difficult to identify shortages once merchandise is placed in stock.

and address of the shipper, the purchase order number, the method of shipment, and the amount of loss or damage. Greg sent the forms to the store's traffic office, which takes care of filing the claim. The store files a claim against the carrier if it is certain that the carrier is at fault. If there is some doubt, the claim may be filed against the vendor (manufacturer or wholesaler).

Distributing Goods

After Greg had become experienced with various types of receiving, checking, and returned-goods procedures, he was introduced to the methods of distributing goods

Checking Method	Procedures Followed	Advantages	Disadvantages
Spot check	Checker selects one or a few packages at random.	Faster, more economical method of checking larger shipments.	Certain errors in quantity or quality of the total shipment may remain undetected.
	Checker compares quantity and quality of random packages with invoice.	Speeds up checking of seasonal items.	Difficult to determine errors if spot checking is not frequent enough.
	If errors are found in the random check, the entire shipment is checked.		
Indirect, or blind, check	Checker completes a dummy invoice based on actual inspection of shipment.	More accurate quantity check is achieved.	It is more expensive and time-consuming as checker has to complete a form and check this form against an invoice.
	Or, checker may receive an invoice with blank spaces to fill in quantity of items received.	Checking can be partially completed before the vendor's invoice is received.	If merchandise is checked without the vendor's invoice and moved to the selling floor, it is impossible to check the shortages when the vendor's invoice arrives.
	Only when the checker completes this form is a comparison made with the quantities indicated on the original invoice.		

to the departments within the main store and to the branch stores in shopping centers. Greg learned that the purchase order shows where goods are to be delivered within the store, since the purchase order shows the department that ordered the goods. If receiving, checking, and marking are done in the same building where the goods are sold, buyers fill out **distribution forms** indicating where each order is to go. When goods are to be sent within a network of stores from a warehouse, a buyer fills out the distribution form. This form indicates the quantity of goods to be sent to each store and the goods to be kept in reserve stock in the warehouse.

If merchandise is presorted in the receiving area, both spot checking and distribution are made much simpler. Courtesy of Electronic Realty Associates, Inc.

After 3 months of employment in the receiving department, it was time for Greg's initial job performance review. During this review, Mr. Moskowitz evaluated Greg's progress and training. He asked Greg, "What's your opinion about your job in the receiving department?"

Would you agree with the answer Greg gave—that the job was certainly more interesting and challenging than he had thought it would be? Possibly yes, because in this chapter you've learned about invoices, inventory reports, claims forms, shipping policies, and receiving books. Also, learning what store managers, salespeople, buyers, and merchandise managers do has given you an idea of the planning and organization required to handle all types of merchandise. So now, like Greg, you should have a better understanding of why management trainees often spend their initial training in the receiving department.

In the next chapter, you'll learn about another processing method that merchandise must go through on its way to be sold—marking.

Trade Talk

Define each term and use it in a sentence.

Apron	Invoice
Bill of lading	Magnetic price ticket
Bulk check	Pallets
Carrier	Purchase order
Consolidator	Quality check
Direct check	Quantity check
Distribution forms	Rack jobbers
Dummy invoice check	Receiving book
	Shipping date
Indirect, or blind, check	Spot check

Can You Answer These?

1. Describe the steps in the typical flow of merchandise from vendor to sales floor.

2. What are the advantages of beginning a retailing career in stock handling and receiving?

3. What services does the consolidator offer the retail store?

4. What are three examples of receiving records that should be kept? Describe how each is used.

5. What should be checked in a shipment? Describe this generally as well as specifically for several retail items.

Problems

1. Rule a form similar to the following. In the left column, list five items of merchandise with which you are familiar, either as a consumer or a seller. Discuss your completed list with your employer or a retailer to identify additional features to inspect. Assume that you are responsible for inspecting incoming goods. In the right column, record the features of this item that you would inspect.

Item	Inspection Features
Example: Transistor radio	Damage to case, working condition, sound

Marking Merchandise

CHAPTER 19

Communications & Human Relations
Economics & Marketing
Merchandising
Selling & Technology
Advertising & Display
Operations & Management

Since Cathy Pastore had been on her job for just 2 weeks, she realized that she had a lot to learn. She wondered, for example, what the number and letter markings meant on the various merchandise tags, tickets, and labels. She recognized the department number and the selling price. The other markings meant nothing to her.

Fortunately, Cathy's store had a training program that used group training sessions, individual on-the-job department-level training, and self-instruction reading assignments. Cathy noticed that the topic of marking merchandise would be covered at the next group training session.

The Importance of Marking Merchandise

At the group training session, Mr. Bjornsson, the store merchandise manager, began by defining marking and its importance. He described **marking** as the process of placing a retail price and other important identifications on each merchandise item. These identifications may include costs of the merchandise, manufacturer number, department number, size, style, color, date received, selling season, and locations in the store or warehouse.

This information is like a story or history of the individual item. The information may be useful in reordering merchandise, in identifying the most profitable merchandise lines, and in determining pricing and promotion strategies to sell the merchandise. It may tell the buyer how many items are in stock and whether a price reduction should be made. It helps salespeople in adjusting returns and dealing with complaints. And it helps prevent the misquoting of prices and assists the cashier (especially in self-service stores) by giving the price. The customer depends upon the ticket to reveal the price and size of an item. So, if any items are mismarked (wrong price, size, location, etc.), serious mistakes in ordering, pricing, and selling can occur. Customer dissatisfaction naturally results from these errors.

A marking system must be designed to keep the merchandise moving. It must be quick and efficient. Marked merchandise on the shelf, display fixture, rack, or in the bin must be checked often to keep buyers and salespeople up to date on the availability of stock. As items are sold, they must be replaced in the selling area. In small stores and in those stores where stock sells rapidly, such as supermarkets, marking is done on the selling floor. In other stores, marking is done in the area where goods are received and checked. In any case, marking must be completed before the merchandise is ready for sale. And it must be completed as soon as possible after the goods are received to avoid being out of stock and losing sales.

Managerial Decisions Related to Marking Merchandise

Management must make a number of decisions before the actual process of marking articles can occur. Some of these are policy decisions, such as whether the cost of the item to the store is to be indicated by a code on the ticket. Other decisions must be made each time an item is to be marked. Among the important decisions are the following:

1. What is the retail price?
2. Who sets the retail price?
3. What information, such as the inventory control code, is to be marked on the item?
4. Is each article to be marked, or is a shelf or bin label to be used?
5. What type of marking will be hard to remove (making the switching of prices between two items impossible) and yet not damage the item?

6. Can a manufacturer or wholesaler handle any part of the marking?

The most important single piece of information that the process of marking puts on an item of merchandise is the **retail price**, which is the amount that the store charges the customer for the item. In a large store, determining the retail price is usually the responsibility of the buyer or merchandise manager. In a small store, it's usually the responsibility of the store manager. The retail price is determined either when the goods are ordered or after the goods have arrived and have been inspected.

Preretailing

Preretailing is the practice of determining prices and placing them on a copy of the purchase order at the time that goods are bought (orders placed). Preretailing is possible because the buyer usually thinks in terms of the retail price when purchasing the merchandise. The price is usually written on the duplicate copy of the purchase order that's sent to the receiving room. Then the merchandise can be price-marked as soon as it's received. Preretailing is widely used for **staple goods** (goods that should always be kept in stock). Preretailing is useful because it enables merchandise to be marked and moved onto the selling floor rapidly. However, it's not as practical for goods whose prices are changed frequently or for goods that must be inspected by the buyer after their arrival.

Premarking

Some staple, nationally branded merchandise has a price that is nationally advertised. The manufacturer may mark the standard price along with other information right on the package to save the store the time and energy of marking. This is called **premarking**. It's also used for items that might be difficult to mark in the store.

Buy Brut Lotion and receive travel size lotion **Free** | 11.50 Value for 7.00 Limited Time Only

FABERGÉ
BRUT

Some manufacturers premark the price of their merchandise. Art Zollo/Fundamental Photographs

Another form of premarking is done by most chain stores that set retail prices in their central headquarters. The price is usually uniform throughout the chain. And the marking is done at the warehouse before the merchandise is shipped to the individual store units. Sometimes a list of prices may be sent to local store managers, who then do their own marking and may be allowed to adjust the prices of some articles to reflect local market conditions.

There are benefits for the retailer who premarks. If merchandise arrives in the store completely marked, it speeds up the flow to the selling floor. This allows more sales of the product and thereby generates more reorders. If merchandise has to be delayed in the receiving room to be marked, however, the sequence of events breaks down.

To the retailer, either large or small, there are other definite advantages to premarking. The first is simply the significant reduction and sometimes complete elimination of store marking costs, not just in terms of labor costs but overhead costs as well. As overhead expenses are also incurred in a nonselling area, most retailers try to keep nonselling space to a minimum. Premarking can reduce marking-area requirements substantially.

Pricing Merchandise in the Store

Frequently, merchandise is priced after it arrives in the store. The person who sets the price at this time has the advantage of up-to-date market information on which to base that price. Also, a shipment of newly arrived merchandise items, such as jeans, can be inspected for variations in style and quality and then priced accordingly. The items can also be sorted into different price groupings based on their sales appeal.

Identifying Basic Information on the Price Ticket

"After this discussion of the importance of marking and the various locations where marking is done, you're probably wondering what all those letters and numbers on the ticket mean," said Mr. Bjornsson. So he went on to explain elements contained on basic tickets used in the store.

"The markings on the ticket usually include such information as the merchandise classification, department, manufacturer, style, model, color and size, and the selling season in which the merchandise was received into stock."

Mr. Bjornsson pointed to a price ticket with several letter and number codes. (See page 148.) Then he explained what each code meant.

"The NRMA classification is used for this type of apparel (R 1843). On this ticket, the classification identifies a woman's jacket. The manufacturing season is indicated by the last number (2) of the NRMA classification. This number represents the selling season for which the manufacturer shipped the merchandise to the retailer. In this case, the number (2) indicates the summer selling season. The manufacturer is specifically identified by the letter and numbers P 142. The color and size code are presented in both coded (M 25 636) and decoded formats (CAMEL 14) on the price ticket. These two provide coded input data for the terminals (electronic cash registers) and decoded information for the customers.

"If the retailer wants to indicate the cost of merchandise on the ticket," Mr. Bjornsson continued, "a cost code is used. A **cost code** is usually a code word or phrase of ten letters and related numbers. The following example shows a typical cost code:

$$\begin{array}{cc} \textbf{M O N E Y} & \textbf{T A L K S} \\ \textbf{1 2 3 4 5} & \textbf{6 7 8 9 0} \end{array}$$

If this code is used, the letters NAY on a ticket would mean that the item cost the retailer $3.75. An eleventh letter, such as X, may be added to represent a decimal point. In this case, the coding for $3.75 would change to NXAY, and $375 would be NAYX."

Elements contained on a basic price ticket. Why are color and size presented in both coded and noncoded formats?

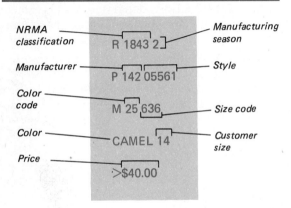

Understanding the Computer-Based Marking Systems

Mr. Bjornsson explained that Cathy's store used a computer-based **Universal Vendor Marking (UVM)** system on its price tickets. The word "universal" means that many manufacturers, suppliers, and retailers have agreed to use a common coding system that can be understood by the various companies buying and selling goods. The UVM system is used primarily by manufacturers, suppliers, and retailers of general merchandise items. The Universal Product Code (UPC) system is used mainly by manufacturers, suppliers, and retailers of food and drug items. Some products are marked with both a UVM and a UPC marking. Certain stores will use one or the other of these markings. Such markings are usually premarked by the supplier.

Computer-Based Marking Systems

A computer-based marking system may use several futuristic-appearing devices. One of these is an **automatic reading scanner,** also called an optical scanner, which resembles a futuristic ray gun. This scanner sends a variety of merchandise information from the magnetized ticket to an electronic cash register, often called a terminal. In turn, the terminal feeds this information to either a minicomputer located in the store or to a larger computer located at a regional headquarters. Information from the computer tells retailers the following:

1. What and how much merchandise is selling
2. When and how much merchandise to reorder
3. The sales productivity of individual salespeople
4. The percentage of cash versus credit sales
5. The results of various comparisons between past and present sales
6. Other types of desired merchandise information

UPC SYSTEM

Guard bars to assure readability of UPC and symbols.

0 = grocery item
(3 = drug item —— 0
5 = coupon)

2 1275 13500

Manufacturer's 5 digit number, coded into symbols.

Product identification, size, flavor, color, etc.

UVM SYSTEM

STORE NAME
●
16½

SHORT SLEEVE

DEPT CL SEAS
‹12312123

MFR   STYLE
P12312345
COL SIZE
M12123

›$19.95

Examples of UPC system and UVM system markings. UPC markings courtesy of Grey Advertising, Inc.

In certain cases, after a predetermined level of inventory has been reached, the computer can be programmed to write automatic reorders of needed merchandise.

The UPC System

Mr. Bjornsson distributed samples of both UPC and UVM price tickets. He explained the UPC price ticket by calling attention to a set of numbers and lines that are both thick and thin. "The ten numbers across the bottom of the symbol," he explained, "provide the same information as the lines in the symbol. The automatic scanner reads the meaning of the lines into the cash register. You can interpret the numbers accordingly: the first set of five lines and numbers identifies the manufacturer. The second set of five lines and numbers identifies the product. The price of the merchandise is stored in the computer. When the scanner reads the price ticket, the computer identifies the product and the price is recorded on the cash register."

The UVM System

Mr. Bjornsson continued, "The UVM price ticket resembles the more common price tickets. If you look closely at the numbers and letters on this price ticket, you'll notice that the shapes of the markings are different from normal printing. These shapes are in the form of standardized **optical character recognition (OCR)** markings. These are magnetically coded markings that can be read by many different scanners, electronic registers, and computers. An advantage of the UVM system is that it can be read by automated scanners as well as by the human eye."

Using Different Marking Methods

Marking may be done by hand or by machine. A variety of methods may be used, including ink stamps, colored pens, grease pencils, and various kinds of tickets, tags, and labels. The method that's used is determined by the kind of equipment the store has available and the kind of merchandise to be marked. In some cases, every item is not marked. Instead, the price is indicated on the shelf or bin where the item is stored or is shown on a price list.

Item Marking

Price marking with a rubber stamp saves time and is used on fast-moving, lower-priced items in supermarkets and self-service stores. A colored pen, crayon, or grease pencil is used to mark goods by hand in small stores and for some merchandise in large stores. China, glassware, and canned goods are examples of products that are often marked in this fast, inexpensive manner.

Price tickets and tags can be printed and punched with the required information either by hand-operated or automatic equipment. Some ticket markers will not only print the required information on the ticket but also pin that ticket automatically to certain kinds of soft goods.

Nonmarking

When the price is not put on the item itself but appears on a price list or on a shelf or bin holding the item, the system is known as **nonmarking.** Some retailers have eliminated the marking of many items, such as packaged groceries, drugs, notions, and small hardware items. Instead, retailers put these items in containers, trays, or shelves that show the price. Also, for goods such as tires and storage batteries, retailers may post price lists in the area where the goods are sold. Nonmarking saves time, labor, and the cost of price tags. It's also useful in times of rapid price increases because it eliminates the need to re-mark merchandise when a price adjustment is made.

Vendor Marking

More and more, suppliers or vendors pre-mark merchandise with the appropriate price and item identification information before delivering the merchandise to the store. This premarking service offered by some suppliers or vendors is called vendor marking, or **preticketing.** In some cases, the store supplies the prepared tickets and the vendor puts them on the merchandise. In other cases, the vendor both prepares and attaches the tickets. Sometimes the price is a nationally advertised one that the manufacturer has printed on the package.

When a vendor prepares the price tickets, the store's code or the vendor's own code, which the store then adopts, may be used. The tickets may be prepared with all the necessary information on them, or they may have space to insert code numbers, which the store adds when it receives the shipment. In either case, the service speeds up the flow of merchandise onto the selling floor by eliminating some of the preparation work the store needs to do.

In addition, marking at the vendor level is much more accurate than marking at the store level. In stores, too many different types of equipment and too many different people can be involved in the production of the tickets. There is neither uniformity nor continuity. But at the level of the wholesale supplier, a single marking machine operated by a single operator produces the same ticket in long continuous runs for merchandise shipped to all stores, whether in New York or California.

Re-Marking

Changing a price or replacing a ticket that has been removed or a mark that has become illegible is known as **re-marking.** Re-marking is required, for example, when merchandise is returned by a customer with the price ticket removed.

Merchandise may be re-marked by (1) putting new tickets on the merchandise, (2) removing the old price and showing only the new price, or (3) using the original ticket and showing both the old and the new price. Store policy determines the method of re-marking. If merchandise was marked down for special sales such as bargain days, holiday sales, or store anniversaries, the unsold items may be re-marked with their original prices. Re-marked tickets must contain the same information as the original tickets and keep the same season numbers or letters, so that there will not be any confusion about the length of time the merchandise has been in stock.

In a small store, the manager decides which merchandise should be re-marked. In a large store, the buyer or head of the

Kinds of price tickets.

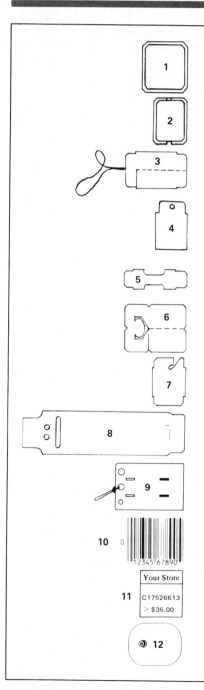

1. **Pin tickets** are used on towels, washcloths, and similar merchandise because they cannot slip off.

2. **Gummed labels** are used on cloth, leather, plastic, and unpainted wood.

3. **String tickets** are used on many kinds of items.

4. **Hole pin tickets** are used on paired items, such as gloves.

5. **Ringseal tickets** in a small size are used on items such as jewelry. A double size is used for lampshades.

6. **Wedge tickets** are used on delicate fabrics such as hosiery.

7. **Button tickets** are slipped over a button. They are used on shirts, jackets, and blouses.

8. **Folding pin tickets** are used to mark heavier merchandise such as rugs, jackets, and overcoats.

9. **Punched tickets**, often attached by a plastic string, are used on many types of goods. They feed inventory control information directly into an automatic data processing system.

10. **Universal price-coded (UPC) tickets** are printed with a special kind of type that can be read by machine. They also feed inventory information directly into a data processing system.

11. **Universal Vendor Marking (UVM) tickets** have a special kind of type that can be read by the human eye as well as by a computer.

12. **Shoplifting detection wafers** are firmly attached to goods and must be removed with a special device. If the goods with the wafer are taken out of the departments or store, they set off an alarm that signals store personnel.

department must fill in a form regarding the change in price. Salespeople may do the re-marking under the supervision of the head of the receiving department or the buyer. Re-marking machines are used by some stores to do the work faster and more economically than it can be done by hand.

Mr. Bjornsson concluded the training session with these comments: "Now you should understand that marking involves various types of decisions and procedures. The accuracy and timeliness of the marking functions are critical if the merchandise is to flow smoothly from the supplier to the consumer. Modern computerized technology can assist all of us in performing this necessary merchandising function."

Trade Talk

Define each term and use it in a sentence.

Automatic reading scanner
Cost code
Marking
Nonmarking
Optical character recognition (OCR)
Premarking
Preretailing
Preticketing
Re-marking
Retail price
Staple goods
Universal Vendor Marking (UVM)

Can You Answer These?

1. What decisions must be made before an item is marked?

2. In what ways is preretailing an advantage?

3. Name the various methods of price marking and give examples of goods for which each method would be desirable.

4. What are the differences between the UPC and UVM price ticketing systems?

5. What is the major advantage of the OCR marking system over the regular printed or marked price tickets?

6. When does merchandise need re-marking?

Problems

1. Your department head has requested that you use your creativity in designing a distinctive price ticket for a new line of merchandise. You may select a merchandise line that you are familiar with for this assignment. Your department head requests that the ticket design reflect the basic identity of your merchandise line. In addition, the layout of the price ticket should provide for manufacturer identification, merchandise classification, department, cost code, size, style, color, and selling price.

2. Several types of price tickets are described in the figure on page 151. Rule a form similar to the following. In the left column, write the letter of each of the following types of price tickets: (0) pin tickets, (a) button tickets, (b) wedge tickets, (c) string tickets, (d) ringseal tickets, (e) hole pin tickets, (f) gummed labels, (g) folding pin tickets, (h) print-punch tickets, and (i) optical-font tickets. In the middle column, list two different kinds of merchandise that would be marked with each type of price ticket. Do not use the same merchandise examples discussed in the figure. In the right column, give your reason for choosing each specific piece of merchandise to be marked with each price ticket.

Type of Price Ticket	Kinds of Merchandise	Reason
Example: (0)	Towels	They cannot slip off the merchandise.

Stockkeeping and Safety

CHAPTER 20

Communications & Human Relations

Economics & Marketing

Merchandising

Selling & Technology

Advertising & Display

Operations & Management

Vince Esposito is beginning his first day on the job as a retail salesperson in Marx's Home Furnishings Store. Mr. Lamont, his department head, is taking him on a tour of the store. They stop in the employee lounge for a quick break. Vince notices the following housekeeping rules posted on the employee bulletin board:

If you open it, close it.
If you move it, put it back.
If you turn it on, turn it off.
If you make a mess, clean it up.
If it belongs to someone else, get permission to use it.
If you use it, take care of it.
If you borrow it, return it.
If you break it, repair it.
If you don't know how to operate it, leave it alone.
If you can't fix it, call someone who can.

Mr. Lamont commented, "You would be surprised, Vince, how an otherwise good salesperson can quickly earn a negative reputation by violating any one of those rules. Sometimes, in the hustle and bustle of our work, we just forget to return borrowed items, straighten up stock, or clean up our mess. We intend to do the housekeeping later. Unfortunately, our memories fail us or we're distracted by other tasks. The consequences of our neglect can cause poor human relations with our fellow employees and our supervisors. These ten helpful rules apply to all retail workers from beginners to top management. They are among the most important aspects of a retail worker's code of behavior. And when they are followed by all retail workers, they can help to ensure prof-

itable business operation. They are especially important for beginners, because those who ignore them are unlikely to remain employees very long."

To remain in business, today's retailers must maintain well-kept places of business that are safe for both customers and employees. And those retailers who carry out this responsibility usually get their fair share of the market's business. Excellence in stockkeeping, also called "housekeeping" in some stores, and safety depend on the complete cooperation of all employees.

Stockkeeping

When given the choice of businesses in which to shop, do you choose those that are neat, clean, and attractive and avoid those that are not? Like most people, you probably prefer businesses where there is good stockkeeping. Good stockkeeping means keeping the entire stock of merchandise neat, clean, and accessible at all times.

Customers usually prefer businesses that practice good stockkeeping because it makes them feel important. And because it presents the business in the best way, good stockkeeping also gives customers confidence. For example, it tells them that the business is run efficiently and that therefore service will be efficient. So good stockkeeping is good business because it attracts customers. But it's also good business because it saves employee labor, reduces losses from stock damage and pilfering, and is a strong factor in maintaining employee morale. These results of good stockkeeping are discussed below.

Selling-Area Stockkeeping

The impression customers get of a retail business's physical shopping environment is formed by many factors. For example, lighting, background music, and attitudes of salespeople are all important. But a well-kept selling area is the most important. From the moment customers enter a place of business, they are confronted with its appearance. The overall impression they form as a result of the appearance influences their buying behavior. Progressive retailers realize this. So, to maintain desired appearance standards, they use checklists like the following:

- Are the floors clean and free from litter?
- Are the garment racks neat and free from extra hangers?
- Are the aisles clear of carts, boxes, and merchandise?
- Are the counter tops neat and clean?
- Are the fitting rooms free of merchandise, hangers, and rubbish?
- Are the wrapping desks and checkout counters orderly, with quantities of supplies on hand?
- Are under-the-counter areas neat and free from personal belongings?
- Is trash removal supervised and spot-checked?
- Are free-standing displays and open displays neat, dust-free, and orderly?
- Are the signs fresh and clean?
- Have any soiled or torn price tags been replaced?
- Are unused signs, sign holders, and display fixtures stored away and not left lying around?
- Is all the merchandise protected from sun damage?

Behind-the-Scenes Stockkeeping

Stockkeeping behind the scenes of a retail business is that done in any place other than the selling floor. These places include stockrooms, receiving and marking areas, and display departments.

General housekeeping should also be extended to parking lots, rest rooms, and employee lunchrooms. The exterior of the building should also be kept neat and clean, including the display windows, awnings, and signs.

Not long ago, many retailers insisted that all new workers start in jobs at the bottom of the ladder, behind the scenes of a retail business. This meant pushing a broom, washing windows, and doing stock work. One reason for this practice was to make all employees aware of how even these seemingly unimportant tasks help to make a business successful. A second reason was that those who moved up the ladder would be prepared to supervise those less prestigious tasks and maintain high standards.

Though starting all new workers at the bottom of the ladder is less popular today, attention to small details like maintaining clean environments is as important as ever in the operation of a retail business. So if you want to advance in retailing, doing your fair share of stockkeeping tasks behind the scenes may be time well spent.

Stockkeeping duties behind the scenes vary with the characteristics of the work being done. In all kinds of work, there are general maintenance duties to be shared among the members of a department. Some maintenance tasks, though, are not fun to do. Occasionally a worker, knowingly or unknowingly, neglects the not-so-much-fun-to-do, and this often results in strained relationships with coworkers and supervisors. To solve this problem, some companies use a schedule that indicates who is to do certain tasks and when they are to be done.

In the following pages, you'll learn why

Behind-the-scenes stockkeeping helps to make a business successful. Michael Weisbrot

behind-the-scenes stockkeeping is important in caring for stock and in economizing, or keeping business expenses low.

Caring for Stock. When shopping, do you accept soiled or damaged merchandise at the regular price? Because of poor stockkeeping, merchandise is sometimes damaged in areas behind the scenes before it reaches the selling floor. For example, if you work behind the scenes of a business and fail to clean up in the receiving, marking, or stock area, merchandise will become soiled, dented, or scratched. Merchandise that is not clean and properly maintained is difficult and frequently impossible to sell. When goods become dirty or damaged, retailers may have to lower the price and possibly take a loss. Proper care of stock can reduce markdowns and increase profit. It can also improve worker morale.

When shopping, do you bother to find what you want on a table that is a jumble of merchandise? Or do you go to one where the goods are neatly piled or stacked and you can find what you want without delay? Here again, proper care of stock can greatly reduce lost sales and help increase profit. What's more, neatly displayed merchandise reduces the chances of damaged goods, ticket switching, and shoplifting. It's much easier for dishonest customers to operate when stock is not neatly displayed.

Economizing. Retailers are in business to make a profit. To ensure a profit, every employee has to be part of a team. So all employees must work together to use supplies efficiently, keep accurate records, take care of the merchandise, and be alert to shoplifting. All these tasks help retailers keep costs low and profits high. **Economizing,** which is the management and thrifty use of materials, is one way employees can help retailers in keeping costs low.

While at work, employees perform many tasks that involve using supplies and equipment. The careful use of these supplies and equipment will save money. Have you ever seen an employee take home pens, hangers, boxes, or supplies that are used frequently on the job? Many employees don't realize that when they do this, it means considerable losses for the business. And one reason retailers have to increase prices on merchandise is to make up for this loss. Supplies, no matter how insignificant they seem, add up. A good employee will remember this and take care when using supplies and equipment.

One way retailers economize is by using an accurate recordkeeping system. The careful use of supplies, marking of sale merchandise, taking of markups and markdowns, and maintenance of accurate credit records are necessary to keep a business operating smoothly. Every employee can help with recordkeeping by taking a little extra time and being accurate when doig inventory counts, checking in merchandise, marking down price tickets, and making sales. All these tasks are part of planning and control, and careful employees are the key.

Good records are only one way to control expenses. Expenses can also be controlled by reducing the number and causes of sales returns, the amount of sales allowances, and the breakage of merchandise as well as by practicing proper stock control.

Salespeople can help the most in reducing sales returns and allowances. For example, when a salesperson takes care and makes a sale that fulfills the customer's needs, it is less likely that the merchandise will be returned or that an allowance will be given. Also handling, cleaning, and keeping track of the stock will reduce the expense of breakage or damage to merchandise. By taking care of supplies and merchandise, all employees can help retailers keep costs low.

Safety

Adam Singman was asked to place on shelves several boxes of shoes that were left in the aisles. Before Adam could take care of them, a little boy tripped on the boxes and injured his leg. Adam didn't know what to do. Would you have known how to handle this accident? How could you have prevented it from happening? **On-the-job safety** refers to the procedures and practices followed at work to ensure the well-being of both employees and customers. Employers have the responsibility of maintaining both safe and pleasant working conditions for their employees. Employers are also responsible for the well-being of customers while they are on the business premises. Employers are usually insured against accidents that occur on their property, but there are several safety measures that both employers and employees will want to observe. A basic safety precaution is being alert to conditions that could lead to an accident. The following is a list of common places where accidents have occured in retail establishments:

♦ Counters with sliding doors or glass tops
♦ Elevators, escalators, and other moving equipment
♦ Water coolers
♦ Interior displays of merchandise—for example, mannequins, stands, and props
♦ Electrical outlets
♦ Stairs, balconies, and railings
♦ Swinging doors and two-way doors

General Safety Practices

In recent years, government safety regulations have become an important concern of retailers. The government has established rules and regulations regarding safety programs and provisions for employees and customers in case of an accident. Both employees and employers will want to become acquainted with these local, state, and federal regulations.

The government organization that coordinates federal safety programs is called the **Occupational Safety and Health Administration (OSHA).** OSHA was created in 1970 to protect 60 million workers in over 5 million places of business. The major

Safety regulations should be posted where they can be seen by all employees. Courtesy of U.S. Department of Labor

---

job safety and health protection

The Occupational Safety and Health Act of 1970 provides job safety and health protection for workers through the promotion of safe and healthful working conditions throughout the Nation. Requirements of the Act include the following:

Employers: Each employer shall furnish to each of his employees employment and a place of employment free from recognized hazards that are causing or are likely to cause death or serious harm to his employees; and shall comply with occupational safety and health standards issued under the Act.

Employees: Each employee shall comply with all occupational safety and health standards, rules, regulations and orders issued under the Act that apply to his own actions and conduct on the job.

The Occupational Safety and Health Administration (OSHA) of the Department of Labor has the primary responsibility for administering the Act. OSHA issues occupational safety and health standards, and its Compliance Safety and Health Officers conduct jobsite inspections to ensure compliance with the Act.

Inspection: The Act requires that a representative of the employer and a representative authorized by the employees be given an opportunity to accompany the OSHA inspector for the purpose of aiding the inspection.

Where there is no authorized employee representative, the OSHA Compliance Officer must consult with a reasonable number of employees concerning safety and health conditions in the workplace.

Complaint: Employees or their representatives have the right to file a complaint with the nearest OSHA office requesting an inspection if they believe unsafe or unhealthful conditions exist in their workplace. OSHA will withhold, on request, names of employees complaining.

The Act provides that employees may not be discharged or discriminated against in any way for filing safety and health complaints or otherwise exercising their rights under the Act.

An employee who believes he has been discriminated against may file a complaint with the nearest OSHA office within 30 days of the alleged discrimination.

Citation: If upon inspection OSHA believes an employer has violated the Act, a citation alleging such violations will be issued to the employer. Each citation will specify a time period within which the alleged violation must be corrected.

The OSHA citation must be prominently displayed at or near the place of alleged violation for three days, or until it is corrected, whichever is later, to warn employees of dangers that may exist there.

Proposed Penalty: The Act provides for mandatory penalties against employers of up to $1,000 for each serious violation and for optional penalties of up to $1,000 for each nonserious violation. Penalties of up to $1,000 per day may be proposed for failure to correct violations within the proposed time period. Also, any employer who willfully or repeatedly violates the Act may be assessed penalties of up to $10,000 for each such violation.

Criminal penalties are also provided for in the Act. Any willful violation resulting in death of an employee, upon conviction, is punishable by a fine of not more than $10,000 or by imprisonment for not more that six months, or by both. Conviction of an employer after a first conviction doubles these maximum penalties.

Voluntary Activity: While providing penalties for violations, the Act also encourages efforts by labor and management, before an OSHA inspection, to reduce injuries and illnesses arising out of employment.

The Department of Labor encourages employers and employees to reduce workplace hazards voluntarily and to develop and improve safety and health programs in all workplaces and industries.

Such cooperative action would initially focus on the identification and elimination of hazards that could cause death, injury, or illness to employees and supervisors. There are many public and private organizations that can provide information and assistance in this effort, if requested.

More Information: Additional information and copies of the Act, specific OSHA safety and health standards, and other applicable regulations may be obtained from your employer or from the nearest OSHA Regional Office in the following locations:

Atlanta, Georgia
Boston, Massachusetts
Chicago, Illinois
Dallas, Texas
Denver, Colorado
Kansas City, Missouri
New York, New York
Philadelphia, Pennsylvania
San Francisco, California
Seattle, Washington

Telephone numbers for these offices, and additional Area Office locations, are listed in the telephone directory under the United States Department of Labor in the United States Government listing.

Washington, D.C.
1977
OSHA 2203

Ray Marshall

Ray Marshall
Secretary of Labor

U. S. Department of Labor
Occupational Safety and Health Administration

provisions of OSHA relate to safety and health standards. The most common violations by retailers have to do with the accessibility of portable fire extinguishers, the guarding of floor and wall openings and holes, the handling of material, compliance with the electrical code, misuse of power transmission apparatus, and the use of personal protective equipment.

Ensuring Safety. A safety checklist for retail employees follows. As a future retail worker, use it to help ensure safety at your place of business:

1. Know where to find and how to prepare employee and customer accident report forms.
2. Keep stairways clear of any debris or obstructions.
3. Make sure that exits have been marked properly and exit lights are not hidden.
4. Keep stock drawers closed when they are not in use.
5. Keep places in or near elevators free from obstructions. Make sure escalators are operating properly and that customers and employees are using them with care.
6. Check to make sure that the exit doors are unlocked when people are in the building.
7. Make sure that training received in the use of power equipment such as forklifts is followed carefully.
8. Check fire doors to be sure they are not blocked and that they work properly.
9. See that the no-smoking rules are enforced.
10. Keep floors clean and free of grease and spills.

Let's think for a minute about daily routines that can be hazardous if proper precautions are not taken. For example, while dusting the china, you drop a plate and cut yourself. Or you're checking merchandise and get a pin in your finger. Or when stocking merchandise on the shelves, you strain your back by lifting something too heavy. All these situations can occur.

What would you do and what type of insurance does your employer provide to cover injury? Find out what benefits your employer provides in case of injury or hospitalization or both.

Federal Legislation. The government has helped employees with job injuries by passing the Worker's Compensation Law. This law provides for some or all of the following:

1. Payment of a major part of medical expenses
2. Subsistence income for those unable to work
3. Continuation of payments for permanent disability for a specific time or until no longer needed
4. Death benefits to dependents

The Occupational Safety and Health Act and the Worker's Compensation Law have been passed to help prevent accidents and to assist in the possible event of accidents. As an employee, ask your supervisor about the procedures for ensuring safety and securing benefits.

What to Do in Case of an Accident. Adequate safety precautions will help to prevent accidents, but accidents do occur in every business. How should they be handled? When an accident does occur involving an employee or a customer, follow these steps:

1. Report it to your supervisor or manager.
2. Do not move the injured person.
3. Get a full report of the accident from the injured and a verification by a witness.
4. Do not volunteer personal opinions concerning the accident.
5. Be accurate in reporting accidents; remember that the employer would like to avoid a lawsuit.
6. Make sure that the accident is reported to insurance companies.

These steps will help with taking care of injuries. But you will also want to follow any additional regulations that your company has set up.

It is important to make sure that both customers and employees observe the no-smoking regulations. Kip Peticolas/Fundamental Photographs

Here is an important point to remember: if you are not trained in first aid, then don't attempt to give aid. Do contact individuals who can administer aid properly. Improper first aid can make an injury worse, and this could result in a lawsuit. If a first aid course is offered by your company, take it.

Fire Safety

Knowledge of fire procedures is part of every employee's job; it can save people's lives. If there is a fire, stay calm and assist in getting customers out of the building. As an employee, the first thing you should know is the location of the fire exits and fire extinguishers and how to use the extinguishers.

Observe basic fire-prevention regulations. For example, observe the no-smoking regulations, and make sure that customers also obey this rule. Use proper electrical connections. Store all boxes and flammable cleaning equipment properly.

Read procedure booklets carefully and follow instructions given by your employer and supervisors. You can prevent many accidents by observing regulations and making safety part of your responsibility. Employers, of course, must also make safety their responsibility. The completion of daily stockkeeping duties and alertness to safety will lessen the causes and likelihood of accidents.

In this chapter, you've learned the basic tasks and responsibilities of stockkeeping and safety that all beginning retail workers must perform. You've also gained an understanding of why the tasks and responsibilities of stockkeeping and safety are important to the success of all retail businesses.

In the next chapter, you'll learn how retailers try to keep costs low, or to economize, by preventing stock shortages and theft.

Trade Talk

Define each term and use it in a sentence.

Economizing
On-the-job-safety
Occupational Safety
  and Health
  Administration
  (OSHA)

Can You Answer These?

1. Why is good stockkeeping important to a retail business?

2. How can employees help their company economize?
3. How can employees assist their employer with safety practices?
4. What is the Worker's Compensation Law and what are its provisions?
5. What steps should be followed in the event of an accident?
6. How can an employee help prevent a fire from occurring?

Problems

1. Rule a form similar to the following. In the left column, list five stockkeeping duties. Then determine what benefits are derived by the retail company from the practice of these duties.

Stockkeeping Duty	Benefit to Company

2. Rule a form similar to the following. In the left column, list ten safety practices. In the appropriate columns at the right, list the benefits of each practice to the business and to the customer.

Safety Practice	Benefit to Business	Benefit to Customer

Preventing Shortage, Damage, and Theft of Stock

CHAPTER **21**

Communications & Human Relations
Economics & Marketing
Merchandising
Selling & Technology
Advertising & Display
Operations & Management

Dorothy Kimura was startled. She had just finished ringing up a sale for a customer and was prepared to assist a second customer. But the second customer had vanished along with an expensive cashmere sweater! Dorothy had just placed the sweater on the display rack this morning. She thought that the second customer must have stolen it while she was at the cash register. She decided to report the matter to Mrs. Omerjee, her department head.

Mrs. Omerjee responded to Dorothy's report by saying: "Your immediate reporting of theft is very important so that we can rapidly alert management and sales personnel to the presence of shoplifters. The worst thing any of us can do

is to ignore shoplifting or not take it seriously. If a store is negligent in the detection and prevention of shoplifting, the word spreads to potential thieves. I'm sure that you'll find our next employees' meeting very informative and helpful. It's about preventing stock shortage, damage, and theft."

Here's how Mr. O'Leary, the store manager, introduced the employees' meeting: "As you know, we'll soon be entering the holiday season. During this 2½-month season, sales will account for over 35 percent of the total sales for the year. It's also a time when our store can experience high

160

losses due to stock shortages. We consider **stock shortages** to be the difference between the amount of merchandise that we believe we should have in stock according to our records and the amount of stock that our physical inventory actually reveals to be in stock. To identify this difference or shortage, we take a physical inventory immediately following the holiday season. In past years, such shortages have run between 1.5 and 2 percent of total retail sales each year. Since our store now earns only 3 to 4 percent net profit each year, you can better appreciate how important it is for all of us to control losses due to stock shortages and theft."

Finding Causes of Stock Shortages and Damages

Most stock shortages are the result of either (1) mistakes that have been made in keeping track of the inventory, which means that the discrepancy is due to a recordkeeping error or (2) actual theft of merchandise. Some bookkeeping errors are bound to happen because people make mistakes. Far more serious, though, is theft by employees or by customers. Stock damage is greatest during the holiday season and during special sales when customers are rushed and handle merchandise carelessly.

Maintaining Effective Stockkeeping Practices

Stockkeeping practices are those practices that employees are expected to follow to help the store keep track of stock. These practices protect stock from becoming shopworn or damaged and also from being exposed to possible theft. Shopworn or damaged merchandise can result in losses as great as those caused by theft because the affected merchandise cannot be sold. Therefore, the following practices are suggested:

1. Handle merchandise carefully and with clean hands when demonstrating its use.
2. Tactfully assist customers in handling stock and trying on garments so that merchandise will not be damaged.
3. Cover textile merchandise at night to reduce damage from dust.
4. Dust and clean stock and fixtures such as display cases before the store opens and during slack periods.
5. Keep stock neatly arranged in its proper order.
6. Return merchandise to its proper place after each transaction.
7. Be sure price tags have not been switched.

Warehouse employees are directed to handle stock carefully and to make sure that all shipments are put into protected storage locations as quickly as possible. Goods left in the receiving, checking, or marking areas are open to theft.

Stock shortages can also be prevented by employees who take care in counting, weighing, and measuring. For example, suppose that the fabrics department of a store purchased stock with a retail value of $1,000. The sales records for 2 months shows sales of $800. The inventory records indicate a stock on hand of $200. However, a physical count of the stock shows an amount having a retail value of $175. The stock shrinkage is therefore $200 minus $175, or $25. It may be that this amount of merchandise was damaged, spoiled, or stolen. But it may also be that the salesperson did not measure the fabric accurately.

Detecting and Preventing Theft

Mr. Ivanov, the security officer at Dorothy's store, began the discussion of theft detection and prevention by asking the group, "What is shoplifting? How serious do you think it is in this store and in stores across the nation?"

The group offered several descriptions of shoplifting, which Mr. Ivanov summarized. "**Shoplifting** is a crime that occurs when a person, usually a customer, steals merchandise from a business." Mr. Ivanov explained that when an employee steals merchandise from the company for which he or she works, the crime of **larceny** is committed. The theft of money by an employee is called **embezzlement.** And **pilferage** is a type of stealing done by hiding small amounts of merchandise in shopping bags, purses, pockets, and so on. Theft in whatever form, regardless of what is taken or who takes it, is a crime punishable by law.

Next, Mr. Ivanov gave the group an idea of the extent of **internal theft** (thievery by employees) and **external theft** (thievery by amateur and professional thieves). "In a recent national report," he said, "merchandise losses and extra security costs add an average of 2 to 3 percent to everything sold by major department stores and grocery and drug chains. And shoplifting appears to be growing. Current estimates point out that over $8 billion a year is stolen from retailers in this country."

Professional Shoplifters

Mr. Ivanov told the group that professional shoplifters are people who enter a business knowing what and how they plan to steal. They usually have a customer, or "fence," for the stolen merchandise. Sometimes they work in teams. One-fourth of all shoplifting is done by professional shoplifters. Included in this group are drug addicts, who may have to steal between $100 and $300 worth of merchandise daily to support their drug addiction.

Professional shoplifters use a variety of sophisticated techniques. As sleight-of-hand experts, they can, without being noticed, snatch items from counters and pass these items to accomplices. Shoplifters come equipped with coats and capes that have hidden pockets and slits or zippered hiding places. By reaching through the slits in their clothing, shoplifters can

Retailers must always watch for shoplifters. Mimi Forsyth/Monkmeyer

snatch up articles directly from open displays without being seen. Often, the open coat itself prevents the shoplifter's actions from being seen.

To all appearances, professional shoplifters are average, polite customers who don't like to take chances. If they fear discovery or conditions are not favorable for shoplifting, they won't try to steal but will wait for a "sure thing."

Kleptomaniacs

A **kleptomaniac** is a person with an abnormal impulse to steal. Kleptomaniacs often have no control over this desire, and many of them are very practical and skillful thieves. Medical or physical treatment is sometimes required for kleptomaniacs.

"Thrill" Shoplifters

Some people steal not for real gain but because they get excitement from the very act of stealing. Sometimes they steal "for kicks" or because they have been dared to do so. They may enter stores in gangs to distract salespeople. When salespeople are suspicious of a group, they should request assistance from associates or managers.

Employees

Employees have been known to steal cash as well as merchandise. This type of thievery is discussed in Chapter 31.

Mr. Ivanov reminded the group that regardless of the type of shoplifter, the common answer that many shoplifters give when caught is, "I have never done this before." But failure to prosecute "first offenders" encourages shoplifting. Some stores operate on the theory that a person who steals will also lie. When a store follows a policy of prosecution, the word gets around, and professionals will avoid the store. Amateurs will think twice before yielding to the temptation to steal.

Protecting Stock from Theft

The size of a store, its type of merchandising operation, and its lines of goods determine where stock is kept. Merchandise on the selling floor is called **forward stock**. Usually some merchandise is kept in **reserve stock**, typically in a stockroom or warehouse. When reserve stock is kept in drawers or shelves on the sales floor, it is called **under-the-counter stock**. In some departments, such as those selling dresses, coats, suits, and shoes, only one sample of each item may be displayed on the selling floor.

Retailers have to protect all merchandise, regardless of where it is located, because stock is stolen from warehouses,

selling floors, and stockrooms alike. Four methods are usually used together in a security system:

1. Employees are trained in effective customer service practices that help reduce the opportunities for theft.
2. Apprehension and arrest policies are set up and explained to all store employees.
3. Surveillance systems are set up to keep all stock under constant or periodic observation.
4. Store layouts are set up to discourage shoplifting.

Following Customer Service Practices

At this point during the meeting, several salespeople asked Mr. Ivanov what they should do to better detect and prevent shoplifting. Mr. Ivanov said that employees must continually watch merchandise and people and:

1. Keep in mind that ordinary customers want attention while shoplifters do not. When busy with one customer, salespeople should acknowledge other customers with a polite remark such as, "I'll be with you in a minute." While such attention can make a shoplifter feel uneasy, it pleases ordinary customers. Remember that shoplifting is more likely to occur during the busy, rush periods of the day or week.
2. Always give a receipt. If store rules require that you staple a customer's receipt to a bag or box, do so without fail. This prevents shoplifters from obtaining refunds and credits on stolen items.
3. Observe customers carrying unwrapped packages. Offer to wrap or bag the merchandise. This will not offend a true customer. It will, however, discourage a shoplifter.
4. Do not give the impression that you distrust customers, but always be alert to their movements. If possible, never turn your back on customers, even when seeking merchandise for them.
5. Be alert to people who wear loose coats, capes, or bulky dresses. Also, watch in-

Examples of (left) forward stock, (middle) reserve stock, and (right) under-the-counter stock. Elizabeth Richter

dividuals who carry large purses, packages, umbrellas, and shopping bags. Those who push baby strollers and collapsible carts also bear watching.

6. In clothing departments, beware of the "try-on" shoplifters. They try on an item for size, as it were, and then, if they feel no one has seen them, walk out wearing the garment. Salespeople should keep a check on the number of garments carried into the fitting rooms. Thieves often try to sneak in extra garments, beyond the number permitted.

7. Be especially alerted for "teams"—thieves who pretend not to know each other. One of the team will attract the clerk's attention away from the partner. One team member will cause a fuss, ask unreasonable questions, create an argument, or even stage a fainting fit while a partner picks up the merchandise and escapes.

8. Know your stock. Keep your stock in good condition. By paying attention to new stock and the orderly appearance of your displays, you can more readily detect missing stock. A messy department attracts shoplifters. Thieves will assume that the salespeople will not be able to miss the item in time to catch them before they leave the store.

9. Know how to obtain authorized help promptly if you suspect someone of being a shoplifter. Most stores have a way of letting other personnel know of a suspected shoplifter. Some have security personnel whom you can call, while others have a special number that can be used to alert the manager.

Observing Apprehension and Arrest Policies

A question salespeople often ask is "What should I do if I actually catch a shoplifter stealing merchandise?"

Most stores have specific store policies regarding the responsibilities of employees and managers with respect to apprehending shoplifters. Salespeople should check with their managers to get a clear understanding of the store's policy.

Managers should also instruct employees about what they are to do when they observe a theft by a shoplifter. This training should be given periodically, at least once every 3 months. The knowledge will help prevent legal problems in addition to catching offenders.

There are certain principles and practices that many stores follow regarding shoplifting apprehension and arrest. But the most important guideline to follow is to be certain; otherwise you will risk a false-arrest lawsuit. So, never accuse customers of stealing or try in any way to apprehend shoplifters. When you see what appears to be a theft, keep the suspect in sight and alert your manager immediately. The police or the store security personnel should also be notified.

Many states have passed "shoplifting laws" which, among other things, deal with apprehending shoplifters. Apprehension in many states doesn't necessarily have to begin outside the store. Sometimes, shoplifters can be apprehended if they are observed in the process of concealing merchandise. Shoplifters are generally apprehended in the store if the merchandise involved is of substantial value.

Certain store policies recommend apprehending shoplifters outside the store. For one thing, apprehension of this kind strengthens the store's case against a shoplifter. Then too, a scene or any type of commotion that a shoplifter may cause interferes with the store operation. In most cases, store security or management personnel will handle these types of apprehensions. It's very important for employees to inform such personnel immediately so that apprehensions can be made before the shoplifters escape. If necessary, when supervisory or designated antishoplifting personnel are not available, a good approach to use when stopping a suspect is to speak to the person and identify yourself. Then say: "I believe you have some merchandise on your person or in your bag that you've forgotten to pay for. Would you mind coming back to the store to straighten this matter out?" Never touch the suspect, because the contact could be considered as roughness or rudeness.

Some organizations in large cities have control files on shoplifters who have been caught. The retail merchants association can inform retailers about the services available in their area. These files can be checked to see whether the person caught has a record. As mentioned earlier, shoplifters often claim to be first offenders. And they are likely to remain "first offenders" if retailers allow them to leave the store without obtaining positive identification or referring names to the police and local retail merchants' association.

Using Surveillance Systems

Mr. Ivanov explained that the store security department now uses a closed-circuit television system to monitor sales areas, entrances, exits, and storage areas. He went on to say that, periodically, security guards use selected observation posts and one-way mirrors that allow them to watch activities on the sales floor without being detected. Occasionally the security guards assume the role of customers to check sales and stockkeeping security practices.

"One of the newer security systems that

the store has installed to protect merchandise," Mr. Ivanov continued, "involves electronic detection equipment.

When this equipment is used, each article is tagged or labeled with a plastic device. When the article is paid for, this device,

Closed-circuit TVs, mirrors, and electronic detection equipment are among the security devices now being used by retailers. Courtesy of Burns International Security Services, Inc. (upper left); Jane Hamilton-Merritt (upper right); Charles Gatewood (lower left); courtesy of Knogo Corporation (lower right)

which is often hidden, is removed or deactivated by the salesperson. If the customer attempts to leave the store with the article without paying for it, the hidden device will trigger an alarm as the customer passes through the electronic detection equipment.

"However," emphasized Mr. Ivanov, "keep in mind that there is a legal danger in using electronic devices. If the cashier forgets to remove the pellet device, an innocent shopper may be stopped outside and falsely detained. At the very least, it can be a very embarrassing incident for both the customer and the store."

Preventing Ticket Switching

Next, Mr. Ivanov explained the methods used to prevent ticket switching. They include the following:

1. Tamperproof gummed labels that rip apart when an attempt is made to remove them
2. Hard-to-break plastic string on soft-goods tickets
3. Special staple patterns recognizable to store personnel for all stapled tickets
4. Extra price tickets concealed elsewhere on merchandise

If a store uses simple and basic pricing methods, it shouldn't mark prices in pencil. Instead, a rubber stamp or pricing machine should be used.

Improving Store Layout

"Stores such as ours," Mr. Ivanov explained, "take a number of preventive measures against theft. Shoplifters like crowds, open counters, and displays near exits or in corner areas. A store's layout can discourage or encourage shoplifting. For example, high fixtures and tall displays that give visual protection to shoplifters will encourage theft. To destroy such protection, set display cases in broken sequences.

"Keep small, high-priced items out of reach, preferably in locked cases," Mr. Ivanov continued. "Keep valuable and easy-

to-hide items at counters where salespeople are in attendance. Or, better yet, encourage the customers to ask a salesperson to show such items from the display fixtures."

Mr. O'Leary, the store manager, ended the employees' group meeting by making these comments: "Most people are honest. Most customers wouldn't consider taking merchandise they hadn't paid for, nor would they steal money out of an open cash register. Most store employees are just as honest. However, a few customers and employees are not as honest, and they are responsible for a significant amount of theft. Theft and stock shortages can be significant because, you will recall, these losses can account for up to 50 percent of our net profit. We all have a responsibility to prevent, detect, and control these needless expenses."

Now that you have completed this unit, you should have a good understanding of the many different tasks that have to be done before merchandise is ready to be sold to customers, who does these tasks, how they are done, and why they are done. You should also have gained an understanding of why all retail employees must observe stockkeeping and safety practices and store policies regarding stock shortages and theft.

Trade Talk

Define each term and use it in a sentence.

Embezzlement	Pilferage
External theft	Reserve stock
Forward stock	Shoplifting
Internal theft	Stock shortages
Kleptomaniac	Under-the-counter
Larceny	stock

Can You Answer These?

1. What are the differences between larceny, embezzlement, and pilferage?
2. Name the major types of shoplifters. What

type do you think is responsible for the largest losses? Why?

3. What are the main ways of protecting stock from theft?

4. What recommendations were given to salespeople concerning effective customer service practices that can reduce shoplifting?

5. What recommendations were given concerning the apprehension of suspected shoplifters?

Problems

1. You are a new salesperson in a retail store. Your manager has requested that you prepare a checklist of tasks that you will perform each day and week to maintain the newness, freshness, and appearance of your stock.

Rule a form similar to the following. In the left column, identify the stock maintenance tasks you will perform. In the remaining columns, check whether these tasks would be performed daily and/or weekly.

Stock Maintenance Tasks	Daily	Weekly
Example: Conduct count of stock		

Activities and Project

UNIT

7

Retailing Case

On a separate sheet of paper, rule a form similar to the merchandise receiving report on page 169. Use the following to complete the entries.

1. **Receiving No. 1411:** Purchase order 6-711 for 12 hair dryers from the Sunbeam Company. Dryers weigh 5 pounds each and were shipped via UPS freight, No. 7862 from Chicago. Transportation costs, $4.50, will be charged to Department 60.

2. **Receiving No. 1412:** Purchase order 6-715 for six cartons of Christmas candles. Only three cartons were delivered. One of the three cartons was damaged. You accept the shipment but indicate the problems on the receiving record. The shipment weighs 80 pounds and originated in Minneapolis via Viking Transport. Transportation costs of $12 will be charged to Department 61. (Note: Receiving problems are noted by drawing a diagonal line in red across the receiving number.)

Working with People

You have just been hired as a salesperson in the record store of a shopping mall. On the first Saturday afternoon, your store is very busy, as a special record promotion is being offered. While assisting a customer, you observe two customers studying a record album. Suddenly, one of the customers slips the album under a trench coat and rapidly walks out the door. You try to hurry through the crowd of shoppers to catch the "customer." By the time you reach the door, the individual has disappeared.

You report the theft to two of the other, more experienced salespeople. Their response shocks you about as much as the theft.

"Oh, that happens all the time. We have

to expect some thefts. The management anticipates it; they just add a percentage for stock shortages and theft to the markup. The cost is just passed on to the customers. The last time a shoplifter was prosecuted, the judge threw the case out of court because of lack of evidence. Besides, we shouldn't get involved in all the hassle for a mere $4.95 album."

1. What do you consider to be the major attitude problems that exist in this store?
2. What are the important facts to be considered?
3. What are possible solutions to the problem that managers and employees can work together on?
4. How could the results of each solution be evaluated?

Project 7: Planning a Receiving and Marking Department

Your Project Goal
Given a retail store of your choice, identify what activities must be done to properly receive, check, mark, and distribute merchandise to the selling floor.

Procedure
1. Design a physical layout of the receiving and marking department for the above functions. Include within your layout the following areas: (*a*) receiving dock, (*b*) receiving room, (*c*) checking area, (*d*) marking area, and (*e*) stockroom or warehouse storage area. Keep in mind the logical flow of merchandise from the receiving dock to the storage or selling area.
2. Also include within your layout needed equipment such as overhead distribution tracks, conveyor belts, storage bins or racks, tables, marking machines, or other related equipment.
3. It is recommended that you draw the plan on a large sheet of paper using an appropriate scale.
4. Study the receiving and marking department of your firm or other businesses to obtain ideas for your project. Contact your instructor for additional references, if necessary, to complete the layout plan.

Evaluation
You will be evaluated on the completeness and appropriateness of your layout plan for the kind of store and merchandise line you selected.

A sample merchandise receiving report.

colspan RECEIVING REPORT

RECEIVING REPORT

This form is to be filled out and sent to the purchasing agent the day that material is received. If this report indicates a partial shipment, a supplemental receiving report should be prepared showing materials yet to be received on this order. Provide full particulars if material is unacceptable for any reason.

Rec. by	Shipper	Shipped from (City only)	Carrier	Carrier's No.	Items Rec.	Wt.	Chgs.	Dept.	Rec. No.	Date Rec.

Report loss or damage immediately to the purchasing division.
Retain container and contents for inspection.
Furnish damage report on form supplied by purchasing department.

Partial Shipment_____   Order Completed_____

UNIT 8

Learning How to Sell

Analyzing the Product

CHAPTER 22

Communications & Human Relations

Economics & Marketing

Merchandising

Selling & Technology

Advertising & Display

Operations & Management

In a large, well-known New York City department store, there was an extraordinary young menswear salesperson whose daily sales volume was always nearly twice that of any of the 14 other salespeople in the department. George Vance had a higher average sale record than any of his coworkers. He also had a smaller percentage of returned merchandise than anyone on the floor.

George wasn't the most handsome man on the sales force, but he dressed well and was well groomed. He was friendly but not overly so. He wasn't especially talkative—he didn't spend a great deal of time with each customer. Yes, he was honest and reliable. What made George such a successful salesperson?

George's achievements may be credited to his superior knowledge of the products he sold and to his ability to match the features of the product with the needs and wants of his customers. He was heading for a promotion.

Why do shoppers return to the same store and often to the same salesperson time after time? Why do some retail businesses succeed while others fail? Of course, there are many factors that lead to success in selling and in operating a retail business. But essential to both is the ability to analyze a product in terms of the needs and wants of customers. A **need** is an unfilled requirement not necessarily demanding immediate supply, while a **want or desire** is a craving or urge to have a particular product or service.

To serve customers properly, salespeople, buyers, merchandise managers, and advertising personnel must be able to analyze the products they sell in terms of sales potential and customer needs and wants. Advancement in career level and pay depend largely on this competency.

When you begin your retail career, your first responsibility will be to master information about the stock—its benefits and features. This is one reason why, as a beginner, you may be assigned to stock work. Being familiar with the stock on hand and where it's located is an advantage in selling and building steady customers.

As well as improving your sales and merchandise abilities, product analysis will also offer you personal satisfactions. For example, you'll get to know the merits of various brands and models. And you'll learn how products should be used and the benefits customers will get from their use, which will give you a sense of social service in a people-oriented field like retailing. It will help you develop self-confidence and a sense of personal worth.

Types of Products

To understand fully the purpose and procedure of product analysis, you must know the three general categories into which retailers group merchandise: convenience goods, shopping goods, and specialty goods. These categories are based on the customer's viewpoint, and each type of goods calls for its own sales approach.

Consumers seldom want information from a salesperson about **convenience goods.** These are items such as candy and toothpaste, that customers usually buy wherever and whenever it's convenient. Customers, however, do want information and advice when purchasing **shopping goods,** such as dress clothing and electric drills, because these are products that they generally compare and shop for before purchasing. Certainly, an experienced homemaker wants no help when buying coffee but may require much information when purchasing an electronic oven. **Specialty goods** are those that attract consumers for some reason other than price. Customers will usually go out

of their way to visit a retail store where this merchandise is sold and to purchase it without shopping around. Some typical specialty goods are very high quality watches, famous-label clothing, and certain brands of fine china.

Of course, not everyone has the same purchasing habits. Some people buy automobiles only after shopping carefully for them; then cars are shopping goods. Others decide upon the "make" or brand of car they want and go directly to the dealer that sells it—these cars are specialty goods. However, when classifying goods for merchandising purposes, retailers are concerned mainly with the majority of customers.

Selling Convenience Goods

Most convenience goods are presold through mass media—magazines, newspapers, television, and radio—and through point-of-sale displays. Preselling reduces the need for person-to-person selling. Nevertheless, employees assigned to the sales floor must be able to identify and locate items for customers and answer their questions about merchandise.

Selling Shopping Goods

All those who sell shopping goods—particularly the salespersons—must have complete product information. Competition in this field is based largely on strong buying appeals to consumers. These buying appeals are made through national magazine and TV advertising, local advertising, personal sales service, and store displays. Merchandising personnel using any of these methods must thoroughly understand the products they sell in order to compete for the shopper's favor.

Selling Specialty Goods

To maintain the prestige of specialty goods, retailers continuously make their customers conscious of the product's unique features. So, selling specialty goods usually requires even greater product-analysis competencies than does selling shopping goods.

Product Analysis

Product analysis is based on consumer needs and wants. The logical way to analyze a product is to answer the questions that customers might consciously or unconsciously ask themselves during the buying process. This approach to product analysis provides a framework that is helpful to all types of retail workers, from beginning sales and stock workers to top management. It consists of the following nine basic questions. These questions may be organized into an analysis checklist that can be modified to fit a particular product or group of products.

Can you identify the convenience goods, shopping goods, and specialty goods? Gary Gladstone/Image Bank (upper left), courtesy of Sears, Roebuck and Co. (upper right), Kip Peticolas/Fundamental Photographs (lower left)

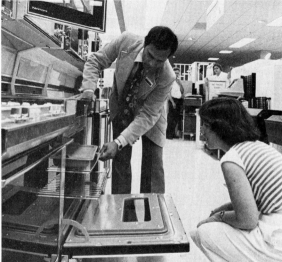

1. Is the product primarily a convenience good, a shopping good, or a specialty good?
2. *Who* uses the product? (*consumer characteristics*)
   a. Age, sex, marital status
   b. Approximate income level
   c. Occupational, social, and cultural background
   d. Fashion-consciousness
   e. Other consumer characteristics
3. *What* do consumers want from the product? (*satisfactions or needs*)
   a. Appearance
   b. Comfort
   c. Distinctiveness
   d. Economy
   e. Prestige
   f. Protection
   g. Seasonability
   h. Security
   i. Sentiment
   j. Suitability
   k. Trade name
   l. Other satisfactions
4. *How* does the product satisfy user needs and wants? (*advantages and disadvantages*)
   a. Regular uses
   b. Advantages of each use
   c. Special or unusual uses
   d. Relationship of use to other merchandise
   e. Objections to the product
   f. Disadvantages or limitations of the product
   g. Other advantages
5. *Why* does the product satisfy consumers' needs? (*proofs*)
   a. Materials and methods used in manufacturing
   b. Quality of workmanship and construction
   c. Special features, processes, and finishes
   d. History of the product
   e. Availability of replacements
   f. Guarantee or warrantee
   g. Other proofs
6. *How much* should be spent for the product? (*price*)
   a. Savings from product use

b. Potential value compared with other products
   c. Saving through cash purchase
   d. Cost of upkeep or maintenance
   e. Competitors' prices
   f. Payment arrangements
   g. Market-price behavior
   h. Other price factors
7. *Where* should the product be purchased? (*source*)
   a. Company policy on customer satisfaction
   b. Customer services
   c. Quality of personal selling
   d. Other source factors
8. *When* should the product be purchased? (*time*)
   a. Time(s) when product is available or in season
   b. Stage of the fashion cycle
   c. Duration of sale or reduced price
   d. Anticipated price change
   e. Time required for delivery
   f. Dates of related holidays and relevant events
   g. Other time factors
9. *How* should the product be used, cared for, or maintained? (*use*)
   a. How to assemble the item
   b. Regular uses or applications
   c. Special uses or applications
   d. Other products with which the product may be used
   e. Product care and maintenance
   f. Availability of repair service
   g. Other use and care factors

Acquiring Product-Analysis Competencies

What motivates superior merchandising personnel—salespeople in particular—to learn the basic facts about a product and keep on learning after the basic facts are mastered? Where do they obtain the essential information? How do they develop skill in recalling and applying their

Successful salespeople analyze the products they sell so that they will be able to answer any questions their customers ask. Jane Hamilton-Merritt

knowledge when it's needed? The following sections answer these questions.

Learning to Like Product Analysis

First, the superior performers like, *or learn to like,* the merchandise they handle. This feeling grows as they gain more information about the products. Knowledge creates enthusiasm. Salespeople receive personal satisfaction from being authorities on the products they sell. What may at first seem to be a bothersome responsibility becomes an enjoyable challenge as they seek new sources of knowledge. So liking product analysis is a matter of getting started on the right foot—assuming a positive attitude toward it from the start.

Sources of Information

The five basic sources of product information are direct experience with the product, other people, formal training, consumer education information, and promotional material and information.

Direct Experience. Direct experience means personal contact with the product. The most effective direct experience is personal use of the article. Salespeople who use a product themselves are usually better informed and more enthusiastic about it. This is one reason employers offer their staff discounts on the products they sell.

Another kind of direct experience is examining the product—comparing the various grades, styles, or models. This helps merchandising personnel to explain the differences to customers. Products may be studied while one is doing regular sales or stock duties, during business lulls, or during personal shopping trips.

Studying labels is also a good way to learn product information. As a modern merchandising tool, labels save time for both customers and salespeople.

Visits to factories and wholesale houses, when possible, provide valuable product information. When salespeople know how products are made and distributed, they develop confidence in the product. Also, it gives people the ability to offer technical information to customers, which can help increase company profit as well as sales.

Other People.   Discussing products with other salespeople can provide a variety of viewpoints. It can also help salesworkers make sales presentations and meet customer objections with greater confidence and flexibility.

One of the best ways to get product information is by talking to customers. Good salespeople encourage their customers to share their buying problems and their experiences with a particular product. By doing this, they learn why customers prefer certain brands, models, and colors.

Another way salespeople learn product information is by talking to their friends. They frequently can learn from them what services customers expect from an article, the uses to which a product is put, how to care for it, and its advantages and limitations.

Many successful salespeople improve their product knowledge by talking with coworkers. Most salespeople, if properly approached, are willing to discuss a product and to talk about their successful sales and perhaps even their failures.

Experienced salespeople know and beginners soon learn that when it is done tactfully, asking their supervisors about a product brings good results. Successful buyers and department managers spend part of their time on the sales floor selling and helping the salespeople. Assistant buyers usually spend most of their time on the sales floor helping the sales process. Buyers and managers have product information that is not available from other sources.

When possible, questioning of vendor sales representatives can be an excellent way of getting product information. New ideas and information about products may be obtained from these sales representatives because they come into contact with a variety of sales situations. A Chicago manufacturer of baked goods requests his sales reps to spend some of their Saturdays behind the counters of retail stores so that they will be able to offer advice to the storekeepers they serve.

Formal Training and Supervised Study. Some salespeople can take a shortcut to learning product analysis if they work for a company that offers courses in the subject. Large department and specialty stores, franchising companies, and chain stores usually offer such courses. Public schools also offer these type of courses. They are taught by well-qualified instructors who design the content to meet the needs of class members. Instructors preselect the necessary reading material, which saves learners the time they would need to do this themselves. This type of guided study shortens the route to mastery of product analysis. Also, students are able to evaluate what they have learned and fill any gaps in their knowledge.

Studying Consumer Education Information.   The consumer movement has given rise to many ways of informing consumers about buying and using thousands of products. Consumer organizations; federal, state, and local governments; newspapers; radio; TV; and the marketers and merchandisers themselves engage in consumer education programs.

Studying Promotional Material and Information.   Because product information is always changing, only the advertising and sales promotion media can supply the information a person would need to stay knowledgeable in a particular product area. Virtually all types of consumer advertising and displays are potential sources of information for product analysis. Their value lies mainly in the creativity used to persuade prospective customers.

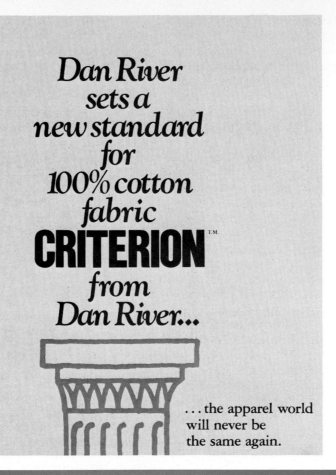

Dan River
sets a
new standard
for
100% cotton
fabric
CRITERION T.M.
from
Dan River...

...the apparel world
will never be
the same again.

One of the basic sources of product information is promotional material. *Courtesy of Dan River*

When one is using a biased source such as promotional material, it is necessary to separate facts from propaganda. In learning to identify basic product information, however, beginners in product analysis usually find the major mail-order catalogs to be a good starting point.

For their sales staffs, large manufacturers and some retailers prepare special sales training materials ranging from simple product manuals to costly visual materials. Programmed individual instruction may be available to retail personnel. Most business and industry sales training materials relate to specific products. Usually they are very effective.

Now that you have an understanding of product analysis, you can see why it is so important for retail salesworkers to master this skill. It's also important for them to master the skill of analyzing retail selling, which you'll learn about in the next chapter.

Trade Talk

Define each term and use it in a sentence.

Convenience goods   Specialty goods
Need   Want or desire
Shopping goods

Can You Answer These?

1. Why should retail salespeople, as well as management, understand the differences among convenience goods, shopping goods, and specialty goods?
2. What product-analysis information should retail personnel know to answer customers' questions concerning the need for a product?
3. What information is needed to answer customers' questions about price?
4. How do successful retail workers learn to like product analysis?
5. What are five good sources of product-analysis information? Explain the advantages of each.

Problems

1. Rule a form similar to the following. In the left column, write the letter of each of the following products: (0) candy, (a) tennis racket, (b) greeting card, (c) bread, (d) knit shirt, (e) flowers, (f) perfume, (g) lamp, (h) shoelaces, (i) toaster, and (j) motorcycle.

Place a check mark (√) in one of the columns to the right to indicate the type of good each product is.

Products	Convenience Goods	Shopping Goods	Specialty Goods
Example: (0)	√		

2. Rule a form similar to the following. In the left column, write numbers 2 through 9 of the product-analysis questions at approximately 3-inch intervals. Then choose three nationally advertised products: a convenience good (for example, Coca-Cola), a shopping good (for example, Sherwin-Williams A-100 Latex House Paint), and a specialty good (for example, a particular model Cadillac automobile). Write the names of the items in the appropriate column heads. Then, in the columns, record two or three items of information called for by each of the nine questions. Compare the information for the three types of goods.

Product-Analysis Question No.	Type of Goods		
	Convenience _____ (Name of item)	Shopping _____ (Name of item)	Specialty _____ (Name of item)

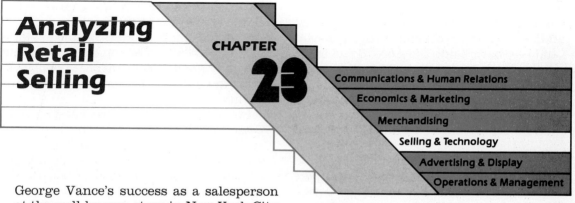

Analyzing Retail Selling

CHAPTER 23

Communications & Human Relations
Economics & Marketing
Merchandising
Selling & Technology
Advertising & Display
Operations & Management

George Vance's success as a salesperson at the well-known store in New York City is not due to his superior product knowledge alone. It is also a result of his understanding the basic beliefs of retail selling.

Basic Beliefs of Retail Selling

A *customer* is not a cold statistic but a flesh-and-blood human being with feelings and emotions like our own.

A *customer* is a person who brings us needs and wants—it is our job to fill those needs and wants.

A *customer* does us a favor when calling on us—we are not doing our customer a favor.

A *customer* is not an interruption of our work but the purpose of it.

A *customer* deserves the most courteous and attentive treatment we can give.

A *customer* is part of our business—not an outsider.

A *customer* is the most important person in any business.

These basic beliefs about customers are the essence of all retail sales transactions. No matter what the type of retailing, selling begins with customer service foremost in mind.

In today's retail market, everybody sells something. Selling is a teamwork task in which some workers utilize persuasive skills while others create and maintain an inviting shopping environment. Even customers take part in selling when they tell their friends or relatives to buy a certain product or shop at a certain store.

A large part of current retail selling is making it easy, pleasant, and economical for customers to buy. All retail workers help set the stage for the sale—few sales would be made without this contribution. Some work in advertising to bring potential purchasers into the store. Some make displays that help sell merchandise. Some provide customer services such as credit. Some keep records, take care of stock, and do stockkeeping. And, of course, salespeople serve customers during the final act of the selling process.

All retail workers should understand how their jobs help to make sales take place. So even those retail workers who don't come into direct contact with customers should understand the basic beliefs of retail selling. And they should know enough about the selling process to cooperate with those whose main job is selling. Remember, the main goal of the retailer is profitable sales.

Types of Retail Selling

In the past, when retail selling was limited mainly to over-the-counter contacts with customers, it was relatively easy to analyze. But the selling practices of today, which depend on the customer's self-selection of products, have changed the roles of many salespeople and changed the way customers shop. This change has affected mainly the area of convenience goods. Advertising and display now pre-sell many products, so customers don't need as much assistance from salespeople. These changes have made it necessary to view retail selling in two different ways: (1) as personal selling and (2) as mass merchandising or selling.

Personal selling is person-to-person selling to individuals. Salespeople are included in the selling process. **Mass selling** is nonpersonal selling to groups of potential purchasers. It is the preselling of goods through various forms of advertising and display without the use of salespeople. However, even though the aim of mass selling is to presell goods, some assistance from salespeople might be needed by customers when they are actually in the store. And, of course, salesclerks are needed at the checkout counter.

Both personal and mass selling are used in the distribution of some shopping and specialty goods. Convenience goods, however, are usually presold through mass selling.

Both types of selling are based on competent product analysis. The results of such analyses, however, are organized and applied in different ways. Both types of selling require the basic beliefs discussed at the beginning of this chapter. But the ways in which those beliefs are applied to the mass and personal selling processes are very different.

Mass Selling

Let's look at mass selling first, since it applies to a broad range of merchandise. One form of mass selling is advertising. Other forms are displays of all types and free samples. Advertising is placed in newspapers and magazines, on television and radio, and carried through the mail by the U.S. Postal Service. Some types of displays that are used in mass selling are signs, showcards and posters, window displays, and sound-slide projections. Mass selling also uses the public address system to call attention to bargains. Various kinds of remembrance advertisements such as calendars are also used.

These mass-selling sales devices all have some elements in common that influence the way in which sales goals are achieved. How this works is explained in the following pages.

Characteristics of Mass Selling

As mentioned earlier, mass selling appeals to groups of people rather than to individuals. Compared to personal selling it allows advertisers more time to think through a sales message. And mass selling lends itself to market research. But once an ad is released, it's difficult to retract or change—although a display can be changed relatively soon. Finally, except for mail orders, mass selling does not close very many sales.

All these characteristics suggest a broad, general approach when selling to large groups of customers. The mental stages experienced by a customer during a purchase, which are usually referred to as **AIDCA,** offer a sales approach that fits mass selling.

AIDCA Sales Analysis

Regardless of how long it takes them to buy, customers pass through a series of mental stages. But all these stages do not necessarily occur at the time of purchase.

They are (1) attention, (2) interest, (3) desire, (4) conviction, and (5) action.

♦ *Attention.* The first mental stage takes place when a prospective customer notices and pays attention to a product or service being offered for sale. Headlines and illustrations, displays of merchandise, and signs frequently attract attention to the merchandise for the first time.

♦ *Interest.* Customers reach the interest stage when they continue to give attention to the product or service and become motivated by a concern or curiosity about it. They may study the copy in the ad. They may sense some kind of unconscious response to the ad.

♦ *Desire.* Desire is developed the moment that customers feel that they will be lacking something if they can't have the product or service.

♦ *Conviction.* Conviction grows out of a desire for the product or service. It's a mental stage at which prospective purchasers believe that there's more to gain by making the purchase than by not doing so. They are convinced that they should buy.

♦ *Action.* This mental stage occurs when customers indicate a readiness to buy. They may place the article in their shopping cart, place an order, send in a coupon, or tell the salesperson that they'll "take it."

Sometimes an additional stage, "satisfaction," is added as a final mental stage. Satisfaction may be described as a feeling of enjoyment or contentment regarding the purchase itself, the merchandise acquired, or the business firm and the salesperson who served the customer. If a customer is satisfied, repeat sales are usually made.

If you begin your retailing career in personal selling, you may find it difficult to use AIDCA to analyze your sales. It may be helpful for you to think of the mental stages as general objectives to be achieved as a sale progresses rather than distinct steps of a sales transaction. AIDCA has

high value in analyzing mass selling. If you become employed in that area, it will help you identify your role in the total retail distribution process.

Personal Selling

Contrary to common opinion, personal selling in the distribution of shopping and specialty goods is more important than ever before. And personal selling will continue to improve its position in retailing as long as invention and technology increase the number and complexity of products and services on the market. As consumer purchasing becomes more complex, consumers will step up their demand for more and better-trained retail sales-workers to help them buy wisely. This trend can be noted in shopping centers, where there is a growing number of specialty shops that don't use self-service.

Although mass selling has changed the role of the salesclerk, it is raising the competency standards of all salesworkers in personal selling. For example, advertising and a pleasing shopping environment may provide the initial attraction to consumers. But salespeople, by the competencies they possess, still play a large part in making customers want to return. Today's customer has so many stores in which to shop and so many kinds of merchandise from which to choose that buying has become more of an emotional than a rational process. "Satisfying" the customer is not enough, and it is being replaced with a commitment to *please* the customer.

Wise consumers like to feel thrifty and clever when shopping in a discount house or catalog showroom. And they also like to feel secure and confident when shopping in a specialty store. So the consumer's selection of retail outlets varies between service and self-service outlets. So as long as our economic system exists to offer these choices, there will always be a need for skillful personal selling.

Buying-Decision Sales Analysis

Skillful retail salespeople, consciously or without realizing it, use the customer's buying decisions as a tool in analyzing their sales and serving their customers. Here's how the system works. Every customer must make five major buying decisions during a purchase or there will be no sales transaction. Here are the decisions the customer must make and the questions that must be answered:

♦ *Need decision*—What type of product or service do I need to solve this problem?
♦ *Product decision*—Which product (and brand) should I buy?
♦ *Price decision*—How much should I spend on the product?
♦ *Place decision*—From which source should I buy it?
♦ *Time decision*—When should I buy it?

It will be easy for you to learn the five buying decisions because you have made them many times—perhaps without realizing it. Note that the questions are similar to a number of those in the product-analysis checklist in Chapter 22.

Sequence of the Decisions. Unlike the fixed sequence of the customer's mental stages (AIDCA), the order in which the five buying decisions are made varies a great deal. The need decision is nearly always the first, but the other decisions may be made in any order. The product decision is often made as soon as a need is recognized and when the customer has a strong preference for a particular brand. The place decision can be made at the time the need is recognized, or it can be delayed until the moment the purchase is actually made. The time decision may follow the need decision or be postponed to the end of the transaction, and, of course, the price decision may be made at any time after the need is realized.

Where the Decisions are Made. A purchaser's buying decisions may be made almost anywhere. However, they are usu-

"It's hard to find knowledgeable salespeople today. But at J.B. Hudson, they're terrific!"

Steve Andersen
Minneapolis

"At today's prices, I want to feel confident I'm getting what I'm paying for... and I know the people at J. B. Hudson will advise me honestly in my decision. That's why I shop at J. B. Hudson. They never try to sell you something you can't afford. They tell you the difference between one item and another. They stand behind everything they sell... that's very important to me.

And I think it's obvious from their gift selection they spend as much time selecting affordable pieces as they do selecting $2000 watches."

You'll find other things to like about J. B. Hudson, too. Like our expert service department, the convenience of our own credit plans... and the option of using major credit cards.

J.B. Hudson
JEWELERS SINCE 1885

770 ON THE MALL, 375-2840

SOUTHDALE—BROOKDALE—ROSEDALE—RIDGEDALE—BURNSVILLE—ST. PAUL, 7th & CEDAR—ROCHESTER, 210 FIRST AVENUE S.W.

USE OUR CONVENIENT CREDIT TERMS OR AMERICAN EXPRESS. MASTER CHARGE OR VISA ally made at the point of sale or in the home, depending on the type of product or service. When purchasing low-priced convenience goods, customers have frequently made all five buying decisions before entering the place of business. This happens because the customer has usually already purchased the item many times before. Purchases are made quickly and at low cost to the retailer. On the other hand, most of the buying decisions for shopping goods are usually made in the store. The larger the investment in a product, the more difficult the decisions become and the greater the need for personal assistance with buying decisions.

Applications of the Buying-Decisions Sales Analysis. Manufacturers spend millions of dollars persuading consumers that they need certain types of products (need decision) and that they should buy a particular brand (product decision). Retailers do the same, but they also spend large amounts in satisfying consumers' price, place, and time decisions. Within retailing, salespeople spend a great deal of time helping their customers arrive at all five of the necessary buying decisions—to complete those that they have not yet made. So, all types of distributors and all levels of retail workers find the five buying decisions to be useful. It is a customer-

This supermarket tries to help customers make a buying decision on eggs— without a clerk's assistance. Is this typical for convenience goods? Courtesy of *Chain Store Age Supermarkets*, Lebhar-Friedman, Inc.

based system of sales analysis that is especially useful in our country, where customers cast economic votes both for products and for distributors who meet their needs and wants best.

Levels of Retail Selling Occupations

A final item in building your foundation for learning the techniques of retail selling deals with the levels of retail selling occupations. In Chapter 9, you learned about the three categories of in-store retail selling occupations and something about outside selling jobs. You will recall that the main differences among the levels of in-store jobs is the amount of "persuasive" selling responsibility—buying assistance usually needed by customers. Note the relationship between the five buying decisions and the sales levels in the list that follows:

♦ *Salesclerk:* Customer makes all five buying decisions, usually without assistance.
♦ *Salesperson:* Customer usually makes the need, product, and time decisions but needs help with item and price decisions.
♦ *Sales representative:* Customer may need help with all five decisions because the product or service requires a large investment.

This information explains, in part, the reasons underlying the differences in pay associated with the levels of sales occupations.

Additional information about the application of the customer's mental stages (AIDCA) and the five buying decisions is given in later units of this book. You should now be prepared to learn how to take the first step of the personal selling process—opening the sale. Find out how by reading the next chapter.

Trade Talk

Define each term and use it in a sentence.

AIDCA   Personal selling
Mass selling

Can You Answer These?

1. To what extent can mass selling be applied in selling convenience goods? Shopping goods?
2. What types of advertising and displays are used in mass selling?
3. What mental stages does a customer pass through when purchasing a product?
4. What decisions are included in the buying-decision sales analysis?
5. In which buying decisions does a salesclerk usually participate? A salesperson? A sales representative?

Problems

1. Rule a form similar to the following. In the left column, write the letter of each of the following statements: (*a*) I know Steele's has beautiful shoes, but I can't get there without a car. (*b*) My mother would be upset if I spent that much on a blouse. (*c*) I'm sick of wearing the same winter jacket winter after winter. (*d*) Only 6 more shopping days until Christmas. (*e*) I like the blue in that rug, but I know my wife prefers green. In the right column, indicate whether the statement relates to a need, time, place, product, or price decision.

Statement	Buying Decision

2. Rule a form similar to the following. In the left column, list the five mental stages of a purchase (attention, interest, desire, conviction, and action). In the remaining columns, indicate as accurately as possible the situation in which you experienced each mental stage during a recent purchase of a product or service—where you were, what you thought, and what you did.

After the individual charts have been completed, let the class tabulate, on a master chart similar to the individual charts, the information regarding which type of advertising or display motivated each mental stage. Draw conclusions concerning the interaction of the advertising and display and how they work together in producing sales.

Mental Stage	Advertising	Display	Personal Selling

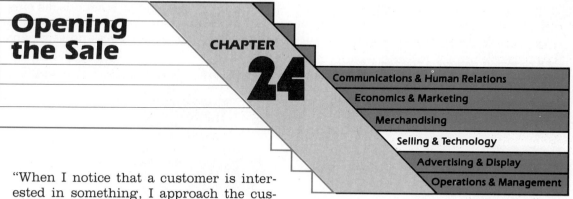

Opening the Sale

CHAPTER 24

Communications & Human Relations
Economics & Marketing
Merchandising
Selling & Technology
Advertising & Display
Operations & Management

"When I notice that a customer is interested in something, I approach the customer, and in a pleasing voice I say, 'May I help you?' It seems that nine times out of ten the customer says, 'No thanks, I'm just looking,' and walks away. I suppose that I should be used to it by now, but it still burns me up."

Why does the salesperson relating this experience get "burned up" because customers nearly always walk away? Why do this salesperson's customers walk away?

The salesperson doesn't approach customers in an effective manner and feels angry because they leave before a sale can be completed. The chances are that the customers are trying to make up their minds when the salesperson interrupts their "Should-I-or-shouldn't-I" debate with "May I help you?"—a poor sales approach in this situation. Such an approach frequently makes customers afraid that the salesperson will talk them into a sale they may later regret, so they walk away.

Successful salespeople understand how customers like to be approached, the best time to approach them, and what to say and do while opening the sale. They realize that opening the sale calls for zeroing in on their customers' thoughts and feelings and carefully identifying their needs and wants.

If you decide to become a salesperson, your entire outlook on selling may depend on your ability to start a sale off right, because what happens later depends largely on how you opened the sale.

Consider the Customer's Feelings

Customers usually enter a store with a purchase in mind, but sometimes they are only interested in getting ideas for a possible future purchase. Occasionally they are just looking around to find a bargain.

Always Be Courteous

Nearly all customers think of themselves as being important, at least when shopping. When they have money to spend, they like to feel that they are appreciated. Regardless of the appearance or manner of a customer or the quality of merchandise asked for, a salesperson should treat him or her with respect and courtesy.

Good salespeople apply this practice to children as well as to adults.

Build Trust in Your Service

Most customers feel that they work hard for their money and want to get as much as possible for it. For this reason they prefer a salesperson who dresses properly, seems competent, and takes a genuine interest in their problems. They like to believe that the salesperson is able and willing to help them select the merchandise that, within the limits of their pocketbooks, will best meet their needs.

Give the Customer Prompt Attention

Even though they are just looking around, customers like to feel that their presence is known and appreciated. Attention is a subtle form of flattery. Time your approach to the customer's actions, as effective salespeople do. When customers enter the department hurriedly and seem anx-

All customers deserve a courteous salesperson. Jane Hamilton-Merritt

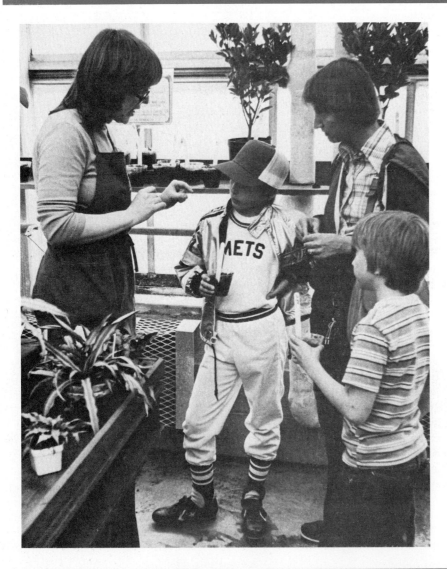

ious to buy, approach them briskly. This will indicate that your real desire is to satisfy them quickly. On the other hand, when customers come in and wander around in a leisurely way, approach them in an unhurried manner but with unmistakable interest. If customers just want to look around, encourage them to do so.

Types of Approaches

The **approach** is the first direct contact with the customer during those few seconds when the salesperson and the customer meet. If a salesperson is stationed behind a counter, the customer usually comes to the salesperson. Otherwise, the salesperson is free to move around a given area and usually goes to any customer who enters the area.

There are three basic approaches: the greeting approach, the service approach, and the merchandise approach. Salespeople choose an approach according to the circumstances.

The Greeting Approach

As its name suggests, the **greeting approach** involves addressing a customer—either with a general greeting such as "Good morning" or with a greeting and by name—before the customer has shown interest in any particular kind of merchandise. Either the customer has just come to your station or counter or has just entered your department.

Words are only part of making your customers feel welcome, important, and confident in your ability to serve them well. The tone of your voice, your facial expression, and your inflections and gestures show your attitude and can help you make a natural, friendly approach.

Treat your customers as if they were guests in your home. Greet them by name if you can. Usually, the appropriate form of address to use is based on relative age: the first name for children; the social title (Mr., Dr., and so on) for persons older than yourself. First names may be appro-

Customers should be made to feel as welcome as a guest in your own home. Jane Hamilton-Merritt

priate for people your age in some stores, such as men's specialty shops. If you don't know your customer's name, you may say "Sir" or "Madam" or just "Good afternoon," or "Good evening." Customers will usually return your greeting and indicate what merchandise interests them. If you know your customer's name, use it throughout the sale.

After you have greeted your customer, wait. Don't move and don't say anything for about 4 seconds. This gives your customer a chance to respond. Within those 4 seconds, most customers will tell you what merchandise has drawn them to the department, thus putting you in a good position to continue the sale.

The Service Approach

When you ask a polite question that indicates your willingness to be of service, you are using a **service approach.** Some firms that distribute mostly convenience goods insist on a service approach and usually encourage a greeting to go with it. However, "May I help you?" or "What can I do for you?" can become monotonous to customers and also making selling routine and uninteresting. "How can I help you?" is an open-ended question that is much better.

The Merchandise Approach

When competent salespeople notice a customer paying attention, indicating interest in an item, they make a comment or ask a question that helps move the customer from the interest stage to the desire stage. This reference to the product is called a **merchandise approach**. If the salesperson at the beginning of the chapter had used this approach, the customers might not have walked away. When skillfully applied, the merchandise approach is an effective tool to increase personal sales. For example, a fitting remark to a customer examining a pair of curtains made of Fiberglas might be, "Those Fiberglas curtains will look just as fresh after they have been washed many times." A few more comments may convince the customer to take action.

The effectiveness of a merchandise approach depends on the appropriateness of your opening comments and how well they match what the customer is thinking at the time. You can usually get clues by observing the customer's behavior. For example, a customer who is examining a price tag is likely to be interested in price or size. One who is reading a label may be concerned about material, construction, or warranty. One who is handling an article may want to know about the quality of workmanship and material.

In the absence of a definite clue, you can direct the customer's attention to more general interests such as (1) popular items, (2) special values, and (3) items with unusual appeals. Opening words should contain a special appeal to the customer's needs and quickly get the customer to transfer attention from the salesperson to the merchandise.

When to Approach the Customer

Usually, the time to approach a customer is as soon as the customer enters the department. However, you may be busy serving another customer. In most cases it is wise to wait on customers in order of their arrival.

Even if you are busy with another customer, you should still acknowledge the arrival of the second customer. Exactly how you do this depends upon which buying stage the first customer has reached.

If the first customer is just about ready to buy and requires your full attention, simply look up at the second customer, smile, nod, and concentrate on completing the first sale.

If the first customer still needs your attention but is not quite ready to buy, say to the second customer, "I (or somebody) will be with you in a moment."

If the first customer is still at an early buying stage and doesn't need your constant attention, excuse yourself from the first customer for a moment, greet the second customer, identify the latter's need, and then return to the first customer.

Sometimes you'll be able to wait on several customers at a time. For example, you may find this necessary when you're selling garments that need to be tried on or products that the customer may want to consider carefully, such as wallpaper. However, you would begin to serve only as many customers as can be handled at once. A customer who feels neglected is likely to depart quickly—and often permanently.

Identifying Customer Needs and Wants

In today's retail market, the most important task of both mass selling and personal selling is to determine what the customer needs and wants. Helping customers identify their individual needs and defining their wants or desires are major purposes of personal selling. No customer will be pleased with a purchase that doesn't satisfy his or her personal desires.

If you question the customer and listen to what is being said, you will shorten the time spent on a sale and please your customer. Also, in all likelihood, your customer will be more receptive to your suggestions throughout the sale.

If customers were always aware of their needs and knew exactly what they wanted, self-service would be sufficient. However, frequently customers have latent needs (those that they don't realize or think about when shopping) as well as conscious needs (those that they recognize). If a customer's awareness of a need is strong enough to make him or her want to do something about it, it is called a want or desire. Customers can be divided into three groups according to their awareness of their needs and the strength of their wants.

1. Those who know exactly what they want
2. Those who have a general idea of what they need and want
3. Those who have needs but are not aware of them

Each type of customer requires a different sales procedure.

Serving Customers Who Know Exactly What They Want

It is easy to serve this type of customer if you have the requested item. You can quickly get the article for your customer and find out whether some related product is needed. However, certain precautions may be necessary.

Verifying the Specifications. Sometimes a customer wants a specific product but forgets one of the necessary specifications. Or you may suspect that one of the

specifications is wrong—shoe size, for example. In either case, the specifications should be verified, for if the customer takes home the wrong product, you will not have succeeded in making a satisfactory sale.

Selling Substitute Products. Most customers like to be served quickly, especially when they want a specific item. If you don't have the item they ask for, they will often accept your suggestion for something to take its place. Selling a product or brand other than that requested by the customer is called **substitute selling.** When you do substitute selling, remember the following rules:

♦ Be sure that the article you suggest as a substitute will serve the customer's needs as well as or better than the article requested.
♦ Don't criticize the article originally requested. If you hint that the requested article is inferior, the customer might interpret your statement as an insult.

Here are six actions that you might take to sell a substitute for the specific item requested:

1. Make a sincere attempt to locate the requested article if the store carries the line of merchandise.
2. Bring out the substitute merchandise.
3. Tell the customer that it is not the brand requested.
4. Inquire about the intended use of the article.
5. Point out the features that are similar to those in the requested article.
6. Point out additional features if the substitute article is of a better grade.

Serving Customers Who Have a General Idea of Their Needs and Wants

Many customers have only a general idea of what they want to buy. For example, a customer may be interested in buying a typewriter without having any particular size, model, or brand in mind. Here is how

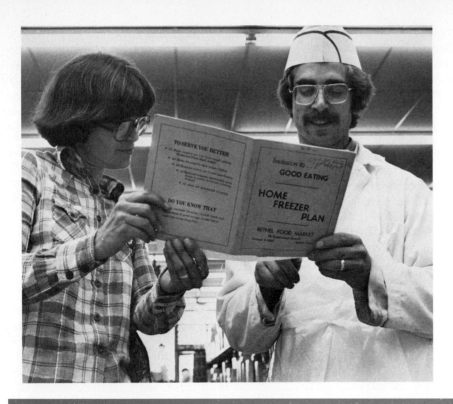

Always verify any specifications a customer gives you. Jane Hamilton-Merritt

you would help this type of customer define needs and clarify wants.

Asking the Right Questions. Success in serving an impartial customer depends largely upon asking the right questions in the right way. There is certain information that you'll always need before being able to select the merchandise to show the customer. For example, you'll need the size when selling some kinds of clothing. Questions about the use of the product are usually opening questions. They create the impression that you're interested in solving the customer's problem and not trying to dismiss him or her.

Take care to avoid the impression of cross-examining the customer. Don't ask too many questions—you may lose the sale before you've even have had a chance to show the merchandise. Don't ask a long series of questions such as, "What size?"

"What color?" "What kind of material?" and "About how much would you like to spend?" Here are the dangers of these kinds of question:

- They may force the customer to make a snap decision concerning a point to which little thought has been given.
- The answers to specific questions of this type usually restrict the variety of merchandise that may be shown.
- Numerous direct questions increase the danger of being out of stock or of the store's not carrying the product.
- The customer may feel that you don't want to show a broad selection.

Listening Carefully. Listening will be one of your most valuable skills as a salesperson. It is important throughout the sale and is especially critical when you are identifying customer needs and wants.

Many times you will be able to appraise your customer's desires by listening carefully to what is being said and particularly to how it is said. If you're alert, the speed of speech, tone of voice, inflection given to certain words, and even the accent will be meaningful. The art of listening, which requires discipline and practice, is discussed in Chapter 13. A customer's silence isn't necessarily a sign of disapproval. A silent customer is communicating too. Silence may be another way of saying "Go ahead, I'm listening." Pause occasionally so that you don't miss the message.

Observing the Customer. Pay attention to your customer with your eyes as well as your ears. Customers may not say what they think or feel. Often you can gauge what might interest your customers by telltale signs such as where they look, the position of their hands, the raising of an eyebrow, or the clearing of a throat.

Serving Customers Who Are Unaware of Their Needs

Customers who are unaware of their needs present an interesting challenge, even if you're an experienced salesperson. They really don't plan to buy. If you go to their homes or try to sell them something, you may have to try hard just to gain their attention. Their attention may be more easily won if they come to your store, but you still have to spark their interest.

You have to convince such customers that they have a need and explain to them how your product can satisfy that need. Most people are open to suggestion and do become aware of their needs once those needs are brought to their attention. Suggestion selling, which deals with customers who are unaware of their needs, is discussed in Chapter 44.

In this chapter, you've learned the first step of the selling process: how to treat and approach customers and how to iden-

tify their needs and wants. But to be a successful salesperson, you'll also want to know how to present products to customers effectively and how to answer their questions and objections. Also, you'll be interested to learn how you can increase your sales and finally close the sale. These steps are discussed in Unit 14.

Trade Talk

Define each term and use it in a sentence.

Approach
Greeting approach
Merchandise
  approach

Service approach
Substitute selling

Can You Answer These?

1. When should a salesperson use a greeting approach? A service approach? A merchandise approach?
2. How does an effective salesperson judge when to make a merchandise approach or how to phrase his or her opening remarks?
3. What should a salesperson do to acknowledge a customer when busy serving another customer?
4. What are two rules to follow when one is practicing substitute selling?
5. What type of questions should salespeople ask customers who have only a general idea of what they want? What type of question should be avoided?

Problems

1. Rule a form similar to the following. In the left column, write the letter of each of the following situations. The customer asks for: (0) "A pair of Wand shoes, No. 34-4, size 8, red." You have only dark brown. (a) "Cardigan sweater in light blue." You have it in pink and white; you also have a pullover sweater in light blue. (b) "XYZ brand toothpaste." You are out of it but you have ABC and DXO brands, which are similar in price. (c) "Brass door

hinges." You have bronze, chrome, and white enamel hinges. (*d*) "Clock radio that was advertised as a special at $39.95." You are sold out but have a new model at $49.95 or an AM-FM radio at $39.95. (*e*) "Apple pie á la mode." You are out of apple pie; you do have cherry, blueberry, lemon, and peach pies. In the right column, write an appropriate statement that could be used to sell a substitute item.

Item Situation	Substitute Selling Statement
Example: (0)	"I'm sorry, sir, but we only have that size and style in dark brown. Try on this pair and see how well they fit."

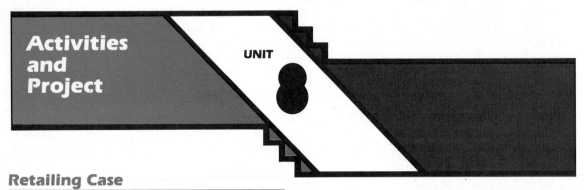

Activities and Project

UNIT 8

Retailing Case

After graduating from the Marketing and Distributive Education Program at his high school, Ari Moustakas took a position as a salesperson in a large sporting goods store that advertised extensively. Opportunities for advancement appeared to be excellent, and he looked forward to a prosperous future with the firm. However, during his first week on the job, Ari was disappointed with the attitudes of the other salespeople. Some of them actually seemed to avoid waiting on customers. They withdrew to the stockroom and often continued with their stock work even after a customer arrived. Sometimes they would continue to chat with one another in the customer's presence. They didn't smile when waiting on their customers and appeared disinterested in their customers' problems. This behavior was particularly noticeable when teenagers or people who were not well dressed were being served. The salespeople didn't spend much time with them.

1. Was Ari right when he decided to join the company?
2. Now that Ari is an employee of the firm,

should he engage in good selling practices and the behaviors he learned in school?
3. What might happen if Ari consistently sold more than the other salespeople in the department?
4. Should Ari talk to his supervisor about his negative feelings toward the other salespeople? What else might he do?
5. Should Ari try to find another job?

Working with People

Ellie Olson was disappointed because she was assigned to stock work rather than to a selling position in a high-fashion women's wear specialty shop. She had prepared herself for sales work, hoping someday to own or manage a shop. When she was hired, the manager had said that it was store policy to start all sales and merchandising personnel in the stockroom. Ellie thought that the idea was old-fashioned, but she took the job anyway.

1. Should Ellie take a position about which she is not enthusiastic?

2. Will her attitude toward her job reflect in her work? How?
3. What are the possible reasons why the management assigns new personnel to stock work?
4. How can stock work help Ellie to prepare herself for a selling job?
5. What activities should you recommend that she engage in regarding product analysis? Regarding customer buying decisions?

Project 8: Preparing the Merchandise Approach

Your Project Goal
Given two products and a product-analysis sheet, interview five customers and determine whether, in each case, their reasons for buying revolved around a product feature or a personal benefit. Prepare an effective merchandise approach for each product.

Procedure
1. Consult your teacher about your selection of two products that are suitable for your product feature analysis. Students who work in retail stores or service businesses should preferably choose products and services they sell on their jobs.
2. Construct two product-analysis sheets like the one on page 173. Put one of the products you've chosen on each sheet.
3. For each product, interview five customers who have just purchased the product from you. (Students who are not employed in sales work may interview friends and relatives.) Ask each customer why he or she bought the product. If the reason is based on a product feature, record the particular feature in the right column; if it pertains to a benefit, record the particular benefit in the left column.
4. Circle those benefits and product features that occur more than once.
5. Compare your lists with those of your classmates who selected the same product. On a separate sheet of paper, list all these circled items and rank them in order of their popularity.
6. Write as many effective opening remarks about the product as you can for use in making a merchandise approach. In doing so, use the most popular features and benefits.
7. Prepare a brief skit in which you assume that the customer is interested in either or both of these products. Have the salesperson use a merchandise approach that stresses the product benefits and features that you have found to be most popular in this project.

Evaluation
You will be evaluated on your ability to match product features with customer benefits in a merchandise approach that gets the customer's prompt attention and makes the customer feel welcome, important, and confident in you.

Sales Promotion

CHAPTER
25

Communications & Human Relations

Economics & Marketing

Merchandising

Selling & Technology

Advertising & Display

Operations & Management

Magda Kruger and Frank Caruso, both high school juniors, had just been listening to a guest speaker from a local service club address the students on careers in retailing. Frank turned to Magda and said, "That was an interesting session all right, but I think the speaker went overboard on sales promotion. I'm planning on being a supermarket manager someday. I don't want to be bothered with a lot of Mickey Mouse jazz on display and advertising. Supers thrive on their merchandising abilities, and pricing is their bag."

Magda, who had a flair for art and fashion, was surprised by Frank's remarks. "I don't understand you, Frank. Today a supermarket manager, or any other kind of retail-store manager for that matter, has to be good at sales promotion. I'm looking forward to running a dress shop, and I know that promoting sales and goodwill will play a major role in its success." Magda also told Frank that she thought sales promotion skills would be salable in other fields as well as in retailing.

Did Frank really understand what sales promotion is all about? Would he need sales promotion skills if he were to become a supermarket manager? How is sales promotion today different from that of a generation ago? Was Magda right about the salability of sales promotion skills in other fields? Think about these questions as you study Chapters 25, 26, and 27.

Successful retailers know that most products and services do not sell themselves. The marketplace today is highly competitive. Retailers have to use a large variety of methods to attract customers and build sales.

The NCR Corporation (in *Retail Terminology*, 1977, page 35) defines sales promotion as follows:

Sales Promotion. In a very broad sense, all activities and devices that are designed to sell more merchandise and create goodwill, directly or indirectly. Also those activities and devices whose primary function is that of inviting, persuading, and otherwise encouraging and stimulating trade. In a more restricted sense, the selling activities that supplement both advertising and personal selling, coordinating them, and rendering them more effective.

Sales promotion efforts may be classified as (1) nonpersonal activities such as advertising, display, and press releases and (2) personal contact activities such as selling and participation of personnel in community projects. In retailing, this includes ideas and activities that relate to products, a department, the store itself, or store personnel.

Categories of Sales Promotion

There are two general categories of sales promotion activities in retailing. They are merchandise promotion and institutional promotion.

Merchandise promotion deals directly with selling products storewide or selling products of single departments. It involves using various forms of advertising, display, and other promotion media.

Institutional promotion deals only indirectly with selling products by building goodwill for the store (institution). Its activities focus on the entire store and use devices such as image-building newspaper ads and various customer services.

Both kinds of sales promotion may employ nonpersonal and personal methods of communicating with their audiences. Also, they may utilize the same vehicles to reach potential customers and supporters.

Communication Vehicles

There are literally scores of ways for merchants to communicate their sales and goodwill messages to the wide variety of customers they serve. These ways of com-municating take on many forms and appeal to all the five senses. They can be arranged into five groups: (1) advertising, (2) display, (3) publicity, (4) personal selling, and (5) customer services.

Advertising

Nonpersonal paid messages about merchandise, services, or ideas that retailers wish to communicate to customers and potential customers is called **advertising**. The vehicle that advertisers use to communicate their messages is called an **advertising medium**. (The plural of "medium" is "media.") Common media are print, broadcast, and direct mail. The store pays for these services. Advertising accounts for the largest share of a retail store's promotion budget.

Print. The most commonly used advertising medium is the newspaper—daily, Sunday, and weekly; local, regional, or national. Advertising makes newspaper publication possible. This is so because without advertising revenue, a paper would cost two or three times the selling price. Other printed media include magazines, shopping reminders, the Yellow Pages, handbills, circulars, and billboards.

Broadcast. Some stores advertise on television and radio by sponsoring a specific program at a scheduled time. Others use short spot announcements between programs. National chains, franchisers, discount houses, and specialty stores use television regularly. Many smaller retailers advertise on local TV stations.

In a way somewhat akin to radio and TV advertising, some stores use their intercom systems to call the customer's attention to special sale items and various customer services. Loudspeakers may be used by concession operators at sporting events and other recreational functions.

Direct Mail. Any form of advertising that is sent through the mail—such as promotional letters, samples, catalogs, circulars, and announcements—is **direct-**

Specialty items printed with the advertiser's name and a brief message are a good way of keeping the business in the customer's mind. Richard C. Tapio

mail advertising. Promotional material, unlike the ads in newspapers and magazines, can be sent to specific segments of the market without competing with other ads. Often, promotional enclosures are sent along with end-of-month statements to charge-account customers at no additional cost in postage.

Display

Selling through display is a part of "visual merchandising," which includes all visual ways of promoting the store and the merchandise it sells. Stores make extensive use of displays, especially for the special items featured each week. Largely through the imaginative use of window and interior displays, stores show their products in ways intended to stimulate interest and help customers make their selections.

Window displays invite customers into the store. And once they are in the store, interior displays take over the selling task, in part or in total, depending on the extent of self-service practiced.

Many retailers, such as automobile and boat distributors, exhibit or display their products at fairs and trade shows.

Publicity

Any mention of a firm, a product or service, or store personnel in the mass media in any form other than an advertisement is called **publicity.** Stores use two types of publicity: free publicity and special feature publicity. You have only to read the daily paper to find some publicity items about a retailer. The newspapers sometimes obtain this information from publicity or news releases. Large stores usually employ professionals to prepare these releases. Small stores depend more on a reporter employed by the medium to do the job. Such publicity may relate to merchandise promotion or aim at building goodwill for the institution.

Here are some examples of publicity items:

♦ A family-page article about an imaginative storewide special event
♦ A society-page item about a fashion show conducted by a local specialty shop for the United Way
♦ A story in the business section describing a chain of clothing stores that has become famous for its low markups

All these are **free publicity** because they are published without charge to the store.

Special-feature publicity costs the store money. This type of publicity includes fashion shows, educational programs, demonstrations, parade floats, calendars, and various gifts that usually advertise the store.

Personal Selling

"As a salesperson, I'm one of the most visible parts of the company." This statement by a successful sales representative for a large distributor suggests the importance of the sales staff in promotion activities. Success in promoting sales depends on the cooperation of the sales staff in particular, because they supply the expertise in selling the products or services to be promoted.

Personal contact with customers offers excellent opportunities for promoting sales. This is especially true when the sales staff is coached for its promotional role in advance of a special sales event. Through wearing promotional badges, placing telephone calls, giving good service, using package inserts, and so on, the sales staff can put the finishing touches on a promotion event.

This store-sponsored Thanksgiving Day parade is an example of a special feature publicity. Courtesy of J. L. Hudson Co., Detroit, Michigan.

Customer Services

Prompt, efficient, and courteous performance of customer services is one of the most effective sales promotion vehicles in today's retail marketplace. Often the products offered for sale are much the same in several different stores, so the customer chooses the store that offers the services he or she wants most. Returned-goods policy, complaints and adjustments, alterations, delivery service, wrapping and packing of merchandise, repair service, store hours, rest rooms, shopping climate of the sales floor, parking facilities, convenient floor layout, and consumer credit—to name only a few—are usually offered at cost, less than cost, or free of charge in order to attract and hold customers.

During the past decade, consumer credit has become a powerful sales promotion vehicle. Charge-account customers are often favored by retailers because a debtor-creditor relationship tends to play a key role in maintaining customer relationships with the store. So credit managers work with the sales promotion and merchandising divisions in seeking new charge accounts and in keeping charge-account customers happy.

Sales Promotion Techniques

To encourage sales during slow selling periods, to introduce new products or services, or to bolster the sale of certain products or services, retailers use **sales promotion techniques.** These techniques include premiums, contests, special price reductions, free samples, and other incentives to buy.

Premiums

Something that retailers offer to customers free or at a nominal price to induce an actual sale or to promote interest in a product is called a **premium.** The premiums most commonly offered by retailers are coupons and trading stamps.

Coupons are certificates that allow customers to get a discount on a product. Retailers use them to encourage customers to try a new product or continue to buy one they are already using. Many supermarkets, drugstores, and variety stores include coupons in their newspaper advertisements. Grocers often tie in with national coupon offers made by manufacturers.

Trading stamps are printed stamps that retailers offer to their customers in return for making purchases at the place of business. Customers save the stamps by pasting them in books and then redeem them for merchandise supplied by a trading-stamp company. Trading-stamp companies may be either independently owned or owned by a group of retailers. These companies usually sell stamps to retailers at a cost of between 1.5 and 2 percent of total sales.

Contests

A common type of contest is one that calls for some degree of skill on the part of the customer—for example, a retailer-sponsored Mother's Day contest in which children paint pictures of their mothers. By distributing entrance forms and awarding prizes within the store, retailers increase customer traffic in their establishments.

Special Price Reductions

The two types of sales-promotion techniques that offer customers special price reductions are (1) special sales events or special price offers and (2) combination offers.

When a retailer features merchandise at a reduction in price, it is called a **special sales event.** The white sales and furniture sales in January and August are sales events that generate interest in buying

THE BRITISH DAILIES
Plan ahead for your best Fortnight ever!

Step into our magical, marvelous world of make-believe. From the Design Centres of London and Glasgow to N-M. China dolls, Cheshire cats, pink piglets, geese, soldiers, trucks and ducks and dozens more. All winners of the coveted Design Index for excellence. Toy Shop, Fifth Floor

Walk away with a winning pair of shoes from our complete Cole-Haan shoe collection — renowned for classic design and superb workmanship. Today, special envoy Mr. Mark Goodwin will be on hand to take your special orders. The Man's Store, First Floor

Trace the course of history with six splendid table settings representing a series of reigns — Queen Elizabeth I, Queen Anne, King George III, Queen Victoria, King George V and Queen Elizabeth II. The Galleries, Fourth Floor

Plan your next trip to Britain via N-M's Travel Service, Fifth Floor. British Airways, our official Fortnight carrier, will take you there. And we'll fill you in on all those fascinating little spots to visit.

Neiman-Marcus used a variety of promotional categories in its "A celebration of Britain" promotion. Courtesy of Neiman-Marcus, Dallas, Texas

sheets, pillowcases, towels, and furniture. The months of January and August were buying slumps before these two sales were started. "Dollar day" sales, clearance sales, and anniversary sales are other sales events that increase store traffic and result in greater sales volume.

Through **combination offers**, retailers allow customers to buy two products at a price that comes to less than the combined prices of the items purchased separately. Supermarkets, variety stores, and drugstores often make combination offers. For example, a dairy store may offer a package of cookies free with each purchase of a gallon of ice cream.

Free Samples

To encourage customers to buy new or improved products, some retailers give free samples of the product. For example, a food retailer might offer customers samples of a new type of cheese, or the cosmetic department of a large store might give its customers free samples of a new perfume or powder. Depending on the product, retailers will either offer the free samples in the store or mail them to customers.

Public Relations

Store activity performed for the direct purpose of building goodwill rather than sales is called **public relations**. This function is increasingly important in the minds of progressive retailers. In no other field of distribution is success or failure so dependent on public attitude. So retailers engage in many public relations activities that, along with merchandising policies, encourage customers to patronize a store regularly. Common public relations activities include (1) institutional advertising and publicity releases, (2) improvements in store plant and facilities, and (3) contributions to community welfare.

Institutional Ads and Publicity Releases

People need to be told what the store does for its customers and for the community. So ads are run and publicity releases are prepared to make the community aware of the achievements and concerns of the firm.

Store Plant and Facilities

Many customers identify with a store because of its appearance and the good feeling they have when shopping there. Attractive, easily identifiable storefronts and signs; clean, comfortable, and attractive interiors; and a store layout designed with the customer in mind are public relations activities that are worth costly expenditures.

Contributions to Community Welfare

Retailers realize that their success is dependent on the community. So, wisely, they improve their image by contributing to worthy causes, supporting community projects, serving as leaders of cultural movements, and supporting better business bureau and consumer activities. By supporting service clubs such as Rotary, Kiwanis, and Lions and in many other ways, retailers demonstrate their concern for the people of the community.

Deciding on the Promotional Mix

Deciding which combinations of promotional categories and communication vehicles will be most effective in reaching the desired consumers or target group requires careful judgment by retailers. When they want to reach more than one kind of consumer market, they may find that it is best to use several kinds of communication vehicles. The combination of communications vehicles that retailers use during a promotional program is called a **promotional mix.**

The promotional mix varies widely, depending on the product or service being promoted, the characteristics of the desired consumer market, and the size of the promotion budget.

Who Handles Sales Promotion?

Within a retailing organization, the responsibility for promotion is determined by both the size and type of organization. Many retailers, both large and small, use the services of outside specialists.

In Small Stores

In a small store, the owner or manager usually handles promotion planning. The local newspaper frequently provides help in preparing ads. Small signs may be made by machine or by a local art service. The manager or one of the salespeople may build the window displays, or a free-lance display specialist may do the job. A free-lance display specialist is not employed permanently, or full-time, by any one store. This type of display specialist works for several stores and is paid a fee for each display built.

In Chain Stores

Most chain-store organizations have a central or regional promotion director. It is this person who decides what promotional activities will be used throughout the chain or region. This person is also responsible for carrying out these activities. He or she is assisted by a group of advertising, display, and sales training specialists who take part in planning sales campaigns, take responsibility for window and interior displays, and sponsor sales training programs for all stores in the chain. These plans are supervised by regional supervisors and carried out by the local store manager. In some situations, an advertising agency may handle the advertising.

In Large Department Stores

Large department stores usually devote a significant number of people and careful attention to the promotion of sales. They usually have their own sales promotion staffs. Heading the staff may be a sales promotion manager and an advertising manager, and there also may be someone in charge of publicity and someone else in charge of display. A department store usually has its own artists and display specialists and prepares all its promotional material itself.

In Shopping Centers

Stores and service businesses in many shopping centers cooperate in promoting the shopping center as a whole. Large centers employ a promotion director. This person coordinates the overall publicity and advertising activities of the center and may also plan special shows and events to gain publicity for the center. This coordination enables the center to compete with downtown retailers and other local distributors in attracting customers. It is also of special benefit to the smaller stores in the shopping center because they are able to take part in all the centerwide promotions, which are planned by experts.

Now that you have a general understanding of the forms of sales promotion, you're ready to study two promotion vehicles more closely, advertising and visual merchandising. You can do this in Chapters 26 and 27. And don't forget, while you're studying these chapters, to think of the different retailing career opportunities that sales promotion activities have to offer. Perhaps you have skills and abilities you could use in this field of retailing.

Trade Talk

Define each term and use it in a sentence.

Advertising	Premium
Advertising medium	Promotional mix
Combination offer	Publicity
Direct-mail	Public relations
advertising	Sales promotion
Free publicity	techniques
Institutional	Special-feature
promotion	publicity
Merchandise	Special sales event
promotion	

Can You Answer These?

1. What is the purpose of sales promotion in the broad sense of the term?
2. What are the five broad classifications of communication vehicles used in retail sales promotion?
3. What sales promotion techniques are used to introduce new products or to bolster sales of regular merchandise?
4. In what ways do retailers go about improving their public relations?
5. What factors influence the retailer's decision when choosing the most appropriate promotional mix?
6. Who handles sales promotion work in small stores? In chain stores? In large department stores? In shopping centers?

Problems

1. Rule a form similar to the following. In the left column, list the letter of each of the following promotional categories: (a)

print advertising, (b) display, (c) contest, (d) personal selling, (e) publicity, (f) public relations, and (g) telephone promotion. Leave about 2 inches between each category. In the next column, write two retailing activities for each category. Then choose a line of merchandise with which you are familiar and write the name in the space provided. Decide whether or not you think each sample activity is appropriate or inappropriate for the line of merchandise and place a check mark (√) in the correct column on the right.

Line of merchandise: _____

Promotional Category	Activity	Appropriate	Inappropriate

2. Rule a form with six columns across it. In the left column, write the letter of each of the following examples of promotional activities or items: (a) fashion show, (b) display theme suggested by sales promotion manager for downtown store, (c) advertisement run simultaneously in many large city newspapers, (d) hiring a free-lance display specialist to put in a Halloween window, (e) mailing out pictures with lists of props and merchandise for special Christmas displays, (f) letter sent to preferred customers with coupon offering discounts on items priced over $200, (g) offer of a free pamphlet on automobile care, (h) development of an ad for new franchised product with help of local newspaper, and (i) sponsoring an antique automobile fair. Label the next five columns across as follows: small store, service business, chain store, department store, and shopping center. Place a check mark (√) in the appropriate column or columns to the right to indicate whether the activity or item would be used by a small store, a service business, a chain store, a department store, or a shopping center.

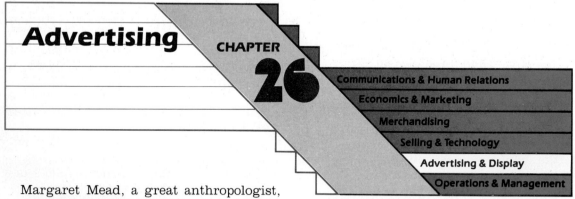

Advertising

CHAPTER

26

Communications & Human Relations

Economics & Marketing

Merchandising

Selling & Technology

Advertising & Display

Operations & Management

Margaret Mead, a great anthropologist, once blamed many of our trying problems on the advertising industry's sales tactics. But she also viewed consumer advertising as essential, saying that "you really can't live without advertising." She also referred to the problems the Soviet Union had when it started producing consumer goods without advertising them. Because the goods weren't advertised, Soviet consumers didn't know that they were available. And they didn't buy them. So finally the Soviet government had to launch advertising programs.

Advertising is viewed as a controversial but essential service. As a retail worker, you should be aware of the criticisms made of advertising. But a retailer's very livelihood depends on how well he or she identifies and satisfies consumer needs and wants—and advertising helps the retailer do this.

Who Sponsors Consumer Advertising?

First, let's look at consumer advertising to see who uses it and why. Knowing who sponsors consumer advertising will help you get an overview of the advertising industry and enable you to see where retailing fits in the advertising process. Sponsors of consumer advertising range from a seller who places a three-line want ad in a local newspaper to an industrial giant such as General Motors who uses many advertising media. Sponsors of consumer advertising may advertise independently, or they may combine their promotional efforts with other sponsors. The three main types of consumer advertising are (1) manufacturer and wholesaler advertising, (2) cooperative advertising, and (3) retail advertising.

Manufacturer and Wholesaler Advertising

Many manufacturers and wholesalers of national brands spend large amounts of money on advertising their own brands. They spend some of that money on advertising to encourage retailers to stock their products or buy their services. But most of that money is spent on advertising that encourages consumers to buy the products from retail outlets. The purpose of this national consumer advertising is to persuade consumers to buy a particular product or service wherever it is sold. It is the product or service, not the store, that is important to the manufacturer or wholesaler. Nevertheless, retailers get an important free boost from the advertising done by manufacturers and wholesalers.

Retailers can do little to influence the amount of national advertising that their suppliers prepare and purchase. However, learning which items the suppliers

are planning to promote—and when and how they plan to do so—can help a retailer decide what to order and how much additional promotion, if any, should be given to these products.

Cooperative Advertising

Advertising in which the cost is shared by the retailer and the supplier of the product

Cooperative advertising benefits both the supplier and the retailer.   Courtesy of SOA Shoes, Inc.

The old soft Shioux.™

In case you think we've gone a little soft, we have. The "Old Soft Shioux" is done in the most superbly supple kidskin. It's hand-lasted and has an innersole that will float your foot on air, and an outersole of genuine natural Plantation Crepe. The entire combination is pure walking pleasure. Made by Sioux of America for men whose feet prefer gentle going.
In a slip-on or tie.

$**00**

STORE NAME

is called **cooperative advertising**. In a program of cooperative advertising, the supplier may support the retailer's advertising according to the amount the retailer purchases from that supplier. Or the supplier may pay a set percentage of the advertising cost. By law, a supplier must offer the same program to all retail customers.

Cooperative advertising saves the retailer money. It also means more promotion for the supplier at a lower cost, because retailers are usually able to get lower rates for advertising in local media.

Cooperative advertising has become a somewhat touchy subject for retailers. Some retailers feel that agreeing to accept cooperative advertising tends to influence both their buying plans and their promotion plans. They feel that their buyers may be more influenced by the amount of promotional money a supplier offers than by their own estimation of what the store's customers want.

Retail Advertising

The chief purpose of a retailer's ad is to attract buyers to a particular store. Of course, to do this successfully requires the promotion of national products. But essentially the retail ad says, "Come to my store first."

Most retailers prefer to depend mainly on their own efforts to attract consumers to their store. They plan and prepare their own advertising, with or without help, and pick the media most likely to reach their target group of consumers. An individually tailored advertising campaign telling specific consumers about a specific store and its products or services is expensive. But it's more effective than any kind of tie-in advertising.

Other Advertising Sponsors

Manufacturers, wholesalers, and retailers are not the only sponsors of consumer advertising. Many other agencies, organizations, institutions, and individuals compete for the consumer's dollar also. Included are people who place newspaper want ads to sell their goods and services, movie theaters, professional athletic associations, travel agencies, banks and savings and loans, trade groups, colleges and private schools, and many others. Today, even dentists and lawyers advertise. Most of these sponsors compete for a share of the consumer's discretionary income, which is personal income that is not required for the purchase of the basic necessities of life. Alert distributors of products and services realize that their advertising must compete with the appeals of these advertising sponsors.

Advertising Benefits

Most of us don't realize the extent to which advertising influences our way of life. For example, the variety of products and services available to us and our ability to enjoy their use before paying for them in full is a result of mass production, selling, and credit. But mass production and credit wouldn't survive very long without advertising to sell—or distribute—the products and services to us, the masses. So you can see that advertising, the critical element in mass selling, is necessary to keep the wheels of industry from coming to a halt. When properly used, advertising benefits everyone.

Benefits to Consumers

Advertising can help consumers with their purchasing decisions by making them aware of their needs and wants. It offers useful information about products and services, enabling shoppers to compare quality and prices with those of different businesses. It may also assist consumers in getting greater satisfaction from the use of their purchases. And, of course, it pays for much of the cost of entertainment, news, and other information received through the print and broadcast media.

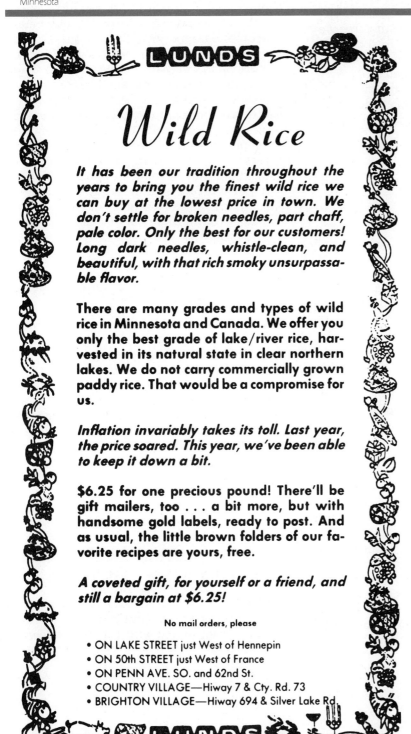

Wild Rice

It has been our tradition throughout the years to bring you the finest wild rice we can buy at the lowest price in town. We don't settle for broken needles, part chaff, pale color. Only the best for our customers! Long dark needles, whistle-clean, and beautiful, with that rich smoky unsurpassable flavor.

There are many grades and types of wild rice in Minnesota and Canada. We offer you only the best grade of lake/river rice, harvested in its natural state in clear northern lakes. We do not carry commercially grown paddy rice. That would be a compromise for us.

Inflation invariably takes its toll. Last year, the price soared. This year, we've been able to keep it down a bit.

$6.25 for one precious pound! There'll be gift mailers, too . . . a bit more, but with handsome gold labels, ready to post. And as usual, the little brown folders of our favorite recipes are yours, free.

A coveted gift, for yourself or a friend, and still a bargain at $6.25!

No mail orders, please

- ON LAKE STREET just West of Hennepin
- ON 50th STREET just West of France
- ON PENN AVE. SO. and 62nd St.
- COUNTRY VILLAGE—Hiway 7 & Cty. Rd. 73
- BRIGHTON VILLAGE—Hiway 694 & Silver Lake Rd.

Benefits to Sales Personnel

As a salesperson, advertising can help you increase your sales volume in three ways: (1) it brings more people into the store, (2) it presells the consumer, and (3) it can be used as an effective sales tool.

Both merchandise and institutional advertising bring more people into the store. Shoppers may enter the store to see a particular advertised article. Or they may be convinced to shop at the store because an institutional ad convinced them to do so. In either case, the extra traffic provides an opportunity for you to increase your sales volume.

Preselling means convincing consumers, through advertising and other promotional activities, to buy a product or service before they enter a store. An advertisement by either the manufacturer, the retailer, or both is so convincing that the customer places a telephone order for the product or purchases it without the help of a salesperson. It saves time for the salesperson as well as for the customer.

As a professional salesperson, you'll learn to use advertising as an effective selling tool. It provides you with timely, believable information and gives the product visibility and prestige. You'll find it much easier to suggest additional merchandise or to sell a higher-priced article if the customer has seen the product advertised. Likewise, institutional advertising will help you by establishing positive consumer attitudes.

To get the most benefit from their advertising, many stores post copies of ads in the department where the advertised items are sold. Or they provide sales personnel with copies of those ads. In some stores, buyers or department heads hold sales meetings to discuss the advertised merchandise.

Why Retailers Advertise

For retailers, the function of advertising is to communicate with customers, potential customers, and others—to give them messages that will build sales and goodwill for the sponsor. **Potential customers** are consumers who live in the trading area and use the products sold by the store. Mass media are used to reach them. Others include people such as community leaders, legislators, certain government officials, and educational, religious, or other social groups. The goodwill of these people is essential in effective and efficient retailing. Advertising can expand present markets and develop new ones. It is an important factor in creating a product or company image, a brand image, or a store image. (Store image is discussed in detail in Chapter 63.)

Advantages of Advertising

Advertising has three unique features as a promotional aid:

♦ It reaches out to customers. No matter where a person is, there is likely to be advertising—newspapers, magazines, radio or television commercials, outdoor advertising, and many other kinds of advertising.

♦ It can fill a retailer's area with news about a firm and its products and services. For example, an ad in a local newspaper will be noticed, consciously or unconsciously, by most people who buy the paper.

♦ It can reach long distances. An ad in a national magazine may produce orders from Miami to Seattle and from abroad.

Goals of Merchandise Advertising

The main purpose of merchandise advertising is to persuade people to buy products and services at the sponsor's store. But each advertisement is usually planned to achieve one or more of the following goals:

♦ *Increase sales volume.* This is a goal of all merchandise advertising. Additional sales volume increases the profit on the products and services sold.

♦ *Bring shoppers into the store.* Products are

often offered at a reduced price to attract consumers who will then see and buy other merchandise at regular prices. The reduced item is called a **leader.**

♦ *Attract new customers.* Advertising can be used to attract a different group of customers or to enter a new market. For example, it may appeal to teenagers, young adults, or new residents.

♦ *Introduce new products or ideas.* The promotion of new fashions, new product lines, or new customer services is often the aim of merchandise advertising. Ads are also used to inform consumers about new uses for established products.

♦ *Reinforce user satisfaction.* Advertising is often used to remind product users of the satisfactions they receive from a product or service. Beverage advertisements usually have this goal. They aim to build pride of ownership in a product.

♦ *Even out levels of sales volume.* These ads aim to persuade customers to shop at times when store traffic is light. For example, Mondays at supermarkets and Wednesdays at department stores.

Goals of Institutional Advertising

Institutional advertising, as a part of institutional promotion, is usually classified as either service advertising or prestige advertising. **Service advertising** informs the public of the ways in which the store serves customers. Such service would include the availability of credit terms, delivery service, personal shopping ser-

Advertising in a national magazine reaches audiences all over the country. *Courtesy of Garden Way and The Fish Market*

Home Canners

64 PAGES BIG!

FREE CATALOG!

SHOWS OVER 500 HARD TO FIND FOOD PRESERVING TOOLS AND KITCHEN UTENSILS

• PRESSURE CANNERS • JUICERS
• FOOD AND GRAIN MILLS
• BLANCHERS • DEHYDRATORS...
...EVERYTHING FOR KEEPING THE HARVEST!
PLUS CHARTS, GUIDES, SPECIALS... PLEASE INCLUDE 25¢ TO HELP COVER POSTAGE. WRITE:

GARDEN WAY CATALOG
DEPT. A104F
CHARLOTTE, VT. 05445

Philadelphia's upscale seafood restaurant.

The Fish Market

*Well-bred fish, fresh daily.
Luncheon. Dinner. Drinks. Reservations.
18th & Sansom Streets. 567-3559.*

vice, free parking, and many other things. **Prestige advertising** is used to impress customers with the "personality" of the store as a way of convincing them that this is the store in which to shop. It may stress such distinctive store characteristics as quality products, varied assortments of merchandise, or the store's position as a fashion leader. Although service and prestige advertising do help to sell goods directly, they also improve and maintain the store's good image in the eyes of the buying public.

How Advertising Motivates Consumers

Advertising deals with mental processes during a purchase. You will recall from the discussion of mass selling in Chapter 23 that there are five mental stages through which a person passes during the course of a sale: attention, interest, desire, conviction, and action. Here is how advertising guides or directs a purchaser through these stages.

♦ *Attracting attention.* In order to attract attention, advertisers use sharp contrast through illustrations, white space, color, motion, sounds, position, time slots, and so on.

♦ *Stimulating interest.* Appealing to the self-interest of the consumer is a common way of developing interest. This is achieved through headlines, illustrations, radio messages, and TV commercials.

♦ *Building desire.* Appeals to the emotions as well as to reason are used to lead the customer from an interest in the product to a desire for it. In advertising, this is done through copy, script, or demonstration.

♦ *Gaining conviction.* Advertising may convince interested customers to buy by reinforcing claims that are made for the product or service advertised. A guarantee, warranty, testimonial, or illustration may convince a prospective customer to make the final decision to buy.

♦ *Inducing action.* Advertising may call for

immediate or future action. Incentives to action may take the form of coupons, announced time limits, trading stamps, offers of something free, and a warning of a limited supply of a product or service. Retailers always include their store name and location to prompt customers to buy from them rather than from a competitor.

Advertising Standards

Advertising as we know it today started with the first newspapers. In 1846, Volney B. Palmer established the first advertising agency in Boston. During these

Service advertising helps to improve a store's image by informing consumers of the services offered by the store. *Courtesy of Bachman's*

early days, there was no code of ethics and few, if any, restrictions concerning advertising. Patent medicines, soap, and railroad travel led the list of advertised products and services. Anyone of national prominence in any field, from the president down, was fair game for those who were willing to go to any length to sell their products and services. More than one well-known figure lent his or her name, willingly or not, to products. Even President Grover Cleveland endorsed a brand of North Carolina cigarettes.

Advertising has come a long way since those early days. Many federal and state laws attempt to define "false" or "misleading" advertising. And organized business associations have worked out codes of ethics. These codes are attempts to end practices that might be considered wrong, or unethical, even if they are not technically illegal.

Better Business Bureaus

Local commercial organizations, such as the better business bureaus, have drafted codes that set standards of advertising practices. Every sponsor of advertising should use the Association of Better Business Bureaus' publication *A Guide to Retail Advertising and Selling* as a reference when preparing for promotional events. These codes help reduce unethical advertising practices. Unethical practices include offering "free" goods, making exaggerated claims about merchandise, giving misleading information, giving false list prices for marked down merchandise, and bait-and-switch advertising. This type of advertising brings consumers to stores to buy the advertised product with the intention of switching them to another item. In addition, the American Association of Advertising Agencies has a code of advertising ethics that sets standards for both its members and their clients.

Federal Trade Commission

The Federal Trade Commission (FTC) issues orders to stop firms from engaging in unethical advertising practices. It also fines persistent violators of the many laws and regulations governing truth in advertising, labeling, and selling in interstate commerce. Some of the laws under the control of the FTC are the Federal Food, Drug, and Cosmetics Act, the Fair Packaging and Labeling Act, and the Textile Fiber Products Identification Act.

Advertising is one of the most valuable promotion tools that retailers can use to inform consumers about a store's products and services. So it is important to maintain advertising standards that will keep the public's confidence. These laws and codes are guidelines for the store's advertising—and for its protection against less reputable competitors.

Now that you know more about the role of advertising in retailng, would you agree or disagree with Margaret Mead that we "really can't live without advertising"? If you agree, could you, as a retail worker, defend your position against the critics of advertising? If you disagree, how would you argue that we *can* live without advertising? No matter what field of retailing you're interested in, you'll probably find yourself asking and being asked these questions. So be prepared.

Trade Talk

Define each term and use it in a sentence.

Cooperative advertising	Potential customers
	Prestige advertising
Leader	Service advertising

Can You Answer These?

1. Why is advertising so critical in the distribution of products and services?
2. How do consumers benefit from advertising?
3. In what ways do sales personnel benefit from consumer advertising?
4. In what ways does advertising guide po-

tential customers through the five mental stages of a sale (AIDCA)?

5. What is being done to maintain good advertising standards?

Problems

1. Prepare a form like the following. Clip the first and last three ads in a local or regional newspaper of your choice. Write the name of the newspaper in the space provided. In the left column, list the purposes of advertising found in Chapter 26 under the headings "Goals of Merchandise Advertising" and "Goals of Institutional Advertising." According to the number of the ad, indicate with a check mark (√) the purpose(s) of each. Try to find ads for each of the purposes that were not checked on the form.

Name of newspaper: _____

Purpose of Advertisement	1	2	3	4	5	6

Visual Merchandising

CHAPTER 27

Communications & Human Relations
Economics & Marketing
Merchandising
Selling & Technology
Advertising & Display
Operations & Management

Fran Adelman was thumbing through a copy of the latest issue of *Visual Merchandising*. She had just read an article on fashion forecasting prepared for the National Association of Display Industries. (She wondered why her teacher had suggested an article in a "display" magazine, because her report was to be on spring fashions.) There were articles on display techniques, the use of mannequins, and sign making—and plenty of ads by fixture and prop manufacturers. But there were also articles on fashion, store decor, how computers serve customer needs, ad logotypes, and merchandising in Paris. Later, Fran said to her teacher, "I always thought that 'visual merchandising' was just another name for 'display.' Evidently, it's much more than that."

Visual merchandising includes everything visual that is done with, to, or for products, services, and their surroundings to help sell the products and services. This includes merchandise and service displays; print, broadcast, or film advertising and publicity; store layout; store decor; and any other visual means of communication. It also includes any modification or packaging that is intended to help sell products and services. And it includes the use of a variety of motion and audiovisual devices to show a product in use. Visual merchandising takes into account store layout and interior trimming and decorating. And it implies that the visual merchandising manager takes part in sales promotion planning. The store planning and layout aspect of visual merchandising is discussed in Chapter 70.

Development of Visual Merchandising

At one time, the word "display" would have been an accurate description of the way retailers showed their products. But marketing conditions and practices have changed, and so have the methods retailers use to promote sales. Much progress has been made since the late 1900s, when manufacturers first began to package their products and sell them under brand names.

Self-Service Retailing

Since the introduction of self-service retailing, visual merchandising has grown a great deal. The main reason for this growth is that self-service merchandise must sell itself in the retail store. Products must compete with one another in the selling area. They must sell themselves before the customer reaches the cash register, which may happen fast.

This situation creates strong competition among manufacturers in designing and packaging products that will not only be given good display space in retail stores but also win the customer's favor. In response to this competition, there has been

In self-service retailing, attractive visual merchandising helps products to sell themselves.
Courtesy of Lebhar-Friedman, Inc.

rapid advancement in product design, product packaging, and point-of-purchase (POP) displays. Fortunately, science and technology have provided new materials and machines to make self-selling practices possible. For example, think what the plastic bubble attached to a card has done for the visual merchandising of small hardware items.

Full-Service Retailing

Visual merchandising in self-service stores, especially supermarkets, has had a strong influence on the promotional activities of many full-service stores. Consumers often carry over into other purchasing tasks the shopping habits they formed when they shopped in self-service stores. Progressive full-service retailers noticed this trend and created more hands-on displays. They also learned to use colors in ways that enhanced the merchandise and came up with more creative window displays.

The New Role of the Visual Merchandiser

The window trimmer, dresser, or decorator of the past was usually the last person to be considered during sales promotion planning sessions. The visual merchandiser of today, however, may be an important part of the decision-making team and is frequently included at the beginning of the planning process. What special talents must a visual merchandiser have in order to be included in the planning team? If this area of retailing interests you, think about whether you have or want to develop any of these talents.

The special contributions to retailing of visual merchandisers are in the area of art and design. Creativity, imagination, and selling ability are their specialties. While shopping, a customer's attitude and impression of the store has much to do with what the store looks like inside. So the visual merchandiser has an important responsibility in maintaining a consistent, positive image of the store. This means, as one visual merchandiser expressed it, "liaison between merchant and display, as well as with the fashion director . . . and close cooperation with store planning."

As in the past, a display manager's work entails the use of space, color, line, design, light, movement, and location. But today, because visual merchandising goes much beyond these appeals to the sense of sight, display managers must use nearly all types of human perception. For example, they are frequently responsible for sound (background music and acoustics), cleanliness in the shopping areas, various types of aromas, and any other nonpersonal appeals to the senses.

Visual merchandising involves both display and drama. Live models are used more and more to dramatize the use of products. Visual merchandising entails the coordination of store interior decoration to support the theme of a promotion and keep the store atmosphere in tune with the sound and look of the times.

Display Objectives

The main objective of all visual merchandising activities is to increase the sale of merchandise and services. Usually the approach is direct, through a display of merchandise. But much visual merchandising effort is directed toward the creation of goodwill that, it is hoped, will result in future sales.

Promotional Displays

Displays that are used to increase the sales of specific merchandise and services are called **promotional displays**. Retailers realize that customers buy more when they see merchandise displayed in an appealing way. A good display prompts the impulse to buy. It reminds shoppers of things they want to buy. It announces new products and the arrival of the latest fashions. And it suggests new uses for familiar products and builds pride of ownership among product users.

Institutional Displays

Displays that are used to build goodwill for the store in the minds of regular and potential customers are called **institutional displays** because they sell the institution or store as a whole. Some large department stores, public utility companies, and banks have displays during holiday periods that reflect the holiday spirit rather than promoting their goods and services. Other institutional displays dramatize such themes as civic fund-raising drives, high school clubs, or the work of social organizations.

Functions of Display

In addition to increasing the store's sales volume, display serves four other functions: (1) reinforcing the store's image, (2) generating the atmosphere of a promotional event, (3) speeding up sales transactions, and (4) protecting the store's merchandise.

Each kind of store has individual characteristics. A supermarket, for example, is easily distinguished from a prestigious dress shop by the way it displays its merchandise. Some supermarkets appeal almost exclusively to the economy motive. Other supermarkets attract customers because of their broad selections of quality products. Good displays contribute to the store's desired image through the atmosphere or climate they generate.

A promotional theme is projected to customers through the atmosphere generated by displays and through store decorations and trimmings. Thus, the idea of gift-giving is conveyed at Valentine's Day, Mother's Day, and so on.

Certain displays—in supermarkets, for example—speed up transactions. Self-selection and self-service, along with well-marked prices, save time for the customer and allow the store to serve more people.

Theft of and damage to merchandise is very important in a number of product lines. Poor display fixtures can hurt sales and even cause damage to the merchan-

Christmas windows in the main store of Lord & Taylor on Fifth Avenue in New York City have become an annual attraction. This one shows the Staten Island ferry. Cosmo Photographers, Inc.

dise displayed. Cluttered merchandise often causes store personnel much inconvenience and wastes the customer's time. Frequently, it leads to the switching of labels and damage to the merchandise. Jewelry stores and camera shops usually display costly items in glass showcases.

Types of Displays

Store displays may be divided into two basic groups according to location: window displays and interior displays. Window displays carry out the first two parts of the visual merchandising task—attracting attention and arousing interest. Interior displays help clinch the sale—they develop desire and lead to action. Of course, there are situations in which either of these types of display accomplishes the sales task alone, but usually they act together.

Think of visual merchandising as a series of road signs. These road signs direct the potential purchaser from the store window, through the front door or opening to the sales floor, and into the department where the merchandise is presented for sale. The item or idea that the window display expresses is sometimes reinforced by a series of reminders along the customer's way to the sales location. These reminders at key traffic points may take the form of signs or interior displays that keep the customer moving toward the point of sale.

Window Displays

A window display is a picture that is quickly passed by the average pedestrian. So this picture must be attractive and magnetic enough to stop potential customers and bring them into the store.

Window displays can be classified by the

Can you identify these two types of window displays? Kip Peticolas/Fundamental
Photographs (top), Rhoda Galyn (bottom)

UNIT 9 ♦ Learning about Sales Promotion

type of background they have: (1) a full background, which means that the window is closed off from the rest of the store; (2) a partial background, which allows customers to see inside the store; or (3) an open background, which presents no restrictions to a total view of the main sales floor. Each type has its own advantages and its own set of problems for the display specialist. The types are further discussed in Chapter 48.

Full Background.   The full-background or closed window provides an attractive setting for a main theme. A display placed against a full background often gets more attention from a customer because there is no distraction by merchandise or activity within the store.

Partial Background.   When people look at a display with a partial background, they see other people in the store. So they may follow an impulse to join the crowd and see what the people are buying.

Open Background.   This type of window is more difficult to dress because it must blend in with the rest of the store. But it gives the front of the store an air of spaciousness and beckons the customer to come in and see the rest of the store.

Interior Displays

Once the customer has entered the store, interior displays take over the visual merchandising task. An effective interior display must sell ideas that result in sales. And it must be strategically located within the store and department. It must be easy for the customer to reach the display, particularly in self-service stores. Aisle space is just as important as display space because the customer must be able to get to the display and stand there while looking at the merchandise.

Five types of interior displays are used by retailers. They are (1) open displays, (2) closed displays, (3) built-up displays, (4) shadow boxes, and (5) ledge displays.

The choice of type of interior display depends mainly on the type of merchandise and the space available.

Open Displays.   Merchandise in an open display is arranged so that customers can touch it and examine it. Merchandise may be displayed openly on a counter or rack, shown on a mannequin, or placed on a decorative **display prop,** which is a fixture used to support displayed goods.

Closed Displays.   In addition to high-value merchandise, such as jewelry and photographic equipment, fragile and easily soiled articles must be protected in a closed display. An example is expensive figurines. Kinds of merchandise that are dangerous for children to handle should also be kept in closed display areas.

Built-Up Displays.   Built-up displays are those in which merchandise is placed on platforms or built-up props to make the article displayed more attractive and to enhance the general appearance of the store. These displays are found at important traffic points in the store, as at the end of the aisle in a supermarket, in front of the elevator, or in full view of the escalator of a department store.

Shadow Boxes.   A small display area that resembles a shallow box open on one side is called a **shadow box.** It is usually found in the interior of a store, but a shadow box is also sometimes used in a display window to highlight a featured item. The three-dimensional effect of a shadow box creates the impression of a stage set with a desirable piece of merchandise.

Ledge Displays.   Sometimes, merchandise is displayed on ledges, store walls, or partitions. These areas may also be used for decorations during holiday seasons or other special occasions. Displays in these areas make the store interior look inviting and do not clutter the aisles.

Effective interior displays result in sales. Can you identify the types shown here? Kip Peticolas/Fundamental Photographs (upper left and lower left), Richard Megna/Fundamental Photographs (upper right and middle), Ken Karp (lower right)

Full-Service Store Displays

In department and large departmentalized specialty stores, each department usually has one or more displays featuring timely, attractive merchandise sold in the department. These displays are usually located at heavy traffic points, frequently at or near the most used entrance to the department. Sometimes, departmental displays are also located on ledges and tops of fixtures or in shadow boxes recessed into the wall. Counter and showcase displays are also popular in these stores. The way merchandise is grouped and the informative signs that describe the items aid both customer and salespeople by showing what is new or fashionable.

Displays in the interiors of department and large specialty stores may be designed by personnel from either the display department or the sales department. Simple displays on counters and in showcases are usually built by sales-department personnel. Complex displays are built by professional display artists.

In stores where clothing is sold, related items of apparel and accessories may be displayed together in an **ensemble,** which is a group of articles that are worn together. If a customer buys a jacket she has seen on a mannequin, she usually buys the blouse and skirt shown with it. She may also buy the shoes and handbag shown on the mannequin.

Self-Service Store Displays

Visual merchandising is more highly developed in the supermarket than anywhere else. This is not surprising if you consider some facts and figures about the grocery business. The typical supermarket sells more than 7,000 items, and the average shopper spends about 26 minutes in the store. This means that an item has to catch the shopper's eye and sell itself in a split second. For this reason, super-

markets have been called "battlegrounds of display."

Point-of-purchase (POP) displays, also known as "impulse displays," are displays made from props and signs supplied to the retailer by the manufacturer. They are used to promote the manufacturer's products where the goods are sold. POP displays include posters, counter cards, window-display reminders, backdrops, price cards, cutouts, stands, racks, and barrels. These displays often repeat the advertising message that has been used in magazines or on television because such repetition increases sales.

Retail food stores often use POP displays at the ends of the aisles for products such as canned goods, paper napkins, and cookies. Many department and specialty stores use POP displays to sell cosmetics, packaged socks, and other small items. POP displays are frequently found at the checkout counters of all types of self-service stores.

Much of the impulse (unplanned) buying of customers is motivated by POP displays. Impulse items—such as magazines, chewing gum, candy, and razor blades—are displayed in special racks. Sometimes POP displays of new items are placed in locations away from the place where merchandise is usually sold. This location is at a point reached by the customer after planned purchases have been made. So the item is added to the intended purchases rather than becoming a substitute for an item already in the customer's shopping cart.

You may recall the discussion, at the beginning of Chapter 25, that Magda Kruger and Frank Caruso had about promotion. Turn back to Chapter 25 and re-read their discussion. Do you understand what promotion is all about? Would Frank need promotion skills to become a supermarket manager? Can you explain how the forms of promotion have changed and developed? Apart from retailing, in what other fields could you use promotion skills?

Point-of-purchase displays are provided by the manufacturer to the retailer. Courtesy of Thermos Division of King Seeley Thermos Co.

If you can answer these questions then you'll be interested to learn how promotion workers achieve the effects they want.

Trade Talk

Define each term and use it in a sentence.

Built-up displays
Display prop
Ensemble
Institutional displays
Point-of-purchase (POP) displays

Promotional displays
Shadow box
Visual merchandising

Can You Answer These?

1. Why did the introduction of packaging and brand names stimulate the development of visual merchandising?
2. How has the scope of visual merchandising increased during recent years?
3. What are the four functions of a merchandise display?
4. How do the displays of full-service stores differ from those of self-service stores?
5. Who usually prepares POP display materials? Why are they so effective?

Problems

1. Rule a form similar to the following. In the left column, write the letters of each of the following types of interior displays: (*a*) open display, (*b*) closed display, (*c*) built-up display, (*d*) shadow box, and (*e*) ledge display. Then visit several stores in your neighborhood to find an example of each type of display. In the middle column of your form, write a short description for each display type; in the right column, record the type of store in which you saw it.

Type of Interior Display	Display Description	Type of Store

2. Rule a form similar to the following. In the left column, write the letter of each of the following types of stores: (0) hardware, (a) drugstore, (b) music, (c) shoe, (d) clothing, (e) sporting goods, (f) variety, (g) florist, and (h) jewelry. In the middle column, for each type of store, give an example of one product that could be sold effectively through POP displays. In the right column indicate a suggested location in the store for such a display.

Type of Store	Product Sold through POP Display	Location of Display in Store
Example: (0)	Flashlight batteries	Checkout counter

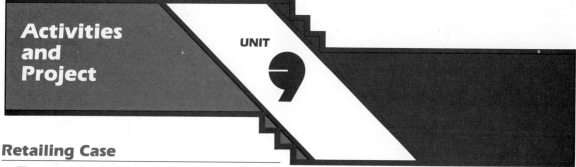

Activities and Project

UNIT 9

Retailing Case

The retailing class was just about to wind up a discussion of the forms of retail sales promotion when Frankie Martinez beamed with an idea. "Why couldn't we plan a promotion for our marketing and distributive education program along the lines used by one of the fast-food franchisers? We have an excellent program, and it's too bad that more kids don't know what it really is and take advantage of it. We could get help from our merchants, I'm sure, and we'd learn a lot and have fun."

1. What types of retail sales promotion could benefit the high school MDE program? Advertising? Display? Publicity? Others?
2. What are the differences in the clienteles of retailers and your classmates?
3. What advantages of the program to students would you promote?
4. What media would you recommend to communicate with potential members?

Working with People

Mavis O'Brien had been a salesperson at the Jones Department Store for nearly a year before John Chu joined the staff. These two young people started a discussion about the need for sales promotion in our economic system today. They discussed advertising at length.

"We would be better off without advertising," John said. "This extensive use of commercials has simply spoiled TV and radio, and the newspapers are so full of ads that you can't find the news. Magazines are almost as bad; they're so crammed with ads that you have to look through half the issue before you come to the reading material." Then he went on to say, "People today are intelligent enough to know what they want. They can make their own selections without the 'help' of ads that only confuse them and make them buy things they really don't need. And don't forget that the consumer pays for it all. I say let's get rid of all of it."

There wasn't much Mavis could do but listen as John went on and on. Finally she managed to say, "I can't agree with you entirely, John. I'll grant that commercials can be a real nuisance, but every company has to advertise its products if it wants to stay in business." Assume that you are Mavis. How would you handle this difference of opinion tactfully?

1. Identify the true problem.
2. What are the important facts to be considered in this problem?
3. List several possible solutions to this problem.
4. Evaluate the possible results of each solution.
5. Which solution do you recommend? Why?
6. Do you think that advertising benefits the consumer? Why or why not?

Project 9: Surveying Promotion Methods

Your Project Goal
Given one area of retailing, survey a sample of the particular kinds of sales promotion methods used by businesses in the area; conduct the survey; collect, classify, tabulate, and interpret the data; and prepare a written report on your findings.

Procedure
1. Choose one of the areas of retailing listed below:
   a. Apparel and accessories
   b. Automotive, recreational, and agricultural vehicle and accessories
   c. Finance and credit services
   d. Floricultural, farm, and gardening supplies
   e. Food marketing
   f. Food service
   g. General merchandise
   h. Hardware and building materials
   i. Home furnishings
   j. Hotel, motel, and lodging services
   k. Petroleum
   l. Real estate
   m. Recreation
   Ask your instructor to approve your selection so that unnecessary duplication of areas may be avoided.
2. Locate a partner who is interested in the same area of retailing or a closely related area and select a shopping area for your study. Get your instructor's approval of the shopping area.
3. Make a checklist of all the sales promotion and publicity methods mentioned in Chapters 25, 26, and 27 under the following headings: Advertising, Display, Personal Selling, Publicity, and Other Methods.
4. Prepare a simple interview schedule similar to the following:

Sales Promotion Survey

Area of distribution	_____
Name of business firm	_____
Primary method of sales promotion	_____
Primary medium used	_____
Reason for using this medium	_____
Secondary medium	_____

5. Plan the sales promotion methods survey.
   a. Determine the number and size of the firms to be contacted; for example, three large and three small.
   b. Prepare a time schedule; check it and your plan with your instructor.
   c. Plan the way the data and information are to be tabulated.
   d. Plan your introductory remarks for the interviews.
6. Conduct the survey and tabulate the data.
7. Prepare a written report on the sales promotion methods used and the reasons for their use. If possible, use graphs and charts of the data and include interesting information from the interviewees.
8. Compare and contrast your findings with those tabulated from related areas of distribution and with those tabulated from unrelated fields. Report to the class according to a plan which you have worked out with your instructor.

Evaluation
You will be evaluated on the completeness and accuracy of your survey, on the interest generated by your written report, and on the contribution your oral report makes to the understanding of promotional media and methods.

Keeping Track of Merchandise

Recording Sales

CHAPTER

28

Communications & Human Relations

Economics & Marketing

Merchandising

Selling & Technology

Advertising & Display

Operations & Management

"I don't know why you go to all that bother," remarked Janet Meislin to Andy Devane as he finished checking a department number before recording a sale on the cash register. "When I'm not sure of a department number, I usually make one up. Other times I group two or three items together and add the prices in my head. That way I can ring one department number and the total price. It's a lot faster. It's our responsibility to keep the customer happy. And they certainly don't want to stand around here waiting for me to check some silly number."

Janet's attitude toward recording sales will lose many more customers for the store than it will gain. And it may well be a violation of store policy. Grouping items together and adding prices in her head could easily cause her to over- or undercharge the customers. Or it could make it impossible for customers to return or exchange merchandise. Contrary to what Janet may think, accurate department in-

formation recorded at the time of the sale is essential if the store is to have useful records. Janet's way of recording sales can lead to faulty buying and management decisions. And these faulty decisions can eventually lead to large financial losses for the store.

Types of Sales

The two most common types of sales transactions are cash and charge sales. Retail salespeople may also handle COD sales, layaway or will-call, sales, and discount sales.

Every transaction requires the use of a sales check, a cash register, or both. A **sales check** is a form on which the details of the sale are recorded at the time of the sale. The appearance of sales checks and the types of cash registers vary from store to store. Salespeople must be trained in the procedures used in their individual stores. The cash register and sales checks are covered in more detail later in this chapter.

Cash Sales

When a customer pays for merchandise with money or a check, the transaction is a **cash sale.** Each store has its own procedure to use when accepting checks. In most cases, the customer is asked for one or more forms of identification. Some reliable identification documents are a driver's license, a company identification card, a passport, a credit card, and a check guarantee card. A **check guarantee card** is a card issued by a bank that insures the store against loss provided that the check doesn't exceed a specified amount.

The cash sale is almost always rung up on a cash register. The slip of paper from the cash register roll that is ejected from the machine and shows the dollars-and-cents amount of the sale is called a **sales slip.** It's usually given to the customer as evidence of the purchase.

Often, a sales check may be used to record a cash sale. Sometimes the store wants to collect more information than is recorded on most cash register tapes. Sales checks are also used to record a customer's address and delivery instructions. Another use for a sales check in a cash sale is to provide a more detailed receipt for the customer. The receipt is either a copy of the sales check or a small portion of it, known as the "stub." Stores that use sales checks for cash sales often use the cash register to stamp the sales checks. This way the cash register tape becomes an accurate record of all the business done each day.

Charge Sales

Most stores offer some form of credit service. When customers buy on credit, they charge merchandise to their accounts and pay for it later. In a **charge-take sale,** cus-tomers take the merchandise with them at the time of the sale. In a **charge-send sale,** the merchandise is delivered to customers.

Because charge customers have the use of store's merchandise before they pay for it, stores require some form of customer identification in every charge sale. In the most common type of charge transaction, the customer presents to the salesperson a charge plate or **credit card.** This is usually a plastic card with the customer's name and account number printed on it in raised letters. It's valid only when signed by the customer. The salesperson uses the card to imprint the customer's name and account number on a sales check. Then the salesperson asks the customer to sign the sales check. It's the salesperson's responsibility to compare the signature on the charge plate or credit card with the one on the sales check.

In some small stores, the customer is known personally by the sales staff. Because of this personal identification, no further proof of identity is needed.

There is usually a limit to the amount a customer can charge without authorization from the store's credit department or the credit card company that issues the card. This is called the **floor limit.** For purchases below the floor limit, the salesperson has the important responsibility of personally authorizing the sale.

COD Sales

If a customer pays for merchandise when it is delivered, it is called a **COD (cash on delivery) sale.** Customers usually use the COD service when ordering goods by telephone or mail. Some customers may also use COD service when they are actually shopping in a store but would rather pay for a purchase at the time it is delivered. It is the salesperson's responsibility to establish the fact that someone will be there to accept the merchandise when it is delivered. Some stores require a deposit on COD sales to ensure that the customer will accept the goods when they are delivered.

In addition, there may be a delivery charge for COD items.

Layaway or Will-Call Sales

If a store withdraws an item from stock and holds it in storage for a customer, it is a **layaway or will-call sale**. In return for this service, the customer must leave a deposit and must pay the total price plus tax within a certain amount of time. When the payments are completed, the customer obtains the merchandise. If the customer does not complete the payments within the time allowed, the merchandise is returned to stock.

Discount Sales

A **discount sale** is a reduction in price to special classes of customers. The most common discount sale is the employee discount. It's usually a reduction in price of between 10 and 25 percent. When a discount sale is made, the sales check is made out in the usual way. Then the discount is subtracted from the recorded price before the sales tax is added. Employees and any other customers who qualify for a discount must properly identify themselves to receive it.

The Cash Register

There are a number of different cash register models with many different features. The simple ones are like adding machines with drawers. The more complex ones are electronic and may be connected to a computer. One type of computerized register has a small hand-held wand that is passed over specially coded price tags. With the help of this wand, the register "reads" the tags and rings up the sales automatically. Computerized registers can also give the salesperson information about customer credit and about inventory. On one type of register, a charge sale cannot be completed if the customer's credit is not acceptable for some reason.

You may have seen the type of computerized register that is often used in su-

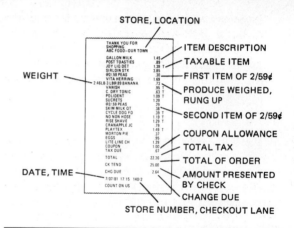

A computer-assisted checkout sales receipt. Courtesy of Gray Advertising, Inc.

permarkets. It produces a sales slip that lists by name each item the customer has purchased. Another computerized register that's used by department stores produces a completed sales check instead of a sales slip.

No matter what model of cash register a store has, as a salesperson who works with the register, you'll have these duties: first, you must follow some general rules for cash register use; second, you must learn the opening and closing procedures for the cash register; and third, you have the important job of guarding the store's money against possible theft.

General Rules for Cash Register Use

♦ *Keep Your Cash Drawer Orderly.* Arrange your cash drawer, which is also called a **till,** so that all the bills are face up and in the same direction. One common way to arrange bills is to place the $20 bills in the first compartment on the left. Then the $10 bills go in the compartment to the right of the $20 bills, next the $10 bills, and then the $5 bills, and finally the $2 and $1 bills. Because the $2 and $1 bills share the compartment on the far right, place the $2 bills, if you must handle them, underneath the $1 bills. It's always a good idea to crumple new bills and

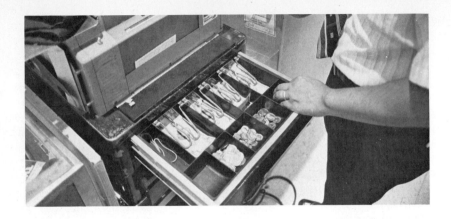

One of the most important duties of someone who works with the cash register is making certain the cash drawer is always kept orderly. *Art Zollo/ Fundamental Photographs*

straighten them out so that you won't accidentally give out two bills instead of one. The coins should be arranged in the cash drawer in a similar manner, with the silver dollars and half-dollars in the first compartment on the left. Then the quarters to in the next compartment, followed by the dimes, nickels, and pennies.

♦ *Always Have Sufficient Change.* Make sure early in the day, when you are less likely to be busy, that you have enough coins and bills in your cash drawer to make change. This will help you avoid unnecessary delays that annoy customers. If you need change, be sure to follow the store procedure for buying change.

♦ *Record Sales Carefully and Accurately.* Take care to accurately record all the information that your store needs to collect, not just the dollar amount of the sale. You may be asked to record such things as a salesperson number, department numbers, product codes, prices, tax, and an amount tendered. The **amount tendered** is the amount received from the customer.

If you should happen to make a mistake in recording a sale, be sure to correct it immediately, following your store's procedure.

♦ *Do Not Group Sales.* Most stores require that each sale be recorded separately. If you ring several sales together, store rec-

ords become inaccurate. They show that one customer was served instead of several. The grouping of sales may also reflect unfavorably on your honesty.

♦ *Be Very Careful in Handling Receipts.* The receipt, or sales slip, is very important because it is an official record of the sale. It provides the customer with proof of the purchase in case the merchandise has to be returned or exchanged, and it protects the store against accepting returned goods that were purchased elsewhere. It also gives charge customers accurate records of what they purchased when they are asked to pay their bills. Follow the required procedure for handling the receipt. Some stores enclose it with the merchandise, others attach it to packages, and still others hand it to the customer. If a customer will not wait for a receipt, ring up the sale immediately and comply with store policy regarding the receipt.

♦ *Build Customer Goodwill.* How? Make a habit of looking at customers as you thank them, smile, and call them by name if you've seen the name on the credit card. Show customers that you're pleased to serve them and that you hope they return soon. Remind them of the store's return and service policies, but—if possible—give them reasons why they will be happy with the merchandise. Invite them back. "Your new quartz watch will give you the accuracy you need, Dr. Malkowitz. Enjoy wearing it and come back again."

Opening and Closing Activities

At the start of each day, the employee in charge of opening the register must get the change fund from the store's accounting office. He or she must then count the money to be sure that it's the correct amount. If it's over or short, this fact should be reported to the person in charge.

The money must then be arranged in an orderly way in the cash drawer.

At the end of each day, each salesperson and each cashier are expected to account for the day's sales and money. They prepare a summary of the sales handled during that day and submit it to the proper store department. A record or summary of sales made during the day is known as the **tally**. Salespeople using books of sales checks keep a daily tally of all sales. Each time a sales check is written, the sales in-

A tally is a record of all sales made in a day.

	TALLY		
NUMBER	DENOMINATION	AMOUNT	
41	Pennies		41
12	Nickels		60
11	Dimes	1	10
4	Quarters	1	00
12	Half-dollars	6	00
25	$1 bills	25	00
7	$5 bills	35	00
6	$10 bills	60	00
5	$20 bills	100	00
4	Checks	83	00
6	Charge sales	310	00
	Cash in drawer	622	11
	Plus cash paid out	4	07
	Total cash	626	18
	Less change	50	00
	Cash received, cashier's count	266	18
	Cash received, detailed audit strip	263	07
Cash proved ☐ Cash over ☑ Cash short ☐		Amount of cash short or over	3	11

formation is entered on a tally sheet. Then, at the end of each day, the salesperson adds up the tally sheet and gives it to the department manager together with the carbon copies of the sales checks.

In many stores the cash registers keep an automatic tally of the sales punched into them. An employee in charge of a register writes down this amount, counts the money in the till, and fills in whatever report forms the store requires. The employee also removes the machine's tape and sends it to the accounting office. In any case, all cash is bagged and taken to the cashier's office or picked up by the cashier's staff. Often the change fund for the next day is bagged separately from the day's receipts. That way the change fund is ready for the next day's business.

Protecting Money Against Theft

If possible, everyone in a store should be trained to prevent theft of money and merchandise. Theft hurts the retailer, the employees, and the customers. Shortchange artists and counterfeiters, for example, are constantly trying to cheat retail business firms.

Cash registers play a vital part in recording sales. As an employee who handles a cash register, you should know how to recognize and deal with potential thieves. Some of the tips stores give their cashiers follow.

Never Leave Your Cash Drawer Open. Whenever you leave the register, be sure that the drawer is closed and latched. If you have a key to lock the register, be sure to use it. An open drawer invites a dishonest person to steal. It's also very easy for a thief to ring the register and steal the contents of the cash drawer.

Watch for Customers Who Try to Confuse You. Shortchange artists may try various tactics to confuse you when you're making change. They hope that you'll make mistakes in their favor. Such a person may, for example, interrupt while you're counting change and ask that a larger bill be changed. Another shortchange artists may use the ploy of remembering some small item to add to his or her purchase or of wanting to exchange one purchase for another.

Ignore Interruptions. The best way to protect yourself against shortchange operators when you're handling cash is to ignore all interruptions. Always finish counting change first, no matter what question is asked of you. if a customer asks to add another item to the sale or to make an exchange, treat it as a new transaction. Follow the store's procedure at all times and don't try other methods of cashiering that customers may suggest.

Beware of the Marked Bill. You may have difficulty with shortchange artists who work in pairs. Often, they try the marked-bill trick. One member of the team may buy an item and pay for it with a $5 bill that is marked with an ink blot or some other distinguishing mark. Later the other team member may buy some article for a small amount and pay for it with a $1 bill. After you have put the $1 bill in the register, the second customer may try to convince you that he or she had presented a $5 bill. The customer can identify it as having a certain mark. When you look in the till and find the $5 bill with that mark, you may believe you have made a mistake. So make a habit of examining both sides of every bill you handle. If there is any unusual mark or tear, call the customer's attention to it. This indicates to the customer that you are well trained and that the shortchange attempt had better be dropped because it will probably be unsuccessful.

Be Alert for Counterfeit Money. Counterfeiting is on the rise, so you should be prepared to receive and reject counterfeit money. In order to guard against accepting counterfeit money, you should (1) become more familiar with what genuine money really looks like and (2) learn how to recognize money that is counterfeit.

There are several places to look on paper money for signs of counterfeiting. One of the more obvious is the portrait with the oval background. The portrait should be lifelike and stand out sharply from the background. The lines in the pattern of the oval background should be sharp and unbroken. They should look like a fine screen. If the portrait is dull, blurry, or lifeless and blends in with the background, the bill may be counterfeit. This is also true if the lines in the background of the oval are broken. A second obvious thing to look at on a bill is the paper it's printed on. The paper used for genuine currency has tiny red and blue silk fibers mixed in with the paper.

Stores usually advise their employees specifically on how to spot counterfeit money. Pay attention to what you're told to look for. Also, make sure that you know the procedures for dealing with someone who's passing counterfeit money, whether intentionally or unintentionally.

Never Accuse a Suspect.   Finally, no matter how sure you are that someone is trying to commit a theft, never accuse that person of the attempt. Instead, notify a supervisor or a member of the store's security force at once. These people are trained to know what to do and should be able to handle the situation discreetly.

Sales Checks

Most retailers use sales checks in addition to cash registers to record sales. A sales check has these two main purposes. (1) It gives the customer a receipt that's useful in case the merchandise has to be returned. (2) It gives the retailer information that's vital to the operation of the store.

The information recorded on the sales checks is used by a number of departments. Buyers use the information to help them decide how much and what kind of merchandise to order. The credit department uses the information to bill charge customers. The people in charge of delivery use the information to determine what merchandise to deliver to whom. The accounting department uses the information to update records, prepare tax reports, and prepare reports for management's use. Inventory records may be updated from information recorded on sales slips. If these departments are to understand and use the information on sales checks, all salespeople must be familiar with the forms and use orderly procedures in preparing them.

Sales-Check Procedure

The procedure that a store uses to complete sales checks depends on the type of sales check that it has and on store policy. Every time a salesperson writes up a sales check, all the appropriate blanks for that type of sale should be filled in. Details should never be left to be filled in later. Most salespeople develop a set order in which they put down the information on a sales check. By following this order faithfully, they avoid leaving out any of the information needed.

Each sales check is numbered and should be used in the proper order. If a salesperson makes a mistake on a sales check, the check must be voided or nullified by an authorized person. Then, it is turned in at the end of the day with the store's copies of the sales checks. Sales checks must never be destroyed unless this is specifically authorized by a supervisor.

Sales Books.   Some stores use sales books that contain three copies of each sales check. The original is kept by the store for its records and the duplicate is the customer's copy; it goes with the merchandise. The triplicate copy is the tissue-paper copy that remains in the sales book.

Sales Register.   Other stores and a large number of service establishments use sales registers instead of sales books. The salesperson or order clerk fills out the sales check, which is in the register. When the check is completed, the handle on the side of the register is turned. The complete sales check then rolls out, a carbon copy is retained in the register, and a new blank sales check rolls into place for the next sale.

Credit Cards and Charge Plates. When a customer uses a credit card or charge plate to make a purchase, the salesperson inserts a special sales check into an imprinting machine along with the credit card or charge plate. The machine imprints the customer's name and account number on the sales check. In some stores, the machine is connected to a computer that holds credit information about the customers. The machine reads the customer's account number from a magnetic strip on the back of the credit card or charge plate. At the same time, the

There are almost as many different sales-check forms as there are stores that use them. Courtesy of Chemical Bank, Harvey's Chelsea Restaurant, Montgomery Ward & Co., and Budget Uniform Center, Inc.

salesperson presses the amount of the sale on a small keyboard. If the customer's credit is not acceptable for some reason, the sale cannot be completed. In other stores, if the sale is over the floor limit, the salesperson must telephone for authorization before the sales check may be imprinted.

If, like MasterCard, a credit card can be used nationwide, the salesperson may be required to check a **credit-card bulletin** before completing the sales check. The bulletin is issued on a weekly basis and lists the numbers of credit cards that shouldn't be accepted for charge sales. Don't automatically assume that a customer's credit is bad if the card imprinting machine won't work or if his or her account number is in the credit-card bulletin. The cardholder may only have reported a credit card missing and forgotten to call when it was found.

Trade Talk

Define each term and use it in a sentence.

Amount tendered	COD (cash on
Cash sale	delivery) sale
Charge-send sale	Credit card
Charge-take sale	Credit-card bulletin
Check guarantee	Discount sale
card	Floor limit

Layaway or will-call sale — Sales slip
Sales check — Tally
— Till

Can You Answer These?

1. Name the types of sales transactions and describe the differences between them.
2. Describe some special features of computerized registers and show how each feature can save time for the salesperson.
3. What are some general rules to follow when handling a cash register?
4. Describe the typical opening and closing activities for the salesperson who deals with the cash register.
5. What are some tips for protecting money against thefts?

Problems

1. Rule a form similar to the following. In the correct places on your form, record the following items as if you were preparing a sales check: 2 blouses, style 486, size 34, at $19.00 each; 1 pair of jeans, style 6140, size 10, at $29.94; and 1 scarf, style 1129, at $9.50. Sales tax rate is 5 percent.

			Amount	
Quantity	Description	Price	Dollars	Cents

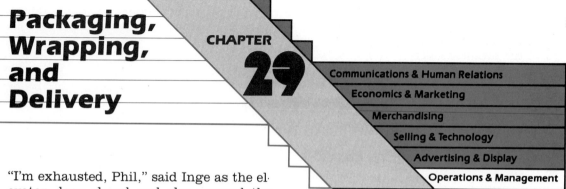

Packaging, Wrapping, and Delivery

CHAPTER 29

- Communications & Human Relations
- Economics & Marketing
- Merchandising
- Selling & Technology
- Advertising & Display
- Operations & Management

"I'm exhausted, Phil," said Inge as the elevator door closed and she pressed the sixth-floor button. "Only one more stop and we can get something to eat."

Inge and Philip Lindstrom had been shopping for hours. Their first stop was the furniture store where they carefully selected the comfortable recliner they'd been saving for. It was to be delivered the next week. Then they went to a large department store where their purchases included peppermint candy in a cylindrical can, tissues in a decorated pop-up box, pantyhose in a plastic egg, and earrings in a hinged box covered with blue velvet. All their purchases had been put in well-designed bags in the departments where they had selected them. In addition, the store had gift wrapped the earrings.

The elevator door opened at the sixth-floor toy department, where they decided on a talking baby doll for their niece's birthday. It was packaged in an attractive bright-pink box with a clear plastic window. The box was designed so that the customer could pull a string and hear the doll talk.

Preparing Merchandise for Delivery

Packaging, wrapping, and delivery each played an important part in Inge and Phil Lindstrom's shopping trip. But chances are that Inge and Phil didn't even realize it. **Packaging** is the protective and decorative covering that the manufacturer adds before merchandise is sent to the retailer. Although the practical purpose of packaging is to protect the merchandise from damage, a major purpose today is to attract the customer's attention and help sell the product.

The cylindrical candy can, plastic pantyhose egg, pop-up tissue box, velvet earring box, and pink doll box are all examples of packages designed by the manufacturers to sell their products. Retailers often give a great deal of attention to the way a product is packaged when they buy merchandise for their stores.

Wrapping is enclosing the merchandise in an attractive protective cover after the sale has been recorded. It includes bag-ging, boxing, wrapping in paper, gift wrapping, and other methods of preparing merchandise for delivery to the customer. The earrings Inge and Phil purchased were gift wrapped, and all their other department store purchases were bagged by salespeople in the store.

Attractive, well-wrapped packages are a visible sign that a store is concerned about giving its customers good service. Furthermore, wrappings may carry the store's name and serve as advertisements for it. Stores spend large amounts of money on well-designed and attractively decorated boxes, bags, ribbon, and other wrapping supplies because of their advertising potential.

Delivery of merchandise to customers' homes used to be taken for granted as part of the normal retailing procedure. Now many stores are self-service, and many customers are used to carrying their own packages home. But delivery still plays an important role in certain types of retailing. There are some items, such as Inge and Phil's recliner, that may be too bulky or heavy to carry. Then too, there are some customers who cannot make the trip to the store. And there are still others who do not wish to carry packages. Also, as the energy crisis worsens, it may be cheaper to call in an order and have it delivered than to come into the store and carry one's purchases home.

Employees in charge of wrapping and packing merchandise for home delivery must protect goods from possible damage during the delivery process. If not packed and handled carefully, furniture may become scratched or chipped, china may be broken, and frozen foods may become spoiled.

Packaging

What makes a self-service customer select one product over another of equal price and quality? Often, one reason is the appearance of the package. In fact, many manufacturers believe that the package sells the product; therefore they spend millions of dollars on packaging.

What Makes a Package Successful?

The customer's choice of one product over another often takes place in the retail store. For this reason, most retailers are careful to consider those factors that will attract the customer's attention to a particular package and will stimulate the desire to own. Here are some of the questions retailers may ask themselves when they are evaluating possible packages for their stores:

1. Does the package look valuable enough for this product? The package should tell the customer that it contains something valuable.
2. Does the design of the package give the right impression of the product? If the product is to be used by young people, for example, does it project a youthful image? Retailers also want to know whether the package is deceptive or honest.
3. Will the package look attractive when it is in the store? In a store, customers will probably be seeing the product sideways or at an angle. The package should look attractive from all different angles, not just from the front. Also, a unique shape may add to the excitement of the product.
4. Is the package convenient to use? If the package or container holds a product that will be used up gradually, it should be convenient to open and reclose. For example, the stay-fresh linings that are sturdy enough to be reclosed easily are practical features of cereal boxes.

What Is Multiple Packaging?

Multiple packaging is the grouping of merchandise for the convenience of the customer and the retailer. Oranges are

What are the advantages and disadvantages of multiple packaging? Ron Tanner/Progressive Grocer (left), Jeanne Hammond (right)

sold in bags of a dozen, T-shirts are sold in packages of three, drinking glasses are sold in sets of 4, 6, 8, or 12, and china is sold in single place settings or services for 4, 8, or 12. Multiple packaging for the supermarket may be done at the local store or at chain headquarters. For other types of retail stores, it may be done by the manufacturer or wholesaler. This practice is especially common for breakable items.

When the manufacturer carefully packs such items as glasses and china in multiples, most of the retailers' packaging work is eliminated. A box can be prepared for delivery by just adding a mailing label, or it can be handed to the customer without repacking.

Both individual and multiple packaging have been completed long before the sale begins. Wrapping and delivery, however, take place after the sale has been recorded.

Wrapping

Many retailers take the opportunity to advertise their store names on the street and on trains and buses by having it printed on attractive bags, boxes, and shopping bags. Of course, the kind and quality of wrapping materials varies widely from store to store.

Only in recent years have some retailers dared to eliminate the wrapping service.

A few of the newer discount supermarket chains ask customers to supply their own bags and boxes, to pay cash, to do their own bagging in return for substantially lower prices.

Where Goods Are Packed or Wrapped

There are three types of wrapping and packing systems: salesperson wrap, department wrap, and central wrap. Some large stores may use all three. Smaller stores usually expect the salesperson to wrap or pack goods.

Salesperson Wrap. In small stores and in some departments of large stores, the salesperson wraps the customer's package. Many customers like the personal attention of this system. After a friendly salesperson has helped the customer make a selection, recorded the sale, and wrapped the package, the customer leaves the store with a feeling of having been respected and well treated.

Department Wrap. Sometimes wrapping is done at a special location in or near the department where the merchandise is sold. Personnel assigned to wrapping may also work at the cash register, or they may do only wrapping and packing.

The department-wrap method saves time for salespeople and reduces the amount of

Fragile or easily crushed items should be placed at the top of the grocery bag. Courtesy of National Cash Register Co.

space needed to wrap merchandise. Also, wrapping is usually done efficiently, because wrappers have been specially trained for this work.

With this method, after a sale has been rung up, the salesperson may take the merchandise to the wrapping section to be wrapped and then bring it back to the customer. Or the salesperson may escort the customer to the wrapping section and then go on to help other customers. In some stores, customers are expected to take their own purchases to the wrapping section.

Central Wrap.   There are two types of central wrapping systems. One is used in stores where most of the merchandise is delivered to customers rather than carried home by them. The customers' purchases are sent in bags or boxes to a central packing room. There, packers wrap the merchandise and sort it according to delivery localities. This system is efficient because it uses specialists in packing, can make use of special wrapping equipment, and saves the salesperson's time.

The other type of central wrap is used in supermarkets and self-service stores, where it is located near the store exit. The cashier or a bagger places the customer's purchases in a bag or a box. In nearly all supermarkets, bagging is an important customer service. Customers expect bags to be strong, and they expect special protection for all items that could be damaged in transit.

How to Wrap and Pack

Wrapping may seem a routine kind of job, but it requires skill and knowledge. It is the close of the sales transaction, and as such must make a final good impression on the customer. The five following practices should be observed in wrapping packages:

1. Prepare the merchandise. Before you begin to wrap, inspect the goods to make sure they are in perfect condition. Check the price tag; remove it from gifts. Then carefully assemble the articles, making sure that heavy items are on the bottom.

2. Select the type of wrapping suited to the merchandise. Use paper, a bag, or a box, and use the proper inner wrap if one is needed. Be sure that the merchandise is completely covered.

3. Use durable wrapping materials. If possible, fold soft merchandise so that it protects itself to some extent. Protect breakable goods with corrugated board or padding. When folding clothing, use tissue paper to keep the garment from wrinkling. Use plastic bags to wrap frozen foods or products that might spill. Use paper and twine that are strong enough for the goods being wrapped. Use double paper or bags if necessary. Fold the edges and ends of the paper well to make a strong package. Use enough twine to give maximum support. If necessary, provide a handle for easy carrying.

4. Practice both speed and economy in wrapping. Put as much as you safely can into one package. Avoid wasted motion by keeping wrapping materials in a convenient place. Use the correct amount of paper and twine and cut the twine close to the package. Always try to wrap parcels correctly the first time.

5. Observe safety practices. Use proper supplies, tools, and equipment, and return them to their proper places after use. Keep the surface of the wrapping table clear, and keep the wrapping area orderly: clean the floor, close doors and drawers, restock bins, and place refuse in proper containers.

Gift Wrapping

Many stores offer gift wrapping as a service. Gift wrapping can be a matter of simply putting merchandise into a gift box. At other times it can involve wrapping packages elegantly in special paper tied with brightly colored ribbon. Store personnel who do gift wrapping are usually trained in the art of creating attractive, eye-appealing packages. In small stores, salespeople may be in charge of gift wrapping for their own customers.

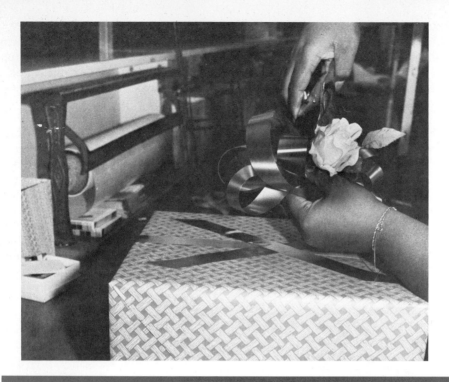

Gift wrapping is a popular customer service; it may or may not be provided free of charge. Elizabeth Richter

Some high-quality shops wrap gifts without charge. But gift wrapping is expensive, and most stores now charge for this service. Some stores have solved the expense problem by giving collapsible gift boxes with each gift purchase so that shoppers can do their own wrapping. Other stores give free gift wrap for merchandise costing over a certain amount, say $75.

Delivery

Whether a retailer offers delivery service depends on store policy. This policy is influenced primarily by the kind of service customers expect at the store and by what the competitors are doing.

Most supermarkets and discount houses do not offer delivery service so that they can maintain low prices. With increasing delivery costs, some retailers are trying to reduce the delivery of small items by encouraging customers to take small packages with them. Many stores have adopted a policy of charging fees for delivering merchandise priced under $10, for COD orders, or for delivering outside a certain area. Some suburban stores that have to compete with shopping centers and downtown stores still deliver merchandise free of charge as part of their sales promotion strategy.

Retailers have formed many systems and practices to provide efficient delivery service at a lower cost. The types of delivery most commonly used are (1) individually owned and operated services, (2) consolidated delivery, and (3) the U.S. Postal Service.

Individually Operated Systems

In an individually operated delivery system, the store operates its own service. Some stores own their own cars or trucks; others rent them from a trucking firm.

Stores that rent their equipment can also obtain extra vehicles when they are needed during heavy selling periods such as Christmas.

There are two important advantages to a privately operated delivery system. First, a store can display its name on its trucks for advertising purposes. Second, the store can carefully select its own delivery staff and employ people who will represent the store effectively. Courteous, helpful delivery people can help reduce the number of customer complaints and can also report any customer dissatisfactions. Another advantage, particularly to a small store, is that the person who does the delivery work usually performs other duties around the store when not making deliveries.

The most obvious disadvantage of an individually operated delivery system is the cost. The store must bear the expense of hiring, training, and supervising the drivers. It must also pay for equipment which, because the number of packages varies from day to day, may stand idle part of the time.

Consolidated Services

A **consolidated delivery service** is a private business that delivers parcels for a group of local merchants for a fee. Examples of this type of firm are the United Parcel Service (UPS) and Emory Air Freight.

This type of service has several important advantages. It eliminates duplicate routes and thus reduces mileage costs. The store does not have to invest in equipment. And the services usually have trained personnel who are courteous and efficient.

But such a system also has certain drawbacks. The store loses direct contact with customers and usually finds it difficult to discover and settle delivery complaints. It has little control over delivery

Businesses that have individually operated delivery systems can use their trucks for advertising purposes. Jane Hamilton-Merritt

schedules. And it can't use trucks for advertising purposes.

U.S. Postal Service

Some retailers send packages via the U.S. Postal Service to customers who live outside the store's delivery area. Stores may choose between two ways of mailing packages. They may mail first class, which is also called **priority mail** when the package weighs over 1 pound. Or they can mail fourth class, which is also called **parcel post.** Priority mail is more expensive than parcel post, but it's faster.

A small store may use the mail even for local deliveries. And mail-order firms depend almost entirely on the U.S. Postal Service.

Is the salesperson's responsibility ended when the sale has been recorded, the merchandise wrapped, and the customer has taken it home or had it delivered? Not always. Sometimes customers change their minds and return their purchases to the store. In Chapter 30, you'll learn how to handle returns and adjustments.

Trade Talk

Define each term and use it in a sentence.

Consolidated delivery service
Multiple packaging
Packaging
Parcel post
Priority mail
Wrapping

Can You Answer These?

1. What are some questions that manufacturers ask themselves when they are evaluating possible packages for their products?
2. What are the advantages and disadvantages of each type of wrapping system?
3. What are the five general practices to observe when wrapping packages?
4. What are the advantages and disadvantages of offering delivery service?
5. Name the basic types of delivery systems. What kinds of stores might profitably use each type?

Problems

1. Rule a form similar to the following. In the left column, write the letter of each of the following products: (a) breakfast cereal, (b) bar soap, (c) chewing gum, (d) toothpaste, and (e) candy bar. In the center column, list one brand name that comes to mind when you think of each of the products. Then, in the right column, indicate whether or not you can readily recall what the package for that product looks like. (Do you remember the size, shape, and color of the package?)

Product	Brand	Do You Recall Package?	
		Yes	No

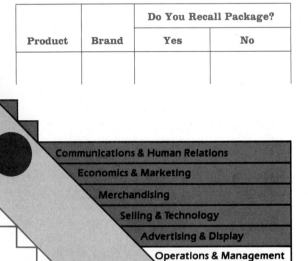

Returns and Adjustments

CHAPTER 30

Communications & Human Relations
Economics & Marketing
Merchandising
Selling & Technology
Advertising & Display
Operations & Management

As Michael Reilly turned the key in the front door, he heard the sound of the stereo. "Jenny, I didn't expect to find you home so soon. I thought you were going to Brighton's after work to exchange that blender your brother gave us." Michael draped his jacket over the nearest chair and walked into the kitchen where his wife Jennifer was opening a large box.

"I couldn't believe it, Mike. I did go right after work and they didn't give me any hassle at all. Here's the new blender. And this one works. They even tried it for me in the store."

Jennifer continued to unpack and set up the new blender as she talked. "You know, while I was at Brighton's I saw an automatic coffee maker we should think about getting. It's on sale this week."

"I thought you didn't like to go all the way over to Brighton's to shop," said Mike as he inspected the new blender.

"I've changed my mind. They were so nice about exchanging the blender that I think I'll start shopping there. It's not too far away."

Brighton's Department Store has just gained two new customers because the store has a policy that makes it possible for customers to return merchandise without a great deal of difficulty. Most retailers believe that the cost of allowing a reasonable amount of returns is a good investment. There is "profit" in settling complaints properly and building customer goodwill. Customers telling their friends about the pleasant treatment they received at a store is actually word-of-mouth-advertising.

If you talked to a number of retailers, you would find that policies on merchandise returns and adjustments vary widely. Some stores are quite liberal regarding complaints and returned merchandise. They make adjustments quickly and without asking any questions. Such practices stem from a belief that a liberal policy builds customer goodwill. As a result, some large department stores have as much as 20 percent of their merchandise returned, and they may have refunds or credits equal to more than 10 percent of their sales. At the other extreme are stores that have eliminated adjustment services

to keep prices low. Some of these stores have a no-return policy because they carry merchandise with a manufacturer's guarantee. They expect customers to settle any complaint directly with the manufacturer.

No matter what type of return and adjustment policy a store has, it can profit from listening to customer complaints. The reasons customers give for returns can provide valuable clues to ways of improving store operations.

Reasons for Returns and Adjustments

A **merchandise return** is an item brought back by a customer to the seller because it is not wanted or is in some way not satisfactory. The customer is seeking some sort of **adjustment,** which is a settlement of a customer's complaint about an item. There are four major reasons besides the product itself for customer complaints and returns: store personnel, the customers themselves, the manufacturer, and store policy. Gift exchanges, while not actually complaints, are also a source of returned goods.

Store Personnel

Poor selling on the part of salespeople is the largest contributor to returns. Salespeople often neglect to find out what customers really need before selling them a product. If customers buy merchandise that doesn't satisfy their needs, they will probably return it.

Some salespeople do not take time to learn about the merchandise they are selling. And if they do not understand the merchandise, they may misrepresent it to customers unknowingly. This can also result in returns. And sometimes, salespeople who do know their merchandise well do not take time to explain it to customers. This often leads to returns because customers do not know how to use the merchandise or how to take proper care of it.

Other salespeople tend to pressure customers, either knowingly or unknowingly. If these customers later realize that they do not really want the merchandise, they return it. This is another important reason salespeople should never sell customers more than they want or need.

Sometimes, salespeople make errors in filling out sales checks. This is particularly true when a customer orders merchandise that has to be shipped out of reserve stock from a sales check made out

Pressuring customers to buy something they do not really want may lead to returns. Philip Teuscher

on the selling floor. Complete information about the merchandise being ordered is essential. Correct delivery information is also very important.

Other store personnel may also be responsible for complaints and returns. Careless or improper wrapping can result in damaged merchandise, incomplete shipments, or lost sales checks. Errors in billing or crediting accounts may occur, which results in customers being overcharged or not credited with payments. Delivery personnel may also be the cause complaints by not staying on schedule, by mishandling merchandise, or by confusing parcels or payments.

Customers

The oversights or mistakes of customers are another cause of returns. At times, customers select unsuitable sizes, colors, or models—even though the salesperson may have advised them to do otherwise. And occasionally, customers buy merchandise in a hurry and don't realize that they've made a mistake until they examine the merchandise at home. They may buy on impulse and later realize that they have made the wrong decision. In some cases, customers simply change their minds. And in a few cases, their intention is only to "borrow" the merchandise for a special occasion, like a party.

Manufacturers

Manufacturers may also be responsible for the return of merchandise. Some items shrink, fade, spoil, or break down under ordinary use. When this happens, the fault may lie with the materials they are made of or with the manufacturing process itself. Most often, stores accept the returns from customers and then send the unsatisfactory items back to the manufacturer.

Store Policies

It is probably obvious that stores with more liberal policies regarding returns and exchanges can expect to receive more

UNIT 10 ♦ *Keeping Track of Merchandise*

returns and complaints. However, these liberal policies can often result in increased sales.

Some stores regularly sell merchandise to customers on approval. An **approval sale** is a cash or charge transaction made with the understanding that the customer can try out the merchandise and return it for a full cash or credit refund if it is not satisfactory.

If a retailer allows a high volume of selling on approval, a large number of returns can result. Nevertheless, some merchandise is best sold if the customer can take it home and try it. The retailer must decide what kinds of goods the store will sell on approval and should make the policy clear to all customers and salespeople.

Retailers must also expect some returns of COD sales because customers often change their minds after seeing the merchandise in their homes. Some retailers add an additional charge on COD orders so that the customer will think twice before placing such orders.

Another store policy that can lead to adjustments is known as a **price guarantee**. This is a promise that a store will not be undersold. For example, one chain of pharmacies advertises a national guarantee of prices on prescriptions. This means that if a customer purchases a prescription anywhere in the United States and pays less for it than the store charges, the store will refund the difference. This refund comes in the form of a merchandise certificate mailed to the customer from the store's national headquarters.

Types of Adjustments

The methods that retailers use to handle adjustments vary widely, depending on the type and size of business. Regardless of the method followed, retailers usually agree that, in most cases, the customer must be satisfied. The four kinds of adjustments that retailers make most often are (1) cash refunds, (2) exchanges, (3) credit refunds, and (4) partial allowances on

the original price. Gift exchanges are an additional type of adjustment.

Cash Refunds

Most stores prefer to avoid giving cash refunds if they possibly can. The major reason for their reluctance is to discourage potential shoplifters. They do not want to make it easy for shoplifters to exchange their stolen merchandise for cash.

Another reason why stores are reluctant to issue cash refunds is that customers who receive cash will probably spend it elsewhere. But if customers receive credit or other merchandise in exchange, the store hasn't lost a sale.

Many stores now require customers to have a receipt or proper identification to get an immediate cash refund. If the customer doesn't have either, the store may issue a check by mail a week later. This delay satisfies legitimate customers but discourages shoplifters who are trying to exchange stolen goods for instant cash. As a further means of control, many stores require their salespeople to get a supervisor's signature before they issue cash refunds over $50.

Exchanges

Sometimes customers want to return an article and select another. If the price of both articles is the same, it's an **even exchange.** In some stores the salesperson may make this exchange without issuing a new sales check. In other stores, the exchange must be approved by a floor manager or some other authorized person, and a new sales check must be written.

When the price of the returned article and that of the exchange are not the same, the transaction is called an **uneven exchange.** When the price of the goods returned is less than that of the new goods given in exchange, usually a new sales check must be written. On the new sales check, the price of the returned merchandise is deducted from the price of the new merchandise. If the new merchandise costs less than the returned goods, a refund

Many stores choose not to give cash refunds. Richard Megna/Fundamental Photographs

must be made and a new sales check must be written for the new merchandise. The approval of a supervisor is usually needed in an uneven exchange.

Credit Refunds

When customers making a return have a charge account with the store, the full cost or a set percentage of the cost of the merchandise returned (allowance) may be credited to that customer account. Another way stores can give customers credit for returned merchandise without giving them a cash refund is to present them with a due bill. This is also known as a merchandise certificate or script coupon, and in some stores it's called "play money." Customers can use a **due bill** instead of cash for the purchase of other merchandise from the store.

Partial Allowances on the Original Price

Some stores offer customers a partial price allowance on items they return. Usually, stores do this when they feel that the customer's reasons for returning an item are not good enough for a total refund. Such instances would, for example, include returning items that have been used and returning items a long time after their purchase. Some stores also offer a form of price allowance if an item is returned because of a manufacturing fault. The amount of the allowance granted may depend on the length of time the item has been in use. This is often the case with clothing and utensil returns. Or the amount of the allowance may depend on the degree of use to which the item has been subjected, as is the case with tires. The date of purchase is very useful information in determining how large an allowance should be granted. This is so because the customer almost always thinks that the time elapsed is a great deal less than is actually the case.

Stores that offer partial allowances must make sure that customers know about them. Customers often think that the item they are returning has hardly been used and can easily be resold. So when the store offers them what they see as only a fraction of item's worth, they may feel insulted.

Stores may suffer a substantial loss if the returned article looks shopworn, doesn't have its original package, is no longer carried in stock by the store, or is missing some parts or accessories. If stores accept these goods as returns, they must sell them at a loss or throw them away.

Gift Exchanges

Customers return gifts throughout the year, but the largest volume of gift returns occurs right after Christmas. Some stores even advertise their willingness to accept returns and make exchanges in the few days right after Christmas. A few stores are even willing to exchange gifts purchased in other stores. Doubleday, a book chain, has this policy.

Most stores won't give cash refunds for gifts. There are three reasons for this. First, through cash refunds of gifts the store may lose potential customers. If cash is immediately refunded, the customer won't have the opportunity to become acquainted with the store's merchandise or services.

Second, the giver didn't intend a cash gift. If the giver had wanted to give cash, he or she would have done so in the first place, and it might have been an amount different from the cost of the gift.

Third, the store wants to influence old customers and attract new customers. There is an opportunity to interest the customer in exchanging the gift for better-grade merchandise or for additional purchases. The "buying climate" is favorable because the merchandise being returned costs the customer nothing. If these customers are treated tactfully and pleasantly, some of them who had not been familiar with the store before will return as regular customers.

Adjustment Policies and Procedures

A store's adjustment policies and procedures have one major purpose—to satisfy the customer. These policies and procedures are guided by the fact that 95 out of every 100 customers returning merchandise to a store think they are right. Stores cannot afford to lose customers over issues in which the customers feel they are right.

Many retailers feel that it's better to be generous than to drive away the trade. When dealt with properly, most people try to be fair. Often, customers will propose solutions to their complaints that are more moderate than the salesperson would have proposed. In the interest of satisfying the customer, some stores make an adjustment even when the store is not at fault. This type of adjustment is called a **policy adjustment.**

Procedures for Handling Adjustments

In a small store, the owner or manager usually takes care of returns or other adjustments. Simple cases are usually handled on the sales floor. More difficult situations are handled privately. In large stores, adjustments are sometimes handled on the sales floor and sometimes in a separate department called the **adjustment department** or customer service.

In many stores, simple exchanges of merchandise are made by salespeople on the sales floor. Some stores feel that an adjustment can be made promptly and satisfactorily on the selling floor becuase being on the selling floor makes it easier to encourage customers to buy other merchandise. Procedures may vary as to which types of exchanges can be made by part-time salespeople and which types can be made by experienced regulars. In addition, the types of transactions requiring authorizations may also vary from store to store.

The adjustment department in a large store is a centralized complaint or customer service department. Personnel in this department must understand customers and have tact and patience. They have the authority to maintain a liberal

Employees in the adjustment department must be understanding and patient. Art Zollo/Fundamental Photographs

return and adjustment policy. The adjustment department also maintains records of the adjustments that are processed. This department prepares regular reports for management on merchandise returns and customers who habitually return and complain about merchandise and about store service.

Policies for Reducing Returns

Retailers can often reduce the number of returns made in their stores by setting a policy that places reasonable restrictions on returns caused by the customers themselves. Some of these policies are as follows:

♦ Stating a time limit after purchase when returns may be made
♦ Requiring proof of purchase, such as a sales receipt or register tape
♦ Not permitting return of some types of goods that cannot be resold after wear or use

♦ Eliminating cash refunds and permitting only exchanges

Retailers can also help to reduce returns if their advertisements inform customers of how much returns cost the store. This cost must be passed on to the customers. Salespeople should also be instructed to remind customers of the store's return policies when they are making sales.

Procedures for Satisfying the Customer

A store's policy governs the way in which a return is settled. The store doesn't want to lose money, nor does it want to lose the customer. But it is difficult to reach an acceptable agreement if the customer is angry or upset. Some methods that retail workers use to maintain a pleasant relationship with customers while settling disputes follow.

- *Place the customer in a good frame of mind.* The first step is to get complaining customers in a good frame of mind so that they will be capable of reasoning calmly and sensibly. If possible, customers should be invited to sit with the adjuster and should be given all the time they want to explain their point of view. One rule of thumb to follow is "Let the customers fully express their feelings before you say anything at all."
- *Never argue.* Do not blame customers or argue with them. Assure them that you will try to make adjustments, thus demonstrating that you recognize their rights and opinions. Usually, when customers see that the retailer is trying to be fair, they try to be fair as well.
- *Abide by policies and follow recommended procedures.* Customer complaints can be handled satisfactorily only if definite policies concerning the complaints are laid down. It's also important that all employees who are involved in handling complaints be kept fully informed of the policies. These policies will be controlled by the firm's basic attitude toward complaints. Established policies and procedures in serving customers with complaints help to assure customers of consistent and equal treatment.
- *Always consider each customer's feelings.* When customers have legitimate complaints, the store is obligated to correct each problem and should be glad to do so. But even when complaints are not justified, the store, in order to protect its reputation, must consider each customer's feelings and act accordingly. In both situations, customers should be satisfied that the firm is interested in serving them personally. As a result, they may become "boosters" for the store and recommend it to their friends, who may become good customers too.

Many salespeople fear handling a return. But the professionals realize that if handled in the right way, each return can (1) increase the size of the sale, (2) create additional sales, (3) help develop steady customers for the store, and (4) increase the number of customers who prefer to deal with the salesperson personally.

Reducing the number of returns is only one good way to save money for the store. Another effective way is by reducing employee theft. In Chapter 31, you will learn about dishonest employees and how to minimize the losses caused by them.

Trade Talk

Define each term and use it in a sentence.

Adjustment	Even exchange
Adjustment department	Merchandise return
	Policy adjustment
Approval sale	Price guarantee
Due bill	Uneven exchange

Can You Answer These?

1. What are the four major reasons for customer complaints and returns?
2. Why do retailers prefer not to give cash refunds?
3. How can retailers reduce the number of returns made by customers?
4. What are four procedures for satisfying the customer who is returning merchandise?
5. Professional salespeople realize that if it is handled in the right way, each return can be turned into an opportunity. Explain.

Problems

1. The following are some situations that could arise over the sale of jeans priced at $20.95: (*a*) customer returns jeans, selects $12.95 shirt, and asks for $8 refund; (*b*) customer has worn jeans, which were purchased on charge account, and wishes to return them for credit; (*c*) customer claims jeans were defective and wishes to have them replaced with jeans of same type and price; (*d*) customer returns jeans and selects jacket priced at $38.95;

(e) customer returns jeans and asks for due bill; and (f) jeans were given as gift, and recipient wants full cash refund.

Rank each of these claims on a scale from 1 through 6 in the order in which you feel the store would receive the greatest benefit. The most beneficial action to be taken should be ranked 1, the second choice 2, and so on down to 6, which would be the least beneficial action. On a separate sheet of paper, write the letter of each action and after it the number you assign to that action.

2. The following is a list of typical customer complaints: (a) "I bought these cherries yesterday. When I got home, I discovered that most of them were spoiled." (b) "I'm getting tired of bringing this car back. I still have the same oil leak." (c) "I received this chair as a gift, and it just does not fit in with my other furniture and color scheme." (d) "I bought this electric drill for heavy-duty use. It burned out the first time I used it to drill a steel plate." (e) "The salesperson told me this large handbag was sturdy and would hold a lot. Look, this strap broke the first time I used it." On a separate sheet of paper, write the letter of each statement and after it note what you would actually say to the customer who made the complaint in each case. Your statements should be specific and realistic.

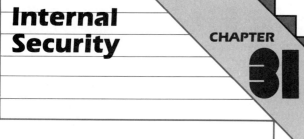

Internal Security

CHAPTER 31

Communications & Human Relations
Economics & Marketing
Merchandising
Selling & Technology
Advertising & Display
Operations & Management

As Linda Durand was leaving for her lunch break from her job as a salesperson in the cosmetics department, she picked up her purse and slipped a $10 bottle of perfume into it. "After all," she thought, "this is a big department store; they can afford it."

Linda went to a nearby fast-food restaurant where her good friend Tom Jansen worked. When she ordered her food, Tom charged her for a regular $1.50 burger instead of the $2 superburger she received. With a knowing smile, she thanked him. After all, he had just "saved" her 50 cents.

When Linda returned to the store, she stopped in the jewelry department to buy earrings. With tax, the bill was $3.12. Linda had the exact change. The salesperson, Jenny Snyder, rang up only $2.12 on the cash register. Later, Jenny intended to take the $1 "underring" out of the register and pocket it. She felt that the store owed it to her because she was being underpaid and treated unfairly by her supervisor.

Linda hurried back to her department. She was already almost 20 minutes late, but she didn't have to worry because she had asked a friend to punch her time card.

Linda, Tom, Jenny, and Linda's friend who punched her time card are all, of course, dishonest employees. And they are all cutting into their employers' profits.

Losses Cut Into Profits

Stock shortages and theft by customers, mainly from shoplifting, were covered in

Chapter 21. So you'll remember that this type of loss is called "external theft." Internal theft, you'll recall, results from the dishonesty of employees in terms of merchandise, cash, and time. Losses due to employee dishonesty are of serious concern to retail owners or managers because they cut into profits.

Most employees are honest, but those who aren't can account for losses in the billions. In a recent year, retailers lost $8 billion due to all types of inventory shortages. Although it's difficult for retailers to distinguish between merchandise losses due to external theft and those that result from internal theft, it is estimated that over half of all merchandise shortages are related to employee theft.

While the exact amount of loss varies depending upon the type of store and the department within it, the amount of loss from internal theft is about 1 percent of sales. In the retail business, the average net profit is 3 percent, or 3 cents of every dollar of merchandise sold. In other words, the store would make a net of $9 on sales of $300. But if an article costing $10 were stolen, that $9 profit would be more than wiped out.

Employee dishonesty regarding merchandise, cash, and time are discussed in the pages that follow.

Theft of Merchandise

Theft of merchandise may range from the simple pocketing of an item to larger-scale stealing concealed by accounting manipulations. The most common types of theft by retail employees include:

♦ Taking merchandise from the store
♦ Passing out merchandise to accomplices
♦ Conspiring with employees in other departments—such as the warehouse, stock-

Most employees are honest and want to help their employers prevent both internal and external theft. *Courtesy of Thalhimers, Richmond, Virginia*

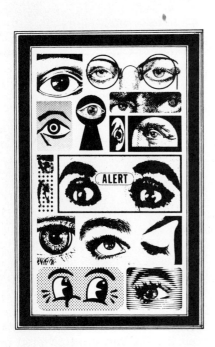

room, dock, and other nonselling areas—
to remove goods

♦ Giving discounts to friends or other unauthorized people
♦ Giving unauthorized markdowns to themselves or others
♦ Writing a fake sales slip and picking up merchandise on the receiving dock
♦ Smuggling goods out of the store in trash or refuse
♦ Eating food without paying for it
♦ Switching the price ticket of lower-priced merchandise to a higher-priced item before purchasing it
♦ Taking supplies and equipment, such as a wrench or a roll of tape

Theft of Cash

Cash in a retail business is handled by salespeople, cashiers, bookkeepers, and credit department personnel. There are many opportunities for dishonest employees to steal. Dishonest employees usually steal cash by doing the following:

♦ *Making an underring.* An **underring** occurs when a cashier rings up the merchandise for an amount less than the price and later pockets the cash given by the customer.
♦ *Ringing a no-sale.* A **no-sale** occurs when a cashier voids the sale after the customer has left and pockets the cash given by the customer.
♦ *Overcharging.* Overcharging the customer means charging more than the regular price or charging regular prices for sales merchandise so that the cash overages can be taken.
♦ *Making false entries or setting up false credit accounts.* Such errors in the store's records and books serve to conceal thefts.
♦ *Making improper refunds.* Giving refunds to accomplices or recording ficticious refund slips.
♦ *Taking cash.* Cash can be taken from the cash register or from petty cash.
♦ *Falsifying payroll records.* Pay rates and number of hours worked can be faked.

Theft of Time

The misuse of time by employees can be as costly to a business as is the theft of merchandise or cash. Suppose that an employee's hourly rate is $3.50 and the employee is 5 minutes late each morning as well as after rest and lunch breaks. The resulting loss would total over $200 for just one year. Other examples of the misuse of time include (1) excessive absenteeism; (2) fraudulant claims for worker's compensation, which is payment received for job-related illnesses or accidents; and (3) punching time cards or signing out for other employees.

Why Employees Are Dishonest

Employees have many motives for being dishonest. Sometimes they steal for no other reason than that they are unable to resist the wide-open opportunity given them by a trusting manager.

At other times, employee morale is a factor. As a rule, losses go down when morale is high and increase when morale is low. For example, stealing may be the employee's method of correcting what he or she regards as a pay injustice. The employee makes up for the difference between what the pay is and what he or she thinks the pay should be by stealing in some way.

Employees may also steal because they don't have a clear understanding of what theft really is. For instance, employees may not consider that they're stealing when they do such things as stamping a parking validation, taking supplies for personal use, or using time for personal business.

Employees often don't fully understand the difference between gross profit and net profit. They may believe, for example, that since an item that has a selling price of $1 and only cost the business 60 cents, the profit is 40 cents. But that 40 cents is the gross profit. The net profit, which is

Always punch your own time card; in many firms, punching someone else's time card is cause for dismissal. Jim Anderson

the profit after all expenses are paid, is only 2 or 3 cents. Employees who misunderstand this may be led to believe that the business is making much more money than is actually the case, and they then think that the business can well afford a minor loss.

Some employees steal to help themselves through some financial emergency, regarding their theft as a temporary measure. The chances are, though, that this temporary thing will become a regular one once employees get into the habit of stealing; and they often come to think that they can't do without the extra cash even after the financial emergency has passed.

Loss Prevention Techniques

A loss prevention program by a firm includes all security measures taken by management to discourage and prevent employee dishonesty. In a large business, this security function is likely to be carried out by the owner or manager. But it's important that each employee in a supervisory capacity be trained in internal security systems.

It's especially important for small businesses to have an effective loss-prevention program. They suffer more than three times the stock and cash losses of larger businesses, and are much less able to absorb these losses.

Retailers have found that the best way to control internal loss is to eliminate the opportunity for employee dishonesty. Four simple guidelines they use are to:

1. Watch for signals indicating employee theft
2. Set up and follow routine security measures
3. Build positive employer-employee relations
4. Take action in every case of employee dishonesty

Watch for Signals Indicating Employee Theft

There is no such thing as a typical dishonest employee. In fact, the dishonest person is often the person least likely to be suspected. But an alert manager will be aware of the following signals or characteristics of employees who may become thieves.

♦ Employees who have financial problems
♦ Employees who have spending habits that could not be covered by their earnings alone—for example, expensive clothes, gambling, or an expensive hobby
♦ Employees who arrive early or stay late when there is no need
♦ Employees who are unhappy, dislike the boss or company, and complain about being underpaid or overworked
♦ Employees who place merchandise or materials in unusual places, such as near exits, close to rest rooms, or in concealed corners
♦ Employees whose cash register records frequently show discrepancies in cash funds
♦ Employees who make many alterations in inventory records, void slips, refund receipts, and other documents

Follow Routine Security Measures

To make sure that their loss prevention program is effective, retailers follow these routine security measures:

1. Keep good records.
2. Permit no employee to make sales to themselves.
3. Require all employee purchases to be checked.
4. Restrict all employees to a single exit, if possible.
5. Use care in allowing employees free access to stockrooms and service areas.
6. Have a good system of controls in nonselling areas such as service areas, stockrooms, and credit departments.
7. Have definite rules for refunds and the voiding of sales tickets.
8. Investigate carefully all inventory and cash shortages when they show up.
9. Make periodic checks of time-card areas at check-in and check-out times.
10. Take regular inventories of all merchandise, supplies, and equipment.
11. Change all locks and combinations when employees who have used them are no longer with the firm.
12. Check the possibility of using an outside firm to "shop" the employees and check them for inefficiency and dishonesty.
13. Use an electronic surveillance system in the receiving area and stockrooms.
14. Pretend a dishonest employee is in every job slot and try to imagine what that person might do to steal. Then set up an effective countermeasure.
15. Have employee entrances and exits monitored at all times by security guards.
16. Control and audit duplicate copies of sales slips for employee charge or layaway purchases to be certain that records of amounts due the store are not destroyed or changed.
17. Check all incoming shipments carefully.
18. Carefully record all orders being delivered.
19. Check the store's trash bins for stolen merchandise periodically. Dishonest employees often hide stolen merchandise in trash bins and pick it up after the store is closed.
20. Have cashiers record on a special form all information about purchases paid for by check.

Some retailers hire outside firms to evaluate employees on their efficiency and honesty. Courtesy of Dale Systems, Inc.

ALCO-DUCKWALL STORES, INC.

GENERAL SERVICE ANALYSIS

FIRM _____ DATE _____ TIME _____ A.M. P.M.

ADDRESS _____ CITY _____ STATE _____

QUAN	SIZE	TYPE OF CONTAINER	BRAND & ITEM	PRICE	DESCRIPTION OF EMPLOYEE			
					SEX	APPR. AGE	HEIGHT	BUILD / HAIR
					Wearing Glasses Yes No	S.P.'s No. or Letter	DEPT.	FLOOR
				TAX	SPECIAL FEATURES			
					PERCENTAGE EVALUATION			%
				TOTAL	# OF CHECKSTANDS OPERATING			

		YES	NO
10%	Was employee wearing a badge?	____	____
5%	Was employee well groomed?	____	____
10%	Did employee greet customer?	____	____
10%	Did employee call prices audibly?	____	____
5%	Did employee correctly charge prices?	____	____
5%	Did employee charge correct amount of tax?	____	____
5%	Was cash register drawer closed until money tendered?	____	____
5%	Did employee call amount tendered?	____	____
5%	Did employee count back customer's change?	____	____
10%	Did employee issue customer a receipt?	____	____
10%	Did employee thank customer?	____	____
5%	Did employee bag items properly?	____	____
5%	Did employee perform work quickly?	____	____
5%	Did employee have a pleasant attitude?	____	____
5%	Did employee give complete attention to customer?	____	____

REMARKS _____

_____

_____

_____

_____

_____

_____

21. Have cashiers clip the price ticket so that the store half of the ticket falls into a locked box which cashiers take with them when they change shifts.

Build Positive Employer-Employee Relations

A sense of honesty and loyalty to the firm in all employees helps to prevent employee theft. Many managers are reluctant to tackle internal security problems because they are afraid of bad publicity. Some feel it would cause poor employee relations. But honest employees will not be outraged by efforts to curb dishonesty. An alert manager will have definite personnel policies, such as:

♦ Screening new employees carefully and insisting on references that can be checked
♦ Informing all prospective employees of an active internal loss prevention program
♦ Establishing a program to show that management views dishonesty as both immoral and illegal
♦ Urging employees to be alert for illegal activity and to report it to management, perhaps through a "secret witness" program

Take Action in Every Case

When managers discover dishonest employees, they should deal with the situation swiftly and very visibly. Managers should take this action to discourage other employees from similar actions. Most businesses have a fixed course of action to be followed, which might include:

1. Having fixed policies about discipline for dishonesty.
2. Apprehending suspects in strict accordance with the law—the police department may be of assistance.
3. Terminating employment and proceeding with prosecution of the employee.

Crime consists of three basic elements: a criminal, a victim, and an opportunity. With internal loss in business, the criminal is a dishonest employee, the victim is the business, and the opportunity is as large as the owner or manager will permit.

Now that you've completed this unit, you should understand that keeping track of the merchandise is an important retailing task. It involves the many procedures that retail workers must follow in recording sales; in packaging, wrapping, and delivering products; and in return and adjustment policies and procedures it also involves an awareness of internal store security, which you read about in this chapter.

Trade Talk

Define each term and use it in a sentence.
No-sale
Underring

Can You Answer These?

1. Is internal theft a real problem for retailers?
2. What are the three types of losses caused by internal theft?
3. Describe the different ways by which employees can steal merchandise.
4. What are some of the common types of cash thefts?
5. What are some of the common ways employees misuse time?

Problems

1. List at least eight measures a manager can take to help minimize internal theft.
2. Imagine that you are a retailer employing, say, 100 people; outline the techinques you would use to reduce internal theft. You may want to rule a form similar to the following. In the left column, list the following types of internal theft: merchandise, cash, time. In the right column, outline the procedures you would use.

Types of Internal Theft	Techniques to Minimize Internal Losses

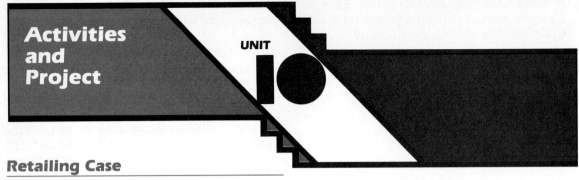

Retailing Case

You are a salesperson at Town and Country Fashions, where you have worked for about 6 months. Dawn Moulin joined the company the same week you did and has been working as a salesperson in another department. You have been casual friends with her since you both started at Town and Country, and you occasionally have lunch together.

This morning you were both reassigned to work in the new ski and skate shop that has just opened. In this new department, you and Dawn are sharing a cash register. When you rang up your first sale this morning, you noticed that the register had been left unlocked. When the cash drawer came open so you could make change, you noticed that all the paper money and coins were mixed up. There were $5 bills in with the $10 bills, and upside-down $20 bills were among the $1 bills. The coins were as mixed up as the paper bills. You took time to organize the cash drawer after your customer left the department, but the next time you rang a sale, the cash drawer was disorganized again.

About an hour later you saw Dawn make a mistake on the register. Instead of voiding the incorrect sales slip, she crumpled it up and threw it away.

It is now 11:30 a.m. and for the first time all morning there are no customers in the ski and skate shop. This is your chance to talk with Dawn about her use of the cash register.

On a separate sheet of paper, write exactly what you will say to Dawn. While you are talking with her, it would be a good idea to remind her about both the general rules for using a cash register and the usual procedures for protecting money against theft. But remember, she is a coworker and friend. You are not her supervisor.

Working with People

Cheryl Rodriguez is a full-time employee in the stationery and book department of Linden's Department Store. She works with Jared Friedman, who came to Linden's about a month ago. He is friendly and seems to be a good salesperson. However, for the last three weeks Cheryl has noticed that Jared has been staying alone in the department for a few minutes each evening after the rest of the employees have left the department.

Last week, as she was leaving, Cheryl noticed Jared slipping an expensive pen set into his pocket. A few days later she noticed him placing a calculator into his lunch bag under the cash register. And yesterday she saw him slip a book into a friend's shopping bag without ringing up a sale.

The store has a security department, but so far they haven't seemed to notice Jared's activities. Cheryl is having difficulty deciding what to do about the activities she has observed. She doesn't want to get Jared into trouble and have him lose his job, but she believes that what he is doing is wrong. She is also concerned that when the department's inventory shortage is finally discovered, it could make her look dishonest as well as Jared.

1. Identify the true problem.
2. What are the important facts to be considered in this problem?
3. List several possible solutions to this problem.
4. Evaluate the possible results of each solution.
5. Which solution do you recommend? Why?

Project 10: Surveying Policies for Returns and Adjustments

Project Goal
Given a survey form, interview managers or experienced employees from five stores to determine their policies on returns and adjustments. Then compile the results and analyze them.

Procedure
1. Select five stores from your community.
2. Using the following survey questions, interview the manager or an experienced employee from each of the stores. (It is a good idea to use a separate sheet of paper in recording the answers for each of the five stores. You can use one neatly printed or typed master question sheet.)

a. Who handles customer complaints and adjustments in your store?
b. Does your store give cash refunds? What documents must the customer have to get a cash refund?
c. If a customer returns merchandise that has manufacturing faults, do you take it back or have the customer deal directly with the manufacturer?
d. Does the store ever give refunds or credit when the store is clearly not at fault?
e. Do some customers try to abuse your policies for returns and adjustments? If yes, please give a few specific examples. What do you do when this happens?
f. What steps does your store take to reduce returns and adjustments?

3. Use a blank sheet of paper to compile your answers. Then prepare a brief report comparing your findings from the five interviews. List additional suggestions for reducing returns and adjustments if you can think of any that are not being used by these stores. Is there any evidence that a more generous policy of returns and adjustments builds customer goodwill?

Evaluation
You will be evaluated on the completeness of your survey and the reasons you give in your report.

BECOMING A MASTER EMPLOYEE

One day I was rapping with the other guys on the swimming team, and they began to gripe about their part-time jobs. I got to thinking about my job—and you know, I realized I've got a pretty good deal. I know a lot about the retail sporting goods business now and am really getting into it more every day. In fact, I can actually see a career goal for myself.

My marketing and distributive education teacher helped me chart some of the steps upward so I could plan a way of getting ahead. Retailing is for me! As the teacher said, it fits my "lifestyle" and makes the most of my abilities and interests—especially my love for sports and my ability to work with people.

One specialty I learned on the job was to help customers get the best tennis rackets for their skill level and budget! In school I learned a lot more—about better selling, about using displays, and about what makes people buy. Calculating prices and learning about credit policies were tough, but I managed. I also learned some ways to get along better with my supervisor. Things began to look really good.

Remember when I wasn't keen on retailing? Well, I've changed my mind.

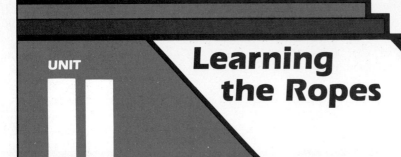

Company Policies and Employees

CHAPTER
32

Communications & Human Relations

Economics & Marketing

Merchandising

Selling & Technology

Advertising & Display

Operations & Management

If you had been employed by Carson, Pirie, Scott & Co. in Chicago in 1856, you would have been expected to follow the company rules shown here.

Rules to Employees

1. Store must be open from 6:00 a.m. to 9:00 p.m.
2. Store must be swept, counters and base shelves dusted, lamps trimmed and filled and chimneys cleaned, a pail of water, also a bucket of coal brought in before breakfast, and attend to customers who will call.
3. Store must not be open on the Sabbath Day unless necessary and then only a few minutes.
4. The employee who is in the habit of smoking Spanish cigars, being shaved at the barber shop, going to dances and other places of amusement, will surely give his employer reason to be suspicious of his honesty and integrity.
5. Each employee must not pay less than $5.00 per year to the church and must attend Sunday School regularly.
6. Men employees are given one evening a week for courting and two if they go to prayer meeting.
7. After 14 hours of work in the store, the leisure time should be spent mostly in reading.

Signed: THE MANAGEMENT

Of course, company rules in retailing are not as strict today as they were in 1856, but rules do exist in every retail firm and all too often employees don't know about them. To help keep employees and customers out of trouble and prevent misunderstandings, retailers must have rules.

Rules that guide employees in making decisions are known as **company policies**. Policies give direction to the activities of a retail firm. For example, retailers may decide to give cash refunds on items returned by customers because they feel that this policy increases goodwill and, in the end, profits. Good company policies are designed to build goodwill between a business and its customers, employees, suppliers, competitors, and surrounding community.

It's easier to work in a retailing firm where everybody knows and follows company policies. Company policies help do the following:

1. Reduce confusion and disagreement among employees
2. Maintain high employee morale
3. Keep employees from having to make decisions that may be difficult to defend
4. Ensure that appropriate action is taken when the need arises

Company policies, then, provide the entire staff with basic guidelines for making decisions. Most important, though, company policies help ensure that every employee treats customers in the same fair manner in every situation.

Retail Policies

People know you by your reputation. Your friends know that they can depend on you to do certain things in certain ways. Similarly, consumers want to be able to rely on the stores with which they do business. As you've just read, one way retailers are able to achieve this is by developing company or store policies.

If you work in a business owned by one person, you'll usually find that there are no *written* policies. In such a business, the owner-manager is able to discuss procedures with you and all new employees to make sure everybody acts in the same way. But in a larger store (one in which the owner cannot personally supervise

Some stores establish and enforce store policies for all members of the sales staff. *Courtesy of Carson Pirie Scott & Co.*

A Checklist of Actions and Attitudes For Selling Associates

STORE POLICY

. . . enables all Associates to work together in making our Company profitable and pleasant . . .

— Do I follow the Door Policy?
— Am I careful about being on time and ready to work as scheduled?
— Do I notify my supervisor when I find that I will be absent or late?
— Is my dress and manner confident and business like?
— Do I wear my ID badge visibly at all times I am working in the store?
— Am I always courteous to customers and fellow associates?

— Do I smile and make the customer feel welcome? Do I remember that the customer gives me a job?
— Do I follow all store procedures in completing sales, exchanges and returns?
— Do I observe and help enforce all No Smoking and safety regulations?
— Do I stay alert and notify Security of any suspicious activity in my area?
— Do I allow security personnel to remain anonymous when I see them on the selling floor?
— Do I refrain from discussing Company business in front of customers?

— Do I help new Associates by making them feel welcome and by giving them positive assistance and information?
— Am I following the directions given to me by my supervisors and managers?
— Do I allow customers to enter elevators and escalators ahead of me?
— Do I have proper ID cards when shopping with my discount?
— Do I always get my packages sealed before going to my work area?
— Do I keep all my personal belongings in my locker?

A "YES" answer to all these questions is a "must" for all of us.

each worker) there's a need to communicate thoughts in a more formal way, so you'll usually find that policies will be passed along to you and other employees in both spoken and written form. These policies become the guidelines or rules for the operation of the firm.

Many stores also establish guidelines for achieving the goals of meeting competition and gaining the desired profit. More and more firms are also establishing policies for dealing with routine matters such as what is to be stocked and how much will be charged for each item.

Sometimes policies are changed. A firm may reconsider its policies because of competition, changing customer needs, changing company goals, new laws, or for other reasons.

Learning and Following Policies

Your first few weeks or months on a job are usually a "tryout" or "probationary" period. During this time, you learn to follow the company's policies that apply to your entry-level job. Then, as you progress to the master-employee level, you'll find that there are additional policies and rules to learn. So learning the firm's policies is a never ending task, and it will be to your benefit to develop a system for keeping up to date and following the policies and rules of the firm for which you work.

Learn Essential Policies First

Learning about the company and its policies means becoming thoroughly familiar not only with written rules and regulations but also with the unwritten ones. Make your first objective that of getting in step with the company and its policies. While you're learning, be extra alert to make quite certain what management expects of you. When you have an understanding of this, then concentrate on using more initiative. Policies and procedures

vary from firm to firm. Among the essential policies that you should learn about the business first are:

♦ Hours of work and procedure for checking in and out
♦ When and how you will be paid
♦ Lunch periods, coffee breaks, and leaving job at other times during assigned work hours
♦ Employee discount privileges and how to make purchases
♦ Employee benefits
♦ Dress and other behavior, such as eating, drinking, smoking, or chewing gum
♦ Channels of communication
♦ Requesting a change in your work schedule or hours
♦ Health and safety programs, including what to do in case of an accident
♦ Use of the telephone for personal business
♦ Policy about friends visiting you on the job
♦ Policies for the protection of merchandise and money
♦ How and where to enter and leave the business
♦ Things that you can and cannot make decisions about
♦ Handling shoplifters

You'll usually be able to find this sort of information in an employee manual, fact sheet, or handbook, which will either be given to you when you are hired or on your first day of work. If you don't receive any written or spoken instructions, ask about the various policies.

Let Your Employer Help

Many large retailers have training departments that prepare manuals and teach employees about their policies. Training handbooks often cover both general policy and topics such as cash register procedures and the granting of credit. To make sure that all the staff learns about new procedures, many retailers now conduct training classes for experienced employees as well as for newcomers. Training sessions may include films, demonstra-

Many retailers conduct training classes for their employees. Courtesy of Gino's, Inc.

tions, programmed instruction, television, flip charts, talks, actual practice on the cash register or in selling techniques, and tests.

Following Directions

Research has shown that the two most important things that retailing employees should be able to do are (1) to accept and follow company policies and procedures and (2) to follow directions. Once you've learned the written policies, your next major task is to follow your supervisor's instructions for carrying them out. Supervisors may also give spoken instructions on various policies that are not in writing, such as how to deal with a fire or other emergency situation. Follow these instructions just as carefully as you follow written ones.

You can improve your ability to follow directions by listening, asking questions, and taking notes.

Learn to Be a Good Listener

The Greek philosopher Epictetus observed, "Nature has given to men one tongue but two ears, that we may hear from others twice as much as we speak." What percentage of the time do you listen? Do you learn more while you're talking or listening? Some people enjoy listening; others are bored by it. Those who really enjoy listening usually are the ones who are interested in people. They respect the other person's right to express an opinion. Good listeners are also interested in comparing points of view and in learning from others rather than in defending their own position. And good listeners are patient.

Good listening is good manners; people will think more of you when you listen to them attentively. There is an added bonus in good listening: when you listen well, you encourage others to listen to what you have to say.

Intelligent listening requires a willingness to hear and to understand. You can't understand spoken directions unless you're willing to listen to them. So when you're being given directions, do the following:

- Stop talking. You can't listen if you're talking.
- Put your supervisors at ease by making them feel that they are free to talk.
- Show your supervisors that you want to listen by looking and acting interested.
- Give your supervisors plenty of time; don't interrupt them.
- Don't argue or criticize. This would put your supervisors on the defensive, and you don't want to win the argument at the risk of losing your job.
- Try to see your supervisors' point of view.
- Ask questions to clear up points which you don't understand; don't ask inappropriate questions that would sidetrack your supervisors.
- Control your temper. Try not to get angry; an angry person often misinterprets meaning.

Learn to Ask Questions

As long as you hold your job, you can be sure that you'll make mistakes. Everyone does—and it's often a good way to learn. Don't try to cover up your mistakes. It's much better to admit them and say, "I'm sorry about that. I'll try to do better next time." But be sure you know what caused the mistake so that you don't make it again.

One way to avoid mistakes is to ask questions. Many people on a new job are afraid to ask questions because they think their employers will consider them stupid. But that's not so. Rather, asking about things is a sign that you're interested and thinking. Intelligent people ask a lot of questions, and they listen to the answers.

When you ask questions, ask the right person. Sometimes a coworker may know the answer—but if it's an important question, ask your supervisors. Don't bother your supervisors with constant questions and interruptions, but if a question must be answered right away, ask it. If it

doesn't need immediate attention, save it and keep your eyes and ears open. You may find the answer before you have to ask.

Learn to Take Notes

New workers often get information on the job. For example, there are directions from supervisors, tasks to be completed, and forms to fill in. It's easy to forget some of these facts and instructions.

Instead of trying to memorize all this information, get a pencil and a small notebook that you can keep with you. Write down the things you're supposed to remember. Your supervisors will be pleased to find that they only have to tell you something once. And save those notes! They will be helpful in training the worker who takes your place when you go on to a better job.

Interpreting Policy

Large firms spend a great deal of money to communicate policies to their employees, their customers, and the businesses with which they deal. They use brochures, manuals, meetings, company newspapers and magazines, advertisements, and letters to tell everyone about their policies. Nevertheless, as a member of a retail firm, you have a major share of the responsibility for interpreting policies to the public.

Policies can be carried out successfully only if every employee is aware of them and accepts the responsibility for carrying them out correctly. The more effectively you learn how to carry out company policies, the more valuable you'll be to the company. And this could lead the way to increased responsibilities and larger paychecks.

Courteously explain policies to any customer who questions them. Neither the customer nor your employer will appreciate remarks such as, "Don't ask me, I just work here," or "They don't ask me when they make rules like that." Make sure that your answer shows good judgment.

It's a good idea to take notes when your supervisor explains things. Kip
Peticolas/Fundamental Photographs

Sometimes you'll be faced with a problem for which there is no established policy. If so, it's wiser to report the problem to your supervisor than to make your own decision. For example, in a business with a policy of meeting low prices, salespeople are not expected to lower the price of an article if a customer reports that another business is selling it for less. Instead, the employee reports the claim, and often comparison shoppers are sent to the competing business to verify it.

Businesses that succeed have effective policies to protect their employees and give them guidelines for action. Policies should be welcomed rather than dreaded.

Throughout this book, and as you gain experience in retailing, you'll learn about policies that relate to areas such as credit, merchandising, security, sales, promotion, pricing, service, public relations, personnel, and employment.

In the next chapter, you'll have an opportunity to learn about the person in your company who will be responsible for telling you about many of the company's policies—your supervisor. First you'll be given an idea of what it takes to be a supervisor. (Rate yourself as you read—would the work of a supervisor be for you?) And then you'll be given some ways to help you develop a smooth-working relationship with your supervisor.

Trade Talk

Define this term and use it in a sentence.

Company policies

Can You Answer These?

1. Why do retail firms have policies?
2. Who is responsible for carrying out the policies of the business?
3. Where can you learn about the policies of a retail firm?
4. What are some of the policies you will want to learn about first when you take a job in retailing?
5. What is the first step in becoming a good listener?

Problems

1. Rule a form like the following. Under each category, list three examples of information that all employees should know about the retail business for which they work.

Store Policies	Merchandise Carried	Free Services Offered
Example: Pierced earrings may not be returned.	Men's shoes: One popularly priced and two expensive brands.	Free delivery on items over $5.

2. Rule a form like the following. List five questions about store policies for which you would need the answers in order to effectively carry out the job of salesperson in the shoe department of a large store. Also indicate where or to whom you might go for help in answering each question.

Question	Source of Help
Example: What is the return policy on shoes that have been worn?	Store policy handbook

Working with Your Supervisor

CHAPTER 33

Communications & Human Relations

Economics & Marketing

Merchandising

Selling & Technology

Advertising & Display

Operations & Management

The longer you've been employed, the more you'll realize that just about everyone who works for a living has one or more "bosses." And you'll also realize that almost everyone whom you'd regard as a boss has a boss of his or her own. Even the president of a large corporation has a boss—the board of directors. And, in turn, the board of directors is accountable to the stockholders.

As a retail worker, your boss may be a supervisor, department head, manager, buyer, or owner. And as an entry-level employee, you must recognize right from the beginning that you will be supervised. But if you're wise, you'll welcome supervision simply because you'll learn from it.

Employees who respect and get along well with their supervisors are usually happier on the job. One way to get along with your supervisor is by remembering that your supervisor's attitude toward you is usually a reflection of your attitude toward him or her. Of course, you'll find that some supervisors perform certain duties more skillfully than they do others. But remember that just as you are learning through your work, so your supervisor is learning through his or her work. Show respect for your supervisor. Help her or him to perform the job by cooperating and understanding. Then, you'll not only earn your supervisors appreciation but also develop a smooth-working relationship.

The Role of Supervisor

Supervisors are the people responsible for getting things done. They must be able to perform the important roles of teachers, leaders, and counselors. More than anything else, supervisors must be leaders. They are responsible for the happiness and productivity of all the employees reporting to them. But as well as being able to motivate their staff to work hard, they must also earn their staff's respect.

Supervisors are responsible for achieving the three broad goals of (1) getting things done—which contribute to profit, (2) keeping expenses to a reasonable limit, and (3) building group spirit. To achieve these goals, they must have the abilities and competencies that are discussed below.

Supervisors are necessary in any company's organization, and being a supervisor calls for a wide range of abilities. Apart from having good judgment and being able to plan effectively, supervisors must also:

♦ Have been successful as regular employees

♦ Know the jobs and the people they supervise
♦ Know basic policies and rules
♦ Work with and handle people well
♦ Improve job methods and increase production
♦ Teach the employees they supervise the different job tasks

What does it take to be a supervisor? A study involving 500 "leaders" and 15,000 "followers" in various group and supervised situations answered this question. The study showed that the most essential duties of successful leaders can be grouped into the six categories given in the following list. Some examples of workers' comments that illustrate each category are also given.

♦ Setting group goals with group members: "Our boss asks our opinions frequently."

Success in supervision depends on how well the supervisor performs these six leadership functions.

"We have frequent group rap sessions on work problems."

♦ Helping the group achieve its goals:

"Our boss always sees that we have good equipment and materials on hand when we need them."

"She always helps us out when any of us are swamped."

♦ Promoting coordination:

"She gives us all a chance at choice jobs—no playing favorites."

"He lets us help each other and doesn't mind when we share workloads."

♦ Helping members fit into the group:

"Our boss understands the way we feel about things."

"He gives me a chance to do the work I do best."

♦ Showing an interest in the group:

"My boss is really good about getting us overtime and raises."

"She'll always stick her neck out for one of us."

♦ Being a personable and responsive human being:

"She's fair in enforcing rules and in asking us to take on assignments."

"He always tells us when we've done a good job."

These, then, are the qualities that it takes to be a supervisor. But, as you'll find out, some supervisors are more likeable than others and will be able to meet your expectations more effectively. No matter who your supervisors are, however, learn to understand them and try to help them achieve their goals, because many of their goals will be the same as yours.

As a promotable employee, you'll be better off working with a supervisor who can help you reach your potential and who is more demanding than a lenient supervisor, who might not be as useful to you. Also, you can probably assume that most supervisors are self-confident and have a strong personality, because those are the qualities needed to become a supervisor. Something else to keep in mind is that being a supervisor is quite a heavy responsibility and that supervising other people is never easy.

Developing a Working Relationship with Your Supervisor

There are ten ways in which you can develop a good relationship with your supervisor. And when it is developed (in the ways explained below), the employee, the supervisor, and even the company will benefit. You may find that some of these ways are already part of your relationships with your family or teachers. Others will be new to you and thus a challenge for you to develop.

Be Sold on the Aims of the Business

Employers have three basic aims: (1) to make a profit on their investment, (2) to attract and keep satisfied customers, and (3) to develop and maintain an effective organization. As an employee, you should be fully aware of these aims and be in agreement with them. If you can't accept these aims, you'll find it very hard to perform well and should seek other employment.

Make Good Use of Constructive Criticism

It's a supervisor's job to suggest to staff members better methods of performing a job. When your supervisor offers you such suggestions, remember that you aren't being criticized as a person. Rather, your supervisor is making suggestions concerning your actions as an employee. So take these suggestions and adjust your business conduct accordingly. Don't take criticism personally—keep your emotions out of the situation.

At times, you may encounter a supervisor whom you believe to be an unjustly harsh critic. But if you develop a sensitivity to other people's feelings, you'll usually be able to tell the difference between

When a good relationship is developed between the supervisor and the employee, the employee, the supervisor, and the company all benefit. *Courtesy of Peoples Gas Magazine*

a criticism that is offered for your improvement and one that is not. As you gain experience on the job, you'll also learn to distinguish a criticism that is justified from one that is not. If you consider your critic's complaint to be unfounded, don't let the situation get out of hand by dwelling on it. Defend yourself politely and briefly; then let the quality of your work prove your point.

Respect Supervisor Authority

Supervisors have the right to be treated with respect—they carry a sizable responsibility. It's the supervisor's job to direct the work of other employees; their experience has taught them how to assign duties in a way that will benefit the entire staff. When a supervisor asks you something, respond willingly—as you would in selling. Always address your supervisor by his or her last name unless you're told to do otherwise.

Be Loyal to Supervisors

Always be loyal in dealing with supervisors. Being loyal means supporting the decisions of your supervisor in front of others. If you think the decision can be improved, see your supervisor in private and offer your suggestions. Don't gossip about the decision with others.

As a loyal employee, also recognize the right and responsibility of your supervisor to direct activities and make decisions, even though some of those decisions may not always be to your liking. For example, you might want Friday evening off, but your supervisor may know that you are really needed and schedule you to work. Finally, loyalty means holding no resentment toward your supervisor and not encouraging any resentment shown by coworkers.

Carry Out Responsibilities

A supervisor's job is to direct the work of others. To do this job effectively, a supervisor must expect that workers will assume the responsibilities she or he assigns. And a supervisor also has the right to expect these responsibilities to be carried out as skillfully as possible. A cooperative and conscientious attitude on your part, as a worker, will earn your supervisor's appreciation and help get the job done. For example, you may not want to work the hours required in taking annual inventory; however, taking inventory is part of the job. Your supervisor is responsible for getting the job done and is counting on you to carry out your responsibilities.

Recognize Supervisors as Individuals

Because supervisors are individuals, they are subject to varying moods. They have their own problems both at work and in their private lives. Recognize that as your supervisor reacts to such problems, his or her attitude toward you may vary from day to day. Remember that the moods of your supervisor, like your own moods, will not always be consistent, and adapt your behavior accordingly. For example, if your supervisor's daughter is home ill from school, it may be that your supervisor won't have much time to talk to you about what you learned in your marketing and distributive education class that day.

Contribute New Ideas

Retail management seeks creative ideas. If you have a new idea, discuss it with your supervisor; the supervisor's experience can help make a good idea a superior one. But as a newcomer to any job, be cautious about suggesting new ideas or changes before you've become fully acquainted with the store policies and operation. Suggestions that are not well thought out can be mistaken for unfair criticism. For example, talk to your supervisor before you decide entirely on your own which merchandise you will feature in a center aisle.

Have a Venturesome Spirit

A venturesome spirit—the courage to try new things—and good judgment are qualities that good employees should possess. The people who succeed in retailing are almost always those who seek to advance by their own efforts rather than depending on breaks, "pull," or seniority. If you're venturesome, you'll probably be a self-starter and have an inquiring mind, a resourceful personality, and an active imagination. You'll have the courage to stick with these convictions while remaining open-minded and willing to discard unsound ideas.

Profit from Instruction

Although some supervisors are very good teachers of new workers, not all have been trained in how to instruct. Frequently they are so busy with other duties that they can't devote the proper amount of time to training. Consequently, as a worker, you may sometimes feel neglected. Several guides that you can use to gain the greatest benefits from supervisory instruction follow:

- Be prepared and at ease. You will have every opportunity to learn.
- Stand or sit where you can see clearly.
- Study instructions by repeating each step to yourself and connect what you are learning with what you already know.
- Learn steps in logical order—not too many at once.
- Ask your instructor to repeat or explain doubtful points.
- Be sure you know why, when, where, and how you are to do the job you are assigned.
- Perform the job as well as you can.
- Ask the instructor to watch you if it's necessary, and tell the instructor each step as you perform it.
- Make new knowledge or a new skill a part of you by thinking or talking about it.
- Strive for production.
- Strive for accuracy—speed will follow.
- Ask questions whenever necessary.
- Work on your own as much as possible.
- Make a list of the steps in your job and refer to your list to check yourself.

Communicate with Your Supervisor

Many of the human relations problems that exist between employees and supervisors are caused by poor communication.

In order to profit from instruction, an employee must be able to clearly observe what is being shown.

Almost every situation involving more than one person requires that those involved communicate with each other. It's quite easy to misunderstand what is being communicated. And when this happens, it's even easier for confusion and hard feelings to arise between people. So, developing the skills needed for effective communication is essential. These skills are speaking, writing, listening, and reading. (They are discussed in detail in Chapter 13.)

When your supervisor is speaking to you, don't hesitate to ask questions if there is any doubt in your mind about his or her meaning. Similarly, observe your supervisor as you're speaking to him or her. If you notice any signs of confusion or hesitation, offer a fuller explanation of what you were saying. Communicating effectively with your supervisor, along with attending to the nine other principles

discussed here, will do much to promote a workable and pleasant relationship between you and the person who supervises you.

Learning how to work with the person who supervises you is perhaps the most important thing for you to achieve in any job. As a beginning worker, however, to really learn the ropes, you'll want to find out as much as you can about how your particular job relates to the jobs of other employees, how your company is organized, and how to join a labor union. You can learn about all these things by reading the next chapter.

Trade Talk

Define this term and use it in a sentence.

Supervisors

Can You Answer These?

1. Why are people usually chosen for supervisory positions?
2. What are three broad goals a supervisor is responsible for achieving?
3. What are the ten ways to develop a good working relationship with your supervisors?
4. What are the ways in which employees can be loyal to their supervisors?
5. What can workers do to help improve communications with their supervisors?

Problems

1. Choose one of the following tasks that a supervisor might teach you: (*a*) taking an order over the phone, (*b*) selling a sweater, (*c*) filling out a customer charge slip, or (*d*) using a cash register. On a separate sheet of paper, write a paragraph giving the guides to follow in profiting from the on-the-job instruction given by a supervisor.

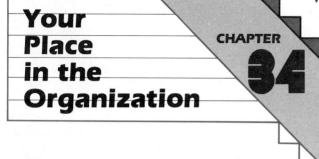

Your Place in the Organization

CHAPTER 34

Communications & Human Relations

Economics & Marketing

Merchandising

Selling & Technology

Advertising & Display

Operations & Management

"May your association with us be both pleasant and rewarding in every way. . . . Your company has long recognized this basic truth: a company is only as good as its employees, as successful as its individuals are successful."

These are statements appearing in the employee handbook of a retail firm. They indicate that progressive retailers are interested in their personnel not only as employees but also as individuals. Such employers know that if their employees are satisifed and like being a part of their company, they are more likely to do a good job and stay with the firm. So many employers do all they can to keep their employees satisfied with their jobs.

Employers invest a part of their resources and the future of their businesses when they hire you as a new employee. Similarly, you invest a part of your future when you agree to join a firm. If your investment is a sound one, it should help you to fulfill the beginning goals of your career plan.

If you're happy in your work and feel that your investment is paying good returns, you'll probably look forward to continuing as an employee of the firm. A satisfying relationship between you and your employer will continue to exist as long as you both act responsibly.

All retailers have some type of organization to achieve their goals. An **organization** is a group of employees united for the purpose of achieving the goals of the firm. The objectives of retailers are to satisfy consumer wants and needs while making a reasonable profit.

Learning Your Job

An **organization chart** shows levels of authority and the relationship of each employee to the operation of the business. It enables you, as an employee, to see how you relate to your coworkers, supervisors, and management. To fully understand your job duties, however, you need a job description. A **job description** is a written summary of specific duties, responsibilities, and the relationship of your particular job to your supervisor and coworkers.

When you begin a new job, there will be many things to learn. One way to learn and master a new job quickly is to find out why things are done in certain ways. Don't be satisfied with merely knowing how things are done.

List the Tasks

Here's how you can understand the tasks involved in learning a new job. First, list every task the job calls for. You needn't follow a particular order. Each time you receive a new assignment, add it to your list of tasks until the list is complete. While you are making your list, don't worry about how small the task seems to be; if in doubt, list it anyway. For example, figuring a sales check is a task, and so is determining the proper color scheme for a display. The best source of help is your supervisor. Your coworkers may also give you valuable information.

Categorize the List

After you've completed your list of job tasks, categorize the listing so that it's more meaningful. Just as a store is divided into departments where similar kinds of merchandise are kept together, your tasks should be grouped into categories of similar kinds of work. For example, the tasks involved in selling scarves might be grouped as follows:

♦ Group 1: Assist customers in selection of scarf, suggest related merchandise, and prepare sales checks.
♦ Group 2: Construct counter displays, and build window displays.
♦ Group 3: Prepare advertisements.
♦ Group 4: Take inventory, arrange stock in stockroom, maintain stock controls,

receive and mark price on scarves, care for stock on scarves, and care for stock on sales floor.
♦ Group 5: Perform clerical duties.

Analyze the Tasks

After you've categorized your list by grouping related items together, you're ready to break the tasks down further. Note that in the chart on page 270 the employee has taken the task of constructing a counter display for scarves and broken it down into various parts. The employee has also listed the information or skill need for each step.

Gain Knowledge and Practice

Now you're ready to begin to gain knowledge about those job tasks that you don't know enough about. First, you'll probably want to learn about those tasks that are performed most often. Your firm may have instructional training materials to help you, or you might ask your marketing and distributive education teacher-coordinator to assist you. You may need to ask one of your coworkers or supervisors to assist you. Once you've gained the needed knowledge, you're ready to practice until you can do the job task to your own satisfaction and that of your supervisor.

Learning How the Firm Is Organized

It's important that you be able to identify the type of organization your firm operates under and where you fit in that organization.

Some retail firms have an informal organization. With this type of organization, the relationship of employees' job activities to the goals of the firm is not always clear and precise. Other retail firms have a carefully planned formal organization. Most firms establish a **line of authority,** which is the organization pattern that tells who is responsible for what and who reports to whom. Without any type of organization, there is no clear un-

CONSTRUCT COUNTER DISPLAY FOR SCARVES	
What I Do	**What I Need to Know**
Choose kind of goods to display	Current fashions
	Seasonal demand
Choose scarves to display	Color harmony
	Customer needs and wants
	Features of the items
Select theme	Current season
Prepare show card	How to write show-card copy
Clean counter	Uses and location of cleaning materials
Assemble goods and props	Uses and location of props
	Location of stock
Prepare props	How to clean and adjust props
Place scarves on form	How to dress forms
Place goods, props, and sign in position	Display selling principles

derstanding of responsibilities. And in this situation misunderstandings and errors or duplication of effort may result.

Small Retail Firm Organization

If you work in a small firm, such as a paint or a shoe store, you and all the other employees may report directly to the owner or manager. In this way, a fixed line of authority is established. This system is referred to as a line organization. A **line organization** is a chain of authority in which each person reports to a specified supervisor who, in turn, reports to a higher supervisor. Final responsibility rests with the owner or manager. Several people may perform similar tasks, but usually each person has sole responsibility for certain operations. All employees may have specific assignments, such as buying, selling, or stockkeeping.

Large Retail Firm Organization

If you work in a large retail firm, you'll find that it has a more complicated organization than a small firm. This is neces-

sary because large firms have greater specialization and wider varieties of merchandise and services. Large firms generally organize under a line-and-staff system. In a **line-and-staff organization,** each employee reports to a single supervisor; in addition, however, there are specialists within the organization who act as advisers in certain areas. For example, a firm might employ a fashion coordinator, a display manager to assist with displays, or a personnel manager to assist with hiring and training employees.

Frequently the lines of responsibility in an organization are shown in a chart or diagram. These organization charts show graphically the overall organizational pattern and the responsibility assigned to each position in the firm. The organization chart on page 271 shows how a large department store is organized to perform five major retailing activities: merchandising, store operations, control and credit, personnel, and sales promotion.

The organization chart on page 272 is typical of the structure of a large national general merchandise chain. This is the chart of J. C. Penney, a chain with 190,000 employees.

The organization chart for the typical national retail chain includes both an organization plan at corporate headquarters plus successive layers of organization (as shown in the bottom of the chart on page 272), depending on the size and scope of the firm's operations. This chart shows the layers of organization and illustrates the staffing patterns of the vice presidents, directors, and local store managers.

Note that chain-store organizations lean toward centralized management. That is, the functions of buying, promotion, personnel, and control are typically performed in the central or perhaps the regional headquarters. Selling, on the other hand, is likely to be the only purpose that the individual stores are responsible for. This is called a "decentralized" function.

Today, the trend in management is to achieve the advantages of both centralization and decentralization. Management is striving to achieve the cost savings offered by the centralization of mass buying, promotion, personnel, and control while allowing the individual stores to respond and adjust to local selling conditions.

Gaining Acceptance

One of the first things you'll want to do when you begin a job is to gain the acceptance of those with whom you work as a member of the firm's organization. To gain this acceptance, you must show concern and friendliness toward other employees—especially those who help you to learn the job. Also, take on all your new duties enthusiastically. The following suggestions may help you to become a master employee.

♦ *Approach your new job with enthusiasm.* Show people that you're glad to be with the firm and that you're going to enjoy working with its members.
♦ *Spend full time on the job.* Don't be afraid

This organization chart shows how the responsibilities in a large department store are divided. It also traces lines of authority for the executives in the divisions. Note that the Director of Research and Development has a staff position.

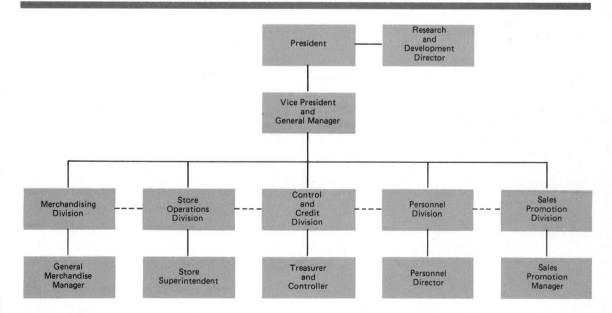

Organization chart of J. C. Penney Co., a large national retail chain.

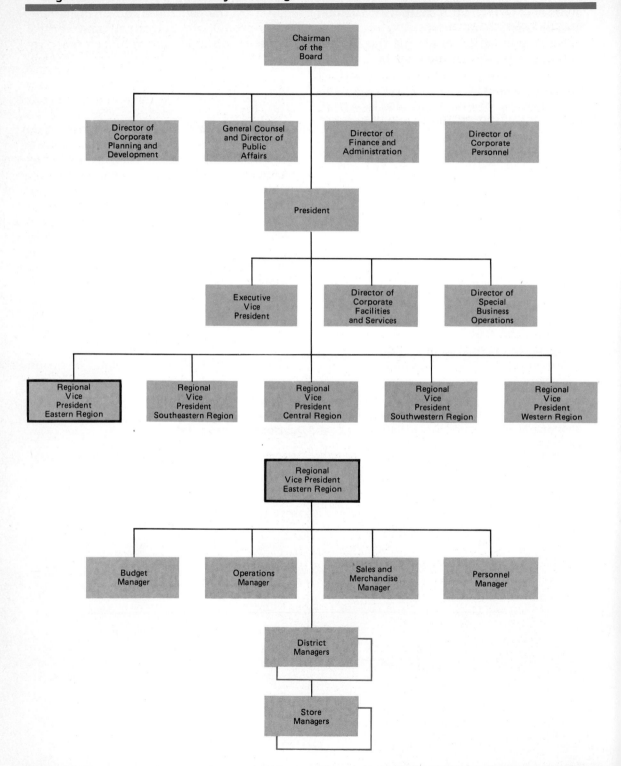

to earn the full value of your salary. This means arriving on time and returning promptly from lunch and breaks.

♦ *Respect the know-how of older, experienced employees*. The know-it-all becomes unpopular very quickly. But the person who expresses appreciation for advice and who compliments fellow employees when they do a good job gains valuable friends.

♦ *Be friendly.* Don't be afraid to smile and show your eagerness to belong to the firm. Show an interest in other employees by learning their names. But don't be too quick to use first names, especially with other workers. Listen attentively when your coworkers talk about their jobs and themselves. But don't pry into their personal affairs or take sides in disagreements between others. Adopt a pleasant and cooperative attitude toward everyone.

Joining a Labor Union

You can't work for very long in this country without hearing about unions, because about 17 million workers belong to them. A **labor union** is a group of workers who have banded together for common purposes of maintaining and improving employment conditions. Unions are becoming increasingly common in retailing, particularly in food distribution and in service businesses such as hotels and restaurants. The main reason for which unions are organized is to improve working conditions, salaries, and fringe benefits for workers. Some of the benefits unions have obtained for their members are improved vacation and holiday pay, retirement pensions, and health and welfare services. Unions have also become involved with other types of issues. These

Labor unions have helped to improve working conditions for all employees.
Courtesy of ILGWU (International Ladies Garment Workers Union)

IF YOU DON'T COME IN SUNDAY DON'T COME IN MONDAY.

THE MANAGEMENT

That's the way it used to be. If you were told to come in, you did! If you wanted to keep your job. But unions like the International Ladies' Garment Workers' changed that. The shorter work week, paid holidays, paid vacations, higher wages — all came about because unions worked and fought for them. The signature of 450,000 ILGWU members is the union label, sewn into women's and children's apparel. It is our symbol of progress made; and more to come.

LOOK FOR THIS LABEL
When You Shop For
WOMEN'S AND CHILDREN'S APPAREL

include additional pay for overtime work, grievance procedures (the steps to be taken when a worker feels he or she has been treated unfairly), and length of employment as a consideration in determining promotions and layoffs.

Collective Bargaining

A union may act as a recognized bargaining representative for a group of workers. Discussions between organized labor and management for the purpose of solving problems is known as **collective bargaining.** Under collective bargaining, labor and management discuss what they expect of each other. When an agreement is reached, a labor contract is signed by representatives of both labor and management. Such contracts are usually written for periods of 1 to 5 years. Collective bargaining requires that each side be willing to give a little. If one side refuses to compromise, agreement is not reached. In an effort to force management to agree to its demands, a union may strike.

A **strike** is a refusal by employees to work, causing a loss of business. Employees on strike receive no wages. But they may receive strike benefits from the union, which includes some money and other provisions. If employees strike without the approval of the union, they receive no strike benefits. This is known as a **wildcat strike.** Workers on strike usually picket the entrance of the business against which they are striking, carrying signs with the words such as "unfair" or "on strike." During the past 10 years, only a fraction of 1 percent of total people-workdays was lost because of work stoppages resulting from labor-management disputes.

Why Employees Join Unions

Employees often join unions because they believe that in this way they will be able to bargain more effectively with their employer for improved wages and working conditions than if each were to act alone. For example, if one or two people threaten to strike because of unsatisfactory conditions or low wages, their absence may not be felt. But if a majority of the workers leave the job, their absence is greatly felt and can even force the business involved to close.

But unions also serve their members in another important way. They give each individual a feeling of belonging. Union membership gives workers the assurance that they belong to a group that will back them up and come to their aid if necessary.

There are several unions in retailing. All are affiliated with the American Federation of Labor-Congress of Industrial Organizations (AFL-CIO). In recent years, these unions have included the Retail Clerks International Union (RCIU); Retail, Wholesale, and Department Store Union (RWDSU); Service Employees International Union (SEIU); and Hotel and Restaurant Employees and Bartenders International Union (HREBIU).

Before deciding whether to join a union or not, you should get all the facts and compare the advantages and disadvantages by talking with both your coworkers and supervisors. If you do join a union, you can be a good union member by paying your dues, going to meetings, voting at meetings, and taking part in union activities.

In this last chapter of Unit 11, you've been given some ideas on how you can speed up the process of learning a new job. Also, you gained an understanding of why firms have to have some type of organization, the main types of retail firm organizations, and how you can become accepted as a member of the company in which you'll work. In this chapter, you also learned how labor unions help workers.

Now that you've finished this unit, you should have a good understanding of what will be expected of you in your retailing job and how you can meet these expectations. In other words, you should have a good idea of what "learning the ropes" is all about. If you have a part-time job, put this knowledge into action now. If you don't, take notes so that you can use what you've learned in the job you plan to get.

Trade Talk

Define each term and use it in a sentence.

Collective bargaining
Job description
Labor union
Line-and-staff
    organization
Line of authority
Line organization
Organization
Organization chart
Strike
Wildcat strike

Can You Answer These?

1. Why do retail employers want satisfied employees?
2. What steps should an employee follow in learning a job?
3. How do the organization patterns of large and small firms differ?
4. What are the principal reasons unions are organized?
5. What six suggestions can a new employee follow in learning a job?

Problems

1. Rule a form similar to the following. In the left column, write the letter of each of the following actions: (0) telling the manager how to create an advertisement when you have no previous training, (a) dressing appropriately for job, (b) having coffee with the department manager and talking about how you need a raise, (c) staying ½ hour after work to help arrange merchandise for a sale the next day, (d) arriving at work and back from lunch on time, (e) offering to empty trash cans and sweep the floor after a busy day, (f) asking another salesperson how best to handle a difficult customer, (g) working a few extra hours for a fellow worker who went home ill, (h) siding with two other employees who want to complain to the boss about a fellow worker, and (i) taking a joke—someone put play money in your cash register. In the right column, indicate whether you think each action would help you gain acceptance on the job. Give a reason for your opinion.

Action	Behavior Evaluation
Example: (0)	No. Would be considered the behavior of a know-it-all.

2. Imagine that you have just become a salesperson in either the sporting goods or music department of a store. Using the list on page 269 and the chart on page 270 as models, make a list of tasks for the job that you have chosen. Choose one of the tasks and break it down into its various components.

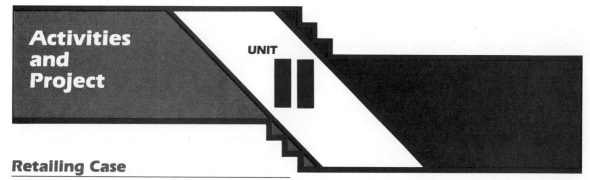

Activities and Project

UNIT II

Retailing Case

A new salesperson, Len Holentzka, was assigned to the suit department at Lieland's, an exclusive menswear store in a shopping mall. It was a hot day in August and the air-conditioning system malfunctioned. It turned out that there couldn't have been a worse time for the system to fail. All the mall merchants were promoting a Crazy Daze sale and the place was mobbed.

Len was particularly busy during his supervisor's lunch hour. He was rushing around the department waiting on customers as fast as he could. Naturally, Len got pretty warm and he decided to take off his suit coat and loosen his tie. Len's supervisor came back from lunch, noticed that Len had removed his suit coat, and said, "Get that suit coat back on and tighten your tie! You know the rule—you don't wait on customers in this store without dressing properly. That means wearing your suit coat and having your tie neatly tied at all times." Len was shocked because nobody had told him how to dress and he assumed that because it was so hot it was all right to remove his coat and loosen his tie.

1. Was the supervisor's reprimand to Len justified? Why or why not?
2. What lesson did Len learn about company policies?
3. If you were Len, what would you have done?

Working with People

Ms. Moustakas owns a small drugstore that carries many different lines of merchandise with a limited stock in each. You have been working for her for 4 months. She is a rather stern employer. She means well but is quick to criticize your work when it is not up to her standards. She seldom compliments you even though you have done a good job. Today was an extremely busy day. You made several sales of items like hair dryers and electric shavers, which take a lot of salesperson's time. You also handled some difficult customers.

It is now after 5 p.m. and business has slowed down. You are marking boxes of candy to put on the counter. After doing about a dozen boxes, you discover that you have been marking the boxes 69 cents instead of 96 cents. You ask Ms. Moustakas

how you should correct the error, and she again begins to criticize your work. She points out that you should have started on the daily stock work earlier.

1. Identify the true problem.
2. What are the important facts to be considered in this problem?
3. List several possible solutions to this problem.
4. Evaluate the possible results of each solution.
5. Which solution do you recommend? Why?

Project 11: Reviewing Articles on Supervision

Your Project Goal
Given three articles on supervision selected from newspapers, manuals, or trade journals, read each article, prepare a written review, and determine how you could apply the concepts you read about to on-the-job situations.

Procedure
To assist you in learning more about supervision in retailing, complete the following project.

1. Read three articles on the subject of getting along with your supervisor. Select these from magazines, newspapers, or trade journals. Note: You may want to ask your teacher, librarian, or retailer about possible sources of such articles.
2. Write a 100- to 200-word review of each article. Include information such as: (a) title or headline, (b) author, (c) source of the article, (d) content of the article, (e) your opinion of what was said, and (f) how you would apply what you learned from the article to promote better relations on the job.

Evaluation
You will be evaluated on (1) how clearly you can show that what you read in the article can help you to become a valuable member of a retail organization and (2) how thoroughly you complete Step 2 above.

276

Free Enterprise and Profits

CHAPTER

35

Communications & Human Relations

Economics & Marketing

Merchandising

Selling & Technology

Advertising & Display

Operations & Management

Jack had worked for Mrs. Scarpella in her stereo and music shop for about a year. He enjoyed working and learning about the latest music and stereo equipment. He noticed that Mrs. Scarpella often worked long hours, especially during holidays. Jack wondered why Mrs. Scarpella didn't just get a job and work for somebody else and not have to worry about her business and all its day-to-day business decisions. He decided that he would talk to her and find out why retailers go into business.

Mrs. Scarpella likes her job for several reasons, most of which are personal. But, like so many people in retailing, she has a sense of social service too and gets satisfaction from pleasing her customers.

From a personal viewpoint, she likes to "do her own thing"—being her own boss, performing a variety of tasks. She enjoys the freedom to use her abilities as she wishes and to exercise her creative talents. The opportunity to work with people, being in a pleasant work environ-ment, and enjoying a certain amount of social status are pleasing. Also, from the economic viewpoint, she likes the way she is compensated for her work—being paid for her creativity and the risks she takes.

From the standpoint of society, Mrs. Scarpella serves two groups of people: her customers and her employees. Her customers receive products and services for the money they spend. Her employees are given an opportunity to earn a living. In her role as a retailer, Mrs. Scarpella stands between the producer and the consumer. If her business is to succeed, it must respond to the needs of its customers. Survival also depends on the productivity of the workers who serve those customers, for prices must be competitive and a profit must be made.

Our Economic System

The American economic system is sometimes called the **modified free enterprise or private enterprise system.** It's called "free" because individual freedoms are an important part of it. It is called "private" because most businesses are privately owned and operated, or not run by the government. It is called "modified" because the government controls some of its actions. For example, it is against the law to sell goods that are harmful to people, such as narcotics. Other names used for our economic system are "capitalism" and "market-centered economy."

Economic Freedom

Many of our freedoms are economic freedoms. Individuals have the freedom to go into business if they wish. Employees have freedom to bargain with their employers. Workers have the freedom to choose the type of work they do. (You may decide to go to school in order to obtain a better job.) We have the freedom to own private property; business and individuals can buy or sell property without government permission. As consumers, we have the freedom to purchase the goods and services we want. So, the free enterprise system gives businesses as well as consumers many freedoms.

Freedom in Retailing

Retailers have the freedom to compete with each other for consumer dollars. They have the freedom to make profits, and they can do various things with those profits.

As a retailer, Mrs. Scarpella has many economic freedoms. She can buy goods and services of her own choosing. She can develop advertising techniques to suit her needs. Lowering or raising her prices are her own decisions. And, as well as going into business, Mrs. Scarpella can go out of business if she chooses.

Competition

Competition is the force that makes the American free enterprise system work. It constantly generates improvements in the ways retailers distribute goods and services to their target customers. Retailers compete with one another in satisfying the changing needs of consumer groups. And they try to get consumers to buy products and services from their particular business. Retailers do this by special advertising, various types of sales promotions, lowering prices, improving services, and various other activities. So the name of the game is: "The right products and services at the right time, at the right place, and at the right price."

The Role of Government

In our free enterprise system, the major role of government is to protect our individual rights, ensure fair competition, and promote public welfare. In recent years, the role of government in our economic system has grown. Over the past 70 years, government on all levels—federal, state, and local—has become an increasingly important part of our economic system. The Employment Act of 1946 made the federal government even more responsible for the care of our economic system. This act called for the government to encourage a healthy economy and good business conditions. The purpose of the legislation was to encourage as many people as possible to have jobs with incomes at increasing levels.

Government often affects a nation's economic system. For example, the Soviet Union doesn't consider consumer likes and dislikes when making economic decisions. Instead, it has special committees to decide what and how much to produce and sell in retail firms. The same is true of the People's Republic of China and other communist countries. These countries use government policies to decide who gets

Many local governments charge fees for vendor licenses. Kip Peticolas/Fundamental Photographs

certain goods and services and where they are sold.

Retailers in our economic system deal with government in a number of ways. Minimum wage laws require a certain wage rate for employees. Other laws require periodic inspection by health officials if a retailer sells food or beverages. To go into business, in certain cities, one must pay a fee for a license. Retailers must be aware of ever-increasing government rules affecting their businesses. The role of government in retailing is discussed further in Chapter 56.

The Circular Flow

Jack, who was curious about Mrs. Scarpella's love of business, might wonder how an economic system functions. He could look at his parents going to work, or Mrs. Scarpella stocking her shelves, or a city

ambulance going to a hospital. All these activities represent economic activities. But what does the whole economy look like? How do the many different parts of an economy work together? How does money function in the economy? These and many other economic questions can be answered by studying the circular flow in the market economy.

There are three main groups of people in the circular flow: business, consumers, and government. Businesses consist of all producers and sellers of goods and services. Consumers are all people who buy and use goods and services. There are three levels of government: federal, state, and local.

Here is how these groups work together. Among businesses, consumers, and government, both money and goods and services change hands. For example, consumers exchange money in payment for goods and services supplied by business. Wages flow from businesses to consumers in payment for labor services.

How does government fit into our picture of an economic system? Government performs two activities in our economy: it collects taxes and it provides services.

Different levels of government collect different types of taxes. The local, or city, government may collect water and sewer taxes from Mrs. Scarpella. The local, or county, government may collect a property tax based upon the value of her store. Income taxes are collected by the federal government and sometimes by the state government. Also, most states have sales taxes, which Mrs. Scarpella collects from customers.

What does the government do with the taxes it collects? It provides goods and services, which include fire and police protection, education, public health programs, the maintenance of competitive markets, highways, bridges, airports, and public parks. These are just a few of the many types of goods and services the government provides.

Now you have seen how our free enterprise system works. Each of its parts is important to our country's strength. But, what keeps the system going? For example, why do retailers want to keep providing us with products and services? And why do people go into business? Some of these questions were answered briefly at the beginning of this chapter. The next sections answer them in greater detail.

The Roles of Profit

Our country has many different kinds of businesses. Some are large, like Sears, United Air Lines, or General Motors. Others are smaller, owned by one person such as Mrs. Scarpella. Some businesses like a car wash, sell only services. Others, such as large department stores, may sell both products and services. Why were these businesses started? What keeps them going for many years?

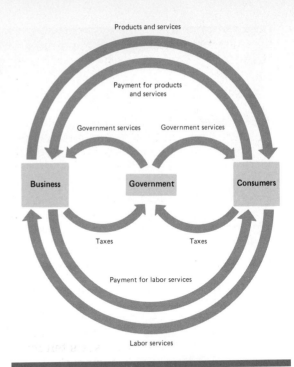

The picture of our economic system.

As mentioned earlier, there are two basic reasons for going into business. One is the personal satisfaction of being in charge of a business that a person can call her or his own. A second reason is the desire to earn profits. What are profits?

Let's go back to Mrs. Scarpella's stereo and music shop. Profit starts with income. Mrs. Scarpella receives money from her customers when she sells them records, tapes, and stereo equipment. This is called **income.** Is this profit? No, because as Mrs. Scarpella owns a business, she has to pay out money from that income. She must pay rent on the store building. The store uses electricity, for which she pays the power company. Wages to her salespeople are another cost of doing business. She must also pay for the merchandise she sells to her customers. All these costs are called **expenses. Profit** is the amount of money left over from income after subtracting expenses. A business must have profits or it will eventually close its doors.

Profits can be measured and evaluated

in three ways: as a percentage of sales, as a percentage of assets, and as a return on investment. Each way serves a different purpose.

Profits on Sales

Profits as percentage of sales can tell management the ability of a business to control expenses and get the most sales profit for each dollar spent on the sales effort. For example, if Mrs. Scarpella earned profits of $15,000 after selling $300,000 of stereo equipment and records last year, her profits as a percentage of sales would be 5 percent. She would calculate it this way:

$$\frac{\text{Total profits}}{\text{Total sales}} = \frac{\$\ 15,000}{\$300,000} = .05 = 5\%$$

Profits on Assets

Profits as a percentage of assets tell management how well the business's assets are contributing to its well-being. As men-

tioned earlier, **assets** are things the business owns, such as the store fixtures and stock. This measure of profits tells if a business is getting its money's worth from what it owns. Are all the store fixtures, sales representatives' cars, and neon signs contributing to profits, or are they unnecessary for the business to own? If Mrs. Scarpella's store assets were worth $150,000 and she had a $15,000 profit last year, her profit as a percentage of assets would be 10 percent. She would calculate it like this:

$$\frac{\text{Total profits}}{\text{Total assets}} = \frac{\$\ 15,000}{\$150,000} = .10 = 10\%$$

Profits on Investment

Another way to measure profits is in relation to the amount of money the owners have invested in the business. This measure of profits is called **return on investment.** Suppose Mrs. Scarpella had invested $75,000 of her own money and had

Mrs. Scarpella was pleased to see that her business had made a profit.

also borrowed $25,000 from a bank to start her business. If she had earned profits of $15,000, she would figure her return on investment as follows:

$$\frac{\text{Total profits}}{\text{Total investment}} = \frac{\$\ 15,000}{\$100,000} = .15 = 15\%$$

Mrs. Scarpella earned 15 percent on the money she invested in her business.

Results of each measure of profit can be used in a number of ways. For example, Mrs. Scarpella could compare them to last year's figures. She could also compare them to the figures of similar businesses to see how she is doing in terms of her competition. These measures of profit provide guideposts to Mrs. Scarpella on how well she is doing. They provide owners and managers with a "thermometer." They let managers know if they are on the right track in effecting good retail management.

What Profits Represent

Mrs. Scarpella prefers the freedom of owning her own business. Because she is the owner, she can do what she wants with the profits of her store. She may want to return the profits to the business, using them, perhaps, to expand it. This is called **reinvestment,** or returning the profits to the business, Or she might wish to keep the profits for her personal use, perhaps to buy a new car.

Profit, then, represents the money that business owners receive in return for the money they risk by going into business. Rather than investing their money in a business, they could put it into a savings account and be assured of earning interest. Business profits, however, usually provide the owners with a larger amount of money than the interest they could earn in a savings account. But first, of course, they have to be willing to take the risk of owning a business. Profit is never a "sure thing" for business. Owners always have to live with the possibility that their business may make no profits. In fact, if their business expenses are greater than their income, they would not only fail to make any profit but would also suffer a loss.

Factors Affecting Profits

What things determine whether a business will make a profit or take a loss? Mrs. Scarpella will have to make sure her prices are high enough to cover her expenses. But she must also be careful not to price her goods too high. Why? Her customers might go to other music stores. She must also watch her expenses. If they are too high, she may not have enough income to make a profit. Profit is a reward for the risk of running a business.

Retail businesses are a very important part of our economic system. They provide us with both goods and services. Retail businesses hire people to work for them and serve as sources of income. Yet, to have businesses, there must be profits. Profits are the reward for the efforts and risks of owning a business. Without profits, few or no businesses would exist. Profits are the lifeblood of our free enterprise system. The source of profits is income from the sale of goods and services after expenses are paid. When consumers buy goods and services from Mrs. Scarpella's shop, they provide her with a reason to stay in business. Consumers, by deciding to buy a particular brand name at a particular store, are an important force in our market-centered economy. Profits provide the basis of future economic growth when owners reinvest them in their businesses. Profits are a means of providing a higher standard of living for all.

In the next chapter, you'll learn about the different types of ownership that retailers can choose from in a free enterprise system.

Trade Talk

Define each term and use it in a sentence.

Assets   Expenses

Income
Modified free
   enterprise or
   private enterprise
   system

Profit
Reinvestment
Return on
   investment

Can You Answer These?

1. What is the major purpose of business?
2. What are the three economic questions discussed in the chapter about the use of economic resources?
3. Why is the American economic system called the modified free enterprise system?
4. List the three main groups in the circular flow.
5. Are profits good or bad?

Problems

1. Rule a form similar to the following. Then interview local retailers and ask them:

(a) who their competition is and (b) why? Record the results on your form, as shown below. Be prepared to discuss your findings in class.

Store Name	Competition	Why
Example: Discount Gas	Joe's Standard	Across the street

2. Rule a form similar to the following. Then select a shopping area in or near your community and make a list of the retailers located there. Record each store's name in the left column of your form. For each store, indicate whether it offers just products, just services, or both by placing a check mark (√) in the appropriate column(s) at the right of your form.

Store Name	Products	Services	Both
Example: Vandermeer's Dry Cleaning		√	

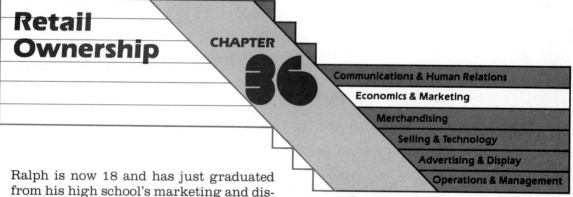

Retail Ownership

CHAPTER 36

Communications & Human Relations
Economics & Marketing
Merchandising
Selling & Technology
Advertising & Display
Operations & Management

Ralph is now 18 and has just graduated from his high school's marketing and distributive education program. He plans to remain at his training station to learn more about the business so that someday he can own his own pet store.

Julie has just graduated from college with a degree in marketing and secured a job with a large national grocery chain. She plans to own her own large chain of stores eventually. Julie knows that she needs experience, maturity, and money before she can achieve her career goal.

Wayne, age 46, has worked his way up to executive vice president in a firm that

owns six hardware stores. The president wants to retire and Wayne has agreed to buy the business by the end of the year.

Who Goes into Business?

Ralph, Julie, and Wayne will soon be entrepreneurs. **Entrepreneurs** are individuals who organize, manage, and assume the risk of a business for the purpose of making a profit. People of all ages and backgrounds go into business for themselves. Being one's own boss, being independent, and making money are reasons that motivated individuals such as James Cash Penney, Richard Sears, Rowland Macy, Aaron Montgomery Ward, and F. W. Woolworth to become entrepreneurs. Most people who are successful entrepreneurs have saved money and gained experience before going into business for themselves.

Small-Business Ownership

Statistics show that since the turn of the century over 85 percent of retail businesses in the United States have been one-store operations. And these have accounted for 60 percent of all retail sales. In fact, over 75 percent of all retail businesses since 1900 were operated by firms with no more than five employees.

Large-Business Ownership

In Chapter 7, you looked at the 20 largest retail businesses. Sears is the largest retailer in the United States. It has sales of almost $18 billion and employs over 420,000 people. Most of the 20 largest retailers operate in the general merchandising and food store areas of retailing, while small retailers operate most commonly in areas such as music stores, clothing stores, bookstores, service stations, and restaurants. See page 53.

Forms of Ownership

Each form of business ownership has advantages and disadvantages. Although no one form is better than another, a particular form of ownership may be better for certain types of owners and certain types of businesses.

There are three major types of retail ownership: the individual proprietorship, the partnership, and the corporation. How these work is shown in the following story about Wendy Medov, who became an entrepreneur. Besides the three major types of ownership, there are other ways to become an entrepreneur. These forms of business ownership are defined and explained later in this chapter and in Chapter 37.

Individual Proprietorship

While she was in high school, Wendy Medov worked in a pet store. She liked the work so much that she decided to make a career in retailing and stayed with the store after graduation. Wendy had begun to dream of owning her own store. She was determined to go into the retail pet business for herself. She wanted to be her own boss, try out some of her own merchandising ideas, and earn more money than she felt she could make by working for someone else. She saved as much money as she could, borrowed money from a local bank, and established credit with several suppliers. These resources enabled her to buy a small pet store in the southeast section of a large city.

Characteristics of an Individual Proprietorship

The type of ownership Wendy chose is called an **individual proprietorship,** which means that one person owns the business alone. Most businesses are started as individual proprietorships. What appeals to many people about the individual proprietorship is the chance to be one's own boss and, if the business succeeds, to earn a handsome profit.

Most individual proprietorships are small because it takes a great deal of money—sometimes millions of dollars—to start and operate a large business. A small business can be started with a modest investment plus credit from banks and suppliers. Most individual proprietorships are owner-operated. Although other employees may work in the business, most owners of such businesses cannot afford to hire many additional employees. The owner works in the business and supervises its operation. Because this results in personal contact between customers and owner, individualized service is often a feature of individual proprietorships.

Pros and Cons of an Individual Proprietorship

After her initial excitement over owning her own store, Wendy began to discover some realities about being an individual owner. She found that she had less time to relax and was seeing less of her family and friends because she had to work very long hours. She also found herself doing a good deal of worrying about the success of the store and often wondered whether it would provide adequate income and security.

Wendy saw that in many ways, working for someone else had been less troublesome than being her own boss. There were fewer responsibilities and worries involved. Nevertheless, every time she considered her situation, Wendy was pleased with being on her own. She had found that there were the following advantages to being an individual owner.

Simple Organization. There was little red tape to organizing the business that Wendy started. There were few legal problems and no negotiations with outside parties. She simply obtained the necessary capital and began her operations. Ease of organization is one of the reasons most businesses start out as individual proprietorships.

Freedom of Action. Wendy could make her own decisions; it was not necessary to ask anyone when she wanted to try something new or give up something that was not profitable. She had complete freedom.

Unshared Profits. If Wendy succeeds in her store, she can keep all profits herself; she does not have to share them with anyone. One main attraction of an individual proprietorship is the opportunity to make money. However, if the business fails—which is a possibility—Wendy must suffer the loss.

Taxes. While Wendy had to pay taxes on her income, the individual proprietorship is not taxed in the same way as more complex types of businesses. For example, the individual owner does not have to pay an income tax on the business separate from personal income tax. The total amount of tax paid, therefore, tends to be a good deal smaller than that paid by more complex businesses.

Personal Pride of Ownership. Many people like to be their own boss. The owner of a business can take pride in the fact that success in the venture is a personal one. The person can say "This is mine—I did it myself." Pride of ownership can be one of the most rewarding aspects of being on one's own.

Partnership

When Wendy's pet store started to make a sizable profit, she began to think in terms of a larger store. She knew that she had almost reached maximum sales volume with her present amount of store space and merchandise lines. And there was one way Wendy was certain she could increase her sales. The store didn't carry high-price aquariums. Yet customers continually asked for these aquariums and the exotic fish to go inside them, and Wendy knew that she could sell both if she carried them. Establishing an aquarium department would require expanding the store and installing water and temperature control systems and display facilities. This would cost a great deal of money. Also, Wendy knew very little about buying and promoting aquariums or the exotic fish to go inside them; this would require a specialist, someone who had had good experience. The more Wendy thought about it, the more convinced she became that an aquarium department was necessary if she was going to expand her business. But she lacked the necessary capital and know-how, so she began to think of forming a partnership. This is a form of business

Pride of ownership can be one of the most rewarding aspects of being on your own. Courtesy of Liberty Mutual Insurance Company

much like an individual proprietorship except that it has two or more owners.

After a good deal of searching and inquiring, Wendy met Marsha Johnson, a person with experience from another town. Marsha had some money saved up and had long hoped to go into business for herself. She and Marsha decided to form a partnership. They agreed on the amount that Marsha was to invest in the business, how the responsibilities were to be divided for operating the store, and how the profits were to be distributed between them. These decisions were put in the form of a contract—called articles of copartnership—and both Wendy and Marsha signed it. They were in business.

Characteristics of a Partnership

When two or more people combine to own a business jointly, the venture is known as a **partnership.** Many retailers form partnerships rather than start individual proprietorships because two or three people can usually assemble a great deal more money than one person. Then, too, each partner can contribute to the business a special skill the other may not have. In many partnerships, in fact, each partner is a specialist and takes care of the different aspect of the business. In Wendy's and Marsha's store, it was agreed that Marsha would run the aquarium department because she knew more about it than Wendy. This experience and know-how were just as important to Wendy as the money that Marsha had invested. In the typical partnership, all partners share in managing the business, and all have a say in any decisions that are made.

Pros and Cons of a Partnership

Both Wendy and Marsha discovered that there are certain drawbacks to being someone's partner. To begin with, they found that they did not always agree on how their business should be run. Being involved in a partnership means sharing authority with someone who does not always see things from your point of view. It also means taking a chance on your partner's honesty, willingness to work, and ability to do what the partner promises to do.

Being someone's partner, then, means an end to total business independence; each partner is dependent on the other in important ways. In a partnership, each partner is responsible for the business decisions made by the other. An agreement made by one partner is binding on all other partners. This means that if one partner makes a poor decision, the other partner faces the consequences as well. Each partner is also liable for the debts of the other as far as the business is concerned. The death, serious illness, or withdrawal of one or more partners can strain a business to the point where the owners are forced to dissolve it. The law requires that a business be reorganized whenever partners leave the business or whenever new partners are added.

In spite of these disadvantages, both Wendy and Marsha were mature enough in their attitudes toward each other and conscientious enough in their attitudes toward their partnership to have a successful relationship. As they worked together, they were pleased to discover that

In a partnership, each partner contributes a specific skill, such as selling ability or mathematical aptitude.

a partnership offered the following advantages:

More Capital Available.   Two or more people can usually assemble more capital than one person can. This makes it possible to start a larger business, have more capital for expansion, and have reserve funds to fall back on. Likewise, if the business suffers a loss, both partners share the burden of the loss.

Better Management.   Each person in a partnership usually has a special skill that the other lacks. One may be a specialist in accounting and finance, another in advertising and promotion, and still another in buying and merchandising. These combinations of skills lead to better operating procedures and better management.

Greater Interest in the Business.   When a person becomes a partner, there is a much keener interest in the success of the business than when a person is merely an employee. For this reason, partners usually work harder, make a greater effort to keep costs down, and use their imagination more creatively.

Relatively Simple Organization.   It is not difficult to organize a partnership as compared with a corporation. There are few regulations to be dealt with, and the cost of setting up the partnership is relatively small. A lawyer usually prepares a legal document stating the agreements made by each partner.

Low Taxes.   Just as in the individual proprietorship, a partnership enjoys a tax advantage, for the business is not separately taxed on its income.

Corporation

Wendy and Marsha prospered in their partnership. The aquarium department made a handsome profit. They remodeled and expanded the store, and they also added several new lines of merchandise that turned out to be profitable. But they were still not satisfied. They knew that they would do a much greater volume of business if they started an additional store in a new shopping center. However, this would require a great deal more capital than Wendy and Marsha could raise, even if they sold their present store (which they did not want to do). The additional store would require a good deal of money not only for the fixtures but also for the merchandise. Moreover, a large staff would be required to operate the store—salespeople, bookkeepers, cashiers, and department managers would have to be hired. Wendy and Marsha would also have to hire someone to manage the present store.

It would be extremely difficult for Wendy and Marsha to borrow a sum large enough—$100,000 or more, for example—to start and to organize such an operation. If, however, they were to find 20 people willing to invest $5,000 each (with the expectation of making a profit on their investment), their problem would be solved. So, to raise the capital for the new pet store, Wendy and Marsha decided to form a corporation.

Characteristics of a Corporation

A **corporation** is a form of business ownership that operates under a charter issued by the state in which it is located. The charter permits the corporation to sell shares of stock, each share representing part ownership of the business. The shareholders, or owners of the business, elect a board of directors to decide upon the policies of the business. The elected board of directors has the responsibility of appointing the top executives to manage the firm.

Whereas the individual proprietorship is owned by one person and the partnership by two or more, a corporation may have any number of owners. Some corporations have only a few shareholders, often members of the same family. Other corporations have as many as 100,000 or more shareholders (also called stockholders). Since Wendy and Marsha are now accountable to other shareholders, they will no longer be as independent as when they were partners—they actually become employees of the corporation. However, they will still have a major voice in the business, will draw attractive salaries, and will share in the profits of the business by receiving dividends on their investment in the stock.

Pros and Cons of a Corporation

Before Wendy and Marsha formed a corporation, they found that corporations have several advantages over the partnership form of business. There are fewer corporations than individual proprietorships and partnerships in the total number of businesses in the United States. But, in terms of sales volume and the number of people employed, the corporation is the largest form of business ownership. The corporate form of ownership is increasing in popularity. Some of the advantages involved in this form of ownership follow.

Limited Liability.   Each stockholder is liable for debts only to the extent of the original purchase of stock. In contrast, in a partnership, each partner is responsible for all obligations of the firm.

Designated Officers Make Legal Contracts. As partners, Wendy and Marsha could make agreements for which the other partner was responsible. Since there is no one owner in a corporation, only designated officers can make a contract that will bind the company and all its owners (shareholders).

Continued Existence.   When an individual proprietor or a partner dies, the business is often forced to close. This is not true of a corporation. The life of a corporation is not affected by death or disability of an owner; a corporation continues to exist for as long as it operates at a profit.

Growth Possibilities.   A corporation can usually expand rather easily. If the firm wants to build new stores or take on new lines and needs a great deal of money to do so, it can offer stock or sell bonds to the public and obtain the capital needed.

Expert Management and Economic Operations.   The large corporation can afford to hire a variety of skilled personnel. The large corporation can also save money by purchasing goods in large quantities and by organizing its various operations efficiently.

Consumer Cooperatives

Cooperatives are not a legal form of ownership; rather, they are a business orga-

A consumer cooperative is a retail business that is owned and directed by its customers. *Courtesy of Metro Newspaper Service*

nization that is owned and directed by its own customers. The customers are members and owners of the organization. All cooperatives operate under a set of basic principles. They are set up to meet the specific needs and problems of the membership and they share operating costs and profits with the membership based on some predetermined formula.

A **consumer cooperative** is a retail business owned and directed by its own customers, who are known as members. Consumer cooperatives normally develop where existing retail facilities are viewed as being inadequate for some reason. They may also develop in areas where consumers suspect retailers of getting excessive profits from the prices they charge. Essentially, however, a consumer cooperative can be formed any time a large enough group of people decide to compete with existing retailers or to perform a service that is not currently being performed by someone else.

The oldest consumer cooperatives in this country are those that were formed by farmers in rural areas of the north central United States. The farmers formed them to serve their needs for various types of economical farm supplies and services. On or near some college campuses, students operate bookstore cooperatives in competition with other bookstores. There are also food cooperatives and health cooperatives operating in various sections of many large cities. Credit unions, travel co-ops, and child day-care centers are other examples of cooperatives. Because profits are returned to the members in the form of lower prices, the desire to save money seems to always be the main reason for beginning a cooperative.

Choosing a Form of Ownership

There are several factors to consider when choosing a form of ownership. These factors include (1) the type of business, (2) the degree to which the owners wish to take part in the management of the business, (3) the amount of capital needed for the business, (4) the extent of risk or liability the owners wish to assume, and (5) the entrepreneur's management experiences.

In this chapter, you learned about the four different types of retail ownership. However, these types of arrangements aren't the only choices available if you have the ambition to branch out on your own. Some ownership-management combinations will also give you this opportunity. Ownership-management combinations are discussed in the next chapter.

Trade Talk

Define each term and use it in a sentence.

Consumer cooperative
Corporation
Entrepreneurs

Individual proprietorship
Partnership

Can You Answer These?

1. What are the advantages of the type of ownership called an individual proprietorship?
2. Why would people choose to organize a business as a partnership rather than as an individual proprietorship?
3. One advantage of a corporation is limited liability. Why is this so important?
4. What type of organization is best if a business requires a large amount of capital? Why?
5. What form of ownership is least common in the retail industry? What are some advantages of this form of ownership?

Problems

1. Rule a form similar to the following. In the left column, list ten retail businesses in your community; in the middle column tell what kind of business each is; and in the right column, indicate how each business is organized—that is, whether it is

an individual proprietorship, a partnership, a corporation, or a cooperative.

Name of Business	Kind of Business	Form of Organization
Example: Munson's Dairy	Small grocery store	Individual proprietorship

2. Rule a form similar to the following. In the left column, write the letter of each of the following business organization characteristics: (*0*) two or more people combine their money and skills, (*a*) a board of directors is elected, (*b*) a contract is drawn up on how responsibilities and profits will be shared, (*c*) the owner is boss, (*d*) the business is formed more easily than other forms of business, (*e*) capital is obtained by selling shares of stock, (*f*) the business is dissolved upon the death of an owner, (*g*) only designated officers can make a contract, (*h*) the owner assumes all risks, and (*i*) the business requires a written state charter. In the right column, give the appropriate form of business organization for each characteristic listed.

Business Organization Characteristic	Form of Business
Example: (0)	Partnership

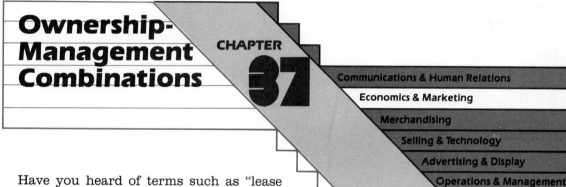

Ownership-Management Combinations

CHAPTER 37

Communications & Human Relations
Economics & Marketing
Merchandising
Selling & Technology
Advertising & Display
Operations & Management

Have you heard of terms such as "lease dealership," "franchise," "manufacturer-owned chains," "leased department," and "corporate retail chains?"

In retailing, as in most fields, special terminology is used. In this chapter you're going to get acquainted with various ways in which retailers can choose to own or manage their businesses. You may find out that you have even worked in a retail firm that is like one of those described.

Development of Ownership-Management Combinations

Over the years, retailers have created various ownership-management combinations in an effort to gain an advantage over their competitors. During the 1930s, large retailers grew because they could sell their products and services more cheaply than could smaller retailers. During the years that followed, smaller retailers joined together. Also, other retailers designed various ownership-management combinations to compete with the larger retailers and gain increased consumer acceptance. The advantages and disadvantages of the following ownership-management combinations are discussed in the order of their development: corporate retail chains, manufacturer-owned chains, voluntary chains, leased departments, leased dealerships, and franchises. They were also discussed briefly in Chapter 3.

Corporate Retail Chains

As you'll recall from Chapter 3, a **corporate retail chain** is a group of two or more businesses linked together under one management and owned by stockholders. The businesses in the chain are centrally owned and managed and usually sell similar products and services. A well-known example of a corporate retail chain is Sears, Roebuck and Co.

The chain-store movement began to grow rapidly in the late 1930s and now accounts for almost 40 percent of the nation's total retail trade volume. In some kinds of retailing—groceries, gasoline service stations, variety stores, department stores, drugstores, furniture stores, and mass merchandisers—chain stores account for over 60 percent of the total sales volume. Corporate chains have obtained a growing share of the total retail sales volume.

Corporate retail chains have prospered because they have certain advantages not available to the independent retailer. The one major advantage of the corporate chain is its central management. Central management can provide many services at very little cost to the individual business. For example, the chain can offer a complete advertising plan for all its locations, and the cost of administering the plan can be shared by all the units in the chain. Centralization also means that corporate chains can afford to hire staffs of specialists that most retailers have neither the time nor the money to hire. In addition, individual businesses in the chain also benefit from the credit and sales promotion plans developed at central headquarters.

Corporate chains are also able to reduce their expenses by several means. For one thing, because they buy the same merchandise and supplies for several businesses, they can enjoy discounts given for buying in quantity. Also, the headquarters staff is trained to buy and control the inventory very carefully.

Chain retailers can spread their risks. Merchandise that does not sell well in one location can be moved to a site where it is well received. A business that is doing poorly in one location can be closed and the cost of its loss absorbed by the other businesses in the chain.

Manufacturer-Owned Chains

When two or more retail stores that are owned and managed by a manufacturer primarily to sell the products of that company we have what is known as a **manufacturer-owned chain.** There are many such firms. Goodyear Tire and Rubber Company and Firestone Tire and Rubber Company are examples of manufacturer-owned chains. Approximately 60 percent of the sales in the shoe business are handled by manufacturer-owned chain stores such as Thom McAn and Flagg Brothers.

With this type of arrangement, the manufacturer has complete control over the distribution of the company's products, but it takes a large amount of capital to build and operate the necessary retail outlets. It is for this reason that many manufacturers cannot or do not wish to own their own outlets.

Voluntary Chains

A **voluntary chain** is an organization of independent retailers who own and operate their own stores. Voluntary chains exist mostly in the food distribution business to meet the competition of large corporate chains such as Jewel, A&P, and Safeway.

Sometimes, voluntary chains are owned and financed by the member retail stores. Associated Grocers is an example of this type of chain. More often, voluntary chains are organized by wholesalers such as Independent Grocers Alliance (IGA). When food retailers join the independent Grocers Alliance, they agree to buy all or a major part of their merchandise from the wholesaler in return for management services. Such services include pooled advertising, accounting system aids, assistance in store planning, employee training, and equipment and display materials. Sometimes wholesalers finance a new independent business completely.

Leased Departments

Have you purchased shoes, automotive supplies, photographic equipment, optical goods, or jewelry from a corporate chain store? If so, chances are that the department you shopped at was not owned or operated by the store itself. It was probably a **leased department,** one that is rented by another retail organization that specializes in a particular line of goods or services.

Retailers have found the leased department to be an effective way of offering more goods and services to customers at minimum risk and with less expenses for operating costs. The lessee benefits too by reaching customers who have been attracted to the chain store. The lessee must obey all the rules and regulations of the store. The lessor (retail store) usually receives a percentage of the income from the department.

A leased department specializes in a particular service that the lessor wants to provide at minimum risk and with lower operating costs.   Elizabeth Richter

Leased Dealerships

A **leased dealership** is an arrangement whereby a supplier leases a business establishment to a retail operator. The retail operator, or lessee, rents not only the building and land but also major equipment. The retail operator has the right to manage the business and sell certain goods and services. In return for these rights, the dealer agrees to follow operating procedures established by the supplier for running the business.

Major oil companies have, in some cases, found it best to own service stations and lease them to dealers who operate them under the company's guidance and control. The station operators must buy their own merchandise from the company leasing the station. The station operator must also buy small pieces of equipment and tools needed for the station operation.

Franchises

A **franchise** is an agreement that gives the owner of a business the right to use a certain business name or sell certain products and services. Most franchise businesses are managed by the person who owns them. This means, for example, that if you wished to open a Dairy Queen fast-food operation, you would first have to enter into a legal agreement with that franchise owner.

During the past 20 years, franchising has been one of the fastest-growing forms of retailing. More than 466,000 outlets account for 30 percent of all retail sales. Among the larger franchise businesses are Baskin-Robbins, McDonald's, AAMCO automatic transmissions, and Holiday Inn.

Perhaps the major reason for the growth of franchising is that it offers people the

Franchise opportunities are available in a wide variety of retail businesses.

CARVEL

opportunity to own their own businesses while still enjoying many of the advantages of the corporate chain operation. Some of these advantages are group buying power, promotional support, financial aid, help in finding a good location, detailed product information, the use of a well-known name, managerial training, and supervision.

In return, the franchisor receives a return from the franchise in one or more of the following forms:

1. A straight fee for the use of the name of the firm
2. A percentage of the gross sales
3. Profits from the sale of equipment, supplies, or finished products or services to the franchisee

Advantages of Franchising

According to the U.S. Small Business Administration, the franchise has several advantages over the independent retailer. These are as follows:

♦ *Initial Investment*. It usually takes less money to start a franchise business than a nonfranchise one. Moreover, the franchisor often provides the franchisee with financial assistance.
♦ *Working Capital*. It takes less money to operate a franchise business because the franchisor provides the franchisee with good inventory controls and other means of reducing expenses. When necessary, the franchisor may also provide financial assistance for operating expenses.
♦ *Reputation*. In an established and well-known franchise system, the new franchisee does not have to work to establish the firm's reputation. The product or service being offered is one that the public has already accepted.
♦ *Experience*. The management assistance provided by the franchisor makes up for the new store owner's inexperience.
♦ *Management Assistance*. The owner of a small independent store has to be a jack-of-all-trades, and even an experienced re-

tailer may not be an expert in all aspects of financing, recordkeeping, marketing, and sales promotion. The better franchising companies provide the franchisee with continuing assistance in these areas.
♦ *Profits*. Assuming reasonable franchise fees and supply arrangements, the franchisee can usually expect a reasonable margin of profit because the business is run with the efficiency of a chain.
♦ *Motivation*. Because the franchisee and the franchisor both benefit from the success of the operation, both work hard to achieve it.

Disadvantages of Franchising

There are also disadvantages for the retailer in franchising. The Small Business Administration lists the following drawbacks:

♦ *Fees*. The fees the franchisor charges for the use of the firm's name, the prices charged for supplies, and other charges may be too high for a particular locality. So they may result in losses or low profit margins for the retailer.
♦ *Less Independence*. Because the franchisee must follow the franchisor's pattern of operation, the retailer loses some independence.
♦ *Standardization*. Procedures are standardized, and franchisees don't get much of a chance to use their own ideas.
♦ *Slowness*. Because of size, a franchisor may be slow to get in on a new idea or adapt methods to meet changed conditions.
♦ *Cancellation*. It's difficult and expensive to cancel a franchise agreement without the cooperation of the franchise company.

Employee-Ownership Participation

Retailers have learned that the more their employees take part in the planning and operation of the business, the more dedicated they are. So some retailers own a number of franchises that they allow their employees to buy into on a cooperative ba-

Standardization is both an advantage and a disadvantage of franchising. Courtesy of McDonald's Corporation

sis. Also, some retailers offer their employees the opportunity to enroll in profit-sharing plans and have found such arrangements to be profitable for both the store and the employees.

Now that you've finished this unit, what can you conclude about the many different ways our economic system—free enterprise—allows those who are willing to take a risk to start a business and make a profit? After you've successfully learned the ropes of a retailing job or jobs and had enough experience in different retailing areas, you might want to consider starting your own business or forming a partnership with someone else. But remember, to be an effective retail worker and to build a successful business, you must have enthusiasm and develop into the type of person who makes things happen!

Trade Talk

Define each term and use it in a sentence.

Corporate retail chain
Franchise
Leased dealership
Leased department
Manufacturer-owned chain
Voluntary chain

Can You Answer These?

1. What are the advantages of operating a corporate retail chain store?
2. Why do manufacturers sometimes own and operate stores?
3. In what kinds of businesses do voluntary chains predominate?
4. How can a leased department benefit a department store retailer?
5. Why would a person choose to operate a store under a franchise agreement rather than becoming an independent retailer?

Problems

1. Rule a form similar to the following. In the left column, list ten retail businesses in your community; in the middle column, tell what kind of business each is; and in the right column, indicate how each business is organized.

Name of Business	Kind of Business	Type of Organization
Example: Flagg Bros.	Small shoe store	Manufacturer-owned chain

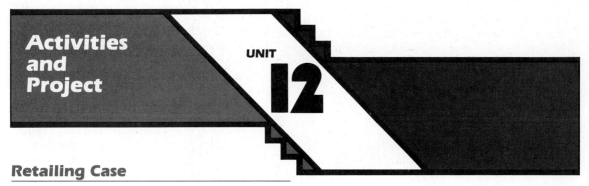

Activities and Project

UNIT 12

Retailing Case

Sheila Greenspan, owned a small neighborhood apparel store in Detroit. The business, operated as an individual proprietorship with two full-time employees in addition to Sheila, was profitable and well established.

Terry Zilinski, a long-time friend of Sheila's had been employed by a specialty mail-order house for 5 years when he suggested that he and Sheila start a mail-order business of their own, to be called the Green-Z Company. Since Sheila had already been considering expanding her business, she agreed to Terry's proposition.

A verbal understanding was reached to the effect that Sheila would be paid back the money she put into the business before a 50-50 sharing plan was begun. Terry quit the mail-order house where he had been working and devoted all his time to the preparation of a catalog and mailing list and to similar duties. He did an excellent job of getting current price quotations from potential suppliers of the articles listed in the catalog. No effort was made, however, to obtain firm price commitments on any given quantity of goods or for any specified period of time.

For several years preceding Sheila's and Terry's venture, prices had been fairly stable with a slight tendency to decline. However, just as their last catalog was mailed, conditions changed, the prices rose because of inflation. The Green-Z Company received orders that emptied out its small inventories within a week. It soon became clear that many of its goods could no longer be obtained at prices allowing any profit. So the closing of the business was inevitable.

Forms were quickly printed to accompany refunds on all future orders, and notices of dissolution were sent to the entire mailing list. Sheila paid the printer and all expenses connected with winding up the affairs of the company. Her total loss was close to $5,000, half of which they agreed would eventually be repaid by Terry.

Fortunately, Sheila was able to settle the

company's obligations without seriously harming her own financial position or endangering her retail store business. Terry soon had another job. Both had learned a lesson about partnerships.

1. Since Terry was the mail-order expert, was it fair for Sheila to suffer the entire financial loss?
2. What would you have done had you been in Sheila's position?
3. Under the circumstances described in the case, should the Green-Z Company have been incorporated? If it had been, what effects would that have had on the outcome of the business?
4. What lesson did Sheila and Terry learn about partnership?

Working with People

David Espinosa, owner of Espinosa's Sporting Goods, recently developed financial problems in his company. At that time, Dave's friend Mike McCrary offered to invest in the business. Dave accepted the offer and a partnership was formed. Now that Mike is a partner, he wants to change the name of the store to McCrary and Espinosa, change some of the suppliers used, and begin an advertising program. Dave told Mike that he had no right to come in and start taking over, and he refused to make the changes that Mike suggested. Mike said he would go to see a lawyer if Dave didn't reconsider.

1. Identify the true problem.
2. What are the important facts to be considered in this problem?
3. List several possible results of each solution.
4. Evaluate the possible results of each solution.
5. Which solution do you recommend? Why?

Project 12: Analyzing Types of Business Ownership

Your Project Goal
Given descriptions of the individual proprietorship, partnership, corporation, and franchise, read three articles on business ownership from current magazines, newspapers, or trade journals. Then interview a person who represents each of the different ownerships. Based on your reading and interviews, write a report on what type of ownership would offer the greatest opportunity for success in today's marketing economy.

Procedure
Review Chapters 36 and 37, which discuss the different types of business ownership. To help you learn about ownership and management, complete the following project.

1. Read three articles on the subject of different types of business ownership. Select these from magazines, newspapers or trade journals. (You may want to ask your teacher or librarian about possible sources.)
2. Interview one person for each of the various ownership styles. Ask the following questions during your interviews:
   a. What is your previous business experience? Why did you choose that type of ownership?
   b. What are the advantages of this business?
   c. Have you had any problems with this type of ownership?
   d. What advice would you give a potential business person about this type of ownership?
3. Write a 500 word report on the type of ownership that would offer the greatest opportunity for success in today's marketing economy. Base your report on your readings and interviews. Submit the report to your teacher.

Evaluation
You will be evaluated on (1) the reading you accomplish, (2) the information received from the interviews, and (3) how thoroughly you complete Step 3.

298

Keeping Merchandise Moving

Stock Turnover

CHAPTER 38

Communications & Human Relations

Economics & Marketing

Merchandising

Selling & Technology

Advertising & Display

Operations & Management

Ed Marias, an appliance-department head of stock, was wondering how he might best allocate space to various products. He realizes that some merchandise moves fast but doesn't bring much profit. So he wondered whether he should give it more space in hopes of increasing profit or try to replace it with a more profitable item. Also, there is other merchandise that sells infrequently, but Ed doesn't really know whether it's worthwhile to continue stocking it.

Ed's questions are not unusual for either a small- or a large-store retailer. Knowing what merchandise to carry in stock is basic to good merchandising decisions. If a store or an individual department within a store is to be successful, sales and inventory should be reviewed periodically to determine:

1. How rapidly the merchandise is selling
2. How much floor or counter space should be given to the merchandise
3. The amount of return on investment that's being realized on certain merchandise

How to Calculate Stock Turnover

Several basic tools of inventory control can be used to help a retail salesperson like Ed Marias make the above decisions. For example, to identify how rapidly clock radios are selling for a 3-month period, Ed could calculate the **stock turnover** or "stockturns," as it is often called. This is the number of times a quantity of stock, or inventory, is turned into sales during a given period of time. Stock turnover can be figured for a week, a month, a selling season, a year, or any other period. It can be calculated for the store as a whole, for each department within a store, for each classification of merchandise, or occasionally for a particular item of merchandise. Stock turnover is calculated in terms of units or dollars or both.

Determining Stock Turnover by Units

Stock turnover by units is the number of times that the average units of stock on hand have sold out and been replaced during a selling period. "Average units of stock on hand" means the usual amounts of stock that are kept on hand during the selling period. (Various methods of computing average stock are described later in this chapter.) The rate of stock turnover by units can be computed by dividing the total units sold by the average number of units of merchandise in stock. This calculation is illustrated as follows:

$$\text{Stockturn in units} = \frac{\text{sales in units}}{\text{average units of stock on hand}}$$

Let's determine the unit stockturn of Ed's clock radios for the past year. From the inventory and sales records, the following information is computed:

Average units of clock radios on hand	= 20
Total units of clock radios sold	= 80
Number of unit stockturns for the year	= 4 (80 ÷ 20)

Ed knows that the clock radio inventory has been turning over at the rate of 4 times a year. He can use this number to identify the lines of merchandise that have turned over at a faster or slower rate. In certain cases to obtain increased profit, Ed may decide to order more stock that has been selling at a faster rate. In other cases, he may decide to reduce or eliminate slower-selling merchandise.

Computing Average Stock

Determining total net sales volume for the period is a simple matter of referring to the sales records. Determining what the average stock on hand is during a particular period requires more effort. The general formula is:

Beginning inventory + ending inventory ÷ 2 = **average stock**

If Ed Marias's beginning inventory was 16 units and the ending inventory was 20 units, then the average units of stock on hand was 18 units, (16 + 20 ÷ 2 = 18). Suppose Ed Marias had a beginning inventory of $1,600 and ended the year with $2,000 worth of goods. Adding the figures $1,600 + $2,000 and dividing by 2 would give an average dollar value of stock on hand of $1,800. These two examples illustrate how the average stock can be computed both by units and by dollars.

These calculations would be satisfactory methods to use if the period of time concerned were short enough. It would give accurate enough data when figuring stock turnover for a week or a month. However, it would not be an accurate method to use when figuring the average inventory for a period longer than a month, such as a quarter, a season, or a year. In the case of a year, for example, most retailers try to carry their smallest inventories at the end of the year, particularly if those inventories are subject to tax.

A more useful way to figure an average inventory for a period of a year is to use the inventory figures for the beginning of each month in that year. The 12 monthly figures plus the ending inventory for the last month of the year are added, and the resulting sum is divided by 13. This method is more accurate because the monthly changes in inventory are taken into account. This consideration of monthly variations is important. In some stores, for example, the amount of inventory changes widely because of the seasonal nature of sales.

Determining Stock Turnover by Dollars

Stock turnover by dollars is a measurement of the number of times during a given period that the retail dollar value of the average inventory is sold and replaced. To determine the stockturn in dollars, the following calculation is used:

$$\text{Stockturn in dollars} = \frac{\text{dollar sales of merchandise for the period}}{\text{average retail dollar value of the merchandise on hand}}$$

Note that in this calculation, the average dollar value of the merchandise must be at the retail, or selling price, value if the correct stockturn in dollars is to be obtained.

Ed can calculate the average dollar value of his inventory by reviewing the inventory records. The beginning inventory of clock radios was valued at $1,600 and an ending inventory was valued at $2,000. The average dollar value of merchandise can be calculated to be $1,800. Ed determines from his records that the dollar sales of clock radios for the period was $7,200. By using dollar figures rather than unit figures, he can also determine that the stockturn for the clock radios was 4 ($7,200 ÷ $1,800 = 4).

Using the Retail or Cost Method of Inventory Valuation

Some retailers keep records in terms of cost figures; others keep records in terms of retail figures. Stock turnover can be figured either in terms of cost figures or retail figures, depending on the kind of bookkeeping the retailer uses.

Many small stores use the **cost method of inventory valuation** rather than the retail method. This means that all records are kept on the basis of the actual cost value of the merchandise. This is the older of the two methods. It's popular among retailers with very rapid turnovers of merchandise, such as supermarkets, where retail prices may change several times within a given week. For small stores, it's

the easier of the two ways of keeping records. Less information needs to be collected and calculated when the cost method is used.

Most retailers use the **retail method of inventory valuation**. This means that records are kept on the basis of the retail value of the merchandise. This method enables retailers to record a more current estimate of the value of the inventory. The current retail selling price is usually a realistic price, the price that retailers believe customers will pay for the merchandise. This price is adjusted upward or downward on the basis of such factors as economic conditions, supply of and demand for the merchandise, and competition. For these major reasons, this method is widely used by retailers.

Determining Stock Turnover by Retail and Cost Methods

The following examples show how the rate of stock turnover can be determined by the retail method and by the cost method. You'll recall that to determine the rate of stock turnover by the retail method, retailers divide total net sales for the period by the average inventory. For example, if net annual sales are $60,000 and average inventory at retail is $6,000, then:

$$\frac{\text{Net sales (\$60,000)}}{\text{Average inventory (\$6,000)}} = 10 \text{ stockturns per year}$$

Calculations by the cost method are a little more involved. First, the net sales must be known at cost figures. This is found by figuring the cost of goods as follows:

Beginning inventory	$ 6,000
Add purchases	24,000
Total goods available for sale	$30,000
Deduct ending inventory	5,000
Costs of goods sold	$25,000

Supermarkets prefer to use the cost method of inventory valuation because they have very rapid turnover of merchandise. Ron Tanner/Progressive Grocer

Now divide by the average inventory at cost (assume that it's $5,000 here):

$$\frac{\text{Cost of goods sold} (\$25,000)}{\text{Average inventory at cost} (\$5,000)} = 5 \text{ stockturns per year}$$

Analyzing Stock Turnover Rates

Turnover rates themselves are of little importance unless retailers know what they mean and how to analyze them. For example, the rate of stock turnover within a store or any of its departments can be compared from one year to the next. And this comparison will suggest whether the right items are being bought and promoted. Retailers can also compare rates of stock turnover with the rates of similar stores. If turnover rates are different from the average of other similar stores, it's necessary to determine why. Retailers can get average turnover rates for various types of stores and lines of merchandise from trade journals, reports of trade associations, and organizations such as Dun & Bradstreet.

Variations in Turnover Rates

Turnover rates can and do vary. Successful retailers attempt to get the best turnover possible within the merchandising policies they establish. A jewelry store, for example, may consider a turnover rate of about 1 acceptable. But a supermarket may set the rate at 50 or more. The rate depends upon a number of factors. First, what assortment does the store wish to carry? Some stores carry huge assortments with many items that sell very slowly. Customers expect to find whatever they want and expect to pay a price for this service. Some stores carry only a limited line of goods that are best sellers. And they expect to lose some sales when they don't have everything customers want. Some stores are located near suppliers and can get stock replacements quickly. Others are not, so they must order far in advance.

Advantages of Increased Stock Turnover

If retailers can increase stock turnover at a rate that's good for business, these are some of the advantages:

1. An increase in total profits, which usually results when sales volume rises.
2. The ability to use capital more efficiently. With increased turnover, a smaller capital investment in stock can be made to produce a satisfactory volume of sales. If the rate of turnover is increased, so that $10,000 in sales can be made with an in-

vestment in stock of $2,000 instead of $4,000, the extra $2,000 can be used to buy other lines of merchandise or can be invested in some other way.

3. A decrease of expenses. Some store expenses are fixed; they do not vary with sales. Examples of fixed expenses are rent and property taxes. But when a store increases its rate of turnover, such expenses (and usually other expenses as well) are decreased in proportion to sales.

4. A decrease in markdowns. When there is a rapid rate of turnover, goods remain in stock for a short time. They do not spoil or become shopworn or obsolete.

5. The ability to buy new merchandise without exceeding planned closing-stock levels. This is especially important in fashion goods. These goods often change rapidly in customer color and style preferences.

6. The ability to keep merchandise fresh. This increases sales because customers like to buy fresh merchandise and salespeople like to sell it.

Which of these two stores has the higher stock turnover rate? Why? Paolo
Koch/Photo Researchers, Inc. (top), Jane Hamilton-Merritt (bottom)

Disadvantages of a High Stock Turnover

A store may lose sales and decrease profits if it tries to maintain too high a rate of turnover. If the inventory becomes too low or too restricted in variety, the store may often be out of stock on some items. Sales and customer goodwill will be lost. To keep a complete assortment of goods, most retailers also stock some items that sell more slowly. While this leads to a slower turnover for the complete stock, the store satisfies its customers and maintains its sales volume. A high rate of turnover may also increase the costs of ordering and receiving because more frequent orders and shipments are made. Finally, retailers may lose quantity discounts if only small quantities are ordered.

Determining Profit According to Selling Space

As well as obtaining a desirable stock turnover, retailers must also be concerned with realizing maximum profit from available selling space. Rent for retail stores is often charged per square foot of selling space.

As a head of stock, Ed Marias must still consider the space costs of doing business. This space is either owned or rented. Such costs as interest on borrowed money, rent payments, maintenance expenses, and heating and lighting expenses must be paid from the sales realized from the space available.

Stock turnover is directly related to the profit-per-square-foot calculations. Retailers must periodically analyze the profit per square foot in relation to the stock turnover of the various lines of merchandise. All retailers must be concerned with realizing maximum profit from available selling space. The calculation of profit per square foot provides an indication of how much profit was realized on an item of merchandise from each square foot of sell-

ing space it occupied. This calculation helps to determine how much space should be allocated to each item.

Calculating Profit Per Square Foot

As the term suggests, **profit per square foot** is calculated by dividing the gross profit of an item—or merchandise line—by the area of selling space for that item. The procedure for computing profit per square foot is as follows:

$$\text{Profit per square foot} = \frac{\text{gross profit on item or merchandise line}}{\text{square feet of selling space}}$$

Assume that Ed Marias's department made $4,000 in gross profit last year on hair dryers. The selling space for the line was 200 square feet of shelf and floor space. What is the profit per square foot for the hair dryers? It can be figured as follows:

$$\text{Gross profit per square foot} = \frac{\$4,000 \text{ gross profit}}{200 \text{ square feet of selling space}} = \$20$$

Allocating Selling Space on the Basis of Profit Per Square Foot

To obtain the highest profit from available selling space, retailers must study each merchandise line to determine which provides the highest, as well as the lowest, profit per square foot. To do this, they figure the profit per square foot for the fastest- and slowest-moving items. The difference in these profits is called a **profitability range**. For example, Ed Marias discovered that his most profitable line of merchandise generated $30 gross profit per square foot of selling space. He also discovered that his least profitable line generated only $5 per square foot of selling space. Ed would use this profitability range to increase and decrease selling space on the basis of the profitability of merchandise lines.

Retailers can increase overall profitability by taking the following courses of action for low-profit items:

304

- Promoting the merchandise more effectively
- Reducing the space alloted to the merchandise
- Replacing the merchandise

In certain cases, even the low-profit items may be yielding a sufficient profit per square foot. But retailers can still increase the profitability of such items by:

- Increasing promotion and merchandising efforts for individual items
- Expanding the selling space
- Taking both courses of action

Before retailers decide to replace low-profit items from merchandise lines, they usually determine that the manner of merchandising them isn't the problem. In many cases, for example, they can improve sales volume by promoting products. At other times, however, it's obvious that little can be done to increase sales of a given product. Some items just don't lend themselves well to promotion. In such situations, gradual replacement may be the best strategy.

How to Increase Stock Turnover

The decisions that retailers make concerning average stock on hand and sales-space allocations have a direct effect on stock turnover. Also, the following merchandise strategies can help to increase stock turnover.

Improved Buying

When buyers know what customers want and follow an appropriate plan, stock turnover will increase. Buyers can find out what customers want by spending time on the selling floor, consulting with customers and salespeople, and by studying reliable market information. And by carefully following a plan, buyers can purchase goods in sufficient quantities without overstocking a department or store.

Better Pricing

The pricing of goods at too high a figure leads to slow stock turnover. If this situation occurs, buyers or retailers should

One way to increase stock turnover is to mark down the price of merchandise. Kip Peticolas/Fundamental Photographs

immediately mark down the goods to a price that will cause customers to buy.

Accurate Stock Control

Accurate stock control helps to increase turnover. It shows which items are selling well and which are not. Stock control also indicates the maximum number of items that should be in stock. This eliminates the buying of too large a stock, which reduces stock turnover.

Efficient Stockkeeping

Turnover can be increased by efficient stockkeeping practices that reduce damages in handling and assembling. Proper stockkeeping procedures protect merchandise from soiling, spoilage and water, heat, or age damage—all of which prevent rapid turnover. Prompt restocking of shelves will prevent the store from running out of floor stock and keep turnover rates high.

Coordinated Promotion

Stock turnover can be increased by buyers who use a coordinated plan for advertising, display, and personal selling. Advertised items that are both displayed in store windows and promoted by sales personnel on the selling floor arouse the customer's interest and increase sales. To ensure that salespeople give correct information regarding promotional campaigns, retailers should offer their sales staffs training in selling techniques. Promotions lose their effectiveness when the sales staff is not adequately trained or informed.

Obviously, stockturns are only general guidelines. There are certain reasons why retailers can't strictly adhere to them with respect to specific items. These reasons include the following:

1. Minimum quantities of an item may have to be purchased. Because of such purchases, the average inventory cannot be reduced enough to maintain the stockturns desired.

2. An opportunity to obtain quantity dis-counts on large volume purchases may exist. In cases where it pays to take the discount, the average stock on hand will be larger, causing the stockturns to be smaller than desired.

Ed Marias, as well as other retailers large and small, must keep informed of the turnover of merchandise. With today's frequently changing customer preferences for new product models, styles, and colors, retailers can't tie up their selling space in yesterday's outdated merchandise "dogs." Stock-turnover analysis is a valuable merchandising tool that helps retailers to make buying, pricing, and space-allocation decisions.

In this chapter, then, you've learned about the importance of stock or inventory turnover. And in the next chapter, you'll find out about the steps retailers must take to control stocks or inventory so that they get the desired amount of turnover.

Trade Talk

Define each term and use it in a sentence.

Average stock
Cost method of
 inventory
 valuation
Profit per square foot
Profitability range
Retail method of
 inventory
 valuation

Stock turnover
Stock turnover by
 dollars
Stock turnover by
 units

Can You Answer These?

1. How is the average stock figure calculated for a year period?
2. How is stock turnover by dollars calculated?
3. How can stock-turnover calculations be related to profit-per-square-foot calculations?
4. What advantages are there to a retailer in having a high stock turnover? What risks?

5. How is the profit-per-square-foot figure calculated?

Problems

1. Ed Marias's appliance department recorded its total sales and stock inventory from January 31 to June 30 as follows:

Date	Sales	Stock
January 1	$20,000	$30,000
February 1	26,000	32,000
March 1	36,000	30,000
April 1	42,000	60,000
May 1	48,000	60,000
June 1	55,000	50,000
June 30	50,000	55,000

On a separate sheet of paper, calculate the stock turnover for the period from January 31 to June 30.

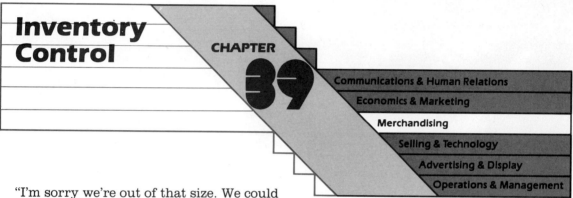

Inventory Control

CHAPTER 39

Communications & Human Relations
Economics & Marketing
Merchandising
Selling & Technology
Advertising & Display
Operations & Management

"I'm sorry we're out of that size. We could special-order it for you, but it may take 3 weeks to receive the coat."

"That's too bad, I need the coat for a party next week. I'll look somewhere else."

How often is an exchange like this conducted between salespeople and customers in stores throughout the country? "Too often" is probably the answer. A retailer may want to sell and a customer may want to buy, but if the merchandise isn't on hand, no sale will be made. A good inventory control system can minimize this problem.

Inventory Control Systems

Inventory control is the coordination of the supply, storage, distribution, and recording of goods. Retailers have such systems to maintain quantities adequate for current needs without too much oversupply or loss. And successful retailers organize an inventory-control system to provide this information for a certain elapsed period, such as a month, a selling season, or a year. Such a system also provides retailers with information concerning the condition of the inventory at a specific date—the end of the month, for example.

Importance of Inventory Control

Recent merchandising trends have made careful inventory control more important than ever before. Reliable inventory control provides retailers with information for meeting competition, regulating the amount of stock, and calculating taxes. Intense competition has increased the need for retailers to find out exactly what customers want today and to determine what they are likely to want tomorrow. Only by identifying and measuring customer demand, as indicated by what sells and what doesn't, can retailers offer attractive merchandise to their customers.

Today, to devote the maximum amount

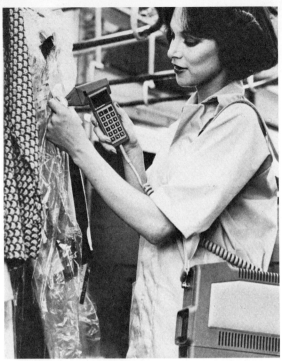

Careful inventory control is very important to retailers. Here, inventory is being checked on a supermarket floor (left) and in a warehouse (right). *Courtesy of Recognition Products Inc. (left) and NORAND (right)*

of space to selling, more and more retailers are reducing the size of their storage and other nonselling areas. They are keeping their reserve stock in warehouses in low-rent areas and shipping to the store or directly to customers as required. Chain stores are relying with increasing frequency on central warehouses rather than keeping their reserve stock in the store or a neighborhood warehouse. When retailers keep less stock at the retail outlet, they need close inventory control to make sure that the store doesn't run out of stock.

Retailers usually pay federal and state income taxes on the basis of net profit earned. Some state and local governments also collect personal property taxes on the inventory on hand. But only when inventory records are properly organized will state and local government accept them as a basis for figuring taxes. So, obviously,

the lower the inventory, the less tax retailers have to pay.

Inventory Control Systems by Units and Dollars

Unit control is an inventory control system based on the number of items of merchandise rather than on the dollar value of the merchandise. This system shows how many items (units) of each type of merchandise are on hand or on order or have been sold. This information may be classified by type of merchandise and by size, color, style, model, and so on. Since the increased use of computers, retailers can keep track of many classifications of merchandise information.

Dollar stock control is an inventory control system that records data about merchandise in terms of money. This system identifies how much the goods are worth in terms of either cost or retail prices. Such information is very important because buyers must know the dollar value of stock on hand and on order when making decisions about the funds required to reorder needed merchandise.

In actual practice both unit control and dollar stock control are necessary if buyers are to have sufficient information for inventory control decisions. This chapter focuses on unit-control systems.

Information Provided by Unit-Control Records

Buyers rely on unit-control records to give them up-to-date information regarding merchandise and sales. Unit-control figures can help answer the questions below.

Question 1: How can an adequate assortment of merchandise be maintained?

Answer: Unit control makes it easier for buyers to maintain an adequate assortment of merchandise because the records show when a minimum stock quantity has been reached. **A minimum stock quantity** is the level at which goods must be reordered. It's based on the number of units sold during a past sales period. By ordering goods in advance, buyers avoid being out of stock on any item. An adequate assortment of merchandise is thereby maintained.

Question 2: Which reorder should be increased and which should be decreased?

Answer: When a store carries a number of brands, buyers may find that unit-control records reveal only a few bestsellers. In this case, buyers can reduce the number of brands without hurting sales and profits.

Unit-control records also indicate sales by sizes, styles, colors, and price lines. By analyzing this information, buyers can identify changes in customer preferences.

By being aware of these changes, buyers can increase or decrease the size of certain orders.

Question 3: Which best-selling items or slow-selling items should be promoted?

Answer: By referring to unit-control records, buyers can see which items were offered during previous promotions. Decisions can be made concerning whether the best-selling items should be promoted again or whether a promotion should be used to get rid of certain slow-selling merchandise.

Inventory Control Stock Lists

A department or store that's often out of stock finds itself constantly ordering small quantities on a rush basis or losing sales. The rush orders involve extra expenses, such as telephone and delivery charges. There are two kinds of inventory control stock lists that keep a buyer informed so that rush orders or out-of-stock conditions can be avoided: model stock lists and basic stock lists.

Model Stock List

A **model stock list** is a list of items, established by store or department policy, that are always kept in inventory. Model stock lists reflect store policy concerning the number of variety of assortments. They indicate whether a store aims to carry a full range of styles and brands or only the most popular items. For example, many prestige department stores have rather extensive model stock lists in keeping with their policy of offering customers a broad selection. This policy is designed to attract discriminating customers who like a variety of choices and are willing to pay for this service. On the other hand, mass merchandisers usually have very limited model stock lists. These limited lists are based upon a policy designed to attract customers who prefer lower prices and are willing to forego wide merchandise assortments and services.

Basic Stock List

Many retailers dealing in stale goods—such as groceries, hardware, drugs, cosmetics, and stationery—use basic stock lists to maintain tight control over merchandise. A **basic stock list** shows the minimum amount of stock that should be on hand for each type of goods sold and the quantity that should be reordered when ordering is done. A basic stock list identifies the items that should never be out of stock. This is quite different from a model stock list, which shows the range of goods that should be carried.

At regular intervals—either daily, weekly, or monthly—buyers or assistant buyers count each item and enter the amount for each item on the basic stock list. By checking the quantity on hand against the minimum amount that should be in stock, buyers can determine when and how many units to reorder.

Physical Inventory Systems

Under a **physical inventory** system, buyers take an actual count of merchandise to determine the exact quantity on hand. In addition to keeping records of the unit sales of each item, buyers obtain the sales figure by adding any merchandise received to the opening inventory and subtracting the closing inventory. This sales figure is based on an actual physical count of the merchandise. The count may be lower than the sales figure obtained from a perpetual inventory record, such as a cash-register tape. The difference between sales recorded on a tape and sales based on a physical inventory is usually due to shortages from theft, improper checking of income merchandise, errors in cash-register operation, or damaged and unsalable merchandise. Some of the more commonly used physical inventory systems are (1) tickler control, (2) reorder control, and (3) visual control.

Tickler Control

A system by which buyers figure the entire inventory for a given period by counting portions of the stock at regular intervals is called **tickler control**. The term "tickler" comes from another system that buyers use called a tickler file, which reminds them when to take stock counts for each type of merchandise. Tickler control is also referred to as a "rotated inventory" because the stock counts occur on a rotated, or staggered, basis.

Tickler control is used most often for staple merchandise. The unit-control card usually shows the maximum amount of stock that should be on hand and on order when goods are reordered. Each time buyers take a count or inventory of an item, an order is placed to cover the difference between the maximum stock and the amount of stock on hand and on order. For instance, maximum stock for an item can be 20 pieces, and the buyer may take a count every month. If the monthly count shows that there are 15 pieces in stock and none on order, the buyer places an order for 5 pieces.

Maximum stock	20
Stock on hand	15
Stock on order	0
Stock to order	5

Reorder Control

A type of physical inventory system that doesn't involve regular counting of stock is called **reorder control**. Buyers may use it to control items such as hosiery, gloves, blouses, and shirts that are stocked in boxes, bins, or drawers. A card, slip, or gummed label containing necessary reorder information is used to mark the minimum stock point under reorder control. When the stock reaches this level, the reminder card, slip, or label appears and is removed and sent to the buyer, who makes use of the data in reordering.

BASIC STOCK LIST

Store 30　　Dept. 7　　Effective Date 4/15　　Page 2

Vendor: Westco Apparel
Address: 924 Belmont
Chicago, Illinois

Representative: Sandra Baker
Address: 416 Harris Boulevard
Oakland, California

Phone: 286-5188

Coverage Period: 7 Weeks

Delivery Period: 2 Weeks

Method of Count: [XX] Group Mgr. [ ] Vendor

_____ 1. First Week
　x　 2. Second Week
_____ 3. Third Week
_____ 4. Fourth Week
_____ See Additional Information Below

Additional Information

Emergency Orders:
[XX] Call Vendor
[ ] No Emergency Orders

Requisition must be mailed from store by Wednes. of count week

Minimum Model Allowed

Item Description	Style	Size	Color	Pkg.	Retail	Min Qty	Max Qty	A
Men's over-the-calf	63	small	black	2/pkg.	4.98	4	12	1
100% nylon stretch			gray	2/pkg.	4.98	4	12	2
socks			brown	2/pkg.	4.98	4	12	3
			navy	2/pkg.	4.98	4	12	4
		medium	black	2/pkg.	4.98	6	16	5
			gray	2/pkg.	4.98	6	16	6
			brown	2/pkg.	4.98	6	16	7
			navy	2/pkg.	4.98	6	16	8
		large	black	2/pkg.	4.98	5	14	9
			gray	2/pkg.	4.98	5	14	10
			brown	2/pkg.	4.98	5	14	11
			navy	2/pkg.	4.98	5	14	12
								13
								14
								15
								16
								17
								18
								19
								20
								21
								22
								23
								24
								25

A basic stock list.

Visual Control

Visual control by **color coding** is another control technique that can assure good rotation. With this method, a record is kept of the date on which a shipment of merchandise was received and a color is assigned to the shipment. The price tag or label placed on the item will be the assigned color. For example, the first shipment may have blue tags, the second one green tags, and so on. When a price is applied directly to the merchandise by a marking pen, the color used is the same as that assigned the shipment.

Once the system has been in operation for more than one shipment, buyers can tell at a glance which merchandise has been in stock the longest time. Besides helping with stock rotation, such color coding helps to reveal slow- and fast-moving items, thereby identifying merchandise ready for reduced-price sales.

Perpetual Inventory Items

Taking a physical inventory is a tedious and costly job. This is why many retailers take inventory only once or twice a year. Even so, to market goods competitively, retailers need information about sales and stock on hand that is much more current than the figures obtained in the last physical inventory. For most categories of merchandise, a monthly updating of inventory information is important. For some categories, such as food and apparel, weekly and sometimes even daily updating is needed. A perpetual inventory system produces this kind of updated information. The aim of this system is to keep inventory records in agreement with inventory actually in stock.

A **perpetual inventory system** always begins with a physical inventory. The figures obtained in the physical inventory are entered in the books. They are updated regularly in accordance with current orders, receipts, and returns (additions) as well as sales, shortages, and damages (subtractions). Some stores update their perpetual inventory records with the help of electronic equipment to keep records current within 24 hours. How frequently retailers need to add new information to the inventory records depends upon the kind of merchandise they sell. Retailers can manage fast-moving goods and fashion merchandise more efficiently with information that shows what happened yesterday than with last month's data.

Operating a Perpetual Inventory System

The table entitled "Operating a Perpetual Inventory System" lists the responsibilities of those retail workers who are involved in making sure that a perpetual inventory system operates correctly and efficiently.

One example of a stock record system that provides considerable information is the **perpetual unit-control record,** which is shown on page 313. The record illustrated provides sales, cost, and inventory information for periods of 2 weeks to 5 months.

The following information is readily available from this perpetual unit-control record:

♦ Items currently in stock
♦ Sales trends over a 3-month period
♦ High and low sales months
♦ Comparative figures for the previous year
♦ Wholesale costs and retail prices
♦ Delivery information: what has been ordered, what is in, and how long it takes to obtain a fresh supply
♦ Minimum quantities
♦ Ordering quantities

In this perpetual unit-control record, the size referred to is 15½   36 (that means

OPERATING A PERPETUAL INVENTORY SYSTEM

Retail Workers Involved	Responsibilities	Information Records
The buyer	Sends a copy of each purchase order to inventory records department.	Purchase order information is recorded on perpetual unit-control records as "on order."
The receiving department	Records information concerning the number of items received and the date on which items were received.	Receiving record information is recorded on perpetual unit-control records as "received" (added to inventory records).
Sales personnel	Records sales and returns from sales checks, price tickets, reserve requisitions, credit slips, and cash register tapes.	Sales and returns are recorded on perpetual unit-control records as "sold" or "returned."

PERPETUAL UNIT-CONTROL RECORD

Style Men's knit golf shirt

Size 15½ 36

Minimum Order Quantity 8

Unit Cost 5.95

Delivery Time 1 week

Date	Qty. On Hand	Qty. On Order	Qty. Recd.	Qty. Sold	Qty. Returned	Balance
4-7	28			3		25
4-21	25			1		24
5-5	24	8			2	26
5-19	26		8	4		30
6-2	30			3		27
6-16	27		2	1		28
6-30	28				1	29

15½-inch neck size and 36-inch sleeve length). The minimum quantity the retailer wants to keep in stock is eight units. When stock reaches this minimum quantity, reorders are placed.

Sources of Perpetual Inventory Information

There are a number of methods that retailers use to obtain information about sales for perpetual-inventory purposes. But whatever system they use, it records every sale made and identifies the merchandise sold by style, size, color, price, or other relevant classification. Retailers usually get this information from sales checks, price tickets, reserve requisitions, or cash-register tapes.

Sales Checks. In some stores, the salespeople record quantity, items, sizes, colors, and similar information for each sale on the sales check. Duplicates of the sales checks are used to transfer the information to the inventory records. The success of this method depends on the accuracy

and completeness of the information on the sales checks.

Price Tickets. Many stores use premarked price tickets to record merchandise information in code. Because the information is already attached to each item at the time it is sold, the salesperson does not need to spend time writing a detailed sales check and the possibility of error is reduced. In stores with large sales volumes, it is especially convenient to use code-punched price tickets that are suited to a mechanical system of recordkeeping.

Reserve Requisitions. When inventory sales come from requisitions made against reserve stock, individual sales are not recorded. A **reserve requisition** is a request for the shipment or sale of merchandise that is located in a reserve or warehouse area. A quantity of individual items are requisitioned from the reserve stock for the selling floor. The total number of units requisitioned is subtracted from the inventory records as if the items had been sold.

Cash-Register Tapes. With cash register tapes as with sales checks, information is recorded when the sale is made. However, information on the cash-register tapes can be coded for automatic transfer to punched tapes that can be fed into a computer for a final report. If sales are recorded accurately on the cash register, the rest of the process is accurate and fast. Certain stores have invested in automatic scanners or "magic wands" that automatically record the price-ticket information. Cashier errors can thereby be reduced.

Which Inventory System Is Best?

As mentioned previously, both unit and dollar stock-control systems are necessary to provide the buyer with sufficient inventory control information. This is also the case regarding physical and perpetual inventory systems. Both systems are necessary. Each system offers the "best" information in certain circumstances.

The main advantage of the physical inventory system is that it is more accurate in determining inventory quantity and value at a particular time. Its chief disadvantages are that (1) it is costly and time-consuming and (2) it can only provide accurate information right after the inventory is completed.

The main advantage of the perpetual inventory system is that records can be updated frequently and at any time. It's also readily adaptable to the use of automated and computerized information systems. Its chief disadvantages are that the system is dependent upon the accuracy of the information provided and that it's expensive to maintain the necessary records. A perpetual inventory system doesn't reveal shortages, damaged merchandise, or losses due to shoplifting.

For these reasons, retailers usually rely on a perpetual inventory system for keeping track of staples and merchandise of

lower unit cost. For controlling high-unit-cost items, retailers usually use both a periodic physical inventory plus a perpetual inventory. Also, they usually use both these inventory systems for controlling fashion merchandise. When you go on to read the next chapter, "Merchandising Fashion," you'll get a better idea of why inventory control is especially important for retailers who sell fashion items.

In this chapter, then, you've learned that the ideal inventory control system for any retailing operation is the one that produces all the information retailers need (and no more) to merchandise goods efficiently. Unnecessary additional information is not only confusing but wastes the time and money spent in collecting it. The ideal inventory control system also produces information when the retailer needs it—neither too early, which would mean that money was being spent with unnecessary speed, nor too late, which would mean that only outdtated and useless information was being produced.

Trade Talk

Define each term and use it in a sentence.

Basic stock list	Perpetual unit-control record
Color coding	
Dollar stock control	Physical inventory
Inventory control	Reorder control
Minimum stock quantity	Reserve requisition
Model stock list	Tickler control
Perpetual inventory system	Unit control

Can You Answer These?

1. What trends in retailing cause inventory control to be more important than ever?
2. What information can a unit-control system provide?
3. How does a model stock list differ from a basic stock list?
4. A tickler system for the control of physical

inventory obtains its name because of what function it performs?

5. What are principal advantages and disadvantages of a physical inventory control system? A perpetual inventory control system?

Problems

1. You are an inventory control specialist who is posting daily transactions for March 2 to the perpetual unit-control record. From the following information, determine the stock on hand at the end of the day for a line of size 9 men's ski boots.
   a. March 1—quantity on hand: 25
   b. March 2—quantity ordered: 5
   c. March 2—quantity received: 5
   d. March 2—quantity sold: 4
   e. March 2—quantity returned: 1
2. Choose any mail-order catalog (for example, Sears, Wards, Penneys). Assume that you are a buyer for your own small store. Also assume that the mail-order catalog represents the supplier from whose stock you can make your selection. Develop a merchandise assortment plan for a line of products of your interest. In developing your assortment plans, consider that:

   a. Sales volume for your product line is forecast at $10,000.
   b. Your merchandise assortment should be planned according to four or five characteristics of the line (for example, sweaters could be classified according to prices, sizes, colors, styles, and materials).
   c. Merchandise units and amount of dollars should be allocated for each product characteristic that you select.

   A form like the one below will assist you in planning your merchandise assortment.

Product line: _____

Product Characteristic	Merchandise Units	Amount

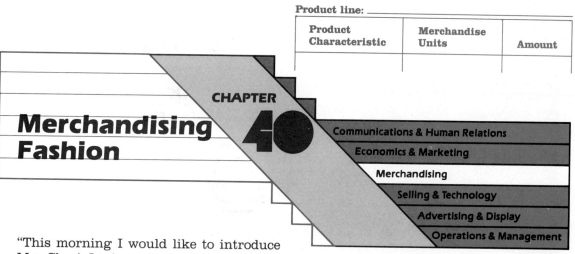

Merchandising Fashion

CHAPTER 40

Communications & Human Relations
Economics & Marketing
Merchandising
Selling & Technology
Advertising & Display
Operations & Management

"This morning I would like to introduce Ms. Sheri Levine, the buyer for junior sportswear at the Emerson Stores, and Mr. John Hofmann, Emerson's menswear buyer," Mrs. McCoy, the marketing and distributive education teacher-coordinator said. She continued, "Since we've been studying fashion merchandising, I'm sure that you'll find Sheri's and John's talk very interesting. They'll discuss how merchandisers use fashion concepts when planning, coordinating, and evaluating the marketing of a variety of products or services. Let's welcome them to our class."

What Is Fashion?

"Good morning," said Ms. Levine. "Now first, let me ask you a question. Just what do you believe fashion really is—the 'in' thing . . . what everyone wants . . . the latest style . . . where it's at . . . ?

"Fashion is all that and more. Let's consider several definitions offered by fashion authorities," said Ms. Levine.

Here are some definitions of **fashion**:

♦ A style that is accepted by many people.
♦ The currently accepted, widespread style that is generally established and adopted by certain types of individuals.
♦ The prevailing style during a particular time.

It appears from these definitions of fashion that "style" also needs to be defined. **Style** refers to the characteristic of a garment or other product that distinguish it from other items of the same type. For example, pants come in many different styles—bell bottoms, painters' pants, and Western jeans. And furniture is offered in many styles—Early American, French provincial, or contemporary.

Styles that stay in fashion year after year are known as **classics.** They are simple in design. This simplicity ensures their popularity because they can be combined with current fashions. The blazer jacket, the cardigan sweater, and the trench coat are all examples of classics. Certain kinds of homes such as the Cape Cod, the colonial, or the ranch style are examples of styles that maintain their popularity.

Styles or designs that gain and lose popularity in a short time are called **fads.** Compared to classics, fads are often extreme in a certain characteristic. An example of a fad is the "hot pants," or short pants, which were introduced in 1971. They were very popular during the spring and summer of 1971. And even though short pants are not generally worn as "dress up" apparel, the hot pants were worn in the evening. But by fall, their popularity had declined. Often, gift or novelty

Fads are styles that are in and out of fashion very quickly. John Dominis/Life Magazine © Time Inc.

items are fads. Several years ago, Pet Rocks were promoted as a gift for the individual who had everything. Fads come and go rapidly, so retailers have to be especially alert to market trends when handling fad merchandise.

Why Fashion Is Important

Next, Mr. Hofmann wrote on the chalkboard the following question: "Why is fashion important to our nation's economy?" His discussion of this question is summarized below.

Economic Value of Fashion

In our free enterprise system, the consideration of fashion and style is very important to manufacturers, distributors, and consumers. The acceptance or rejection of a certain style by consumers can make the difference between profits or losses in many businesses. Through their purchases, consumers, in effect, decide whether specific designs, colors, appearances, or models of products that are offered in the marketplace should be continued or dropped. Also, new products and services motivate consumers to earn the necessary income to satisfy a variety of wants and needs.

The design, manufacture, and distribution of these new products and services create and maintain jobs for individuals throughout the nation. For example, the combined producers of fabrics and finished apparel represent one of the largest fields of employment in the United States—about 2½ million people. The auto, home building, sporting goods, and furniture industries, to name a few, are economically very dependent upon consumer acceptance of the styles of their particular products.

Value of Fashion in Retailing

Mr. Hofmann wrote the next question on the chalkboard: "Why is fashion important to retailing?" He related his answers to the history and development of retailing in the following way.

"In the early years of our nation, retailing was a comparatively simple function. Retailers sold what was available to consumers, and selection of merchandise was often limited to what was available from local manufacturers or suppliers. But because of improved transportation, communication, and production facilities, retailers today can offer a greater variety of goods to consumers. Now consumers can choose between many styles of products. If a certain retailer doesn't offer the selections of merchandise that are desired at the moment, there are competitors who do. There is no consumer market that belongs exclusively to any one retailer."

How Fashions Change

"We've asked you the questions so far," remarked Ms. Levine. "Now why don't you ask us any questions you might have about fashion?"

"Ms. Levine," responded a student, "I read an article that criticized fashion changes. The writer said that businesses purposely design products that will go out of date so that we buy what we may not really need. And the writer called this practice **planned obsolescence**." Ms. Levine emphasized the following points in her reply.

The Need for Newness and Variety

The human need for newness and variety is a powerful force that strongly influences fashion change. There is always a movement toward new and different ideas, attitudes, and values. Sometimes it's only when we look at the past that we realize the differences. Try this exercise. Recall the oldest movie that you've seen on television. What kinds of clothing, cars, houses, and even language did the movie portray? What turns us off when we watch an older movie? We no longer accept many of the styles that we see.

The fashion cycle.

Life would be dull and boring if all our products were suddenly frozen in place like a stop-action television scene. But it's true that some of our products may still have serviceable life in them even if they are out of style. At the same time, though, if products seldom or never changed, we'd have to pay the price of boredom.

Fashion Cycles

"Let's identify what effects fashion cycles have on consumer purchases," Ms. Levine told the students. "But before we do that, let's define what a fashion cycle is. Basically, a **fashion cycle** consists of the phases that a fashion goes through. These phases repeat themselves for many different types of products."

To describe the phases, Ms. Levine drew a curve on the chalkboard and divided it into four sections or "phases," as she called them. The first stage of the fashion cycle is the **creation phase**. In this phase, the styles are new, limited in number, high-priced, and handled by exclusive specialty stores. These creation styles are accepted by a few so-called fashion leaders, or what retailing terms **early acceptors**. The second stage of the fashion cycle is called the **limited acceptance phase**. During this phase, the style has gained greater acceptance by the **early followers** of the fashion leaders. The style is more readily available at specialty or department stores handling medium- to high-priced lines. Later, during the third or **mass acceptance phase**, the style becomes fashionable to the largest consumer group, the **later followers**. The styles are available in many different kinds of retail establishments at lower prices. In the final, fourth stage of the fashion cycle, the **fashion abandonment phase** or decline phase, the style is sold at the lowest markdown prices to customers sometimes called **style laggards**.

Geographic Migrations

One interesting thing about fashion cycles is that they often migrate geographically across the United States. Historically, styles moved from east to west as the pioneer settlers migrated across the nation. Now, because of the influence of movie and television productions (originating from both East and West Coasts) and because of the sizable migration to Southern and Western Sun Belt states, many styles appear to move from these areas to the central areas of the nation. Also, rapid communication via television, radio, movies, and the printed media has tended to reduce geographic influences on fashions. In many areas of the nation, however, retailers must still decide whether a certain fashion is ahead of its time in terms of sales acceptance in their trading area.

Factors Influencing Fashion Change

Mr. Hofmann then took over the discussion and wrote the following words on the chalkboard: "income," "social attitudes," and "technological innovations." "These," he said, "are the three powerful influences that affect fashion. Retailers need to consider all of them in order to merchandise any fashion item properly." Mr. Hofmann then discussed each of these influences.

Income

Fashion, in many cases, is a luxury. In the United States, many consumers have sufficient discretionary income to seek a higher social status through the products and services they purchase. (You'll remember that "discretionary income" is income that consumers have left over after they have paid for essential products or services such as food, clothing, and shelter.) With discretionary income, consumers are able to replace products before they are completely worn out. So retailers must continually analyze the features and benefits of products and services that can satisfy more than just the basic needs of consumers. For example, a fashion item can't effectively be promoted on serviceability or durability because customers who buy such items really want prestige, recognition, and public acceptance. Fashion-minded customers are willing and able to spend the necessary money to satisfy needs of this type.

Social Attitudes

The social attitudes of a region or country have a strong influence on fashions. Country-western styles, for example, were once looked upon with distaste by certain social groups. But now the popularity of certain tastes associated with the country-western way of life—for instance, music—has made those social groups find these styles acceptable. What a popular television, sports, or political leader may wear also has an influence on socially acceptable fashions. Often a group of individuals such as rock stars will influence hairstyles, speech, dress, and even lifestyles.

Today's society places a higher value on leisure activities. The 40-hour work week, less homemaking drudgery because of time-saving appliances, and an increased number of 3-day-weekend holidays makes more leisure time available to more people. Fashion merchandisers are alert to the increased consumer interest in leisure activities. Now fashionable items are a "must" for consumers who wish to feel properly attired or equipped for such socially accepted activities as jogging, tennis, boating, or camping.

Technological Innovations

Space-related technology has produced television satellites that instantly send images of the latest fasions from Paris, Rome, and New York. Supersonic jet transportation brings people from all nations into personal contact with the world's markets. By using computers to analyze the market tests of styles in selected areas, retailers can better predict the success or failure of a specific product. Today's buyers follow fashion trends daily because of these technological innovations. A certain style can gain swift publicity and acceptance because of technological developments in communications and distribution. Technological innovations involving production, transportation, communications, and distribution will affect fashion trends even more in the future.

How Are Fashion Concepts Used in Retailing?

Ms. Levine then took over and said, "We've discussed many concepts of fashion. But now, let's discuss how you can use several of these concepts in fashion merchandising."

The Fashion Merchandising Approach

The fashion merchandising approach is related to the definition of merchandising. And applied to fashion, "merchandising" involves the retailer's decisions concerning the selection of the right styles of goods in the right assortment, in the right quantities, at the right prices, and at the right time—based upon consumer wants. Retailers as well as fashion designers use the fashion merchandising approach when predicting what the right merchandise selections and assortments should be. Examples of such predictions were presented in a recent article in *The New York Times* entitled "Fashion Speaks Softly, But Carries a Big Classic Look into the 1980s." These predictions include the following:

1. A new mood of individuality will develop,

Changes in social attitudes influence fashions. Cosmetics for men, for example, are becoming increasingly popular. Irma Schorell, Inc.

rather than one particular look. A freer and more fun-loving approach to apparel will result.

2. We are just beginning a new knit-fashion cycle.
3. Weekend clothes that can be worn for dress or sport will be the hit of the 1980s.
4. Because of the unstable economy, customers are more concerned about investing in clothes that will last.

Wise retailers must rely upon various factors such as customer moods, the state of the economy, different fashion cycles, and changing lifestyles when using the fashion merchandising approach. All the "right" decisions (styles, assortments, quantities, prices, times) cannot always be made correctly. Considering these decisions in as thorough a manner as possible can, however, aid retailers in the merchandising of fashion.

How Salespeople Use Fashion

The selling of fashions is often based on emotional appeals. An effective sales presentation encourages customers to improve their image. Cosmetics, hairstyling, health-spa memberships, and self-improvement programs are based upon such universal desires as looking fashionable, staying young, or feeling fit. Salespeople must recognize that customers often want to be reassured concerning their fashion choices. Often customers want reassurances that they are making a wise buy, that the style is "in" this season, or that they will enjoy and be pleased with their selection. Salespeople must be knowledgeable about the appropriate styles to suggest to customers.

What Are the Opportunities in Fashion Careers?

"What type of career do you normally associate with the term 'fashion'?" Ms. Levine next asked the class.

"A fashion buyer," responded a student.

"You're right," said Ms. Levine, "The fashion buyer is usually mentioned. Often this career is associated with glamour, buying trips to New York or Paris, fashion style shows, excitement, and so on. These associations are correct to some degree. It should be noted, though, that the fashion buyers' job demands long hours, hard work, and certain pressures. The individual jobs vary depending upon the size of the organization and the type of products or services handled. There is a variety of fashion-related careers available, such as boutique store owner-manager, fashion coordinator, bridal consultant, department head, display specialist, fashion salesperson, fashion designer, interior designer, fashion model, and photo stylist."

"What would you say that you like best about your job, Ms. Levine?" a student asked.

"It's difficult to identify any one aspect of my job that I like best. A fashion career can provide opportunities for personal growth and satisfaction." She then summarized these opportunities as follows:

1. The daily challenge of dealing with professional colleagues and customers.
2. The satisfactions realized from planning and conducting a successful fashion promotion or sale.
3. The opportunity to observe and learn about people, styles, and fashion trends.
4. The avoidance of boredom. Because of the variety of fashion merchandising duties, no 2 days are alike.
5. The chance for a good income, promotions, training, travel, and associations with exciting individuals.

Ms. Levine concluded the discussion by recommending that "If any of you are interested in this area of retailing, study fashion merchandising in a high school, community college, or college program. Obtain occupational experiences in a fashion-related part-time job or training program. If you do, you can be on your way to a rewarding career. Thank you for inviting John and me to your class today."

Trade Talk

Define each term and use it in a sentence.

Classics
Creation phase
Early acceptors
Early followers
Fads
Fashion
Fashion cycle
Fashion
  abandonment
  phase

Later followers
Limited acceptance
  phase
Mass acceptance
  phase
Planned obsolescence
Style
Style laggards

Can You Answer These?

1. What is the difference between a style, a fashion, and a fad?
2. What economic benefits does fashion provide?
3. What are the four phases of a fashion cycle?
4. What merchandising decisions are made with respect to the fashion merchandising approach?
5. What are the requirements for success in fashion careers?

Problems

1. Select a fashion career of your choice. Contact your teacher for career reference materials that describe the particular fashion career. If possible, arrange for an interview with a person employed in the fashion position of your interest. Prepare a summary of the career information that you obtained. Include within your summary such information as job entry requirements, major job duties performed, education or training required for entry and advancement, rewards and satisfactions possible, and any interesting career information found. Be prepared to share this information with your classmates.

2. Rule a form similar to the following. In the left column, identify three fashion items. In column 1, identify by name a type of store or a department within a store in your community that would first carry the item. Follow the same procedure for columns 2, 3, and 4 with respect to stores identified as early followers, later followers and style laggards.

Fashion Item	(1) Early Acceptors	(2) Early Followers	(3) Later Followers	(4) Style Laggards
Example: Men's suits	Ye Olde English Clothing Shoppe	John's Mod Shop	B. J. Meyers	Ajax Surplus Store

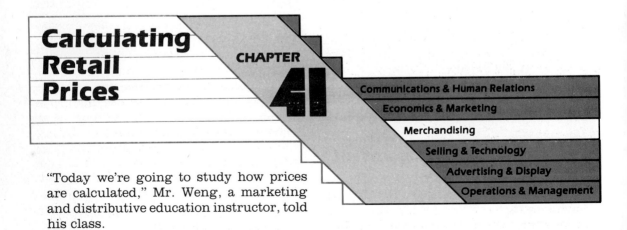

Calculating Retail Prices

CHAPTER 41

Communications & Human Relations
Economics & Marketing
Merchandising
Selling & Technology
Advertising & Display
Operations & Management

"Today we're going to study how prices are calculated," Mr. Weng, a marketing and distributive education instructor, told his class.

"Oh, no," thought many of the students, "I hate doing math."

Realizing that his students might be having such thoughts, Mr. Weng explained, "We'll use a building-block approach, and this will help you understand how the various elements of pricing are related. I'll show you on the chalkboard how these elements can be visualized."

Understanding Pricing

Pricing is a course of action that involves setting a price or changing a price upward or downward to achieve a marketing objective. Such objectives may include attracting larger numbers of customers, reducing excess amounts of stock, introducing new products, or closing out year-end stocks of merchandise. Most retailers use the following pricing calculations: (1) initial markup, (2) additional markup, (3) markup cancellation, (4) markdowns, and (5) markdown cancellations. In addition, retailers must also make decisions about whether to base markup on the cost or on the retail selling price of the merchandise.

Initial Retail Price and Initial Markup

Initial retail price is the cost of merchandise plus the initial markup. The resulting sum is what customers pay. **Markup** (or margin) is the difference between the cost of merchandise to the retailer and the retail price charged. **Initial markup** is the difference between the cost of the merchandise and the initial, or first, retail price. This initial markup, sometimes called "markon," must be sufficient to include not only the cost of the goods sold but also the expenses of doing business and a reasonable profit. (Pricing goals and strategies are discussed in more detail in Chapter 58.)

Mr. Weng suggested using a simple example to illustrate the elements that are considered when determining the initial retail price and initial markup. He said

that these elements could be viewed as building blocks, because one depends upon the other for support. The first element, or building block, is the cost of the merchandise. For example, assume an item cost $30 as represented by this block.

```
┌─────────────────────┐
│                     │
│                     │
│                     │
│     Cost of         │
│  merchandise: $30   │
│                     │
│                     │
│                     │
└─────────────────────┘
```

The second building block is the initial markup of $20, which is added to the "cost" building block. These two blocks added together equal the initial retail price.

Initial retail price = $30 + $20 = $50

```
┌─────────────────────┐
│                     │
│      Initial        │
│   markup: $20       │
│                     │
├─────────────────────┤
│                     │
│     Cost of         │
│  merchandise: $30   │
│                     │
└─────────────────────┘
```

Additional Markup

In certain cases, the initial markup may not be adequate to cover the cost of the merchandise expenses and the desired profit. In such cases, an additional markup is calculated. **Additional markup** is a price increase made after the initial markup is established. These additional price increases (markups) are common during periods of inflation, when a product is in short supply, or when its wholesale cost has increased. This type of markup follows (reading from the bottom up):

Second retail price = $50 + $10 = $60
Initial retail price = $50

Additional markup: $10
Initial markup: $20
Cost of merchandise $30

Markup Cancellation

Markups may not only be increased but occasionally also reduced. A **markup cancellation** is a reduction in the retail price of an item some time after an additional markup has been made. Retailers sometimes make such changes because of a competitor's price reductions, too much inventory on hand, or resistance of customers to higher prices. A markup cancellation of $5, using the same pricing figures as in the previous illustration, follows (reading from the bottom up):

Final retail price = $60 − $5 = $55
Second retail price = $60
Initial retail price = $50

Markup cancellation: − $5
Additional markup: $10
Initial markup: $20
Cost of merchandise: $30

Markdowns

A **markdown** is a reduction of the initial retail price. Retailers mark down for a variety of reasons, the most common of which are to attract customers, to move slow sellers, and to clear out odds and ends of stock and shopworn goods. The need to mark down goods is a frustrating problem to retailers. All of them would like to sell their goods at their initial markup prices. Still, they recognize that a certain percentage of markdowns is inevitable.

As with markups, markdowns can be stated in percentages. The **markdown percentage** is computed by dividing the initial retail price into the markdown allowed:

$$\frac{\text{Markdown}}{\text{Initial retail price}} = \frac{\$10}{\$50} = 20\%$$

A markdown may be illustrated using the building-block concept, as follows:

Second retail price = $50 − $10 = $40
Initial retail price = $50

Markdown: − $10
Initial markup: $20
Cost of merchandise: $30

Markdown Cancellations

A **markdown cancellation** is an upward price adjustment on a markdown already taken. The most common example is when a price is restored to its initial retail level after the goods have been marked down temporarily for a special sales event. In the illustration below, the $30 cost of merchandise was added to the $20 initial markup, resulting in a $50 initial retail price. Then a $10 markdown was subtracted from the $50 initial retail price, resulting in a $40 second retail price. The $10 markdown was then canceled, which restored a $50 final retail price.

Final retail price = $40 + 10 = $50
Second retail price = $50 − $10 = $40
Initial retail price = $30 + $20 = $50

Markdown cancellation: $10
Markdown: −$10
Initial Markup: $20
Cost of merchandise: $30

$$\frac{\text{Markup}}{\text{Cost of merchandise}} = \frac{\$20}{\$30} = 66.6\%$$

You'll notice that percentage of markup based upon the retail price (40 percent) is lower than the percentage of markup based upon cost (66.6 percent). In either case, the calculation of a percentage figure for markups makes possible comparisons of markups for several items or lines of merchandise even though the individual cost and retail prices may be different.

Markup Percentages Based on Cost or Retail

Large retailers usually express markup as a percentage of the retail price rather than the cost price. Small retailers or stores that will bargain on prices may state markup percentages on the basis of cost. Markup percentages are usually based on retail prices because expenses and other items such as profits are commonly expressed as a percentage of retail sales.

If markup percentages are expressed in the same way, they can be compared with markup figures in other departments of the store or with other stores in the same line of retailing. The National Retail Merchants Association (NRMA) publishes an annual report of average markups and expense percentages for many different stores in the nation. By using markup and expense figures based on the retail price, retailers can compare a store's operations with national average reports such as the NRMA's.

The markup percentages based on the retail price and the cost of the merchandise are computed accordingly:

Cost of merchandise ($30) + initial markup ($20) = initial retail price ($50)

Markup based on retail price:

$$\frac{\text{Markup}}{\text{Retail price}} = \frac{\$20}{\$50} = 40\%$$

Markup based on cost of merchandise:

Establishing Markup Goals

The figuring of markups and markdowns may be viewed as the strategy of pricing translated into mathematical terms. It is very important mathematics, because retailers measure success or failure by goals—cost goals, sales goals, price goals, expense goals, and profit goals.

To establish markup goals, retailers begin with their "income statement," which they prepare at regular intervals. This statement, which they complete at the close of a period such as a month or a year, helps retailers to plan sales, costs, and desired profit for the coming period. And this information allows retailers to determine the markup goals needed to arrive at retail prices. Income statements are discussed in depth in Chapter 72.

A term retailers use to evaluate the realization of various pricing goals is the **maintained markup,** or net markup. This markup is the difference between the cost of the merchandise and the actual price at which it's sold. This actual selling price may include various markups and markdowns. The following example shows how goals and maintained markups are used.

To arrive at the selling price that will yield a profit, a certain retailer begins by establishing sales goals. Suppose that this retailer's estimated sales goals for the coming year are $100,000; that the cost of the merchandise to be purchased is

$60,000; that the total estimated operating expenses are $36,000; and that a net profit of 4 percent on sales is desired.

Category	Volume	Percentage
Income from net sales	$100,000	100
Less cost of merchandise sold	60,000	60
Gross profit on sales	$ 40,000	40
Less operating expenses	36,000	36
Net profit	$ 4,000	4

The retailer now knows the gross profit on sales that must be achieved to make the desired profit. ("Gross profit on sales," or "gross margin," is a bookkeeping term that expresses the difference between net sales and net merchandise costs. This and other bookkeeping terms are discussed in detail in Chapter 72.) In this example, the retailer needs to realize a maintained markup of 40 percent to earn 4 percent profit. This is a markup goal that must be considered when the amounts or percentages of individual markups and markdowns are being determined.

Determining Markups on Individual Items

When they are pricing individual items, retailers don't always use the same markup needed to meet expenses and realize a profit. Instead, they take into consideration the pricing strategy required for each item or category of merchandise. Some items—such as fashion goods, jewelry, or delicatessen foods—will provide a higher-than-average markup. Other goods, such as staple merchandise, will be priced below the uniform markup. Individual markups are set so that the total gross profit they will produce equals the total amount of the projected maintained dollar markup for the store.

For instance, suppose the store with projected net sales of $100,000 and a projected markup of 40 percent carried the following three main categories of goods, with projected sales for each category as indicated:

1. Goods having considerable fashion appeal, projected to net $60,000 in sales
2. Goods made up of steady sellers, expected to produce $30,000 in sales
3. Goods consisting of a small selection of very competitively priced items, projected to produce $10,000 in sales

On the basis of this pricing strategy, the retailer might decide to apply a markup of 45 percent to the first category, 35 percent to the second category and 25 percent to the third category. The following examples show how the prices would be computed:

Projected Goals

Net sales	$100,000
Markup (40 percent)	.40
Gross profit on sales	$ 40,000

Category Goals

Goods 1:

Net sales	$ 60,000
Markup (45 percent)	.45
Gross profit on sales	$ 27,000

Goods 2:

Net sales	$30,000
Markup (35 percent)	.35
Gross profit on sales	$10,500

Goods 3:

Net sales	$10,000
Markup (25 percent)	.25
Gross profit on sales	$ 2,500

Summary of Gross Profit Goals

Goods 1	$27,000
Goods 2	10,500
Goods 3	2,500
Total	$40,000

Taking Markdowns

It's difficult for someone new in retailing to decide when markdowns should be taken. Sometimes, retailers who delay this decision a few days find that the goods that were to be marked down can now be moved only by being offered below cost. And if retailers continue to wait, the goods may deteriorate, become shopworn, and tie up space and money that could be more wisely invested in new stock. Through experience, retailers learn to mark down goods quickly when there is evidence that they are not going to move.

Automatic Markdown System

Some stores use an automatic markdown system. An **automatic markdown system**

Retailers take into consideration the pricing strategy required for each item of merchandise. *Courtesy of Stewart's*

is a plan that sets a time period during which an item is offered at its original price. If the item isn't sold at the end of that time, it must be marked down by a given percentage. For example, a well-known department store in Boston, Massachusetts, offers merchandise in several price lines on different floors of the store. If merchandise retailing for $29 doesn't sell, it's moved to the next-lowest floor, featuring merchandise for $19. If it still doesn't sell, it's moved to a lower-price floor—and this process continues until the merchandise is sold on the basement floor or finally given to charity.

Markdown Plans

Certain retailers, particularly supermarket owners, use a **multiple pricing plan** for markdowns. This means that the price is reduced when several items are sold at the same time. For example, soap may be sold at 30 cents a bar or at 59 cents for two bars.

Experience and observation help retailers to determine the percentage of markdowns that must be taken. Usually the markdowns must be large enough to move the goods. One large markdown is generally more effective than several small ones.

Using Markdowns as a Selling Tool

Markdowns hurt retailers because they cut into the amount of markup planned for an item and therefore, eventually, into the net profit earned by that item. However, no retailer has yet found a way to avoid markdowns. So experienced retailers plan for markdowns when the original price is established. The original price is set high enough to include anticipated markdowns as well as operating expenses.

Even though they cut into gross profit on sales, markdowns are really a useful marketing tool, for they will usually speed up the sale of goods. Advertised markdowns attract customers into the store to buy regular items. Markdowns also clear slow-moving stock out of the store so that new merchandise, which will be more profitable, can be purchased.

Now that you've finished this chapter, which completes Unit 13, you should have a good understanding of the many different methods that retailers must use to keep merchandise moving. Retailers must be concerned about stock turnover; inventory control, especially as it relates to fashion items; and the calculation of retail prices.

Throughout this unit, you've learned in what ways these methods of moving merchandise may relate to your present or future job as a retail worker and why pricing is a function that all retail workers must be concerned about, not just store owners or managers.

Trade Talk

Define each term and use it in a sentence.

Additional markup	Markdown
Automatic	cancellation
markdown system	Markdown
Initial markup	percentage
Initial retail price	Markup
Maintained markup	Markup cancellation
Markdown	Multiple pricing plan
	Pricing

Can You Answer These?

1. What is the difference between initial and maintained markups?
2. Why do most stores calculate markup as a percentage of retail price rather than as a percentage of cost price?
3. How does an automatic markdown system operate?
4. Which is generally more effective—taking several smaller markdowns or one larger markdown? Why?

A change in the law may lead to an abrupt change in a retailer's markdown plans! Frostie/Woodfin Camp & Associates

5. How can retailers plan for markdowns when setting the original price?

Problems

Use this example to help you answer the problems below.

You know that an initial markup of 40 percent is needed for your line of stereos to provide a required net profit. Because the retail price is 100 percent (based on retail), the wholesale cost of the stereo should not be more than 60 percent of the retail price (100 percent–40 percent). Therefore, if you wish to handle a line of stereos selling at retail for $300, the maximum wholesale cost you can afford to pay for the stereos is 60 percent of $300, or $180.

Using this example as a guide, determine costs and retail selling prices in the following problems:

1. You purchase a line of swimsuits that you wish to retail at $14.95 per suit. You need to have an initial markup of 30 percent. The cost of each suit must not exceed 70 percent of the retail price. What is the maximum wholesale price that you can pay for the suit?

2. You visit the central market where you locate bicycles that you believe you can sell at retail for $140 each. If you desire an initial markup of 30 percent, what is the highest price you can pay for the bicycles?

3. An electric fan that costs you $9.60 is to be given a markup of 40 percent of retail. What should the retail selling price be?

4. A dress that you wish to add to your $49 retail price line is offered at a wholesale price of $39. You need to realize a 40 percent initial markup. Would the wholesale price of this dress be low enough to meet this requirement?

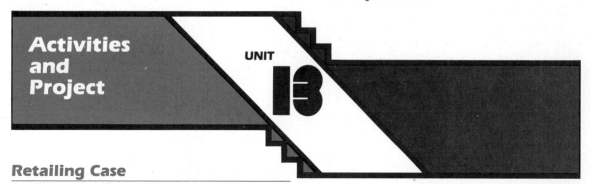

Activities and Project

UNIT 13

Retailing Case

You are discussing with your supervisor the courses that you are enrolled in at your school. You mention that you have just studied merchandise turnover and stock-sales ratios. Your supervisor says: "Oh! Let's see if you can compute several stock turnover problems." You accept your supervisor's challenge.

1. For the year, the sporting goods department had net sales of $200,000. The average stock during this period was $25,000. What was the rate of stockturn?

2. Find the average stock and the turnover for this period.

Sales		Stocks at Beginning of Month	
January	$10,000	January 1	$13,000
February	8,000	February 1	12,000
March	14,000	March 1	17,000
April	16,000	April 1	19,000
May	12,000	May 1	15,000
		June 1	18,000

Why is it necessary to use the June 1 BOM stock in your calculations?

3. What were the stock-sales ratios for each of the months in Problem 2?

Working with People

Having worked in the sportswear department for over a year, you have just been given additional responsibilities by Mr. Caruso, the buyer for all clothing (soft lines) in the store. You are now responsible for selecting the coming season's sportswear fashion lines. You have analyzed the latest fashion trends in the metropolitan markets. In addition, you have studied the styles that the leading sportswear manufacturers will be featuring during the upcoming season.

You present your plans for a new, more exciting sportswear line to Mr. Caruso. After reviewing your plans, he responds by saying that your selections are too advanced for the store and the area. He suggests that you "go back to the drawing board" and resubmit your fashion buying plans. Initially, you are very disappointed, but you are determined to propose certain needed new lines.

1. What additional information could you use to prepare a revised fashion merchandise plan that Mr. Caruso would probably accept?

2. How could you present your plan in a persuasive, effective manner?

3. What marketing strategies could you propose to evaluate the success of your revised fashion merchandising plan?

Project 13: Analyzing Inventory Control Forms

Your Project Goal

Given a retail store of your choice or the store in which you are currently employed, determine the types of inventory control forms that are currently being used.

Procedure

1. Select one line of merchandise that is being handled by the store being considered.

2. Interview the department manager, buyer, or your supervisor concerning the inventory control forms that are to be used to record orders, sales, markdowns, returns, etc.

3. Write a brief report describing the inventory control method used. Include in your report examples of the various business forms used. Indicate how and when entries are recorded on these forms.

4. Be prepared to present an oral report to the class describing the inventory control forms and entries made on the forms.

Evaluation

You will be evaluated on how accurately and completely you have described the inventory control forms.

Why People Buy—Or Don't Buy

CHAPTER

42

Communications & Human Relations

Economics & Marketing

Merchandising

Selling & Technology

Advertising & Display

Operations & Management

Two people were doing their weekly shopping in a supermarket. While passing through the cereal aisle, one of them put an attractive, brightly colored package of cereal from an eye-level shelf in her shopping cart and went quickly on her way. The other shopper stopped, compared the weight of the contents and prices of the various brands, checked the store coupons, chose the best buy, and checked "cereal" off his shopping list.

The differences in the shopping habits of these two customers may seem unimportant to most people. But to retailers, the shopping habits of consumers are important. Retailers analyze consumer shopping habits to find the reasons why people buy. Knowledge of the satisfactions customers seek from a given product and the priorities given to those potential satisfactions is the key to retail selling and sales promotion. These preferences are **buying motives,** or the needs and wants that cause people to buy.

A working knowledge of consumer buying motives will help you understand why an individual buys a product. It will also give you a good start on a career in retailing. Applying consumer buying motives to retail activities is a basic competency, or skill, that all retail workers need, from entry-level to top-management positions. Mass merchandisers and fast-food franchise businesses are highly dependent on research findings concerning customer buying motives in today's fast-changing markets. So the time you spend in the study of why people buy will offer a good return on the time invested.

Consumer Buying Motives

Most of us do not always understand why we behave as we do in the marketplace.

We like to think that we make sensible buying decisions. But who hasn't regretted an impulsive purchase? There are many known and unknown forces that influence our buying motives. One known force is our value system.

Every customer has a different system of values. **Values** are convictions about things one considers good, important, or beautiful. Values may be moral, social, aesthetic, cultural, or economic. They are learned from parents, teachers, friends, peers, clergy, and so on. Values are involved in every situation calling for a choice. They determine the origin, intensity, and priority of consumer needs and wants.

Internal Influences on the Consumer

Consumer buying procedure starts with a variety of mental forces and activities. These are needs, wants, motives, perceptions, judgments, and thoughts. As mentioned earlier, buying decisions are influenced by the customer's personal values. These values come from three types of influences: cultural, group, and individual.

Cultural Influences. Every person is a product of his or her culture. As members of society, we learn to live by its rules, which include customs, laws, and sanctions. Almost without our awareness, our culture affects our everyday actions and decisions. Since customers usually come from a variety of cultural backgrounds, retailers cannot impose their values on them.

Group Influences. Most people identify with a number of groups—at home, at work, at school, at their place of worship, and in the community. Within these groups, people learn how to conform and how to act in a certain way. For example, the family often provides standards of behavior. As infants, we learn through imitation. As we grow older, our imitation becomes selective, and the people whom we imitate when we make purchasing de-

cisions may be outside the family. But often, children are influenced by their parents' values. If a parent enjoys fishing, the child, too, may learn to enjoy it and to buy all the equipment. Through pressure to meet group standards, groups influence not only a person's present behavior but also his or her plans for the future.

Individual Influences. All people view the world about them in their own particular way. Their decisions are made in conformity with their unique views of reality. So their decisions to consume given products (to choose one brand over another) are guided by what they perceive, what they have learned, and their attitudes.

External Influences on the Consumer

Internal influences on the consumer's buying procedure represent only one side of the retailer's problem. The other side relates to the external forces in the consumer's environment. Most of these forces are difficult for the consumer to control. Six common external influences that directly or indirectly affect consumers are:

♦ *Income:* The consumer's income usually limits the amount to be spent.
♦ *Product availability:* The number of available goods and services is generally limited.
♦ *Factual information:* The accessibility of unbiased information may vary from place to place.
♦ *Time:* The time that can be spent on shopping is usually limited.
♦ *Fashion:* Fashion moves rapidly and styles may soon be outdated.
♦ *Source location:* Some retail outlets may be more easily reached, in terms of time and effort, than others.

These and many other external influences are on the consumer's mind when he or she is planning a purchase, and some of them persist during the buying process.

Types of Buying Motives

In selling, understanding buying motives is as important as knowing your mer-

How does this scene reflect group and individual influences on the choices of purchases? Susan Berkowitz

chandise. Buying motives can be divided into three groups: rational, emotional, and patronage motives.

Rational Buying Motives. When consumer purchases involve careful, calculated reasoning, they are based on **rational buying motives.** They include such considerations as economy, efficiency, dependability, and the saving of time, money, or space. Rational motives are always conscious. Many purchases are definitely based on rational motives. For example, the purchase of prescription drugs, men's socks, or carpentry tools is nearly always based on rational motives.

Emotional Buying Motives. When consumer purchases involve feelings such as pride, comfort, and romance, they are based on **emotional buying motives.** These may occur either independently or together with rational buying motives. The customer is not conscious of them. Emo-

tional motives may have a more important influence on buying decisions than do rational motives. In fact, many customers convince themselves that they are using rational motives while actually justifying an emotional purchase. For example, a customer may claim to be buying a Cadillac car for reliable performance when the real reason is prestige; here an emotional purchase is obviously being justified with a rational argument.

Patronage Buying Motives. So far in this chapter we have discussed the customer's motives for buying a certain product. But when the same or equally suitable products can be purchased in several stores, the customer selects one of the sources for patronage reasons. **Patronage buying motives** are those that cause a customer to buy from one store instead of another. Patronage buying motives may be either rational or emotional.

Patronage buying motives stem from the firm's image in the trading area. In the mind of a consumer, a business firm's image may be judged on the basis of his or her value system or past experience with the company. For example, a customer may shop a certain store first because it is easy to return goods there.

The table below lists various patronage motives together with examples of customer benefits associated with the motives.

Patronage Motive	Customer Benefit
Customer policies	Satisfaction with goods and services, returns, and adjustments
Integrity	Fair dealing, truthful advertising, and reliability
Fashion cycle	Up-to-date merchandise and suitable styles
Quality of merchandise	Purity, freshness, and excellence of goods
Shopping atmosphere	Store layout, decor, noise factor, cleanliness, and lighting
Assortment policy	Number of lines stocked and adequacy of selection
Courteous treatment	Courtesy of sales staff and other personnel
Customer services	Credit, delivery, gift wrapping, and carry-out service

The percentage of sales completed in relation to the number of shoppers entering the store is related to the strength of a firm's appeal to the patronage motive. It's difficult to estimate what the percentage of sales closed should be; so much depends on what is being sold to whom. However, a rule of thumb is that over 50 percent of the customers who enter the store should be sold something, and 70 to 80 percent is not an uncommon achievement.

Impulse Buying

Unplanned purchasing based largely on an on-the-spot decision is called **impulse buying**. To avoid impulse buying would be *not* to make a spur-of-the-moment decision. The real issue about impulse buying isn't whether the purchase has been planned in advance but whether the decision seems to be wise or foolish later on. Many impulse purchases prove to be good investments. Many meet an unclarified but real need. A customer may see something he or she had not planned to purchase, but this may be the exact item that, at some time in the past, he or she has considered for future purchase. Upon seeing the item, the customer is reminded of this earlier thought or plan and is prompted to act on it.

In some cases, the customer may feel the need of a mental lift that the purchase of a given product might offer. Sometimes people are afraid to admit to their inner needs because it's difficult to rationalize many of them. But often these inner needs are being satisfied when an item is bought impulsively.

Human Needs— What Comes First

For a long time, psychologists have known that people assign priorities to their needs and alter their values when conditions change. Psychologists identify these evaluations as the process of clarifying and ordering human needs. Knowledge of this concept will help you tailor your sales presentations to your customers' needs and wants.

Everyone has certain physical and psychological needs that are vital to happiness. A. H. Maslow named the following needs in order of their importance:

1. *Physical needs:* Food, drink, sex, and shel-

AESTHETIC
Beauty, art, literature, and music

KNOWLEDGE
Learning and understanding

SELF-FULFILLMENT
Rewarding work

SOCIAL
Affection, acceptance, and friendship

SAFETY
Security, family stability, and protection from danger

PHYSICAL
Food, drink, sex, and shelter

A. H. Maslow's hierarchy of needs.

ter are the needs that people try to satisfy first.

2. *Safety needs:* Next, the individual seeks security, family stability, and protection from danger.
3. *Social or love needs:* These include the need for affection and acceptance.
4. *Self-fulfillment needs:* These needs can be satisfied by doing work that is rewarding.
5. *Knowledge needs:* People are curious and they seek knowledge and understanding.
6. *Aesthetic needs:* This need is to enjoy beauty and to appreciate art, literature, and music.

Psychologists believe that as soon as one of our needs is satisfied, another demands to be fulfilled. As long as a person is hungry or thirsty, for example, he or she will not spend time and energy seeking social acceptance. But when the physical needs have been met, social needs will become important motivators.

From your experience, you can realize that people usually try to satisfy their needs on several of these levels at the same time. Also, the needs on any given level are seldom satisfied completely; people are always ready to accept more affection, more security, and more money.

Consciously or unconsciously, each consumer develops needs and wants and places them in order of importance. Consumers base their lists of needs and wants on personal concepts of value and efficiency. When consumers make intelligent choices, they allow for emotional as well as rational buying motives in satisfying their needs and wants.

A consumer's priorities may shift with each succeeding purchase of a product because every new purchase affects his or her value system. Every purchase increases the consumer's desire to buy and consume more. And often, consumers make purchases in terms of the relationship of the product or service to an earlier transaction. If the experience was positive, chances are that consumers will try to repeat it. This is why management stresses patronage buying motives in sales training and in advertising. These motives build repeat sales.

Motivation and the Life Cycle

The ways in which consumers interpret and satisfy their needs and wants depends upon many factors. Factors such as age, climate, cultural background, customs, group affiliations, income, occupation, resource availability, and personal values and goals are all important. But as these factors change, of course, consumers needs and wants also change. Among the most consistent and rapidly changing areas of consumer needs and wants are those associated with the life-cycle stages.

As the age, income, and marital status of a consumer change, different needs and wants emerge. These changes in needs and wants are reflected in consumer buying patterns—the combination of products and services consumed. The table entitled "Major Motivation and Buying Patterns by Life-Cycle Stage" shows the

To what conscious and unconscious consumer needs do these ads appeal? Courtesy of Greg Peterson, president, K. E. Peters Billiard Inc., Minneapolis, Minnesota; Strawbridge & Clothier K. N. Stabeck Company, Inc., and Dayton's

BRUNSWICK

Since 1845

THE NO. 1 NAME IN BILLIARDS

MONARCH

The Monarch table from Brunswick . . . classic styling from a bygone era. Table features a woodgrain finish, burn, stain, and scratch resistant rails, 3-piece matched and registered state, live rubber cushions, wool/nylon blend billard cloth plus 4 cues, balls, triangle, bridge, rulebook and more. Available in traditional pocket style only. Gold cloth.

$799
Includes Delivery & Installation

TRAMPOLINE SALE!!!

K.E. PETERS BILLIARD SUPPLY AND MFG

Authorized Brunswick Billiard Dealer.

SERVICE, REPAIR, RECOVER. HOME OR COMMERCIAL

6150 Lyndale Ave. So.   866-8433

Strawbridge & Clothier

totes® half boots give maximum protection with minimum effort

Hard to believe that such lightweight easy-on boots keep shoes so dry. But they do. And they fold easily to carry in pocket or briefcase. Side zippers make stretch rubber half boots even swifter to pull on and off. Black. S(6½-8), M(8½-9½), L(10-11), XL(11½-13). Like a winter insurance policy. **9.95** Men's Shoes (548) First. All stores.

Take the heat out of the kitchen!

with an
EMBER MATIC™
GASGRILL BY ARKLA

Real "charcoal" flavor with no charcoal mess
Uses natural or bottled gas
Choose from roll-a-round cart, permanent post or patio base models
Grill, bake, fry . . . any kind of food . . . any kind of weather

Distributed by
THE K. N. Stabeck Company, Inc.

Available from the following dealers:

Midwest Fence	Minneapasco	Hearth & Home
525 S. Concord	Appliance Stores	384 St. Peter
South St. Paul	626 Nicollet Mall (372-4601)	St. Paul
(451-2221)	Brookdale (561-1160)	(222-2549)
	Yorktown, 71st & York (831-8464)	

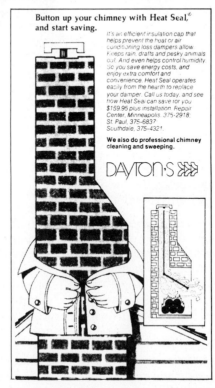

Button up your chimney with Heat Seal,® and start saving.

It's an efficient insulation cap that helps prevent the heat or air conditioning loss dampers allow. Keeps rain, drafts and pesky animals out. And even helps control humidity. So you save energy costs, and enjoy extra comfort and convenience. Heat Seal operates easily from the hearth to replace your damper. Call us today, and see how Heat Seal can save for you $159.95 plus installation. Repair Center, Minneapolis, 375-2918; St. Paul, 375-6837; Southdale, 375-4321.

We also do professional chimney cleaning and sweeping.

DAYTON'S ⧩⧩⧩

needs and wants that are likely to predominate among different consumer age groups along with the products likely to be purchased during each life stage.

Using Buying Motives to Increase Sales

Appeals to customer buying motives are used in all phases of merchandising—all forms of personal selling, advertising, display, and buying as well as in market research. In fact, it is a function of *all* store divisions, both selling and nonselling. Custodians, for example, should be fully aware that their work must meet the customer's desire for cleanliness and safety. This desire causes the customer to return to the store.

Buying Motives and Personal Selling

If you would sell Bill Jones
   What Bill Jones buys.
Then you must see Bill Jones
   Through Bill Jones's eyes.

Personal selling is a fascinating occupation when the salesperson looks at the merchandise through the customer's eyes and sees his or her motives. Putting yourself mentally in the customer's "shoes" raises personal selling to a professional status regardless of your occupational level. Professional salespeople who understand customer buying motives receive great satisfaction from helping customers fulfill their needs and wants. Satisfaction from performing this type of personal service is the reason that many salespeople remain in retail sales occupations.

MAJOR MOTIVATION AND BUYING PATTERNS BY LIFE-CYCLE STAGE

Age Group	Major Needs and Wants	Buying Patterns
Children	Physical comfort and pleasure	Toys, food, and candy
Teenagers	Recognition, satisfaction of curiosity, and pleasure	Clothes, cosmetics, and sports gear
Young adults	Self-fulfillment and social needs	Cars, clothes, and recreational gear
Newly married couples without children and single persons	Social needs and self-fulfillment	Furniture, household goods, cars, and vacations
Young married couples with children	Safety needs and self-fulfillment	Homes, baby products, medicines, washers, TV's, and toys
Middle-aged married couples	Self-fulfillment, knowledge, and aesthetic needs	Fancy foods, new furniture, appliances, travel, and magazines
Older married couples	Knowledge and aesthetic needs	Vacations, luxuries, and home improvements
Retired couples	Physical needs and recreation	Medical care and products
Single older persons	Physical, safety, and social needs	Medical care and products

Recall from the discussion in Chapter 24 that a skillful salesperson inquires carefully about the intended use of a product in order to identify the need. And in doing so, the salesperson is likely to discover clues to the customer's motives and preferences. When such clues are revealed, you, as a salesperson, should follow them up quickly. However, if none appear, you can appeal to what seem to be the most appropriate buying motives in order to help your customer reach a decision to buy. When you are appealing to those motives, usually some signal from the customer will let you know that you have struck a responsive chord. You can try rational, emotional, and patronage appeals to help encourage a decision to buy.

Buying Motives and Mass Selling

Appealing to various buying motives in nonpersonal selling is a subtle and profitable art used by manufacturers and wholesalers as well as by retailers. Mass merchandisers depend almost entirely upon buying motives in their carefully researched advertising and sales promotion campaigns. Fast-food franchisers use striking TV commercials appealing to a wide variety of buying motives. Mail-order houses and catalog showroom distributors use colorful illustrations and catalog copy based on the reasons people buy. Manufacturers appeal to rational buying motives through informative labels and point-of-sale display props. And they appeal to emotional buying motives through magazine advertising.

Why People Don't Buy

Consumers may choose between one brand or another *or* they may decide not to buy at all. Selling is an interpersonal relationship. In this relationship, the purchaser's fears, prejudices, and attitude toward the store or the salesperson are just as important as his or her feelings about the product or service and its price. If customers have any of these doubts, they may decide not to buy. For example, customers may fear that a product will not look nice or perform as well as it did in the store. They may also fear that they will look foolish in the eyes of a spouse or friends, or that they might have bought it for less elsewhere, and so on. Any of these fears may prevent customers from buying.

Most customers fear the salesperson's expertise at the same time that they seek help. Right or wrong, your customers believe that you know more about your merchandise than they do. Also, they know who pays your salary and believe that you will place your employer's interest above theirs. Your task, therefore, is to convince customers you are on their side, believing that there is more to be gained from satisfying them than from the profit of a single sale.

In this chapter you've learned about the causes of different types of buying motives and how they make consumers buy. You also learned that an understanding of human needs is important in determining why people buy and how you can use buying motives to increase sales.

In the next chapter, you'll find out about the next two choices that consumers make when they decide on a purchase—that is, determining *how* and *when* to buy.

Trade Talk

Define each term and use it in a sentence.

Buying motives	Patronage buying
Emotional buying	motives
motives	Rational buying
Impulse buying	motives
	Values

Can You Answer These?

1. What uses can be made of a working knowledge of buying motives?
2. What is the relative importance of each of the three general categories of buying motives in personal selling? In mass selling?

3. How do people assign priorities to their needs?

4. How does mass selling make use of the buying motives? How do fast-food franchisers use them?

5. Why do some consumers decide not to buy?

Problems

1. Rule a form similar to the following. In the left column, list the six needs named by A. H. Maslow. In the right column, list two examples of products and services that a consumer would buy to satisfy each need.

Need	Products and Services

2. Rule a form similar to the following one. In the left column, write the letter of each of the following statements: (a) "Half boots give maximum protection with minimum effort." (b) "First time ever—Lucille's French rug yarn." (c) "Dress for success—a fashion show for men and women." (d) "Select now for Christmas giving." (e) "Picture yourself in mink." (f) "Take the heat out of the kitchen." (g) "Button your chimney with heat and start saving." (h) "For the times you want to remember." (i) "Since 1945, the No. 1 name in billiards." (j) "No down payment, easy credit terms, 90 days same as cash." Place a check mark (√) in the appropriate column at the right to indicate whether each statement makes a rational, emotional, or patronage appeal to the customer.

Statement	Rational	Emotional	Patronage

How and When People Buy

Communications & Human Relations

Economics & Marketing

Merchandising

Selling & Technology

Advertising & Display

Operations & Management

Here is what a top-ranked salesperson of a leading specialty chain store told a researcher about retail selling procedure:

Consumers are very different in their likes and dislikes and in the way they buy. The kind of selling attitude that would make me feel comfortable might offend a customer. What you have to do certainly is *not* to treat them exactly the same way you want to be treated, but rather to find out—as well as you can—how each customer wants to be served and then do it that way whether it's your way or not.

You make things harder for yourself if you don't study your customers. There are so many little things one notices that tell you right away how to act. For instance, the way they walk, what they look for, and how they talk. You can see a lot without your customer's knowing it if you know what to look for.

It's important for everyone in retailing to understand that everyone has changing moods and attitudes toward buying. Sometimes we hunt for the best price, gladly walking a mile to save a dollar. At other times, all we want is to save time.

And then there are occasions when we want reassurance about quality and taste, and in our minds only certain retail firms can satisfy this need. Yes, all retail workers should take these changing customer behaviors into account.

You will recall from Chapter 22 that consumers act differently when buying convenience goods, shopping goods, and specialty goods. Also, it makes a great deal of difference whether they are in a hurry or can take their time. They act differently when purchasing a product they haven't used before or one that is new on the market. And they act differently when buying for themselves rather than for someone else.

Without doubt, the salesperson quoted at the beginning of this chapter gave sound advice when suggesting that the first thing to do in retail selling is to find out how each customer wants to be treated. Knowing how people buy is an art and a science. The information that follows will help you cultivate the art and introduce you to the science of how and when people buy.

How People Buy

How people buy is of great concern in both personal and mass selling. All retailers strive to keep track of ever-changing consumer behavior, not just in what is bought but also in how it is bought. Once a change in consumer buying behavior becomes evident, retailers compete to meet the newly identified consumer preferences.

Sometimes the change in consumer buying preferences is so great that it affects the entire retail industry. For example, consider the increasing popularity of full-service specialty stores with wide assortments in a single product line. These types of specialty stores have become popular because retailers have responded to consumer dissatisfaction with self-service merchandising in certain product lines such as toys, sporting goods, and building supplies.

Most changes in the buying behavior of a store's customers are very gradual. As old customers move away or change their buying loyalties, new ones with different value systems and buying behaviors take their places. A store that is sensitive to its customers' buying behavior makes the necessary adjustments in its services.

The answer to successful retailing rests with the ability of a store's policymakers to identify changes in customer behavior and, of course, to make suitable adjustments in its services. Computers can tell retailers what products and services customers want. But the matter of sensing changes in how people buy rests largely with alert salespeople, buyers, or managers who spend time on the selling floor and credit workers who contact customers directly.

You may have heard an experienced salesperson say, "Customers aren't what they used to be." How true it is! However, the critical question is, "How are they different?"

You will recall from your study of Chapter 23 that customers go through five mental stages during a sale—attention, interest, desire, conviction, and action. You'll also remember that all purchases require five buying decisions—on need, product, price, place, and time. Then, in Chapter 42, you learned about buying motives (why people buy). These three types of consumer buying analyses offer insight into the matter of how and when people buy goods and services. Now let's explore consumer buying further. We'll do this by studying some of the forces that cause customers to act differently when they are buying. Such knowledge makes selling and merchandising more interesting and effective.

Who Makes the Purchasing Decisions?

Who determines the need for a product or service and who does the buying makes a great deal of difference in how and when the purchase is made. (And, of course, it makes a difference in the way goods and services are promoted and sold.) Most consumers make their own decisions to buy and do the actual purchasing. However, family decisions to purchase are frequently made by more than one family member, and one family member does the actual purchasing.

The purchase of costly products and services that affect a number of family members requires careful thought. On the other hand, buying decisions on less expensive items that are not as important are made without hesitation, usually by one person. Most joint purchases are influenced by the person who knows the most about the goods or services being considered. As a salesperson, your job is to identify the decision maker and direct your appeals to that person.

The Decision-Making Process

The consumer decision-making process during a purchase can be explained best with the aid of the following figure. It shows what factors enter into a customer's decision to buy.

Note that there are two main groups of factors to be brought together: (1) consumer needs and wants and (2) product features. The goal of retailers is to assist consumers in arriving at satisfying solutions that will bring these two groups together.

Can you see how the need and want factors on the left side of the figure can influence the four remaining buying decisions shown on the right—product, price, place, and time? The better you (or any merchandising or sales promotion divi-

The consumer decision-making process.

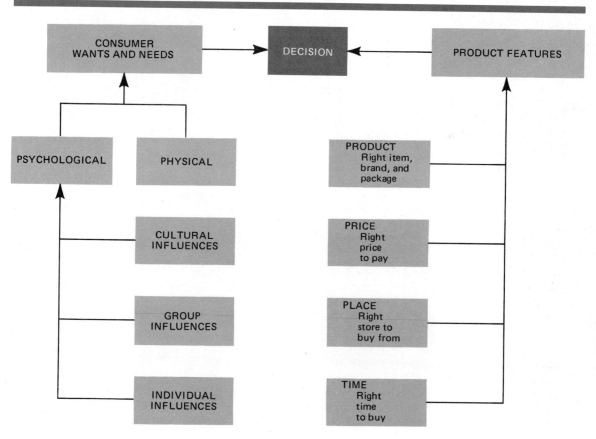

sion worker) understand the factors in the customer's decision-making process, the greater your chances are of completing satisfactory sales.

How Customers Deliberate. Of course, little or no deliberation takes place when consumers buy on impulse. And there is very little thought given to the purchase of many convenience goods. But when financial resources are limited and a sizable expense is involved, consumers often think about a purchase for a considerable length of time.

♦ Step 1: Normally the first step consumers take in solving a purchasing problem is to clarify their need. You will recall from Chapter 24, on opening the sale, that there are customers who know exactly what they want, those who have a general idea of their needs and wants, and those who are unaware of their needs. This is a critical step in the buying process because the remaining steps depend on its outcome.

The consumer decision-making process may be simple or complex. Courtesy of F.A.O. Schwarz

UNIT 14 ♦ *Improving Your Selling Techniques*

The amount of thought given to it varies markedly.

♦ Step 2: The next step consumers take is to identify the alternatives available to meet that need. As in Step 1, the difficulty of this task varies with the complexity of the buying problem. Sometimes there is no alternative product or service available, but often there are many.

♦ Step 3: The third step consumers take is to gather information about each alternative. Consumers may make the operation simple or complex. Its degree of complexity depends on the consumer's sophistication, the availability of accurate information, the variety of products available, and the prices of the product or service being considered.

♦ Step 4: The last step consumers take is to choose the most appropriate alternative and take action. In this step, consumers weigh the evidence, then rank the alternatives on the basis of their concept of personal values and efficiency. When making an original purchase, consumers usually include a series of eliminations, first one item then another, in making this final decision.

How the Ego Is Involved. A very important influence on consumer buying behavior is the consumer's concept of self, or the ego. The way consumers act and the decisions they make in the marketplace reflect what they think of themselves. From a retailer's viewpoint, protecting the customer's ego is law. Witness the old saying, "The customer is always right," which relates to that "law" of retailing.

How deeply a consumer's ego is involved in any given purchase depends on that person's value system, the kinds of products being purchased, and treatment by the store and the salesperson. Some people are more concerned than others with possessing products and become highly ego-involved in a purchase. Rightly or wrongly, many consumers think that they are attractive to others because of their possessions.

When consumers purchase products, such as groceries, that call for little ego involvement, they generally use fewer steps of the decision-making process. But when they purchase products such as fashionable clothing, where there is considerable ego involvement, they may use all the steps of the decision-making process. Regardless of the products being purchased, all consumers are influenced by a salesperson's attitude toward them. And all consumers feel somewhat flattered when a salesperson treats them with respect and shows a sincere interest in their problems.

Salespeople must be able to judge consumers' ego involvement in a purchase and provide the right amount of subtle reinforcement. Insincere bolstering of a customer's ego is almost sure to backfire.

When People Buy

Except in some remote communities, most retailers must be open for business when their customers want to shop. This was not always true. Not many years ago, most stores were open from 9 a.m. to 5:30 p.m. on weekdays and Saturdays and closed on Sundays. Some retailers even drew the draperies across their display windows on Sunday. Competition has changed all that. Survival in retailing today depends largely on the store's ability to serve customers when they are willing to buy regardless of the time or day or evening or the day of the week. Thus a convenience food store in a high-traffic location may stay open 24 hours a day, 7 days a week. And a gift shop may open for only a few hours a day on certain days of the week, with the days and hours depending on the season of the year. During the Christmas selling season, retailers may extend their shopping hours to enable most potential customers to do their shopping.

In many shopping areas, such as shopping centers, the retailers meet to determine which shopping hours would best

Teenagers now account for a large percentage of all customers. Ann Hagen
Griffiths/Design Photographers International, Inc.

serve the needs of the majority of customers. After these hours are determined and agreed upon, all merchants are expected to comply with the agreement. Sometimes such agreements are limited to a single type of store, such as unionized supermarkets.

To know what hours best serve the interests of their actual and potential customers, retailers may study hourly sales records for the weeks being investigated. They may also question their customers directly to find out whether the store schedule is convenient for their needs. Most retailers also watch the practices of their competitors to see whether any change in their own practices should be made.

Maintaining the shopping hours that best meet consumers needs is a challenge that each retailer must meet. There are problems to be dealt with in maintaining such hours. For example, work schedules of employees must be staggered when the store is open more than 8 hours daily. Also, it may be difficult to hire workers who are willing to work during certain hours.

Trends in Purchasing Decisions

The way in which consumers make purchasing decisions is changing, just as individual lifestyles are changing. A number of major trends in consumer purchasing decisions have been detected. Some recent studies on the role of various family members in shopping show that:

- The spending of teenagers far outweighs their percentage of the population in the purchase of many items. Teenage girls, for example, account for the purchase of one-third of the nation's cosmetics. Teenagers also influence a vast amount of adult spending, beyond their own purchases.
- Young husbands and husbands in higher income brackets are more involved in the family purchasing process than are older husbands or husbands in middle and lower income brackets.
- Working women are partly responsible for the fact that, over the last several years, consumers have tended to shift their shopping day from weekends to weekday evenings.

- The high rate of inflation has caused what probably will be permanent changes in supermarket shopping behavior. Seventy percent of consumers will stock up when they find a bargain. An equal percentage buy lower-priced private brands. Fifty-four percent buy in quantity if it is cheaper to do so.
- Men are making more family purchases, women are making somewhat fewer, and children are making slightly more. In addition, more husbands and wives seem to be shopping together. The increase in joint shopping has been seen especially in the areas of home furnishings, automobiles, clothing, and hardware.

Now that you understand the motives underlying consumer buying habits and how and when consumers buy, you're ready to see how, as a retail worker, you can put this knowledge into practice. Chapter 44 explains how to respond to customers' needs and wants. Chapter 45 discusses how you can help customers make buying decisions and finally bring the sale to a close.

Can You Answer These?

1. What causes consumers to act differently at one time as opposed to another? What should salespeople do about these differences?
2. Which retail store workers should be concerned with the way consumers buy?
3. In what ways do consumers change their buying behavior?
4. What kinds of purchasing decisions are made jointly or by a number of family members?
5. What are the two main groups of factors that influence consumer buying decisions? What are the factors in each group?

Problems

1. Using the information in the chart on page 341, analyze one or more of your recent purchases that required a fairly large expenditure. When doing this, consider the following questions:
   a. What physical needs, if any, prompted your decision to make the purchase? What psychological needs?
   b. What cultural, group, and individual influences were involved in your decision to purchase the product or service?
   c. How did you decide on the particular product or service you bought? Did you use the four steps in solving a purchasing problem without realizing it?
   d. How did you arrive at the time decision? The place decision? The price decision?
   e. What help, if any, did you receive from advertising? Displays? The salesperson?
   f. If you were to repeat the purchase, what would you do differently?

Responding to Customer Needs and Wants

CHAPTER 44

Communications & Human Relations
Economics & Marketing
Merchandising
Selling & Technology
Advertising & Display
Operations & Management

Mary Ramoz, a part-time salesperson at a sporting goods specialty store, will soon graduate from high school. Her expression is pleasant, her eyes bright, and her mouth breaks into a smile whenever she speaks to a customer. Mary moves quickly and with assurance and is always full of life, showing in every gesture that she loves her work and enjoys helping her customers.

Mary's attitude is the same toward all her customers. She serves them carefully, willingly sharing her knowledge of products and offering helpful suggestions concerning their use. Without doubt, Mary, though a beginner, is in tune with the purposes and mood of personal retail selling during the 1980s. And she is headed toward a satisfying career in retailing.

This brief sketch of a sincere young salesperson, who knows all about the products and services she sells, contains the secret of all successful retail selling. If Mary can maintain her present positive attitude, she will acquire all the personal and technical skills required in successful retailing. Just as Mary's attitudes toward her occupation and her customers govern the way she responds to them and how she goes about helping them when they shop, yours can too.

Attempting to impose the salesperson's will on customers (high-pressure selling) has always been distasteful to the customer and damaging to the store as well as the salesperson. The key to today's personal selling is empathy—placing yourself mentally in the customer's shoes. Empathy implies the following:

♦ A desire to please each customer
♦ A willingness to consider each customer's buying problem
♦ Respect for the customer's wants and preferences
♦ The ability to talk the customer's language
♦ The ability to apply your knowledge of how customers buy
♦ The ability to help the customer reach a buying decision

Making the Sales Presentation

Many customers need help with their purchasing problems. They need a salesperson who knows about the product or service and who can show them the values or benefits of a product's features. This part of the selling task is called the **sales presentation.** It involves (1) choosing the right merchandise or service to present, (2) dramatizing the product, (3) involving the customer in the presentation, and (4) emphasizing customer benefits.

Choosing Merchandise to Present

In order to choose the right merchandise or service to show a customer, you as a salesperson, must know your stock well. You have to know the general characteristics, the customer benefits, and the price of each item and service you sell as well as the major differences among similar items. No customer will expect you to know everything about every item in the department. But a customer will expect you to be able to locate the desired information quickly.

As a salesperson, you also have to know where stock is in the department. This is not a problem in some kinds of retail selling jobs. But if you handle a large number of different kinds of products, such as hardware, you'll have a large amount of stock to keep track of.

When choosing items to show customers, you have to decide which merchandise to show first and how much to show at one time.

What to Show First. When determining what merchandise to show first, experienced salespeople use the following guidelines:

♦ If a customer asks for a particular style, color, price, model, or brand, show it immediately.
♦ If the customer expresses no preference, inquire about the intended use and show what you think would be appropriate for that use.
♦ If the customer gives no clue concerning price, show the medium price line first.
♦ When in doubt, show advertised or very popular articles first.

How Much to Show. The following suggestions from experienced salespeople will help you to decide how much merchandise to show:

♦ Show enough merchandise to allow the customer a reasonable choice. When selling goods such as shoes, show several styles.
♦ Indicate that you are interested in your customer's buying problem and that you are willing to show all suitable merchandise, but avoid overwhelming the customer with stock.
♦ If you display and describe your merchandise effectively, you will not need to show every item you have in stock. Try to avoid unnecessary steps in getting more merchandise from stock.

Dramatizing the Product

Customers are much more likely to move from the mental stage of interest in a product to the point of wanting to own it if you present the merchandise vividly, bringing out its strong features and dramatizing its uses. Many customers are confused by the number of products they have seen; others haven't really concentrated on any product. Nearly all customers will appreciate it if you show them how one product, or a carefully limited number of items, can meet their needs and wants.

The kinds of dramatization practices that add to the success of a sales presentation are (1) displaying the merchandise effectively, (2) showing the product in use, and (3) using correct grammar with appropriate gestures.

Displaying the Merchandise Effectively. Window and interior displays aren't nearly as helpful to a shopper as the displaying of a product by a skillful salesperson. Displaying the merchandise is an art in itself. It is said that the most effective display prop is the salesperson's hand. The manner in which you handle a product reveals your feeling toward it. For example, if you sell expensive jewelry, or shotguns, carefully select each item from the display case. While showing it to a customer, handle it gently so that the customer feels this to be a very special product, one that the customer would like to own.

If an article is small, separate it from similar items. You may want to hand it to the customer so that attention is concentrated on that single item rather than on the entire display of merchandise. You can even isolate a large immovable major appliance, such as a freezer, by gradually positioning yourself so that the customer's attention is concentrated on one model. If you are selling ready-to-wear, you can highlight the garment by holding it up to the customer in front of a mirror. Or you can hold it against a neutral background such as a wall instead of against the multicolored, confusing background of a rack of other apparel.

Showing the Product in Use. Whenever possible, show your customers how the merchandise will look when used. Show a towel folded over a towel bar, a rug spread on the floor, or a bedspread on a bed. Put records on stereos, sew on a sewing machine, and turn on lamps. These activities help customers to see how the product will solve their buying problems. Showing the product in use is an art too. It is one that merits practice because a poor demonstration often spoils a sale.

Using Effective Language and Gestures. When you make your sales presentation, use simple, accurate language at all times. Avoid slang because it makes a poor impression on customers and sometimes fails to convey meaning. Also, avoid words like "nice," "pretty," "fine," and "wonderful," which have very little meaning. Try to use stimulating adjectives and phrases that carry conviction. How much more effective it is to say, "See how smoothly this jacket fits across the shoulders," than to say, "It's a nice fit."

You can communicate with gestures as well as with your voice. Use your hands, arms, and face to express enthusiasm and to get and keep the customer's interest. Sincere enthusiasm is contagious. Hands

Gestures can communicate the salesperson's attitude toward the merchandise.

play an important role in communication. They emphasize the spoken word, communicate your feelings, and direct the customer's attention to the product.

Involving the Customer

Customers usually like to participate in the sales presentation. Participation allows the customer to "experience" the product. Also, participation can change a customer's interest in a product into a desire for it. How customers act and what they say while participating will enable you to understand their needs and wants better. It will also help you determine the stage of the buying process the customer has reached. To involve customers, encourage them to talk and to participate physically by examining or demonstrating the product, using as many of the five senses as appropriate.

Appealing to the Five Senses. The cus-

tomer's first clue about a product is almost always provided by *sight*. It reveals clues such as size, shape, color, and texture. People remember more of what they see for themselves in a product than of what they hear about it. So it's important that you display the product in a favorable way. As a salesperson, if you understand and apply the principles of color, line, and design in selling, you'll have the advantage because you're able to show the product in an attractive way.

The sense of *touch* is very effective in selling many types of products. By feeling a fabric, a customer can tell whether it's soft or stiff, smooth or rough, lightweight or heavy. When customers can handle a golf club, balance a hammer, or type on a typewriter, their sense of touch tells them whether the product will satisfy their needs.

Retailers use sound in several ways to appeal to the customer's sense of *hearing*.

OPEN IT UP AND HEAR WHAT IT WILL DO

A funny thing happens to some people when they get near a Steinway piano. They get nervous. They stroll into a showroom bold as you please, play other pianos with wild abandon, and then humbly ask permission to play the Steinway.

That's silly. A Steinway isn't a holy shrine. It's the one instrument where playing with wild abandon makes the most sense.

In fact, that's the best way to find out why a Steinway is a Steinway and why other pianos are just other pianos. If there is any reason why playing a Steinway should make you nervous, it's this . . . once you know what a Steinway can do, you'll be spoiled for anything else.

Write or phone for color selection folder.
Open Saturday. Parking facilities available.

STEINWAY & SONS

109 West 57th Street, New York 10019 · 246-1100

They use it through the spoken word of salespeople or through loudspeakers announcing shoppers' specials. They use it through the sounds made by the products themselves, such as stereos and stereo records. And they use it through background music, the purpose of which is to establish a buying mood. The clear ring of a crystal goblet in a quiet atmosphere often helps a customer move closer to a final buying decision.

For hundreds of years, merchants have appealed to the sense of *taste* in selling foods and beverages. Recently, the importance of the sense of taste has been recognized in merchandising mouthwash, toothpaste, and similar items. Many manufacturers introduce a new food or drink by dispensing samples. Many new flavors have been added to product lines.

The sense of *smell* is very important in selling products such as cosmetics, food, and tobacco. As customers head toward the cash register in a large supermarket, the mouth-watering smell of baked bread wafts past them. Weakened, they double back for an unplanned purchase. Stores also try to create a pleasant shopping atmosphere by keeping the air clean and free from offensive odors.

Talking with the Customer. Because customers react differently and say different things, you must vary your responses. Make sure that your comments suit each customer and each situation. If you talk too much, you may make your customers feel that you're more concerned about making a sale than you are about helping them. If you talk too little, you may cause a customer to think that you lack interest in the sale. After making a point, stop and let your customer ask a question. If the customer doesn't respond in some way, try asking a question that will direct attention to the merchandise.

Emphasizing Customer Benefits

Customers think about products in terms of benefits to themselves. What they really want to know is "Will the benefits received from this product be worth the price?"

Customers seldom attach equal importance to the same benefits of a particular product. One customer may be interested in serviceability and economy, while another is looking for appearance and prestige. Other frequently pursued consumer satisfactions are listed in item 3 on page 173.

To be successful, a salesperson must match the product's features with the customer's needs and wants. Select those product features that will appeal to the particular customer. See item 5 on page 173 for guidelines concerning product features that are used to prove that customers will receive the benefits that you claim they will.

A table like the one entitled "Product: Wool Coat" is called a **product benefit analysis.** It matches the product features in one column with the corresponding benefits in the other column. Organizing product features in this manner should help you convince customers that a product will provide the desired customer benefit. A **customer benefit** is an advantage that the product provides for the user. **Product features** are descriptive facts about the product.

Prove your benefits to your customers by using the product features to back up your claims. For example, tell your customer that the child's dress does not have to be ironed and is easy to care for because it is made of a cotton and polyester blend, which can be washed in a machine.

Answering Customers' Questions and Objections

Customers' questions usually are indications that they are interested and sincere. Questions will help you assist your customers with their buying problems. Welcome questions and express your appreciation by saying, "I'm glad you mentioned that point," or "Thank you for bringing that to my attention."

PRODUCT: WOOL COAT	
Customer Benefits (Satisfactions)	Product Features (Proofs)
Attractive appearance	Soft colors. Soft, luxurious nap. Interesting fabric design and texture. Careful tailoring to ensure proper fit.
Easy care	Wool fabric resists soil. Wrinkles tend to hang out.
Comfort and protection	Wool absorbs moisture slowly and holds a great deal of moisture before it feels damp, thereby protecting the wearer from sudden chill. Wool nap keeps warm air from escaping, thereby keeping the body warm in cold weather.
Suitability	Closely woven fabrics are suitable for wearing in cold weather.

Types of Objections

Customers differ in the ways they reveal and conceal their objections to buying. Some are straightforward in expressing their feelings and come directly to the point that concerns them most. An objection based on an honestly felt misgiving about a purchase is called a **sincere objection.** It may have to do with one of the five buying decisions—involving need, product, price, place, or time—discussed in Chapter 23.

Many customers refuse to reveal their true objections. They may be polite or timid. Or they may want you to give some good reason for their making the purchase. Concealing the real objection is called an **excuse.** For example, a customer may say, "I didn't intend to buy today" when they really mean that they are not satisfied with the article.

Dealing with Sincere Objections. A customer's sincere objection offers the salesperson an opportunity to identify areas of doubt and to show the customer additional benefits that relate to the customer's concern. Listen very attentively to a customer's objection. In fact, if a customer obviously hesitates but hasn't voiced any specific objection, try to get the customer to indicate the cause of his or her indecision. Do not ridicule or ignore customers' uncertainties or contradict them directly. Instead, assume that you didn't make your original explanation clear and explain the point again using a different tack. Try using the common ways of meeting sincere objections that experienced salespeople use. They are:

♦ *Asking the customer to explain the objection.* As customers attempt to explain, they often answer the objection or else show that it is not a serious one.
♦ *The "yes, but" method.* Agreeing with the customer but presenting another angle. For example:

Customer: I doubt that these light shoe soles will wear well.

Salesperson: Yes, but they're lightweight so they'll be comfortable.

Dealing with Excuses. Never ignore a customer's excuse. Instead, treat the customer courteously and try to find the underlying objection. The real objection will usually reveal itself as a result of your question or come to light as the sale proceeds. The customer may state it directly, or you may detect it from the customer's remarks and actions. Here is an example of how you can use a question to help a customer complete the five buying decisions.

♦ When a customer says, "I'm just looking," you may say, "Certainly, that's the best

Customers may be reluctant to give their real reasons for not buying.

way to know what we have. Isn't this a great assortment of posters?"

Note that the salesperson followed the excuse with a question concerning a buying decision. The salesperson questioned the source decision. Suppose that the customer had said, "Yes, but I really had something less expensive in mind." It would have been evident that the price decision had not been made, and you would have had to work on that buying decision.

Dealing with Product Disadvantages. It's almost impossible for a retailer to stock an assortment of items large enough to meet all customer needs and wants. So even the best salespeople encounter valid objections. If a customer has a serious objection to a product, it's far better to keep the customer's confidence than to try to force the customer into a sale. When ap-

propriate, present the strong features of the item and show how these points are important. If the customer agrees, then you will make the sale. If the customer is not convinced, you may not make the sale, but the customer will remember your helpful interest in serving his or her needs.

Anticipating Objections

Frequently, the best way to deal with objections is to prevent them from arising. Keep in mind that the customer's very act of raising an objection often strengthens that thought in the customer's mind. And talking about it too much can help increase the customer's negative attitude. Therefore, a good strategy may be to present product knowledge skillfully, answering objections even before the customer has thought of them. If you know your product's benefits and features well, you are bound to know a great deal more about your merchandise than almost any of your customers.

Anticipating objections is particularly important when customers who have used a product for a long time are reluctant to accept a new model. It is your job to educate them about the new model so that they will accept it. This technique contributes to a skillful sales presentation.

In Chapter 24 you studied the first steps of the selling process. In this chapter, you learned the in-between steps: how to make a sales presentation and how to answer the customer's questions and objections. And now, you're ready to study how to increase sales and to bring the sale to a close. These last selling steps are discussed in the next chapter.

Trade Talk

Define each term and use it in a sentence.

Customer benefit   Product features
Excuse   Sales presentation
Product benefit   Sincere objection
  analysis

Can You Answer These?

1. How does a salesperson show empathy for a customer's buying problem? How does such empathy help the salesperson? Help the store?

2. What guidelines do salespeople use in selecting the goods to show a customer?
3. How does a productive salesperson dramatize products for customers?
4. What is the basic difference in procedure between handling an excuse and dealing with a sincere objection?
5. How does a salesperson anticipate customer objections?

Problems

1. On a separate sheet of paper, write the letter of each of the following types of products: (a) automobile, (b) cake, (c) cassette tape, (d) corsage, (e) fire insurance, (f) house paint, and (g) tennis racket. Under each letter, write a selling statement or describe a selling action that would appeal to more than one of the five senses (sight, touch, hearing, taste, and smell). Appeal to as many senses as you can. After completing your list, you can add good statements or selling actions contributed by other class members.

2. Assume that you are selling one of the items in Problem 1. After you have presented the product or service to the best of your ability, the customer says, "I just can't seem to make up my mind. Perhaps I should think it over for a while." On a separate sheet of paper, explain what you would do and say to the customer. Compare your solution to the problem with that of a classmate who has chosen the same product or service.

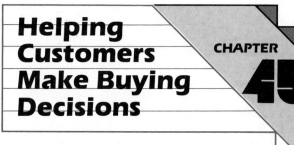

Helping Customers Make Buying Decisions

CHAPTER 45

Communications & Human Relations
Economics & Marketing
Merchandising
Selling & Technology
Advertising & Display
Operations & Management

Fred Kozlowski had been selling retail hardware for about a month when his supervisor said to him, "Fred, you are a hard worker, and we're glad to have you here. You have the qualities necessary to become an excellent salesperson. That's why I'd like to help you improve your sales skills.

"I've noticed that most of your sales checks list only one item, and your average sale is relatively small. You should learn to increase your average sale by encouraging customers to buy better-quality goods when needed and by suggesting additional products. I'll help you if you want me to."

Three weeks later, a customer asked for 6 feet of aluminum half-inch molding. Fred measured the length, hesitated, and then tried to be a real salesperson rather than just waiting on customers.

"Do you have enough tacks left to put this up, sir?" he asked the customer. "It has predrilled holes that call for special ¾-inch tacks."

The customer turned over the molding in his hands. "No, I didn't realize that there were special tacks for this material—and I did have trouble with that last strip I installed. Let me have a box."

"Here you are, sir," said Fred, "and if you do much work like this, you ought to look at our special tack hammers."

By the time Fred had finished, he had sold the customer four items in addition to the molding the customer had come in to buy. And one of those items was the best-quality tack hammer carried in stock! Fred had become a salesperson rather than an order taker; when he closed the sale, he had used both trading up and suggestion selling.

Increasing the Average Sale

Why was Fred's supervisor anxious for Fred to increase his average sale? Simply because higher profit results from larger sales transactions. Higher profit is possible because some business costs—rent and salaries for example—do not rise proportionately when sales are increased, that is, up to a certain point. The example below shows that eight times as much profit before taxes can be made by selling only twice as much merchandise. This example may be slightly exaggerated because it may actually cost a store slightly more in handling costs to transact a second sale. Doubling the sale, however, will still result in a substantial increase in profit.

Sale 1

Selling price of one item	$1.00
Cost of one item	.65
Gross profit	$ .35
Expenses	.30
Net profit	$ .05

Sale 2

Selling price of two items	$2.00
Cost of two items	1.30
Gross profit	$ .70
Expenses	.30
Net profit	$ .40

Fred's supervisor also wanted Fred to sell his customers better-quality goods than they requested (a practice called **trading up**) because a store usually makes more profit on its higher-priced merchandise. Stores make very little profit on their low-priced specials.

Fred was pleased that he had increased his sales. He was pleased not only because of the additional profit this had made for the store but also because of the personal satisfaction he received from helping customers better fill their needs. Fred realized that the least costly items were often not the best value for the money in terms of the customer's use of a product. He also learned that suggestion selling, when properly done, saved his customers time and money and often increased the satisfaction they received from using a product. **Suggestion selling** is the selling technique through which a salesperson gives a customer a buying idea that leads to the purchase of additional items.

Trading Up

Trading up is related to suggestion selling. Many customers may be willing to pay higher prices if they believe that they will receive additional benefits for their money.

Why does a department stock several price lines in some of its product areas? One good reason is to serve customers who buy the product for different reasons or use it in different ways. For example, there are customers who are price-conscious. There are prestige-motivated buyers who insist on deluxe models. And there are those in between these extremes. Another reason for carrying several price lines is that regular customers may put the same product to different uses, and one price line may not serve all customer needs adequately. Therefore, several price lines may be stocked. So salespeople, more than ever before, have to be knowledgeable about more products and features, be familiar with more prices, and be in a position to explain the differences to customers.

You can master the technique of trading up if you follow these rules:

1. Determine the customer's intended use of the product before you try to trade up. This enables you to help your customer find the best buy for the purpose. It also helps keep you from misjudging the consumer values the customer seeks.
2. Do not belittle the lower-priced item by suggesting that it is of inferior quality. If you do and your customer does not want the higher-priced goods, you may spoil your chances of making a sale.
3. Lower-priced specials frequently are less functional, and once the customer realizes this, he or she may not be satisfied. Therefore, indicate the similar features of the

When you are trading up, it is important to point out the additional benefits of the higher-priced merchandise. Ken Karp

better product, and call the customer's attention to its *additional* benefits.

4. If the store advertises a product, be fully prepared to sell and deliver it. Avoid any suggestion of the "bait-and-switch" selling technique in which customers are pressured into buying a higher-profit item. It is unethical as well as illegal. Some customers cannot afford to pay a higher price, and in some situations the low-priced article may be satisfactory.

Selling Additional Merchandise

In many sales transactions, customers need certain products in addition to the ones they came to purchase. They are frequently grateful for suggestions that will save them another shopping trip or a telephone call to the store. Also, many customers are interested in new products and opportunities to save money. They usually welcome useful suggestions from competent salespeople. So place yourself in your customer's shoes, and suggest appropriate additional merchandise.

Types of Suggestion Selling

There are several types of suggestions that you can make to sell additional merchandise. They include the following:

♦ Related products
♦ Larger quantities of an item
♦ New stock and new products
♦ Special values
♦ New or additional uses for products
♦ Products for special occasions

As a salesperson, you have to choose the type of suggestion that is practical for the situation.

Suggesting Related Products. Items that can be used with the article the customer has purchased are called **related merchandise,** or **companion goods.** You'll only succeed with this type of selling if you know what you have in stock and have mastered

product knowledge skills. Related merchandise helps the customer in the following ways:

♦ It may increase the value or pleasure derived from the original purchase. For example, shoe polish protects shoes.
♦ It may be used with the original article. Brushes, paint thinner, and sandpaper are usually used with paint.
♦ It may improve the appearance of the original item. Costume jewelery or a scarf is often used to accent a dress.

Suggesting Larger Quantities. Suggesting a larger quantity of some items can save customers additional shopping trips because they will have a supply of the product on hand. Also, it may save them money. By suggesting a larger quantity of an item, you may be appealing to convenience or economy. For example, if you're a drugstore salesperson, you may suggest a larger bottle of vitamins because such a purchase will save the customer money.

Suggesting New Stock and New Products. Most customers will appreciate your telling them that new merchandise has been received by the store. For example, if you've just finished selling a suit to a customer, you might say, "We've just received our first shipment of fall coats. Would you like to see what they're wearing this year?"

Many customers are interested in hearing about new products that are easier to use or that provide them with some advantage. As a hardware salesperson, you might show the customer a level that can be carried in the pocket or a new lawn edger that is easier to operate.

Suggesting Special Values. Stores often advertise merchandise at special low prices. Customers benefit because they save money and get a bargain. The store gains from the extra profit made on the additional purchase. Furthermore, end-of-season and pre-inventory sales help to empty the

A salesperson may suggest an additional item or larger quantities before the completion of the sale. Customers appreciate suggestions that save them money, more shopping trips, or inconvenience. *Courtesy of Sears, Roebuck and Co.*

store of old merchandise and make room for new. To take advantage of these situations, suggest appropriate unadvertised specials that the customer may not have noticed.

Suggesting New or Additional Uses of Products. Sometimes you can suggest a new use for products that will lead the customer to buy more than one item. For example, if you sell towels, you can show the customer a display featuring a beach robe made of towels.

Suggesting Products for Special Occasions. Sales volume usually increases just before most holidays, such as Christmas and Mother's Day, when people buy gifts. On these occasions, be alert and make appropriate suggestions for gifts; when possible, remind customers of coming events. A special sale in November may be the rea-

son for suggesting that the customer buy the item for a Christmas present.

When to Suggest Additional Products

A good time to suggest additional products is just after a customer has already bought one item, while the customer is still in a buying mood. There are times, however, when you may suggest an additional item before the completion of the first sale. This is when the suggested item might increase the customer's desire for the original product. And in this case, it's advisable to introduce it at an appropriate time during the sale. For example, if a customer is examining a man's dress shirt, an attractive necktie—knotted and laid in position on the shirt—might help the customer visualize the shirt in use.

Timing a suggestion is a matter of sensing your relationship to the customer and using good judgment. Occasionally, suggestion selling is appropriate after the sales check is completed, particularly when there is a lull in business and the customer is waiting for the purchase to be wrapped.

How to Handle Suggestion Selling

A large percentage of successful suggestion sales depend on knowing not only when to suggest but to whom and how the suggestion is to be made. You can achieve good results by making certain that the conditions for making a suggestion are favorable. And you can also succeed by using the tested procedures presented in the following pages.

Conditions for Suggestion Selling. Successful suggestion selling depends on the following conditions:

1. *The customer must need the suggested article.* Training and experience will enable you to sense what is best suited to a particular customer's need. You will be guided by your experience during earlier sales.
2. *The customer's attitude toward you should be positive.* You can pave the way toward acceptance by gaining the customer's confidence. A customer who suspects that you're more interested in making a sale than in being helpful is not likely to accept a suggestion.
3. *The suggestion should exclude opposing ideas.* For example, you would *not* say, "Would you like some shoe polish?" because of the opposing idea that the customer might have some at home. Rather, you might say, "This polish matches the color of your shoes exactly. If you polish them before you wear them, you'll be assured of a long shine."

Recommended Procedures in Suggestion Selling. Here are three rules to follow when using suggestion selling. They will help you avoid any resentment on the part of the customer and will make your suggestions more welcome.

1. *Suggest a specific item.* You might say,

"This cleaning fluid is recommended by the manufacturer of this copying machine." Don't say, "Do you need any cleaning fluid?"
2. *Explain the reason for the suggestion before making it.* Customers are willing to look at additional merchandise if they feel that you're trying to help them satisfy their needs. For example, "Your shoes will keep their shiny finish longer if you use this special polish."
3. *Show and demonstrate the item.* The product will often speak for itself. If the article is handed to the customer, the customer can see it, feel it, and begin to think about owning it.

Closing the Sale

The aim of the entire selling task is to guide the customer to a decision to buy, in other words, to **close the sale.** Frequently the customer says, "I'll take it," thereby ending the sale. But some customers will wait to be asked—even after they have made up their minds to buy— and you will have to close the sale.

Like many new salespeople, you might be afraid to close the sale. It might seem like asking a favor. You may fear that the customer's response will be negative. Or you might not want to hurry the customer and feel that the customer should always take the initiative. With experience, however, you will realize that some customers need help in making decisions, and you will close the sale with confidence.

When to Try for a Close

The best time to try for a close is when the customer seems receptive to making a favorable decision to buy. This may occur in a few minutes. Or it may not occur until the customer has returned several times to examine the merchandise. There are ways that you can tell when to try to close the sale. The process by which you can test the readiness of the customer to buy is called a **trial close.** As an adept salesperson, your aim is to help the customer reach the point when a close can be attempted. Here are some ways you can make that happen.

Identifying Clues to Close. Watching the customer rather than the merchandise will help you to know when a customer is ready to make the final buying decision. Watch for the following clues:

♦ When your customer looks pleased with an article and does not seem to be looking for more, ask for a decision.

♦ When your customer shows interest in an article and appears annoyed if anything else is brought out, try for a decision.

♦ The moment that your customer begins to show signs of weariness or confusion, stop bringing out goods and try for a close.

♦ Listen carefully for remarks such as "This is exactly the style I'm looking for." Or, "I don't like the price, but I do like the desk."

Acting on Closing Clues. When you see that the merchandise will satisfy the customer's needs and wants, select one of the several procedures leading to the close of the sale. Here are the procedures:

♦ Try to identify the questionable buying decision that blocks the decision to buy. Testing for the item decision, you might say, "Those shoes certainly match your coat well, don't they?"

♦ If the customer asks for your opinion, give it without hesitation and state the reason from the customer's viewpoint.

♦ When you see that the customer is inclined toward a suitable article, call attention to its advantages for the customer's need.

♦ Without appearing to hurry the customer, lay aside or put away quietly articles that have not seemed to interest the customer.

How to Try for a Close

How do you go about the ticklish business of getting a customer to decide, of being helpful and yet not pressuring the customer?

First of all, don't be afraid to ask your customer for a decision. Many sales have been lost simply because salespeople have continued to talk when they should have tried to close the sale.

Start your trial close by making a comment or asking a question that invites agreement from the customer. Agreement is a positive reaction. Having made one positive response, the customer is then in the right frame of mind to make a favorable decision to buy. The point should be one that seems to appeal to the customer most.

Once the customer has voiced or nodded an agreement, you may assume that the

Experienced salespeople know that courteous service and a friendly manner after the sale encourage customers to buy from them again. *Jane Hamilton-Merritt*

customer's mind has been made up. So ask for some additional information that is needed to complete the sale. Typical questions are:

- Would you like this to be cash or charge?
- Do you want to take it with you?
- Will a half dozen be enough, or should I send a dozen?

There is always the possibility that the customer will stop short at this point and say, "Wait a minute—I haven't made up my mind." But far more often the customer will take your question for granted and answer it without ever having said, "I'll take it."

What to Do after the Sale Is Made

Part of your selling personality should be a friendly interest in people. This should be as evident after the sale as when you are serving the customer.

First, show your appreciation. When a salesperson says sincerely, "It was a pleasure serving you," the customer is pleased.

Next, make some friendly remarks while completing the paperwork of the sale. Casual conversation helps create a friendly atmosphere.

When appropriate, try a sincere compliment. People like to hear genuine compliments about their children, their property, their taste, their judgment, or anything that concerns them.

What to Do if the Sale Is Not Made

It pays to be courteous, even if the customer doesn't make a purchase. Tell such customers that you were glad to help them. If they didn't find what they wanted, you'll be pleased to serve them when they return. Don't leave or turn away quickly. You may give them your card or your name and ask them to inquire for you.

Remember, your job is to offer service as well as to sell. Providing good service,

regardless of whether it brings a sale today, can result in a future sale.

Now that you've finished this unit, you should have some good ideas on how you can improve your selling techniques.

Trade Talk

Define each term and use it in a sentence.

Close the sale	Suggestion selling
Companion goods	Trading up
Related merchandise	Trial close

Can You Answer These?

1. How does increasing the average retail sale affect the store's profit? Illustrate with figures.
2. What are the four rules to follow in trading up?
3. What are the six types of suggestion selling? Cite an example of each.
4. What actions might you take when your customer gives you a clue to close?
5. How should a salesperson treat a customer who does not buy?

Problems

1. Rule a form similar to the following. In the left column, write the letter of each of the following products: (0) paint, (a) bicycle, (b) electronic calculator, (c) pocket camera, (d) jump suit, (e) microwave oven, (f) ladies' tote bag, (g) barbecue grill, (h) stereo turntable, and (i) automobile tire. In the right column, for each product, list at least three related items that may be suggested to a customer who is interested in purchasing the product.

Product	Related Items
Example: (0)	Brushes, thinner, and sandpaper

2. Statements made by customers may be clues for the salesperson to try to close a sale. On a separate sheet of paper, write

the letter of each of the following statements; then write your reply. (*a*) "I've looked at several pairs of jeans, but I like the first pair I tried on best." (*b*) "What is the guarantee on this?" (*c*) I'm not sure about the style of these shoes—do they look all right on me?" (*d*) "How long would it take to deliver these?" (*e*) "I'm buying a watchband for my father. Do you think he'll like this one?" Add to this list three statements taken from your experience as a customer or salesperson and, after it, your reply.

Activities and Project

UNIT 14

Retailing Case

Lisa Montague had been working at the Burris Department Store for 7 months. To her dismay, just as her confidence in dealing with customers was growing, a reorganization took place and she was transferred to women's blouses on the main floor. On her second morning in the new department, Lisa noticed a woman frowning at one of the racks of blouses. As Lisa approached the woman, she smiled and the following exchange took place:

Lisa: Those blouses do come in a lovely selection of colors, don't they?

Customer: Well, I was just thinking how sick I am of those pale washed-out pastels! Don't they make a rich yellow anymore?

Lisa: You're so right! It's been ages since I've seen any really bright colors.

Customer: I don't suppose you've got anything in bright yellow?

Lisa: Well, I do have this shirt in bright yellow—it has an interesting cut, don't you think?

Customer: That looks like linen.

Lisa: Well, it does look like linen, but according to the manufacturer, it's 75 percent polyester and 25 percent cotton. It requires no ironing and it should hold its shape and color no matter how many times it's washed.

Customer: I don't care what the manufacturer says it is. I can recognize linen when I see it. Don't you know that those manufacturers are out to cheat you blind?

Lisa: Some may be unethical; but our buyers avoid doing business with them.

Customer: I hate linen! It's uncomfortable and always wrinkles. Imagine buying a linen blouse! Someone in this town must sell bright-yellow, no-iron blouses! Good day, young lady.

1. What do you think Lisa's main problem was in dealing with this customer?
2. If you were Lisa's supervisor or friend, what advice would you have given her?
3. Rewrite the dialog. Put yourself in Lisa's place and show how you would have tried to overcome the objections of this customer.

Working with People

Alan Klein was a senior at West High School and a marketing and distributive education student-trainee at Karsten's Men's Clothing Store. Alan liked his work and hoped to pursue a retailing career after finishing high school. So he worked hard and studied salesmanship avidly. His concern for customer buying problems was evident, and he began to develop a steady clientele. His sales volume continued to increase until it was usually higher than that of several of the full-time sales workers. Alan's employer was highly pleased with Alan's work and singled him out for praise at one of the weekly sales meetings.

Soon after that sales meeting, Alan began to encounter difficulties with some of the other sales personnel. He thought that some of them were going out of their way to take sales away from him. He also noticed that two of them were unfriendly and avoided talking to him. One of the older men even seemed to make extra work for Alan.

1. Identify the true problem.
2. What are the important facts to be considered in this problem?
3. List several possible solutions to this problem.
4. Evaluate the possible results of each solution.
5. Which solution do you recommend? Why?

Project 14:
Ranking Sales Occupations

Your Project Goal
Given three sales occupations—one from each of the three major types (salesclerk, salesperson, sales representative) described in Chapter 9—and access to information about them, arrange them in order of your career area preference and justify your ranking.

Procedure
1. Select one salesclerk job situation, one salesperson job situation, and one sales representative job situation. Check your selections with your instructor.
2. Prepare lists of the desirable and undesirable job factors that you find are important to you in selecting a career.

3. Improve your list by doing two things: (a) Ask your teacher or guidance counselor for help in locating information about sales occupations, and add job factors from this source to your lists. (b) Interview one or more sales workers in each of the three categories and add new factors mentioned by them to your lists.
4. On separate sheets of paper, make three forms similar to the following. In the left column, write or type the desirable factors from your list, then fill in the undesirable factors.

Occupational Title: _____ DOT Code Number: _____	• Type of Occupation _____ Salesclerk _____ Salesperson _____ Sales representative		
		Degree to Which the Factor Exists	
Job Factors	**High**	**Medium**	**Low**
a. Desirable factors			

5. On the first form, do the following: (a) fill in the title of the salesclerk situation and the *Dictionary of Occupational Titles* code number; (b) check the type of situation in the upper right corner; (c) draw a circle around the factors present in the situation; and (d) check the degree to which the factor is to be found in the situation.
6. Repeat the process described in Step 5 for the salesperson and sales representative situations.
7. After careful consideration of the information in the chart and of your own inclinations, rank the three occupations in order of their desirability as careers for you. Prepare a brief report (no more than two pages) in which your justify your ranking.

Evaluation
You will be evaluated on the completeness of your list of desirable and undesirable job factors and on the reasons with which you justified the way you ranked your preferences.

Using Design Principles

CHAPTER

46

Communications & Human Relations

Economics & Marketing

Merchandising

Selling & Technology

Advertising & Display

Operations & Management

Inside a store, you can see design principles in use everywhere. You can see them in the merchandise displays, in the products used in those displays, in show cards, signs, posted ads, and also in store and department layout and decorations. And you may be able to recognize good design. But have you ever asked yourself what makes a design good? The answer to that question is what this chapter is all about.

Design principles have many applications in retailing, but in this chapter you'll mainly learn how design is related to building an attractive display. Display is a powerful merchandising tool; if you know how to use design principles to plan and arrange a striking display, you'll have a very salable skill in modern retail merchandising.

The Role of Design

If you merely group items of merchandise together in space, your result will not be an attractive display. But if you place mer-chandise in the display area so that it presents an arrangement that is pleasing to the eye, you'll have what is called **composition**—and that could make an attractive display. Good composition does not just happen. A display is a work of art, and good composition in a display depends upon an understanding and use of the artistic principles of design.

Just as a painter starts with a blank canvas, you, as a display specialist, will start with an empty space. This space may be an entire window, or it may be a counter, shelf, shadow box, or any area commonly used for display. Into this space you must place the merchandise to be displayed and whatever props and signs you think would be useful.

A good display results when an effective arrangement of merchandise is made and design principles are followed. Such a display also has two broad goals, unity and order. **Unity** is achieved by having one main theme or idea as a point of emphasis or dominance, with the other elements in the display contributing to the main idea. **Order** in a display means that all the parts of the display are arranged into an easy-to-understand plan, so that the passerby immediately gets the selling message of the display. The proper blending of all the design principles produces displays that make the customer stop, look, and buy.

Ensuring Unity

Unity is especially important in visual merchandising, where the objective is to increase sales. Viewers may find a display pleasing to the eye, but unless there is a central point of interest that emphasizes the sales message, the display misses its target. So, emphasis is one of five important criteria of good design. The other four are balance, harmony, proportion, and rhythm, which are discussed later in this chapter.

Emphasis refers to the point of a display that appears most dominant. Therefore, the point that is emphasized is the place at which the eye makes contact with the display. From this point, all additional eye movements flow. For example, a jewelry display will show the most important item—such as a necklace—in the center of the display case. Other items like bracelets and earrings will be placed so as to point to or emphasize the necklace.

Locating the Dominant Unit

You may place the dominant element of a display either near the optical center of the composition or in the upper left-hand corner as viewed from the front. The **optical center** is halfway from either side of the display and slightly above the bottom half. When you place the dominant unit at the optical center of a display, the viewer's eye will travel evenly on all sides of the point of emphasis. When you place it in the upper left-hand corner, you can

assume that the viewer's eye will flow from left to right, like that of a reader, and cover the entire display area.

Highlighting the Dominant Unit

You can achieve emphasis in a display by surrounding the dominant unit with appropriate colors and similar or contrasting lines, shapes, and textures. Combining shapes, sizes, and colors so that the difference is emphasized is known as **contrast.** The dominant unit may be larger, stronger, brighter, darker, or lighter than its surroundings. Usually a single point of emphasis is sufficient. Too many areas of special interest in a display may confuse the viewer and result in lost sales. Such displays lack unity. Nevertheless, if your display is to be approached from either side by a viewer, it is well to place a secondary point of emphasis on each wing of the display.

Achieving Order

You can achieve order in a display by meeting the four remaining criteria of good design: balance, harmony, proportion, and rhythm. All these factors contribute to the attractiveness of a display; when one is below standard, the viewer tends to be "turned off."

Balance

There are two types of balance that you can use in the arrangement of displays: formal balance and informal balance.

Formal balance in a display means that the left half of the display is a duplicate of the right half. One or more identical items are placed on opposite sides of the axis, which is the center of the display area. Formal balance can be used in most types of displays and is easy for the beginner to master.

Informal balance results when more weight is placed on one side of the display than on the other. It is used to achieve balance among items that are different in size, shape, or some other element. While

364

The container of flowers is the dominant element as well as the optical center in this display. Larry Fuersich/Retail Reporting Bureau

informal balance can be used to interesting effect, its use requires more skill than that of formal balance.

Harmony

Combining similar lines, shapes, sizes, and textures into a pleasing arrangement is called **harmony.** When there is agreement among these four factors and they blend together, there is harmony.

Line. Every display should have some definite lines, formed by the merchandise itself and the way in which the merchandise is arranged. Strongly defined lines help make a display seem more unified and vivid, while fuzzy lines may tend to blur the projection and lessen the impact of the display.

Specific types of lines convey specific impressions to the viewer. So, as a display specialist, you have to work out the dom-inant lines of a display according to the feeling you want the display to project:

- Vertical lines are considered dramatic, arresting, and vigorous in their appearance.
- Horizontal lines are thought to project a placid, flat, and calm feeling.
- Curving lines are considered soft and gentle.
- Diagonal lines are thought to be abrupt, startling, and demanding.

Shape. When lines are joined, they result in geometric (round, square, rectangular, triangular) or irregular shapes. Similar or like shapes when properly placed produce harmony.

Size. To achieve harmony within a display, sizes should be consistent and kept in proportion to one another. If not, large

Why is this such a pleasing arrangement? *Richard Megna/Fundamental Photographs*

objects will minimize the smaller ones in a display.

Texture. The look or feel of the surface of an object is called its **texture.** Our sense of touch may be stimulated either physically or visually as we perceive roughness or smoothness. Some textures reflect light while others absorb light. A display has consistency and harmony when the majority of the textures in a display tend to be either smooth, rough, reflective, or absorbent.

Proportion

The principle of **proportion** involves the relationship of one item to another with respect to size. The meaning of proportion can be explained by comparing two boxes. A box that is 1 foot wide and 2 feet high and a box that is 2 feet wide and 4 feet high would be in proportion because both boxes have the same ratio of height to width—the ratio involved in each case is 2 to 1.

The size of the display area is determined by the size of the merchandise that is put into it. Small items like jewelry or perfume containers can be displayed in a small area. But large items like men's suits or ladies' dresses require a larger area for effective display. Show cards must be proportionate to the size of the area and merchandise; for example, small cards would be lost in a large area. The props must be in proportion to the merchandise being displayed. A careful consideration of all elements of a display is necessary to achieve the effect of correct proportion.

Rhythm

In a design, **rhythm** is the sense of movement created by repetition, gradation, or interruption. It involves the way the various shapes, lines, sizes, and colors in the display are arranged. **Repetition** is the reproduction of an element of a design more than once. Similar shapes, lines, sizes, or colors may be used several times in a display. A display of gifts for Valentine's Day, for example, could use the same shape (hearts) and the same color (red). Exact repetition is a regular, uniform repeating of one element; it may become monotonous. This would happen if everything in the Valentine's display was heart-shaped and red.

A more interesting effect is created by the repetition of the same shapes, lines, sizes, or colors at regular intervals. In the display for Valentine's Day, for example, square bottles of perfume and round boxes of dusting powder would add interest to the background of red hearts. Smaller hearts attached to ribbon could be used between the perfume and dusting powder to repeat the pattern. Rhythm is more effective than repetition.

Rhythm might also be obtained in a costume jewelry display by arranging the pieces according to size, so that the smallest pieces were in front and the larger ones in back. This would involve **gradation,** or progression, which is the gradual change in size or color of the units in the design.

If the design consists of the same size, shape, or color, the insertion of an item that is different in size, shape, or color produces an **interrupted rhythm.** For instance, an interesting variation of the costume jewelry display could be worked out for an Easter window by placing a porcelain rabbit holding a piece of jewelry into the display.

Choosing an Arrangement

Visual merchandisers use several basic patterns of item arrangement over and over again because they are both flexible and effective. These patterns tend to create rhythm, harmony, and contrast within the display, no matter what types of merchandise are used to form the patterns. Five patterns frequently used in displays are shown below and described on page 369.

The five basic patterns of item arrangement.

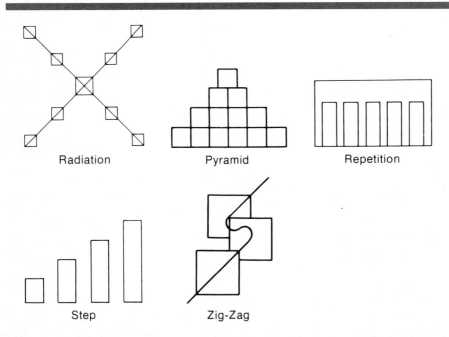

Radiation   Pyramid   Repetition

Step   Zig-Zag

Several basic patterns may be combined in the same display. These displays use both radiation and repetition. They also use a pyramid shape. Ken Karp

Radiation

In **radiation**, the elements of the design are spread out like rays from a central point. This type of design creates interest by having one dominant feature from which the other elements of the display radiate. For example, a men's furnishings window may have a male mannequin as the focal point with various accessories displayed on platforms arranged in a circle around the mannequin.

Step

In a step arrangement, either the merchandise or the fixtures holding the merchandise are arranged in a series of steps going up or down. This is a harmonious type of display that gives the feeling of motion. If a customer looks at a display of shoes arranged on ascending platforms, the customer's eyes will move naturally from one step to the next.

Pyramid

The arrangement shaped like a triangle with a broad base that gradually tapers to a point is called a pyramid. This type of arrangement is used in modified form by supermarkets and drugstores because it is easy to construct. Some cans are usually removed from the pyramid so that customers will not be concerned about destroying the form.

Zig-Zag

The arrangement called **zig-zag** is similar to the pyramid arrangement except that it is not built up directly to the top. It begins with a broad base but zigs its way to the top. Department stores often use zig-zag displays for clothing. It is best suited to light, open displays and is usually limited to three major items, as in a display of shoes, sweaters, and skirts.

The placing of merchandise or props so

that they interfere with or overlap each other is known as **interference**. This technique, which may be used in any of the patterns of arrangement described above, helps to unite or join together the items in a group so that the customer sees all the items at a glance.

Repetition

Repetition, as previously mentioned, is an arrangement that uses items of the same general nature and aligns them in exactly the same manner, as by height, spacing, or angle. Monotony can be avoided by using panels or elevated platforms or by tilting the platform. For example, sweaters or blouses might be fastened in a line on a tilted board so that the viewer can see the different colors that are available.

Even if you don't plan to work in display, you'll find many opportunities to apply the principles of design in other areas of retailing. As a salesperson, for example, you can observe the customer's aesthetic preferences and select articles to complete an ensemble. As an advertising worker or buyer, design will be one of your primary concerns. And regardless of where you work in the store, you are a living example of the use of color, line, and design. You may not realize it, but your appearance affects your relations with your coworkers as well as with the store's customers. As revealed in grooming, choice of apparel, and posture, your appearance is largely a matter of the application of color, line, and design principles.

Trade Talk

Define each term and use it in a sentence.

Composition	Informal balance
Contrast	Interference
Emphasis	Interrupted rhythm
Formal balance	Optical center
Gradation	Order
Harmony	Proportion

Radiation	Texture
Repetition	Unity
Rhythm	Zig-zag

Can You Answer These?

1. What four principles of design are required to produce order in the composition of a display?
2. What factors are considered in creating harmony in the composition of a display?
3. What feelings are suggested by vertical lines? Horizontal lines? Curving lines? Diagonal lines?
4. How does a display specialist go about keeping the elements of a display in proportion to the available space and to one another?
5. How does a display specialist go about creating rhythm when composing a display?
6. What five commonly used patterns of arrangement are used in making displays?

Problems

1. Rule a form similar to the following. In the left column, at quarter-page intervals, write the letter of each of the five display criteria: (*a*) emphasis, (*b*) balance, (*c*) harmony, (*d*) proportion, and (*e*) rhythm. Then select a window or interior display of merchandise in your shopping area or use a picture of a display in this book or another publication. In the right column, write the display specialist's way of meeting each criterion.

Design Principle	Way in Which the Principle Is Followed

Rule a form similar to the following. In the left column, write the letter of each of these merchandise categories: (*a*) food, (*b*) clothing, (*c*) hardware and building materials, and (*d*) sporting goods. Choose an additional category if you wish. Leave

2 inches between each category. Under each category, write first "magazine ad" and then, halfway to the next category, write "newspaper ad." Select one ad from a magazine and one ad from a newspaper for each merchandise category. In the right column, note the design arrangement used by the advertiser (radiation, step, pyramid, zig-zag, repetition), or write the word "other." If "other," try to describe or sketch the ad.

Kind of Advertisement	Arrangement Used

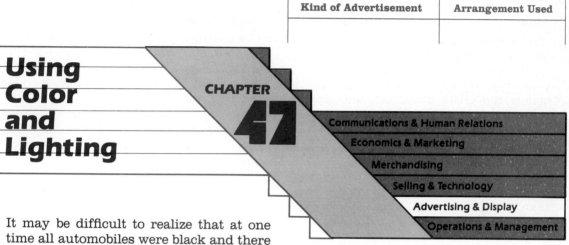

Using Color and Lighting

CHAPTER 47

- Communications & Human Relations
- Economics & Marketing
- Merchandising
- Selling & Technology
- Advertising & Display
- Operations & Management

It may be difficult to realize that at one time all automobiles were black and there was no chromium trim on them. But now, some cars are purchased just because the customer likes a certain color. Color has become a powerful tool for promoting sales.

No one realizes the impact of color on consumer purchasing more than the retailer, because color has invaded almost every merchandise line. Today, the psychology of color should be considered in nearly every merchandising decision. And, like design, knowledge of color is used by retail workers throughout the store, not only in the work they do but in their choices concerning personal appearance. Yes, color psychology is a part of the personality of the retail worker.

Now that you have been introduced to the principles of design in Chapter 46, you are ready to explore the use of color in retailing. Color and design serve most of the same purposes and are inseparable parts of visual merchandising. Although lighting may not be as highly conspicuous as color and design, it interacts with them and is part of the same package. Your un-derstanding of visual merchandising is not complete without a knowledge of lighting and its uses in the promotion techniques of today. The science and use of lighting is increasing rapidly.

In this chapter, you'll learn about the psychology of color, be introduced to the study of color, and be given some basic information about the use of lighting. This chapter will also provide you with some helpful suggestions on the use of these visual merchandising tools.

The Psychology of Color

Each color situation has to be treated individually. No one choice is going to please everyone. In promoting sales, however, visual merchandisers want to attract and please select groups of consumers, those regular and potential customers of the various products they promote. Using their basic knowledge of colors, visual merchandisers pick the color schemes most likely to attract those customers and influence them in favor of buying the store's merchandise.

Warm and Cool Colors

Color stimulates an emotional response—and, as you learned in Chapters 24 and 42, emotions play an important part in the customer's buying decisions. For instance, yellow, orange, and red are warm colors. **Warm colors** tend to come forward and are called advancing colors. They make an object look closer and larger than it is. Red velvet used as a chair fabric makes the chair stand out and appear closer than a chair covered in green fabric.

On the other hand, blue, green, and purple are cool colors. **Cool colors** suggest relaxation and are called receding colors. They create the illusion of space by making objects look smaller and farther away than they actually are. A pair of dark-blue shoes will appear to be smaller than the same size shoes in white.

What Color Suggests

Each basic color usually suggests certain feelings, events, and concepts to people. This does not mean that every person sees colors in the same way or reacts to them in the same way. But it does mean that the majority of people will tend to have somewhat similar reactions to certain colors. As a retail worker, knowing some of the general reactions and associations usually connected with specific colors will help you use color to influence customers.

♦ *Red* is highly visible and suggests strong emotions. Red is traditionally associated with Christmas and Valentine's Day. But it is used best for accents of colors in displays and should be used in small quantities to lead the eye to the main feature of the display.
♦ *Blue* suggests distance, air, water, and quiet, peaceful atmospheres. When used in displays, it often creates a feeling of pleasantness in the person who views the display. Darker blue creates a somber effect.

♦ *Yellow* is a cheerful color suggesting sunshine and life. Yellow used against a dark background stands out more clearly and sharply than any other color in combination. This is the reason that price tags on sale merchandise frequently are yellow. Since yellow is so vivid, it is tiring if used in large quantities. Yellow is often used in a display where the light is poor.
♦ *Orange* suggests Halloween, harvest time, warmth, and vitality. Orange, like red and yellow, is best used in small quantities. It is an appetizing color that makes food and interiors more appealing.
♦ *Green* suggests the calmness and freshness of nature and is very relaxing to the eye. Yellow-green tones combine well with yellow to produce a cheerful atmosphere. The cooler or bluish greens produce a more restful effect.
♦ *Purple* is a deep, rich color that many people seem to associate with royalty, the mysterious, and the serious. Because purple has a rather dull quality, its use is limited. It is used at Easter and sometimes in displays where a dramatic or rich effect is desired.
♦ *Black* and *white* are the neutral colors. Together with brown, they are used in brightly colored displays to soften the bright effects.

Understanding Color

To gain a real understanding of color, you should know something about the components of color and how the colors are combined to create pleasing effects. These points are discussed in the following paragraphs.

Color Qualities

Color has three important qualities that must be considered in planning harmonious combinations: hue, value, and intensity.

Hue is the technical term used to describe color itself—it is another name for color (red, blue, green). We call a valentine heart red in hue, a leaf green in hue.

Value is the lightness or darkness of a color or hue. The words "tint" and "shade" refer to the value of a color. To make a tint, white is added to a pure color. To make a shade, black is added.

Intensity or chroma is the purity, strength, or brightness of a color. A pure red of full intensity gives our eyes the sensation that it is redder than when it is mixed with gray or some other color.

Planning Color Harmony

In the seventeenth century, Sir Isaac Newton looked at sunlight reflected through a glass prism and found that the beam separated into the colors seen in a rainbow. The colors are always the same and appear in the same order: red, yellow, green, blue, purple. The arrangement of these colors from red to purple is called a **color spectrum**. When the colors of the spectrum are arranged in a circle, they form a **color wheel**.

When the colors of the spectrum are arranged in a circle, they form a color wheel. Shades of a color are produced when the color is mixed with black, and tints of a color are produced when it is mixed with white.

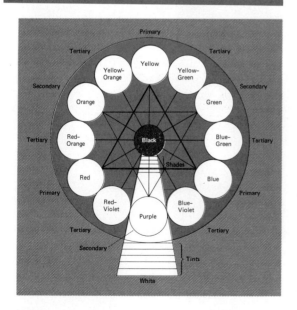

Primary, Secondary, and Tertiary Colors. A color wheel contains primary, secondary, and tertiary colors. The **primary colors**—red, blue, and yellow—are called primary because they are independent. That is, they cannot be produced by combining other colors. But all the other colors of the spectrum may be mixed from the primaries.

Secondary colors are made by mixing any two primaries. Red with yellow makes orange, yellow with blue makes green, and blue with red makes purple. Orange, green, and purple are the secondary colors.

Tertiary colors are derived from combining the primary and secondary colors. They give us six additional colors—red-orange, yellow-orange, yellow-green, blue-green, blue-violet, and red-violet.

The neutral colors, black and white, do not appear as hues in the outer ring of the color wheel. Rather, they serve to make tints and shades for the other colors. Thus, brown is a shade of orange (plus black); beige is a tint of brown (plus white). Brown may also serve as a neutral color.

Color Schemes. As a retail worker, you'll find the color wheel a very useful tool. It will help you in planning color schemes, in deciding what background is best for merchandise display, and in determining what color accents can be used to make a display more interesting. Also, you'll find that the most effective color scheme is a simple one.

The simplest color combinations are **monochromatic color schemes**. In this type of scheme, tints and shades of the same hue—such as navy blue, medium blue, and light blue—are combined.

Analogous color schemes are composed of colors—such as pure blue, blue-green, and yellow-green—that are next to each other on the color wheel. "Analogous" means "neighboring." Usually three neighboring colors are used, but as many as five can be used. These simple color combinations result in a pleasing effect.

Complementary color schemes are composed of colors—such as red and green or yellow and violet—which are directly across from each other on the color wheel. Various shades and tints of two complementary colors can produce color harmony. **Contrasting colors** are the same as complementary colors.

Split complementary color schemes are similar to the complementary pattern but involve three points of the color wheel instead of two. For example, yellow, whose complement is violet, has for its split complement the analogous colors blue-violet

and red-violet. Any two colors equidistant from the complement blue-violet might be used.

Double split complementary color schemes involve four points of the color wheel. For example, the two neighboring colors to yellow (yellow-orange and yellow-green) may be combined with two neighboring colors of red (red-violet and blue-violet).

Triadic color schemes are composed of three colors forming an equilateral triangle on the color wheel. For example,

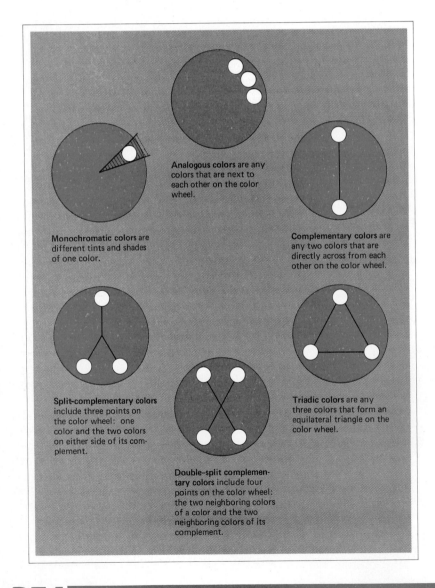

Monochromatic colors are different tints and shades of one color.

Analogous colors are any colors that are next to each other on the color wheel.

Complementary colors are any two colors that are directly across from each other on the color wheel.

Split-complementary colors include three points on the color wheel: one color and the two colors on either side of its complement.

Double-split complementary colors include four points on the color wheel: the two neighboring colors of a color and the two neighboring colors of its complement.

Triadic colors are any three colors that form an equilateral triangle on the color wheel.

This display is made more interesting by the contrast in color and texture between the merchandise and the background. Larry Fuersich/Retail Reporting Bureau

red, yellow, and blue form this type of triangle. These colors should not be used in equal proportions.

Color Tips

Here are some general suggestions that you'll find helpful in dealing with color selection. As a beginner, you should consider these suggestions as rules. As you become more experienced, however, you'll be able to gauge the impact of color more accurately. And then, just as experienced display workers do, you can violate established ways of using color and still produce tasteful effects.

♦ *Keep the color selection simple.* Some of the most interesting displays are those that use a one-color scheme. If you use too many colors, the display may confuse and distract the viewer.

♦ *Look for clues in the colors of the merchan-*

dise, the package, or the container. For example, good color and design may be found in a garment, a cosmetic container, or a cereal package. Make your color scheme suit the product on display.

♦ *Be careful when using bright colors and contrasts.* The more intense a color, the smaller the area it should cover. Too much bright color may attract attention at first, but it soon disturbs the viewer and distracts from the merchandise.

♦ *Try a balance of colors.* If you blend two or more colors so that the effect is pleasing, you have color harmony. The effect can be exciting or subtle. Choose colors that suit the occasion.

♦ *Allow sufficient space around a colorful article.* Beware of clashes. Space serves as a buffer and emphasizes the featured product.

♦ *Light shades are easy on the eyes.* They appear to deepen the display space and seemingly increase the size of the display area. *Emphasize contrast between merchandise and background.* Contrast in texture between merchandise and background makes a display more interesting. Jewelry is at its best when displayed against a background of fabric, such as velvet. If you put two colors of the same value, such as red and green, next to each other, they seem to vibrate and cause disturbing and confusing effects. Every color looks different against a light background and against a dark one. The following table shows the effect of background colors on the color of merchandise.

Remember, customers reject or accept a considerable amount of merchandise on the basis of its color. In much the same way, a display—or a brochure—can be just another interesting arrangement or it can be a magnet for customers, depending upon the way in which color is used.

Light Makes a Difference

Notice what happens to color when you turn on a light at dusk. Intense colors appear brighter in strong light or sunshine. See what happens when you beam a light on an object from several angles. Shadows seem to change the dimensions of the lighted object. Yes, light changes the appearance of things, and it can be a strong sales device when properly used in a display or personal selling situation.

Good display lighting pulls the shopper's eye to the merchandise. The eye is drawn automatically to the brightest spot within its range. Then proper lighting brings out the best features of the merchandise. Colored lamps and soft lights may stimulate the customer's mood—a buying mood, one hopes. Thus, lighting plays an important part in visual merchandising.

Kinds of Lighting

There are three broad categories of lighting: primary lighting, secondary lighting, and atmosphere lighting. **Primary lighting,** sometimes called wash lighting, refers to the general illumination of the store, including that of the aisles, escalators, and so on. Self-service stores usually provide a great deal of light to invite the customer's thorough examination of the merchandise. Specialty shops use softer lights. Discount stores often prefer

EFFECT OF BACKGROUND COLORS ON MERCHANDISE COLORS

Color of Merchandise	Black Background	White Background	Light-Gray Background	Dark-Gray Background
Yellow	Richer	Slightly duller	Warmer	Still brighter
Red	Far more brilliant	Darker and purer	Bright but less intense	Brighter but less intense
Blue	More luminous	Richer and darker	Little more luminous	Brighter
Green	Paler and sharper	Deeper in value	Yellowish	Brighter (gray becomes reddish)
Orange	More luminous	Darker and redder	Lighter and yellowish	More brilliant
Purple	Less strength and brilliance	Darker	Brighter (gray becomes greenish)	(Gray becomes greenish)

376

cool lights. And prestige stores usually have warm white lights. Primary lighting is an important factor in determining the intensity of lighting needed for an interior display.

Secondary lighting provides for the specialized showing of merchandise. Spotlights and floodlights supplement basic window lighting; they brighten shelves, cases, and freestanding displays. Secondary lighting in displays includes down light from the ceiling or wing lights from the side, showcase lighting, and **valance lighting**—lights behind the short draperies or wood or metal facing across the top of the window. Electrified tracks that have directional sockets into which the lights fit permit flexibility.

Atmosphere lighting is special lighting used to create atmosphere or a mood. Twinkling miniature lights (called Italian lights), rotating color wheels placed in front of spotlights, colored lighting, flashing strobe lights, and lighting from the bottom of the display rather than the top and wings are some of the techniques used to establish atmosphere.

Intensity of Lighting

Light is radiant energy reflecting from an object. Intensity of lighting is the amount or degree of that reflection. The more difficult it is to see detail, the more display light is needed. The lighting on a display should be two to five times stronger than the primary lighting. Extra lighting is used in feature displays. It should be 2½ times stronger than the regular lighting of a display. The light should be far enough in front of the featured merchandise to provide effective brightness on all vertical surfaces.

Types of Artificial Light

There are two types of artificial light, incandescent and fluorescent. Incandescent light is flexible and very useful in creating special effects, as with spotlights. It is always used with some type of fitting, such as a track installation or a reflector. In-

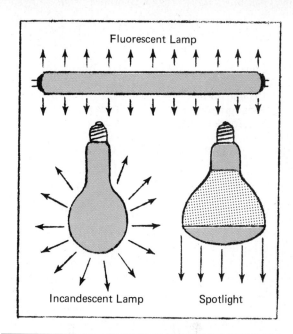

Fluorescent lamps are commonly used for overall lighting, and incandescent lamps and spotlights are used for highlighting small areas.

candescent lights give a warm effect. More energy is used and they are more costly to operate than fluorescent lights.

Fluorescent light provides shadowless light that serves as a general background or ceiling illumination. It is cool and produces little heat.

In Chapter 46, you studied design principles and how visual merchandisers use them in almost every type of display. In this chapter, you learned some of the basics of color and lighting, so that you now have some idea of the knowledge, skills, and creativity that display specialists must bring to their work. In the next chapter, you'll find out how display specialists go about creating a display.

Trade Talk

Define each term and use it in a sentence.

Analogous color   Atmosphere lighting
  scheme   Color spectrum

Color wheel
Complementary color scheme
Contrasting colors
Cool colors
Double split complementary color scheme
Hue
Intensity or chroma
Monochromatic color scheme

Primary colors
Primary lighting
Secondary colors
Secondary lighting
Split complementary color scheme
Tertiary colors
Triadic color scheme
Valance lighting
Value
Warm colors

Can You Answer These?

1. How is color used in stores other than in display and advertising?
2. Which colors are considered to be warm? Which are cool? What are the characteristics of warm and cool colors?
3. What are the colors of the color spectrum?
4. What are the primary colors? Secondary? Tertiary?
5. What are the six color schemes commonly used in a display?
6. What are the three broad categories of artificial light used in stores?

Problems

1. Rule a form similar to the following. In the left column, write the letter of each of these six color schemes: (a) monochromatic, (b) analogous, (c) complementary, (d) triadic, (e) split complementary, and (f) double split complementary. Then select one of the primary or secondary colors and write the name in the space provided. In the right column, write the names of the additional colors needed to complete each of the six color schemes.

Name of color: _____

Color Scheme	Additional Colors

2. Rule a form similar to the following. In the left column, write the letter of each of these types of lighting: (a) primary lighting, (b) secondary lighting, and (c) atmosphere lighting. Visit a retail store of your choice to observe these three types of lighting. Write the name and type of the store in the spaces provided. In the right column, briefly describe the lighting. Be sure to note the intensity and effectiveness of the lighting, whether the lighting is incandescent or fluorescent, and the use of any special equipment or devices. Observe display windows and interior displays as well as general illumination.

Name of store: _____ Type of store: _____

Kind of Lighting	Description of Lighting

Creating a Display

CHAPTER

48

Communications & Human Relations
Economics & Marketing
Merchandising
Selling & Technology
Advertising & Display
Operations & Management

Now that you are familiar with the principles of design and have begun your study of color, you will enjoy trying your

378

hand at creating a display. When creating a display, you'll start with an empty space—a window or an interior area. Display work is especially fascinating because of the many challenges you face when you are combining the principles of design, color, and lighting with the art of silent persuasion in so many different situations.

How Displays Sell Ideas

You will recall from your study of retail selling in Chapter 23 that selling through advertising and display is guided by the mental stages through which a customer passes when making a purchase. These stages, known as AIDCA, are attention, interest, desire, conviction, and action. The purpose of all displays is to guide potential customers through all five mental stages. However, there is one difference in purpose between displays prepared for self-service stores and those used in full-service stores: the goal of the action stage. The action objective of a self-service store display is to get the customer to purchase the item displayed without further assistance from sales personnel. On the other hand, in full-service stores the objective is to bring potential purchasers to the place where a salesperson takes over. The following discussion explains how a display should guide its viewers during the mental stages of the purchasing process.

Attention

There are two kinds of attention: voluntary and involuntary. Voluntary attention exists when window shoppers purposefully view various displays, usually to learn about merchandise that they intend to purchase. Involuntary attention is unintentional observation. It's more difficult to achieve because the display must draw the potential customer's attention away from its existing focus.

Interest

A display will attract attention to itself only if it highlights the product involved

and suggests a reason for continued attention. It must relate in some way to the viewer's interests and concerns. Sometimes a display will tell a story, which is an effective device for holding the viewer's interest.

Desire

To build desire, the featured product must relate to a viewer's needs and wants. Otherwise the display will merely satisfy the viewer's curiosity. Usually, desire is achieved through the theme of the display. And the copy on a show card may help viewers to realize their needs. A poor display fails to persuade viewers that they will be lacking something if they don't have the product displayed.

Conviction

A good display often convinces viewers that they want to own the product. This is especially true when the product is displayed as it would be used. For example, a set of lawn furniture may be shown in a garden-like setting, with attractively dressed mannequins stretched out on the lawn chairs. Viewers could visualize themselves enjoying the furniture in their own back yards. The price on the show card may convince them to buy.

Action

In self-service merchandising, the attractiveness of the item or its package may tip the scale in favor of the merchandise. Also, information on the package or labels may help the customer make a positive decision. Of course, price tags and signs also help customers make the final buying decision.

The goal of most window displays in department and specialty stores is to encourage viewers to enter the department where the merchandise is sold. So such displays must let the customer know where the goods may be purchased and, if possible, offer some incentive for going there. Interior displays in these stores should either help the product sell itself or at least prompt inquiries about it.

Planning a Display

The effectiveness of a display depends on the judgments of its planners. Merchandising-division personnel decide what type of merchandise will sell well at a given time. Visual-merchandising decision makers plan and build displays that will sell merchandise and project the proper image of the firm.

Many factors enter into the judgments of visual merchandisers. While planning, they must constantly keep in mind the following points:

♦ The type of retailing
♦ The store image
♦ The types of consumers wanted as customers
♦ The season of the year
♦ The display cycle of the merchandise
♦ The assigned space to be used

A common sequence of planning steps is described in the following pages.

Check the Display Schedule

Most visual merchandisers have a general idea of what their display space is supposed to feature at all times. A small store may have a very informal method of deciding what products are to be displayed and when to display them. Most medium-size and large stores work on the basis of 6-month and yearly display schedules. These schedules assign specific display space for definite periods of time to selected categories of merchandise. For instance, the schedule may show that the window display of a particular shopping center is to feature spring coats for the next month. Often the display schedule is influenced by special sales events, when displays are coordinated with ads and other forms of promotion.

Select a Theme

Every display, no matter what type it is

or where it's located, should get across to the viewer a clear message or basic theme. The entire presentation should be built around a single idea, and passersby should be able to understand the idea immediately. This is easier to achieve when all the displays in a store are based on the same theme, such as a season or a news event. But when displays are not based on such a general theme, a central idea is particularly needed.

Make a Sketch

When a theme has been chosen, the next step is to create the display—on paper. Large retail organizations with many outlets prepare graphic presentations of proposed displays. These are kept in the central office to assist the organization's store managers in the preparation of important displays. For those who must plan a display without professional help, the following steps are appropriate:

♦ Prepare the floor plan of your display on paper and made to scale.
♦ Indicate the position of props, mannequins, and other fixtures.
♦ Indicate the floor covering and the background materials.
♦ Show the position of the display cards, props, and merchandise on an elevation (vertical) sketch.

Getting Ready

Empty or covered display space results in lost sales. So the installation of a new display must be completed as quickly as possible. As a display worker, you can do this by learning to time your tasks with other display workers so that all merchandise, props, signs, and lighting equipment are ready and assembled before the old display is removed. Then, when the old display is removed and the area has been cleaned, your new display can be installed right away. But time the installation to be done when store traffic is at its lowest.

Every display, regardless of its type or location, should have a clear theme.
Ken Karp

Many stores change displays after the store is closed or just before it opens.

In display installation, the most frequent cause of lost time is poor planning of props, materials, and merchandise. Changes in plans result in lost time. To prevent delays when actually installing a display, you'll find it necessary to check and recheck your completion of the following tasks:

◆ Selecting the merchandise
◆ Choosing the props and materials
◆ Ordering or preparing the display show cards
◆ Removing the old display
◆ Preparing the display area for the new display

Select the Merchandise

The most critical task in creating any merchandise display is the selection of the merchandise to be displayed. No display will sell unwanted goods, so be sure that the most attractive and best-selling items are selected. Of course, the items selected should be representative of the category of merchandise promoted and should emphasize the theme of the display. There also has to be enough of the displayed items on hand to fill customer requests.

Choose the Props

In the construction of a display, several types of props may be used. **Structural props** are the major props supporting other props and merchandise; they include platforms and columns. **Functional props** are used to support merchandise; they include easels, hosiery forms, and mannequins. **Decorative props** are used for decoration. These props include items such as flowers, trees, animals, mirrors, curtains, and scenery.

Structural props create the basic dimen-

Can you identify the structural, functional, and decorative props shown below?

Ken Karp (upper left and upper right); courtesy of Bloomingdale's, photo by Marsha Cohen (lower left)

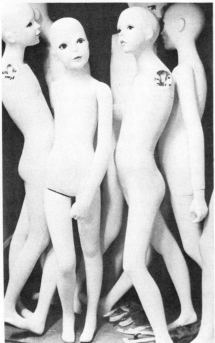

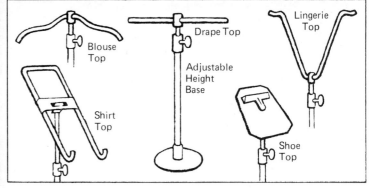

Blouse Top

Shirt Top

Drape Top

Adjustable Height Base

Lingerie Top

Shoe Top

sions of the display. Platforms allow merchandise and decorative props to be arranged at various levels. Columns may be used to frame the display or to give a strong vertical line to its appearance. Panels and screens, which may serve as structural props, come in many varieties—from painted plywood to velvet—and can be used to form walls and background.

Functional props give shape and movement to the merchandise. Easels and stands are used to drape or hang such items as towels or handbags, drapery fabrics, or sweaters. Mannequins and forms show the merchandise in use. A **mannequin** is a full-body dummy. A **display form** is a partial mannequin, such as a torso or a hand. A **millinery head** is a form for displaying hats.

Order the Show Cards

Show cards are important because they answer questions that come to customers' minds when they are attracted by a display. And these answers help customers come to a buying decision. For example, show cards usually answer questions about the price, how the merchandise is used, what its good features are, and why it should be purchased now. In a window display, show cards may also give the store's name and tell where the merchandise is located in the store.

The size of the show card or sign and the information given on it depend upon the kind of display involved. A display of jewelry in an exclusive shop may simply have a small sign reading, "Rubies Set in 18-Karat Gold" and even smaller price signs next to each piece. The display of a single dress from a specialty shop's high-style collection may have a simple sign that says, "Today's Look—North Room, Fourth Floor."

If a display calls for more informative signs, however, here are some rules for preparing the copy:

♦ Concentrate on one thought or idea so that the customer gets the message quickly.

♦ Be informative. Tell about the latest fashions and newest products. Give the uses of a new product or new uses for old products.

♦ Word your copy to attract the largest group of customers.

♦ Make your copy persuasive enough to encourage customers to buy.

♦ Be accurate when you give information.

♦ Use trade names, trademarks, and names of authorities to increase customer confidence.

Installing a Display

Display procedures and practices vary widely depending on the type of store, the merchandise promoted, and the purpose of the display. Contrast, for example, installing a display in a corner window of a large department store with making a produce display in a supermarket. Nevertheless, in installing a display, there are certain common steps. For example, it's always necessary to dismantle the existing display, prepare the space to be used, assemble the new display, and check to see that the job has been done properly. Here are some other general tips on each of these steps.

Dismantle the Current Display

When a display is being dismantled during store hours, it's wise to conceal the activity as much as possible so as to maintain privacy and avoid interruptions. Use curtains or screens for this purpose.

Always take care in removing the merchandise from the former display so that it's not damaged and can be returned to its proper place for sale. If you don't return goods quickly to the home department, their absence could contribute to inventory shortages. For this reason, you'll find that many stores will require you, or whoever was responsible for borrowing the products, to sign a list of the items used in the display. Likewise, systematic display departments keep accurate rec-

No matter where a display is being installed, a last-minute check of the details is important. Courtesy of J. C. Penney Co.

ords of the location of display fixtures and supplies that must be returned to their assigned places, so that they will be available for future use.

Prepare the Display Space

After removing the old display, the next very important step is to make sure that the space to be used is fresh and clean. Soiled or damaged surroundings or a smudged window will divert the viewer's attention. So, as a display builder, check the background, walls, and ceiling for blemishes. Remove nails, staples, adhesive tape, and other distracting materials. Clean the floor and windows and check the light bulbs and fluorescent tubes.

Assemble the Display

Assembling a display also calls for careful completion of the tasks involved. Damaged merchandise and props not only cost money but waste valuable time. As a display builder, you'll first place the structural props in position, then the functional props, and then the decorative props. Your next step is to prepare the mannequins, forms, and merchandise before they are put in the window or inserted into an interior display. If your display uses cartons, cases, or boxes, make sure that they are neatly opened before placing them in position. Your final task is to add the accessories.

But you haven't finished creating a display until you've checked it closely. Check to ensure that everything is in its proper place—merchandise, props, and signs—that tags do not show, and that the lighting works as intended. Usually it's a good idea to get someone else's opinion of what you have done. Things you may not notice are often obvious to another viewer.

After the Display Has Been Installed

Successful visual merchandising calls for accurate records of each display's contribution to sales. Equally important, good display records are used in alloting display space for the following year, selecting products to be displayed, and providing a source of ideas for new displays.

In supermarkets and self-service stores, customers make their selections from the merchandise displayed. This calls for frequent replacement of stock in order to maintain the selling power of the display. Poorly stocked shelves don't attract favorable attention. This situation is almost the opposite from that of the customer who insists on purchasing the particular garment in the display window of a high-fashion shop. Retailers who run this type of store find it necessary to establish policies relating to the sale of items from window displays.

Finally, a display must be kept fresh and clean throughout its life. Long gone are the days when the general-store window trimmer put clean flypaper in the windows once a month and did little more.

Competency in creating a display is not learned in a few easy lessons; it is developed a step at a time, progressing from the simple to the complex. With only average artistic ability—and much patience—a person can become a good visual merchandiser. So if your first efforts don't meet your expectations, don't be disappointed. Keep in mind that the demand for display skills is high and that the effort you spend in learning how to display merchandise can help you a great deal in your retailing career.

Trade Talk

Define each term and use it in a sentence.

Decorative props   Mannequin
Display form   Millinery head
Functional props   Structural props

Can You Answer These?

1. Why is the theme of a display so important?
2. What is the function of the show card in a display? What information should be included?
3. What are the steps in installing a display? What precautions should be taken in performing the tasks of installation?
4. What tasks follow the installation?

Problems

1. Rule a form similar to the following. In the left column, write the letter of each of the following subjects for a display: (*0*) lawn seed, (*a*) school supplies, (*b*) top ten records, (*c*) ladies' hats for Easter, (*d*) towels, (*e*) bargain sale on lingerie, (*f*) ice cream, (*g*) tape recorder, (*h*) special sale on costume jewelry, (*i*) ice skates, and (*j*) end-of-season sale on boats. In the right column, give a general theme for an appropriate display to feature each product.

Product	General Theme
Example: (0)	Think green for spring.

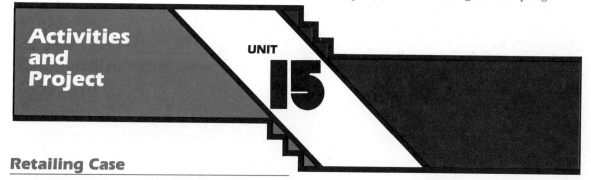

Activities and Project

UNIT 15

Retailing Case

Until recently, most retailers, when attempting to increase sales, have stressed "external" promotional efforts (such as advertising) while neglecting "internal" efforts (such as display). Discount stores, many of which were first established in windowless buildings, are giving more attention to interior displays. Recently, a study of the shopping habits of discount store customers in a small city revealed some information for use in planning interior displays. Some of the findings are given in the table below entitled "Customer Characteristics."

In addition, the following data were gathered:

♦ Sixty-five percent of the regular customers shopped in the store several times per month.

♦ Seventy-five percent of the customers compared prices and merchandise in several stores.

♦ Thirty-eight percent of the customers came to the store without a definite purchase in mind.

Assume that you are the display director for this store and have been asked to formulate a policy on visual merchandising on the basis of the information given here.

1. What important conclusions about interior display can you draw from each of the four categories above?
2. What visual merchandising policies would you recommend to the store management?

Working with People

Diane Sung had been selling at Nygren's, a shopping center women's wear shop, for nearly a year when one of the regular customers asked to see a sweater that was displayed in the window on the mall. The sweater, which was on a simple form, could easily be removed from the window, so Diane took it to show the customer. The customer decided to buy the sweater. Diane wrapped it and wrote up the order and the customer left the store.

After the customer had gone, the store manager, who happened to witness the sale, asked Diane to meet him in his office. He said that he would like to discuss the sale with her.

1. What is the problem? Why does the manager want to talk to Diane?
2. If salespeople were allowed to take merchandise from windows and other displays built by display artists, how would it affect sales? The attitudes of other salespeople? The display artist? The store image?
3. Since the store manager was close at hand when the customer asked to see the sweater, what should Diane have done?
4. Other than talk to Diane, what else could the store manager have done?
5. What should the store manager say to Diane when he talks to her?

Project 15: Preparing a Display Rating Form

Your Project Goal
Given four displays related to your career interest and information provided by four display artists, design a display rating form tailored to the particular type of merchandise you have chosen.

Procedure
1. Select a partner who is interested in the same field of retailing as you are or who

CUSTOMER CHARACTERISTICS

Age	Percentage	Education	Percentage	Income	Percentage
18–24 years	23	Some high school	18	Under $6,000	11
25–34 years	27	High school graduate	37	$ 6,000–$ 9,999	10
35–44 years	23	Some college	16	$10,000–$14,999	25
45–54 years	15	College graduate	17	$15,000–$19,999	19
55–54 years	8	Advanced degree	12	$20,000–$24,999	23
65 years and over	4			$25,000 and over	12

is interested in a closely related field. Ask your teacher to approve the selection.

2. Together with your partner, choose one of the areas of distribution from the fields listed in Project 9, "Surveying Promotion Methods," on page 220. Check your choice with your teacher.

3. Using the Yellow Pages of the telephone book, locate the stores in the area of distribution you have chosen. Select at least four of them for your study of display evaluation and decide which partner will visit each.

4. Prepare a display rating form incorporating all the points covered in Chapter 48 of your text. Make enough copies so that there are two for each store and several additional copies to use as work sheets.

5. Find out who is in charge of display in each of the stores to be included in your survey and request a 10-minute interview. Ask your teacher for information on interviewing if you need help.

6. Explain the purpose of the interview and cover the following points:

a. What factors the person interviewed considers important in evaluating a display.

b. Whether he or she has a display rating form that is now being used.

c. Show the interviewee your form and ask whether the points alloted to each category are appropriate for use in this person's area of distribution. If they are not, ask him or her how they should be changed. Record the suggestions.

7. Prepare a new form based on the information acquired in the survey above. Present your new form to the class and compare it with those of other classmates working in both related and unrelated fields of retail distribution.

Evaluation

You will be evaluated on the completeness of the interview information gathered and on the completeness of the new display rating form that you prepared.

UNIT

16

Keeping Up with Credit

Types of Customer Credit

CHAPTER 49

Communications & Human Relations

Economics & Marketing

Merchandising

Selling & Technology

Advertising & Display

Operations & Management

"Starting now, you can shop with your Baker's Holiday Dollar Shopping Card." This heading on an invitation that contained a special credit card, mailed in mid-November, invited the charge customer to shop until Christmas and not be billed until the regular billing date in February of the following year—and with no finance charge. All the charge customer had to do was to sign the card and then present it with the store's regular charge card when making purchases up to a total of $1,000. And if the customer wished additional amounts of holiday dollars, he or she could check with the store's credit office.

This use of credit as a sales promotion device spurred Jack Mills, who had started at Baker's last June and was fast becoming a master employee, to look into the entire matter of consumer credit. Why would a retailer make such an offer? How could the store afford to do this? What should he, Jack, know about credit in his position as a salesperson?

This unit will provide you with basic in-

formation about the rapidly expanding area of consumer credit, which has become such an important institution in our way of life. This chapter explains the function of consumer credit, its advantages to consumers and retailers, and the different types of credit offered by retailers and other consumer credit sources. Chapter 50 deals with the credit policies of retail stores and explains the operation of a credit department. And Chapter 51 describes the bookkeeping procedures, billing practices, and collection methods used by retailers.

Uses of Credit

The use of credit is not new—but the extent to which credit is used is new. Not many years ago, "cash on the barrelhead" and "neither a borrower nor a lender be" were still commonly held values. The average consumer probably had a monthly credit account with a few local stores and may have financed an automobile purchase by using credit. Today that same consumer probably has a wallet stuffed with cards and plates that authorize him or her to buy merchandise and services from firms such as retail stores, public utilities, and special credit-granting companies.

Two types of credit are vital to retailers. The first is commercial, or **trade credit,** which is extended by manufacturers and wholesalers to merchants who buy from them. The second type is **consumer credit,** which is used by individuals to obtain merchandise or services for which they agree to pay at a later date. Trade credit is discussed in Chapter 61. This chapter deals with consumer credit as it relates to retailing. Knowing why consumers use credit so freely and why so many stores promote it is the kind of knowledge that helps workers like Jack Mills become master employees.

Why Consumers Use Credit

Consumers vary greatly in the extent to which they use credit. Some use it almost all the time, some only in emergencies. Some use it mostly for big-ticket items, some for everyday staple goods. Some use credit only when purchasing from a few stores, others have credit accounts everywhere—at department stores, drugstores, banks, and automobile service stations. Credit has become popular because it appeals to consumers for the following reasons:

♦ *Convenience.* Many customers like the convenience of paying for an entire month's purchases at one time. Using credit also avoids the necessity of carrying cash on a shopping trip. Moreover, having a charge account or a credit card makes it easier for customers to shop by telephone.

♦ *Immediate use of product or service.* Credit is a boon to many people because it gives them the opportunity to enjoy and use costly items while spreading out the payments. This enables many people to own appliances and automobiles much sooner than if they had to save to buy them.

♦ *Possible savings.* In some cases, using credit may enable people to save money. By using their charge accounts or credit cards at a time when they lack cash, customers may be able to buy items being sold at reduced prices.

♦ *Preferred treatment.* Some customers use credit because they feel that as charge customers they receive better service. For example, they find that at many stores it is much easier to return credit merchandise than cash purchases. Also, sometimes charge-account customers receive advance notice of sales and thus have the first choice of merchandise on sale.

♦ *Preservation of savings.* Sometimes purchases can be made by drawing upon savings or other financial assets. Customers may, however, wish to conserve their savings and obtain interest income from them. They therefore choose to use their charge accounts rather than use their savings.

♦ *Income tax records.* Another advantage of using credit is that complete records of expenditures can be obtained for income tax reporting purposes. Such records indicate the items included in a purchase as

Credit customers receive advance notice of sales.

well as the amount of the purchase itself. For this reason, many people who have business expense accounts use credit receipts to justify their tax deductions.

Why Retailers Offer Credit

Credit has become so important to the American way of life that about one-third of the nation's retail sales volume is based on credit. Retailers feel that credit gives them a number of advantages.

♦ *Charge accounts create customer loyalty.* Cash customers tend to shop in a number of stores. People who have charge accounts, though, tend to be loyal to the stores that let them buy without cash.

♦ *Credit customers may be less price-conscious.* Consumers who have a charge account are less likely to hunt for bargains. They will buy an article because they want it now. The average sale to a credit customer, therefore, is larger than that to a cash customer.

♦ *Credit customers buy more freely.* Credit customers like the convenience of saying "charge it" without worrying about whether they have enough cash on hand to pay for their purchases. They can often be sold by point-of-purchase displays and may do impulse buying. They are also open to suggestion selling of related items.

♦ *Credit may attract a preferred trade.* Credit privileges may attract customers interested in quality, service, and style rather than those interested in price alone.

♦ *Credit builds goodwill.* For some customers, the fact that the store has sufficient confidence in them to grant them credit builds confidence in the store. In smaller firms, salespeople often know the charge customer by name, which is flattering to the customer and a big factor in building confidence and goodwill.

♦ *Credit helps smooth out business peaks.* Cash shoppers tend to buy heavily on certain days when they get paid and lightly on other days. Credit customers, on the other hand, tend to buy whenever products and services are needed. Peaks in business volume are costly, and credit tends to smooth them out.

Benefits to Society

Now that you know the motives of those who use and those who offer credit, let's see how it benefits society. As a master employee, you need to understand the two major benefits of credit: social and economic.

Social Benefit

Think of how few people would be able to purchase an automobile or a home if credit were not available. As mentioned earlier, credit provides the privilege of enjoying a purchase while it is being paid for. Consumers can start using something needed at once instead of being forced to wait until they save enough money to pay cash. This opportunity causes people to buy and use more products and services, thereby raising their standard of living. So the use of credit has been one of the most important factors in the continuous rise in the American standard of living.

Economic Benefit

Few people realize that the liberal use of credit by both business and consumers is one of the most important factors in the constant economic growth of our country. The United States is renowned for its leadership in producing, distributing, and consuming products and services. Our enviable position among nations has been achieved through mass production, mass distribution, and mass credit—the "three M's of American business." Keep in mind that were it not for credit, mass distribution could not survive and production would come to a halt.

On the other hand, execessive use of credit by consumers can contribute to inflation. So when the inflation rate rises excessively, government restrictions are placed on loan credit as they were in 1980.

Extensive Use of Consumer Credit

Both charge accounts and installment credit are receiving acceptance by increasing numbers of consumers. Buying on the installment plan has become a way of life in American homes, to the point where a high percentage of people are never out of debt and another large proportion seldom are. Many families consider it worth the interest cost to use someone else's money and have the earlier use of a product or service. About one-third of the nation's retail sales volume is based on credit; more than one out of every two American families owes an installment debt.

The following reasons explain the expansion of credit:

1. Most consumers have more earning power.
2. More consumers have better financial security through health insurance, social security, unemployment compensation, retirement pensions, and the income of a second family member in the labor force.
3. There is more regularity of consumer income, since our economy is now dominated by service industries where employment is much steadier.
4. Young people are eager to acquire without delay the things that other families have and credit is being extended to younger age groups.
5. Attitudes toward debt have changed.

Sources of Credit

The most economical way for consumers to buy products or services is to pay cash for them. They can shop around for the best buy. They don't tie up future income. They are well aware of how much they are spending. And they are not tempted to overbuy. However, there are good reasons for borrowing, most of which were mentioned earlier in this chapter. The advantages of credit usually outweigh the disadvantages of the cost of credit and possible extravagance.

After deciding on the use of credit, consumers have a number of sources to chose from. Consumers may be able to borrow from friends and relatives, their employer, full-service commercial banks, credit unions, life insurance companies, or pawnbrokers. Or they may use one of the credit services of the store where the purchase is made. It may pay to shop for credit.

Consumer Credit Services

Two general types of credit services offered by retailers are charge account credit and installment credit. The differences between the two types are based on two criteria:

1. Who owns the purchased item after the purchase agreement has been made
2. Whether the credit arrangement covers any purchase the customer wishes to make or whether it's limited to a single purchase

Charge Accounts

Charge account credit is **open-account credit,** which means that the customer's account remains open, permitting the purchaser to make any number of purchases at any time, up to a predetermined amount specified in the account. With this type of credit, the purchaser usually is not asked to sign a contract or provide additional security. The articles bought on open account credit belong to the purchaser as soon as the purchase is made. The retailer doesn't retain ownership of the goods.

Retailers may offer one or more of six types of open charge accounts: (1) the open 30-day account, (2) the 90-day charge account, (3) the revolving charge account, (4) the 30-day sales contract, (5) the budget account, and (6) the coupon credit plan.

The Open 30-Day Account. With an **open 30-day account** or regular account, customers have to pay the full balance of the

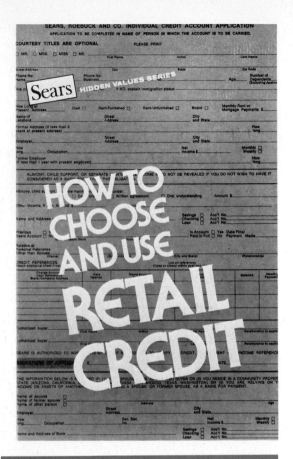

Retailers explain the various credit plans they offer to customers. *Courtesy of Sears, Roebuck and Co.*

account at the end of the month or within 30 days. However, the account remains open for future purchases. Some stores place a limit on the amount customers can charge. The stores base their estimate on the customer's ability to pay. Usually, stores don't charge interest on this type of account.

The 90-Day Charge Account.

Department, furniture, and apparel stores commonly offer the 3-month or **90-day charge account** for large purchases such as clothing, appliances, and furniture. Instead of paying the full amount at one time, customers may pay one-third of the amount each month for 3 months, after which the account is closed. Some retailers limit these accounts to certain items or to items

that cost more than a certain amount. Most stores don't charge anything extra for this service. Others may charge a percentage of the unpaid balance (usually 1 to 1.5 percent a month) or a fixed amount, depending on the unpaid balance.

The Revolving Charge Account.

A **revolving charge account** enables customers to charge all purchases up to a specified dollar limit and pay only part of the total amount due at the end of the month. Stores usually make an interest charge of 1 to 1.5 percent on the balance at the end of the month. Once customers have reached the limit, they can't charge any more purchases until they make a payment.

The 30-Day Sales Contract.

With a **30-day sales contract,** customers receive a due bill that is good for a special amount of merchandise. After shopping, customers bring the goods to the credit desk, where their limit is verified, their purchases are totaled, and the carrying charge (normally 10 percent) is added. If customers pay within 30 days, there's no carrying charge and stores won't bill them.

The Budget Account.

With a **budget account** (or flexible account), customers' monthly payments to the store are based on the size of the account balance, and the store charges interest on the unpaid amount. For example, if an account balance is $100, the customer might be expected to pay $25 monthly.

The Coupon Credit Plan.

With a **coupon credit plan,** stores give customers "credit coupons" that may be used in the store as cash; such coupons are generally paid for over 6 months or so. This eliminates a monthly billing to the customer and the nuisance of detailed bookkeeping by the store.

Installment Credit

Installment credit is the second major kind of credit offered by retailers. The selling of consumer goods on credit with a provision for regular periodic payments after an initial down payment is known as **installment credit.** The loan is for a specific amount of money, therefore it's closed-end credit. Installment credit differs from charge-account credit in four ways: (1) the buyer must usually sign a contract agreeing to pay for the purchase; (2) a **down payment,** which is a certain percentage of the total price paid at the time the merchandise is received by the customer, may be required; (3) interest and a carrying charge are paid for the use of installment credit; and (4) periodic payments must be made until the goods are paid for.

Installment sales are usually made either by a conditional sales contract or a chattel mortgage. The difference is very important to both the seller and the customer. In a **conditional sales contract,** the seller retains title to (ownership of) the goods and may take the article back (repossess it) if the buyer fails to make a payment. A **chattel mortgage** differs from a conditional sales contract in that the title to the goods goes to the buyer immediately. The seller, however, has the right to bring legal action to regain the title and repossess the goods if the buyer fails to fulfill the contract by not making payments. Firms would rather be paid than be forced to repossess the goods. They take goods back only as a last resort, because the value of the goods decreases as they become worn.

Credit Cards —The Facilitators

As you know, a credit card is an identification card permitting the holder to charge products and services simply on the holder's signature. Its purpose is to simplify the purchasing process through the use of a plastic or metal card that can be inserted into a machine to print the owner's name and identification number on a sales check. This card authorizes the charging of a purchase to the customer's account, which may be with the store where the products or services are purchased or with

Some retailers accept many different credit cards.
Elizabeth Richter

another credit-granting agency. Credit cards may be classified in three ways: (1) single-purchase cards, (2) travel and entertainment cards, and (3) all-purpose cards.

Some retailers operate their own credit plans, which have been discussed. Other retailers recognize that various nationwide and international credit organizations can help them offer credit. Sometimes a firm will honor as many as six or seven different credit plans, only one of which is its own.

Stores that don't want the expense and trouble of setting up and maintaining a credit system find outside systems very useful. The service costs the store a fee, but the sponsoring organization assumes the responsibilities of collecting the accounts and maintaining a bookkeeping system.

Single-Purpose Cards

Single-purpose cards are issued by all kinds of businesses—department stores, oil companies, motel chains, car-rental agencies, telephone companies, and the like. Customers don't have to pay a fee to the issuer, and they are allowed to charge their purchases, paying all or a part of the cost when billed. Customers are charged interest on the remaining unpaid balance if they don't pay the entire bill. The purpose of this kind of card is to encourage customers to buy only from the company that issued the card.

Travel and Entertainment Cards

Travel and entertainment cards—like Diners' Club, Carte Blanche, and American Express—are used mostly by business people and travelers, although anyone may apply. Holders of these cards pay a yearly fee to the issuer. Retailers who honor these cards bill the credit-card company monthly. The credit-card company charges the retailers a percentage of the bill to cover handling and collecting expense. In turn, the credit-card company

bills the card holder monthly, when the full amount usually has to be paid.

All-Purpose Bank Credit Cards

Large banks operate credit plans in which member retailers agree to honor credit cards issued to individuals. All-purpose bank credit cards, of which VISA and MasterCard are the best known, operate in much the same way as travel and entertainment cards. The bank issues a card after checking the applicant's credit rating. Usually, the card holders pay no fee. If they are willing to pay an interest charge, then the holders of a bank credit cards can pay bills in monthly installments as in a revolving charge account, an option that's not possible with all credit-card plans. If the bill is paid in full within the billing cycle, there's no interest charge.

Lost Credit Cards

According to federal law, the maximum liability to a credit-card holder for fraudulent charges on any kind of credit card is $50 per card. Also, the holder has no liability under the law unless the credit-granting agency has taken several steps. It must (1) have informed the card holder of the $50 liability and sent him or her a stamped, self-addressed envelope with which to notify it of the loss; (2) be able to prove that unauthorized charges up to $50 were made before the card holder notified it of the loss; and (3) ensure that the credit card displays the card holder's signature, photograph, or some other means of personal identification.

The Consumer Credit Acts

The consumer movement in general and consumer credit in particular received much attention in Congress starting with the Truth-in-Lending Act of 1968. This attention continued throughout the 1970s. As the credit industry grew and became organized, rules regarding what credit-granting companies should or shouldn't do developed. These were translated into law with the help of creditor trade associations and Associated Credit Bureaus, Inc., an international association serving the credit industry.

Starting in 1968, several consumer credit laws were passed. These laws provide the source of regulations for the consumer credit industry. The Truth-in-Lending Act is discussed in this chapter. Other important consumer laws concerning credit are discussed in Chapters 50 and 51.

The Truth-in-Lending Act of 1968

This law requires that the grantor of credit tell borrowers (1) the total amount of the finance charge and (2) the annual rate of interest to be paid for the credit. This includes the basic finance charges as well as additional fees such as credit investigation fees, service charges, or required insurance premiums. **Credit life insurance** is a type of term life insurance required by some lenders such as automobile dealers. It pays off a loan in the event of a borrower's death. The law also protects credit-card holders against unauthorized use of their credit cards, as mentioned in the discussion on lost credit cards.

The law also regulates the advertising of credit terms. It says that if a business is going to mention one feature of credit in its advertising, such as the amount of the down payment, it must also mention all other important terms.

Now that you know about the various types of consumer credit available in retail stores and why they are offered and used, you are ready to explore retail credit policies, which the next chapter covers. You'll find out why some retailers offer credit and others don't, why some stores have liberal credit policies and others have strict credit rules, and how retailers gather information about credit applicants and evaluate their applications.

Trade Talk

Define each term and use it in a sentence.

Budget account
Chattel mortgage
Conditional sales contract
Consumer credit
Coupon credit plan
Credit life insurance
Down payment
Installment credit

90-day charge account
Open-account credit
Open 30-day account
Revolving charge account
30-day sales contract
Trade credit

Can You Answer These?

1. Why do consumers use credit? Why do retailers offer it? How does it benefit society?
2. What are the characteristics of each of the six types of open charge accounts discussed in this chapter?
3. Who has title to the goods in each of the two types of installment sales?
4. What are the three main types of credit cards? Who uses each type, and why do they use it?
5. In what ways does the Truth-In-Lending Act protect users of consumer credit?

Problems

1. Rule a form similar to the following. In the left column, write the letter of each of the following products and services: (0) automobiles, (a) groceries, (b) homes, (c) men's clothing, (d) restaurants, (e) TV sets, (f) cosmetics, (g) appliance repair, (h) pets, (i) notions, and (j) housewares. Place a check mark (√) in one of the three columns to the right to indicate whether sales of each of the products or services listed in the first column would be greatly reduced, somewhat reduced, or remain about the same if credit were eliminated.

Goods or Services	Greatly Reduced	Somewhat Reduced	Remain about the Same
Example: (0)	√		

Credit Policies

Communications & Human Relations

Economics & Marketing

Merchandising

Selling & Technology

Advertising & Display

Operations & Management

Jennifer Lamont, who owned and managed a small dress shop, was upset. She realized that the money she had tied up in customer credit services had almost doubled during the past year and that too much time was being spent in managing and operating her credit accounts. At lunch, she confided to her friend, Charles Schwinn, "I wonder how many of my charge customers will ever pay me the money I have lent them through credit. I'm beginning to question whether I should be offering credit at all."

Charles managed a cash-and-carry sporting goods store in a neighboring shopping center and was thinking of offering some kind of consumer credit to improve sales volume. His response was, "I'd think twice before discontinuing credit services, Jenny. People just don't seem to want to pay with cash anymore. It's surprising the number of people who walk right out of our store when they're told that we don't accept credit cards. They say, 'Why should I pay cash when I can go almost anywhere and buy all I want on credit?' "

Why do some stores offer credit and others sell only for cash? Why do some firms honor certain credit cards and reject the use of others? Why do some retailers have strict credit and collection policies while others seem to extend credit to just about anyone? Where do retailers get information about the payment records of credit applicants, and how do they evaluate such information? This chapter discusses consumer credit from the retailer's point of view, so that you can understand the differences in credit policies of various firms and support those of the company for which you work. It deals with the factors retailers must consider if they want to offer credit and the types of credit and collection policies they use. The chapter also explains the sources of information retailers use to check credit applicants, the way they evaluate this information, and the procedures they use for granting credit.

Credit—A Selling Tool

For a long time, retailers granted credit only when a customer requested it. Since World War II, however, credit selling has swept the nation. When retailers realized the powerful volume-building potential of credit as a merchandising tool, they actively encouraged consumers to open credit accounts. At times they even allowed slow-paying charge customers to buy more and more beyond reason.

As part of their promotion campaigns to increase sales, many retailers and other credit-granting firms mailed credit cards to potential customers who hadn't requested them. However, because mailing lists were checked hastily, cards were sometimes sent to people who had died; to young children; and, more unfortunately for retailers, to people who were poor credit risks.

The careless granting of credit also proved to be bad for consumers. Consumers who had little experience in using credit and who were already facing difficulties in meeting payments were often led further into debt when they used unrequested credit cards. During the 1970s, this situation prompted a number of federal laws favoring credit users. Whereas debtor laws in this country used to be severe, the new legislation favors the debtor. And the regulations governing credit and collection are very strict.

Even though the laws concerning consumer credit are so complex that without legal training it is difficult to interpret them, and despite the limitations placed on loan credit, the fast pace of consumer credit promotion persists. And the advantages of EFT (Electronic Fund Transfers) to the retailer make consumer credit an even more attractive selling tool. (See the discussion of EFT in Chapter 11.) This system may replace the familiar check with a plastic "debit" card. When the card is inserted into a retailer's computer terminal, the bank computer tells the operator whether there is enough money in the cardholder's account for the purchase.

When Should a Firm Offer Credit?

In the opening story, Jennifer Lamont wondered whether she should cut back on credit services while her friend Charles was thinking about offering credit for the first time. What information would they need if they decided to pursue their concerns? Here are some important questions that Jennifer and Charles should be able to answer about offering customers credit:

1. What are the consumer credit offerings in this line of retailing? (Usually, the lower the price of goods, the more likely the firm is to have a cash-only policy.)
2. What credit services, if any, do competitors offer?
3. What effect will granting credit have on **cash flow**—the money coming in and going out of the business?
4. What effect will granting credit have on **working capital**—funds used to operate the business? Money used to finance credit cannot be used for the purchase of inventory or other business purposes.
5. To whom should credit be granted?
6. How much credit, if any, should be granted?
7. What would be the cost in expenses and effort to grant the credit?

In addition to answering these questions, Jennifer and Charles should also check, from time to time, whether credit does really bring the benefits it's expected to bring. And if credit is granted, what system should be used? It could be, for example, that Jennifer has problems because she's not using the best system for her type of business.

Credit-Card Systems versus Direct Credit

Retailers can grant credit in either or both of the following ways:

1. They can honor one or several established credit-card systems.
2. They can grant credit directly to customers through their own credit arrangements.

Their choice depends on their needs.

External Credit-Card Systems

If retailers choose the external credit-card system, they have two options: the all-purpose bank route (for example, VISA or MasterCard) or the travel and entertainment card route (for example, American Express, Carte Blanche, or Diners' Club multipurpose cards). And if retailers have an automobile-related business, they may choose one of the major oil company card systems. The more credit cards retailers honor, the more paperwork they will have to do.

Credit granted with external credit cards greatly reduces the number of decisions to be made by retail personnel in making a charge sale. And since credit-card companies assume much of the responsibility for collecting payment from the customer, their fee of 3 to 6 percent of the amount purchased (usually called a discount) may well be worth while, since it means no collection problem.

Along with the discount rates, the credit-card company establishes a store's authorization line. The **authorization line** is the maximum amount that a credit card company allows a customer to charge to his or her account without special approval by the credit-card company. Thus, when a customer wishes to make a purchase on a credit card, the usual procedure is first to check to be sure that the credit-card number has not been listed in the latest credit-card bulletin, which is a list of lost, stolen, or withdrawn cards.

If the card number is not in the bulletin and the purchase amount doesn't exceed the store's authorization line, the sale may be charged to the card. However, if the amount the customer wishes to purchase exceeds the store's authorization line, then the salesperson must call the credit-card company in order to gain approval for the sale. At this time, the credit-card company checks the customer's balance and decides whether or not to allow the customer credit for the purchase. If the charge is approved, the credit-card company will give the store an authorization number for the sale. Should a store fail to obtain an authorization number for a large credit-card purchase, the store rather than the credit-card company must bear the loss if the customer fails to pay. The store is also responsible for checking that the customer's signature on the slip matches the one on the credit card itself.

In many areas of the country, retailers who check customer credit frequently install a small direct-access computer in their store. The salesperson punches on the terminal the amount to be purchased, and the computer checks to see whether the card has been withdrawn and whether the credit company's files show that the customer still has enough credit to cover the purchase.

A salesperson must call the credit card company when the price of the purchase exceeds the store's authorization line. Courtesy of VISA, U.S.A.

Direct Credit

After considering answers to the seven questions about whether to offer customers credit, retailers may decide to do so and to offer direct credit. Such a move might result in lower costs and more loyal customers. Retailers would then offer one or more of the credit services discussed in Chapter 49 and select an appropriate credit policy.

The appropriateness of the store's credit policy depends on these factors:

♦ The profit margin on the merchandise
♦ The line of business and its customers

- The policies of competitors
- The phase of the business cycle that prevails at the time
- The competitive position in which the store finds itself
- The financial and other circumstances peculiar to the business

Businesses with similar merchandise, similar customers, and similar images usually have similar credit policies. When two firms have different merchandising policies, that difference is usually also reflected in their credit policies. Credit policies may be divided into four main categories, which are described below.

Liberal Granting and Liberal Collection. The point of this policy is to extend credit to consumers with "excellent," "good," and "average" credit ratings as well as to those with just "fair" or "poor" credit standing. The retailer's aim is to achieve the highest credit sales volume possible and avoid using pressure when collecting.

Liberal Granting and Strict Collection. Under this policy, retailers extend credit to all classes of risks, including those who are considered poor risks. Usually the granting of credit is liberal because the owner feels that the firm is a better collector than competitors.

Strict Granting and Liberal Collection. With this policy, the firm doesn't charge or write installment contracts for poor-credit-risk customers. But the firm isn't strict when it collects payments from customers. The owner justifies this approach by the careful selection of the credit customers, who, he feels, can generally be trusted to pay their bills.

Strict Granting and Strict Collection. By stressing prompt payment of bills, the business seeks to minimize collection expenses and to keep customers in a position to make new purchases.

Sometimes retail firms find it necessary to adjust their credit granting and collection policies. When the sizes of the losses in their consumer credit divisions balloons because of the cost of borrowing money and other operating expenses, they become more selective in adding new accounts and more strict in collecting overdue payments.

Obtaining Information about Applicants

To decide whether an applicant is an acceptable credit risk, credit grantors collect information through questionnaires, interviews, and the reports of credit bureaus, making sure that they obey the regulations regarding equal credit opportunity. Then they evaluate the applicant's credit rating on the basis of their firm's credit policy.

The Equal Credit Opportunity Act of 1975 (ECOA)

This federal law says that everyone has the right to apply for credit without fear of discrimination on the basis of sex or marital status. This means that an application will be judged only on the basis of the applicant's "creditworthiness." The two most important factors that determine creditworthiness are the applicant's income and credit history. So, in most states, questions about sex designation and marital status have been removed from application forms.

Sources of Information

When retailers have known a customer for a long time and know something of the customer's background, they do very little checking into the customer's credit status. On the other hand, if there is a question about the customer's creditworthiness or ability to pay, they check the customer's credit status thoroughly. They may use all the following sources.

Credit Application Forms. Usually, credit application forms are used to start the information-gathering process. The applicant is asked to fill in a questionnaire that provides basic information to help determine whether he or she will be a good credit risk. Credit-card companies usually use mail questionnaires. Questionnaires generally call for information that contributes to knowledge about the applicant's character, capacity, and capital within the limits of the ECOA regulations. Specifically, the most important information on an application for credit is as follows:

♦ *Employment*—A credit applicant's ability to pay is usually based on the capacity to earn a steady income. The length of time a person has been employed and the position held indicate ability to pay.
♦ *Income*—An applicant's ability to pay may include income from other sources such as social security, pensions, and alimony.

Credit card companies give information to applicants as well as get it. Here the billing system is explained to potential customers. Courtesy of The Chase Manhattan Bank, N.A.

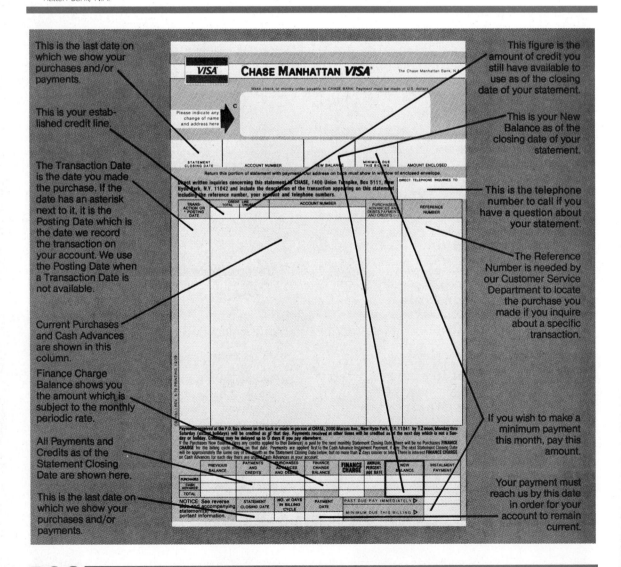

This is the last date on which we show your purchases and/or payments.

This is your established credit line.

The Transaction Date is the date you made the purchase. If the date has an asterisk next to it, it is the Posting Date which is the date we record the transaction on your account. We use the Posting Date when a Transaction Date is not available.

Current Purchases and Cash Advances are shown in this column.

Finance Charge Balance shows you the amount which is subject to the monthly periodic rate.

All Payments and Credits as of the Statement Closing Date are shown here.

This is the last date on which we show your purchases and/or payments.

This figure is the amount of credit you still have available to use as of the closing date of your statement.

This is your New Balance as of the closing date of your statement.

This is the telephone number to call if you have a question about your statement.

The Reference Number is needed by our Customer Service Department to locate the purchase you made if you inquire about a specific transaction.

If you wish to make a minimum payment this month, pay this amount.

Your payment must reach us by this date in order for your account to remain current.

Most businesses use the total income to determine the authorization line.

♦ *Capital assets*—An applicant's sense of responsibility is usually indicated by whether he or she owns property, has a savings account, and carrys insurance. Applications for credit usually ask whether the applicant owns or rents his or her housing and the name of the applicant's bank.

♦ *Outstanding obligations*—If the applicant is heavily burdened with financial obligations, that person may not be eligible for additional credit. The applicant is asked to list the names of loan and finance companies with whom he or she does business.

Credit Interviews.   In many businesses, potential credit customers, after filling in a questionnaire, are interviewed by trained personnel. The interview is conducted in a pleasant, tactful manner so that the necessary information is obtained without offending the customer. Questions about marital status are avoided, and interviewers are careful to avoid statements that can be interpreted as indicating a sex bias.

Credit Bureau Reports.   Many retailers depend on credit bureaus for information about a customer's credit credentials. A **local credit bureau** is a central office that gathers information about the credit habits of consumers and provides this information for a fee to firms and individuals who intend to use the information in permissible ways. Local credit bureaus are often members of regional and national associations such as the Associated Credit Bureaus, Inc., in Houston, Texas. Some local bureaus are privately owned. Others may be nonprofit organizations operated by the members. Besides the membership fee, there is usually a small charge for each inquiry on a credit applicant.

Credit bureaus obtain information from three sources: (1) credit applications; (2) creditors with whom the applicant has done business; and (3) public records such as bankruptcies, court judgments, dispositions of lawsuits, marriages, deaths, and divorces.

Credit bureaus don't rate how good a credit risk the applicant is. They simply collect information from the three sources mentioned and report it to their clients or members. The lenders then decide whether the applicant is a good risk. The activities of credit bureaus are subject to the rules generated by the Fair Credit Reporting Act of 1971.

Credit bureaus can be friends of both consumers and businesses. Both benefit from the ease with which a credit transaction can be made, a charge account opened, or a new credit card issued. This is made possible by the voluminous files of 2,500 credit bureaus throughout the country and to the large number of local merchants' associations. The consumer credit reporting industry processes from 125 to 150 million credit reports yearly.

The Fair Credit Reporting Act of 1971 (FCRA)

This law represents an effort by Congress to regulate the gathering of information on individuals in order to protect their privacy. Before the law was passed, a consumer didn't legally have the right to know what was in his or her file. And credit grantors were not as limited in the purposes for which they could gain access to a person's record. Here are some of the essential features of present consumer rights:

♦ Upon the consumer's request and proper identification, the credit reporting agency must disclose all information in the consumer's credit file and inform the consumer about the sources of the information.

♦ If an account is in dispute, the credit bureau will reinvestigate any item that the consumer questions. If it's found to be inaccurate or can no longer be verified, the item will be deleted.

♦ If the reinvestigation doesn't resolve the question, the consumer may file a brief statement reporting his or her side of the issue that will be included in any future reports containing the item in question.

- ◆ Whenever consumers are denied credit on the basis of information in a credit report, the credit company must inform the consumer of the decision and also provide the name and address of the credit bureau supplying the information.

- ◆ The law limits to 7 years the reporting of adverse information. The only exception is bankruptcy, which may be reported for up to 14 years after the event.

- ◆ Credit bureaus are limited to providing credit reports to credit grantors for specific purposes: extending credit, review or collection of an account, employment purposes, underwriting insurance, or in connection with some other legitimate business transaction such as an investment.

Evaluating Credit Applications

Guidelines for evaluating credit applications vary from lender to lender, as discussed earlier. Two retailers with different credit policies may take completely different points of view about the same

Credit bureaus compile reports like these to help retailers evaluate applicants for credit. In this report, the applicant's credit history is given in the code shown. Courtesy of Associated Credit Bureaus, Inc.

NAME AND ADDRESS OF CREDIT BUREAU MAKING REPORT

Credit Bureau of Elytown
1234 Paloma Drive
Elytown, Texas   77036
Telephone: 214-555-8701

☐ IN FILE REPORT   ☐ SINGLE REFERENCE   ☐ TRADE REPORT
☐ EMPLOY & TRADE REPORT   ☒ FULL REPORT   ☐ PREVIOUS RESIDENCE REPORT

CONFIDENTIAL Factbilt® REPORT

FOR   First National Bank of Elytown

Date Received 5/2/8-
Date Mailed 5/5/8-
In File Since 8/1/6-

This information is furnished in response to an inquiry for the purpose of evaluating credit risks. It has been obtained from sources deemed reliable, the accuracy of which this organization does not guarantee. The inquirer has agreed to indemnify the reporting bureau for any damage arising from misuse of this information, and this report is furnished in reliance upon that indemnity. It must be held in strict confidence, and must not be revealed to the subject reported on, except by reporting agency in accordance with the Fair Credit Reporting Act.

REPORT ON (SURNAME): Velez	MR., MRS., MISS, MS. Mr.	GIVEN NAME: Robert Luis	SOCIAL SECURITY NUMBER: 123-44-5678	SPOUSE'S NAME: Margaret

ADDRESS: 921 Third Avenue	CITY: Elytown	STATE: Texas	ZIP CODE: 77043	SINCE: 10/7-

COMPLETE TO HERE FOR TRADE REPORT AND SKIP TO CREDIT HISTORY

PRESENT EMPLOYER: Elytown Morning Herald-News	POSITION HELD: Circulation Manager	SINCE: 8/7-	DATE EMPLOY. VERIFIED 5/4/8-	EST. MONTHLY INCOME $1,875

COMPLETE TO HERE FOR EMPLOYMENT AND TRADE REPORT AND SKIP TO CREDIT HISTORY

DATE OF BIRTH 5/5/40	NUMBER OF DEPENDENTS INCLUDING SELF: 2	☒ OWNS OR BUYING HOME ☐ RENTS HOME ☐ OTHER (EXPLAIN)

FORMER ADDRESS: 606 Encina Street	CITY: Austin	STATE: Texas	FROM: 8/6-	TO: 9/7-

FORMER EMPLOYER: City Publishing Co.	POSITION HELD: Manager-Bindery	FROM: 3/6-	TO: 7/7-	EST. MONTHLY INCOME $1,600

SPOUSE'S EMPLOYER: Elytown Oil Co.-Branch Office	POSITION HELD: Exec. Secretary	SINCE: 11/7-	DATE EMPLOY. VERIFIED 5/4/8-	EST. MONTHLY INCOME $800

CREDIT HISTORY. INCLUDE ALL PUBLIC RECORDS, COLLECTIONS AND REPORTS FROM OTHER BUREAUS

KIND OF BUSINESS	DATE REPORTED	DATE ACCOUNT OPENED	DATE OF LAST SALE	HIGHEST CREDIT	AMOUNT OWING	AMOUNT PAST DUE	TERMS OF SALE AND USUAL MANNER OF PAYMENT
O 825	5/73	5/64	9/80	53	53	00	O-1
D 155	4/73	1/63	9/79	181	23	00	O-1
C 312	3/73	9/65	6/75	68	00	00	O-1
S 231	3/73	2/67	2/77	48	00	00	O-2
C 381	3/73	3/65	9/76	200	60	00	I$5-1
B 451	5/73	8/64	8/78	25,000	19,600	00	I$150-1
H 403	5/73	11/66	8/81	260	156	00	R-1
B 451	3/73	8/72	Med 3 fig ckg				
B 707	3/73	10/75	Low 4 fig savs				

MEMBER
Associated Credit Bureaus, Inc.

FORM 100

YOUR GUIDE FOR USING THE COMMON LANGUAGE FOR CONSUMER CREDIT

TERMS OF SALE
Open Account (30 days or 90 days) .... O
Revolving or Option (Open-end a/c) .... R
Instalment (fixed number of payments) I

USUAL MANNER OF PAYMENT	TYPE ACCOUNT		
	O	R	I
Too new to rate; approved but not used	0	0	0
Pays (or paid) within 30 days of billing; pays accounts as agreed	1	1	1
Pays (or paid) in more than 30 days, but not more than 60 days, or not more than one payment past due	2	2	2
Pays (or paid) in more than 60 days, but not more than 90 days, or two payments past due	3	3	3
Pays (or paid) in more than 90 days, but not more than 120 days, or three or more payments past due	4	4	4
Account is at least 120 days overdue but is not yet rated "9"	5	5	5
Making regular payments under Wage Earner Plan or similar arrangement	7	7	7
Repossession. (Indicate if it is a voluntary return of merchandise by the customer.)	8	8	8
Bad debt; placed for collection; skip	9	9	9

If Account is Disputed, indicate DISP.

Applicants for credit are evaluated in terms of their character, capacity, and capital. *Courtesy of GMAC*

credit credentials. Nevertheless, they do have some common goals.

There are three major factors that retailers or credit managers consider when evaluating a credit application: (1) the applicant's ability to pay, based on income and obligations; (2) the applicant's willingness to pay, determined from his or her credit history; and (3) the potential profitability of the account. When the credit manager has analyzed the information about the applicant, a decision is made to accept or reject the application and decide what limit, if any, should be put on the account that is accepted.

Underlying the credit evaluations are the **three C's of credit:** character, capacity, and capital.

The Three C's of Credit

Character is the most important of the three C's. It is based on the individual's sense of responsibility in meeting finan-

cial obligations. A person who has always paid bills promptly rates high on this standard. A person who has sufficient money to pay bills but doesn't feel an obligation to pay them promptly is not considered a good character risk.

Capacity usually refers to the person's ability to earn money. It frequently means that the applicant has job skills to keep a steady job at a wage level sufficient to meet financial obligations. Wage earners who may be subject to layoffs or who already have more financial responsibilities than their earnings will safely cover are examples of those who are rated low on the capacity standard.

Capital refers to the wealth of the applicant. This means the physical and financial assets the applicant possesses. If a person owns property or has savings or other investments that can be put up as security for an indebtedness, the person's credit potential is usually good. To most retailers, it's the least important of the three C's.

Limiting Credit Sales

When a decision is made to accept a credit application, the final decision is whether or not a credit limit is to be set on the account. If a business decides to put a limit on the amount a customer can charge, some guidelines that help determine what this limit should be are:

♦ The applicant's income and that of the other members of the family whose incomes will be used to repay the account and the number of dependents of the applicant
♦ Other financial obligations that the applicant must meet, such as house mortgage payments and car loans
♦ The amount that the customer can be expected to buy during the account month

Businesses try to prevent customers from overcharging by requiring that the salespeople check with the credit department for the credit rating of any person making a purchase above a specified amount. This amount, called a floor limit, varies both according to the department and according to the season. Just before Christmas, for instance, when sales volume is very high, floor limits are set somewhat higher than their usual levels. Some credit cards are marked in code with the limit that the customer may charge without special authorization. If the customer wishes to make a purchase above this amount, the salesperson must get authorization.

When customers apply for credit, they often wish to make a purchase immediately. Some retailers will give the customer a courtesy account with a special credit limit. This account allows the applicant to make purchases up to that amount. It is granted on the basis of the information contained in the application or from information received directly from a credit bureau. This practice is called **spot credit approval**. It is temporary. The usual full credit investigation is made before the account is finally approved.

Rejecting Credit Applications

If a decision is made to refuse a credit application, generally the person is informed by a tactful letter. Such a letter usually states that the person's application is not acceptable "at the present time." If the customer requests the reason for rejecting the application, it must be given. For example, the business must tell the customer that the reason the credit application was denied was "based on information received from the XYZ Credit Bureau." The person can then contact that bureau for specific details about the reason for the rejection and can ask to see the credit record on file with the credit bureau. The applicant can then discuss the information in the credit file with the bureau and have included in the file any corrected information.

Once retailers have decided to grant credit to customers, they must set up a system to keep track of all charge purchases and payments made by their customers. And they must also have some method of collecting payments that are overdue. All these things are covered in the next chapter.

Trade Talk

Define each term and use it in a sentence.

Authorization line	Spot credit approval
Cash flow	Three C's of credit
Local credit bureau	Working capital

Can You Answer These?

1. How does credit function as a selling tool?
2. What are the questions that should be answered by a retailer who is debating whether or not to offer credit?
3. What services does a credit-card company offer the retailer?
4. Describe each of the three C's of credit.

5. What are the most common questions included in an application for credit?
6. When evaluating a credit application, what does a credit manager look for?

Problems

1. Assume that you are working part-time and are applying for a charge account at a local music store to buy a guitar. You have been asked to supply certain facts in a credit application. Obtain a blank credit-card application from a local retail store, and—after reading the entire form carefully—fill in the necessary information. Make certain that your writing or printing is clear and legible. Because this is assumed to be your first major credit purchase, the credit manager has asked you to write a paragraph to justify your borrowing $500. Write this paragraph on a separate sheet of paper.

2. Rule a form similar to the following. In the left column, write the letter of each of the following questions: (0) Do you have a savings account? (a) How many jobs have you held during the past 5 years? (b) Do you own an automobile? (c) How many years of education have you completed? (d) Will you supply the names of two personal references? (e) How long have you worked for your present employer? (f) What are your present financial obligations? (g) Have you ever been turned down for credit? (h) How much life insurance do you carry? (i) What is your social security number? Place a check mark (√) in one of the columns to the right to indicate whether the credit interviewer is attempting to gain information regarding character, capacity, or capital by asking the questions listed in the first column.

Question	Character	Capacity	Capital
Example: (0)			√

Controlling Accounts Receivable

CHAPTER 51

Communications & Human Relations
Economics & Marketing
Merchandising
Selling & Technology
Advertising & Display
Operations & Management

Since Jane Schmidt was sincerely interested in credit work and had potential for a career in the credit field, Mr. Melendez, the credit manager, did his best to help her get a good start. His strategy was to help Jane see the store's credit services from the managerial viewpoint and become a master employee. This is the way he explained credit to Jane:

Like merchandise, Jane, credit services cost the customer money. Even when open charge accounts are paid within 30 days and no interest is charged, the cost of financing the sale until payment is made—as well as the oper-

ating expenses—are reflected in the selling price of the merchandise or service. So our credit operation must be effective and efficient in order to keep costs of merchandise and services down and maintain our position in this competitive industry. Mistakes in promoting credit services, granting credit, recordkeeping, billing, and the collection of outstanding accounts not only raise operating costs but frequently result in lost customers.

Mr. Melendez went on to explain the importance of understanding both customer and retailer viewpoints in relation to each aspect of credit.

Keeping Track of Credit Sales

As Mr. Melendez indicated, good credit account management calls for meaningful, accurate records—records that keep track of what happens following a credit sales transaction. Of all such records, none is more important than the **accounts receivable ledger** or "customers' ledger," which is a record of all charge purchases and payments made by customers. The reason is that cash flow is essential to business survival. For example, often retailers have already paid the suppliers for merchandise before the sale is made to the credit customer. And if the business is to continue, retailers must get paid by the customer. In other words, there must be enough cash coming in daily to cover the expense of doing business and to pay for the goods ordered. This is cash flow.

The Accounts Receivable Ledger

When customers buy goods on credit or return them, the information from the sales records has to be collected, checked, and entered in various other records. For billing purposes, the important entries are those made in the accounts receivable ledger.

Small firms generally use simple methods of recording charge sales. Some firms clip the sales checks of each customer together and file them alphabetically. Most stores enter customer charges and payments directly in the accounts receivable ledger, which contains a ledger sheet or card for each customer, arranged alphabetically. Each customer's ledger sheet should contain the following information:

- Customer's name and address
- Maximum amount of credit allowed
- Date the item was purchased
- Items purchased, quantity, and price
- Amount of purchase

- Payments received and outstanding balance

In larger firms, charge sales checks are usually sent to the sales auditing department first, where extensions (quantities of each item and unit price) and totals are checked and verified. Sales checks are listed on tallies to be sure that each one has been accounted for. Any missing sales checks are traced and located. The sales audit department may also make various summaries of the sales figures—including summaries by salesperson, by merchandise category, or by department, depending upon what kind of figures the store needs.

Charge sales checks are sent from the sales audit section to the accounts receivable section. Here they are filed in the customers' ledger and posted to the proper account.

Computerized sales registers have eliminated many of the manual tasks of preparing accounts receivable ledgers. Sales and payment data are sent directly to a computer, then the computer automatically enters the data on each customer's account card at the same time the store's record of the charge is reported.

Billing

Each charge account customer is usually sent a monthly statement or invoice showing the sales, interest charges if any, and previous payments made.

Cycle Billing. Many retailers use **cycle billing,** a system by which billing is spread throughout the month instead of being done at one time. Each customer's account is assigned alphabetically to one of some 20 sections that represent a different day of the month when the customer is billed. Regardless of when the bill is sent during the calendar month, it contains details about the customer's transactions for the previous 30 days. The cycle method of billing has the advantage of spreading the work of sending out statements and receiving payments over the entire month,

This customer used her charge plate (top) to make a purchase, which was recorded on a sales check. The purchase was entered in the accounts receivable ledger, and she was later billed for the merchandise (bottom).

	DATE	DEPT.	CLERK NO.	INITIAL	SEND	✔
	5/20/–	16	32	E.P.	TAKE	

6140 005 253

NORMA E. SIMPKIN

QUAN.	CLASS	ARTICLE	UNIT PRICE	EXTENSION	
1	23	Winter coat	159.95	159	95
			SUB TOTAL	159	95
		AUTHORIZATION CODE	TAX	6	40
			TOTAL	166	35

SALE CONFIRMED AND DRAFT ACCEPTED
Norma E. Simpkin
PURCHASE ACCEPTOR SIGN HERE

KEENEY'S CLOTHING STORE

B3478-56

Name *Norma E. Simpkin* Account No. *6140-005-253*
Address *1806 Driftwood Lane, Wichita, KS 67217*

DATE	EXPLANATION	POST. REF.	DEBIT	CREDIT	BALANCE
19– May 20		B3478-56	166 35		166 35
24		B3479-32	13 52		179 87
26		CH 3528		13 52	166 35

KEENEY'S CLOTHING STORE
Meadow Walk Mall   Wichita, KS
67210

Norma E. Simpkin
1806 Driftwood Lane
Wichita, KS 67217

STATEMENT OF ACCOUNT

6140 005 253

BILLING DATE 5/28/––

AMOUNT PAID $

Please detach and return this stub. Your canceled check is your receipt.
When paying in person present entire statement. You may pay your total balance at any time, in any Keeney's Clothing Store.

Previous Balance	Charges (+)		Credits (–)		Finance Charge (+)	Account Balance	Amount Now Due
0.00	5/20	166.35				166.35	
	5/24	13.52				179.87	
			5/26	13.52		166.35	166.35

so that office equipment and personnel are used more efficiently.

Statement Forms. In addition to using the cycle method, a store may choose to use country-club billing or descriptive billing. **Country-club billing** is a system whereby the customer receives a copy of each sales check with the statement. **Descriptive billing** is a system in which the statement itself includes identification of the transactions involved. The transactions are usually identified by date, amount, and a code letter indicating the department in which the transaction took place.

Consumer Billing Laws

Just as federal laws protect debtors from misleading information about credit costs and from discrimination on the basis of sex and marital status, so they guard against erroneous and deceptive billing. Again, these laws were supported by credit association members.

The Fair Credit Billing Act of 1975. This law sets up billing-dispute procedures for all types of open-end charge accounts, but it doesn't include installment purchases. Customers can now withhold payment of any balance that's due on defective merchandise or services purchased with a credit card provided that a good-faith effort to return the merchandise or resolve the problem has been made. If the card was issued by an all-purpose credit-card company, the purchase must have been made within the state or within 100 miles of the customer's current address. Creditors must give notice summarizing the dispute-settlement procedure. Also, while the investigation is being conducted, no collection threats or actions to get the disputed amount are allowed.

The Electronic Fund Transfer Act of 1978. This law establishes the basic rights, liabilities, and responsibilities of consumers who use electronic money-transfer services or financial institutions that offer

The Fair Credit Billing Act of 1975 covers disclosures of terms about all types of open-end charge accounts. Courtesy of Woolworth/Woolco

F. W. Woolworth Co. (Woolworth-Woolco) **RETAIL INSTALLMENT CREDIT AGREEMENT**

In consideration of the extension of credit to me, I agree to the following regarding all purchases made from time to time by me, my family or others authorized to use my F. W. Woolworth Co. Retail Installment Credit Account.

1. You are to send me a statement each month which will show the previous balance on my account, **FINANCE CHARGE**, current purchases, payments, credits and the minimum monthly payment.

I agree to pay at least the minimum monthly payment shown on my statement upon receipt of each monthly statement. The amount of such minimum payment shall be in accordance with the following schedule:

If the New Balance is:	$.01 to $10.00	$10.01 to $200.00	$200.01 to $300.00	$300.01 to $400.00	$400.01 to $500.00	$500.01 to $600.00	OVER $600.00
Your Scheduled Monthly Payment Will Be:	Balance	$10.00	$15.00	$20.00	$25.00	$30.00	ADD $10.00 FOR EVERY $100.00

REQUESTED PURCHASE LIMIT					
I Request An Account Permitting Purchases Up To:	$200.00	$300.00	$400.00	$500.00	$600.00
Scheduled Monthly Payment Check (√) Desired Amount	$10.00	$15.00	$20.00	$25.00	$30.00	All Amounts Exceeding $600.00 Add $10.00 For Every $100.00

2. I will make the monthly payment as set forth above before the next closing date as shown on your monthly statement. If I fail to make any payment in full when due, you may declare the full remaining unpaid balance immediately due and payable.

3. If I elect to pay the New Balance as shown on your monthly statement before the next closing date, I will not incur any additional **FINANCE CHARGE** on such balance. The next closing date shall be one month from the closing date shown on your statement as indicated in the Schedule of Closing dates below:

SCHEDULED CLOSING DATES								
Last Name Starts With	A-B	C-D	E-F-G	H-I-J	K-L	M-N-O	P-Q-R	S	T-Z
Closing Date	2nd	5th	8th	11th	14th	17th	20th	23rd	26th

4. The **FINANCE CHARGE** shall be determined by the periodic rate applied to the **AVERAGE DAILY BALANCE** as indicated in the schedule below.

SCHEDULE CODE	F
ON AMOUNT OF AVG. DAILY BALANCE	TOTAL
PERIODIC RATE	1.5%
ANNUAL PERCENTAGE RATE	18%

The **AVERAGE DAILY BALANCE** is determined by dividing the sum of the balances outstanding for each day of the monthly billing period by the number of days in the monthly billing period. The balance outstanding each day of the monthly billing period is determined by adding purchase and debit adjustments and subtracting payments and credits from the previous day's balance.

5. No **FINANCE CHARGE** WILL BE MADE:
(a) During a monthly billing period for which there was no previous balance.
(b) In a monthly billing period during which payments and/or credits equal to or exceed the Previous Balance.

6. The Credit Identification Card issued to me remains the property of the F. W. Woolworth Co. and may be reclaimed at any time.

7. If any payment remains in default more than 10 days after its due date, and if permitted by law, I agree to pay (a) a delinquency and collection charge in an amount equal to 5% of each payment due or $5.00, whichever is less and (b) court costs and other expenses incurred by you in the collection or enforcement of this agreement or such other amounts prescribed by law.

8. The F. W. Woolworth Co. has the right to amend the terms of this agreement as to all purchases. Notice shall be given in accordance with applicable law.

NOTICE TO THE BUYER: DO NOT SIGN THIS AGREEMENT BEFORE YOU READ IT OR IF IT CONTAINS BLANK SPACES. KEEP THIS AGREEMENT TO PROTECT YOUR LEGAL RIGHTS. YOU HAVE THE RIGHT TO PAY IN ADVANCE THE FULL AMOUNT DUE WITHOUT INCURRING ANY ADDITIONAL CHARGE FOR PREPAYMENT.

SEE REVERSE SIDE FOR IMPORTANT INFORMATION REGARDING YOUR RIGHTS TO DISPUTE BILLING ERRORS.

these services. Electronic fund transfers are any exchanges of funds that are initiated through an electronic terminal, telephone, computer, or magnetic tape for the purpose of authorizing the financial institution to debit or credit an account. A debit increases a firm's assets, while a credit decreases them.

Analyzing Accounts Receivable

Retailers must keep a constant check on their credit accounts. They know that the longer an account remains unpaid, the more difficult it is to obtain payment. A successful credit or collection policy requires that all problems be identified and acted on as early as possible. Many small stores check their customers' ledger once or twice a month to identify overdue accounts. Larger stores usually examine their accounts receivable as a whole first and then check individual accounts if necessary.

Problem Identification. An indicator of the effectiveness of a credit and collection policy is the average collection period. The **average collection period** is a ratio that expresses the total amount of receivables outstanding in terms of an equivalent number of average daily credit sales:

$$\frac{\text{total accounts receivable}}{\text{average daily credit sales}} = \begin{array}{l}\text{average} \\ \text{collection} \\ \text{period}\end{array}$$

For example, if a store had average monthly credit sales of $6,000 and outstanding accounts receivable of $9,000, the collection period would be calculated as follows:

1. Average daily credit sales =

$$\frac{\begin{array}{c}\text{average monthly} \\ \text{credit sales}\end{array}}{30} = \frac{\$6,000}{30} = \$200$$

2. Average collection period =

$$\frac{\begin{array}{c}\text{total accounts} \\ \text{receivable}\end{array}}{\begin{array}{c}\text{average daily} \\ \text{credit sales}\end{array}} = \frac{\$9,00}{\$200} = 45$$

This indicates that, on the average, customers are taking 45 days to pay their accounts. The average collection period can be compared to any of the following bases: (1) payment terms—usually 30 days, (2) past history—experience during earlier periods, or (3) the industry average—experience of comparable firms.

The extent of the excess of a store's average collection period can be measured by comparing the actual receivables with a target level set by the store—for example, 30 days or the industry average.

Aging of Accounts Receivable. Information on the average collection period measures accounts receivables problems in total. But immediate corrective action requires the pinpointing of individual problem accounts, which can be done by the aging of accounts receivable. **Aging of accounts receivable** divides each customer's account into amounts that are 0 to 30 days old, 31 to 60 days old, 61 to 90 days old, and so on. It is often useful to calculate the percentage of total accounts in each account-age group to alert the credit manager whenever overdue accounts become excessive.

Establishing Internal Collection Procedures

Collection policies vary among retailers. Also, a retailer may have different policies for different customer groups. Nevertheless, a carefully planned internal collection procedure is essential for consistent treatment of credit accounts. Included are the following:

♦ *Prompt action.* Any delay that lengthens the span of time between sale and payment causes accounts receivable to grow and increases the risk of uncollectable accounts.
♦ *Invoice promptness and accuracy.* Customer disputes and returning the invoice for correction lead to time-consuming and costly controversy.
♦ *Specified cash discounts.* Cash discounts speed up payment and reduce the amount of capital tied up in consumer credit.

- *Easily understood statements.* Complete statements showing the beginning and ending dates of the statement as well as clear descriptions of items charged, dates of purchases, payments made, amount due, and terms of payment reduce misunderstandings and delay of payment.
- *Delinquency charge, if any.* Usually 1 to 1½ percent per month (12 to 18 percent per year) on all balances more than 30 days past due are assessed.
- *Rapid follow-up of overdue accounts.* The best time to start pursuing an overdue account is immediately. As an account gets further behind, the balance increases, while chances of collection decrease.

Collecting Delinquent Payments

Credit customers may be classified into three general groups: those who pay promptly, those who are slow in paying, and those who do not pay at all. The term "collection" does not apply to those who pay on or before the agreed upon time. If such customers are occasionally late in payment, the store may give them additional time to pay because of their good past record. Sometimes good customers experience temporary financial difficulties. A tactful credit manager can work out a series of partial payments.

Of course, there are usually a few debtors who do not respond to the store's communications about overdue payments. Then, depending on circumstances, management may turn the account over to an independent collection agency or take legal action.

Communicating about Overdue Accounts

Communications about overdue accounts can be divided generally into three stages: (1) formal notification, (2) reminder, and (3) discussion. Some customers need only to be notified that their account is overdue, others need to be reminded, and a few require persistent personal follow-up.

Formal Notification. Any bill not paid within 30 days should be followed up. This may be a statement informing the customer of the overdue amount. It would indicate that finance charges have begun and the rate being charged.

Sending Reminders. For all accounts that are more than 30 days overdue, a personal letter usually accompanies the statement. The letter asks the customer whether the bill has been overlooked and whether there is any problem. It is worded so that the customer will realize that it is automatically sent to all customers who are slow in paying. There are many valid reasons why a bill may not have been paid: it may have been lost in the mail, the customer may have been away or ill, or the customer may simply have forgotten about the payment. The retailer does not want the reminder to upset the customer.

Discussions. Once a bill is 90 days old, more forceful collection activities are essential. Usually a personal telephone call is made at either the 60-day point or no later than the 90-day point. If the customer still does not pay, a strong letter is sent. Sometimes it is written over a lawyer's signature. Usually it says that action will be taken if payment is not made.

Engaging a Collection Agency

If the retailer's own collection efforts fail, the next step is usually to engage an outside collection agency. The main advantage that collection agencies offer is their superior knowledge of persuasive collection techniques. Also, the debtor is usually anxious to clear an account referred to a credit agency rather than further damage his or her credit rating. The disadvantage of this method is its expense—the cost ranges from 25 to 50 percent of each account collected. It is also difficult to locate collectors who combine tact and persuasion in their collection methods. Because of the pressure tactics used by some, independent collection services are now strictly governed by federal law.

The Fair Debt Collection Practices Act of 1978 (FDCPA). Credit grantors should be familiar with the requirements of the FDCPA because the methods practiced by their independent collectors will result in much resentment against their firm; in addition they may, without realizing it, legally become "third-party collectors."

The purpose of this law is to provide national standards to protect consumers from a host of unfair, harassing, and deceptive practices. The act prohibits such practices as the use of violence, harrassment, telephone calls at inconvenient times, the impersonation of government officials, and misrepresentation of the legal rights of consumers.

Under the law, consumers have the right to know exactly with whom they are dealing at all times. They must be informed of their right to dispute the validity of a debt, and if they do so within 30 days, the collector must stop collection efforts until verification from the credit grantor, in writing, is received. And consumers can sue for damages sustained through a collector's unlawful actions.

Credit grantors must provide collectors with certain accurate information on the consumers involved—the consumers' locations, the specifics of the consumers' debts, and the credit grantor's intentions of further action if the debt isn't paid. A collector who threatens any action that's not going to be taken or is not likely to be taken risks being sued by the debtor.

Taking Legal Action

If the collection agency fails, the last recourse is to start court action. The problem may be resolved in a small-claims court if the amount owned by the delinquent account customer is small, usually up to $700. For larger debts, the retailer must file suit to collect. Either case is a costly and time-consuming procedure.

Now that you've completed this chapter, which ends this unit, you've learned that to avoid losses in consumer credit operations, all retailers must have:

- A credit and collection policy stated, communicated, and followed
- Detailed records and a regular review of the credit status of accounts receivable
- A thorough collection procedure

Trade Talk

Define each term and use it in a sentence.

Accounts receivable ledger
Aging of accounts receivable
Average collection period
Country-club billing
Cycle billing
Descriptive billing

Can You Answer These?

1. What is the role of consumer credit in keeping a store financially solvent? Of sales promotion?
2. What information should be included in an accounts receivable ledger?
3. What protections are consumers given in the Fair Credit Billing Act?
4. How do credit managers identify problems in accounts receivable?
5. What protection are consumers given in the Fair Debt Collection Practices Act?

Problems

1. Mr. Simon, credit manager of a local department store, was interviewing Mr. Lyons, who owed the store $640. Mr. Simon was trying to develop a plan for bringing Mr. Lyons' delinquent account up to date. During the interview, he obtained the following information about Mr. Lyons' financial situation: his monthly salary after deductions was $1,170, he made a $150 car payment each month, his gas and electric bills averaged $70 each month, he paid $24 per month on a TV set, he paid $320 per month on his mortgage, his telephone bill averaged $18 per month, and he spent $280 per month on food for his family. Here are some ques-

tions about Mr. Lyons's financial situation: (*a*) What is the amount Mr. Lyons pays for fixed obligations? (*b*) What is the total amount he pays out each month? (*c*) Can he maintain his present monthly expenditures on his present salary? (*d*) What items could be reduced in amount? (*e*) If you were Mr. Simon, what would you advise Mr. Lyons to do? On a separate sheet of paper, write the letters of each of these questions and a brief answer for each.

2. The need for cash flow and working capital caused Mimi Nakata to examine her credit sales and compare her store's average collection period with those of similar dress shops. She found that the average collection period for the industry was 40 days and that her average monthly credit sales were $15,000. Her accounts receivable currently totaled $25,000. Here are some questions facing Mimi's credit business operation: (*a*) What are Mimi's average daily sales? (*b*) What is the average collection period? (*c*) How does Mimi's average collection period compare with those of similar businesses? (*d*) What should Mimi's next step be in finding the cause of the problem? (*e*) After identifying the problem, what should she do? On a separate sheet of paper, write the letter of each of these questions; after them, write a brief answer for each question.

Activities and Project

UNIT 16

Retailing Case

Olaf Jansen was the owner-manager of a new marina that sold pleasure boats and parts and offered repair services in a high-income suburb. After a few months in business, he decided to engage the services of an outside company—either a bank credit-card service such as MasterCard or VISA or a travel and entertainment charge-card company such as American Express, Diners' Club, or Carte Blanche. Being the owner of a new firm, he realized the necessity of a good cash flow—cash income and outgo. His main concern, however, was to maintain the goodwill of present customers and, of course, to attract new ones. He estimated that the cost of services plus his bookkeeping expense for bank credit cards would be from 5 to 7 percent of gross sales and for travel and entertainment cards would run from 7 to 10 percent.

Olaf characterized his customers as follows: (*a*) the majority were in high income-tax brackets, (*b*) they traveled extensively at home and abroad, (*c*) they were above average in economic understanding, (*d*) their family size was above average, (*e*) all seemed to be status-conscious, and (*f*) they responded to personal services.

1. What else should Olaf know about his customers?

2. What are the advantages of bank credit cards for his customers?

3. What benefits would travel and entertainment cards offer them?

4. What would Olaf gain from an affiliation with each type of service?

5. What other questions should Olaf answer before making a choice?

6. Which type of service would attract more new customers?

Working with People

Kathy carried a family travel and entertainment credit card, but she wrote a check for her hotel room. For doing so, she was given a 5 percent discount.

In the United States, federal law prohibits merchants from passing on to consumers the 3 to 6 percent fee that credit-card companies charge the merchants. However, if customers pay in cash, as Kathy did, merchants can offer a cash discount of up to 5 percent.

After this experience, Kathy wondered why her local department store didn't offer such cash discounts.

When Kathy returned home, she asked the credit manager of the department store if she could have a cash discount on the new fall wardrobe she wanted to buy. The credit manager told Kathy that the store policy didn't allow cash discounts.

Assume that you are the credit manager:

1. What is the basic problem?
2. How would you explain to Kathy's satisfaction the reasons why store policy does not include cash discounts?
3. How could you keep Kathy's goodwill?

Project 16: Controlling Consumer Credit

Your Project Goal
Given a list of types of stores and a declining economy, make appropriate recommendations for improving income from accounts receivable.

Procedure
Assume that you are a managerial consultant to retailers. As the economy slumps, charge customers are taking longer to make payments. Stung by high interest rates and rising debts themselves, retailers find it necessary to tighten consumer credit and to increase their income from accounts receivable. Several of them ask you for recommendations to cope with the problem. You survey current practices used to handle this problem and come up with the following suggestions: (a) discontinue delayed billing of Christmas purchases; (b) scrutinize new credit applications; (c) charge an annual fee for credit service, like some credit-card companies do; (d) step up credit counseling efforts; (e) approach delinquent customers earlier and more forcefully; (f) increase the frequency of billings, using firm notices; (g) send credit customers a booklet on credit; (h) increase the required minimum payment on credit-card balances; and (i) follow the practices of your strongest competitor.

1. Choose two areas of retailing from the list in Project 9, "Surveying Promotion Methods," on page 220—one selling products and the other selling services. Ask your teacher to approve your selection.
2. Rule a form similar to the following. Write the names of the retailing areas you have chosen in the spaces provided. In the left column, write the letter of each of the credit practices listed above. If you recommend the credit practice to the product area retailer, write "yes" in the center column. Do the same for the service business. Attach a separate sheet of paper on which you give your reasons.

Credit Practice	Product Area: _____	Service Area: _____

3. Identify two people in charge of consumer credit in each of the selected areas of retailing and ask your teacher to approve your selections. Ask the retailers to check your recommendations. Then revise them as you see fit. If convenient, ask a bank employee who works with commercial credit for his or her opinion.
4. Compare your recommendations with those of your classmates who investigated credit practices in other areas of retailing. See whether any generalizations can be made.

MOVING TOWARD MANAGEMENT AND OWNERSHIP

n class I read that out of all the millions of people in retailing, almost 25 percent of them are either owners, managers, or supervisors. That got me to thinking— 25 percent is a one-to-four chance. That means the odds of my moving up to manager are good. So I decided that I'd better start to learn about management, even though it might be a while until I got to manage anything or anybody. It just seemed like a good idea to learn about buying merchandise and making plans for what to sell. There was also more to know about customer relations, promoting sales, and controlling expenses. And I even got into how government regulates businesses and why. Last summer these would have sounded like tough things to learn—and I couldn't have seen any reason to learn them, either.

Now it's different. I'm not the manager and I don't own the place, but I do supervise two new employees. One of my jobs is teaching the new kids what to do and seeing that they get things done. And I'm beginning to understand the problems managers face and what it takes to run a retail business. What's next? Well, I'm already on my way to a career in retail management. And maybe, someday, even my own sporting goods store.

Motivating Retail Employees

CHAPTER
52

Communications & Human Relations

Economics & Marketing

Merchandising

Selling & Technology

Advertising & Display

Operations & Management

In this unit, you'll learn more about what it takes to be a successful retail worker. Employee motivation, which is discussed in this chapter, is something that all retail workers—management, supervisors, and employees—need to understand.

Ask anyone in retail management, "What is your No. 1 problem in store operation today?" and the reply will probably be "The people problem." A retail firm is only as good as the people who work there. But today, management is faced with ever-increasing labor costs, lower profits, and tougher competition. And managers are asking: "Where can we hire career-minded men and women to fill our positions?" "Who will be our key employees 5 to 10 years from now?" "What can we do now to ensure that our firm will have the trained personnel we need in the future?" So, solving the people problem by hiring and keeping motivated workers is important to the management of stores of all types and sizes.

To achieve the goal of getting things done, supervisors must understand why employees work. And workers must understand motivation to appreciate the behavior of supervisors and of their coworkers.

Why People Work

If you have a part-time job, have you ever thought about what motivates you to work? Think about it, and you'll probably find that, like most people, you work for two basic reasons: to earn money so that you can satisfy your human needs and to receive the satisfactions that the job offers.

To Earn Money

You will recall from Chapter 42 that there are seven levels of basic human needs.

These are (1) physical needs, (2) safety needs, (3) social or love needs, (4) ego or esteem needs, (5) self-fulfillment needs, (6) knowledge needs, and (7) aesthetic needs. Most people are motivated to work to earn the money they need to satisfy these needs.

But the needs that a person wants to satisfy today may not be the same as those the person wants to satisfy 5 to 10 years from now. Take yourself for example. Right now, what's motivating you to work part time may be the desire to earn enough money to satisfy some of your physical needs. In a few years, though, when you're working full time, you'll probably want to earn enough money to satisfy more than just physical needs. You may also want to satisfy your ego or self-fulfillment needs. So it's important to choose a career goal that will satisfy your future needs as well as your present ones. And it's important that you and your supervisors are always aware of the changes in the needs of the people with whom you work as well as your own.

To Receive Job Satisfactions

Even though earning money to satisfy their human needs is the reason most people work, there are other equally important rewards from work that are related to the worker's quality of life while on the job. After all, as an employee, you should be able to enjoy life during working hours as well as away from work. So try to find work that you like and can do well, just as employers try to find workers who are competent and will be well satisfied with their jobs.

Job satisfactions can be grouped into two broad categories: satisfactions gained from the work itself and satisfactions gained from the work environment. As an employee, you may be well satisfied with the firm for which you work but very unhappy about the tasks to be performed, or vice versa. Management's responsibility is to correct the situation, if possible, by

providing both kinds of satisfaction. Maintaining high employee motivation calls for carefully planned programs of worker selection, placement, training, and supervision in addition to various fringe benefits.

How Workers See Their Jobs

Not all employees have the same career ambitions. So the importance that workers attach to their employment varies a great deal. An employee's motives or reasons for working often explain his or her attitude toward work and provide clues for supervision and training strategies.

Employees can be grouped into four categories on the basis of the importance they attach to their employment: (1) those who think of their work as just a job, (2) those who are task-oriented, (3) those who identify with their occupation, and (4) those who are career-oriented.

Job-Oriented Workers

Some workers in this category take full- or part-time positions in stores solely to earn money and perhaps take advantage of employee discounts. Others may work just to have something to do with their time. Some are moonlighters (people who work at a part-time job, often at night, as well as working at a full-time job). Members of this group may be good or poor workers, but they have one thing in common—they see their employment only as a job. It's a living.

Task-Oriented Workers

Employees in this group come from a variety of educational backgrounds. They have positions at many different occupational levels. Regardless of the task assigned to them, they enjoy working and take pride in being hard workers. The common element among these workers is that they think of their work as a series of tasks. They have no particular concern for advancement.

Occupation-Oriented Workers

These employees take great pride in their occupation—being a craftsperson, a salesperson, a display artist, and so on. They maintain high standards of performance in their fields. Their identification with their occupation is stronger than that with their employer, regardless of the prestige of the firm for which they work. Their common tie is a fondness for the occupation.

Career-Oriented Workers

These are the "professionals" of their field. They love their work and usually feel strongly that they're making a good contribution to society through their work. They see a task through even if the closing bell rings. They have a strong commitment to their "profession" and work hard and willingly for the advancement of the profession, even if it's not a recognized one.

Supervisory and managerial personnel who know and understand the orientation and work objectives of employees are in an excellent position to motivate them. And they often help employees to remove the drudgery from their work.

Understanding employee orientation and work objectives can also help you as a beginning worker. For example, if you have a part-time job now, you probably know some coworkers who fit the four categories of work orientation. And when you know your coworkers' work-related goals and values, you're in a position to judge what they say and do and to decide whether to take their advice when it is given.

Employee Motivators

Motivating employees means providing them with the opportunity to get what they want in exchange for what the employer wants them to do. Let's see what both parties to an employment agreement want.

Jobs call for certain skills and offer certain rewards or satisfactions. As a worker, you possess certain skills and seek certain rewards or satisfactions. So if the employer and you want to reach an agreement, you must both have a clear under-

Can you identify a person in each of these categories?

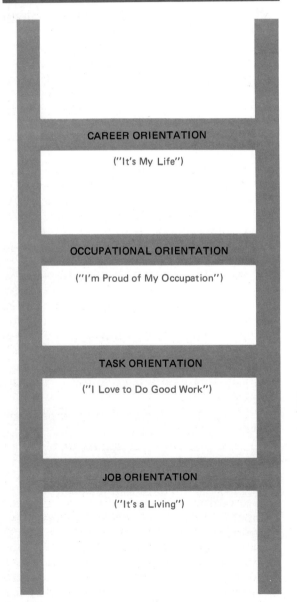

CAREER ORIENTATION

("It's My Life")

OCCUPATIONAL ORIENTATION

("I'm Proud of My Occupation")

TASK ORIENTATION

("I Love to Do Good Work")

JOB ORIENTATION

("It's a Living")

standing of what skills the job requires and what rewards or satisfactions it offers. And the employer and you must also have a clear understanding of the skills that you possess and the satisfactions and rewards you want from the job. Let's see how a clear understanding of these points can help you develop as a well-adjusted employee.

Employment Adjustment

When there is agreement between the skill requirements of the job and the skills you have to offer, the chances of your being satisfactory to your employer are good. But, of course, if you can't perform well, the chances are poor. Likewise, if your job provides the satisfactions that you expect of it, the chances that you'll be satisfied are good. But, of course, if you don't receive the satisfactions you want, your chances of satisfaction are poor. So for strong agreement in your relationship with your employer and vice versa, you must be satisfied with your job and your employer must be satisfied with you. This is called **employment adjustment**.

Of course, the achievement of complete satisfaction is only an ideal, but it's an ideal worth striving for. And if you understand employment requirements and if your employer understands what you want from employment, your motivation and productivity will improve. The main difficulties in achieving such an understanding lie in poor communication between you and your employer and in the ever-changing needs both of you face.

Let's look at some of the kinds of satisfaction employees want and what employment situations may offer. A knowledge of some of these should help improve communication.

Kinds of Employment Satisfaction

Recent studies of worker motivation have identified 21 different kinds of rewards or satisfactions that workers receive or want from their jobs. Here is a list of these sat-

isfactions, with a brief explanation of each:

1. *Ability utilization*—the job makes use of my abilities.
2. *Achievement*—the job gives me a feeling of accomplishment.
3. *Activity*—I am kept busy all the time.
4. *Advancement*—the job provides opportunities for advancement.
5. *Authority*—I can tell other people what to do.
6. *Autonomy*—I can plan my work with little supervision.
7. *Company policies and practices*—the company administers its policies fairly.
8. *Compensation*—the wages or pay compare well with those of other workers.
9. *Coworkers*—my relations with coworkers are friendly.
10. *Creativity*—I can try out some of my own ideas.
11. *Independence*—I can do the work alone.
12. *Moral values*—I can do the work without feeling that it is morally wrong.
13. *Recognition*—I can get recognition for the work I do.
14. *Responsibility*—I can make decisions independently.
15. *Security*—the job provides steady employment.
16. *Social service*—I can do things for other people.
17. *Social status*—I'm regarded as being somebody in my community.
18. *Supervision: human relations*—my supervisor backs me up with top management.
19. *Supervision: technical*—my supervisor trains workers well.
20. *Variety*—I have something different to do every day.
21. *Working conditions*—the place where I work is comfortable and pleasant.

Keep in mind that some of the satisfactions you want may be the same as those of other workers. But since you are an individual, they can vary just as much as your personal characteristics do from those of others. Also, remember that the degree to which you or others want a certain satisfaction ranges from high to very low. For example, having friendly relations with your fellow workers (item 9, coworkers) may be very important to you. But working alone (item 11, independence) may be of little importance to you.

Satisfaction Assessments

Now that you're aware of the 21 satisfactions that employees want from their jobs, let's see how this information can be obtained from an employee and measured.

Worker-Needs Profiles. A chart that shows the importance a worker attaches to each of the 21 satisfactions is called a **worker-needs profile.** Obtaining the necessary information for a worker-needs profile may be compared to finding out about a customer's needs and wants in personal selling. The purpose in both activities is to help the person being questioned. The accuracy of the measure in both situations depends on the person's ability and willingness to give the accurate information.

Worker needs may be assessed formally or informally. Most assessments are made informally, either by the worker or by a supervisor. Of course, your coworkers assess your work needs unconsciously all the time. There are also formal questionnaires, but at present only professional counselors make use of them.

Employees often make a self-assessment of their work needs when they have to solve problems involving career decisions. Progressive supervisors may use worker-needs profiles as guides in making job assignments. And training directors may use them in determining what to teach and how to motivate their trainees.

Job-Satisfaction Profiles. You can make a profile of your work needs by estimating the importance of the various satisfactions you want from your employment. And you can also make a profile of how much satisfaction you're receiving from your job in each of the 21 satisfaction

areas. Simply ask yourself whether your job gives you high, medium, or low satisfaction with respect to each area.

Information about the satisfactions a job offers an employee is valued by supervisors for its use in dealing with the employee and in dealing with management.

The People Problem

You'll recall that we mentioned the people problem at the beginning of this chapter, and you'll remember the statement that a retail firm is only as good as the people who work there. All types of businesses have people problems, but it's more visible in retailing. And it's especially visible in areas like personal selling, where employees come in contact with the public. Maintaining high employee morale is a team responsibility, starting with top management. And it's a complex operation. It begins with the recruitment and selection of employees and continues throughout their tenure.

Dealing with the People Problem

Look again at the four classifications of the ways people view their employment (as a job, as a task, as an occupation, and as a career). This will give you an idea of why it's necessary to advertise job openings in a manner that will attract suitable applicants. You'll also see the wisdom of careful selection of applicants. Don't forget that one disgruntled employee can affect the productivity of an entire department or even a store.

Look again at the reasons why people work. Then concentrate on the motive to make money. Most workers are unable to satisfy all their human needs with the money they earn, so they strive for promotions to make their earnings larger. This is a positive drive. But some workers become frustrated with their real or imagined inability to earn more, and they carry their frustrations to the work place. Usu-

A worker-needs profile for a car salesperson.

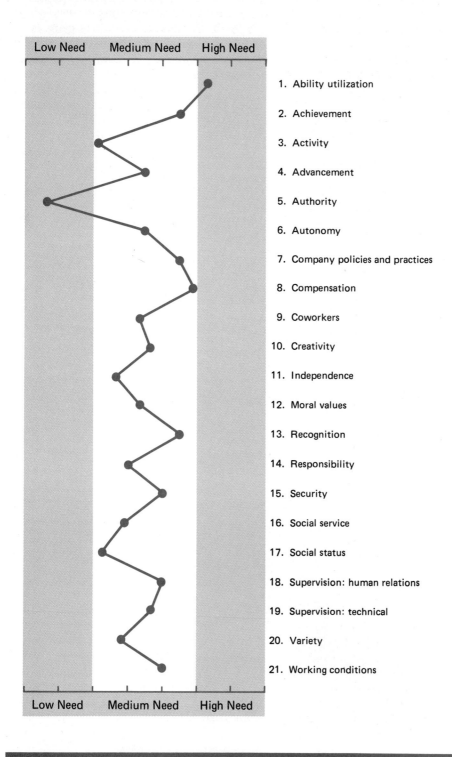

1. Ability utilization
2. Achievement
3. Activity
4. Advancement
5. Authority
6. Autonomy
7. Company policies and practices
8. Compensation
9. Coworkers
10. Creativity
11. Independence
12. Moral values
13. Recognition
14. Responsibility
15. Security
16. Social service
17. Social status
18. Supervision: human relations
19. Supervision: technical
20. Variety
21. Working conditions

ally, superiors or coworkers can't do much about these situations.

Look again at the matter of receiving satisfactions from employment. This is an area that the employer—and the employee—can do something about. It may not be easy, however, because employees' needs change as their situations in life change. Also, be alert to changing social values and attitudes toward work. Employee motives are very dynamic—a fact to be recognized and coped with. In the face of these conditions, the retailer's best means of maintaining a highly motivated work force is to strive continuously for maximum employment adjustment among the firm's employees.

Perspective

Fortunately for progressive firms whose leaders keep pace with social change, researchers are continuously discovering better ways of identifying worker needs and job satisfactions and of improving employer-employee relationships. Of course, these innovations must meet the requirements of labor and human rights laws, which is one of the topics discussed in Chapter 56, on the government regulation of retailing.

The next two chapters in this unit discuss other aspects of employee motivation. Chapter 53 deals with supervision from the managerial point of view and Chapter 54 deals with the training of employees.

Trade Talk

Define each term and use it in a sentence.

Employment
  adjustment
Worker-needs profile

The employer can help employees receive satisfaction from their work by cheerfully answering their questions. Ron Tanner/Progressive Grocer

Can You Answer These?

1. What is the No.1 problem in store operation today? What are the questions managers ask relating to this problem?
2. What are the two main reasons people work? Describe each of them.
3. What are the two broad categories of job satisfactions?
4. What are the four ways in which workers view their employment? Explain the viewpoint of each type of worker.
5. How is job satisfaction assessed?

Problems

1. Rule a form similar to the following. In the left column, write the letter of each of the following wants: (*0*) to earn money to buy clothing, (*a*) to be asked to go for coffee with the group, (*b*) to get better lighting that will cause less eyestrain, (*c*) to use creative ability in a sales presentation, (*d*) to be complimented for doing a good job, (*e*) to obtain shorter working hours in order to obtain more leisure time, (*f*) to obtain hospitalization insurance, (*g*) to have the best sales record in the department, (*h*) to get money to rent a better apartment, (*i*) to make use of artistic abilities, and (*j*) to fit in and be accepted by other employees. In the right column, tell whether each want is an example of a physical, safety, social, ego, or self-fulfillment need.

Worker Want	Type of Need
Example: (0)	Physical

2. Prepare a form similar to that on page 421, but omit the profile shown and include the scales (high, medium, and low) at the top and bottom of the form. Using the list of satisfactions and descriptions on page 419, estimate your own need for each of the 21 satisfactions and place a small x at the appropriate point on the scale. Then connect the x's with straight lines to form a profile of your own needs, which gives you a profile of the satisfactions your ideal job would offer you.

Supervising Retail Workers

CHAPTER 53

Communications & Human Relations
Economics & Marketing
Merchandising
Selling & Technology
Advertising & Display
Operations & Management

Read the following statement about employee satisfaction that was made by an executive of a rapidly expanding West Coast chain of specialty stores:

We feel that the key to our rapid growth is the best use of people. What can happen in the future will be limited only by the limitations of people, people at all levels. People development, we believe, is the key to expansion. Maximizing the satisfaction of people is our greatest asset.

Now read a different viewpoint, which was expressed in an article published by a large Midwestern newspaper. The heading read, "Satisfied Worker May Not Be the Best, Research Indicates." And in the article, a professor of industrial relations was quoted as follows:

When people are too satisfied, they look for ways to minimize their effort. It's a holding pattern. The best thing for both employer and employee is creative dissatisfaction which involves: (1) High standards set by the supervisor's example. High standards are not a happy thing. They're pressure. But people find ways to deal with them. (2) Frequent reinforcement for people who meet those standards. Most organizations don't allow for this. They are set up to be efficient and don't give you time to honestly appraise and reward people.

Which viewpoint is most fitting in a given situation at a given time? As a beginning worker, what would you think? As a store manager, what would your opinion be? Then as a supervisor, what position would you take? As you can see, a supervisor is often faced with tough situations in dealing with employees. This chapter deals with the supervisor's role in retailing. And, as you learned in Chapter 33, supervisory techniques play a most important part in the success of a business.

What Is Supervision?

Dividing the word "supervision" into two parts—"super" and "vision"—gives some idea of its meaning. "Super" means superior. "Vision," in this context, means perspective as applied to a task to be performed. So **supervision** means the management, direction, and overseeing of others. As you learned in Chapter 33, supervisors are the people responsible for getting things done. But you'll get a fuller understanding of the word "supervisor" when you read the following discussion of a supervisor's job.

A retail supervisor's job may be divided into three main categories of supervision—technical, human relations, and leadership. Each category is essential in achieving the goals of the store.

Technical Supervision

Obviously, in order to supervise the performance of a task, supervisors should understand why the job is to be done and what the outcomes should be. That is, they must know the technical side of each job well enough to assign it to a capable worker and to evaluate the outcome.

Human Relations Supervision

Employers are very concerned about an applicant's potential in the area of human relations. One reason for this attitude is that good human relations in a department increases productivity. But a department is only one unit in a retail firm, and supervisors must deal with their own superiors and with other supervisors on a similar level. So a supervisor also needs good human relations skills to function as a member of a team.

Leadership Supervision

Supervisors may possess technical know-how and enjoy excellent relations with co-workers on all occupational levels and still not succeed. The missing quality is leadership ability. Without leadership ability, supervisors usually lose out to those who do have it. Without doubt, supervisory performance is evaluated largely in terms of the achievements of the unit supervised. And this depends on leadership abilities, such as the qualities discussed in Chapter 33.

How Supervisory Decisions Are Made

When problems arise with merchandise, with data, or with people, supervisors must face them promptly and try to solve them as soon as possible. This means that they must make decisions. A decision-making process that many supervisors and other workers find helpful can be broken down into five steps: (1) identifying the problem, (2) getting the facts, (3) considering possible solutions, (4) selecting the best solution, and (5) trying out the planned solution. Experienced supervisors go through these steps automatically. As a result, they are able to solve problems quickly and efficiently.

The steps are explained below. Read them carefully, for you'll find that, regardless of your employment level, you'll be able to put them to use.

Step 1: Identifying the Problem

When they encounter a problem, supervisors ask themselves "What is really the matter?" At this stage, they know it's important to distinguish between the symptoms (signs or indications) that have brought the problem to light and the cause of the problem itself. As an example of the difficulty of separating the symptoms from the causes, consider employee morale. Is unhappiness among a group of workers the real problem—or is the low morale a symptom of the cause of the problem, such as poor supervision or dissatisfaction with wages? To help separate symptoms and causes, supervisors ask questions such as: "How else might the problem be stated?" "What else is involved?" "Are there similar problems elsewhere in the company?" "Is this a problem or a symptom?"

Timing is part of the job of defining a problem. So supervisors ask, "How soon does it have to be solved?" And they know that, while decisions shouldn't be hasty, failure to act in time may be as bad as not acting at all. So wise supervisors set a deadline—a time by which they must reach a decision.

Step 2: Gathering the Facts

Once supervisors have defined the problem, they gather all the facts related to

Supervisors must be able to identify the real problem.

it—not just those that will lead to the conclusion they hope to reach. They consult other people and study reference material. And then they check the facts they have gathered, because the quality of their decision will depend on the accuracy of the facts collected. Supervisors must have complete information to reach a wise decision.

Step 3:
Considering Possible Solutions

Most problems can be solved in more than one way. To reach the best decision, supervisors make sure that they know and consider all possible solutions. They jot down everything that comes to mind—even the things that at first glance seem irrelevant. And they study every possible alternative.

At this point, supervisors measure each possible decision in terms of its costs and its benefits. The benefits gained from a solution may be outweighed by its costs in time, money, or employee morale. Supervisors ask questions such as these about each possible solution: "Will it work?" "What will be the reaction of the parties involved?" "How will it affect customers?" "Does it relate to company policy?" "What will the probable consequences be?"

Step 4: Selecting the Best Solution

There are several dangers that supervisors try to avoid in selecting the best solution. They try to avoid assuming that because a particular solution solved a previous problem, it will work again. Perhaps it would if the circumstances were identical, but they rarely are. It's far safer to consider all possible solutions to the present problem than to rely entirely on past experience.

Supervisors also try to avoid assuming that it's better to make no decision at all than to take the chance of making a wrong one. All decisions involve a certain amount of risk. Supervisors must have enough self-confidence to face the possibility that the decision may be a bad one.

Step 5:
Trying Out the Planned Decision

Every decision requires an action plan that spells out who has to do what and when, why it must be done, and where everything will be done. The people expected to take the action must be willing and able to take it. Supervisors communicate their decisions to everyone involved. Also, they know that it's necessary to follow up at regular intervals to see if the correct decision was made and if it's being carried out as intended.

What a Supervisor Does

Nearly all retail workers above entry-level positions have some type of supervisory responsibility. Of course, the extent of these responsibilities varies with the employment level of the position. Nevertheless, all supervisory tasks can be grouped into four broad categories: (1) planning and organizing work, (2) on-the-job training, (3) liaison duties, and (4) evaluations. Here is a brief description of each category, with some tips on how successful supervisors approach these tasks.

Planning and Organizing Work

Careful planning pays off in terms of a smooth-running operation and good morale. Successful supervisors schedule their planning time as well as other duties. Here are some of a supervisor's planning and organizing activities:

◆ *Prepare task analyses.* Supervisors must know exactly what each worker has to do so that the department's goals can be reached.
◆ *Plan a personnel budget.* The cost of personnel is an item that supervisors and managers can control through careful budgeting.
◆ *Schedule employee working hours.* Determine the right number of workers for each station; schedule meal and refreshment breaks, shifts, and vacations.

- *Assign duties*. Select the right person for each job.

On-the-Job Training

In effect, training and supervision are different sides of the same coin in that the purpose of both is to assist employees in becoming satisfactory and satisfied workers. Each function helps the other: good training makes supervisory tasks easier, and good supervision reduces the amount of training needed.

Instruction by Example. Much of on-the-job training is instruction by example. So when selecting supervisors, management tries to find good models for workers to follow. There is an effort to avoid appointing someone whose outlook is "Do as I say, not as I do." A good example, set by a supervisor gets excellent results from those supervised. And the opposite usually results when the supervisor is disliked.

Giving Directions. The ability to give good directions has a lot to do with the supervisor's attitude toward the worker. Most people don't like being ordered to do something. But they do usually respond willingly to a courteous request. So supervisors should give orders only when the use of authority is necessary.

Good supervisors deliver their directions in a clear, concise manner so that the employee can follow them without hesitation. And they also encourage questions and comments.

Correcting Errors. Correcting errors is a form of instruction. It's one of the most important supervisory skills because it has so much to do with maintaining employee morale. When correcting errors, supervisors generally strive to do the following:

- Assume an attitude of helpfulness and avoid showing authority.

A good supervisor instructs by example. Jane Hamilton-Merrit

- Find the cause of the error, if possible, before talking to the employee; the error may be beyond the worker's control.
- Avoid making judgments while an employee is explaining an error; try to be a good listener.
- Give advice in a friendly manner and share the responsibility for errors.
- Make the cause of the error clear to the worker, show or explain the right way to avoid it, and substitute the right course of action.
- Correct the employee in private.

Liaison Duties

Liaison means connection, or serving as a connecting link. Supervisors are the connecting links between management and employees. They communicate management's policies and concerns to employees and convey employee concerns to management. Liaison involves the five activities discussed below.

Interpreting Management Policies. The purpose of management policies is to ensure the same employee behavior throughout the firm. So accuracy in the interpretation of policies is very important. Supervisors must understand the policy and interpret it in a straightforward, meaningful manner. The interpretation of store policy is especially important when new workers are being trained, and it may be a sensitive task when employees don't follow policies.

Explaining Employee Problems to Management. Excellent relations with both management and employees and good verbal skills are needed to communicate from the bottom up. Explaining employee problems to management is an important supervisory function because profits depend so much on worker productivity. And if employee problems aren't solved, productivity is likely to decrease.

Suggesting Changes to Management. In retailing, excellent ideas often come from lower-level employees because they are closest to the customer. And some of the best ideas for improvements come from supervisors who have an overview of worker operations. As an arm of management, a supervisor is in an excellent position to explain the need for change and its possible beneficial results.

Hearing Complaints. Dealing with complaints frequently requires liaison—liaison between workers and management or liaison within the work force. Or an employee may be personally unhappy about some aspect of assigned work. Supervisors can handle both kinds of complaints effectively by using the decision-making process with emphasis on the first step—identifying the problem. This calls for careful listening in some private place where both parties can be relaxed and calm. Following the identification of the problem, supervisors try to get the facts and then follow the remaining steps in the decision-making process.

Dealing with Grievances. A **grievance** is a real or imagined injustice or wrong. Grievances frequently develop from the repetition of an annoyance. Supervisors try to prevent a grievance by taking care of annoyances before they become grievances. Early attention to complaints is very important, because a grievance may spread to other employees and explode into a serious problem.

Supervisors handle grievances like complaints, using the decision-making steps. Sometimes they must call for advice from other workers and supervisors, from higher level management, from union representatives, or—in some instances—from outside counselors, medical advisers, or other specialists. A complete understanding of the cause of a grievance will point the way to solving it.

Evaluations

Supervisors must evaluate not only employee performance and characteristics but also themselves. Since supervisors are a major element in the supervisory process, it's clear that supervisory self-evaluations are important.

Supervisory Self-Evaluations. Self-evaluation involves gathering information from a variety of sources and rating the achievement of supervisory goals. It includes collecting the opinions of the workers supervised, of other supervisors, and of managers. It may include ratings of customer-contact employees by professional shoppers and department heads. And it usually includes facts and figures related to a department's goals, such as sales volume. In some stores, job satisfaction profiles of employees are used. A supervisor's self-evaluation may consist of any device that provides reliable information about a supervisor's performance in the four categories of supervisory tasks—planning and organizing, on-the-job training, liaison duties, and evaluation.

Evaluation of Employees. Supervisors use both formal and informal methods to determine how well employees perform assigned tasks and how well they are adjusting to work with the firm. The general purpose of employee evaluation is to improve job performance and job satisfaction. But evaluations may also be used when employees are being promoted or reassigned to more appropriate duties.

Supervisors make informal employee evaluations by observing the day-to-day behavior of the workers they supervise. For example, they watch how workers perform tasks and make a mental note of their attitudes toward the work and the firm. They note how workers respond to suggestions and directions and observe how they get along with coworkers. And they also listen to remarks about workers from others—customers, coworkers, and so on.

Listening and paying careful attention can stop a problem before it becomes critical. Courtesy of Cunningham & Walsh Inc.

Every so often, supervisors are called upon to make formal evaluations of employees under their supervision. Many firms provide forms for rating employees so that the ratings can be compared easily. Such forms may ask for information regarding the employee's productivity and call for ratings of the worker's personal qualities and characteristics.

The most important part of a formal employee evaluation is the supervisor's interview with the worker after the form has been completed. This includes talking with workers about their strengths and weaknesses and getting their suggestions for ways of improving their weak points. All workers are entitled to know where they stand in the minds of their supervisors and what they can do to improve their standing.

Now that you've finished reading this chapter, can you answer the questions asked in the first paragraph? Which of the two viewpoints about maximizing employee satisfactions would you favor as a worker? As a supervisor? As a store manager? What are your basic beliefs about the supervisor's job? And do you have what it takes to be a supervisor? From this chapter, you've learned about the supervisor's job in greater detail, so you have more information on which to base your answer. What do you think?

Trade Talk

Define each term and use it in a sentence.

Grievance
Liaison
Supervision

Can You Answer These?

1. What are the three main categories of retail supervision? How does each category affect worker productivity?
2. What are the four steps involved in making decisions?

3. What are the three main ways in which a supervisor performs on-the-job training?
4. What are the five functions of a retail supervisor in carrying out liaison responsibilities?
5. What means are used in a supervisor's self-evaluation? In the evaluation of employees?

Problems

1. Rule a form similar to the following. In the left column, write the letter of each of the following supervisory activities: (a) correct an employee's error in cash-register operation, (b) compliment a worker on good task performance, (c) set an example by being at work on time, (d) show a new worker how to change a price ticket, (e) exchange work shifts with another supervisor, (f) speak to management on behalf of employees, (g) make out a purchase order, (h) help out a worker who is swamped, and (i) conduct a discussion session on work problems. Place a check mark (√) in the column that best fits the supervisory category on the right. Be prepared to justify your decisions.

Job Duty	Technical Supervision	Human Relations Supervision	Leadership Supervision

2. Rule a form similar to the following. In the left column, write the letter of each of the following directions: (0) "Get that order out in the next 10 minutes." (a) "I want you back from lunch by 12:30 p.m." (b) "If we all get at it, we can have the boxes priced in an hour." (c) "The boss says nobody may park in his space." (d) "Stock these shelves fast. We're short-handed this afternoon." (e) "You'd better increase your daily sales volume. There's only 3 days left to meet your quota." (f) "I'm sorry, but you'll have to wear dresses to

Direction	Good	Fair	Poor	More Effective Direction
Example: (0)			√	"Can we get this important order out in the next 10 minutes?"

work, no slacks." (*g*) "I want every employee in the store by 8:30 a.m. each morning." (*h*) "Please select the extra hours you would like to work during the sale." (*i*) "Everyone in the department will attend the training meeting at 7 a.m. Monday." Rank each direction as good, fair, or poor by placing a check mark (√) in the appropriate column to the right. If you rank a direction fair or poor, rewrite it in the last column.

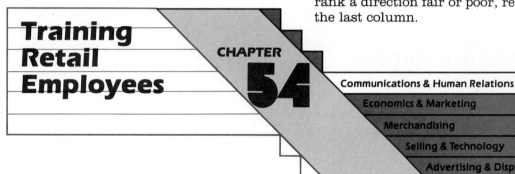

Training Retail Employees

CHAPTER 54

Communications & Human Relations

Economics & Marketing

Merchandising

Selling & Technology

Advertising & Display

Operations & Management

Twenty-five years ago, two young men graduated from the same high school. They were very much alike. Both had been better-than-average students. Both had pleasant personalities. And both were ambitious.

Recently, these men returned to their high school for their 25th reunion. Although they still seemed very much alike, there was a difference. After graduation, they had gone to work for the same retail firm and were still there. But one of the men was manager of a small department of that company. The other was its president.

Have you ever wondered what makes this kind of difference in people's business lives? It isn't always intelligence, talent, or dedication. It isn't that one person wants success and the other doesn't. The difference lies largely in what each person knows and how he or she makes use of that knowledge.

You were *not* born with knowledge and the ability to make good use of it. But you do live in a country where it's possible to gain the knowledge you need and learn how to make use of it when you have it. Taking advantage of the training opportunities offered by your employer is one of many ways in which you can get the knowledge you need for a job and advancement in retailing. It's just good business sense to learn all you can about the retailing field. And remember that for the most part, luck is being ready to seize an opportunity when it presents itself.

Now let's look at employee training from the manager's or owner's point of view. Nearly all firms—whether self-service or full-service—have some type of training program. Whenever a new worker is employed, someone has to explain the job to be done. Small firms usually take care of this with on-the-job training. But in larger firms (those with 100 or more employees) training is systematized, responsibility for training is specific, and a training budget is provided.

Reasons for Employee Training

Retailers usually look at training in terms of costs and benefits, just as they would consider any other operating function. Some firms follow a policy of promotion from within the company and invest heavily in training programs. Others hire workers with retail or related experience and provide little employee training. Training policies vary according to the employment level of the job, the expected tenure of an employee, the type of training given, and the attitude of management toward training.

When they weigh the benefits of employee training, retailers usually have two broad objectives in mind: the reduction of operating costs and improvement in employer-employee relations.

Reducing Operating Costs

One way to reduce labor costs is to improve the effectiveness and efficiency of labor. Better customer service with less errors and reduced payroll expense due to time saved are two important results expected from employee training. Another is the reduction of the need for close employee supervision. This saves supervisory time and releases supervisors for other duties. When employees have been trained to treat customers and handle merchandise properly, there are fewer complaints and returned merchandise and more satisfied customers to build sales.

Improving Relations with Employees

A good training program helps all employees to understand the firm's policies and practices. And this results in less misunderstandings regarding those policies and practices. So employees have a unity of purpose. And, of course, this means that the employees project a consistent store image.

Well-trained employees are more self-confident, less defensive, and easier to deal with than untrained workers. Also, they usually have greater respect for the firm and its management, for the positions they hold, the customers they serve, and the merchandise they handle. And generally, well-trained employees receive more satisfactions from their work. This situation tends to make for contented workers, and contented workers are easy to supervise.

Types of Training Programs

To design an employee training program that will meet the needs of all workers in a firm, retailers must understand the different types of training programs available. To help them understand this, training programs have been classified in the following ways.

Occupational Levels

Employees on different occupational levels need different types of training. For example, as an entry-level retail worker, you'll need instruction about most of the daily tasks you'll have to perform. But as a new supervisor, you'll need a different type of training to help you perform your job duties. You'll need training in such things as supervisory techniques and employer-employee relations. So in developing training programs, management must consider the occupational levels of all their employees—from part-time workers to top executives.

Management must also consider the purposes of the training they give to employees at different occupational levels. These are discussed below. See the table on page 433, which provides training for ski shop employees with different needs.

Initial Training. Just about every firm provides some kind of initial training, whether formal or informal. Such instruction is necessary to inform entry-level workers about store policies and regulations as well as the store systems. Many stores call training of this type **systems training,** since it has to do with store systems in completing sales checks, operating cash registers, and so on. The length of training varies with the complexity of the worker's assignment. In very small stores, it takes place on the job.

Updating. **Updating** is bringing employees up to date on the knowledge and skills needed in their present jobs. Because retailing is an ever-changing industry, updating is a continuous process. It involves training employees to use the job compentencies they have mastered in a different way. This is usually because of a change in store procedures or policies. Updating also includes information about new products or services, the firm, its relations with employees, and changing government regulations and economic conditions. Individual personal instruction ranging from management announcements to correspondence courses may also be given.

Supervisory Training. Supervisory training is probably the most critical type of instruction because it has a strong effect on the work force. Also, it occurs at a crucial time for young supervisors. Many of them make up their minds to carry on or end their retailing careers at this point. Supervisory training often consists of training and experience in supervisory techniques, methods of on-the-job instruc-

TRAINING PROGRAM FOR SKI SHOP EMPLOYEES*
(Program incentive: free lift tickets at completion of training)

Employee	Training Method	Instructor	Date for Completion	Ability at Completion Date	
				Pass	More Training Needed
Training Need: Binding Installation					
Jim	Class and on-the-job	Bob	10-1	✓	
John	Class and on-the-job	Bob	10-1	✓	
Ed	Class and on-the-job	Bob	10-1		Make up 10-7
Training Need: Ski and Boot Selling					
Jim	On-the-job	Bob	10-15	✓	
Sally	On-the-job	Bob	10-15	✓	
John	On-the-job	Bob	10-15	✓	
Training Need: Ski Release Check					
Jim	On-the-job	Ski Rep.	10-20	✓	
Ed	On-the-job	Ski Rep.	10-20	✓	

* Here, the training needs are listed for all employees on one plan, in order of their importance for these employees, from learning how to install ski bindings to learning how to check ski releases. The training method selected for the first two skills was a brief class and on-the-job training administered by skilled employees. Since the last training need involved learning how to use a new machine, a representative from the binding-machine company was called in to instruct the employees.
Source: Small Business Administration, *Business Basics: Training and Developing Employees* (self-instruction booklet; Washington, D.C.: U.S. Government Printing Office, 1953).

Updating is a continuous process in the retailing industry.   Courtesy of Gino's, Inc.

tion, employer-employee relations, and the interpretation of store policies and regulations.

Upgrading.   **Upgrading** is designed to prepare trainees for promotion to higher positions. Most managerial training programs fit this category. But upgrading also focuses on workers who have been selected for better positions regardless of level. Upgrading instruction may provide greater depth in specific technical competencies and in leadership and human relations.

Executive Development.   Executive development is designed to enable certain operating and administrative managers to keep up with the times in retailing and to encourage their creativity. It may involve marketing, economics, finance, communications, sociology, anthropology, civic responsibility, community welfare, and other studies and experiences related to retailing and marketing. Executive development may also consist of con-

ferences, retreats, courses of study, travel, lectures, and any other activity considered relevant to leadership in retailing.

Administration of Training Program

Training programs may also be classified according to the way they are administered and controlled. The two basic ways of administering training programs are by centralization and decentralization. **Decentralized training** is on-the-job training. As mentioned earlier, small-store training is usually done on the job. Large stores also use on-the-job training in combination with **centralized training,** which takes place in a classroom or at some other location away from the job station. Centralized training is usually done by staff members of the personnel department.

Whether large stores use centralized or decentralized training depends on the purpose and content of the instruction. For example, the personnel department staff may be able to teach general subject matter such as selling techniques, the salescheck system, and employee policies better than it could be done in the department. On the other hand, facts about merchandise and merchandising practices can be better learned on the job.

Competencies Taught

Training programs may also be classified according to the competencies they teach. The checker-cashier training program, the selling-techniques program, and the merchandise math program are all examples. They are often classified this way when a store enters into an arrangement for training with the public schools, colleges, or universities.

Designing a Training Program

Let's assume that you've been asked to help design a training program to meet the needs of a group of employees who require updating. What steps would you follow in preparing the plan? The following discussion outlines the steps that most retailers use.

Surveying the Need

The object of this step is to learn what the

employee or group of employees must learn to perform better on the job. With a new worker, it's just about everything, but experienced workers have some knowledge and skills to begin with. So the task is to find out what the workers need to know and what they already know. One useful tool for determining this is a **knowledge-skill profile,** which is simply a list of all categories of competencies required for a job. This can be prepared by referring to a job description. (See Chapter 34.) It need not be very detailed.

Once a knowledge-skill profile has been prepared, it's fairly easy to review the employee's proficiency in various competency areas. If some competency areas are more important than others, employees should be given training in those areas first.

Analyzing Performance Problems

The lack of ability to do the job properly is a common cause of problems in performance. Lack of training, however, is not the only reason employees don't do things the way they should be done. For this reason, an analyzer must study performance problems before a training program is started. This is particularly true in updating training. Here are some of the rea-

Is this a centralized or decentralized training program? Courtesy of K Mart Corporation

sons for poor performance other than lack of training.

Some workers feel that the quality of performance doesn't matter. This attitude is common when good performance is not recognized and poor performance is equally rewarded, leading workers to think that nonperformance is rewarding. This may arise when a superior performer is given more work to do but is not compensated in added wages for the extra load. There are also some situations where the work force sets the performance standards and makes the employees who perform above those standards feel like outsiders. Other obstacles to proper performance may be poor scheduling, improper flow of information, or poor materials or facilities. All these things can hold up work and create problems. Additional skill training will not solve these problems.

Developing a Training Plan

After identifying the learning needs of the workers, setting priorities for training, and analyzing performance problems, management can prepare specific training plans. A complete training plan should consist of the following:

♦ Identification of those training needs that must be met first
♦ The instructional system that should be used to satisfy each need, including the selection of the person or organization who will accept the responsibility for each part of the plan
♦ The date on which each part of the plan is to be completed
♦ Selection of the person who can provide the help and guidance during the entire training process
♦ Follow-up on each item to see that learning has taken place
♦ Help and remedial training where indicated by the follow-up
♦ Follow-up to ensure that what has been learned is being properly applied to the job

♦ Recognition to the employee for achievements in learning
♦ Arrangements for coaching so that the more sophisticated aspects of the job can be learned

Instructional Systems. The most widely used instructional systems are (1) on-the-job training, (2) company training classes, (3) public and private school courses, (4) correspondence courses, (5) job rotation, and (6) coaching or supervision. All these methods may be familiar to you; however, job rotation may need some explanation.

With **job rotation,** an employee is placed into a different position and is expected to perform in that position or to learn it as if he or she were a new employee. At the end of a limited period, the employee is able to perform most of the duties of that job. Job rotation is particularly suitable in situations where employees have to perform in several positions or when employees are being prepared for advancement.

Selection of Training Personnel. If formal lecturing or conference leadership is needed, many retailers hire professional instructors. The successful on-the-job instructor is always aware of the trainee's attitude. After the program gets under way, one of the instructor's first steps is to gain the trainees' respect and confidence. So attitude toward others, particularly younger people, is an important thing to look for when training personnel are being selected.

Instructing

The secret of successful instruction, whether of individuals or a group, is to focus on the learner. It is for this reason that instructors explain why the learning is necessary. When the trainees have learned something, instructors remember to praise them for a job well done. And they offer to provide help when it becomes obvious that there is difficulty in learning. Most of all, instructors keep in mind that learning will be accepted more readily and retained longer if it's directly related and applied to the job.

In on-the-job training and in the instruction of groups, the four-step method of teaching a competency is frequently used. To get the best results, instructors follow the steps that are explained in the following table.

THE FOUR STEPS OF ON-THE-JOB TRAINING*

Step	Purpose	How Accomplished
1. Prepare the learner.	To relieve tension. To establish training base. To arouse interest. To give him/her confidence.	Put him/her at ease. Find out what he/she already knows about task. Tell relation to task to mission. Tie task to his/her experience. Ensure that he/she is in a comfortable position to see you perform the task clearly.
2. Present the task.	To make sure he/she understands what to do and why. To ensure retention. To avoid giving him/her more than he/she can grasp.	Tell, show, illustrate, question carefully and patiently, use task analysis. Stress key points. Instruct clearly, completely, one step at a time. Keep your words to a minimum. Stress action words.
3. Try out learner's performance.	To be sure he/she has right method. To prevent wrong habit forming. To be sure he/she knows what he/she is doing and why. To test his/her knowledge. To avoid putting him/her on the job prematurely.	Have him/her perform the task and do not require that he/she explain what he/she is doing the first time through. If he/she makes a major error, assume the blame yourself and repeat as much of Step 2 as is necessary. Once he/she has performed the task correctly have him/her do it again and this time have him/her explain the steps and key points as he/she does the task (most frequently neglected). Ask questions to ensure that key points are understood. Continue until you know that he/she knows.
4. Follow up.	To give him/her confidence. To be sure he/she takes no chances and knows he/she is not left alone. To be sure he/she stays on the beam. To show your confidence in him/her.	Put him/her on his/her own; praise as fitting. Encourage questions; tell him/her where he/she can get help. Check frequently at first. Gradually reduce amount of checking.

* This chart is used by the U.S. Army to guide on-the-job training of civilian employees.

Evaluating a Training Program

A training-program evaluation is used to determine whether the training has resulted in learning, whether the methods being used are the most effective, and whether the cost of training is worth the results.

An evaluation can take various forms. Sometimes it's worthwhile to give a formal test, either in writing or verbally, to see how much has been learned. Trainees should understand that the purpose of the test is to identify what hasn't been learned and not to evaluate competence.

Usually the best way to evaluate whether training has resulted in learning is to observe the employee as he or she performs a task or to check carefully the work that has been completed. Because the purpose of training and learning is to improve job performance, gearing follow-up procedures accordingly provides the most direct way to measure success.

When training methods are being evaluated, it's worthwhile to keep track of which learning methods produced desirable results and which methods did not. The cost of the training method in terms of the employee's time, the staff's time, and the money spent on the training effort should also be noted.

This information can be very valuable in planning future training programs. For example, suppose the evaluation reveals that it would take store personnel about 20 hours of on-the-job instruction to teach a new employee a given skill, but the skill could also be acquired through a series of evening school classes at a vocational school or college. In this case it would, of course, be more efficient to choose the latter alternative.

In this chapter, to get an overview of the subject, you've learned about training employees from the manager's or owner's point of view rather than from yours. But think about how you can put this knowledge to use in your retailing career. For example, as an entry-level worker, you might find that your supervisor has enough confidence in you, after your initial training, to let you perform your job tasks without constantly checking your work. What does this tell you about how you're progressing on the job? What does it tell you about the training abilities of your supervisor? What about your contribution toward reducing operating costs? And what does it tell you about your chances of advancement in the company? Think about it.

Trade Talk

Define each term and use it in a sentence.

Centralized training
Decentralized training
Job rotation

Knowledge-skill profile
Systems training
Updating
Upgrading

Can You Answer These?

1. What are retailers' main reasons for investing in employee training programs?
2. What are the five types of retail training programs based on occupational levels?
3. When a retail training program for experienced employees is being designed, why is a survey of need for training necessary? Why is it necessary to analyze performance problems?
4. What should be included in a complete retail employee training program?
5. What are the basic reasons for evaluating a retail training program? How are program outcomes measured?

Problems

1. Planning an on-the-job training program: Assume that you've been selected as a training sponsor for a classmate who has just joined the firm for which you work and that the friend has little or no experience in the line of work involved. If you wish, you may use your present job or one

438

you have held recently. Your assignment is to outline a step-by-step, on-the-job training program for your trainee using information from this chapter and other sources. Set your own time limit and be sure to include the problem of determining the need for training as well as the content to be mastered. Rule a form similar to the following and record your information on it.

Title of position: _____ Name of trainee: _____

Steps to Be Taken	Method to Be Used	Person Assigned	Learning Time

Compare the training program you have developed with that of a classmate who has outlined a program for a similar kind of job; then revise your plan if you see fit to do so.

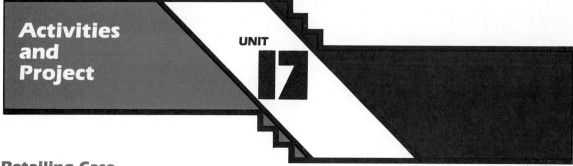

Activities and Project

UNIT 17

Retailing Case

Ann Friedman, assistant manager of a store selling sporting goods at a shopping center, complained to a friend how difficult it was to train workers these days. "No matter how many times I show Dick how to install ski bindings or tell Angela how to close a sale, they always seem to forget something along the way and botch things up. The schools just aren't teaching them the right things these days. What am I going to do? They're both good employees. I'd certainly hate to lose either of them."

1. What is Ann Friedman's attitude toward Dick and Angela?
2. Whom does Ann blame for the problems in training today's workers?
3. Whose fault is it that Dick and Angela can't seem to learn well?
4. Which of the four on-the-job training steps could help Ann improve her instruction?
5. What suggestions would you make to help improve Ann's teaching? How could Dick and Angela help Ann?

Working with People

Sam Skouras was promoted to assistant manager of the Apollo Supermarket largely because of his good record as a merchandising trainee. He'd spent the normal amount of training time in various departments of the store, and the manager had confidence in his merchandising abilities. Everyone in the store seemed to welcome his promotion.

At first, things seemed to go very well; but after a few weeks, workers began to complain about various little things such as parking problems. Absenteeism increased, and reliable employees were late for work more frequently. One day a department head who had been with the company for several years told Jake that he was going to apply for work with an aggressive competitor, that things just weren't what they used to be at Apollo.

1. Identify the true problem.
2. What are the important facts to be considered in this problem?
3. List several possible solutions to this problem.
4. Evaluate the possible solution.
5. Which solution(s) do you recommend? Why?

Project 17: Preparing a Training Plan

Your Project Goal

Given Unit 17 of your textbook and other literature available from the school and public libraries, prepare a training plan that will enable you and your classmates to sell a product or service to the students of your school.

Procedure

Assume that sales projects are permissible in your school. Choose a product or service to be sold by the members of your class, and have the choice approved by your instructor. Then do the following:

1. Prepare a product or service analysis by ruling a form similar to the following one. Then in the left column, list the features or facts about the product or service. In the right column, opposite each feature or fact, list the benefits to prospective purchasers or the selling points. On the back of the sheet(s), write the answers to these questions: (*a*) Who uses the product or service? (*b*) What needs and desires does it satisfy? (*c*) What proof is there that it

will satisfy these needs? (*d*) What are its advantages and disadvantages? (*e*) How does the price compare with competition? (*f*) Where should it be purchased? (*g*) When should it be purchased? (*h*) How should it be used?

Product or service analysis of: _____

Features and Facts	Benefits or Selling Points

2. Design a plan for surveying the need for training. Determine what each classmate already knows and what skills each possesses. Try to measure how proficient they already are in selling the product or service. Assess their attitude toward selling it to students outside the classroom.
3. Develop a training plan based on the training needs revealed in the survey. Set priorities for each competency area. Determine the approximate dates by which each competency area is to be completed.
4. Device a system for following up each competency area to be sure that learning has taken place. Provide help and remedial training when needed. Ensure that what has been learned has been applied to the job.
5. Describe your plan for recognizing the achievement of learners.

Evaluation

Your complete plan for training will be evaluated on the completeness of the information you supplied in each of the five steps above, the feasibility of implementing these steps, and the appearance of the written report.

Serving the Consumer

Retailers and the Consumer Movement

CHAPTER

55

Communications & Human Relations

Economics & Marketing

Merchandising

Selling & Technology

Advertising & Display

Operations & Management

Golden Rules for Better Business:

- ◆ Serve the public with honest values.
- ◆ Tell the truth about what is offered, and reveal facts in a clear and concise manner so that they can be understood by all customers.
- ◆ Tell customers what they want and need to know so that they can make intelligent buying decisions and obtain maximum satisfaction from purchases.
- ◆ Honor promises made to customers and don't quibble on any guarantee offered.
- ◆ Avoid all tricky devices and schemes that make customers believe they are getting a bargain when they really aren't.

These five rules for business were adapted from *The Ten Golden Rules for Better Business,* prepared by the Council of Better Business Bureaus.

Retailers on the local, state, and national levels are increasingly becoming aware of the impact that the consumer movement has on them and their busi-

nesses. In 1977, the National Retail Merchants Association (NRMA) adopted a policy statement on consumer affairs. And that statement spells out the changing role of the retailer in the consumer movement:

Traditionally, the retailer was able to provide a high level of satisfaction by concentrating on the quality, variety, and price of goods available for sale. Retailer responsibility in today's world extends beyond this traditional and essential role. The retailer also has a stake in and a responsibility for the protection of the consumer's right to free choice, adequate information in understandable language on which to make informed buying decisions, safety in products sold, and redress for unsatisfactory purchases.

Discussing the consumer movement, consumerism, and the role of government, a former presidential special assistant for consumer affairs stated:

Consumerism is nothing more and nothing less than a challenge to business to live up to its full potential—to give consumers what is promised, to be honest, to give people a product that will work, and that is reasonably safe, to respond effectively to legitimate complaints, to provide information concerning the relevant quality characteristics of a product, to take into consideration the ecological and environmental ramifications of a company decision, and to return to the basic principle upon which so much of our nation's business was structured—"satisfaction guaranteed, or your money back."

Both these quotations, while coming from very different sources, are in general agreement as to the role of the retailer in the consumer movement. The only difference between the two viewpoints, if any, is reflected in the consumer advocate's reference to the "ecological and environmental ramifications of a company decision."

The nature and scope of the consumer movement was described in Chapter 17. In this chapter, you'll gain an understanding of how retailers have responded to the consumer movement. But first, here is how retailers stand in the consumers' eyes.

Consumer Concerns

Although there is much agreement between retailers and consumers about the role of the retailer, this doesn't mean that all retailers always meet their responsibilities. There will always be a few firms that don't.

Unfair Selling Practices

A survey funded by the U.S. government showed that the following selling practices were most frequently identified by consumers as being unfair:

1. Aggressive selling methods
2. Unclear advertising or packaging claims or both
3. Advertised items not available in stores

4. Pressure to pay for repairs or services never received
5. Poor or hard-to-read warranties
6. Overcharging—making customers pay more than necessary
7. Deceptive product demonstrations

On the other hand, in another survey, consumers indicated that banks and department stores do the best job of serving customers. At the bottom of the quality-of-services list are car manufacturers and auto mechanics. So to understand the quality of consumer service, it's necessary to look beyond retailing as a whole, to its various parts.

Need For Personalized Services

Consumers also seem to be indicating a concern about the automation of retailing. For example, a major complaint of consumers is the growing impersonalization of businesses. Consumers feel that some retailers don't treat them as individuals. However, few consumers would trade the advantages of today's retail stores for the Mom-and-Pop stores of the "good old days."

Government programs dealing with the problems of consumers provide impersonal answers to what are often personal problems. Yet it's to government that the consumer will turn if retailers fail to offer solutions to their problems. Only retailers can effectively restore that personal, local touch—no law can.

Retailer Concerns

Most retailers accept their responsibilities for improving consumer welfare. They believe in the slogan "Retailer—Purchasing Agent for the Public." And they defend consumer rights when dealing with manufacturers and other suppliers. However, retailers also have to take on further responsibilities. The NRMA (1977) has also said that:

Devising effective ways to meet rising levels of consumer expectations in the increasingly complex retail marketplace while sustaining an environment of healthy competition, innovation, and economic growth is a major challenge confronting retailers, government, and consumers. . . .

But many retailers are concerned about how they will be able to meet these responsibilities. Their concerns are explained in the following discussion.

Less Productivity

Many retailers believe that there is too much government regulation of business and that this increases the cost of production and therefore the prices of products and services sold. For example, every time a government agency introduces new regulations that companies have to follow (on product safety, job health, or employment practices, for instance) it usually results in less productivity. That is, it takes more time for employees to complete their jobs, which in turn increases the costs of running a business. To cover these increased costs, retailers usually increase the price of products and services. So higher prices represent the "hidden tax" of regulation, which is passed on to the consumer. Retailers object to the increasing amounts of paperwork that many regulations require, which also increases costs. They say that both these costs stimulate inflation.

Auto mechanics have been singled out by consumers as offering poor service. A good estimate and bill form will often prevent complaints.

PARTS	TIRES	BATTERIES	ACCESSORIES			
QTY.	PART NO.	DESCRIPTION	UNIT	ESTIMATED AMOUNT	ACTUAL AMOUNT	
1		Driving & fog light		30 00	29 95	
1	PF-7	Oil filter		4 50	4 75	

REPAIR FACILITY NUMBER: 978D WAIVER SIGNED YES ✓ NO
NAME: MANUEL VELEZ DATE: 7/30/8—
ADDRESS: 173 RED OAK CIRCLE DENVER, CO PHONE: 555-1496
YEAR AND MAKE: '79 BUICK TYPE OF MODEL: SKYLARK MOTOR NO. SERIAL NO.
SPEEDOMETER: 41,900 LICENSE: PJ201 PROMISED: 5:30 PM PHONE WHEN READY ✓ YES ☐ NO

SERVICES TO BE PERFORMED	APPROX. TIME	ESTIMATED AMOUNT	ACTUAL AMOUNT
Replace driving & fog light		2 50	2 50
Lubrication		3 00	3 00
Change oil filter		free	—

TOTAL PARTS: 34 50 34 70

OUTSIDE REPAIRS: NONE

TOTAL OUTSIDE REPAIRS

SIGNATURES OF MECHANICS
REPAIRS PERFORMED BY: 1. Tom McArdle 2.

YOU ARE ENTITLED BY LAW TO THE RETURN OF ALL PARTS REPLACED, EXCEPT THOSE WHICH ARE TOO HEAVY OR LARGE, AND THOSE REQUIRED TO BE SENT BACK TO THE MANUFACTURER OR DISTRIBUTOR BECAUSE OF WARRANT WORK OR AN EXCHANGE AGREEMENT. YOU ARE ENTITLED TO INSPECT THE PARTS WHICH CANNOT BE RETURNED TO YOU.

NOT RESPONSIBLE FOR LOSS OR DAMAGE TO CARS OR ARTICLES LEFT IN CARS IN CASE OF FIRE, THEFT OR ANY OTHER CAUSE BEYOND OUR CONTROL.

AUTHORIZED INCREASE IN ESTIMATE BY: $ APPROVED PER:

x Manuel Velez

GASOLINE, OIL, GREASE	ESTIMATED AMOUNT	ACTUAL AMOUNT			
GALS GAS @					
6 QTS OIL @ 1.50	9 00	9 00	TOTAL LABOR	5 50	5 50
TRANS/DIFF			TOTAL PARTS	34 50	34 70
ATF @			TOTAL GAS, OIL AND GREASE	9 00	9 00
TOTAL	9 00	9 00	OUTSIDE REPAIRS		
— CERTIFICATION —			OTHER		
			SUB-TOTAL	49 00	49 20
			SALES TAX	3 43	3 44
			TOTAL	52 43	52 64

ALL REPAIRS AND PARTS LISTED WERE FURNISHED IN COMPLIANCE WITH MICHIGAN AUTO REPAIR ACT NO. 300 P.A. 1974 AS AMENDED
X SIGNATURE OF MECHANIC

REPAIRS WERE UNABLE TO BE MADE SEE EXPLANATION ABOVE.
X SIGNATURE OF MECHANIC

Growth of Government Control

Many people in both large and small businesses are concerned about the amount and quality of certain federal regulations involving business practices. They know that federal agencies are intended to act as government "watchdogs," their chief purpose being to protect the public by curbing the abuses of business and industry. But today, people question whether that purpose is being met. Many retailers believe that some of the older regulatory programs have outlived their usefulness. And they feel that instead of encouraging competition, the programs only discourage it.

Many business people, including retailers, criticize federal government control from various viewpoints. They say that innovation and entrepreneurship are discouraged by too much regulation and by delays in obtaining permissions and approvals. They claim that federal regulation reduces economic growth by imposing increasingly heavy taxes on businesses and by creating uncertainty about future regulations. And they point to the cost of the extra training that employees must receive in order to comply with government regulations.

So these are some of retailer concerns about being able to meet their increasing responsibilities to consumers. And because of the growing resistance to government regulation, additional ways must be discovered or rediscovered to protect the rights of consumers.

Improving Relationships with Consumers

What better way is there to involve consumers than through the promotion of face-to-face discussions between business and the consumer, with each side listening as well as talking about consumer problems? It's important that this dialog between business people and consumers be conducted in terms that are meaningful and useful to both. Some consumers need more information than they now have about business practices and activities. Others need the opportunity to air their complaints, offer suggestions, and ask questions. Business efforts to increase consumer goodwill should always include the opportunity for business people and consumers to meet.

Personalizing Relationships

Owners and managers of small retail businesses soon know their customers personally. They can greet them as friends, listen to their requests and complaints, and explain their business policies to them personally. In large businesses, employees who come in contact with the public have a similar role to perform. Every time store employees act warmly and courteously to customers, they are personalizing business procedures. Every time workers report customer complaints or unmet needs to management, they are taking a step toward making retailing operations more responsive to the public. Salestraining programs can emphasize that salespeople are usually the only representatives of companies that customers deal with. So salespeople must assume the responsibil-

Efforts to increase consumer goodwill may include the opportunity for consumers to meet retailers and their staffs. *Courtesy of Don's Food Market, Missoula, Montana*

Don's Food Market is happy to support Co-op Ed.

IN

AND SEE

Co-op student Colin Price and the crew at . . .

STOP

DON'S FOOD MARKET
1500 W. Broadway

444

UNIT 18 ◆ Serving the Consumer

ity for making shoppers regular customers of their businesses.

But some large firms need a more direct line of communication between management and the consumer. Some local department stores and retail chains maintain their own advisory panels.

Consumer Rights and Retailers

In Chapter 17, the following consumer rights were described in detail: the right to safety, the right to be informed, the right to choose, and the right to be heard. The National Retail Merchants Association lists the following consumer rights:

♦ To purchase merchandise that will work
♦ To purchase merchandise that is safe
♦ To shop in a store that is honest and ethical
♦ To shop in a store that supplies needed information
♦ To receive exactly the product or service promised
♦ To shop in a store that guarantees satisfaction or refunds money
♦ To be treated courteously

Retailers can respond effectively to the consumer movement by:

1. Being familiar with local, state, and federal legislation affecting consumers and taking appropriate steps to ensure that all employees have the information they need. Consumer-information meetings, bulletins, and letters can help to keep employees informed.
2. Using various types of advertising media and flyers to inform customers of their rights and of company policies and making sure that employees know how to help customers.
3. Offering seminars and sponsoring meetings to help make customers more intelligent consumers by teaching them about their rights and responsibilities.
4. Carefully selecting the products of reliable manufacturers and other vendors and buying only from those firms who will honor their warranties and guarantees.

Consumer Rights and Manufacturers

Manufacturers, too, are responding to consumer needs. Among them are:

♦ The Whirlpool Corporation, which spends $500,000 annually to provide consumer services. Customers can call free of charge 24 hours a day from anywhere in the country to register complaints (right to be heard), ask about services, or get information about products (right to be informed).
♦ The Polaroid Corporation, which maintains a 300-person consumer services department to do such chores as rewriting ads that might mislead buyers and dropping in on Polaroid camera repair centers to check on quality. And—because small stores sometimes evade customer complaints—the department makes sure that Polaroid's free-service phone number is printed in big type on every product.
♦ The Shell Oil Company in Houston, which has circulated 225 million booklets of driving and car-care tips in a "Come to Shell for Answers" campaign. This effort has resulted in more than 200,000 letters from users.
♦ The Pennsylvania Power & Light Company, whose consumer and community affairs department sponsored the country's first utility-consumer conference.

Many manufacturers have also simplified the language in their guarantees and warranties. A warranty, as defined in Chapter 17, is an agreement that the seller will be responsible for any defects in a product and will replace or repair the faulty product. A **guarantee** is an assurance of a product's quality and durability; it promises money back for unsatisfactory merchandise.

Consumer Rights and Trade Associations

The Association of Home Appliance Manufacturers, the Gas Appliance Manufacturers Association, and the National Retail Merchants Association all sponsor the Major Appliance Consumer Action Panel. It is an organization devoted to ensuring that the consumer's right to be heard is recognized. It consists of a group of independent consumer experts voicing consumer views at the highest level of the major appliance industry. MACAP receives comments and complaints from appliance owners, studies industry practices, and advises industry on ways to improve its services to consumers. The organization also reports to consumers and recommends ways to get the best performance from their appliances. Individual complaints are forwarded to a senior executive of the company that manufactured the product involved. Action taken to resolve the complaint is reviewed. If the action taken doesn't satisfy the consumer, MACAP considers specific recommendations to the manufacturer.

The National Business Council for Consumer Affairs has issued guidelines for advertising to better serve and inform the customer. For example, ads should accurately represent the claims made for the product. Price and price comparisons should be clear enough for the average consumer to understand.

The rise of the consumer movement prompted many companies to set up consumer affairs departments. But consumer advocates have long regarded such moves as public relations gimmicks. Now, though, corporate consumer professionals appear to be developing real power. In a growing number of companies, they have influence on functions ranging from product development to marketing campaigns.

Community Programs

Every city or town needs an organization to encourage two-way communication between consumers and the business community. Such an organization provides an ongoing exchange of ideas between those who sell products and services and those who buy them.

Local chambers of commerce can provide an organization to fill this need. As local business people, chamber members have an interest in satisfying the consumers who are, after all, their customers. As concerned citizens, chamber members prefer to see problems solved locally rather than having new laws passed on the state or national level.

Working together, retailers can establish programs to improve their relationships with the community by doing the following:

♦ Using the media—local newspapers, radio, and television—to provide consumers with information about various topics of concern to them, such as how to shop wisely for their various needs, how to manage money, and how to use credit.
♦ Sponsoring economic education classes with various agencies.
♦ Encouraging high schools, middle schools, elementary schools, and community colleges to add economic education programs.
♦ Conducting sales training programs to make their employees more aware of the needs for good consumer relations.
♦ Employing more specialists to work with consumers and teach them the most efficient and economical ways to use their products.
♦ Forming a credit counseling service to aid consumers who have gone too deeply into debt.
♦ But most important of all, retailers can formulate a business code of behavior.

Business Codes of Behavior

Business codes of behavior are standards of conduct—involving such qualities as honesty, loyalty, and fairness—that business people follow. (The term "business code of ethics" is also used, and there is a discussion of ethics in retailing in Chapter 64.)

As mentioned earlier, consumers have complained that some business people act without concern for the welfare of the customer. Experienced retailers, however, realized that the ultimate success of their business depends on satisfying the customer. Fair and honest behavior is important from the business viewpoint as well as from the moral point of view.

Retailers can compare their practices with the following checklist for proper business behavior, which is based on the Business-Consumer Relations Code adopted by the Chamber of Commerce of the United States.

1. Am I producing and selling goods of high quality at the lowest possible price?
2. Are my products as safe as possible? Have I tried to eliminate harmful side effects, including those affecting the environment?
3. Am I actively seeking out the informed views of consumers and other groups about my products and sales techniques to guard against potential complaints and maximize customer satisfaction?
4. Are my warranties and guarantees clear and simple—and are they honored?
5. Am I providing high-quality repairs and services at fair prices?
6. Are all my transactions honest as well as legal?
7. Do my salespeople know both the capabilities and the limitations of the products I sell?
8. Am I providing my customers with objective information about my products and services to help them make sound value comparisons in their buying decisions?
9. Am I supporting programs of consumer education and using other means to inform consumers about the workings of the marketplace?
10. Am I providing fast, effective ways to

Retailers can provide information showing the ways in which they are assisting consumers in making wise purchases. *Courtesy of A&P*

A new kind of shelf tag lets you make accurate price comparisons at a glance!

Comparison measure

Price per unit use to compare prices

The retail price you pay

Brand and name of item

Weight of item

The Unit Price is always on the left hand side of the tag on an orange background

The larger size— 2 lb. jar is the best buy.

UNIT PRICE
YOU PAY
85¢
42.5¢ PER LB 00
ANN PAGE GRAPE JELLY 2 LB
21690 -12

UNIT PRICE
YOU PAY
49¢
65.3¢ PER LB 00
ANN PAGE GRAPE JELLY 12 OZ
21670 -24

UNIT PRICE
YOU PAY
85¢
42.5¢ PER LB 00
ANN PAGE GRAPE JELLY 2 LB
21690 -12

Commodity code

Number of packages per case

Compare on Value
To compare costs of a product in different sizes or brands, just look at the price on the unit price side of the label . . . then compare that unit price against another, checking price per measure, brand to brand, size to size.

Here Are The Unit Price Measures You'll See—
Items sold by WEIGHTS and MEASURES:
Per Ounce, Per Pound, Per Quart
Most grocery items, frozen food.

Items sold by COUNT:
Number on a package such as napkins, paper towels, paper bags.

Items sold by AREA:
Square feet such as foil, food wrap.

REMEMBER, compare only *like* items to determine your best buy. Don't compare raspberry jam with apple jelly, for example. Compare ounces with ounces, quarts with quarts for accurate information. Because there are so many different items from household products, Health & Beauty Aids to food in liquid and solid state, the same unit of measure cannot be used for all.

Price, of course, is only a yardstick. You also should consider: QUALITY, TASTE, PERSONAL PREFERENCE, CONVENIENCE AND SIZE.

At A&P we feel we have a responsibility to give you as much information about the products you buy in our stores as possible. Isn't it nice to know you have all the facts to make the best possible choice.

satisfy legitimate consumer complaints? Am I taking steps to see that the causes of frequent complaints are eliminated?

In this chapter, you've gained an understanding not only of consumer concerns about products and services but also of the concerns that retailers have about dealing with the ever-increasing government regulations that consumerism has brought into being. You've also been given an idea of the ways in which retailers and other business people are attempting to improve their relationships with consumers.

You'll gain a deeper understanding of why retailers are concerned about dealing with government regulations when you read the next chapter in this unit and discover the many types of laws that retailers have to obey. But you'll also be given an idea of why these laws were enacted. And as a future retail worker, you'll not only have to follow your company's policy regarding these laws but also form your own opinions about them.

Trade Talk

Define this term and use it in a sentence.

Guarantee

Can You Answer These?

1. What selling practices are most frequently identified by consumers as being unfair?
2. What is a major consumer complaint against retail businesses?
3. What are the four ways in which business people can improve relationships with consumers?
4. What are two examples of ways in which retailers can improve their relationships with the community?
5. Which of the national Chamber of Commerce suggestions for promoting business–consumer relations do you feel would work best in your community? Why?

Problems

1. Rule a form similar to the following. In the left column, write the letter of each of the following consumer problems: (0) impersonalization, (a) lack of product information, (b) inaccurate or incomplete explanation of product uses, (c) difficulty in obtaining product exchanges or corrections, (d) aggressive selling methods, and (e) advertising items not available in store. In the right column, state one or more ways in which you as an employee can promote better consumer relations by helping to ease the problem

Consumer Problems	How Employees Can Ease the Problem
Example: (0)	Make customer feel welcome in the store.

2. Rule a form similar to the following. In the left column, list any five of the questions (or parts of a question) from the checklist for proper business behavior, given earlier in this chapter. In the right column, give one or more ways in which retailers can show that they are living up to the code.

Checklist Question	Evidence that the Code Is Being Observed
Example: Are warranties and guarantees clear?	Sit down face-to-face with a customer; have him or her read the warranty, and determine if it's understood.

Government and the Retailer

Communications & Human Relations

Economics & Marketing

Merchandising

Selling & Technology

Advertising & Display

Operations & Management

♦ A woman who wanted to start a small dress shop in her house was denied permission to do so because of local zoning laws.

♦ A business was forced to make a large cash settlement to minority employees after investigation by the state Equal Employment Opportunity Commission (EEOC) proved a pattern of discrimination in hiring, firing, and promotion.

♦ A national retail firm was ordered by the Federal Trade Commission (FTC) to stop advertising a washing machine at a very low price. Evidence showed that the company discouraged sales personnel from selling this advertised product and instead urged them to sell higher-priced washers.

♦ A community was declared a disaster area by the president of the United States, making 25 small retail business owners eligible for low-cost loans to reconstruct their businesses, which had been severely damaged by a flood.

These four different cases show the results of legislation on the local, state, and national levels. They are examples of the roles of government in retailing.

Government involvement in retailing either (1) limits or controls retailers or (2) assists retailers. The purpose of legislation is to maintain free competition and protect consumers as well as other citizens.

In Chapters 17 and 55, you read about some of the most important consumer legislation and what the retailer is doing in response to this legislation. In this chapter, you'll learn about some of the other important government legislation that affects retailers at the local, state, and national levels as well as the assistance that the federal government offers retailers.

Why Government Involvement?

Years ago, our unrestricted free-enterprise system allowed large manufacturers, wholesalers, and retailers to almost put a stop to competition. Businesses were able to get unfair prices on the goods and services they produced and at times they sold products that were unsafe for consumers. Eventually, legislators at various government levels were persuaded to try to pass a series of laws on business practices.

These government laws both assist and control business. So a knowledge of existing government legislation is an important part of any retailer's education. Government laws and legislation affect business location and operation, retail prices, advertising, competition, products and services offered, and the channels of distribution.

Local Government Involvement

Many county, city, and township governments are concerned with making sure that all retailers follow proper business practices. One way governments do this is by issuing business licenses. Other methods governments use include enforcing zoning and building laws and imposing restrictions on direct-to-the-home and on-the-street selling.

Licenses

The **business license,** which is required by many communities, is legal or official permission to operate a business. It is an effective method of local regulation because it can be taken back if the business does not meet the standards of operation that the community requires.

Local officials usually require companies to obtain a license if their business is one that affects the health and well-being of consumers. Examples are restaurants, barber shops, beauty shops, health and reducing studios, and liquor stores. Usually, these types of businesses must pass periodic inspections, and sometimes they are restricted to certain days and hours of operation.

Zoning and Building Laws

Other local ordinances that concern the retailer are zoning and building laws. **Zoning laws** restrict the type of business that may be operated on a particular piece of property or in an area. Such laws may prevent retailers from locating their business on a site they have chosen. So retailers should always check with their local zoning board before deciding where to locate their places of business. Zoning laws also protect individuals located in residential areas from having undesirable commercial firms within the area.

Building ordinances are requirements for the construction or remodeling of buildings. In most communities, a building must meet certain construction standards in such areas as plumbing, electricity, and fireproofing. A building permit

In some places, a restaurant must meet certain standards to qualify for a business license. Courtesy of city of Hartford, Connecticut, Health Department and Bureau of Licenses and Permits

FOOD LICENSE APPROVED BY

NOT TRANSFERABLE

HARTFORD HEALTH DEPARTMENT

DATE ____ APRIL 1, __

TO ____ VISONE'S RESTAURANT ____ (Joseph Visone)

BUSINESS OF ____ RESTAURANT

AT ____ 80 COVENTRY STREET ____ ., HARTFORD, CONN.

REVOKABLE AT ANY TIME

BUREAU OF LICENSES AND PERMITS

M.D., Director of Health

AUTHORIZED DEPUTY OF CHIEF INSPECTOR

EXPIRES

MARCH 31

19--

MUST BE DISPLAYED IN A PROMINENT PLACE

will not be granted if the building plan doesn't meet these standards, which are designed to ensure consumer safety.

Direct-to-the-Home Selling Restrictions

In many localities, retailers who use direct-to-the-home salespeople have to obey additional regulations. Some communities require licenses for such salespeople; others have **Green River ordinances,** which are laws that prohibit salespeople from entering premises without the prior consent of the occupant. Such licensing is intended to protect residents from door-to-door salespeople who practice deceptive selling techniques.

State Government Involvement

State governments have, over the years, passed various types of laws that have affected retailers. Examples of the state legislative efforts include involvement in areas such as sales taxes, unfair trade practices, fraud and usury laws, and licenses and charters.

Sales Taxes

State governments and sometimes local governments use retail sales as a source of tax revenue. In fact, by collecting sales taxes, retailers in some states collect more than half of all the revenues for their state. In some states, local sales taxes are added to the state sales tax. Retailers must collect both these taxes from customers and are accountable to the state and local governments.

Some states try to attract business by lowering their taxes, or they try to keep certain kinds of business out of their territory by raising taxes. State retail sales taxes may also make it difficult for retailers in areas bordering another state to compete with neighboring merchants across the state line. This is especially true if the adjoining state has a lower sales tax on prod-

ucts such as gasoline, food, medicine, liquor, and cigarettes.

Unfair Trade Practices

A wide variety of unfair trade practice legislation has been passed at various times. However, some of the laws are not enforced effectively. The most common unfair trade practice acts now in force are related to minimum markup. These laws, which are in effect in 32 states, require retailers to maintain a stated markup of 6 to 12 percent over their cost price. However, retailers are allowed to lower such markups to meet competition or to close out discontinued or damaged goods. Most of these laws are not strictly enforced, but they must still be considered by retailers.

Most states also have laws to control false and misleading advertising. These laws vary greatly from state to state, but they all make it illegal for advertisers to deceive the consumer. Some states also have **blue laws,** which prohibit the selling of certain types of products, such as alcoholic beverages, on Sunday.

Fraud and Usury

Most states have laws against fraud and usury. **Fraud** is an act of deceit by which someone seeks to gain some unfair or dishonest advantage. **Usury** is the charging of interest in excess of a legal rate. Laws against both fraud and usury have been in existence for many years, and emphasis on enforcing them more effectively has increased.

Licenses and Charters

Some states require certain businesses to be licensed. Among the retailers who have to obtain licenses are real estate agents, barber shop and beauty shop operators, motor vehicle dealers, funeral directors, and pharmacists.

States also regulate the right of entry into certain businesses. For example, banks, insurance companies, and telephone, gas, and electric companies must be chartered by the state. A **charter** is a written document granting the right of organization and other privileges and specifying the form of organization and operation. In most states, the purposes for which these businesses may be formed are limited, and the period of residence of the incorporators and the amount of capital required are specified by law.

Federal Government Control

In response to consumer demand, the federal government has established regulations to control various types of business activities. These services are partially paid for by business itself through taxes. The federal taxes retailers pay include the following: individual income tax, corporate income tax, employment taxes, unemployment insurance, social security payments, and taxes on luxury goods such as jewelry, furs, and luggage. The tax on luxury goods is usually referred to as an excise tax.

Fair Competition

At the close of the nineteenth century, small businesses were threatened by the unfair business practices of large corporations. There were complaints that corporations were seeking a monopoly of trade. (A **monopoly** is the control of the supply of a product or service by one person or group of people.) In response to these complaints, the federal government passed the Sherman Antitrust Act in 1890 and the Clayton Act in 1914. The Clayton Act was passed in an attempt to curb efforts of large organizations to drive smaller ones out of business.

Federal Trade Commission (FTC). In 1914, the Federal Trade Commission Act was passed to set up the legal structure for enforcing the Sherman Act, the Clayton Act, and similar legislation. Retailers can be found guilty of restricting trade if they perform any of the following:

1. Pressuring manufacturers not to sell to competitive retailers
2. Buying out other retail firms to substantially reduce competition
3. Agreeing with other retailers to fix the prices of goods they sell for the purpose of restricting price competition
4. Underselling retailers in one area of the country, for the purpose of forcing competitors out of business, and at the same time selling the same products at higher prices in other parts of the country

Robinson-Patman Act. Another federal law that is of major importance to retailers is the Robinson-Patman Act of 1936. This act was intended to curb the price advantages enjoyed by large retailers. It specifically prohibits manufacturers from giving and retailers from taking the following:

1. Discounts for purchases unless they are justified by a reduction in costs or expenses for the product
2. Discounts in the form of agents' or brokers' fees, unless these are available to all buyers
3. Unequal advertising, display, sales assistance, and other promotional allowances

The Robinson-Patman Act does not make all price differences illegal. For example, it is legal for one retailer to be charged a lower price than another for the same product if the manufacturer can prove that it costs less to sell it to the first retailer. Also, discounts are legal for such practices as prompt payment and buying in large quantity, and it is usually the large retailer who can take advantage of such discounts.

Employee Welfare

The federal government is playing an increasingly important role in supervising the welfare of employees. There are many employee welfare regulations designed to protect or benefit workers, and they all affect the way retailers run their businesses.

Fair Labor Standards Act. The Fair Labor Standards Act of 1938 established a min-

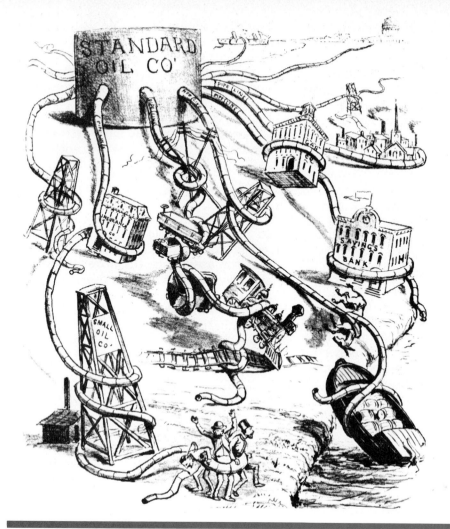

Before the Sherman Anti-Trust Act of 1890, monopolies were driving small companies out of business as this historical cartoon shows. *Courtesy of the Granger Collection*

imum wage, maximum hours, the principle of equal pay for equal work, and child labor laws.

The child labor section of the act states that 14- and 15-year-olds may work in a number of jobs in retailing. They may do clerical, cashiering, or sales work. They may pack and carry orders. They may work in a kitchen, do cleanup work, pump gasoline, and clean and polish cars. But they may only work at certain times if they are employed in a business subject to federal labor laws. In addition they must

obtain a proof-of-age certificate which is sometimes called a worker's permit.

Occupational Safety and Health Act (OSHA).
The Occupational Safety and Health Act of 1970 requires all employers to provide their employees with a safe place in which to work. The act specifies certain safety and health standards which employers must obey. For example, aisles and passageways must be kept clear and in good repair, with no obstructions that could create a hazard. Retail employers should

also eliminate slippery floors, poorly lighted stairways, torn or unanchored floor coverings, and loose wires. The Department of Labor periodically inspects businesses to see that these rules are followed. Violations can be punished by fines and imprisonment.

Social Security Act.　Social security is a federal government program set up under the Social Security Act of 1935. It provides cash payments and hospital care to retired or disabled workers and their dependents. The benefits are paid for by a tax based on the worker's salary. Employer and employee each pay half the tax. Anyone who is engaged in a business must make allowances for the expense of providing these and similar benefits for employees.

Employee Retirement Income Security Act. This act was passed in 1975 to establish guidelines for starting and administering employee retirement funds or pensions. The purpose of the legislation is to ensure that when employees retire, their pension funds will be available to fulfill the contractual retirement agreement.

Wagner Act.　The Wagner Act of 1935, also known as the National Labor Relations Act, guarantees the rights of workers to organize unions, bargain with employers, and choose which unions to join. It outlaws such unfair employer labor practices as penalizing workers for belonging to unions and closing or threatening to close firms if employees join a union.

Taft-Hartley Act.　The Taft-Hartley Act of 1947 modified the Wagner Act by enabling states to adopt right-to-work laws. A right-to-work law is a law under which union membership is not required for employment. This means that in states where right-to-work laws have been passed, neither labor nor management can require an individual to join a union as a condition of employment.

Civil Rights Act.　The Fair Employment Practices section of the Civil Rights Act of 1964 makes it illegal for employers to refuse to hire or promote employees because of their race, color, religion, sex, or national origin. It also outlaws segregation of workers on these grounds. The Fair Employment Practices Law is enforced by the Equal Employment Opportunity Commission.

Federal Government Assistance

So much emphasis is usually placed on federal control and regulation of business that the assistance the government provides to business is often overlooked. Retailing, like any other kind of business, may receive various direct and indirect benefits from the federal government. Some direct benefits are the availability of helpful information through federal bulletins, consultation services, and the training sessions described below. Indirectly, retailers receive the benefits of federally aided state and local programs such as marketing and distributive education. The federal government has become involved in helping small retailers because many of them fail; a little assistance at the right time can make the difference between success and failure.

Small Business Administration

The U.S. Small Business Administration (SBA) provides small businesses with financial, managerial, and technical aid and advice.

The SBA will assist a small retailer in obtaining low-interest financing for construction, expansion, the purchase of new equipment, or the running of the business if their loan requests have been turned down by two lending institutions. The amount involved is usually small, but some SBA loans are very large. The current emphasis is on helping women and minority groups start retail businesses.

The SBA has field offices in major cities

throughout the country. Its staff sponsors conferences and counsels retailers on management problems. The agency publishes a wide variety of bulletins, reports, and pamphlets of value to retailers. Some of the publications are available free from the SBA regional offices, while others can be obtained from the U.S. Government Printing Office in Washington, D.C., for a small charge. The series entitled *Small Marketers Aids* is particularly helpful to retailers; each volume in it contains a discussion of a topic by a specialist in a given area.

Department of Commerce

The U.S. Department of Commerce promotes domestic and foreign commerce. It's also the largest fact-finding organization in the world. Two of its branches, the Office of Field Services (OFS) and the Bureau of the Census, gather information that can be helpful to the retailer.

The OFS maintains three field offices located in major cities. Each office maintains a library of current business publications and is equipped to advise and assist retailers in its own locality. These offices process more than a million inquiries a year and cooperate with local business groups in developing new opportunities for private enterprise.

Can you think of a recent example of local, state, or federal government getting involved in retailing businesses where you live? What was the issue? The outcome? Did the government act to protect consumers or retail businesses or to assist businesses? Read your local newspapers to get an idea of how government does all these things in the town or city in which you live.

Also, by now you should have realized something else. Even though you're planning to be a retail worker, you may not agree with some of the retailer concerns you read about in Chapter 55 and learned more about in this chapter. As a retail employee, you'll probably think that the costs of such health and employment programs are things your employer must be responsible for, no matter what the cost. But as a retail worker planning to start your own business someday—which would, of course, make you an employer—what do you think your obligations would be? Think about the information you've been given from both points of view.

Trade Talk

Define each term and use it in a sentence.

Blue laws	Green River
Building ordinances	ordinances
Business license	Monopoly
Charter	Usury
Fraud	Zoning laws

Can You Answer These?

1. How does government legislation affect retailing?
2. How are local governments involved in retailing?
3. How does fraud differ from usury?
4. Can a group of retailers who agree to sell products at a predetermined price be found guilty of restricting trade? Why? Why not?
5. How can the SBA help retailers?

Problems

1. Rule a form similar to the following. In the left column, write the letter of each of the following kinds of businesses that are required by law to be licensed: (*a*) real estate agencies, (*b*) banks, (*c*) insurance companies, (*d*) funeral homes, (*e*) barber shops, (*f*) restaurants, and (*g*) drugstores. In the right column, give at least two reasons why you think government regulations have been imposed on these businesses.

Kind of Business	Reasons for Government Regulations

Marketing Research in Retailing

Communications & Human Relations

Economics & Marketing

Merchandising

Selling & Technology

Advertising & Display

Operations & Management

Manager: Why do you have those new ski gloves marked to sell for $27? Haven't we been selling them for $24.95?

Buyer: They're a good value, and most customers won't know that they were ever sold for less.

Manager: Why not sell them for the lower price? Won't we sell more?

Buyer: I doubt it; the customer who buys a pair of these gloves has enough money so that the price difference won't mean that much.

Who is right? And what could the manager and the buyer do to determine which of them is right? Could they study the past sales record of differently priced ski gloves? Could they find out the income class of their customers by studying credit records? Could they try out both prices to see which yields the greater profit? Could they visit competitors to find what price they are charging for the ski gloves and at what price the gloves sell best for the competitors? Yes, the manager and buyer could do a number of different things to find out who is correct. In fact, you've probably thought of some ideas that they could try—such as watching customers and then asking those who did buy as well as those who didn't if the price affected their decision. Or, at different times, they might run two advertisements for the gloves, one at each price, and then compare the number of customers who responded to each advertisement. All these are examples of marketing research activities that retailers can perform to help them make accurate marketing decisions.

As defined in Chapter 16, marketing research is the gathering, recording, and analyzing of facts relating to the sale of products and services to consumers. Some retailers have tended to look upon marketing research as something they cannot afford to pay for and could not possibly do themselves. However, marketing research can often be of major assistance to retailers by taking much of the "guesswork" out of making decisions.

Why Use Marketing Research?

Retailers conduct marketing research to obtain information on which to base objective and accurate decisions. They also conduct research to find answers to such questions as: How is the firm doing? What new or different things should the firm be doing? Is something wrong? What? Why? What are the best solutions to the problem?

A study conducted by the American Marketing Association showed that more than half the retailers involved in the study were engaged in the following seven types of research activities:

♦ *Forecasting sales*—How much will a firm make in sales during the following year?

What will customer traffic be like in 2 years?

- *Measuring market potential*—What is the potential for sales in various departments and in geographic areas?
- *Determining the characteristics of a market*—What are the customers like in terms of age, income, occupation, and geographic location, and what kinds and types of firms are competing for their purchases?
- *Analyzing market size*—What is the total sales potential for a product?
- *Making sales analyses*—What kinds of products or services are being purchased in which locations by what kinds of customers because of what types of promotion?
- *Making location analyses*—Is a firm in a good location? Or, if a new location is to be added, where should it be located?
- *Conducting product-mix studies*—Is the quality of a product or service adequate? Is a product packaged properly? Is a brand recognized and approved? What kinds of services should be provided?

Although marketing research is constantly used to solve problems, it is preferable to have answers ready before a problem arises. **Opportunity research** is marketing research that examines what is now being done and tries to determine new and better ways of doing things. Opportunity research can establish guidelines or standards to warn of possible trouble spots. Retailers work to develop control systems that will warn them automatically when something is not going the way it should. This is similar to the way in which drivers watch the oil level of their cars, even when their cars are functioning normally.

Who Does Marketing Research?

Research activities may be performed by retailers themselves, by their employees, or by outside agencies. Today, large and small retailers are spending more time, money, and effort on research than was dreamed of only a few years ago. Much of the research is simple and quite informal.

Retailers in small firms are particularly interested in research that will provide the information needed for making decisions that lead to improved sales and higher profits. For example, the data gathered on sales records may be used as a part of the research. Employees who do recordkeeping, who work with personnel, who serve customers, who deal with suppliers, or who promote products or services all have an opportunity to provide or gather information that will become source data for marketing research. Many retailers rely on stock-control records, customers' complaints and suggestions, records showing reasons for returned goods, and customer service and credit records to improve their merchandise, service, and customer communications.

In large retailing organizations, a department may be established to plan, coordinate, and conduct various types of research activities.

Also, large retail firms are increasing their research on customer attitudes regarding products, services, prices, advertising, and business hours. These firms are particularly anxious to maintain a good public image. The large retail firms also conduct research to determine the ideal locations for new businesses. For example, they take counts of pedestrian and automobile traffic and carefully analyze where people are and will be living. They use information obtained from shopping surveys to select locations for new businesses and to make a number of other decisions.

Progressive retailers of all sizes conduct studies to determine where to locate departments within their businesses and where to place products within the departments. They test various pricing plans, display methods, and advertising techniques to find those that will cause sales and profits to increase. For example, one retailer conducted a study to determine the productivity of salespeople in large and small department stores.

Sources of Research Data

Two major types of data are extremely valuable for marketing researchers—primary data and secondary data. **Primary data** are the original facts that researchers collect. For example, say Mike Pizzaro, owner of a TV business, wanted to know how many people in a particular community were planning to purchase color television sets during the next 3 years. To get this information, he would probably have to conduct his own study. However, before researchers invest time and money on a new study, they usually check to determine whether their questions can be answered by secondary data. **Secondary data** are facts that have already been gathered for other purposes. For example, suppose researchers wanted to know how many people lived in a particular community in 1960, 1970, and 1980. They would look up the information in the *Census of Population,* a report prepared by the U.S. Bureau of the Census, which constitutes secondary data.

Secondary Data

There are two types of secondary data: internal data and external data. **Internal data** are facts, figures, and other information available within the firm, business or industry that a researcher is investigating. There is almost no limit to the types of internal data available. Some of the most common types are salespeople's reports, invoices, records of shipments, statements, and all types of budget reports.

Many firms are starting to use computerized inventory-control systems to store their internal data. When managers and other employees need information on which to base decisions, they can quickly get it from the firm's system.

For example, suppose you are the buyer

Some retailers use computerized inventory-control systems to store their internal data. Courtesy of IBM Corporation

for a department store and you must decide which merchandise should be ordered for the coming season. You have to determine what styles of merchandise should be ordered, how much of each style will be needed, and whether some product lines should be expanded while others are eliminated. You have a great responsibility. Your decisions will be extremely important to the success of the store, for the store needs enough merchandise to meet customers' needs through the entire season. If you order too much, the store will be forced to run a clearance sale at the end of the season to move the unsold items. By consulting internal data, you can make wise and accurate decisions.

A computer has an almost unlimited capacity for aiding retail managers. It can provide not only accurate inventory-control records on stock counts but also information on employee theft, the effectiveness of displays, fashion trends, and so on. More and more, inventory-control systems are being used in making decisions about expanding a product line, identifying potential problem areas, and determining which merchandise should be placed on sale. No matter what a researcher's problem, one very important source of internal data is the firm's inventory-control system.

External data are facts, figures, and other information taken from sources outside a firm or an industry. Examples of external data classifications are:

◆ **Census data**—information collected by the U.S. Bureau of the Census
◆ **Registration data**—information collected and reported regularly through legal requirements or legislative procedure
◆ Project reports published in books, encyclopedias, bulletins, monographs, periodicals, and newsletters
◆ **Commercial data**—information collected

and sold on a subscription basis by companies such as A. C. Nielsen and the Market Research Corporation of America

Primary Data

When retailers cannot find out what they want to know from existing information, they gather their own data. The way they do this depends upon such factors as the information needed and the objectivity and precision required. Often, retailers may know the best method for obtaining the information they need, but they must also consider the time, money, personnel, and facilities available for gathering the information. Taking into account their research objectives and the resources available, retailers may chose one or a combination of three basic methods of gathering primary data: by survey, by observation, and by experimentation.

Some retailers hire firms to provide external data, such as this store audit conducted by the A. C. Nielson Co. Courtesy of A. C. Nielson Co.

The Survey Method. The process of gathering data using a variety of methods such as personal interview, mail questionnaire, and telephone interview is known as the **survey method.** A **sample,** which is a limited number selected from a large group, is drawn when it is not economical to survey the total population. The sample chosen is expected to represent the viewpoints of the total population. The surveys with which many people in the United States are most familiar are the public opinion polls that attempt to predict the outcome of presidential elections. These polls show the usefulness of the survey method for learning people's beliefs, opinions, and personal tastes. Personal interviews, telephone surveys, and mailed questionnaires are three basic techniques used in the survey method for gathering data.

◆ Personal interviewing, though not always practical, is usually the best way to conduct a survey. Collecting information through the personal interview technique allows retailers an opportunity to ask consumers questions while they are in the store and when their thoughts about the business are fresh in mind. Another advantage is that interviewers can ask follow-up questions relating to the consumers' responses to earlier questions. In this way, therefore, it is possible to obtain information that is precise and complete.

One of the most widely used applications of the personal interview technique is the "walkout" study. With this technique, every person leaving the business without a purchase is interviewed about why he or she didn't buy anything.

Another way to get the direct opinions of customers is to establish a consumer panel. A **consumer panel** consists of a selected group of customers who work with the business's management and buyers in helping to make product and service selections. The panel may be a small group that is representative of the firms customers, or it may be a special group, such as teenagers or college students.

Another application of the interview technique is the **shopping-list study.** With this technique, the customer's shopping list is compared with actual purchases. The purchases that were not on the shopping list are studied to find out whether the customer who bought them was influenced by displays and other business motivators. This technique is used a great deal by food stores to measure purchases made on impulse.

◆ **Telephone surveys** can usually be handled less expensively and in a shorter period of time than either personal interviews or mailed questionnaires. As with personal interviews, it is possible to obtain consumer responses on the spot. Because of the relatively low cost of telephoning and the relative ease of administering such a survey, this technique is being used more and more. But a telephone survey may be inaccurate. It is difficult to get a representative sample of the population because some people do not have telephones or have unlisted numbers, while others may refuse to cooperate with survey interviews.

◆ The mailed questionnaire would be an excellent technique of gathering information if respondents would always cooperate fully. Typically, though, only 10 percent of the people surveyed cooperate. An advantage to such questionnaires, however, is that respondents can carefully think through their answers. Also, respondents need not be concerned with impressing the interviewer, so their answers may be more objective. On the other hand, conversation may clarify questions and answers that mailed questionnaires don't. This factor, combined with increased mailing costs and a lack of cooperation that makes the results of mail surveys questionable, has led to a greatly diminished use of the mail-survey technique.

Mail surveys have yielded excellent returns for retailers who immediately follow up services such as delivery, appliance repairs, and carpet cleaning with postcards containing a few key questions.

These brief mailed questionnaires help retailers to keep a constant record of the treatment of their customers and the quality of their service.

The Observation Method. The observation method of obtaining primary data is probably one of the oldest known research methods. For thousands of years, people have been observing others and drawing conclusions from what they see. Small retailers have counted on this method extensively in training their personnel, in determining what they should do to improve their business, and in determining their customer wants.

Creative researchers can think of many methods to use in observing people. Many retailers subscribe to shopping services to determine the effectiveness of their salespeople. With this method, unknown shoppers come into the business, are waited on by the salesperson, make a purchase, pay for the purchase, and leave the store with the purchase. After the shoppers leave the business, they record the salesperson's behavior and any other information they may have been instructed to observe. Retailers use the information received to improve the effectiveness of their salespeople.

Trained interviewers often use observation in combination with personal interviews. Observations of consumer behavior during the interview can be recorded on interviewers' reports, along with answers to the questions asked.

Experimentation. Experimentation is a useful method when retailers want to learn about cause and effect. It is especially useful if they want to test something new, such as a display, a price, a promotional plan, a product, a business layout, or shopping hours. Experimentation has an advantage over observation—experimentation can be conducted under controlled conditions, whereas observation cannot. This enables researchers to identify the reasons for behavior. For example, retail-

ers can observe the number of people who buy a product at a certain price, but they cannot determine whether price is an important reason for buying the product. If they experiment and raise the price while keeping constant other factors such as placement of the product in the business, amount of advertising, and assortment of sizes and colors, they can find out whether a change in price influences the sale of the product.

Because experimentation usually takes place without consultation with the subjects, it is possible to find out what people's true reactions are. For example, if customers are asked whether they are willing to pay a certain price for a new product, they might say yes or no. But if they were to see the product in the business at that price, they might act differently.

There are a number of disadvantages to the experimental method, however. The major problem is that of controlling the conditions affecting the experiment. Some variable factors—such as competition, economic conditions, laws, political conditions, and cultural and social environment—cannot be controlled by researchers. Also, a well-planned experiment may require more time or money than the average retailer has available. The tests and the analysis of the results may take several months. But time is an important factor in retailing, especially when competitors are doing things rapidly. The costs of a retailer's experiment include both the costs of planning and administering the experiment and the costs of the retailing activity being tested.

Putting Data to Work

Once data have been collected, whether primary or secondary sources or both are used, the information must be organized, analyzed, and put to use. No matter how elaborate or simple the project is, the data must be accurate, precise, and easy to understand. For example, a written questionnaire might include a question like the one shown below:

1. Why did you shop in this store for a dishwasher?
   a. Saw newspaper advertisement _____
   b. Advised by a friend _____
   c. Regular customer _____
   d. Other (specify) _____

Researchers may tabulate hundreds of answers to this question—along with other answers in the survey—and may organize the information in tables, charts, and graphs. The responses or observations of the subjects are tallied according to such categories as "shopped in this store because saw newspaper ad" and "regular customer." Then the researchers can calculate the percentage of the sample population that fits into each category.

Once the facts have been assembled, they can be compared and conclusions can be drawn. For example, the owner of an appliance store may check sales figures before and after advertising a dishwasher in the newspaper. The two sets of sales figures do not reveal very much information individually. But when retailers compare them, they can draw conclusions about the effect of their ads on their sales

The analysis or interpretation of data is the basis for decision making, and the purpose of research is, after all, to provide information to guide retailers' actions.

Now that you've finished this unit, what do you think about the retailer's role in serving consumers? What opinions have you formed about consumer concerns, retailer concerns, government regulations in retailing, and the amount of research retailers have to do to satisfy consumer needs and wants? A clear understanding of all these subjects will help you to be not only a successful retail worker but also one who makes things happen!

Trade Talk

Define each term and use it in a sentence.

Census data
Commercial data
Consumer panel
External data
Internal data
Opportunity
  research

Primary data
Registration data
Sample
Secondary data
Shopping list study
Survey method
Telephone surveys

Can You Answer These?

1. Why should retailers try to carry out opportunity research?
2. Name two sources of secondary data.
3. When does a retailer usually gather primary data?
4. Why aren't mailed questionnaries used more frequently?
5. What is the major advantage of experimentation as a method of gathering primary data?

Problems

1. On a separate sheet of paper, list the letter of each of the following pieces of merchandise: (a) stereo, (b) refrigerator, (c) reading lamp for bedroom, (d) sweater, and (e) tennis racket. Then write a paragraph indicating for each item whether you would use a telephone survey, questionnaire, personal interview, or observation as a research method to determine customer satisfaction. Indicate the reason for your choice.

2. Rule a form similar to the following. In the left column, write the letter of each of the following topics: (a) changing the driving habits of shoppers, (b) credit-card usage, (c) customer complaints, (d) impact of displays on sales of coats, and (e) breakage in shipping. In the right column, list the kinds of information that could be gained by conducting research on these topics.

Topic	Information to Be Gained

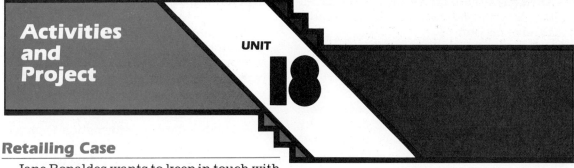

Retailing Case

Jane Ronaldes wants to keep in touch with new developments in the marketing of laundry services and is a firm believer in using facts, not guesswork. Jane realizes that many chages have occurred in the family laundry market during the past 10 years, and she wants to get a current picture of what the market is like. After talking with several business associates and consulting her local laundry association, she found that a survey of the use of family laundry services had recently been published. After reading this survey, she was confronted with the task of interpreting its results.

The survey was based on 500 telephone interviews. The people interviewed were carefully selected to represent a typical cross section of families in the United States. The survey questions and the results obtained are shown in the following table.

TODAY'S FAMILY LAUNDRY MARKET

Of the Families Interviewed, How Many Use a Commercial Laundry?	Percentage
Send all regular family wash to the laundry	10
Send all laundry part of time	15
Used to send wash to laundry, but no longer	30
Have never used laundry service	45
Total	100

What Kind of Service Is Used?	Percentage of Regular Customers	Percentage of Infrequent Customers
All finished	47	56
Damp wash (flatwork ironed)	24	9
Damp wash	10	7
Shirts only	10	18
Fluff dry	7	6
Other	2	4

How Frequently Is Wash Sent to the Laundry?	Percentage of Regular Customers	Percentage of Infrequent Customers
Every week	52	28
Every 2 weeks	41	57
Every 3 weeks	4	3
Every month	3	5
No regular time	0	7

Interpret the facts by preparing a one-page written report describing today's laundry market.

Working with People

Ruth is a marketing and distributive education student employed in the cosmetic department of a store. The department manager is keeping a record of the sales of certain products and has promised to pay each salesperson a commission for selling the products. Ruth notices that her supervisor, Michael Reilly, often writes down the sale of a product after completing a sale at the cash register, even though he did not actually sell one of the "commission products." What should Ruth do?

1. Identify the true problem.
2. What are the important facts to be considered in the problem?
3. List several possible solutions to this problem.
4. Evaluate the possible results of each solution.
5. Which solution do you recommend? Why?

Project 18: Researching a Retailing Problem

Your Project Goal

Given a problem in retailing to be researched, prepare a survey questionnaire, collect data, tabulate your findings, and make recommendations to help solve the problem.

Procedure

Assume that your employer is considering running advertisements in your school paper and she wants to know what to advertise. She has asked you to find out the percentage of teenagers in your high school who shop in a store of the type she runs. She also wants you to find out what products and services they buy. Follow the seven steps outlined below:

1. Decide what data or information to obtain from the students in your high school.
2. Decide what type of survey technique should be used: personal interview, telephone survey, or mail survey.
3. Decide what questions should be asked, and prepare these questions carefully so that they will produce the information needed.
4. Prepare a questionnaire, using good layout techniques, and duplicate the necessary copies.
5. Select 20 students in your school who you feel are typical teenagers and secure their cooperation in providing answers to your questionnaire.
6. Tabulate the results.
7. Prepare a report for your employer containing your recommendations. Include your opinion of whether or not you think she should advertise in the school newspaper. If you recommend that she advertise, specify what goods or services she should mention in her ad.

Evaluation

You will be evaluated on how effectively you can gather data through questionnaires and on the quality of your recommendations.

Developing Pricing Policies

CHAPTER

58

Communications & Human Relations

Economics & Marketing

Merchandising

Selling & Technology

Advertising & Display

Operations & Management

Caroline Cellini is in a difficult situation. She's opening a new arts and crafts shop in a restored downtown area. Several of the merchandise lines are unique, as they include paintings and craft work produced by local artists. Caroline wonders what prices she should assign these items. Because the store is relatively unknown in the area, she's concerned that if she sets the prices too high, she won't attract enough customers. Yet if she sets the prices too low, her sales revenues won't be adequate to meet expenses and realize a profit for the shop.

Caroline decided to consult Mrs. Janick, an experienced arts and crafts retailer. She believed that Mrs. Janick could offer good advice regarding the factors to consider when setting pricing goals and policies.

Mrs. Janick began the meeting with Caroline by suggesting that she first consider the meaning of the term **selling price** from both the customer's and the retailer's

points of view. "The selling price for the customer," Mrs. Janick said, "is the amount of money needed to acquire a particular product or service. Conversely, the selling price for the retailer is the amount of money needed to pay the cost of merchandise and related expenses as well as to realize a reasonable profit. Many conditions, goals, policies, and laws affect both the customer and the retailer with regard to pricing."

This chapter focuses upon the factors that Caroline and other retailers consider when making pricing decisions.

Analyzing Factors Affecting Price Decisions

Caroline, like other retailers, faces the problem of how high or low to set prices.

When retailers set the price of a particular product or service, they usually consider these factors: (1) competition, (2) customer reaction, (3) supply and demand, (4) possible future markdowns, and (5) laws regarding pricing.

In the case of goods that are always kept in stock, these factors don't change very often—and when they do, the changes are seldom radical. So for such well-stocked items, pricing can often be a relatively automatic process. In other merchandise categories, however, the factors can change often. Each change can mean a large difference in what the price should be.

Considering Competition

How far above cost should prices be set? A specific price level will be influenced by competition. Perhaps a retailer's plan is to sell below competition to capture the largest possible share of the market. But there's a delicate balance involved in selling below competition. For example, will the increased number of units sold result in enough additional profit to warrant cutting prices? And will a lower price give the products an unfavorable image? Some firms keep close track of the prices of their competitors so that goods can be advertised to "sell for less." These are the stores that advertise that they "will not be undersold."

When pricing merchandise, retailers must consider the prices that are being charged for the same products by competing firms. A rule of thumb is that retailers should not charge more for a product than is charged by retailers offering similar services. Only when a firm offers extra services, such as free delivery or a liberal return policy, will a higher price seem more acceptable to its customers.

Anticipating Customer Reaction

How will customers react to prices that are higher than those of the competition? Will they recognize the advantages of a product and pay a premium price? Can they be persuaded by salespeople that the product is worth a little more? What if the product is no better than that offered by competition? Or what if there are no significant advantages either in the merchandise or in the service, delivery, or credit terms offered? In this case, how large a price discount will be necessary to attract customers away from competition? How much will it cost to tell the market that this comparable product is offered for a lower price? If prices are raised or lowered, retailers often have to figure on extra promotion costs either to overcome customer reluctance to pay the higher price or to inform the customer of possible savings.

Considering Supply and Demand

When the demand for products and services is greater than the supply, retailers can charge higher prices. But when the supply exceeds the demand, prices should be set low. For example, when seasonal fruits and vegetables first reach the market in the spring, supply is low and people will pay higher prices. But as the year advances and more new produce appears on the market, the price has to be lowered. Sometimes retailers experiment with new products by offering them at introductory discounts. Then, if the demand justifies reordering additional merchandise, they will often set the price at the regular levels.

Planning Possible Future Markdowns

Retailers seldom expect to sell an entire stock of a product at full price. Some items spoil, get damaged, become soiled, or go out of fashion; they must either be discarded or sold at a reduced price. Other items with a fashion appeal or a seasonal appeal have a limited period of popularity. Stock still in the store at the end of that demand period needs to be marked down if it's to be sold. Perishable goods—such as fresh meat, vegetables, and bakery products—are subject to both aging and spoilage. Products that are beyond their

When supply is abundant, people expect to pay lower prices than when supply is scarce. *Grant Heilman*

peak of freshness can sometimes be sold at a reduced price, but spoiled goods have to be discarded.

Retailers may offer three types of price reductions. Using the terminology suggested by the National Retail Merchants Association, these are as follows:

1. A **sale** is an offer of goods at a lower price than the retailer normally charges. Sales may run for a limited time, after which the items return to their higher prices. If the sale is not limited in time, the item should be marked to show that the price was "formerly" or "originally" charged. The use of these terms tells the customer that the items will not be returned to the higher price.
2. A **clearance** is a sale that a retailer uses to remove leftover items from the selling floor. Clearance items are not returned to their former prices.
3. A **special purchase** refers to merchandise

that the retailer was able to acquire at a low cost. Savings are passed on to customers by pricing the goods at less than the customers would expect to pay.

Following Laws Regarding Pricing

There are federal, state, and local laws that apply to pricing. The federal laws are mainly concerned with preventing deceptive pricing and pricing that would tend to kill competition within a given market. State laws may specify the prices below which a retailer may not sell a product. Local laws, when they exist, are likely to reinforce or strengthen the state or federal laws. (See the discussion of unfair trade practices in Chapter 56.)

Setting Pricing Goals

A retailer's pricing goals can include (1) achieving a certain percentage of return on investment, (2) a desired gross profit on merchandise investments, (3) a projected share of the market, or all three.

Achieving Return on Investment

As mentioned in Chapter 35, the dollar amount of the net profit realized for each dollar invested in a business is a company's return on investment. Return on investment is probably the most common goal and yardstick used by retailers. This goal is a much more accurate measure of the effectiveness of any business operation than simple net profit. Two companies can earn identical net profits, but one may have a much better return on investment than the other. For instance, one firm may have $100,000 worth of inventory, equipment, floor space, promotion, and sales force invested in a product line that produces a $15,000 net profit. Another firm may be able to produce exactly the same net profit for an investment of only $85,000. The second firm achieves a greater dollar return on investment because its management controls the relationship of prices, expenses, and merchandise investments more effectively.

Acquiring a Desired Gross Profit on Merchandise Investment

Gross profit on merchandise investment is the gross profit made on every dollar invested in average inventory of a merchandise item or line. It provides retailers with a way of comparing the profitability of various merchandise items. And this enables them to make decisions about whether to increase or decrease the inventory carried or the prices charged.

Gross profit on investment is calculated by dividing the gross profit realized from an item by the dollar amount invested in the average inventory of that item.

$$\text{Gross profit on merchandise investment} = \frac{\text{gross profit on item}}{\text{investment in average inventory of item}}$$

Investment in average inventory of item is determined by multiplying the number of units of average inventory by the cost of a unit. **Average inventory of item** is the midpoint between the highest inventory, which occurs right after a new shipment is received, and the lowest inventory, which usually exists just before a new shipment arrives.

The concept of return on investment to a merchandise inventory is used in the following example:

1. Assume that Caroline Cellini sells $200 of oil paint sets every 3 months.
2. She purchases 10 units once ever 3 months at a cost of $15 each.
3. She prices them for sale at $20 each.
4. There are usually about five sets left over when the new shipment arrives ($15 × 5 units = $75).
5. She then has $225 invested in oil paint sets at the peak of the inventory on hand ($150 + $75).
6. When inventory is at its lowest, $75 is invested in these oil paint sets ($15 × 5 units).

What is Caroline's gross profit and profit on investment for the 3-month period? Gross profit can easily be found from the following calculation:

Total sales of oil paint sets	= $200
Less cost of merchandise sold (10 units × $15/unit)	= $150
Gross profit from oil paint sets	= $ 50

The retailer's investment in average inventory is the midpoint between $225 (peak period) and $75 (low period). The midpoint is then obtained by adding the high and low figures and dividing by 2. In this example, the midpoint is $150; that is:

$$\text{Average inventory investment} = \frac{\$225 + \$75}{2} = \$150$$

The profit on investment can then be calculated as follows:

$$\text{Gross profit on investment} = \frac{\$50 \text{ gross profit on paint sets}}{\$150 \text{ average inventory investment on paint sets}} = 33\%$$

This means that a gross profit of 33 cents is made on every dollar invested in average inventory of this line of oil paint sets. Retailers can compare the gross profit on investment of individual items, lines of merchandise, or the total store sales with past sales periods or with other stores. This comparison enables retailers to evaluate the profit performance, inventory investments, and price levels of certain merchandise. Merchandise lines which have a lower gross profit on investment than other lines may be reduced in quantity or discontinued.

Realizing a Share of the Market

An important pricing objective of retailers is to either get a certain projected share of the market or to maintain the share of the market they currently hold. A **share of the market** is a part of the total sales available for a product or service in a certain sales area, territory, or region. Retailers project or plan to realize a certain share of the total market for a given sales period. This projection is usually expressed as a percentage (10 percent, 20 percent, for example) of the total sales considered to be available in a city, area, or region.

A retailer like Caroline Cellini, with a new product, a new department, or a new store, may price goods at lower levels for a short time to attract customers. While this policy will not result in maximum profit, it may enable a new retailer to build up a share of the market that will eventually lead to a profitable operation.

In somewhat the same way, a retailer may have to set lower prices to keep a share of the market if competitors are offering strong price competition. This, however, is the way price wars begin, and most retailers try to avoid such situations. In a price war, all the retailers involved suffer and none wins.

Determining Pricing Policies

After retailers have considered the various factors that might affect prices and have set pricing goals, their next step is to determine specific types of pricing policies.

Fixed or Variable Pricing

In the majority of stores, the one-price policy is followed. Under the **one-price policy,** goods are sold at any given time to all customers at one price, which is marked on the goods. All customers are treated alike. They do not have a choice of the price they will pay, but they can decide whether or not they want the item at that price. The one-price policy has several advantages. It builds customer confidence in the store, saves time, and can be used in self-service stores.

Under the **variable-price policy,** the price paid by a customer at a given time for a certain item is determined by a bargaining process between the customer and the salesperson. This means that customers may pay lower or higher prices for the same merchandise, depending on how skillful they are at bargaining. Variable pricing is used in some smaller, single-line stores and in sales situations where a trade-in allowance is involved, as with automobiles.

The variable-price policy gives the seller an opportunity to be flexible in dealings with customers. By lowering the price, the seller may attract new customers or increase the volume of sales. In most retail stores, however, variable pricing would disrupt the orderly sales transactions that contribute to the smooth, profitable operation of the store.

Pricing policies are critical in businesses with narrow profit margins, like supermarkets. Do you think that an "early warning system" on price increases would attract customers? Timothy Eagan/Woodfin Camp & Associates

Price Lining

Many stores have definite price lines that are used in pricing merchandise. **Price lining** means setting up a limited number of price points at which merchandise will be offered for sale. For example, a store may sell $79, $99, and $149 suits. The buyer looks for merchandise that meets the standards of quality for each of these three price lines, and cost prices are sought that allow for a sufficient markup.

One of the most apparent advantages of price lining is that it avoids confusing customers with a number of prices; therefore it makes buying easier. Since stores with definite price lines sell goods at the prices that they have found to be most popular with their customers, the stock moves quickly.

On the other hand, price lining may make it difficult for a store to adjust its prices to meet the prices of the competition. During periods of inflation and deflation, the retailer may face the alterna-

tives of changing either the prices of the lines that are carried or the quality of the merchandise within each line.

Odd-Cent Pricing

Some retailers believe that prices have a psychological effect on customers and that **odd-cent pricing** will encourage people to buy. This pricing is based on the belief that customers feel, for example, that $2.95 is much lower than $3 because they pay more attention to the dollar figure than to the cents figure. These retailers also believe that odd prices such as 49 cents or 97 cents will bring in a greater volume of sales than prices of 50 cents or $1. Discount stores and bargain-oriented stores like odd-cent pricing, but prestige stores and stores selling higher-priced merchandise seldom use it except during sales events.

Leader Pricing

To attract consumers into their stores, some retailers often price certain items (called "leaders") just above their delivered cost price. Usually the price covers part, but not all, of the expense of handling the item. A **loss leader** is an article that is actually sold for less than its cost to the store, including the cost of delivery.

Retailers use leaders on the theory that once customers are in the store, they will purchase other items. Some believe that leaders create the impression that all the store's prices are low. Food stores often select items from different departments in the store and use them as leaders: for example, coffee, canned fruit juices, and soaps. Drugstores feature photographic film, over-the-counter drugs, toiletries, and candy.

Sometimes loss leaders are used by a store that actually carries only a very limited stock of the articles advertised at the low price; this practice has been criticized by both customers and manufacturers. Customers object when the small supply runs out and the store tries to sell substitute merchandise at a higher price. National brands are used as leaders because their quality and retail prices are well known. So manufacturers object to the use of their products as "bait" to attract customers.

All retailers must be aware of the ever-changing factors affecting price decisions. There are many ways to evaluate whether certain marketing goals have been achieved by various pricing policies. Obtaining a sufficient profit on merchandise investment and an adequate share of the market are necessary for the continued success of new businesses like Caroline Cellini's as well as for the survival of established retail firms.

In this chapter you've learned about only one part of merchandise planning—all the things that must be considered when pricing policies are being developed. But pricing policies don't mean very much unless retailers also develop a plan that enables the policies to be used effectively. The type of plan that retailers use is discussed in the next chapter.

Some retailers believe that odd-cent pricing will encourage customers to buy. Courtesy of Lebhar-Friedman, Inc.

HOUSEHOLD GADGET RIOT
YOUR CHOICE
58¢

Trade Talk

Define each term and use it in a sentence.

Average inventory of item	One-price policy
Clearance	Price lining
Gross profit on merchandise investment	Sale
	Selling price
	Share of the market
Loss leader	Special purchase
Odd-cent pricing	Variable-price policy

Can You Answer These?

1. What are the advantages and disadvantages of setting prices lower than those of competitors? Higher than those of competitors?
2. What questions should be answered before a retailer decides to set prices below those of the competition?
3. How is the gross profit on investment calculated?
4. How can the gross profit on investment be

(1) Pricing Policies	(2) Firm Name	(3) Merchandise	(4) Reasons for Policy
Variable	Bill's Used Auto	1979 Chevrolet Impala	Customers accustomed to bargaining, value of used cars difficult to determine.

used by a retailer to analyze merchandise operations?

5. What are advantages of each of the pricing policies described in this chapter: fixed pricing, variable pricing, price lining, odd-cent pricing, and leader pricing?

Problems

1. Caroline Cellini sold $2,000 of wood carvings in her arts and crafts store this year. She wishes to determine her gross profit on merchandise investment on these products. Use the following inventory and sales figures to assist Caroline with her calculations:

   a. Merchandise on hand during peak inventory period = $1,000
   b. Merchandise on hand during low inventory period = $600
   c. Cost of wood carvings sold = $1,600

2. Rule a form similar to the one above. In column 1, list the different types of pricing policies commonly used by retail firms: fixed, variable, price lining, odd-end pricing, leader pricing. In column 2, list the names of firms in your community that would likely use each policy. In column 3, give examples of merchandise that would be priced according to each policy. In column 4, state reasons why particular firms would use certain pricing policies for the merchandise named.

Preparing the Merchandise Plan

Communications & Human Relations

Economics & Marketing

Merchandising

Selling & Technology

Advertising & Display

Operations & Management

Charlie Noguchi has a problem. He opened his own bicycle sales and repair shop a year ago. Previously, he'd worked in the bicycle service department of a large sporting goods store. On the basis of his experience in repairing bicycles, his savings, and financial backing from a friend, Charlie decided to pursue his lifelong goal of going into business for himself.

Unfortunately, Charlie had little previous experience with the merchandise planning aspects of retailing. He contacted several wholesalers of bicycles and related parts and accessories, but when asked what his planned sales would be for certain types of bicycles and accessories, Charlie admitted that he had not completed these plans. Consequently, Charlie relied almost entirely upon the recommendations of the suppliers to stock his shop.

After a recent inventory of the merchandise, Charlie realized that he was overstocked in certain lines and out of stock in others. He is now faced with the decision of marking down prices on the overstocked items. Also, he needs sales revenue to supply funds for the replenishment of out-of-stock merchandise.

What Is a Merchandise Plan?

Charlie is determined to follow a merchandise planning system that will provide current information regarding sales, inventory, markdowns, needed markups, and funds available for purchases. Fortunately, Mr. Weisbrod, an experienced wholesale representative, offered Charlie a simplified merchandise plan used by a bicycle retailer in another city. This is how Mr. Weisbrod described the plan to Charlie:

"A merchandise or buying plan is like a road map. It enables you to identify your destination (your planned sales), the route to follow (your planned beginning and ending inventory), and changes in the route that you may have to take (markups, markdowns, and additional purchases).

"A **merchandise plan,** or sales budget, is a projection (or estimate) in dollars of the sales goals of a department, a merchandise line, or an entire store," he continued. "The merchandise plan is usually made for a definite period of time. Included in the merchandise plan are the monthly sales anticipated by the store, the amount of stock on hand at the beginning and end of each month, and the planned amount of reductions, such as markdowns and shortages.

"With this information, you can determine how much money can be used to purchase merchandise. By knowing the amount of money available for purchases and the expected income from sales, you're prepared to take care of financial needs as they arise," Mr. Weisbrod concluded.

In a small business, the owner, such as Charlie Noguchi, is frequently in close touch with all phases of the store's operations. By being on the job, the owner deals directly with customers every day. Owners of small businesses know that their store's success depends on how well it meets customer needs and lives up to customer values. In a single-owner operation, a very basic merchandise plan will guide the merchandising activities.

In a larger business, the merchandising division develops a detailed merchandise plan. This plan helps buyers select merchandise at the right time, thus keeping sufficient stock on hand to meet customer demand. The plan also helps in coordinating the merchandising activities of the various departments in the store so that each department earns a profit. In addition, information from the merchandise plan helps top management judge the efficiency of the executives responsible for the various merchandising operations.

Qualities of a Good Merchandise Plan

One distinguishing mark of a good merchandise plan is simplicity. A good plan contains all the essential information, and it's easy to understand. A simple approach ensures that the plan will be used as a guide to all merchandising activities.

Following Mr. Weisbrod's advice, Charlie Noguchi designed a merchandise plan for each of his lines of merchandise. His merchandise plan for bicycle accessories is shown on page 474.

Who Does the Buying?

In most small stores and service businesses, the merchandise buying is done by the owner or manager. In independent, departmentalized stores, the buying is done by a buyer—a retailing specialist responsible for the purchasing and selling of merchandise in one or several merchandise lines. Usually, each major department, such as women's shoes or sporting goods, has its own buyer. Sometimes three or four small departments carrying related goods may be organized together

NOGUCHI'S BICYCLE SHOP MERCHANDISE PLAN
(Bicycle Accessories)

Factor	Year		Sept.	Oct.	Nov.	Total
Planned sales, dollars	Last year		500	400	350	1,250
	Planned		500	500	400	1,400
Planned stock, first of month, dollars	Last year		100	100	100	300
	Planned		150	200	150	500
Shortages and planned markdowns, dollars	Last year	Markdowns	25	25	20	70
		Shortages	25	25	20	70
	Planned	Markdowns	30	30	25	85
		Shortages	30	30	25	85
Retail purchases, dollars	Last year		550	450		
	Planned		610	510		
Planned initial markup, percent	Last year		40	40	40	
	Planned		40	40	40	

under one buyer. For example, the same person may buy for the apparel accessories department and the rainwear department. In very large firms, the buyers are usually organized under the direction of divisional merchandising managers.

Chain-store organizations buy quite differently. Purchasing is done at the central headquarters by buying specialists in each line of merchandise. From this vantage point they buy in enormous quantities to be distributed to all units of the chain. These specialized buyers concentrate on one kind of merchandise—for example, on toys, paints, appliances, or fresh meats. The manager of the local chain-store unit seldom buys; instead, orders are placed from warehouse stock lists. Occasionally, however, items may be bought locally to meet a stock shortage or to take advantage of a local surplus that results in favorable prices.

In both small and large firms buyers must keep close track of current demand trends. They must pay particular attention to what the store's customers are likely to want. And they must make buying decisions concerning which new products best suit the store image and merchandising policies. Buyers must also understand the place of the store in the fashion life cycle (Chapter 40). And regardless of the buying organization that may exist, buyers must carefully evaluate the prices, quality, construction, and style of merchandise.

Who Prepares the Plan?

Charlie Noguchi's merchandise plan contains the basic parts of a simple plan used by owners of small businesses who do their own buying. In a large store, the buying problems are more complex and therefore require a more detailed, budgeted plan. The merchandising division and the controller's office are usually jointly responsible for preparing a merchandise plan for each department in the store. The controller's office reviews these plans in light of the total funding requests of all departments (merchandising, operations, administration, and so on) for funds. Merchandise plans are often revised depending upon funds available, other costs of doing business, and market trends in the economy.

Elements of a Merchandise Plan

Buyers find the merchandise plan especially useful in making purchases. For example, a detailed plan of the kind used in large stores shows how much money is available for each classification of merchandise in a department by style, size, and color. It also helps buyers to determine how much they can spend for the entire period, as they know how much is left to spend.

Charlie Noguchi's merchandise plan includes certain elements that are found in merchandise plans followed by larger firms. These elements are:

1. **Planned sales**—the anticipated amount to be sold
2. **Planned stock**—the amount to be on hand at the beginning of the month (BOM) and the end of the month (EOM)
3. Shortages and planned markdowns—the reductions in planned sales due to markdowns or shortages
4. Retail purchases—the amounts to be ordered
5. Planned markup—the amount of markup needed

Planned Sales

The first and most important element of a merchandise plan is the volume of sales forecast for the period. All other figures are based on the planned sales figure. If a large error is made when the sales volume is being projected, the entire merchandise plan will be inaccurate.

The reason for beginning the merchandise plan with a sales forecast is that the volume of expected sales often determines such factors as:

1. Changes in **variable expenses**. These expenses, such as sales commissions or delivery costs change in direct relation to changes in sales.
2. Changes in **fixed expenses**. These ex-

Buyers are specialists responsible for the purchasing and selling of merchandise in one or several related merchandise lines. Ken Karp

penses—such as rent, heat, and lighting—do not vary in direct relation to sales. However, if there is a substantial increase in sales, these expenses can increase. For example, a sales increase realized because a new credit program is being offered could affect accounting costs.

3. The need for new funds. Increased inventory and operating funds will be necessary to accommodate projected sales increases.

4. Increases (or decreases) in present resources such as storage space, display area, delivery capability, or needed supervisory, sales, or operations personnel.

When forecasting sales volume, retailers must consider: (1) past sales, (2) general business conditions, (3) the competition, (4) trends in customer demand, and (5) any significant changes in the store's operations or policies.

Past Sales. Analyzing past sales records is useful because they are an indication of what future sales may be. Accurate and complete sales records, including charge accounts, show what types of goods, styles, colors, prices, and quantities customers have bought. Comments regarding why sales on a particular day or period were exceptionally low or high should be analyzed.

Adjustments in planned sales may be made because of unusual weather or business conditions in the previous year. A very rainy period, for example, may have resulted in low sales for the women's sportswear department in June of last year. Dates of holidays can affect anticipated sales. If Easter is in late March, the possibility of cold weather will tend to reduce the sales of spring clothing.

General Business Conditions. When business conditions are good and employment high, sales may increase or remain at the usual level. Sales often decline when customers are worrying about their next paycheck or when they fear a recession may be developing. Retailers can subscribe to

special services that supply them with information on national or regional economic conditions. In addition, they can obtain information from national magazines, such as *Business Week,* and from specialized trade publications, such as *Women's Wear Daily.* Area newspapers and bulletins issued by banks, trade associations, and the chamber of commerce report local business conditions. Large retail firms maintain their own research departments, which prepare reports on both national and local business conditions and on trends in the consumer market.

The Competition. Changes in the nature of the competition affect a buyer's planned sales. For example, if a new bicycle shop opened near Charlie Noguchi's business, he would have to revise his sales estimates. The modernization or expansion of an existing store or a change in a competing store's promotion policy may also reduce a buyer's planned sales. On the other hand, if a competitor loses popularity with customers or becomes financially unable to keep the stock demanded by customers, the planned sales estimates should be increased.

Trends in Customer Demand. Changes in customer tastes strongly affect sales. The trend toward more informal clothing for everyday wear results in an increase in the sales of casual wear and a decrease in the sales of formal clothing. Increased interest in sports means increased sales in sporting goods and active sportswear. From time to time, a fashion trend creates a heavy demand for an item. A buyer should beware of a sudden change in sales. A trend or fad can disappear from the scene as rapidly as it arrived.

Changes in Operations or Policies. Changes in the layout of a store can make one merchandise line more accessible or more attractive to customers and thus open the possibility of more sales. The establishment of a storewide trading-up policy would probably mean a decrease in the sale of lower-priced merchandise and an increase in the sale of higher-priced merchandise. Changes in parking or in a floor plan can also cause more or fewer sales.

The larger the business and the more diversified the stock carried, the more complicated it is to project future sales volume and the higher the risk of predictions being inaccurate. A small business like Noguchi's Bicycle Shop can often feel the "pulse beat" of what customers want and of community changes and other conditions within the market area. A large store, just because of its size, may lose this feel for customer wants and must depend more on reports such as those given by data processing systems.

Planned Stocks

A buyer's next step in preparing a merchandising plan is to determine the stock required to meet the planned sales volume. This is the factor entitled "Planned Stock First of Month" on the merchandise plan for Noguchi's Bicycle Shop, shown on page 474. The buyer wants to have sufficient stock on hand to meet customer demand. At the same time, the buyer does not want to invest more money than is available for such purchases.

Although Charlie Noguchi expects to sell $500 worth of all kinds of merchandise in October, he does not need to have $500 in stock on any given day. He may be able to reorder during the month. Experience has shown him that he must have between $100 and $200 in stock at any given time. Since he expects relatively brisk sales in October, according to his estimate, his first month's stock must be $200. He also plans to have stock worth $150 on hand at the end of the month to carry into November, as the merchandise plan shows.

Planned stock is a key figure, for it will

What effect might this news have on Charlie Noguchi's business?

determine whether the shop has sufficient stock to meet customer demand or whether it may run out of certain stock and lose sales.

Stock-Sales Ratio. To determine, from the planned sales for the period, the amount of stock that should be on hand in a particular month, buyers can use the **stock-sales ratio.** The ratio between the retail value of stock on hand at a particular time during a period and the sales for that period is the stock-sales ratio. This is calculated by using the following formula:

$$\text{Stock-sales ratio} = \frac{\text{retail value of stock at a given time in the period}}{\text{planned sales for the period}}$$

A stock-sales ratio is usually a beginning-of-the-month (BOM) ratio, although an end-of-the-month (EOM) ratio is sometimes used as well. Buyers multiply the planned sales for a month by the stock-sales ratio to figure the amount of stock that should be on hand.

Many buyers determine a stock-sales ratio for each month on the basis of past experience. For example, in Noguchi's Bicycle Shop, .4 is the BOM ratio for October. This figure is calculated as follows:

$$\frac{\text{Planned stock, first of month}}{\text{Planned sales for month}} = \frac{\$200}{\$500} = .4$$

This figure means that 40 percent of stock that is projected to sell during the month (.4) will be on hand at the beginning of the month. The stock-sales ratio helps buyers determine whether the proper amount of merchandise is planned to be on hand at the beginning or end of the sales period.

Inventory Replenishment. To determine inventory replenishment, buyers have to figure out how much to buy to replenish stock up to a desired amount. They do this by establishing an inventory target for any item carried and they express it in terms of so many days, weeks, or months

of sales. For example, assume that a grocery store planned to carry a 5-day supply of apples. If the average daily sales were 15 boxes of apples, a desirable inventory level could be calculated as follows:

$$\text{Inventory level} = \text{days' supply} \times \text{average daily sales}$$
$$\text{Inventory level} = 5 \times 15 = 75$$

If the supply on hand is less than 75 boxes, then more apples must be purchased. If the actual stock is 50 boxes, then the grocer would have to purchase 25 boxes (75 − 50) within the sales period.

In any business, an appropriate inventory level should be calculated by considering expected sales in the coming period. For products that show a steady sales pattern regardless of season or current fads, this can be based upon average weekly or monthly sales.

Shortages and Planned Markdowns

The third section of a merchandise plan involves reductions in sales due to markdowns or shortages. Very seldom, if ever, does the entire stock of each item sell at its original price. For example, Charlie Noguchi knows that he must feature certain accessory merchandise at lower prices to encourage customers to come into his shop. Therefore, he allows $30, or 6 percent of October sales, for planned markdowns.

Seldom, if ever, does a month go by without a few customers taking merchandise without paying for it. Therefore, although Charlie can order stock several times during the month, he still allows $30, or 6 percent of October sales, for shortages due to theft. Thus, his total shortages and planned markdowns for October are $60.

When estimating markdowns, retailers look at past records and again consider general business conditions and price trends—sales events planned, the type of merchandise being sold, the rate at which merchandise is selling, and the markdown policies of competitors.

The planning of markdowns helps retailers to achieve profit in several ways. First, when retailers study the reasons for markdowns, ways of minimizing and even eliminating some markdowns are discovered. Second, the taking of a markdown at the right time can limit more severe markdowns at a later time. The markdown may be considerably smaller than it would have to be at a later date due to style changes, seasonal change, or shopworn merchandise. Third, when markdowns are part of the merchandise plan, the original markup can be made large enough to allow for these reductions in retail price.

Retail Purchases

Careful planning of purchases helps retailers make sure that the right amount of stock is on hand at the right time. No retailer can afford to be either overstocked or understocked. Planned purchases will also vary according to selling season. The decision to buy 1,000 snow tires in April to be sold in May, for example, would be an unwise one.

Let's refer again to the example of Charlie Noguchi's merchandise plan. Planned sales for October ($500) minus the difference between retail stock on the first of October and the first of November ($200 − $150) plus shortages and planned markdowns for October ($30 + $30 = $60) equals the planned purchases for the month of October. Look at the calculations in the merchandise plan. See whether you understand how Charlie Noguchi decided to buy $510 worth of merchandise.

Planned Markup

The planned markup is a guide for pricing merchandise as well as for ordering goods that will sell at a given price. It also helps retailers determine the profit margin. (As explained in Chapter 41, the initial markup is the difference between the wholesale cost and the initial selling price given the merchandise.) The markup is commonly expressed as a percentage of the initial selling price (markup on retail). So if the initial retail price for an individual item is $2 and the wholesale cost is $1.20, the difference is 80 cents. Initial markup is 80 cents, or 40 percent (80¢ ÷ $2) of the initial retail price, $2.

Retailers must be sure that the average markup established for the store is achieved at the end of the planning period. Not all departments in a store operate on the same markup. Highly perishable goods, fads, high-fashion items, and items that have a low stock turnover rate require a high markup. Goods that are highly competitive must be sold at a low markup.

How Open-to-Buy Is Used

Charlie Noguchi planned to buy bicycle accessories worth $510 for October. But

Planned markdowns encourage sales—here are a variety of sales commonly held in October. Courtesy of Metro Newspaper Service

should he spend his money all at once at the beginning of the month? Or should he spend a quarter of his budget each week during the month of October? Should he buy a new bicycle accessory about to hit the market in the hope that it will become a big seller? These are questions he can answer only if he knows what amount he is "open to buy."

Advantages of Being Open-to-Buy

Open-to-buy is a calculation of the amount of merchandise that can be received into stock during any given period without exceeding the planned closing stock level at the end of that period. Most buyers always try to have an open-to-buy amount. It enables them to (1) restock when needed, (2) keep new merchandise coming in to attract customers, and (3) take advantage of an unexpected opportunity to make a good buy. Open-to-buy, for example, helps buyers when some items are selling especially well. If buyers are open to buy, they can place orders immediately. So if they miss an item that customers want, they have funds available to buy a supply.

Calculating an Open-to-Buy

Suppose that, on any given day during October, Charlie Noguchi wants to determine how much money is still available to buy merchandise. To find his open-to-buy, he will need to know the following (refer to the merchandise plan on page 474):

1. The inventory of the merchandise on hand that day (He finds his inventory to be $100.)
2. How much merchandise on order that has not been delivered by the vendors (Outstanding orders for October amount to $300.)
3. Planned stock for the first of November (He wants to end the month with $150 in inventory.)
4. Planned sales for the month (Estimated sales are $500 for the month of October.)
5. Shortages and planned markdowns (Short-

ages and planned markdowns for October are $60.)

What is Charlie's open-to-buy on that particular day in October? The difference between what he has ($100 + $300) and what he plans ($150 + $500 + $60) is $310. So Charlie is still open to buy $310 of the $510 budgeted for retail purchases for all of October.

Converting to Cost Figures

Note that, so far, all the elements of the merchandise plan have been figured at retail. Of course, as a buyer, Charlie does not pay retail prices when he makes purchases. To determine the amount of money that he can spend at cost, he must adjust the retail figure by the amount of initial markup planned. If the initial markup were 40 percent, the planned $310 of retail purchases for October would be multiplied by the complement of the retail markup (that is, 60 percent). In this case, $186 worth of goods could be purchased at cost price ($310 × .60). This is the actual dollar amount Charlie will pay for purchases in October.

If more goods were on hand and more merchandise were on order than Charlie estimated he would need for October, he would be overbought. He would not be open to buy. Until Charlie took some steps to reduce his stock or to cancel a part of the merchandise on order (sometimes this is permitted, sometimes it isn't), he would not be in a financial position to buy anything during the rest of October. This could be disastrous if he began to run low on some of his best sellers.

Benefits of a Merchandise Plan

With a well-planned budget and a well-balanced merchandise assortment, buyers gain many of the following benefits:

1. *Satisfied customers.* With data coming in from stock control, buyers are able to determine the kinds of merchandise cus-

tomers want and can make an effort to keep a sufficient quantity of the right goods on hand.

2. *Increased profits.* A balanced assortment of goods leads to more sales and an increase in store profits. By providing a good selection of merchandise, retailers are less likely to face losses, since items won't remain in stock too long and become shopworn and difficult to sell. Stock control leads to greater profits because it keeps the buyer informed about both fast-selling items that should be reordered and slow-moving items that should be dropped. In addition, good stock control helps buyers plan promotion for goods that will attract customers.

3. *Reliable buying information.* Information provided by stock control helps buyers plan future purchases. On the basis of past experience, buyers can decide what to buy or what not to buy, when to buy, and how much. A practical approach based on reliable information ensures wise buying decisions and helps buyers avoid past purchasing mistakes.

4. *Minimum investment in inventory.* Stock control helps buyers determine how much money should be spent on merchandise. Ideally, buyers make the smallest investment possible in goods that will satisfy customer demands and sell well enough to build up store profits.

In this chapter, then, you've learned why retailers must prepare merchandise plans and how buyers use them in making important buying decisions. For buyers, however, using the merchandise plan is only the first of the four steps of the buying process they must take. Step 2 is discussed in Chapter 60, and Steps 3 and 4 are discussed in Chapter 61.

Trade Talk

Define each term and use it in a sentence.

Fixed expenses
Merchandise plan
Open-to-buy
Planned sales
Planned stock
Stock-sales ratio
Variable expenses

Can You Answer These?

1. Name the elements of a merchandise plan. Why is each important?
2. How does planning markdowns help achieve a profit for retailers?
3. How is the stock-sales ratio calculated?
4. How is the open-to-buy calculated?
5. What information does the open-to-buy figure give the buyer?

Problems

1. You are analyzing the sales and orders for the record department in your music shop. You wish to determine the open-to-buy for the coming month. You project that you will sell $3,000 worth of records during the month. Because the Christams season begins next month, you plan to have a $9,000 inventory at the end of the month. At present, you have a BOM record inventory of $6,000. Orders have already been placed for $2,000 worth of records to arrive during the coming month. What is your open-to-buy for the upcoming month?

2. Select a product line in which you would have an interest as a buyer. Then rule a form similar to the following. In the left column, write the letter of each of the following methods of forecasting anticipated sales for product lines: (*a*) past sales, (*b*) general business conditions, (*c*) the competition, (*d*) trends in customer demand, and (*e*) changes in operations or policies. In the middle column, mention at least one source you might use in obtaining needed sales forecast information. In the right column, identify pertinent questions that you would want answered when using each method of forecasting sales.

Methods of Determining Anticipated Sales	Sources of Information	Questions to Be Answered to Forecast Sales

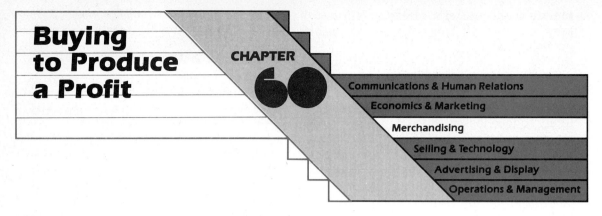

Buying to Produce a Profit

CHAPTER 60

Communications & Human Relations
Economics & Marketing
Merchandising
Selling & Technology
Advertising & Display
Operations & Management

Lydia Romanov is a buyer for Nussbaum's Department Store. She first decided that she wanted to become a buyer while she was studying marketing and distributive education in high school. After graduation, Lydia enrolled in a fashion merchandising program at a nearby community college. She has now completed her management training program at the store and is responsible for buying merchandise for several departments at Nussbaum's. Let's see what Lydia does as she carries out some of her buying duties.

It is 8 a.m. on Monday morning as Lydia arrives at her office. Her desk is already covered with memos, notes, telephone messages, stock lists, and order books waiting for her study and decisions. Above her desk is a sign that reads, "Goods well bought are half sold." She smiles as she remembers what the store's general merchandise manager told her: "Remember, you are a buyer for the store's customers. Don't buy merchandise to satisfy your own personal whims. Concentrate on buying products that will best reflect the store's image, appeal to the store's type of customers, and provide the profit margin desired." Lydia's recollections are abruptly interrupted by the telephone:

"Lydia, Kate Marias here. Have you finished planning the sportswear coat assortment? We need final orders by Wednesday."

"I'll get on it right away," replies Lydia.

Following the Buying Process

Lydia, like other buyers, follows the steps of the buying process. This process can be summarized as follows:

1. Preparing and using a merchandise plan that shows the dollar amounts that can be spent for stock during a selling period
2. Deciding upon the merchandise assortment that will fit the plan and be salable
3. Finding the best suppliers of each item desired
4. Placing the order after determining the most satisfactory terms of purchase and delivery

As the overall merchandise plan has already been developed, Lydia now has to take Step 2 of the buying process—deciding upon a suitable merchandise assortment. Her decision will be influenced by these four major factors: (1) store policies, (2) merchandise planning, (3) customer wants and needs, and (4) the assistance and judgment of people in the industry.

The remainder of this chapter discusses these four factors of Step 2 of the buying process. Steps 3 and 4 are discussed in Chapter 61.

Considering Store Policies

Store policies affect the planning and buying of a merchandise assortment. Store image, brand pricing, and buying policies all affect buying decisions for a store. Each policy is closely related and cannot be overlooked by a buyer, department head, or manager who is determining the makeup of merchandise assortments.

Store Image

Image! Image! Image! **Image** refers to the way customers feel about a store. The image of a store can be compared to the personality of an individual. In deciding upon the price, style, color, quality, variety, and other characteristics of a merchandise assortment, buyers must consider the image that a store wishes to communicate to the customer.

Buyers ask the following questions about image and merchandise assortments. What kind of store are we? Who are customers we want to attract? What type of merchandise are we noted for? What kinds of advertising and display messages do we communicate to the customer? Do we have a definite image, representing specific types of merchandise and service? Is our image blurred by a hodgepodge of confused merchandising techniques and products?

Brand Policies

Buyers have the choice of selecting national, private, or unbranded merchandise or a combination of them. **National brands** are brand-name products of manufacturers. Jantzen, Hart Schaffner & Marx, and London Fog are brand names in the clothing field. Del Monte food products and General Electric appliances are examples of national brands. Retailers who carry national brands know that their customers recognize the brand names and that this will be to the store's advantage, largely because it means that less selling effort will be needed. A disadvantage is that the wholesale cost of such products is usually higher. However, manufacturers of brand merchandise advertise nationally and locally, all of which benefits the retailer.

Private brands carry the label of an individual store. The store usually has a manufacturer make the items for it according to predetermined specifications. The wholesale price for private-labeled merchandise is generally lower than that of nationally branded merchandise. However, private brands must be more extensively advertised by the retailer because they are not nationally known.

Some merchandise may be unbranded or carry a little-known brand name. In the grocery field, a new development is the use of **generic products** (or "no-name" brands). Products are labeled and packaged according to their generic names—that is, their labels say simply "Peanut Butter," "Paper Towels," "Sugar," and so on, and there is no advertising on them. These products are priced lower than national- or private-brand products. Certain customers may question the comparable value and quality of generically labeled products. Other customers, however, will purchase the products because of the price savings.

Buyers must consider the relative percentages of national, private, or unbranded merchandise that will be included in the next season's assortment. Buyers for high-fashion stores usually favor the nationally advertised lines. However, such buyers also seriously consider the private-brand merchandise because it can mean higher profits.

Pricing Policies

Most retailers have a specific pricing policy that sets both minimum and maximum retail price lines for merchandise. Using these price lines, buyers determine whether a particular choice of merchandise at a certain wholesale price will meet planned expense and profit requirements. For ex-

Some supermarkets have developed a line of no-name brands. These products are labeled with just their generic names and are sold at low prices. Courtesy of Pathmark Supermarkets

ample, a supplier offers to sell a lawn mower to a hardware retailer at a wholesale price of $150. Similar lawn mowers have been selling at a retail price of $200. The retailer knows that a markup of 30 percent of the retail price, or $60 ($200 × 30% = $60), must be obtained to cover necessary expenses and obtain a profit. For the $200 price line of lawn mowers, this lawn mower is too expensive unless the wholesale price is renegotiated. By establishing retail price lines, the buyer—in this case the hardware dealer—has a guide to use when selecting individual items or assortments.

Price lining also helps simplify stock control. "Price lining" means setting up a limited number of prices categories for a given type of merchandise. By having an established price line, the buyers can determine the popularity of various types of merchandise. When markdowns are

necessary, customers can more readily identify savings from established price lines. Price lining also reduces confusion in the customer's mind regarding regular and sales prices.

Buying Policies

Considering the variety of merchandise offered by a retail store, the buying of merchandise can be a very complex process. It is simplified and automated wherever possible to enable the buyer to focus upon the more complex buying decisions. Buying policies and procedures vary depending upon whether replenishment or anticipation buying is involved.

Replenishment Buying.   Some types of stores use a basic stock list in preparing an assortment of staple merchandise (goods that should always be kept in stock). When the merchandise on hand reaches this amount, a **replenishment order** (or replacement order) of the goods is made to cover projected sales for a certain future sales period.

Many large retail chains prepare **seasonal information sheets (SIS)** or never-out stock lists for stores in their districts. These lists inform local managers of the quantities and types of preplanned shipments of staple merchandise. Managers can adjust or cancel such shipments if they can offer valid reasons for doing so. With the increased use of electronic cash registers connected with computers in district or home buying offices, staple merchandise is centrally bought and automatically replenished whenever possible.

In voluntary chains or independent businesses, the manager-owner keeps a running tally of the items sold and accumulates a replenishment order from this information. Wholesalers or rack jobbers, who periodically visit stores, take inventories of the items in stock and prepare a replenishment order based on current sales trends. In certain hardware store departments, as much as 80 percent of the inventory may be covered by replenishment buying.

Anticipation Buying. Anticipation buying is acquiring new goods that may not have been previously available for sale. Buying new, high-fashion clothing is an example of anticipation buying. In this situation buyers would not have past sales records to use as a guide in making purchases. So they have to make a logical analysis based on supplier information, articles in trade magazines, recommendations by sales personnel and other buyers, and knowledge of competitors' purchases. For untested merchandise, many buyers are cautious regarding their anticipation buying. They will buy a limited quantity early in the selling season to obtain the reactions of sales personnel and customers. By following this practice, they can avoid being overstocked with slow-selling merchandise. They will still have enough time during the selling season to order additional items for which a strong demand exists.

Analyzing Merchandise Records

A good starting point for planning next season's merchandise assortment is the merchandise records from last year. By reviewing each merchandise classification (amount of sweaters sold at each price, pants or skirts in each type, coats in various styles, and so on) buyers can better determine adequate merchandise coverage and plan stockkeeping-unit ratios.

Merchandise Coverage

Merchandise coverage is the basic amount of merchandise to have on hand and on order to satisfy customer demand. A store may, for example, have a merchandise coverage policy of carrying only the most popular sizes, colors, materials, and brands. Stores that decide to concentrate on a few selected styles and prices are said to have a **depth of stock**. Stores that offer a wide variety in merchandise lines are said to have a **breadth of stock**. Balancing the breadth and depth of inventory without keeping too much money tied up is a central problem for a buyer. A balanced stock satisfies the demands of most of a store's customers and returns greater profits for the amount of money invested.

Stockkeeping Units

To assist buyers in analyzing and planning basic assortments within a product line, the term **stockkeeping unit (SKU)** is used. An SKU is one distinct, individual type of item carried by a store. For example, a gallon of white interior latex paint is one SKU, while the same paint in red is another SKU.

To determine an SKU in men's shirts,

the number of collar sizes is multiplied by the number of sleeve lengths and by the number of colors stocked. The number of SKUs for a man's shirt with an assortment of collar sizes, sleeve lengths, and colors is then calculated as follows:

7 collar sizes × 4 sleeve lengths
    × 4 colors = 112 SKUs

If one unit of this style is ordered, such as red in size 16 × 33, one SKU exists. If 39 more of the identical items are received, there would be 40 units on hand but still only one SKU. If 10 red shirts and 10 yellow shirts in the same size (16 × 33) are ordered, then two SKUs exist. The SKU classification system helps buyers to determine and analyze the sales rates of specific assortments of merchandise according to combinations of sizes, models, prices, colors, and quality offered within each line. For example, with the men's shirts, a buyer could analyze the comparative sales of certain colors of shirts to determine which colors to reorder and which to mark down.

COMPUTING MERCHANDISE ASSORTMENT SKU'S FOR A MAN'S SHIRT

Collar Sizes	Sleeve Lengths	Colors
14 14½	32	White
15 15½	33	Yellow
16 16½	34	Blue
17	35	Red

Assessing Customer Wants and Needs

Buyers cannot rely upon last season's record as a guide in planning merchandise

Buyers must always know exactly how much merchandise is on hand and on order for each SKU they control. *Progressive Grocer*

MERCHANDISE WANT SLIP

Department No. _71_   Name _Jim Watson_

Date _8-4-8-_

The following Requested Merchandise is not in Stock:

Description (Item, Color, Size, Price)	No. of Calls	Buyer's Remarks
Men's washable slip-on slippers, $5-7	3	Carried in Notions Dept. in basement; price too low for shoe dept. to stock

The following Stock is getting low:

Mfr., Style, Color, Price	Pieces On Hand	

SUGGEST A SUBSTITUTE

A salesperson completes a want slip after a customer asks for an item that is not carried in stock. The want slip is given to the buyer, who determines whether the item should be ordered.

---

assortments. Instead, they must assess the current pulse or buying temperature of customers so as to identify preferences and reactions to new and established products. Buyers have two valuable means to make this assessment—want slips and customer contact.

Want Slips

Last year's sales records will not show what items might have sold if they had been in stock. Sales records do not show what might have been. To learn about the demand for items not carried in stock, retailers use want slips. A **want slip** is a written record, completed by the salesperson, that carries a customer's request for merchandise not carried in stock. The key to a successful want-slip procedure lies with the salesperson's careful recording of customer requests. (See the illustration shown above.) Before deciding to buy items appearing on want slips, buyers decide whether such items appeal to enough customers to increase sales and whether they are in line with the type and quality of goods usually carried.

Customer Contact

To get a firsthand idea of current customer wants and needs, buyers visit the sales floor. Here they ask the sales personnel such questions as: What items are and are not selling? What merchandise styles and colors are the customers looking for? What are your reactions to specific merchandise styles, prices, and assortments? In certain cases consumer surveys and consumer reaction panels to new products are used.

Selecting the Actual Merchandise

There are many factors that influence a buyer's decisions concerning merchandise assortments. The final decision, however, will depend on the buyer or store owner-manager's thorough analysis and judgment. The buyer also considers the following questions regarding merchandise selection.

1. *The quality of the products.* Are the products of the quality that the store's customers expect? Is the quality obvious or

must it be explained to the customers? Will the quality result in customer satisfaction or will it bring complaints, adjustments, and additional service calls? Has a testing laboratory evaluated the quality of the merchandise? Is the merchandise quality consistent with the store's image?

2. *The reputation of the manufacturer-supplier of the product.* Does the manufacturer or supplier have a reputation for prompt deliveries? Is the manufacturer's stock large enough to let orders be filled quickly? What credit terms and returned-goods allowances does the supplier offer? Does the manufacturer maintain a uniform quality of goods? Is the firm likely to go out of business and leave the buyer without replacement stock or parts?

3. *The profit potential of the product.* Will the product stimulate repeat business? Can the product be sold at a low markup as a trade builder? Will the product promote the sale of related items? Can the product be sold in large amounts and thus earn quantity discounts that add to profits?

4. *The retail price of the product.* Does the product fit the store's price lines? Will the spread between the retail price and the cost price provide enough margin for adequate profits? Are the retail prices in line with the merchandise plan for the department?

5. *The promotional support needed by the product.* Is national advertising available from the manufacturer (supplier)? Can the firm "tie into" the advertising through local and in-store promotions? Are promotional devices such as coupons, banners, demonstrations, and allowances for local advertising available? How much advertising or other promotional effort must the store provide?

6. *The sales support needed by the product.* Will the supplier provide sales training for sales personnel? Will the item need much effort by sales personnel to overcome sales resistance? Is the item presold?

7. *The package utility of the product.* Does the package have visual sales appeal? Does the packaging protect the goods in storage and delivery? Does the shape of the package make it easy to store and to wrap?

8. *The relationship of the product to existing lines.* Does this item duplicate something in our present line or assortment? Does this item compete with another in price and quality? Should this item be purchased to replace one now carried?

Once a buyer has decided on the merchandise assortment that will produce the best profit, which you learned about in this chapter, he or she must then take the last two steps of the buying process. Do you remember what they are? Read the next chapter in this unit to learn about Steps 3 and 4.

Trade Talk

Define each term and use it in a sentence.

Anticipation buying	Private brands
Breadth of stock	Replenishment order
Depth of stock	Stockkeeping unit
Generic products	(SKU)
Image	Seasonal information
Merchandise	sheets (SIS)
coverage	Want slip
National brands	

Can You Answer These?

1. What are the four major steps in the buying process?
2. What four factors affect the merchandise assortment to be bought?
3. How does store image affect merchandise assortment? Give examples.
4. What is the major difference between replenishment and anticipation buying?
5. How is an SKU (stockkeeping unit) system used to provide an improved coverage of merchandise?

Problems

1. You have been assigned the position of buyer for your school store this month. In reviewing the merchandise promotional

Product assortment analyzed: _____

Names of Competitive Stores Shopped	Competitive Products Carried	Comparative Prices of Products	Products Being Promoted in Store Windows, Displays, and Advertisements	Other Applicable Product Information Obtained

materials received by your teacher-coordinator, you discover an interesting brochure from a national supplier describing monographed T-shirts. The supplier will furnish T-shirts and will imprint slogans or designs requested by the customers. Your store has never handled this line of merchandise before. Develop a questionnaire for potential customers that would aid you in deciding whether to add this product line to your clothing assortment. On a separate sheet of paper, list at least six points or questions you would include in this questionnaire.

2. You have just been hired as a comparison shopper for a large retail store in your community. This store has never employed a comparison shopper before. The store manager is especially interested in obtaining current information about the leading competitors' merchandising strategies for a specific product assortment line (products carried, comparative prices, promotions, displays, ads, etc.). Identify a major retail store and its major competitors in your community. Select a specific product assortment line to analyze (for example, automobiles, bicycles, mens wear or women's wear, or stereo sets) Rule a comparison shopper report similar to the one shown above and record your comparison shopping information.

Obtaining the Best Terms

CHAPTER 61

Communications & Human Relations
Economics & Marketing
Merchandising
Selling & Technology
Advertising & Display
Operations & Management

"You're going along to market next week!" As a buyer-trainee for Carillo's store, you find this statement by Mr. Garcia, the store's most experienced buyer, very exciting. You know that you'll have an opportunity to see the newest merchandise of many suppliers and to take part in the negotiation process to purchase next season's goods. In many respects your responsibility as a buyer is to be a careful

"shopper" for the store. You have to attempt to obtain the needed quality and styles of merchandise with the most favorable prices, discount options, payment arrangements, and delivery schedules possible.

Locating Sources of Supply

The sources of supply that buyers use are called **merchandise resources.** Buyers meet suppliers at one or more of the following locations:

1. Central markets, where resources of similar merchandise are grouped together within an area
2. Trade association shows, where various distributors display and demonstrate their goods
3. International markets, which are located in other countries or are represented by sales personnel in this country
4. Buying offices, where market information and service is provided to client stores
5. Wholesalers, often located in larger, central trade areas, who offer such services as storage, financing, and delivery
6. Manufacturers' sales representatives, who visit the retailer's place of business

While you are preparing for your buying trip, Mr. Garcia stops by your office to explain aspects of the central market, which will include a trade association show. He highlights certain phases of the growing international market as well. Manufacturers and other distributors from the international markets will also be exhibiting at the central market.

Central Markets

Exchanging information with suppliers and buyers from many geographic areas enables a buyer to keep up to date on product trends and merchandising practices. Central markets for apparel are located in Dallas, Chicago, New York, and San Francisco. Furniture central markets are in High Point, North Carolina; Grand Rapids, Michigan; and Jamestown, New York. Manufacturers or wholesalers who are not located in the central market area often rent space in trade exhibit buildings such as the Apparel Mart of the Merchandise Mart in Chicago, where sample merchandise is displayed.

Trade Association Shows

Mr. Garcia offers the following suggestions concerning your attendance at the trade association shows. "When we're at the central market, we'll attend the introductory showings of the new fall product lines. During this introductory show, we'll want to notice the reactions of our competitors and other buyers to detect positive or negative reactions to the new colors, styles, and models. Perhaps we'll be able to determine certain trends so that we can either increase or decrease our planned orders for individual products. We'll need to keep in mind the unique characteristics of our customers and our local market so that we are not overly influenced by the exhibitors or other buyers."

International Markets

Buyers searching for unique, quality merchandise such as electronic products, apparel, sporting goods, china and crystal, and arts and crafts products use international markets as a major source of their supplies.

Buyers who use international markets have a very interesting career touring the markets of various countries, attending the trade shows in world trade cities, and negotiating with suppliers from different cultures. These buyers must be knowledgeable about import regulations, currency exchange requirements, market trends, and different business practices. In certain cases, firms hire an overseas agent or importer to provide international buyer services. Increasingly, exporters are taking part in central market exhibits and trade association shows in the United States. Of special interest are the increasing exchanges of international trade delegations with Russia and China in fields such as electronics technology, food products, and industrial equipment. When purchases are made in foreign markets, more time must be allowed for delivery and the possible influence of world events must be taken into account.

Buyers visit central apparel markets like these in Los Angeles and Atlanta to keep up to date on the latest fashions. *Courtesy of Atlanta Apparel Mart (left) and California Mart (right)*

Buying Offices

Stores cannot afford to send buyers to the central market as often as they would like. So to maintain contact with the central markets, large stores use the services of **resident buying offices.** These offices are located in central market cities and provide information for client stores. There are two types of resident buying offices. The **independent buying office,** sometimes called a "salaried office" or "fee office," is an organization that is independently owned and operated and that actively seeks out noncompeting stores as clients. The **store-owned buying office** is an organization entirely owned by the chain or other stores that it represents.

A buying office is organized in much the same way as the merchandising division within a store. There are merchandise managers, often a fashion coordinator, and market representatives. The **market representative** is a specialist in one segment of the market. This representative learns all about this segment and makes that knowledge known to the buyers of client stores. A market representative usually visits the market daily and often prepares reports on anything discounted that would be of interest to the stores. When a store's buyer is in town, the market representative works with this buyer to locate the most appropriate merchandise.

A buying office also often supplies sales promotion ideas and aids to its client stores, follows up on orders placed by stores, and sends out regular bulletins on prices, merchandise trends, and other market data of interest to the store buyer.

Wholesalers

Small independent retail stores often use the services of wholesalers. Many small-store buyers find it convenient to buy large amounts of goods from wholesalers. Wholesalers buy large quantities of merchandise from manufacturers, store the goods in large warehouses, and sell them to the retailers in the desired quantities. Buyers can save time when buying from a wholesaler because they can purchase a large number of different items at one time. Wholesalers usually give quicker deliveries and better credit terms than manufacturers. (However, because they are intermediaries, their prices are usually higher than those of the manufacturers.) Since most wholesalers do a local business, they can advise retailers on merchandising problems and supply them with useful market information about price trends, new merchandise, and the supply of goods that are in demand.

Sales Representatives

Manufacturers' sales representatives who visit stores can be valuable merchandise resource consultants. These representatives often show samples of the latest merchandise and offer suggestions concerning advertising, display, and sales techniques. Because clients are visited in a geographic area, the sales representatives can often provide current information concerning market trends and may offer predictions. Over a period of time, buyers depend upon certain sales representatives for reliable market information and merchandise supply. These representatives have developed positive relationship with buyers because they have consistently provided dependable product quality, good service, and reliable information.

Evaluating Merchandise Resources

Because of the number and variety of suppliers involved, many stores maintain records evaluating buying experiences with individual resources. These records are called **resource files**. Records of individual purchases are kept on file cards, the card for any given purchase listing the vendor (supplier), the vendor's address, the name of the sales representative, the merchandise offered, and the terms, prices, and delivery schedules involved. There is also a note of whether the delivery was prompt, whether the merchandise was of uniform

---

An accurate and up-to-date resource file is very helpful to a buyer.

```
                                            Dept.  112
                                            Date   8/8/8-


                        RESOURCE FILE

Merchandise: Posters (movie and rock stars)

Resource: Design for Tomorrow, Inc.     Terms: Cash discount - 2/10
          270 Randolph Road                    Quantity discount - 4% per gross
          Paterson, New Jersey  07512          FOB store

Contact: George M. Wilson, President    Prices: See attached price list.
```

Season	1981	1982	1983
Fall	3,000	7,000	9,000
Spring	5,000	8,000	
Total	8,000	15,000	

```
General Comments: Prompt delivery; very cooperative; generous
                  replacement policy, alert to new ideas.
```

quality, and whether it sold well. Finally, any other remarks that might influence future buying from this vendor are added.

Negotiating the Terms of the Sale

At the central market, a buyer may have to negotiate with three different suppliers for a certain line of merchandise that they all offer. It's not necessarily wise to purchase merchandise from the supplier who offers the lowest price. Buyers must consider the following points when negotiating the terms of the sale:

1. *Delivery.* When merchandise arrives on schedule, the store avoids losses due to stock shortages or the rental of extra storage space. Therefore buyers must carefully consider the means of delivery so that the store can save money on transportation.
2. *Discounts.* Buyers can frequently negotiate discounts if they buy large quantities, if they pay cash, or if they buy goods early in the season.
3. *Dating.* The length of time buyers have before a bill must be paid greatly affects the amount of cash needed during the trading process.
4. *Inventory investment.* Buyers can save the store a good deal of money by using special buying methods, such as consignment sales or memorandum buying, which are discussed later in this chapter.

Delivery

Delivery dates are very important because stock must arrive before customers want it. Buyers can also arrange staggered delivery so that stock shipments are scheduled to arrive at various times. Such arrivals don't overtax the store's storage space. The means of shipment determines not only the speed of delivery but also the cost. Large retailers, such as chains, sometimes buy in carload lots so as to save money.

When arranging delivery, buyers try to have vendors pay for transportation so that ownership of the goods is assumed only when they reach the store. With this arrangement, buyers save the cost of insurance expenses to protect the shipment because they are not yet the owner of the goods. Vendors, on the other hand, try to pass these costs on to the buyers' store. So vendors and buyers must bargain over what is known as the **FOB shipping point.** The FOB (free on board) shipping point determines (1) the point from which the buyer pays the transportation charges and (2) when legal ownership of goods, or **title,** passes to the buyer. The FOB shipping point, the FOB city of destination, and the FOB store are the points most commonly used as means of determining who pays for the transportation charges.

When the FOB shipping point is used, the vendor (seller) has title to the goods and responsibility for them until they are delivered to the carrier (the transporting firm). Then the title passes to the buyer, and the transportation charges are paid by the buyer from that point. When the **FOB city of destination** is used as the determining point, the vendor pays all transportation charges to the city in which the buyer is located. When the goods arrive in the city, the title passes to the buyer, who pays the delivery charges from the carrier's freight station to the store. Last, when the **FOB store** is used as the determining point, the vendor pays all transportation charges. The title passes when the shipment arrives at the buyer's store. For large quantities of goods and long hauls, the FOB store point saves the store a great deal of money both in shipping costs and insurance.

Discounts

Manufacturers and other suppliers offer several types of discounts to stimulate business and encourage prompt payment of bills. The immediate availability of cash and the quick movement of goods make the granting of a cash discount worthwhile to the supplier. For the buyer who can meet the terms of the sale, the benefits of a discount are obvious. The four most common types of discounts are cash, seasonal, trade, and quantity. The important characteristics of these types of discounts are given in the table on page 495.

Dating

The term **dating** refers to the length of time for which sellers extend credit to buyers. The length of dating depends on three factors: (1) the length of the marketing period, which is the time it takes the retailer to sell the article; (2) the length of the selling season; and (3) the competitive conditions (for example, a long-established manufacturer may offer different terms from those of a manufacturer who is trying to enter the market).

Buyers must negotiate datings because they are interested in dating that allows a longer period of time for taking discounts or for making payment. And sellers must negotiate because they want prompt payment. The most common forms of dating are ordinary, advanced, extra, EOM, ROG, and anticipation. These forms of dating are given in the table on page 496.

Inventory Investment

As a buyer, you must make buying decisions very much as your customers do. Both of you have limited budgets that call for the evaluation of various means of obtaining merchandise. Two special buying arrangements that can be made are consignment sales and memorandum buying. Both help buyers reduce the buying "budget" required for inventory investment.

Consignment Buying. Goods sold **on consignment** remain the property of the seller. Buyers don't have to pay for the goods until the store sells them. Buyers assume the responsibility for safeguarding the merchandise and maintaining it in a saleable condition. Any merchandise not sold may be returned to the seller. This is a desirable arrangement when retailers don't want to invest money in goods that may not sell. Manufacturers often ship on consignment to encourage retailers to stock their line. New products are sometimes introduced on a consignment basis. Consignment buying also has disadvantages. The price for such merchandise is higher, and there may be difficulties between the retailer and the seller about damages or returns.

Memorandum Buying. When vendors sell goods to buyers on the condition that buyers may return any unsold goods, the goods are said to be sold **on memorandum.** For example, if a vendor ships goods to a store on May 1 "on memorandum until June 15," the buyer may return any unsold goods by June 15. The title of the goods passes to the buyer, but losses are not suffered on items that are not sold. The buyer must, however, pay for the goods when they are billed, and refunds are allowed for goods returned.

Issuing the Purchase Order

After negotiating with several merchandise resources at the central market, you are ready to issue a purchase order. As discussed in Chapter 18, a purchase order is a contract between the buyer and the supplier. This important document must be completed carefully so as to avoid mistakes or disagreements.

The purchase order on page 497 contains the following information:

♦ Purchase order number
♦ Date of the purchase order
♦ Vendor's name and address
♦ Shipping or delivery instructions
♦ Date of desired delivery
♦ Terms of sale
♦ Description of the merchandise, including quantity, stock number, unit price, and total price
♦ Signature and title of the person authorizing the purchase

TYPES OF DISCOUNTS AND THEIR CHARACTERISTICS

Types of Discounts	Description	Example	Benefits
Cash discount	The amount a seller allows the buyer to deduct from a bill if paid within a certain time.	A 2 percent discount for 10 days means that a buyer may deduct $2 from an invoice price of $100, paying only $98 if payment is made within 10 days after the date of the bill. The invoice terms would be stated as 2/10, net 30. If the retailer does not pay within 10 days, the full amount ($100) would be due in 30 days.	The vendor obtains money sooner and reduces credit risks. The store saves money and improves its credit rating.
Season discount	A reduction in price given to those who buy before the usual selling season.	By paying for fall clothing during July, the buyer may deduct 10 percent from the price on the invoice.	The manufacturer or supplier can keep employees working on a regular basis rather than just during the selling season. A seasonal discount reduces the supplier's needs for storage and provides cash for year-around operations. The buyer receives a savings in price.
Trade discount	A reduction in price given to a certain class of buyers who perform a needed distribution function.	A manufacturer gives a wholesaler a larger discount because the wholesaler provides storage and transportation services.	The wholesaler performs needed services that retailers could not supply because of their limited storage and transportation facilities.
Quantity discount	A reduction in price given to retailers who buy in large quantities.	If a gross (144) of an item instead of a dozen were bought, the purchasing retailer might receive a 5 percent discount.	The manufacturer or supplier can save manufacturing, selling, storage, and delivery costs by selling items in larger amounts. The retailer obtains a price savings.

TYPES OF DATINGS

Type of Dating	Description	Example	Benefits
Ordinary dating	The credit period for payment is based on the date appearing on the invoice. Usually the date on the invoice is the date of shipment.	Invoice dated August 15, terms 2/10, net 30. A 2 percent discount may be taken if the bill is paid by August 25. Otherwise, the full payment is due on September 14.	The supplier can obtain payment earlier. The buyer can obtain a savings in price.
Advanced dating	The credit period for paying the invoice is based on a date later than the date of the invoice.	A vendor may state the terms 2/10, as of July 5, on an invoice dated May 1.	The credit period for payment is extended to July 5 rather than the date of the invoice, May 1. The buyer has a longer time to pay the bill.
Extra dating	The buyer is allowed an extra number of days before the credit terms begin to apply.	Terms granted: 2/10, 60 extra. The buyer is allowed 60 extra days before the ordinary discount period of 2/10, net 30, begins.	The buyer is given 70 days from the date of the invoice to take the 2 percent cash discount. Following this, there will be 20 days to pay the net amount.
EOM (end of month) dating	The credit period begins at the end of the month in which the invoice is dated instead of the usual exact date of the invoice. (After the 25th of the month, they belong to the following month.)	If merchandise were invoiced on May 26 with terms 2/10 EOM, the 2 percent discount could be taken through July 10.	The buyer is given an additional period of time in which to take the discount.
ROG (receipt of goods) dating	Credit terms apply from the date that the goods are received by the buyer.	This form of dating is offered to buyers who are located far from their suppliers.	By the time the buyers may receive the goods, the usual credit terms may no longer apply.
Anticipation dating	Payment of an invoice before the date on which the cash discount may be taken. Buyers are often allowed an extra deduction in addition to the cash discount.	The deduction is computed by allowing an interest-rate discount for the number of days the payment was made early.	The buyer is encouraged to make payments earlier than required. The supplier obtains payment sooner and can use the funds for business operations.

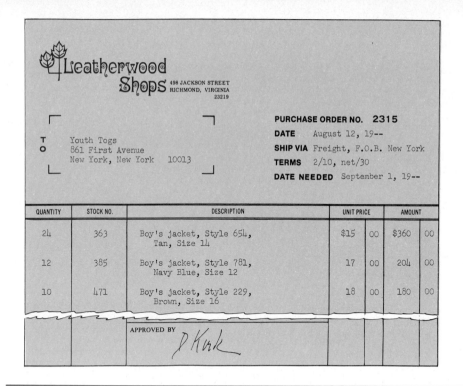

A purchase order is a contract between the buyer and the supplier.

Your experiences at the central market, selecting and evaluating merchandise resources and negotiating the terms of the sale, are challenging and exciting. Now you better realize that there are many factors to consider when making buying decisions for your store and—most importantly—for your customers.

With this chapter, then, you have completed Unit 19, and you should have a good understanding of the many aspects of merchandise planning.

Trade Talk

Define each term and use it in a sentence.

Advanced dating
Anticipation dating
Cash discount
Dating
EOM dating
Extra dating
FOB city of destination
FOB shipping point
FOB store
Independent buying office

Market representative
Merchandise resources
On consignment
On memorandum
Ordinary dating
Quantity discount
Resident buying offices
Resource files
ROG dating
Season discount
Store-owned buying office
Title
Trade discount

Can You Answer These?

1. Name four pieces of information a buyer would record on a resource file.
2. What are four "terms" that a buyer negotiates when purchasing goods?
3. The FOB shipping point determines what two important aspects of the buying contract?
4. What are three kinds of dating that allow the buyer extra time to pay the bill and still take a discount?
5. What are the advantages and disadvantages of consignment buying to a retailer?

Amount of Invoice	Date of Invoice	Terms	Amount Due if Discount Is Taken	Date When Total Amount of Invoice Due
$ 300	Sept. 1	2/10, n/30		
$ 500	Aug. 1	3/10, n/45		
$ 950	Jan. 1	2/10, n/30, 60 extra		
$1,500	July 1	2/10, n/30, EOM		
$ 500	Aug. 1	6/10, n/30, EOM, 60 extra		

Problems

1. At the central market, you are negotiating for discounts and dating terms with suppliers. You wish to analyze these terms to determine:

   a. the amount due if the discount is taken
   b. the date when the total amount of the invoice is due

   Rule a form like the one above, and use it to complete your analysis.

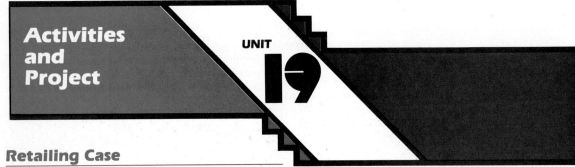

Activities and Project

UNIT 19

Retailing Case

You, as the manager of a variety store, are preparing a 3-month merchandise plan for your stationery department. You are reviewing the actual results of last year's buying plan. This year, you plan sales increases of 10 percent for April, 10 percent for May, and 5 percent for June, You likewise plan similar increases for the planned stock at the first of the month. Because you plan to manage shortages and planned markdowns more effectively this year, you make no changes in these amounts.

Your task is to complete the blank spaces on the following buying plan using the above information. Note that you can only compute retail purchases for the first 2 months. The planned stock for the first of the month has not yet been determined for July. Refer to Chapter 59 to assist you in your calculations.

Working with People

You are a new department manager in a smaller branch store in an outlying suburb. Your main headquarters store is lo-

MERCHANDISE PLAN

Factor	Year		April	May	June	Total
Planned sales, dollars	Last year		1,000	1,200	1,100	3,300
	Planned					
Planned stock, first of month, dollars	Last year		200	300	175	675
	Planned					
Shortages and planned markdowns, dollars	Last year	Markdowns	50	60	50	160
		Shortages	20	25	20	65
	Planned	Markdowns				
		Shortages				
Retail purchases, dollars	Last year		1,170	1,160		
	Planned					
Planned initial markup, percent	Last year		40	40	40	
	Planned		40	40	40	

cated in the inner-city area of a large metropolis. For the past selling season, you carefully prepared a merchandise plan that took into consideration projected sales, necessary purchases, required markups and markdowns, and desired inventories. Toward the end of the selling season, you unexpectedly received a large shipment of merchandise from your counterpart department in the headquarters store. You are informed by this department head that the merchandise is their overstock. It is not selling in the main store. The merchandise was transferred to your store with the directive that you try to sell it. You are very concerned with this unexpected transfer, which has distorted your merchandise plan. Your future promotions and salary increases are dependent on the success of your merchandise plans. Also, you do not appreciate the manner in which this transfer was made.

1. Identify specific problems caused by this transfer of merchandise.
2. What are important facts to be considered in this problem?
3. List several possible solutions.
4. Evaluate the possible results.
5. Which solutions would you recommend? Why?

Project 19: Analyzing Current Merchandising Practices

Your Project Goal
Given magazines, newspapers, trade journals, employer training materials, and so on, prepare a written summary report describing current merchandising practices related to one of the topics covered in Unit 19: developing pricing policies, preparing the merchandise plan, buying to produce a profit, and obtaining the best terms.

Procedure
1. Refer to the "Trade Talk" terms at the end of each chapter in Unit 19 for possible merchandising topics.
2. Contact your instructor or employer for possible reference materials.
3. Organize your report using this outline:
   a. Reference selected for study
   b. Date of reference
   c. Title of article or materials
   d. Merchandising practice described
   e. New, interesting, or unique aspects of the merchandising practice

Evaluation
You will be evaluated on the completeness of your report.

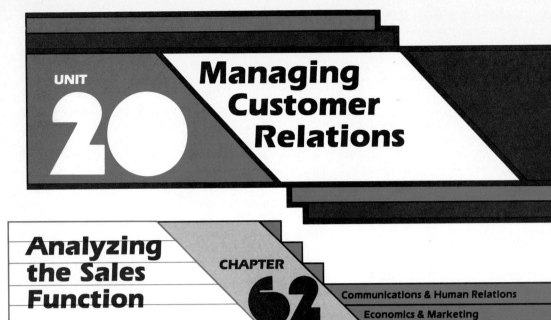

UNIT
20

Managing
Customer
Relations

Analyzing
the Sales
Function

CHAPTER
62

Communications & Human Relations

Economics & Marketing

Merchandising

Selling & Technology

Advertising & Display

Operations & Management

Karen Stromgren's career goal was to be a retail store manager at age 25. She didn't want to waste time, so she took advantage of every opportunity to learn all she could about store management and what makes a manager successful.

Karen's store manager, Mr. Horowitz, had an excellent track record in retailing, having joined the company as a salesperson only 7 years earlier. So Karen asked for an opportunity to talk to him about her career plans. He graciously consented and arranged a meeting.

Early in the interview, Karen asked her key question, "Mr. Horowitz, I realize that hard work and dedication to one's occupation are essential to good store management, but many people meet those qualifications. Can you tell me what helped you most in achieving your superior record?"

The store manager replied, "I suppose that there are many things that enable a

person to become a good merchant or store manager. However, the thing that strikes me as being most essential is to be *sales-minded,* using every opportunity to build sales. A store's success depends on profitable sales. All the people who work for a retailer contribute to those sales whether they realize it or not." He went on to explain the elements of the sales function of retailing from the managerial viewpoint. He then discussed how a good store manager helps employees understand their roles in selling the firm's products and services.

The Exchange Function

"The retailer—purchasing agent for the public." This slogan has persisted for many decades because it expresses so well the concept that governs all retailing. Regardless of the kind of store or shop or its location, this slogan defines the retailer's primary purpose in our economic system. And it gives direction to all retail activities, especially those of the **exchange function,** which consist of buying and selling. Buying and selling in retailing are really like two sides of the same coin; retailers nearly always estimate the salability of merchandise before they buy it for resale.

Let's look at the selling aspect of the exchange function of retailing from a broad perspective, as a progressive retailer sees it. If the slogan opening the paragraph above is true for all retailers, selling must begin long before the consumer enters the place of business. So retail sales really begin in the minds of merchants. They begin when merchants anticipate the products and services their particular "publics" will want and when those publics would like those goods and services to be delivered. Likewise, the sale is not complete until the products or services are consumed or used and the customer is satisfied with the purchase. So the policy of "Satisfaction or your money back" is common in retailing.

This broad perspective of retail selling will enable you to see eye to eye with management on many operational matters. It also offers direction for a satisfying career of service regardless of what type of retail work you do.

Now let's analyze selling from the managerial viewpoint. Here are the factors that produce a retail sale: (1) product or service, (2) place, (3) competition, (4) personnel, and (5) consumer. In the various types of retailing, the mix and makeup of these factors is different, and they have varying effects on each other. How difficult the sales function is in the different types of retailing depends on what these factors consist of and how they affect each other. Certainly, the factors involved in selling groceries contrast sharply with those involved in selling stereos.

The Product or Service Factor

Great retailers are known by the products they sell. This is rightly so, because it is usually the merits of their products that enable them to earn their reputations. Each product category tends to attract workers with certain characteristics and to mold them in certain ways. For example, contrast the traits of a supermarket operator with those of the owner of a prestigious jewelry store. Both are respected retailers, but their thinking seems to be influenced by differences in the type of product (convenience, shopping, or specialty goods) they carry. Other factors that shape them are merchandise turn-

The sales function of retailing. The circles represent the five factors that merchants consider when serving their clientele. The disciplines that support the merchants' decisions are shown as bricks in the foundation.

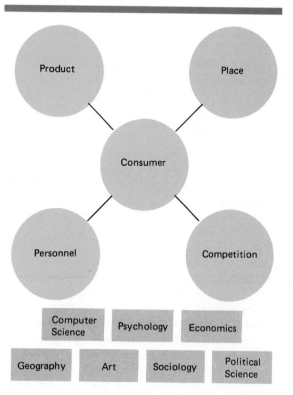

over rate, selling-floor decor, customer services offered, and so on.

Regardless of the form of retailing or the location of the store, the first question retailers ask themselves about a product or service is, "Will it sell well?" So the old principle of "The right merchandise, at the right time, and at the right price," dominates their minds.

As you learned in Chapters 22 and 23, the sales function of retailers in distributing most convenience goods, such as those sold by supermarkets, is relatively simple. This is because the manufacturer usually does most of the job of informing consumers—that is, giving them information through packaging, advertising, and point-of-sale display aids. However, many shopping goods and specialty goods require personal or professional advice. (Refresh your memory on the personal selling task by reviewing pages 181 to 184 in Chapter 23.)

Balancing Supply and Demand

Being able to balance the supply of a product or service with consumer demand for it is vital to retailers. Obviously, there are great differences in the degree of demand for certain types of products. And this is particularly so when fashion or weather influences are involved. Even within a category of goods such as clothing, the differences are great. For example, the demand for hosiery and underwear is relatively stable. But the demand for most outerwear is subject to strong fashion influence. Also, in hardware there is likely to be a steady demand for nails but wide year-to-year differences in the calls for snow throwers. Sometimes, manufacturers fail to make enough of a product, such as electronic games for the Christmas season. This situation makes reordering impossible.

If the store is out of stock in the brand, size, or style of product the customer wants or doesn't carry it, sales (and profits) are lost. On the other hand, overstocking a product reduces profits and often means a loss to the store. So merchants are very much concerned about fast turnover of stock. And they're concerned about the accuracy of stock controls that tell them what kind of product to order and when to order it. Unfortunately, some merchandise may not be available on short notice. In this situation, retailers have to use several different sources to maintain a steady supply for their customers.

Price Considerations

Pricing the product is a complex and critical task. The product's cost to the retailer and the appropriate selling price are taken into account. The risk rests largely with price changes in both wholesale and retail markets. Inflation is a difficult problem for the retailer as well as for the consumer. Retailers know that when consumer benefits other than price are equal, consumers tend to take advantage of lower prices. So the pricing challenge is not going to disappear.

The Place Factor

The second factor to consider in analyzing the sales function is the place where the products and services are available to consumers. This includes the physical plant, its location, and the image of the company in the minds of potential customers. So retailers compete for store locations and they design storefronts and interiors that attract and hold customers. They also offer customer services and try to build an image favorable to their potential customers—it's all part of selling.

The Shopping Environment

Most customers like to shop in a clean environment where there is plenty of light, clean air, and fresh merchandise. They don't like to trip over merchandise or handle soiled goods, and they appreciate a pleasing decor. Many customers like to identify with the store environment. They sometimes prefer one discount department store to another, even though the prices are competitive. So retailers of nearly all types have great concern for the sales function of the physical plant. And they invest wisely in adapting it to the tastes of their customers.

Customer Service Policies

Few stores have identical customer service policies. Each store operates according to what it believes will appeal most to its customers and what will bring in the kind and amount of sales the firm wants. Some retailers favor **hard sell,** which is the use of strong persuasion. Others support **soft sell,** which limits a sales effort largely to supplying requested information. A third policy classification is self-service. In practice, there are a number of different viewpoints within each type of policy.

In some stores, operating costs are held to a bare minimum and rapid sales and large volume per salesperson are strongly encouraged. In prestige stores and often in neighborhood stores, on the other hand, salespeople are usually expected to spend more time with customers. And this is a practice that increases selling costs. Convenience grocery stores are like supermarkets in terms of customer services offered.

The store's method of paying its sales force is usually directly related to the kind of sales practices it prefers. When stores pay straight salary or salary plus a small commission, they usually lean toward the soft-sell approach. When they pay salary plus large commissions or straight commission, they usually prefer the hard-sell method. Automobile dealers, for example, usually pay large commissions on sales.

Promotion Policies

Some stores do a thorough job of promoting sales. Individual products and their prices are promoted strongly in newspaper ads, TV and radio commercials, and displays. In other stores, promotions are less price-oriented and more inclined to stress product lines, customer services, or store image. Continuous sales promotion

usually makes the sales task easier for a salesperson, while low-key promotion usually means a greater challenge. In low-key situations, advertising effort is primarily intended to bring consumers into the store. The salesperson is expected to do the selling job.

The Competition Factor

The third factor of the sales function is competition. It's always in the back of a retailer's mind, raising such questions as: What will the effect of an action have on my competitors? Will it help increase my share of the market? Is it a matter of keeping up with competitors or getting ahead of them? There is a limit to the market for every product, and competition may be strong or weak. When competition is strong, sales efforts are intensified. Competitors feel forced to match their sales practices with those of other retailers, and a contest develops. On the other hand, when there is little competition, selling is much more relaxed.

Retailers welcome legitimate competition—that is, competition that meets consumer demand ethically and effectively. However, retailers resent and fight irregular and malicious competition, the aim of which is to malign or destroy ethical competitors.

You may have wondered what keeps competition alive. The answer is an ever-changing market. Retailers realize that our social and economic structure is constantly changing. Among the underlying changes are new social desires, purchasing patterns, and shopping motivations. And all these factors produce changing concepts of price and non-price competition. For example, discount houses have provided a way of shopping that sometimes gives consumers more product for their money and often permits them to feel thrifty and clever. Many specialty stores have reduced the kinds of merchandise they sell in order to offer broader assortments of those they do sell plus expert consumer services. Catalog warehouse merchandisers display their products in handsome showrooms, and so on. Each kind of business and each store's personnel search constantly for new products and new ways of competing for the consumer's dollar. Each watches the other very closely, and, as a retail worker, you should watch them too.

The Personnel Factor

The fourth factor of the sales function of retailing covers all the firm's personnel. Particular emphasis is placed on those responsible for the last stages of a sale, which take place across the counter. Effective and efficient personnel are the retailer's best sales asset. All workers are responsible for the quality of all customer services. Any one of them can make or break the sale. The goodwill created by the store's reputation can be destroyed in a few seconds. A store's reputation for quality products, fair treatment of customers, civic involvement of executives, institu-

tional advertising, and so on can easily be destroyed by a tactless salesperson, a haughty credit clerk, or a discontented stock worker.

Few employees realize the effect they have, either as individuals or collectively, on the store's sales volume. Very few people are the same from day to day. There are days when a person may be depressed and feel that nothing is going right. And because of such fatigue, the end of the day in particular may be trying. Regardless of the cause, however, the effect on customers and on sales volume is the same. To make matters worse, a bad mood may affect the morale and productivity of other workers. Of course, a positive attitude encourages cooperation from both customers and coworkers. Attitudes are contagious. So, efforts to improve productivity throughout the organization focus on worker morale and the employment of personnel who reflect the firm's image.

The advertising of fast-food franchisers provides evidence of the importance of personnel in the sales function of retail-

Competition helps to stimulate business. Fern Logan

UNIT 20 ◆ **Managing Customer Relations**

Retailers provide for individual needs and wants by catering to special types of trade. Michael Weisbrot

ing. Their TV commercials call the viewing audience's attention—and that of the advertiser's employees—to the treatment salesworkers give customers as well as to the products they sell. A large part of the success of fast-food franchisers can be credited to courteous, well-informed, service-minded personnel. Specialty stores also provide evidence of the importance of personal service and personal selling. They prosper because of the personal services they offer and their informed sales staffs. For this reason, some large department stores are stepping up their training programs.

The Consumer Factor

The fifth factor of the retail sales function, the consumer, is called the "pivotal factor" because the other four factors depend on the consumer's decisions. Much has been said in this book about consumer behavior and how consumers like to be treated.

Wide differences in the tastes, habits, and behavior of individual customers com-

plicate the sales function of retailing. Attempts to provide for individual needs and wants are evident in the variety of retailers catering to different types of trade. So, we have discotheques, natural food stores, stores for tall men or women, prestige-oriented stores, and pushcart retailers. We also have stores for members of consumer cooperative associations, company employees, and the military as well as surplus outlets, direct selling, vending machines, and so on. It is also in order to accommodate individual differences that retailers employ salespeople who can appreciate and serve the customer's individual needs.

As a retail worker, here is how you can handle consumer individuality. Always act and react to the factors involved in the immediate sales situation before you. Remember what you learned yesterday, but tailor your knowledge and skill to today's situation.

Trade Talk

Define each term and use it in a sentence.

Exchange function
Hard sell
Soft sell

Can You Answer These?

1. What is the first question about a product that comes to a merchant's mind? What are the three elements contributing to the answer?
2. What are the three main parts of the place factor? How does each affect the sale of merchandise?
3. From a business viewpoint, why do most retailers welcome ethical competition? What causes competition to continue?
4. Why are retailers so concerned about the personnel factor?
5. Why is the consumer factor referred to as the pivotal factor? Explain the impact of this factor on the other four.

Problems

1. Record your answers to the questions below on a sheet of paper after reading the following:

Neither Ebenezer Scrooge nor Santa Claus can be overjoyed with Christmas 1978.

After strong year-to-year sales gains last Christmas and earlier this year, most retailers are posting modest increases so far this Christmas season. "It isn't spectacular but it isn't the pits either," says a spokesman for Yonkers Bros, Inc., a department store chain in Des Moines.

Shoppers are described as cautious and selective. Among their favorites this year are jogging suits, electric blankets, cosmetics, video games, velour and silk shirts, television sets and 14-carat jewelry. Some items have sold so fast that retailers can't keep them in stock; these include snow blowers, snuggle sacks (for bundling up at home), hot air popcorn poppers and electronic toys. On the other hand, many usually strong gift items—such as most menswear, sportswear, small appliances and outerwear—aren't moving as fast as they did last year. *The Wall Street Journal,* December 19, 1978.

(a) What causes Christmas sales volume to be different from one year to the next? (b) Why do the favorite gifts of Christmas shoppers change each year? (c) What sales function problems do retail toy buyers experience that other types of buyers do not have? (d) What happens when retailers learn that they are overstocked on gift items 2 weeks before Christmas? (e) How does competition affect the activities of a retailer who sells toys or other types of gift merchandise?

2. On five sheets of paper, rule selling function analysis forms similar to the following. Use one sheet of paper for each of the sales-function factors discussed in this chapter: (a) product, (b) place, (c) competition, (d) personnel, and (e) consumer. Fill in the spaces with the name of a product line and the sales function factors. Then, using the information from this chapter and other sources, list in the left column the retailer's concerns about each factor. Compare your list with those of your classmates who analyzed similar products, and enter the additional concerns in the right column.

Name of product line: _____

Sales function factor: _____

My List of Retailer Concerns	Added Concerns from Other Sources

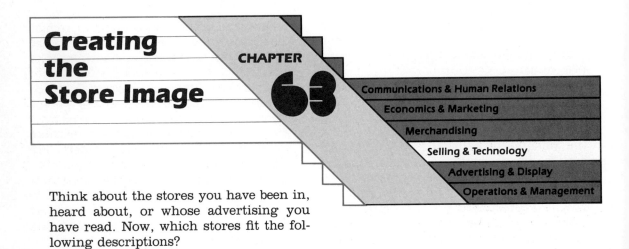

Creating the Store Image

CHAPTER 63

Communications & Human Relations

Economics & Marketing

Merchandising

Selling & Technology

Advertising & Display

Operations & Management

Think about the stores you have been in, heard about, or whose advertising you have read. Now, which stores fit the following descriptions?

- It has real bargains. The merchandise may not be top quality and their displays are average. You have to wait on yourself, but you get a good value for the price you pay.
- They don't have a large selection, but their products are good. They're always friendly and helpful.
- They've got the largest selection in town, and you can charge and have your purchases delivered. Prices aren't the lowest, but they're not the highest either.
- Just go in and let them solve your problem. They're experts, and they give you the kind of attention that's special. Of course, the prices are rather special too, but then you know you get the best there is.

By matching a store you know with one of the descriptions above, you have in part defined its personality. You may not have thought of a store as having personality, but each one does. Just as you have distinctive, individual qualities by which you are known, retail firms also make a general impression on their customers, employees, business associates, and the community in general.

What Is Store Image?

The impression, personality, or mental picture generally called to mind when a store is mentioned is known as the **store image.** It is really the reputation of the store as consumers know it.

Store images are as complex as human personalities. They are the result of a whole series of policies made by management and of the behavior of all store personnel. So, a store's image is the overall impression made by its policies, its personnel, and its physical appearance.

All the following contribute to a store's image: each salesperson serving a customer, each advertisement run by the store, each window or interior display the store shows, each assortment of goods the store offers, and each remark about the store made by an employee (or anyone else). Management sets policy guidelines to help employees get across, during their daily work, the desired store image to customers. All store workers should follow the store's guidelines to create a store image that attracts and holds customers.

Before retailers can begin to create a store image, they must decide on the market, or consumers, they wish to serve.

Market Segmentation

You already know that the quickest way for a retailer to make money is to find out what consumers want and sell it to them. You also know that the surest way for a retailer to lose money is to offer consumers something they don't want. In order to make money and to create a store image, retailers must identify the market or markets that they aim to serve and offer the right products at the right time, price, and place. A sound marketing practice is one whereby management selects a segment, or part, of the total market for the products or services it distributes and concentrates on the potential customers within that segment. Dividing the potential customers (the market) into groups according to their needs and characteristics is called **market segmentation.** A market may be divided according to characteristics such as income level, age, sex, education, or intended use of the product.

One important characteristic of the market is the income level of consumers, which roughly corresponds to four types of stores. So there are basically four major types of retail markets. These markets are those served by (1) the exclusive shop, (2) the specialty store, (3) the popular price store, which has the greatest proportion of buyers, and (4) the discount store. The figure on page 508 shows how the market for men's suits is segmented into four income-level categories that correspond to the four broad categories of stores. Note the overlapping of individual incomes among the categories.

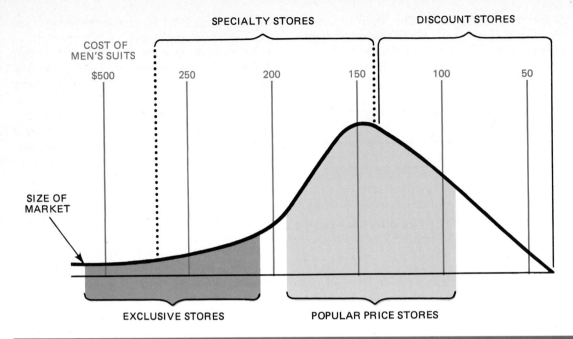

Store strategy and market segmentation.

Shaping the Image

Once retailers have decided on the consumers they wish to serve, they can then change, sharpen, or shape their store image to meet those consumer' needs and wants. To do this, retailers work to make their store policies reflect and reinforce the desired image. For example, suppose a retailer decides to serve customers who like to patronize exclusive shops. The retailer's store, then, would also have to project the image of an exclusive shop. Getting across an image of quality and prestige, which is associated with exclusive shops, can be done by using several methods—such as training the sales staff to give professional assistance and offering a wide variety of services, many of them free of charge. Another method that can be used is to feature a store layout with wide aisles, handsome fixtures, and an air of leisure and luxury. Finally, the most important method that can be used is to offer top-quality goods.

There are four major types of store policies that help create the image of a store: (1) merchandise policies, (2) promotion policies, (3) customer service policies, and (4) physical facilities policies.

Merchandise Policies

The most important factor contributing to the store's image is its merchandise. Therefore, a clearly spelled out merchandise policy is needed. A **merchandise policy** relates to the major lines of merchandise to be carried—including the quality and assortment of goods in each line—and the pricing policy.

Major Lines of Merchandise. Stores are generally considered exclusive, medium-priced, popularly priced, or low- or discount-priced, depending on the quality of the products handled and the pricing policy. With some kinds of products, such as apparel and jewelry, the quality range is great. Retailers must be very careful to select merchandise of a quality that matches the store's image.

Another aspect of the merchandise policy that affects the store's image is the number of brands it carries. Some stores carry several brands to give the customer a wide selection, while others, such as paint and wallpaper stores, may sell only a single brand. Supermarkets and large chain stores frequently offer their own brands in addition to national brands and generic (non-branded) items. Discount stores usually restrict assortments to only those items on which there is a high stock turnover.

Pricing Policies. Relative prices are an important aspect of store image, but prices are not easily controlled. With some types of goods, like many food items, competition brings about nearly uniform prices in a given locality, and there is little retailers can do about it. Customers are not willing to pay more for food in one supermarket when they can pay less for the same food in a neighboring supermarket. For other goods, such as art supplies, the price is determined largely by the cost of business operations. So a store that offers many free services, such as alterations and gift wrapping, has to charge more than a store that offers fewer services.

Sales Promotion Policies

A store projects its image through its sales promotion activities. The frequency of its promotional events, the media through which it advertises, the character of its ads, the quality of its displays, and the services of its salespeople all make a lasting impression on consumers and play a key role in forming the store's image.

Promotional Events. Many customers judge a store largely by the activities it uses to promote sales. There are many variations of the promotion techniques the different stores use; these depend on the merchandise sold, the behavior of the competition, and the aggressiveness of the store's management. A store may do very little sales promotion of any kind. Or it may carry on frequent, aggressive sales campaigns (with

or without the assistance of its suppliers), offer premiums or trading stamps, offer limited-time discounts over the loudspeaker, give style shows or free lessons, and so on. All such efforts contribute to its image.

Advertising. As mentioned previously, stores that carry prestige products put the look and sound of prestige into their advertising. For example, the layout, format, and copy of their advertisements are all worked out to project an image of quality. Stores that feature popularly priced goods use more aggressive and obvious promotional techniques. They try to reach the largest number of people possible. They push price and value for your money. This type of store uses advertisements in which the layout, typeface, and copy reflect the store's image.

A store's promotional policies contribute to its image. *Courtesy of Neiman-Marcus*

THE FANTASIES AND THE FACTS

Neiman-Marcus

FANTASY: Before you buy a gift at N-M, you'd better have a word with your banker.
FACT: We have all kinds of exclusive gifts for men, women, children and houses that won't break the bank. True, some of them do cost a small fortune — but some of them can be yours for under $25. And look like a whole lot more.
We're opening in White Plains on September 8th.

NEIMAN-MARCUS
WESTCHESTER

Display, Personal Selling, and Other Activities. Inside the store, retailers make sure that promotional activities reflect the same image as promotional activities outside the store. For example, discount stores tend to use promotional activities more frequently than prestige stores. Discount stores may use loudspeakers to announce specials and use special interior displays with point-of-sale show cards and other props. In regular stores and specialty shops, salespeople tend to be more aggressive—as, for example, in an automobile dealership during a slack period.

Customer Service Policies

The customer who expects a particular store to have quality merchandise and helpful salespeople also expects that store to have a variety of services available. A **customer service** is any activity, benefit, or satisfaction that is offered for sale or provided with the sale of products. Customer services are so common among large department stores and better specialty shops that they are taken for granted. They include free delivery within a certain area, free parking, a choice of credit arrangements, gift wrapping of packages when requested, and free or low-cost alterations of apparel purchased, plus many others.

Supermarkets, chain drugstores, variety stores, and most discount houses offer only a few customer services. And they often charge a fee for those they do offer. In recent years, however, many chain stores and even discount houses have found it necessary to offer some customer services, such as credit.

Physical Facilities Policies

Although consumers have accepted the automation of retailing, modern consumers still want convenience, comfort, and courtesy when they shop. So the physical environment is an important aspect of the store image. In order to keep their customers, most stores are faced with the choice of becoming more efficient in self-service techniques or more personalized in the services and shopping environment they offer.

The Economy Image. If a store concentrates on popularly priced merchandise, its layout and fixtures should emphasize ease and speed in shopping. Such stores should be bright and cheery. They should have plenty of signs directing customers to the various kinds of merchandise and have well designed self-service units. And such stores should also have conveniently located points where merchandise can be paid for and wrapped or sacked. These techniques are designed to keep the customer on the move and minimize shopping time.

The Prestige Image. If a store's layout and fixtures are to reflect quality merchandise, its aisles should be broad and its counters uncluttered. Many areas of such a store should have carpeted floors, and it should also have many spots where customers can sit down comfortably to examine merchandise. There should be plenty of lighting, but it shouldn't be too bright. The materials used, the colors, and the decorations should all be governed by the store's prestige image.

Chain- and Franchise-Store Facilities. Chain stores and franchises are nearly always particular about the exterior appearance of their outlets. They are almost as particular about this as they are about maintaining the layouts and decor of the selling areas. The reason is that they want customers to be able to identify their establishments quickly when traveling and to feel "at home" inside the store. Some small-town retailers, according to a recent study, experience problems with external store appearance. Such problems may be explained by the financial difficulties that are common to small businesses and to the lack of suitable structures to lease or rent. A related finding of the study was that a number of small-town stores were judged to have confusing names that did not identify their line of business.

Keeping Abreast of Change

With few exceptions, retailers must keep pace with changing customer expectations. They must make appropriate changes in their physical plants and be sure that their customers are aware of their efforts to improve the store image. One exception to the need for constant change was revealed in the study mentioned previously. It relates to small-town retailers who depend on customers from rural cultures where unsophisticated store interiors are common. Such consumers feel more comfortable in a traditional environment and resist change stubbornly. So some, but not all, small-town retailers may be smart to project an entirely different image from that of their city-based counterparts. As a matter of fact, each retail business should strive to create its own image. When stores are very much alike, where to buy makes little difference to a shopper.

In this chapter, you've learned how retailers constantly work at making their store image match the customers they want to serve. You found out that retailers do this by tailoring their merchandise, promotion, customer service, and physical facilities policies to reflect the store image they want to project to consumers.

In the next chapter, you'll learn about another part of managing customer rela-

Some chain stores want to maintain a uniform appearance, while others want a unique look. Geoffrey Gove/Photo Researchers, Inc. (left), courtesy of Gino's, Inc. (right)

tions—dealing with customers honestly and fairly, or the ethics of retailing.

Trade Talk

Define each term and use it in a sentence.

Customer service
Market segmentation

Merchandise policy
Store image

Can You Answer These?

1. Name the four market segments of the retail market.
2. What is the purpose of market segmentation?
3. What four types of store policies contribute to the store's image?
4. What do the store's physical facilities contribute to its image in the customer's mind? In the minds of store personnel?
5. Why do franchisers have strict rules about the appearance of stores associated with their company?
6. Why must retailers keep abreast of changes in the physical facilities involved in their kind of retailing?

Problems

1. Rule a form similar to the following. In the left column, write the names of ten stores representing a cross section of those running ads in one issue of your local newspaper. In the second column, write the kind of store it is—exclusive shop, specialty store, regular store, or discount store. In the third column, write the main image-building appeal(s).

Name of Store	Kind of Store	Image-Building Appeal
Example: Marshall Field & Co.	Exclusive specialty	High fashion Personalized service

2. Rule a form similar to the following. Select a local store that sells clothing or some other commonly used product(s). Write the name of the store in the space provided. Then record the kind of store in the proper space. In the four columns, record your concept of the store's image as to merchandise policies, promotion policies, customer service policies, and physical facilities policies.

Name of store: _____ Kind of store: _____

Merchandise Policies	Sales Promotion and Selling Policies	Customer Service Policies	Physical Facilities Policies

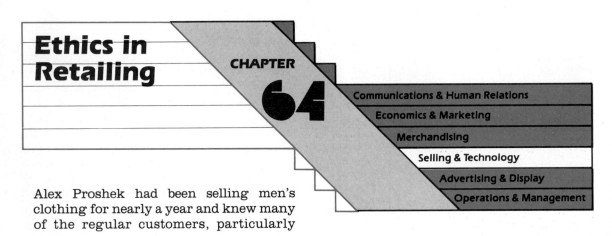

Ethics in Retailing

CHAPTER 64

Communications & Human Relations
Economics & Marketing
Merchandising
Selling & Technology
Advertising & Display
Operations & Management

Alex Proshek had been selling men's clothing for nearly a year and knew many of the regular customers, particularly those who were difficult to serve for one reason or another. When he spotted one of the latter, he would pretend to be busy or leave the floor in order to avoid waiting on the problem shopper.

One day, one of the regular salespeople was on vacation and other members of the department were busy with customers. Alex was stuck with a well-known time-waster who was trying on light topcoats that had just been added to the stock. "Has this garment been waterproofed?" asked the customer. Alex glanced quickly at the coat but didn't notice a tag indicating that the material had been waterproofed. He said, "Of course, it has." Although he had serious doubts about whether the coat had been waterproofed, he wanted to get rid of the customer and wait on a "big spender" who just arrived. However, the "problem shopper" bought the coat and took it home.

When the customer got home, he removed all the tags—*including* the one that indicated the coat had been waterproofed.

Is avoiding certain customers legal? Is it ethical to do so? Was Alex intentionally trying to deceive his customer? Was he acting in the best interest of the company's goal—profitability? Does the fact that the topcoat actually had been waterproofed change the situation? Should Alex be promoted if his sales volume is high?

Ethical problems are not confined to beginners in retailing. Top-level executives often have much more difficult ethical decisions to make. So if you're planning a retailing career—or if you're not—now is the best time to start forming your code of business ethics.

"That's not fair" is not a legal complaint. It is an ethical concern, however, and those on both sides of a controversial problem know what is meant. An ethic is a set of moral attitudes; the field of **ethics** deals with what is good or bad, right or wrong. Ethical practices—or principles of conduct governing an individual or group—are required for a harmonious business operation. That is, a common dedication to honesty and decency is required. Let's look at the honesty factor first.

Ethics in Retailing

From the standpoint of ethical practice, retailing has come a long way during the twentieth century. Only a hundred years ago, many distributors were still following the policy of **caveat emptor** (say ka-ve-at EMP-tor), meaning "let the buyer beware." Some of them even agreed in principle with the philosophy of P. T. Barnum, the circus tycoon, who said "There's a sucker born every minute." Retailers who were situated where competition was weak or nonexistent usually tended to follow the greedy way of doing business. However, the business climate has changed drastically since those early days.

Today, the business climate is usually one known as a buyer's market. A **buyer's market** is one in which the purchasers of products and services are in control because the supply of products and services tends to exceed the demand for them. Even in a **seller's market**, in which demand is much greater than supply, ethical practices usually prevail. They prevail because retailers realize that customers have a long memory and support the firms that treat them fairly regardless of market conditions.

An Informed Public

Long-term profitability and ethical business conduct are now inseparable. (Bad ethics is bad business.) The ethical pursuit of profit is fundamental, a requirement of sound business management. The basic reason for this gradual change in attitude rests with education—education of both buyers and sellers. Thanks to more education for greater numbers of people, and particularly to television and aggressive journalists, the consumer has access to almost unlimited information. As a result, institutions of every description—not just retailing—find their clients more sophisticated, more secure in their challenges, and sharper in their questioning than ever before.

Conflicting Interests

A better-informed public doesn't mean that being ethical is any easier for the retailer—it's not. Balancing the interests of conflicting groups while advancing the company's objectives is becoming more and more difficult. Consumers, employees, stockholders, special need groups, and special interest organizations compete for the retailer's favor. Because of this situation, management has to make decisions it doesn't enjoy. They have to make decisions on such matters as price increases, dividend reductions or omissions, layoffs of personnel, discontinuance of certain lines of merchandise or customer services, and the like. Determining the wisest course of action is often a retailer's most difficult problem.

Another aspect of ethical retail practice involves competition. Managers' consciences, like those of everyone else, are at least partly formed by the forces of their environment. So they are led to believe that if they are to survive, they must meet competitors on the basis of the practices that exist in the retail industry, regardless of ethics.

With access to more information, consumers feel more secure about questioning a business's practices. Courtesy of Florida Department of Agriculture and U.S. Department of Justice.

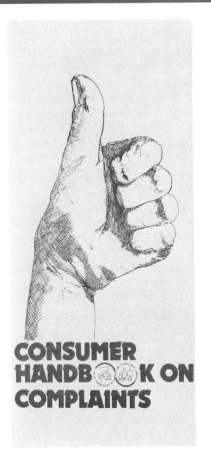

More and more, the new requirements of business are (1) to comply voluntarily with the spirit of the law and (2) to respect the unwritten rules of society; that is, to do what is right simply because it is the right thing to do.

Management's Role in Ethical Practices

Corporations themselves are neither ethical or unethical. But the people who manage them and carry on the daily activities of the business may act in an ethical or an unethical manner. Corporations act only through people. So the moral tone of a business firm is set by the actions of its top executives. Management is the most important single factor in determining employee ethics throughout the organization.

Employees soon learn what kind of company they are working for, and they behave accordingly. They may approve of management's ethical or unethical conduct, cope with it by adjusting their personal behavior, or decide to not work for that particular firm.

Management usually tries to hire people who agree with the company code of ethics. Then it is their responsibility to communicate the company's policies to all personnel through supervisors. Some companies write up their own codes of ethics or guidelines for use by all levels of personnel. Others may use the codes of their trade associations.

Moral Responsibilities in Retailing

In this discussion so far, we have focused on the honesty aspect of ethics and the rationale for honesty in today's retail market. We've also mentioned the complexity of being fair and honest with all parties concerned when management has to make decisions. Now, we'll look at the decency aspect of ethical behavior—the conscience of a retailing business. An ethic tells us what we *may* do among all the things we *can* do. So let's see what retailers may do and sometimes do do.

A New Concept of Purpose

Most retailers today realize that continuing usefulness and profitability depend on a much wider range of relationships. These relationships involve not only stockholders, customers, and employees but other institutions, other businesses, the community, and society as a whole. Sometimes these interest groups are referred to as "stakeholders" rather than strictly shareholders or stockholders. Modern store owners and managers are still concerned with selling products and services at a profit, but they recognize that long-run social and political factors have been ignored. They are committed to our competitive free enterprise system. But they express some fear that if business and industry does not or cannot accept social responsibility, the American system will disappear. And in its place, they fear, a different economic and political structure will emerge. Social standards are changing and business is being sharply reminded that it is part of society and exists only because customs and laws permit it to do so.

The New Viewpoint

In corporations with large numbers of stockholders, earnings (the "bottom line" of the income statement) are the most important indicators to financial analysts or stockbrokers of how well the business performs. Managers of businesses are held accountable for growth in profits quarter by quarter and year by year to boards of directors who answer to stockholders. Is the bottom line *all* that counts?

Directed management, which was once prevalent in this country, says "Yes." **Response management,** which starts with the customer and goes up the line to management, takes the opposite view. Inter-

Burdine's Creed

To be faithful to the high character and honest principles of this business in the words we say and the acts we do.

To treat each customer as we would expect to be treated.

To be content with nothing less than a completely satisfied customer in every transaction.

To insure greater opportunity and future security for all our people by generating dynamic, dominant sales growth with optimum profitability.

To merit good will and confidence by selling fashion-right merchandise which is of the best quality obtainable for the price.

To present stores and shops which are exciting, warm, friendly, and completely customer-oriented.

To believe in the men and women working together here.

To respect the dignity and importance of each one who is helping to build--with energy and enthusiasm--one of the great groups of stores in America--BURDINE'S.

this has been our belief for over 73 years

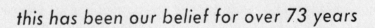

Burdine's Cares

estingly, stockholders, both institutions and individuals, realize that the corporation has to be a good member of the community. They react favorably to companies that are trying to assist their communities—it makes good business sense. Therefore many social-minded managements contribute in many ways to education, health-associated programs, social service organizations, religious organizations, and community betterment projects. Some firms now establish social goals as well as financial goals. In supporting the movement toward more social responsibility of the business community, retailers (being closest to consumers) have been out in front by comparison with other businesses.

How Change Takes Place

Since management is mainly responsible for a firm's ethical conduct, it's important for firms to select, train, and promote workers for managerial positions in our changing world. Schools and colleges prepare people for leadership positions in retailing by instructing them about the social responsibilities of business and the relevant social problems of business and society. Management seminars are increasingly popular for bringing those who are already executives up to date. The number of managerial workers returning to school for advanced work is increasing rapidly. And, of course, many progressive companies conduct their own managerial training programs, drawing on outside resources from various disciplines. Research has shown that formal education usually makes a person more aware of and prepared to talk about ethical issues. But formal education has much less influence on business decisions than the personal conviction that one should behave ethically.

Difficulties in Making Ethical Decisions

Everyone has a different code of ethics. And everyone also has a different set of standards by which he or she judges ethical behavior. This is the basis of one's conscience. So the ethical beliefs of individuals and businesses vary a great deal.

In many business decisions, it is really difficult to determine what is right and what is wrong because of the lack of an acceptable base. Through the ages, philosophers themselves haven't agreed on the bases for determining what is good or bad. Common practices in retailing leave many ethical questions unanswered. And we are all influenced by sayings such as "Let your conscience be your guide" or "The majority rules." Also, managers and employees are exposed to many untruths, such as "Without regulations everyone would be honest." So what can retail managers do to act ethically on their many complex problems?

Approaches to Improving Ethical Behavior

There are no easy answers to management's ethical problems, but there are approaches that will improve managerial ethics:

♦ Managers should rely more heavily on knowledge in the development and execution of policies.
♦ Managers should not let common practices of the organization or the trade become the final guide, taking the easy way out.
♦ Managers should avoid purely personal and emotional values to govern their actions but base their decisions on logic.
♦ Managers should be sensitive to opposing pressures and recognize over-simplified approaches.
♦ Managers should encourage a give-and-take attitude from all concerned and should communicate by setting an example.

With this chapter, you've completed Unit 20. So you should have a good idea of the concerns and problems that retailers have to deal with in managing customer relations. They must understand

Honest, ethical employees keep busy; they feel they owe their company a full day's work for a full day's pay. Courtesy of E.I. Dupont de Nemours Co.

something about analyzing the sales function and developing the store image. And they must deal with the problems of ethics in retailing.

Trade Talk

Define each term and use it in a sentence.

Buyer's market
Caveat emptor
Ethics
Response management
Seller's market

Can You Answer These?

1. From the standpoint of ethics, in what ways has retailing improved during the past century? What caused these changes?

2. What are the conflicting interest groups that compete for the retailer's favor?

3. What part does management play in the ethical behavior of a store's personnel?

4. What are the differences between the qualities of honesty and decency? What moral responsibilities are associated with decency?

5. How do retailers achieve and maintain changes in managerial ethics?

6. What are an employee's responsibilities in achieving employer-employee ethical compatibility?

Problems

1. Rule a form similar to the following. In the left column, write the letter of each of the following groups: (a) customers, (b) employees, (c) community, (d) society as a whole, (e) suppliers, and (f) competitors. Write a policy statement illustrating an ethical practice for each and then give each group a priority based on its probable effect on store welfare. Compare your ratings with those of your classmates.

Target Group	Policy Statement	Priority

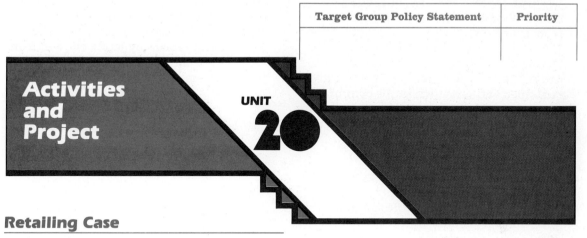

Activities and Project

UNIT 20

Retailing Case

Paul Casals, a young vice president of Vandyke's Furniture, Inc., was in charge of personnel. He was concerned about keeping abreast of the times and wanted to upgrade the performance of his regular sales staff. The store held monthly sales training meetings that dealt with product knowledge, furniture fashion, and selling practices and problems. Paul thought that these meetings were inadequate to meet the demands of changing times.

Paul was convinced that the best way to improve sales performance was to involve members of the sales staff in a training program that was in tune with the times. In light of the consumer movement and favorable economic conditions, he felt that the sales staff would benefit from being involved in the construction of a new type of sales performance rating form, one in which the factors to be rated would reflect the customer's viewpoint.

The store training director did not support Paul's viewpoint. She felt that the traditional training content and procedures were adequate and that the new approach would upset the routines of the experienced salespeople and confuse them. She hinted that the consumer movement seemed to be wearing out and that it would eventually disappear.

1. Should Vandyke's Furniture, Inc., launch a new sales training program more closely geared with the consumer movement? Why or why not?
2. If sales training is to take a new direction, should store image and ethical sales behavior be included along with the consumer movement?
3. Is Paul's idea about personal involvement of the sales staff feasible? Why or why not?
4. What items would you include in a self-rating form based on the consumer's viewpoint?

Working with People

You are the owner of a dress shop. You have the reputation of selling one-of-a-kind dresses, and your typical customer believes that she has a right to expect, from your shop, an exclusive creation at a moderate price. Your styles are not one of a kind, because they would then be too costly for your clientele. Your practice is to order a dress in only one size or color, always keeping to the New York or California markets. However, other stores near you or in nearby towns may also order the same size, color, and style that you have ordered. One of your customers, Mrs. DiVenezia recently purchased a dress from you to wear to a charity ball. At the ball, which was in another city, Mrs. DiVenezia saw another woman with "her dress." Mrs. DiVenezia has been a good customer and is known in the community as being a style-setter. What are you going to do about her angry reaction to this incident?

1. Identify the true problem.
2. What are the important facts to be considered in this problem?
3. List several possible solutions to this problem.
4. Evaluate the possible results of each solution.
5. Which solution do you recommend? Why?

Project 20:
Surveying the Store Image

Your Project Goal
Given two competing retail firms and a structured form, interview ten customers, identifying and classifying the patronage buying motives of each. Prepare a summary report listing suggestions you would offer each retailer to improve his or her business.

Procedure
1. Select two retail firms in your community that are in competition with each other— for example, two department stores.
2. Number each of eight 3 by 5 cards and head each with one of the patronage motives identified on page 334: (a) customer policies, (b) integrity, (c) fashion cycle, (d) quality of merchandise, (e) shopping atmosphere, (f) assortment policy, (g) courteous treatment, and (h) customer services. The first card, for example, would

be headed "customer policies" and would include the examples "satisfaction with goods and services, returns, and adjustments," so that the person being interviewed knows what you mean by "customer policies."
3. On a separate sheet of paper, rule a form similar to the following for each of the two stores. List the patronage motives across the top of the form (by letter shown) from your 3 by 5 cards. List each person interviewed in the left column.

Reasons Why Customers Shop at: _____
Location: _____   Date: _____

Person Interviewed	Patronage Motive							
	a	b	c	d	e	f	g	h

4. Get permission from each store management to interview ten customers to determine why the customers shopped at their store.
5. Standing outside the store, ask the people who are leaving to select the cards that best describe the major reasons why they shop at this particular store.
6. Record the responses on the form that you prepared in Step 3. Shuffle the cards and repeat Steps 5 and 6 until ten customers from each store have been interviewed.
7. Total the results for each store and prepare a report containing (a) a list showing how many customers selected each of the buying motives for each of the stores, (b) a discussion comparing the findings of your interviews for the two different retail stores, and (c) a list of suggestions that you have for each of the retailers on how the retailer could use the information you have gathered.

Evaluation
You will be evaluated on how effectively you gathered data, compared the findings for the two stores, and made recommendations about how the data should be used.

520

Advertising Copy and Illustrations

Communications & Human Relations

Economics & Marketing

Merchandising

Selling & Technology

Advertising & Display

Operations & Management

One Friday evening Rita and Manuel Torres were shopping the ads in preparation for a trip to the Gateway Shopping Center the next morning. Rita wanted some sportswear for the forthcoming family vacation, so she concentrated on department store and specialty shop ads in the women's section of the *Daily Times*. As Rita had been reading national women's fashion magazines and the local newspaper, she had a general idea of what she wanted.

Manuel needed plumbing supplies and wanted some new sports gear, so he read the building supply and sporting goods ads in the business and sports sections of the newspaper and checked the *Post Shopping Guide*. He compared the descriptions and prices of goods in these publications with those advertised in the catalogs of mail-order houses and catalog showrooms. Earlier, Manuel had been impressed with some camping equipment he had seen advertised on television.

This brief account illustrates how con-

sumers use advertising to help them make buying decisions and save shopping time. Of course, advertising saves the retailer time and money too, thereby increasing profit. Manuel's use of several sources of information shows how each advertising medium—print, broadcast, and direct mail—plays a part in carrying out the sales function. Finally, it suggests the need for careful preparation of advertising copy, illustrations, and layout.

Components of Printed Ads

The four parts of a retail advertisement are the headline and **copy** (words), the **art** (illustrations), the **logotype** (identification of the sponsor), and the **layout** (arrangement of copy, art, and logotype). Many ads, of course, consist only of copy and a logotype, and a few only of art and a logotype. Most retail advertising, however, is a blend of copy and art, because retailers know that people are influenced by both words and pictures.

In this chapter, you'll learn about the use of copy and illustrations in preparing an ad. In Chapter 66, you'll learn about advertising layout.

Who Creates an Ad?

In a small store, the owner or the manager decides what merchandise is to be advertised and usually consults the local newspaper's advertising department for help in preparing the ad. Because small retailers know their merchandise and their customers, they can suggest ideas for copy and illustrations and they can judge whether the ads created by the newspaper will result in sales. Some small retailers create their own ads with the help of a representative from the local newspaper. These advertising specialists often suggest ideas for copy and layout. Some manufacturers have ads prepared, so that all the retailers need to do is to add the store's logo.

In larger stores, advertising is assigned by department or category of merchandise. The appropriate buyer or division merchandise manager decides exactly which items are to be featured. Before an ad is to appear, either the buyer or the division merchandise manager fills in a sheet that indicates the merchandise to be advertised and its selling points. The copywriters in the advertising department use this information to prepare ads.

What the Advertising Specialist Must Know

To prepare effective store ads as an advertising specialist, you need the following:

1. An understanding of the store's image and advertising policies
2. Accurate information about the products

or services being advertised
3. An understanding of the medium in which the ad is to be published and what the ad specifications are
4. An understanding of the processes used if the ad is printed

The Store Image and Policies

As an advertising specialist, you'll have an understanding of your store's image and policies if you can answer the following questions: What quality of merchandise do we sell? What image do we want to project? What services do we offer? Who are our customers? What are their tastes? What are their income levels? How does our store compare with the competition? Why do people buy from us?

Accurate Product Information

When you are preparing an ad, you must have complete and accurate information about the merchandise to be advertised. False or inaccurate information in an ad almost always means disappointed customers, loss of goodwill, and even losses to the store. Sometimes, however, mistakes are made. And to correct them some stores run ads apologizing for the inconvenience caused by the mistake in an ad and offering some kind of compensation for it.

To ensure that the product information is accurate, prepare a list of the points to be emphasized in the copy. For example, points such as the qualities of the product, its price, its uniqueness, how it is to be used, and why it is worth special attention. As an advertising specialist, you can obtain information from buyers and sometimes from salespeople. Suppliers' literature can be helpful too. In Chapter 22, on page 173, there was a good format for product analysis that advertising specialists find useful.

The Medium and Ad Specifications

As an advertising specialist, you have to know the medium in which the ad will run

*Sometimes retailers have to run corrections on
their advertisements.*

and the specifications for the particular
ad. You'll also want to know who reads the
publication and the section of the publication in which the ad will appear. Knowing this will help you to match the ad's
appeal to the reader's reasons for buying,
or buying motives. And, finally, find out
the position of the ad on the page; this will
tell you where to start the eye movement
of readers.

The purpose of the ad should always be
clear. Is the objective to create goodwill or
to increase sales? Should the ad tie in with
a promotional event? Should it be directed
to new customers? And so on.

When you know all these things—plus
the ad's size, shape, and running dates—
you're ready to prepare the ad itself. However, there is one precaution you should
take concerning the stock of the product
that you have on hand. Sufficient quantities of the item featured in the ad must
be on hand to satisfy customers responding to it.

The Printing Processes

To make the right decisions about the selection of printers and the preparation of
artwork, you need to understand the characteristics of the printing processes used
to produce advertisements. Three major
printing processes are used today:

1. Letterpress, the oldest process, is used
mainly for producing high-quality materials for magazines and direct-mail
advertising.
2. Gravure is the opposite of the letterpress
process and is also used in producing
quality materials.
3. Offset lithography is a fast process that
accounts for 70 percent of all newspaper
printing.

A fourth process, silk screen, is used
mainly on packages and on show cards
and signs.

In the **letterpress process,** the impressions are made from raised surfaces that
have been inked. An inked plate (either
flat or round) is pressed onto the paper.
The letterpress process includes printing
from line drawings and halftones, which
we will discuss later.

In the **gravure process**—opposite of the
letterpress—depressions are cut, or etched,
in a flat surface. A cylinder rotates through
a pool of ink so that the recessed portions
of the plate are filled. The higher, nonprinting surface is then wiped clean and
the cylinder transfers the impression of
the inked portion to the paper. Gravure is
frequently used to print the Sunday paper's picture supplement, occasionally
called the rotogravure section.

In **offset lithography,** a flat plate does
the printing. The process is based on the
principle that grease and water do not
mix. Since the surface surrounding the
greased design on the plate is kept wet,
ink from the roller does not stick to it. The
plate prints on a rubber blanket which
then transfers the impression to the paper. The use of rubber makes it possible

Berry's

ADVERTISED MERCHANDISE INFORMATION

Advertising information and the merchandise to be illustrated must be in the Advertising Department two weeks prior to the week in which the ad runs in the newspaper.

Department No.	74
Date Ad Runs	June 1, 19—

Item	Regular Price	Sale Price
Cotton canvas tote bags	Bags $18-28	No
Matching webbing belts	Belts $10	

Paper

New York Sunday Times (7 columns full)

List features in order of importance

1. Spacious, weightless, cotton canvas totes for town or travel

2. Five featured styles, wide assortment of colors, darks, neutrals, high shades

3. Webbing trim in contrasting colors, belts in cotton webbing matching bag trim

Sizes Roll: 17x10, $27, Kangaroo pocket, 17x12½, $18, Shoulder: 11½ x 10½, $26, Ring: 11½ x 10, $25, Maxi: 16½ x 13, $28.

Colors Roll: red, navy, black, natural; Shoulder: natural, tan, navy, red; Kangaroo and Ring: natural, black, navy, red, kelly green, pink, tan; Maxi: red, navy, black, natural, tan

Art Instructions Sketch woman's torso showing belt, bags, cascading down length of page

Additional Comments Designer in N.Y. store on 6/7

Submitted by Dorothy Smith, buyer

Date Received in Advertising Department May 15, 19—

Does manufacturer share cost of ad? Yes Is credit claim attached? Yes

Merchandise at Following Stores:

- ☒ New York
- ☒ Manhasset
- ☒ Westchester
- ☒ Short Hills
- ☒ Philadelphia
- ☒ Wynnewood
- ☒ Jenkintown
- ☒ Chicago
- ☒ Oakbrook
- ☒ Cleveland
- ☒ Boston
- ☒ Troy
- ☒ Palm Beach

Reason for Advertising:

- ☐ New Line
- ☒ Season Opening
- ☐ Sale
- ☐ Special Purchase
- ☐ Staple Stock
- ☐ Clearance

Quantity on Hand Date Ad Runs	Date Merchandise will be in Stock	Total Retail value of Merchandise	Use Trade Mark or Label	Is Manufacturer Paying for Ad?	Extra Delivery Charge?	Telephone Orders?	Mail Orders?	Mail Order Coupon?
250 pcs	5/26 complete	$4,450	Yes ☐ No ☒	Yes ☒ No ☐ 20% of Payment	Yes ☒ No ☐ Amount? 75¢	Yes ☒ No ☐	Yes ☒ No ☐	Yes ☐ No ☒

This sheet, prepared by the buyer or the division merchandise manager, contains all the information that the advertising specialist needs to prepare the ad.

to print fine designs and photographs on relatively coarse paper, such as that used by newspaper publishers. The term "offset" refers to the transfer process.

Preparing the Headline and the Copy

Now that you're aware of the information needed to create a retail advertisement, your next task is to understand what copywriting and preparing illustrations is all about. Let's examine copywriting first. Preparing copy (including the headlines) requires skills that are acquired mostly through meaningful practice.

Look Through the Customer's Eyes

"To move your product, you must move people." Copy moves people when it appeals to them personally. As a good copywriter, you will write as if you were talking to the customer and use language that customers can understand. This viewpoint applies to all kinds of copy, including headlines.

Attract Attention with the Headline

With the single exception of a particularly eye-catching illustration, a headline is the most important element in an ad. Effective headlines usually ask a question, make a suggestion, make an interesting statement, or drive home a major selling point or benefit. The table below lists some actual headlines that illustrate these things. Can you identify the underlying motive in each of the headlines in the table?

Buying motives used in personal selling are described in Chapter 42. These same appeals are used in writing advertising headlines and copy, which is actually selling in print.

Hold Interest with Body Copy

If the job of the headline is to catch the reader's attention, the job of the body copy is to create interest and hold it. It does this when it follows the thought of the headline and gets its main point across in the first paragraph. This ad used by Saks Fifth Avenue shows how well the first paragraph may explain the headline:

Saks recommends *yellow for safety* in your son's raincoat and helmet.
He's protected against the traffic as well as the elements when he wears our Safety Patrol Coat—yellow because yellow has the highest visibility in rain, mist, fog.

Copy must also convince customers to buy the advertised merchandise. Repeating the idea helps to convince the customer. Customers are persuaded to buy if the ad gives them a reason to believe that the merchandise should be bought. The concluding paragraph should stimulate the reader to go to the store to buy or to telephone or mail in an order. Here are some examples of copy lines that might convince the customer to take immediate action:

♦ At these prices, you'll be smart to stock up.

TYPES OF HEADLINES

Type of Headline	Real-Life Examples
Question	How's Your Golf Game? (sporting goods store) Time to Put on Something Warmer? (discount store) Need Cash? (savings & loan)
Suggestion	Button Up Your Chimney with Heat Seal and Start Saving (building supply store) Choose Your Favorite Iris Varieties (garden store) Put a Little Magic in Your Meals—And a Little Green in Your Pocket (supermarket)
Statement	Baskets Are Not Just for Picnics (department store) First Time Ever! Milco Radial (tire dealer) The $1 Steak is Back—This Week Only (butcher shop)
Benefit	You're *Really* Going to Save—When Lower-Than-Regular-Price Retailer Lowers His Price (men's clothing store) Relax! Enjoy a Riverboat Sightseeing Trip (excursion) Custom Canvas Awnings—Beauty, Comfort, Protection, *and* Energy Saving (outdoor furniture store)

The copy on a billboard is similar to the headline in a newspaper or magazine ad. Because the message is seen for just a few seconds, all the information must be packed into a few words. Courtesy of Western Airlines

- Now is your best time to buy.
- Your chance to save—this week only.

To get your message across, avoid overworking words and choose those that express the selling idea clearly. And since customers need only one idea to convince them that they should take action, stress one main idea in each paragraph.

An expert in writing advertising that sells prescribes a "B-complex" for copywriters:

- Be human
- Be simple
- Be sincere
- Be specific
- Be informative
- Be enthusiastic
- Be sure you're understood
- And, above all, be believable

Selecting the Illustrations

"One picture is worth a thousand words" is a saying that is sometimes true but sometimes is not. Any illustration in an ad is not worth a thousand words of copy—but a good illustration certainly can be. Although the headline may be the most effective part of an ad, illustrations can communicate more information more accurately than words. That this is so can be seen in catalog advertising.

Most consumers are exposed to pictures far more often than they are to printed copy, and they pay more attention to pictures. Because illustrations are now so commonly used as a means of communication, people have become more critical of what they see. For this reason, advertising specialists have become more skilled in the way they prepare and use illustrations.

Graphics and Artwork

Two terms are often used by people dealing with advertising illustrations: "graphics" and "artwork." **Graphics** refers to the process of producing or reproducing three-dimensional objects on a two-dimensional surface, for example, drawing, painting, and photographing. **Artwork** usually refers only to products of art, such as drawings and photographs. Most people use these terms interchangeably.

No retailer has the time to be a graphics specialist, for that is a full-time job in itself. But all retailers who have something to do with advertising need to know some general facts to do a good job. They need to know how illustrations can be used, what the respective strengths and weaknesses of drawings and photographs are, and what sources they can tap for art talent or for finished artwork.

Uses of Illustrations

A good illustration helps the advertiser communicate with the reader. It contributes to the atmosphere created by the ad. And it can show essential details about the product being advertised. In all these ways, a good illustration acts as a selling tool.

Artwork attracts a reader's attention because people's eyes are directed to drawings and photographs. They are drawn to bold arrows, heavy ruled lines, and other kinds of symbols, designs, and decorations that produce contrast on a printed page.

Many ad illustrations feature the product that is being offered and show it in enough detail that its selling points are clear. Most ready-to-wear ads contain drawings of garments with their style features boldly outlined. Equipment and tools are frequently shown in use. On the other hand, some illustrations are chosen for the general impression they convey. The product illustrated may appear only as a minor element of the ad, or it may not even be shown. Several perfumes, for example, have been advertised very successfully in this way.

Types of Illustrations

The illustrations in an ad start out either as drawings or as photographs. Each type of illustration has its own advantages and disadvantages, depending upon the type of product being advertised and the medium in which the ad is to appear.

Drawings. The illustrations that appear in newspaper ads are usually drawings. An artist can capture both the general impression and the important details of a dress, a suit, or a set of china. But it is difficult to illustrate texture or color variations in a drawing. A **line drawing** consists of black lines and solid black areas with no intermediate tones. The sharp, clear effect of such a drawing is suitable for simple sketches and small illustrations.

Various tones and shades of grey can be achieved by the application of ink or black watercolor with a paintbrush; this results in a **wash drawing**. Wash drawings are particularly suitable for showing texture. A **benday** sheet, which is basically transparent, is printed with patterns of tiny dots in various densities; it can be pasted over any part of a line drawing. The benday method is used a great deal in newspaper advertising. The application of washes and the benday method can be used to overcome the lack of tone in line drawings.

Photographs. Nothing is as truthful as a reproduction of a product in the form of a photograph. Photographs have a "you are there" quality that can make an ad come to life. Photographs reproduce best on "coated stock," which is the hard, glossy paper used for magazines and many mailing pieces. The paper does not soak up the ink the way newsprint does, so small details in a photograph print crisply and clearly. When using a photo in a newspaper ad, plan to use at least a quarter page, so that the photo does not have to be reduced too much.

Halftones. All illustrations and artwork other than line drawings require a photoengraving process because of the variations in tone. **Photoengraving** is a photomechanical process for making line drawings and halftones by photographing an image on a metal plate and then etching with acid. A **halftone** is a photoengraving made from an image photographed through a screen so that the details of the image are produced in dots. The groups of small dots of various sizes produce a variety of tones. A line drawing and a halftone picture can be combined on a combination plate. The photoengraving process used in making full-color letterpress advertisements is basically the same as that used in making black-to-gray half-

A dominant illustration attracts attention, reinforces the headline, and makes people want to read the copy. *Courtesy of Benihana of Tokyo*

YOU COME FOR THE SHOW. YOU COME BACK FOR THE FOOD.

Come to Benihana. Where every meal is an exciting show. And you always have a front-row seat. Because the stage is your own hibachi table.

The stars of our show: carefully selected fillets and sirloins, tender chicken, plump shrimp, and succulent scallops. And — ah yes — fresh vegetables and crisp sliced mushrooms.

The Master of Ceremonies for this oriental feast? Your personal chef.

Watch as he slices with lightning speed. Dices with astonishing precision. Seasons and sizzles your favorite foods into mouth-watering morsels. According to a 1000 year old Japanese recipe.

At Benihana the show always wins your applause.

But it's the food that gets all the encores.

BENIHANA of TOKYO

720 St. Louis St. (Across from Antoine's) 522-0425 / Phone for information on group functions.

tones. Four-color process engraving gets its name from the four colors used in preparing the engravings. When combined in various ways, the four colors will produce all the other colors.

Sources of Illustrations

To obtain advertising illustrations, a retailer can either hire an artist or buy ready-made artwork. Many retailers do both.

Hiring an artist is an expensive way to get illustrations. But this method enables retailers to have illustrations prepared to their exact specifications and gives them the advantage of exclusiveness. Ready-made art is professionally done and relatively inexpensive.

Ready-made artwork can be bought as clip art. The term **clip art** refers to drawings that can be bought for one-time use for a small charge. The drawings are in catalogs that are issued monthly, quarterly, or annually. Sometimes the retailer can buy individual pieces of art; usually the whole catalog is purchased. Most newspapers provide clip-art catalogs for use by their retail clients. Clip art is particularly useful as decorative or mood art.

Advertising photography is a very specialized field. Most retailers turn to professional photographers for their special needs. Numerous free photographs are often available from suppliers.

Does the work of an advertising specialist appeal to you? Do you have any of the skills and abilities needed for this job? If so, you might want to investigate this area of retailing in more detail. You can start by reading the next chapter, which discusses advertising layout and evaluation.

Trade Talk

Define each term and use it in a sentence.

Art	Clip art
Artwork	Copy
Benday	Graphics

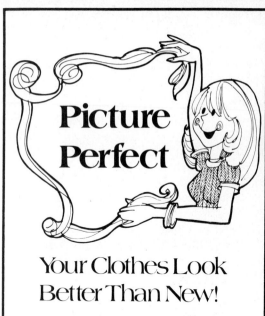

Picture Perfect

Your Clothes Look Better Than New!

Get your clothes Autumn ready! We'll freshen up your entire wardrobe by giving it our special cleaning and pressing treatment! Fast service!

SPECIAL

00

NAME
DRY CLEANERS

Retailers can purchase clip art to illustrate their advertisements. Courtesy of Metro Newspaper Service

Gravure process	Logotype
Halftone	Offset lithography
Layout	Photoengraving
Letterpress process	Wash drawing
Line drawing	

Can You Answer These?

1. Who prepares the advertising in a small store? In a large store?

Basic Facts about Product	Target Group	Major Selling Points	Benefits	Additional Information

2. What important information must copywriters have in order to prepare a good ad?
3. In what ways do copywriters attract attention with headlines?
4. What is the "B-complex" for copywriters?
5. What is the role of graphics in advertising?
6. What are the advantages and disadvantages of using drawings as illustrations in advertising? Of using photographs?

Problems

1. Assume you work for a shoe store that offers merchandise in the medium price range. On a separate sheet of paper, write an example of a headline for an ad that features (a) a pair of loafers, (b) sneakers, and (c) rain boots. Also make a list of the selling points of each product that might be useful in constructing the advertising copy to go with each headline.

2. Select one particularly effective ad for a local store. Rule a form similar to the one above. In the left column, give basic facts about the advertised merchandise. In the columns to the right, list the group of customers the ad tries to appeal to (target group), the major selling points, benefits, and other information given in the ad. Attach the ad to the form.

Advertising Layout and Evaluation

CHAPTER

Communications & Human Relations
Economics & Marketing
Merchandising
Selling & Technology
Advertising & Display
Operations & Management

While Rita and Manuel Torres were shopping the ads in preparation for a visit to the Gateway Shopping Center, dozens of ads competed for their attention. They probably just glanced at some. Several may have held their attention for a fleeting second or two. But a few ads made them stop to give the products offered some thought. What factors entered into their decisions to concentrate on certain ads and disregard the rest?

Certainly, many of the ads were ignored because Rita and Manuel were not interested in the advertised products. (Illustrations and headlines helped the couple to sort them out.) Other ads may have been dropped because the Torres's knew from the store logotype that the store was not in or near the Gateway Center, or perhaps they preferred not to do business with a particular retailer. Rita and Manuel looked for the ads of their favored stores that were promoting the products and brands they were considering.

The ads that held the Torres's attention were chosen because they promoted the products Rita and Manuel were interested in. Also, they provided helpful consumer information that was attractively presented and easy to read. The workers who designed the layout, prepared the illustrations, and wrote the copy had used their knowledge and skills well. So these ad shoppers probably read the entire ad or at least enough of it to make a tentative buying decision.

Layout Rationale

Because a layout is used like a blueprint to communicate a plan for an ad, it is usually prepared before the copy is written. Copywriters may work with the layout artist during the early planning stage of layout development.

The main reason for preparing an advertising layout is to ensure that the proposed ad will fulfill its specific objectives. An advertising layout shows what the elements look like, how they are arranged, and where the emphasis lies. Its role is to attract the attention of prospective customers and stimulate their interest as their eyes are led from one element to the next.

Among the people associated with a layout's development are those who approve the layout and those who prepare it. In retailing, those who have a voice in approving it may include the head of sales promotion, the advertising manager, the merchandise manager of the division in which the advertised items are sold, and perhaps the buyer. Workers participating in the preparation of the layout are the copywriter, illustrators, and, of course, the layout specialist.

Like a picture, the layout tells its viewers many things. The most important of these are:

1. Whether the proposed ad carries out its intended purpose
2. Whether the mood is appropriate for the products
3. Whether the emphasis is justly placed
4. Whether the arrangement guides the viewer's eye advantageously
5. What illustrations, typeface and type size, margins, and borders to use

Types of Layouts

When planning the layout of an ad, a layout specialist automatically thinks in terms of three categories of advertising layouts based on the number of products or services to be promoted. They are one-item ads, group ads, and omnibus ads. Each type has its own characteristics that must be considered by the layout specialist.

One-Item Ads

A **one-item advertisement** stresses only one article. When preparing a one-item ad, the layout artists and copywriters can do a superior sales promotion job because the copy and illustrations are concentrated on one dominant sales message. There is plenty of space in which to describe and illustrate the product or service to be promoted and much flexibility in arranging the elements.

Group Ads

A **group advertisement** shows and describes several related items. Clothing, for example, may be shown with shoes and other accessories, and furniture may be shown with rugs and draperies. This type of ad suggests related items to the customer. It often gives advertising space to more than one department of the store.

Omnibus Ads

An **omnibus advertisement** contains a variety of items that are not closely related. Care must be taken in such ads to avoid a cluttered look. The layout must create a feeling of unity and attract the readers to the variety of merchandise that is being advertised. Also, the layout must be simple and clear. Omnibus advertisements are sponsored by nearly every type of departmentalized store, particularly by mass merchandisers and other promotionally minded stores. They are effective for clearance sales in department stores and specialty stores because a large number of items can be advertised at one time.

How Layouts Are Prepared

Owners of small stores may suggest ideas for layouts, but someone else usually creates them. Their newspaper-ad layouts are done by the newspaper advertising staffs. In preparing layouts for mailing pieces, these retailers depend on the help of the printer's staff.

A large store usually has its own advertising department, which includes layout specialists. These are artists who know

What are the advantages of a one-item advertisement?   Courtesy of Door Store

Night and Day

Door Store - the only one with this exclusive modular grouping. Spacious, elegant seating by day and equally comfortable bedding at night. Removable covers in brown canvas or Haitian cotton. Sofa and loveseat modules also available. Priced from: chair **$95** corner **$99** ottoman **$55** loveseat **$139** sofa **$265**

NEW YORK   210 E. 51 St. 753-2280 (All stores open Sun.)
186 Amsterdam Ave. at 69th St. 873-7115
191 Lexington Ave. at 32nd St. 889-5491
MANHASSET 1579 Northern Blvd (516) 627-4588
WHITE PLAINS   170 E. Post Rd. (914) 682-8417

how to combine copy and artwork in a pleasing, unified design and who understand the basics of the printing process. Advertising agencies and commercial art agencies also have layout specialists available who can help the retailer with advertising layouts.

Stages in Layout Development

Layouts are usually prepared in several stages. The first stage may be a **copywriter's rough,** which indicates roughly what the copywriter had in mind. In many small stores, the copywriter's rough is the only guide for the ad that will be made. It gives the newspaper an idea of what the retailer has in mind.

Frequently, in the first stage of preparing a layout, thumbnail sketches are made. A **thumbnail sketch** is a small, quickly made drawing containing all the elements of a full-size layout. It is used to present one of the several alternative ways of laying out the ad. Details are omitted.

The best of the thumbnail sketches is enlarged into a full-sized rough layout. This rough layout may be drawn many times until all elements of the ad are in the exact size and position desired.

The layout that is shown to the retailer for approval is called a **comprehensive.** It is a nearly exact representation of the final ad, but the type and photographic illustrations, if any, are drawn by hand.

The final layout may be a **mechanical,** which is a pasteup combining the artwork with the proofs of the type. The mechanical shows exactly where each element belongs. It is often prepared in layers or "overlays" to show how line drawings and halftones are to be combined, and—in case of an ad with color—to separate the colors for the printer.

Considerations in Layout Development

Given the product or service to be promoted, the purpose, and the alloted space for the proposed ad, there are several important concerns to keep in mind as the layout is planned. These are the strategy or objective of the ad; the needs, wants, and values of the intended readers; and the mood or atmosphere to be generated by the ad.

Advertising Strategy. An **advertising strategy** is a statement of the specific objective of the ad—the selling problem to be solved. For example, a raincoat ad with the headline "Put Some Sunshine into a Rainy Day" gets to the point and achieves its purpose. It helps keep the thrust of the ad practical and geared toward selling. You can develop an advertising strategy by thinking of the purpose of the promotion. And your strategy can also be used as a guide to see whether the ad achieves what was intended.

Intended Readers. The needs and preferences of potential readers of the ad will have a strong bearing on the amount of emphasis you'll want to give the headline, the illustrations, and the body copy. For example, if you're preparing an automobile ad intended for the average customer, you might plan to have the ad contain more illustration than copy. But if your ad is aimed at a car buff, you might want to give considerable space to detailed copy. So the size of the illustration, the style and size of type in the headline, the use of white space, and so on are chosen in relation to the intended readers of the ad.

Mood of the Ad. As a layout specialist, you must keep in mind the mood that the ad should establish. For example, a festive mood such as that of the Thanksgiving holiday calls for a different layout than one that involves economy. Moods such as joy, excitement, luxury, patriotism, and generosity are suggested through illustrations, headline typeface and size, symbols, borders, and the allocation of white space.

Elements of a Layout

As a layout specialist, you decide how much emphasis each element of an ad is to receive and how these elements should

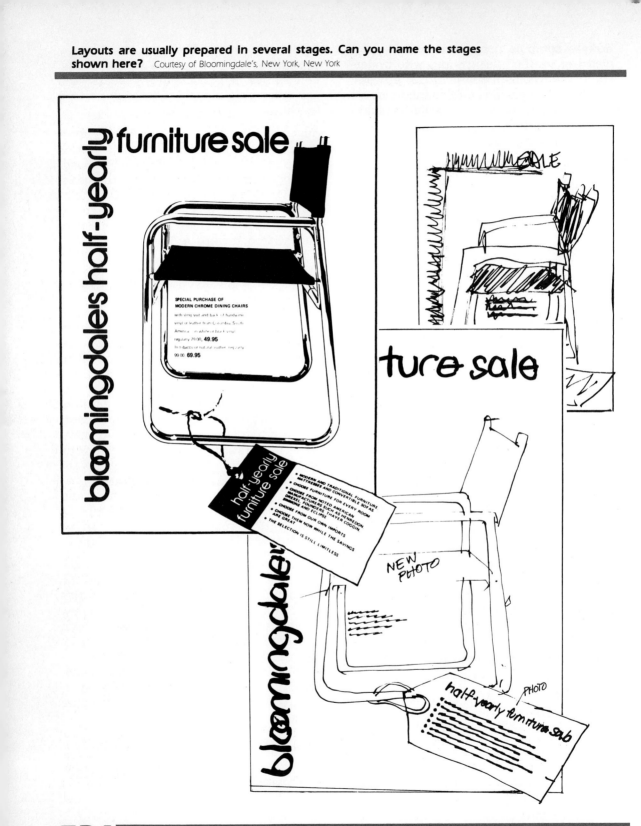

be arranged in the alloted space. Headlines, copy, and illustrations, which were discussed in Chapter 65, are the main elements of a layout design. They are supported by the imaginative use of white space, the size and face of the type, the borders, and the logotype.

White Space.　　The term used for the unprinted areas within the boundaries of an advertisement is **white space.** White space is empty space, but it has its own impact in a design. When a design leaves much white space around the copy, the impression is one of exclusiveness or special importance. This is a technique often used in ads for higher-priced merchandise. When little white space is left and the ad is filled with type and illustrations from border to border, the impression is one of excitement or bargain announcements.

Type.　　Sizes and styles of type, or **typefaces,** are chosen to suit the mood or impression the ad is to give. These are picked from a catalog showing the styles and sizes available from a particular typographer or printer. The right type makes the ad both readable and interesting.

Border.　　Often the borders of an ad are left as white space (newspapers and magazines always put a thin line between ads and editorial matter anyway). But sometimes a layout can be given more impact through the use of a border. The use of the same border for each ad may help readers to identify the sponsor quickly. Borders are especially appropriate for small ads, which may appear on the printed page with a number of other ads. Borders unite the parts of the ad and attract the attention of readers.

Logotype.　　The logotype, sometimes called the "logo," carries the name of the store and frequently a design symbolic of the firm. Many retailers combine other essential information with the logo. They might include opening and closing hours, addresses and telephone numbers of affiliated stores, and a statement about the acceptance of telephone and mail orders.

To many shoppers, the logo serves as a signal as to whether or not the ad is worth reading. A distinctive logo creates an identity and personality for a retailer.

The location of the logo in an ad is usually a matter of advertising policy. The logo appears in approximately the same place in every ad prepared for the store.

Line, Design, and Color

To prepare an advertising layout, a small retailer needn't have the ability to draw. As a layout worker, however, you should have practical art skills along with a command of sales psychology. Adequate layouts can be made by using illustrations cut from existing ads and clip art books, pasting them in place and roughing in the headlines, logotype, and block copy. The preparation of layouts calls for a knowledge of design principles such as contrast, balance, proportion, unity, and movement. These principles are applied in at-

The combination of the right typeface with a distinctive logotype creates a unique advertisement.　Courtesy of The Magic Pan Restaurants

tracting attention, arousing interest, and making the contact with the ad a pleasing experience.

As a layout artist, you must contrast the sizes, shapes, direction of lines, and sometimes colors to dramatize the sales message. Both formal and informal balance may be used. Proper size and intensity relationships among the elements of the layout and of each element to the layout as a whole must be maintained to achieve pleasing proportions. When the elements of a layout are organized so that they blend together to make a single impression, unity is achieved. (All these design principles are discussed in Chapter 46.)

How Advertising Is Evaluated

Evaluation enables a retailer to know which of the techniques and strategies used in an advertisement contributed most to the achievement of the promotional goals and which were least productive. With this information, a retailer is in a position to do better planning—and planning is a continuous process in retailing.

Advertising is a promotional activity that is relatively easy to evaluate. And there are a number of ways to measure the effectiveness of advertising, which usually accounts for the largest part of the promotional cost. Some of the tests of advertising effectiveness are handled by the retailers themselves. Others may be turned over to one of the professional research organizations that specialize in this type of work. In general, the testing takes one of two forms: posttesting or pretesting. Retailers make much greater use of posttesting than pretesting.

Posttesting Ads

The type of research that attempts to measure the effectiveness of an advertisement after it has appeared in a medium is known as **posttesting**. Posttesting can pinpoint the most effective ads for a re-

tailer and can often identify the most appealing features of those ads. This enables stores to improve their advertising and to make use of improved ads the next time they need similar promotional material.

There are three kinds of posttesting generally done in retailing. One kind measures the actual sales results achieved after an ad has been run. Another kind measures audience recognition of ads that have been run. And the third measures audience recall of ads that have been run.

Measuring Sales Results. Nearly every retailer does a posttest of some sort on each ad that is run. In large stores, the advertising department requests a formal report from the buyer or department head. The report tells how many units of the advertised item were in stock before and after the ad appeared, how many were sold, the dollar sales for the advertised merchandise, and the dollar sales for the department. The report also tells weather conditions during the period, what com-

Successful retailers always check the results of their advertising campaigns.

ADVERTISING RESULTS

Department _56 – Toys_

Date of Ad _Oct 14, 198—_

Media _Columbus Dispatch_

3 Day Results _Excellent_

No. of Units Sold _175_

DOLLAR SALES:

Advertised Item _$9,341_

Total Department _$21,637_

Note: *This form must be turned in to Merchandise Manager before noon the 4th day after ad has run. Merchandise Manager will initial and send promptly to Sales Promotion Manager.*

Buyer's Signature _Terry Adams_

Merchandise Manager's Initials _CP_

petitive ads appeared in the medium, and what other types of promotion were used.

In large and small stores alike, each ad that is used goes into an advertising scrapbook, and next to each is noted its dollar cost and the sales results that were achieved by its use. When they are preparing advertising, artists and copywriters look through this scrapbook to see which ads and which techniques have been most successful.

In many small firms, retailers use certain rule-of-thumb devices to posttest their advertising. One of these is to evaluate the immediate response to an ad. **Immediate-response advertising** is designed to cause the potential customer to buy a particular product within a short time—either today, tomorrow, on the weekend, or next week. In weighing the results to these ads, many retailers watch for the number of coupons brought in by customers and for the increase in the volume of traffic in the store as evidence of an ad's effectiveness.

Many retailers are interested in knowing why their ads function as they do. So they go a step further—they measure the degree to which consumers recognize an ad and are able to recall its message.

Measuring Audience Recognition of Ads.
Recognition tests tell the advertiser how readers react to their ads and how their ads compare with other ads in the same publication. The researcher seeks out individuals who say they've read the particular issue of the publication, gives that person a copy of the issue, and goes through the pages with the reader. The researcher then asks the reader to point out each ad he or she remembers and to say whether it made an impression. The ads that the reader remembers are then rated. The weakness of this testing method is that the researcher must accept the reader's statement about the impression made at the time the ad was seen.

Measuring Audience Recall of Ads.
Recall tests attempt to measure what an ad actually communicated to its readers. As in the audience-recognition tests, audience-recall researchers identify only those who say they read the given issue of the publication. In the interview, however, the readers' answers are based entirely on what they can remember about the ads in the publication.

Pretesting Ads

An exploratory test that is run before an ad is published is called a **pretest**. Pretesting is especially useful when a marketer—more often a manufacturer than a retailer—is considering putting a large amount of money into a promotional campaign, theme, or technique. Pretesting helps the advertiser decide whether the effort will be worth the expense; it also allows for necessary changes in a promotional effort before it reaches the public. Two of the more commonly used methods are opinion studies and test-area studies.

Opinion Studies. An opinion study can involve the individual questioning of people or the collective questioning of a group. People are asked to rate ads according to their believability, their ability to command attention and interest, and their power to persuade people to buy. Sometimes those questioned are given several ads to compare and are asked to evaluate them in the order of their merit.

Test-Area Studies. Another way to test an idea for an advertising campaign before putting it into effect is to try out the campaign in a small test-market area. Two test-market areas are chosen, both as similar in size and customer composition as possible. The ad is used in only one of the two areas while the second area serves as a control area. After a specific period of time, the sales records of the two areas are compared and any differences between sales in the test area and sales in the control area are considered to indicate the pulling power of the ad idea.

In Chapters 65 and 66 you learned how an ad comes into being. But preparing ads is only one aspect of the planning of promotional activities. Read the next chapter to find out what other factors retailers consider when they plan to promote sales.

Trade Talk

Define each term and use it in a sentence.

Advertising strategy
Comprehensive
Copywriter's rough
Group advertisement
Immediate-response
  advertising
Mechanical
Omnibus
  advertisement
One-item
  advertisement
Posttesting
Pretest
Thumbnail sketch
Typefaces
White space

Can You Answer These?

1. What is the purpose of an advertising layout? Who uses it?
2. What are the three broad types of advertising layouts?
3. What are the three considerations a layout specialist should keep in mind when planning an ad layout?
4. What are the elements of an advertising layout?
5. What are the three types of posttests used to evaluate ads?
6. What are the two types of pretests used in evaluating advertising campaigns?

Problems

1. Rule a form similar to the following. In the left column, write the letter of each of the following factors in retail ad construction: (a) location of ad in publication; (b) headline; (c) illustration(s); (d) factual copy; (e) interesting copy, (f) store image projection; and (g) eye movement. Identify but do not clip three recent retail newspaper ads of the same type (one-item, group, or omnibus) that promote the same kind of merchandise but are sponsored by different stores. If possible, the ads should be about the same size and appear in the same or comparable medium. Label the ads, "Store 1, Store 2, and Store 3." Then trace the eye movement in each ad with a colored marker. On the basis of your personal feelings, rank each ad (using 1, 2, and 3) on each of the factors above from high to low—1 equals high.

Factor	Store 1	Store 2	Store 3

Planning Sales Promotion

CHAPTER 67

Communications & Human Relations
Economics & Marketing
Merchandising
Selling & Technology
Advertising & Display
Operations & Management

The advertising to which Rita and Manuel Torres were exposed before they visited the Gateway Shopping Center was only part of the promotional activity of the sponsoring firms. The products that the couple wanted call for very different types of promotion. (You will recall that Manuel wanted some plumbing supplies and planned to update his sports gear. Rita, on the other hand, wanted some new sportswear for their approaching vacation.) What are the basic differences in promoting these products?

Most plumbing supplies are staple goods, or products that all households need at some time. And most retailers who handle plumbing supplies seem to think that promoting sales is mainly a matter of letting potential customers know about the availability of those supplies and the quality of their services. Distributors of sporting goods usually try to project an image of reliability too. These distributors, however, are inclined to promote favored brands, and they have seasonal merchandise to contend with. Of the three types of merchandise that Rita and Manuel planned to purchase, sports apparel needs the most promotion to encourage sales. Fashion merchandising demands high sensitivity to rapidly changing consumer preferences and very tactful promotion.

Even though the nature, complexity, and merchandising risks involved in promoting staple, fashion, and perishable goods (such as fresh produce and meat) vary widely, there are elements common to all types of retail promotional activities: each type starts with a budget, each should have a promotion schedule, each requires intelligent selection of merchandise and services to be promoted, and each requires an appropriate promotional strategy.

Promotion Budgets

The volume of sales that a retailer achieves depends in large measure on the amount of promotion that is to be done. So promotional planning must be closely coordinated with the planning of sales volume. As soon as the sales volume totals are set, promotion executives start planning how to reach those goals.

Promotion executives start planning by preparing a promotion budget and a promotion schedule. The **promotion budget** is a plan showing how much money is to be spent on promoting sales during a specific period of time. The promotion schedule is a plan showing the promotional activities to be used during a specific period. The period covered by the budget and schedule is 6 months or a year.

Estimating the Total Budget

Promotion executives use several ways to estimate the amount of money to be spent on promotion. The method they use most frequently is to figure a set **percentage of planned net sales.** The percentage chosen may be taken from the percentage used in other businesses of similar character. Figures are available in trade magazines, Census Bureau reports, Dun & Bradstreet reports, and from other financial and accounting services. Promotion costs usually range from 1 to 5 percent of net sales depending on the type of merchandise and method of distribution.

Another method that promotion executives use to establish a budget is to set aside a fixed sum for each unit of merchandise to be sold. This **unit-of-sales method** is particularly useful in areas where the amount of merchandise available is limited by outside factors, such as the effect of the weather on crops. It's also useful for big-ticket items such as washing machines and automobiles. Thus, a car dealer might plan to sell 500 cars and trucks during the budget period in order to figure the agency's budget.

A third and less-used method that promotion executives employ is the **objective-and-task method.** This method of determining a promotion budget establishes what must be done in order to meet planned objectives. A sample objective might be "Sell 25 percent more of product X by attracting the business of teenagers." Then the next step would be to determine what combination of expenses would best reach this target and to estimate the cost.

Allocating the Budget

General promotion plans are usually made up of several different budgets and schedules. Because advertising is so important to retailers in terms of costs and benefits, promotion executives usually prepare a separate advertising budget and a separate advertising schedule. They may also prepare separate plans for display or for direct mail advertising. Or executives may combine all promotion activities other than advertising into one budget and schedule. In any event, an attempt will be made to coordinate the total effort.

The general promotion budget usually includes the costs of the promotional staff payroll, the advertising payroll, supplies, postage, and distribution. In short, it includes all the expenses involved in all the promotional activities planned. Executives divide the total amount of money in the general promotion budget among categories that correspond roughly to the various merchandising departments, and they subdivide it into monthly or weekly budgets. Usually, they do this in connection with the preparation of the promotion schedule.

Promotion Schedules

Most retailers work out promotion schedules in two stages. First, they prepare a general schedule of promotion for the entire period of 6 months or a year, including advertising, display, direct mail, and so on. Then they work out the detailed monthly schedules one after the other, each one being prepared about a month in advance of its use.

Retailers find that promotion schedules are most effective when they are worked out to accomplish a specific goal. The general goals of promotion are to generate sales and promote goodwill for the store. A more specific goal might be to build customer acceptance of a new line of merchandise during a stated period.

The planned-for goal is more likely to be reached when several types of promotional activities are used. For instance, a retailer could build customer acceptance of a new high-style boutique by planning a promotional campaign that would include advertising, window displays, a mailing to customers, and a special-price promotional event for the first 3 days after the boutique is opened. When retailers use more than one promotional device, however, the coordination of all promotional planning is especially important. Of course, schedules may be changed to feature merchandise that may sell well as a result of changes in the weather or local conditions.

Sales Promotion Campaigns

A **sales promotion campaign** is a series of coordinated promotional activities directed toward certain desired outcomes. With the budget figures and sales promotion schedule firmly in mind, promotion planners give first consideration to the purpose of the campaign and the goals to be achieved. Then they determine the products, services, or ideas to be promoted. (Keep in mind that a promotion campaign may be launched to further institutional goals as well as to promote the sale of merchandise.) After promotion planners have clarified and defined the goals, they make decisions about the specific merchandise, services, or ideas they want promoted. And last, they coordinate the activities of all the promotion departments involved.

Campaign Goals

The goals of a promotion campaign grow out of change. They grow out of changes in economic conditions, the market, social customs, the weather, a firm's merchandising and service policies, and many other factors. Here are some examples of promotion goals that are common in retailing:

♦ To produce immediate sales
♦ To build goodwill for the store
♦ To launch a merchandising season
♦ To reduce the size of an inventory

Breakfast with the Easter Bunny

9:30 a.m. Saturdays,
March 15, 22, 29
Our very own Bunny will host!
Party favors and balloons for
all the children plus an original
mini-musical starring Yvonne Parente
and Tom Brogan in Manhasset and
Diane Lee and Joseph G. Schramm, Jr.
in Garden City. Cost is 2.50 per
child, payable at the door. Be
sure to call in advance for reservations
as seating is limited. Manhasset call
627-3000, ext. 202, Garden City call
742-7000, ext. 2II. In The Cafe, please
use Main Level Shoe Salon Entrance.

The aim of this promotional event is to build goodwill for the store. Courtesy
of Lord & Taylor

♦ To introduce a new product or a new service
♦ To cooperate in the promotion of a shopping center

What to Promote

The most critical step promotion planners must take in conducting a promotion campaign is in selecting specific products and services to be promoted. If a store offers the right product or service at the right time and at the right price, it will make friends as well as a profit. On the other hand, no promotional cleverness will sell unwanted products or services. This principle applies to institutional promotion as well as to the promotion of products and services.

The Right Merchandise. When Rita and Manuel Torres shopped the ads, you'll recall that they skipped over all except those that advertised the products they wanted. This is normal consumer behavior. And this behavior provides retailers with the cue to getting a good return on their advertising investments—advertise fast-selling items that are in high demand.

Certain products and services may be popular at a given time for a number of reasons. They may be near the fashion peak, as could have been the situation with the women's sportswear that interested Rita. Or they may be seasonal merchandise, such as the sports gear that Manuel wanted. Other products that are likely to be in high demand are those which are in short supply at the time, unique items, highly attractive articles, prestigious or distinctive merchandise, and, of course, exceptional values.

Promotion planners often like to promote national brands that attract attention and bring consumers into the store where they buy regular-price goods as well as the specials. Those who sell their own private brands frequently conduct promotion campaigns to help build a steady trade for their product lines.

The Right Price. The price of products and services in our economy is so important that it has recast entire distribution systems—the mail-order house, chain store, discount store, and supermarket. Americans are known to be price-conscious; it's a part of their value system. So in most cases it's good business to let the potential buyer know the price of the merchandise. And often the price is the main buying motive. Generally speaking, price is probably the most powerful competitive weapon.

Price-conscious consumers soon find the most economical sources to fill their needs. They frequently wait for sales so that they can get the most for their money. The retailer obliges with a wide variety of promotion campaigns offering the expected price reductions. Sometimes markdowns are taken to provide a buying incentive, sometimes to meet a competitor's price, and sometimes to beat it. Or the retailer may be fortunate enough to buy a lot of merchandise at a bargain, which can then be passed along to the consumer.

Promotion-minded retailers find many opportunities to attract the attention of economy-minded consumers. They sponsor promotion campaigns offering bargains and buying suggestions to potential customers for reasons such as savings passed along to consumers and the celebration of holidays and various socially oriented events. Some of the themes for these promotions are given in the following table. Some sales events are tied to particular product lines, such as the traditional "white sale," which promotes the purchase of linens, and the August furniture sale.

When to Promote

Promoting sales is said to be the spark used to stimulate action and produce excitement. But if that spark, like the spark in an automobile ignition, is not properly timed, the promotion will sputter—and there will be very little action. Being too late or too early dampens the potential customer's enthusiasm for sale merchandise. So Rita and Manuel would not have wanted the sportswear or recreational gear after their vacation, and they probably would not have been interested a month earlier.

Study Past Records. When planning a promotion campaign, retailers draw on

THEMES FOR SALES EVENTS	
Store-Oriented Events	**Socially Oriented Events**
Grand opening	Back-to-school sale
Anniversary sale	Holiday celebration
Expansion sale	sale
Remodeling sale	Spring and fall
Moving sale	sales
Quitting business	Harvest festival
sale	Mother's Day and
Clearance sale	Father's Day
Pre- and	sales
postinventory	Sports events sale
sales	Teachers'
End-of-month sale	convention sale
	Visiting celebrity
	sale
	Graduation day sale

their past experience, on research findings, and on their good judgment. They try to identify the best month of the year, week of the month, day of the week, and hours of the day. Storewide promotions usually take place slightly in advance of expected important sales periods. For example, back-to-school promotion is started in mid-August. Payday may signal the best week of the month or day of the week. Nonworking hours may be appropriate for certain target-group customers to shop. The secret is to find the time when potential customers are most likely to buy.

Don't Hesitate.   The old saying that "He who hesitates is lost" relates well to sales promotion. As you learned in Chapter 41, modern retailers don't hesitate about taking markdowns. And the markdowns they take are large enough to move the goods. Even a day's delay in advertising a product may be critical in today's highly competitive market. The store that is the first to advertise usually benefits the most in terms of sales and goodwill.

Unfortunately, even the most careful timing may be faulty. Weather and certain other factors such as a competitor's promotional activities, strikes, and unpredictable shortage of supply can interfere with plans.

How to Promote

How a retailer promotes sales and builds goodwill is largely a matter of individual choices. However, such choices are highly dependent upon (1) the type of retailing (for example, supermarket versus exclusive dress shop), (2) the characteristics of the store's customers, and (3) the current competitive situation. As discussed earlier, when the firm's decision makers form promotion policies, they keep one principle firmly in mind. It is that the store depends on *continuing* customer satisfaction for long-run sales volume and maximum profits. So, in promotion, the values of-

fered by the firm must be clear-cut, useful, and have psychological appeal.

Selection of Strategies

Promotional strategies or devices used to increase sales seem limited only by the creativity and good judgment of the retailer. Some are used in cooperation with suppliers. Some are arranged with other retailers, such as a shopping center promotion. But most are independent operations. These strategies may be grouped under the goals of the promotion campaigns listed on page 540. Or, they can be grouped by the type of incentive offered to potential purchasers. These types of incentives are given in the list that follows:

- *Price incentives:* leaders, loss leaders, excellent values, coupons, rebates, trading stamps
- *Product incentives:* premiums, samples, gifts, trading stamps, prizes
- *Service incentives:* credit arrangements, free customer services, free lessons or classes, fashion shows, seminars
- *Recognition incentives:* souvenirs, flowers, contests, courtesy days for charge customers, appreciation letters

Some strategies appeal to more than one kind of incentive. For example, the reward given to a contest winner may take the form of cash, merchandise, or a service, and it also provides recognition for the winner.

Other promotion activities are meant to call attention to the store and project a carnival atmosphere. Some examples are store interior decorations, exhibits, banners, strings of colored pennants, special sales demonstrations, hosting by celebrities, and skywriting.

Practicing Teamwork.   When you were introduced to promotion in Chapter 25, did you realize how complex this retail function really is? Look again at the discussion of the promotion function contained in Chapter 25 and think about the

This promotional strategy uses price incentives.

coordination required to plan and maintain a continuing promotion program. Note the relationship between merchandise promotion and institutional promotion and the position of credit. Also note that the target groups include employees, suppliers, and others in addition to customers and potential customers.

Trade Talk

Define each term and use it in a sentence.

Objective-and-task method
Percentage of planned net sales
Promotion budget
Promotion schedule
Sales promotion campaign
Unit-of-sales method

Can You Answer These?

1. What are the three methods of determining a total promotion budget? What determines which method is used?
2. What is the procedure in preparing a promotion schedule?
3. What is the first task in planning a promotion campaign? Name six broad goals of promotion campaigns.
4. Why is the timing of a sales event so important?
5. What three factors influence a retailer's judgment in deciding how to conduct a promotion campaign? Name some strategies used.
6. Why must successful promotion be a team function?

Problems

1. Rule a form similar to the following. In the left column, list the names of the ten most frequent advertisers in your local newspaper during a 1-week period. In the columns on the right, note the type of firm that sponsors the advertising, the kind of merchandise most frequently advertised, and the day or days that the ads are run. Compare the practices of the different kinds of retailing.

Advertiser	Type of Firm	Merchandise Advertised	Days Ad Is Run
Example: Gateway Supermarket	Super-market	Meat and produce	Wednesday and Sunday

2. Assume that it is September and you are responsible for raising $1,000 for a class excursion in the spring. Your promotion budget is $50. You may buy on consignment the merchandise you need (such as candy or Christmas trees) or you may sell a service performed by your classmates (such as yard maintenance). Your only limitation is that you must confine your sales to members of the student body or their friends and relatives. Now, select a product or service and name the ways and describe the strategies you would use in reaching your goal.

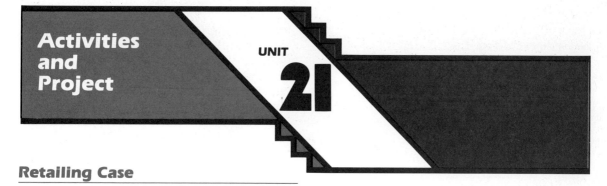

Activities and Project

UNIT 21

Retailing Case

Assume that you have recently been promoted to head of stock in a department because of your superior performance as a salesperson. The merchandise sold by the store is highly competitive, and a large sales volume is necessary for the store to make a reasonable profit. There have been several special sales during the past 6 months and you believe that the sales force has become accustomed to sales promotions to the point where the salespeople have lost their enthusiasm for them.

The department manager calls you into his office to talk over the forthcoming sales event. You become convinced that the values of the merchandise are excellent and that the prices are very attractive. The manager turns to you and says, "I know that we can make our quota and more if you and your salespeople will cooperate in making this sale a success. Will you see what can be done about it? Think it over and jot down some ideas of what you and the sales force can do to make this the outstanding event of the year."

1. What can salespeople do to help make a sales promotion successful?
2. What can the head of stock do to help the salespeople build enthusiasm for the sales event? For the products they sell?
3. What methods and devices would you use to build enthusiasm for a selected event in your chosen area of retailing—for example, a fall festival?

Working with People

Although he was good at running his business, Mr. LeBlanc realized that his English was not fluent enough to let him write effective copy for his gift shop. He therefore asked two of his employees to prepare the copy for his weekly ads in the local newspaper. Jackie had a way with words; she wrote sparkling copy. Barbara had been an "A" student in English in high school. She wrote correct English but rather dull copy. Barbara was obviously jealous when Mr. LeBlanc chose Jackie's copy week after week.

1. What was the real problem confronting Mr. LeBlanc?
2. What else could Mr. LeBlanc have done to solve his problem?
3. What would have been the probable consequences of each alternative?
4. What can Mr. LeBlanc do to maintain the morale and productivity of both girls?
5. Where can copywriters learn to write advertising copy?

Project 21: Preparing an Advertising Campaign

Your Project Goal
Given a product or service commonly purchased by high school students, a marketing and distributive education class, a high school student body, and a school newspaper, prepare an advertising campaign directed toward your high school market for the given product or service.

Procedure
1. Select for possible promotion in the school newspaper a product or service that is usually purchased by high school students. Ask your teacher to approve your selection.
2. Prepare independently a set of questions that will reveal the shopping habits of students in relation to the product or service of your choice. You may include such questions as: Who buys the product or service? How often is it purchased? Where is it purchased? Why is it purchased at this source? Did the customer see it advertised? Did he or she see it advertised in the school paper? Does he or she ordinarily read the ads in the school paper?
3. Check your questions with those of your classmates who are studying the possibility of promoting similar types of products or services. After reviewing all questions, draw up a revised list of questions. Ask a local retailer dealing with the product or service of your choice to check your list and make suggestions for its improvement.
4. Determine the most appropriate way of gathering the necessary information in your school. For example, you might prepare a questionnaire or arrange a series of interviews. Be sure to consider timing, cost, and other factors that may affect how you will gather your information. You may wish to consult with the staff of the school paper or appropriate school officials about the procedures you wish to follow.
5. Design a questionnaire or set of interview questions. Then test the instrument on a sample of five students who represent a cross section of school newspaper readers.
6. Collect and tabulate the data.
7. Prepare a written report of the study. You may obtain assistance from appropriate people such as local retailers, your English teacher, and your marketing and distributive education teacher.
8. Again drawing on the information from your survey, prepare at least two sample ads for your chosen product or service.
9. Pretest your ad using any one of the methods discussed in Chapter 66. Obtain your teacher's approval of the method you propose to use.
10. Prepare a written report of the complete project, giving your findings, conclusions, and recommendations. Consult your teacher regarding the length and specifications for the report.

Evaluation
You will be evaluated on the appropriateness of the questions on which you based your initial survey, on the appropriateness of the method used in your pretest, and on the content and accuracy of your written report.

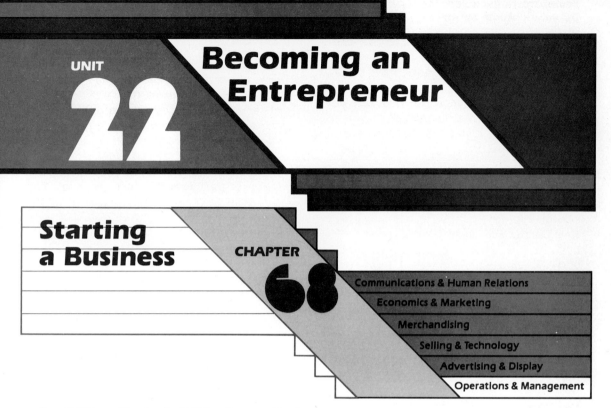

Starting a Business

CHAPTER

68

Communications & Human Relations

Economics & Marketing

Merchandising

Selling & Technology

Advertising & Display

Operations & Management

In 1902, with just $500, James Cash Penney opened his first store, The Golden Rule, in Kemmerer, Wyoming. This store consisted of one room on the street level and an attic in a wooden building without plumbing. This entrepreneur's small beginning has become an international organization with more than 2,000 stores doing over $9 billion worth of business.

In 1954, another entrepreneur, Ray Kroc, talked the McDonald brothers into letting him franchise their restaurant idea nationally. Today, Ray Kroc is a multimillionaire, and the familiar golden arches of McDonald's can be seen around the world.

Not all individuals who go into retail business for themselves are successful the first time. For example, F. W. Woolworth failed three times before he learned to broaden the assortment of merchandise sold and sell 10-cent as well as 5-cent items and to locate his stores in areas where many potential customers would be passing by the store.

Why People Go into Business for Themselves

Each year a quarter of a million new businesses are started in the United States. At least 8 million people, approximately 10 percent of the work force, are owners of small businesses.

In many respects, the small-business owner represents what people around the world believe to be the typical American. These people think that our entrepreneurs possess the basic American traits of independence, self-expression, initiative, inventiveness, industriousness, persistence, and dedication to free enterprise.

The chance to succeed on one's own ap-

Review this rating scale for personal traits important to a business proprietor. Do you think the person who checked this scale is suited for a career in retailing? Now rate yourself on this scale.

Instructions: *After each question place a check mark on the line at the point closest to your answer. The check mark need not be placed directly over one of the suggested answers because your rating may lie somewhere between two answers. Be honest in your answers.*

Are You a Self-Starter?

| I do things my own way. Nobody needs to tell me to get going. | If someone gets me started, I keep going all right. | Easy does it. I don't exert myself unless I have to. |

How Do You Feel about Other People?

| I like people. I can get along with just about anybody. | I have plenty of friends. I don't need anyone else. | Most people annoy me. |

Can You Lead Others?

| I can get most people to go along without much difficulty. | I can get people to do things if I drive them. | I let someone else get things moving. |

Can You Take Responsibility?

| I like to take charge and see things through. | I'll take over if I have to, but I'd rather let someone else be responsible. | There's always some eager beaver around wanting to show off. I say let him. |

How Good an Organizer Are You?

| I like to have a plan before I start. I'm usually the one to get things lined up. | I do all right unless things get too mixed up. Then I stop. | I just take things as they come. |

How Good a Worker Are You?

| I can keep going as long as necessary. I don't mind working hard. | I'll work hard for a while, but when I've had enough, that's it! | I can't see that hard work gets you anywhere. |

How Good Is Your Health?

| I never tire. | I have enough energy for most things I want to do. | I run out of energy sooner than most of my friends seem to. |

peals to many people. In their minds, entrepreneurship usually means an opportunity to gain special compensations—high income, personal growth, the experience of being in charge, a chance to try out one's own ideas, and the opportunity to choose one's own work hours. Other reasons given by people who go into business for themselves include being able to supplement their incomes, to fill an immediate need for a job, to build a business for their children, and to prove their own ability.

What Makes an Entrepreneur Successful?

When this country was in its early stages of development, almost anyone with a little money and some merchandise could make a living running a shop. But this is no longer true. To be a successful retailer takes more than money, resources, and a place to do business. Today's successful entrepreneur must have well-defined traits, competencies, and resources. Some of these qualifications have been discussed earlier. Additional ones are presented in this chapter.

Retailing is a people business. So the needs of people, more than products or services, are the entrepreneur's stock in trade. The first qualification of a successful retail entrepreneur is a genuine interest in what people need. That's the main reason successful retailers make it a point to talk to many of the customers who come into their places of business.

In addition to a deep concern for people, entrepreneurs can be characterized by the following managerial abilities (items 1-6) and traits (items 7-14):

1. Organizing ability
2. Ability to absorb setbacks and bounce back
3. Problem-solving ability
4. Human relations ability
5. Communications ability
6. Ability to make sound decisions and to take full responsibility for decisions made

7. Realistic expectations about the amount of work required and willingness to work long hours
8. Persistence and patience to wait until the business really becomes successful
9. Ambition, energy, and drive
10. Sense of independence and self-confidence
11. Technical knowledge of how to operate the retail business
12. Good health and enthusiasm
13. Willingness to take a chance
14. Common sense

The Small Business Administration has designed the rating scale on page 548. Use the scale to rate yourself on the personal traits that are important for successful entrepreneurs.

Why Businesses Fail

It's a good idea to gain an understanding of why businesses fail in order to avoid some possible pitfalls. Studies show that the greatest number of retail businesses fail during the first 2 years. They also show that if a business operates successfully for 5 years, its chances for continued success are very good. The Small Business Administration estimates that at least 90 percent of all business failures can be attributed to bad management—inexperience and incompetence. The factors that cause businesses to fail can be categorized into the following four areas: (1) inadequate planning, (2) inadequate financing, (3) obsolete methods, and (4) personal factors. Examples of each of these factors were presented recently in a U.S. Office of Education Curriculum Project as follows:

1. Inadequate Planning
   a. Lack of economic knowledge about trading area
   b. Poor selection of location
   c. Failure to foresee major marketing opportunities

d. Failure to plan properly for financial needs

e. Failure to anticipate personnel requirements

f. Inadequate advertising strategy and planning

2. Inadequate Financing
    a. Inadequate working capital to purchase fixed assets
    b. Inadequate capital reserves to withstand slow business period
    c. Insufficient funds to purchase adequate inventory
    d. Insufficient funds to obtain best location

3. Obsolete Methods
    a. Poor expense controls
    b. Poor inventory controls
    c. Poor accounts receivable controls
    d. Poor personnel policy
    e. Poor cost records and pricing methods
    f. Lack of modern equipment

4. Personal Factors
    a. Poor knowledge of business
    b. Unwillingness to accept advice
    c. Unwillingness to work long hours
    d. Content with things as they are
    e. Excessive expenditures in good and bad economic periods

Should You Go into Business for Yourself?

Before answering this question and reading further, you may want to take a few minutes to review what you studied earlier in Chapter 1, "What Is a Career?" and Chapter 12, "Your Attitude." By doing this, you'll be better able to respond to the questions contained in the Small Business Administration's "Checklist for Starting a Business" at the end of this chapter. Each chapter in this unit contains a part of this checklist. Study the items on the checklists and keep them in mind, as they will help get you ready for the project at the end of this unit.

In this chapter, then, you've learned about the first step that all entrepreneurs must take before starting their business. In the remaining chapters of this unit, you'll learn about all the other steps they must take to stay in business and more important, make it grow. These steps are choosing a store site, planning store design, financing the business, and using financial statements.

Note to the Reader

The regular end-of-chapter exercises do not appear in this unit. Instead you will find a checklist at the end of each chapter. Copy the checklists and answer the questions. Choose a retail business that you might like to own and use it throughout this unit. Save your completed checklists as the basis for Project 22.

Checklist for Starting a Business*

1. Are you the type?
    a. Have you rated your personal qualifications using a scale similar to that presented in this chapter?
    b. Have you had some objective evaluators rate you on such scales?
    c. Have you carefully considered your weak points and taken steps to improve them?

2. What business should you choose?
    a. Have you written a summary of your background and experience to help you in making this decision?
    b. Have you considered your hobbies and what you would like to do?
    c. Who wants the services you can perform?
    d. Have you studied surveys and/or sought advice and counsel to find out what fields of business may be expected to expand?
    e. Have you considered working for someone else to gain more experience?

---

* Adapted from Wendell O. Metcalf, *Starting and Managing a Small Business of Your Own* (Washington, D.C.: Small Business Administration, 1973).

3. Should you share ownership with others?
   a. If you need a partner with money or know-how that you don't have, do you know someone who will fit—someone you can get along with?
   b. Do you know the good and bad points about going it alone, having a partner, and incorporating your business?
   c. Have you talked to a lawyer about it?

4. Should you invest in a franchise?
   a. Have you considered how the advantages and disadvantages of franchising apply to you?
   b. Have you made a thorough search to find the right franchise opportunity?

5. Have you worked out plans for buying?
   a. Have you estimated what share of the market you think you can get?
   b. Do you know how much or how many of each item of merchandise you will buy to open your business?
   c. Have you found suppliers who will sell you what you need at a fair price?
   d. Do you have a plan for finding out what your customers want?
   e. Have you set up a model stock assortment to follow in your buying?
   f. Have you worked out stock-control plans to avoid overstocks, understocks, and out-of-stocks?
   g. Do you plan to buy most of your stock from a few suppliers rather than a little from many, so that those you buy from will want to help you succeed?

6. How will you price your products and services?
   a. Do you know how to figure what you should charge to cover your costs?
   b. Do you know what your competitors charge?

7. What selling methods will you use?
   a. Have you studied the selling and sales promotion methods of competitors?
   b. Have you studied why customers buy your type of product or service?
   c. Have you decided what your methods of selling will be?
   d. Have you outlined your sales promotion policy?

8. How will you select and train personnel?
   a. If you need to hire someone to help you, do you know where to look?
   b. Do you know what kind of person you need?
   c. Have you written a job description for each person you will need?
   d. Do you know the prevailing wage scales?
   e. Do you have a plan for training new employees?
   f. Will you continue training through good supervision?

9. What laws will affect you?
   a. Have you checked with the proper authorities to find out what, if any, licenses to do business are necessary?
   b. Do you know what legal and health regulations apply to your business?
   c. Will your operations be subject to interstate commerce regulations? If so, do you know to which ones?
   d. Have you received advice from your lawyer regarding your responsibilities under federal and state laws and local ordinances?

10. Will you keep up to date?
    a. Have you made plans to keep up with improvements in your trade or industry?
    b. Have you prepared a business plan that will be changed as circumstances demand?

Choosing a Store Site

CHAPTER 69

- Communications & Human Relations
- Economics & Marketing
- Merchandising
- Selling & Technology
- Advertising & Display
- Operations & Management

Alison Rodriquez and Phyllis Marx both worked in a craft store full-time since they graduated from the retail marketing program at Harper Community College almost 5 years ago. They finally managed to secure $30,000 (money they saved plus bank and government loans), and planned to meet their shared career goal of opening their own craft store. They knew that their first step was to seek out a good store location.

If Alison and Phyllis were like many retail business owners who select a location, they probably used a combination of factors and methods in making their selection. Some of the things that they considered were personal reasons, such as climate, health, and the need to be close to family and friends. Other things they considered were business and personal contacts in the area.

The five major factors that they investigated in detail were:

1. The community
2. The retail trading area
3. The type of store location
4. The specific site
5. Information sources

Each of these factors is discussed here.

Selecting a Community for a Retail Business

Large companies spend a great deal of time and study on the problem of selecting a new location. Alison and Phyllis and many other small retailers may be unable to do as extensive a study as large companies can in selecting a community for their retail store. Even so, they will want to get answers to questions such as (1) What are the characteristics and size of the population? (2) What are the economic considerations? (3) What is the competition? (4) What are the costs and availability of personnel and other support services? (5) What locations are available?

The chart on page 553 lists the types of information that Alison and Phyllis gathered in the process of selecting a community for their retail business, the craft store.

Defining the Retail Trading Area

To evaluate the potential of prospective geographic areas in terms of the characteristics of the population and the competition, Alison and Phyllis had to define their trading area. A **trading area** is the geographic area from which a business draws its customers. A **store's trading area** is the geographic area in which about 70 percent of the store's customers live.

Measuring the trade boundaries for an existing retail facility is much easier than estimating the trade area for a new business. However, studies of the trading area for similar existing businesses can provide an excellent measure of the probable trading area for a proposed retail business. Firms that are already in the area can analyze credit and delivery records and interview people who live in the area.

Types of Store Locations

Alison and Phyllis, like most prospective retailers, studied these three basic types of shopping areas: the isolated store, the unplanned business district, and the planned shopping center.

The Isolated Store

A free-standing outlet that is either on a highway or a side street is called an **isolated store.** Examples of retailers frequently using this type of location include K-Mart, McDonald's, Kinney Shoes, and Sears. Some small retailers, such as gasoline stations and convenience food stores, also use this type of location. Most small retailers stay away from isolated locations because they are unable to draw and hold customers without the support of other businesses in the area.

The Unplanned Business District

A shopping area that is not a result of prior planning where two or more retail businesses are located together or in close proximity is called an **unplanned business district.** There are four types of unplanned business districts: a central business district, a secondary business district, a neighborhood business district, and a string street.

Central Business District. A **central business district** is the center of retailing in the downtown area of a city. Some of the major strengths of a central business district are access to public transportation, stores with excellent product and price assortments, a variety of services, and nearness to commercial and social facilities. Some of the weaknesses include high rents and taxes, traffic congestion, inadequate parking, failure to improve old stores, and the declining condition of some central cities.

Secondary Business District. A **secondary business district** is a shopping area in a community bounded by the intersection of two major streets. Cities generally have several secondary business districts, and each usually has a junior department store, a variety store, possibly a food store, and several small service shops. The strengths and weaknesses are similar to those of the central business district.

Neighborhood Business District.   A **neighborhood business district** is a shopping area designed to satisfy consumers' needs for convenience-type products and services. A neighborhood business district contains several small businesses with the major retailer being either a department store, drugstore, or supermarket; it is located on the major street of a residential area. This type of store location offers customers longer shopping hours, easier parking, and more relaxed shopping than the central or secondary business district locations.

String Street.   A **string street** is composed of a group of retail businesses located along a street or highway with similar or compatible lines of merchandise or services. Motels and fast-food businesses, car dealers, clothing stores, and antique dealers are examples of retailers that choose this type of location.

The major advantage of a string-street location over the isolated location is customer traffic. It also has many of the advantages of an isolated location, such as low rent, more flexibility, easier parking, and lower operating costs. The disadvantages include limited variety of products or services, higher per customer advertising costs, and higher transportation costs for both customers and employees.

Planned Shopping Center

A centrally owned or managed facility surrounded by parking that includes a group of businesses which complement each other is called a **planned shopping center**. Planned shopping centers have grown to the point that in a recent year

their sales accounted for 36.3 percent of total retail sales. In addition to the emerging subregional malls described in Chapter 11, there are three general types of shopping centers: neighborhood, community, and regional.

Neighborhood Shopping Center.   A **neighborhood shopping center** is a planned shopping area that sells mostly convenience products and services. A neighborhood center serves 7,000 to 70,000 people who live within a 10-minute drive. The largest store is usually a supermarket or drugstore and often includes other businesses such as a bakery, hardware store, hairdresser, and laundry–dry cleaner.

Community Shopping Center.   A **community shopping center** is a planned shopping center that sells both convenience and shopping products and services to city and suburban customers. A community shopping center serves from 20,000 to 100,000 people who live within 3 to 4 miles of the facility. A variety store or a small department store or both is included in the center, as well as the types of retail businesses found in neighborhood shopping centers. Also, much greater control and more long-range planning is used in operating a community shopping center than a neighborhood one.

Regional Shopping Center.   A **regional shopping center** is a planned shopping area that sells mostly shopping-type products and services to customers in a wide geographic area. A regional center serves over 100,000 people who live within 30 minutes driving time of the facility. It has at least one or two large department stores and more than 100 small retail businesses. Regional centers are the result of a planned effort to create the shopping area that has normally been associated with "downtown."

The major advantages of a planned shopping center include:

1. Cooperative promotional planning and sharing of common costs such as advertising, parking, and lighting
2. Carefully planned variety of products and services
3. One-stop shopping
4. Creation of distinctive shopping image
5. Pleasant shopping atmosphere and easy parking
6. Lower theft rates
7. Lower rent and taxes than many central business districts

The disadvantages include restrictions on products and services sold, fixed store hours, rent higher than for locations other than some downtown areas, competition, and being forced to help pay for items that may not help a particular business.

Selecting a Specific Retail Site

Alison and Phyllis wanted to give the selection of a specific retail site the same careful consideration that they gave to the selection of a community and type of store location. Four factors that they studied in making their site selection included (1) traffic and transportation, (2) location in relation to competitors and other businesses, (3) parking and other physical aspects, and (4) terms of occupancy (including taxes and zoning regulations).

Traffic and Transportation

Probably the most important factor in evaluating the desirability of a retail business location is that of both pedestrian and vehicular traffic. Traffic studies usually include an analysis of both the number and types of people going by the proposed site. Fast-food franchises, convenience food stores, and gasoline stations are examples of retailers who use vehicular traffic studies. Pedestrian traffic studies are often conducted by department stores, ready-to-

What factors must a retailer consider when choosing a store site? Courtesy of N.Y. Life Insurance Co.

wear retailers, and other specialty stores that rely on high pedestrian traffic.

Information on transportation facilities needs to be studied most carefully by those retailers who require frequent deliveries of merchandise and whose customers need access to major highways, mass transit, or both to get to their business locations. For example, in downtown areas, closeness to public transportation is particularly important for reaching customers who don't own cars or don't drive into an area with heavy traffic congestion and poor parking.

Nearness to Other Businesses

A location that is too far from competitors can be a problem because it doesn't allow for comparison shopping by potential customers. For example, consumers tend to shop for items such as furniture or automobiles in areas where a number of similar businesses are located. In many cases, it's desirable to locate near complementary businesses in order to draw customers. For example, drugstores are frequently located next to supermarkets.

Parking and Other Physical Aspects

The availability of parking is particularly important in selecting a site. Sometimes, even if adequate parking is potentially available, the spaces may be used by people who are not customers. If additional parking is needed, local ordinances should be checked to make sure that curb cuts can be made and the land used for that purpose.

Other physical aspects that are often considered include the condition of sidewalks and pavements, availability of gas and electricity, and suitability of ground for construction. Also included are the location of industries that might cause air or noise pollution, regulations as to where a building can be placed on a lot, availability of additional land for expansion, and the general condition of the neighborhood where the business is to be located.

Terms of Occupancy

Terms of occupancy include ownership or leasing, operation and maintenance costs, taxes, zoning, and other regulations. One advantage of leasing is that it takes less money to establish a business, which means that more money can be used for operating the business. Another advantage is that the owner-manager can choose not to renew the lease if the location turns out to be a poor one. The advantages of owning a site are:

1. Increased value of the building, if any, belongs to owner.
2. Any desired changes in the building can be made.
3. There is no danger of not being able to renew the lease.

If necessary, some retailers also study the costs of operation and maintenance, such as mortgage or rental payments,

heat, lights, air conditioning, telephone, supplies, and delivery.

Taxes should also be studied, especially if ownership is contemplated. Long-term projections as well as current taxes should be estimated.

Zoning ordinances and other regulations should be considered to make sure that there are no restrictions on building location and type of products or services offered. Most retailers hire a lawyer to help them in checking out such legal matters.

Sources of Information to Use in Selecting a Store Location

Information on selecting a location for a retail business can be secured from a variety of sources. But first, retailers should have an understanding of what it means to serve consumers. Review Units 6 and 18 to refresh your memory.

The local chamber of commerce can offer firsthand information about local business conditions, zoning ordinances, and business trends. The Census Bureau compiles data about the characteristics of the population, and this information is available at most public libraries. Many libraries also have publications such as the *Census of Retail Trade* and *County Business Patterns,* which contain information for analyzing an area both for sales potential and competition. For example, the publications contain information on the number of retail businesses of a given type in an area, information on where consumers spend their money, and national averages on the number of people per store by selected kinds of businesses. The Department of Commerce also issues statistics on the trends of various communities and geographical areas in the United States. The library may also have literature from the Small Business Administration and other sources to help the entre-preneur select a community for a retail business. Magazines such as *Sales Management's Survey of Buying Power* and *Editor and Publisher Market Guide* may also be available in some libraries.

Additional possible sources of information include trade associations, real estate companies, local newspapers, banks, city officials, and personal observations.

Now find out how you'd rate in making the decisions involved in choosing a store site by completing the checklist at the end of this chapter.

Then go on to learn about planning store design, which is covered in the next chapter.

Trade Talk

Define each term and use it in a sentence.

Central business
  district
Community
  shopping center
Isolated store
Neighborhood
  business district
Neighborhood
  shopping center
Planned shopping
  center

Regional shopping
  center
Secondary business
  district
Store's trading area
String street
Trading area
Unplanned business
  district

Checklist for Choosing a Site*

1. Have you investigated general business conditions in your trading area?
   a. Are business conditions good in the city and neighborhood?
   b. Are current conditions good in the line of business you plan to start?
2. Where should you locate?
   a. Have you studied the makeup of the population in the city or town?
   b. Do you know what kind of people will want to buy what you plan to sell?
   c. Do people like that live in the area?
   d. Have you checked the number, type, and size of competitors in the area?
   e. Does the area need another business like the one you plan to open?
   f. Are employees available?
   g. Have you checked and found adequate utilities, parking facilities, police and fire protection, housing, schools, and other cultural and community activities?
   h. Do you consider the costs of the location reasonable in terms of taxes and rents?
   i. Is there sufficient opportunity for growth and expansion?
   j. Have you checked the relative merits of the various shopping areas within the city, including shopping centers?
   k. Have you had a lawyer check the lease and zoning laws?

* Adapted from Wendell O. Metcalf, *Starting and Managing a Small Business of Your Own*, (Washington, D.C.: Small Business Administration, 1973).

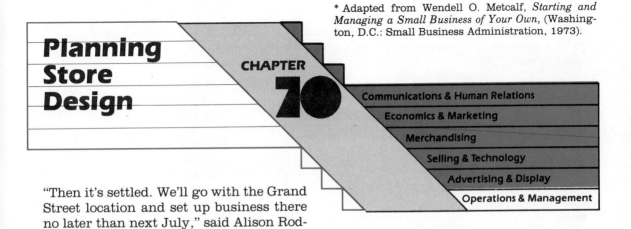

Planning Store Design

CHAPTER 70

Communications & Human Relations
Economics & Marketing
Merchandising
Selling & Technology
Advertising & Display
Operations & Management

"Then it's settled. We'll go with the Grand Street location and set up business there no later than next July," said Alison Rodriguez, co-owner of the Creative Craft Corner. "That location will be great," said her partner Phyllis Marx, "and I've got some ideas about how we should design the store. I'll bet there's enough room there to come up with the rustic kind of look we both liked so much at that little gallery in Smithtown."

"Say Phyl, maybe you're right. And we could even have a separate section for our handmade wooden pieces, like the one they had for the candles. Why don't you do some checking and find out who designed the gallery in Smithtown. Maybe we could use the same designer."

When the co-owners of the Creative Craft Corner set up their business at the Grand Street location, they will remodel the store that's there now to reflect their own store image. The design will tell customers what kind of mood or image the store is trying to create.

Exterior Design

Alison Rodriguez and Phyllis Marx would like to have the Creative Craft Corner designed in a way that will tell people as they look at the storefront, "This is an old-fashioned, friendly store that has unique crafts and handmade wooden gifts. Come in and browse; you're welcome any time." The front of the Creative Craft Corner will be a face that everyone sees. Because first impressions are important, the storefront will play a powerful part in determining what customers will think of the store.

Storefronts attract passersby with easy access, open window displays, and interesting entranceways. Jane Hamilton-Merritt (left), Dennis Rizzuto (right), courtesy of Architectural Record (bottom)

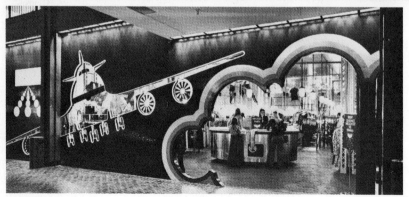

Effective Storefronts

Storefronts achieve consumer appeal in a variety of ways. Some have wide, inviting entrances. Some have attractive window displays. Others are constructed of unique building materials. The type of storefront treatment depends, to some extent, on the location of the store.

In freestanding stores, revolving or swinging doors are common. Some freestanding stores use curtains of warm or cool air that serve as doors during store hours. In covered-mall locations, the open storefront is particularly popular. This design calls for a wide entryway as well as large areas of glass through which the sales floor can be seen. In many shopping centers, the front of the store faces an enclosed mall and is literally open, with no glass separating the store from the mall. The open storefront admits a great deal of light to the store. When the open storefront faces the street, it also draws attention to the store after closing hours, when some interior lights remain lit.

Each storefront should be distinctive as well as in keeping with the kind of image the store is trying to project. Here are some guidelines for creating a storefront that sells.

♦ Entrance doors should be easily identified and invite people to enter the store. They should be placed to facilitate traffic flow. Many stores are creating a second front by placing display windows and entrances at the rear of the store, facing a parking lot.
♦ The sign should be an intergral part of the front and contribute to the distinctive character of the firm. In addition, the store name should be clearly visible at customer eye level, either on the display window or on the door.
♦ Contrast should be created by using both light and dark colors and variously textured materials.
♦ The store should blend with neighboring store designs but still maintain its own distinctive appearance.

Display Windows

Formal display windows, which are more common in downtown store locations, also play an important role in creating the store image. Three different types of display window backgrounds are in common use: the open background, the partial background, and the full background. These three types of window displays are described in Chapter 27. The completely windowless exterior has been used in recent years to reduce air-conditioning and heating costs. In this case, the store sign becomes extremely important.

Interior Design

Another important purpose of store design is to plan the layout and appearance of the inside of the store. Store layout and decor either attract or repel customers—so layout is crucial, especially in shopping centers where dozens of stores compete for the customer's business. The design must allow for the most effective and economical use of the space that's available. It's also important that the design carry out the image and mood that have been created by the exterior store design. Along with these purposes, the interior design should help to reduce merchandise thefts.

Effective Use of Space

Having enough space for every store function is often a problem. Competing for available space are (1) the selling floor; (2) receiving and storing areas for merchandise; (3) store operations such as management, credit, and recordkeeping; (4) plumbing, heating, and electrical systems; and (5) parking for customers and employees—to say nothing of space for future expansion.

An important trend in the 1980s is the construction of smaller stores. Ever-increasing costs have made the effective use of every inch of space a must. Some stores are even leaving empty footage in the rear of the store to reduce the footage that is actually being used.

As a result of the trend toward using less space, there is some reduction of the selling area, but the biggest reductions are in the nonselling areas. An example of this reduction can be seen in apparel chains where, as recently as 1978, 18 to 20 percent of the total store space was devoted to nonselling space. This nonselling space has now been reduced to about 10 to 12 percent of the total space and is often double-decked in metal grill. This reduction may even mean the elimination of office space in some chain-store units.

On the selling floor, well-planned use of space can make shopping easier for customers. And, at the same time, it can reduce confusion by making merchandise easier for customers to find.

Continuation of Store Image

When a store design is carefully carried through to the store interior, customers are reminded of the store image and mood the retailer is trying to create. This has a positive effect on sales because the store image is in keeping with the tastes of the customers it wishes to attract.

Theft Detection

Store design also helps retailers detect and avoid thefts. Some stores build into their designs permanent theft detection devices, such as a two-way mirror in front of the manager's mezzanine desk or security towers with dark glass or two-way mirrors. In addition to depending on such security devices, retailers make special efforts to keep their selling areas orderly, having found that attempted thefts can be discovered more readily in a well-organized space than in a poorly kept area.

Equipment, Fixtures, and Furnishings

Everything within a store aside from merchandise and people falls into the categories of equipment, fixtures, and furnishings. **Equipment** includes a variety of apparatus that is built into or used in the store. Lighting, heating, and plumbing units, elevators and escalators, business and sales machines, storage shelves and bins, and merchandise carts are all equipment. Fixtures are closely related to equipment and are sometimes classified under that general heading. But they are usually considered separately because of their very direct and important influence on the selling effort. **Fixtures** include the shelves, counters, and racks used on the selling floor to display merchandise for sale. **Furnishings** are the furniture, carpeting, and decorative elements within the store. Equipment, fixtures, and furnishings should blend in with the store image and not distract the customer's attention from the merchandise.

Equipment

Lighting, air conditioning, and heating are standard features in offices and factories as well as in stores. In the retail store, however, these types of equipment not only create a comfortable working environment but also give indirect support to the selling effort by making the store attractive to customers.

Perhaps the most important equipment in the store is the lighting equipment. With the increasing costs of utilities, stores have not been able to save money on lighting. Some stores that have experimented with reducing the wattage in their incandescent lights have increased it again because they felt that dull lighting was having a negative effect on business. Good lighting offers these advantages:

♦ It attracts customer attention and makes the interior of the store visible to passersby.
♦ It reveals the true color, texture, luster, and other qualities of merchandise.
♦ It can help to separate sections of the store visually.
♦ It helps reduce mental fatigue among workers and promotes store cleanliness and neatness.

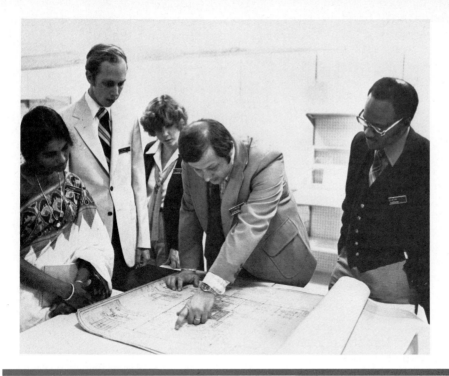

Retailers should pay careful attention to the placement of equipment, fixtures, and furnishings. *Courtesy of J. C. Penney*

♦ It helps create the type of image desired by the management.

Air-conditioning equipment is also standard equipment for almost all stores. Often the installation consists of a joint heating and air-conditioning system. The comfort provided by these heating and cooling systems attracts customers to the store and keeps them there longer. Such systems keep merchandise fresh, largely eliminate dirt and dust, and keep employee fatigue to a minimum.

Equipment also includes the machines that are needed to record, compute, and summarize business transactions and handle inventory control. An important trend in the 1980s is the installation of computerized systems to handle these functions. (See Chapter 11.)

Fixtures

The types of fixtures a store chooses depends upon the type of merchandise to be sold and the merchandising policies of the company. Regardless of type, however, all fixtures perform three general functions: (1) they project the store image, (2) they promote the sale of merchandise, and (3) they provide protection for merchandise. Today, the more portable and flexible fixtures are, the more popular they are.

Fixtures may project a prestige image of an exclusive store where the selling policy calls for the assistance of salespeople. The merchandise in such stores is seldom set out where a customer can examine it without the help of a salesperson. Instead, it's displayed under glass (or in the case of apparel, even kept off the selling floor in a storage area).

An important trend in fashion merchandising is to expose merchandise more fully. This means that increasing numbers of retailers are displaying merchandise so that the front of the item can be seen instead of only the shoulder and sleeve. When as much merchandise as possible is hung on special rods that descend like waterfalls from wall or floor fixtures, the merchandise can face outward instead of sideways. Retailers have found that the probability that a customer will be at least twice as likely to buy a garment if it's hung face-out instead of sideways.

Supermarkets and self-service drugstores put self-service fixtures throughout most of their selling areas and use them for hardware, records, cosmetics, small items of apparel, and other prepackaged goods. There are fixtures with unbreakable glass and steel sidings for very expensive items. Other fixtures display frozen foods while keeping them at the right temperature.

Furnishings

Some furniture, such as desks and file cabinets, is designed to help store personnel do their jobs, but most furniture in the selling area of a store is intended for the comfort of customers. Any store that offers customers a pleasant place to relax will find that people come in to do just that—and that many people will stay to buy. In general, the higher the quality of the goods and the more time and money the customer is expected to spend, the more places there will be for the customer to sit down and relax.

Carpeting also invites customers to stay in a store. It makes shopping easier on their feet, absorbs noise, and looks attractive. Carpeting was once used only by prestige stores because its upkeep was costly and it didn't stand up well under heavy traffic. However, modern carpeting is as durable and easy to maintain as any other kind of floor covering, and many retailers use it.

Decorative furnishings—including the paint or paper on the walls, pictures and murals, dividers, and planters—also attract customers and help to shape the store image.

Layout

The arrangement of the store's equipment, fixtures, and furnishings is known as the **store layout.** It has an important influence on sales activities, since it shows where activities are handled and where equipment, fixtures, and furnishings are located. The development of an efficient layout has always been a challenging task. But in some newer stores it's considerably more challenging because of the trend toward smaller stores and reduced nonselling areas.

There are a few more trends in store layout that are receiving increased attention. The first is the evaluation of the store in terms of sales per square foot. Another is the trend toward the use of more aisle impact in presenting goods. And the third is the improvement of store layout and service accommodations for customers with special needs.

Sales per Square Foot

As you learned in Chapter 38, the layout of the store has a direct relationship to the dollar amount of sales made per square foot. This amount is calculated for the store as a whole and for each department within the store. As costs of operating the store continue to increase, it becomes even more important for each square foot of floor space to be as productive as possible.

Here are a few general rules of store layout that may increase sales per square foot:

- Concentrate stock in the smallest space possible without giving it a crowded appearance.
- Use arrangements that encourage as much self-service as the store and merchandise will allow.
- Place related items within a department and related departments within the store near each other to encourage suggestion selling.
- Put impulse goods near entrances and aisles where traffic is highest. Put con-

This elegant supermarket features wide aisles for easy access to merchandise. The luxurious material and fixtures contribute to a unique store image. Courtesy of Byerly's, St. Louis Park, Minnesota.

venience goods, which customers buy frequently, near high-traffic locations. Put shopping goods, which the customer usually wants to examine carefully, away from entrances and major traffic aisles.

More Aisle Impact

A recent trend in department-store layout is the formation of wider and shallower departments so that goods can be presented with more aisle impact. Wider aisles enable customers to examine merchandise without being jostled or feeling that they are in the way. This trend, in combination with the increasing number of stores that have little room for back stock and the emphasis on more fully exposed hanging merchandise, has reduced the amount of merchandise a store can handle at one time. The result is a faster stock turnover of fewer units of merchandise.

Other general guidelines that should be observed when laying out the selling floor are these:

♦ Remove unnecessary barriers, such as walls and counters, that prevent maximum circulation by customers.
♦ Encourage maximum customer traffic by careful placement of elevators, escalators, customer service areas, and high-demand merchandise that customers will seek out. Locate these away from major traffic aisles so that customers are drawn through the store, past as many types of goods as possible.

Serving Customers with Special Needs

Many stores and shopping centers are now making their buildings more accessible to customers with special needs. This is in response to a federally legislated push to make a barrier-free environment for handicapped customers. Some retail barriers that must be overcome are inconvenient parking, curbs, steps, narrow aisles, difficult traffic flow, small elevators, small or inaccessible restrooms, and poor service and attitude of salespeople.

One of the ways stores have begun to overcome these barriers is by installing special curbside parking for handicapped customers. They have also installed ramps and entranceways that will accommodate wheelchairs. Phone booths have been lowered and special elevators and rest rooms that will accommodate wheelchairs have been installed.

Not all customers with special needs are in wheelchairs. Some have impaired hearing or sight. One example of an attempt to help these customers can be seen at McDonald's, where Braille menus have been built into the counters at some locations. Sears has installed teletype machines at some locations to help deaf customers place catalog orders. Other stores have installed Braille-identified elevator controls and Braille floor signs on the outside of elevator frames at each floor. This way blind customers are able to signal for their floors and to determine at what floor the elevator has stopped.

Retailers setting up new stores need all the designing help that they can afford. They may consult architects who specialize both in designing the basic structure of a store building and in preparing detailed interior floor plans. Manufacturers of equipment, fixtures, and furnishings offer consulting aid in planning interior designs that make use of the products they supply. Making visits to other stores, looking through trade magazines, and talking with trade association experts are other ways in which retailers can obtain new design ideas. It should be remembered, however, that the ultimate success of a design depends on the imagination of each retailer in applying the design ideas to his or her own retailing space.

Retailers are expanding their services to customers with special needs. Courtesy of McDonald's Corporation

The success of each store design also depends on the retailer's financial ability to carry out the design plans. In the next chapter you'll learn how retailers control finances—not only as they relate to design but in terms of the entire store.

Trade Talk

Define each term and use it in a sentence.

Equipment	Furnishings
Fixtures	Store layout

Checklist for Interior Layout and Display*

1. Is your store layout adequate?
   a. Are your fixtures low enough and signs so placed that the customer can get a bird's-eye view of the store and tell in what direction to go for wanted goods?
   b. Do your aisle and counter arrangements stimulate a circular traffic flow?
   c. Do your fixtures (and their arrangement), signs, lettering, and colors all create a coordinated and unified effect?
   d. Before any supplier's fixtures are accepted, do you make sure they conform in color and design to what you have?
   e. Do you limit the use of hanging signs to department identification and sales?
   f. Are your counters and aisle tables overcrowded with merchandise?
   g. Are your ledges and cashier-wrapping stations kept free of boxes, unneeded wrapping materials, personal effects, and odds and ends?
   h. Do you keep trash bins out of sight?
2. What is your merchandise emphasis?
   a. Do your signs referring to specific goods tell the customer something significant about them, rather than simply naming the products and their prices?

---

* Adapted from Wendell O. Metcalf, *Starting and Managing a Small Business of Your Own* (Washington, D.C.: Small Business Administration, 1973).

   b. For your advertised goods, do you have some prominent signs, including flyers at the entrances, to inform and guide customers to their exact location?
   c. Do you prominently display both advertised and nonadvertised specials at the ends of counters as well as at the point of sale?
   d. Are both your national and private brands highlighted in your arrangement and window display?
   e. In the case of apparel and home furnishings, do the items that reflect your store's fashion sense or fashion leadership get special display attention?
   f. In locating merchandise in your store, do you always consider the productivity of space—vertical as well as horizontal?
   g. Is your self-service merchandise arranged to attract and assist customers?
      (1) Is each category grouped under a separate sign?
      (2) Is the merchandise in each category arranged according to its most significant characteristic—whether color, style, size, or price?
      (3) In apparel categories, is the merchandise arranged by price lines or zones to assist the customer to make a selection quickly?
      (4) Is horizontal space usually devoted to different items and styles within a category (vertical space being used for different sizes—smallest at the top, largest at the bottom)?
      (5) Are impulse items interspersed with demand items?

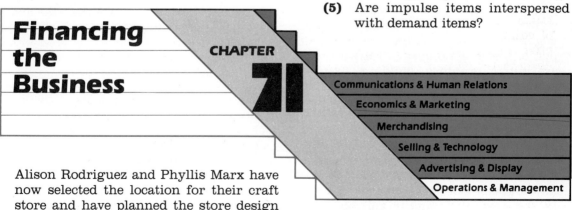

Financing the Business

CHAPTER 71

Communications & Human Relations
Economics & Marketing
Merchandising
Selling & Technology
Advertising & Display
Operations & Management

Alison Rodriguez and Phyllis Marx have now selected the location for their craft store and have planned the store design

---

that they would like to have. But they begin to feel that the $30,000 they have to start their business with is not really going to be enough money. How do they know for sure how much money they'll really need? Where could they go to get more money? If they can't get the additional money they'll need from their friends or relatives and have to borrow from other sources, what kind of information about themselves and their business will they be expected to give these sources?

How Much Money?

The answer to this question deserves careful study and investigation for each new business venture. No average amount can be specified, since every type of retailing business is so different. The amount of money needed varies according to the type of business, kind of merchandise or services sold, size of business, anticipated sales volume, income level of customers, personal finances, and trade connections. The location of the business and general economic conditions at the time of starting are other factors that have to be considered.

The two purposes for which Alison and Phyllis need money to start a new business are operating expenses and start-up costs. **Operating expenses** are the costs —such as salaries, rent, utilities, and taxes—of running the business on a monthly basis. **Start-up costs** are the expenses involved in setting up the retail business; these normally have to be paid just one time. Examples of start-up costs are initial inventory, building, fixtures, and equipment.

Operating Expenses

The first step to follow in attempting to determine operating expenses is to estimate the sales volume. This will depend on the total amount of potential business in the area, the number and ability of competitors, and the owner's ability to

compete for the consumer's dollar. New owners may obtain assistance from wholesalers, trade associations, bankers, and other business people in making their sales estimates.

In estimating the sales volume, it's a good idea not to be overly optimistic, because new businesses generally grow slowly at the start. If Alison and Phyllis overestimate their sales, they might invest too much in equipment and initial inventory and commit themselves to heavier operating expenses than their actual sales volume will justify. For example, the hiring of four salespeople instead of two can make a significant difference in the cost of doing business.

Once the estimated sales volume has been determined and entered into a worksheet such as the one shown in the table on page 567, Alison and Phyllis are then ready to estimate their monthly operating expenses.

There are a number of sources of expense information that they should consult. Among these are Dun & Bradstreet, the Accounting Corporation of America, National Cash Register Company, and various trade associations and libraries.

Alison and Phyllis will, of course, have to study the typical industry figures for their type of retail business and modify them so that they fit into their business plans. For example, their place of business, because of its location, may be less expensive to heat and cool than the average place of business in the industry.

Start-up Costs

One method to estimate start-up costs involves filling out worksheets such as those shown in the tables on pages 568 and 569. Sources for advice on cost and layout and selection of fixtures and equipment are representatives of equipment manufacturers and trade associations.

The total money needed for starting a retail business venture should be a com-

OPERATING EXPENSES WORKSHEET

Monthly expenses	Column 1: Your estimate of monthly expenses based on sales of $ _____ per year	Column 2: Your estimate of how much cash you need to start your business	What to put in column 2*
Salary of owner-manager	$	$	2 times column 1
All other salaries and wages			3 times column 1
Rent			3 times column 1
Advertising			3 times column 1
Delivery expense			3 times column 1
Supplies			3 times column 1
Telephone and telegraph			3 times column 1
Other utilities			3 times column 1
Insurance			Amount required by insurance firm
Taxes (and social security)			4 times column 1
Interest			3 times column 1
Maintenance			3 times column 1
Legal and professional fees			3 times column 1
Miscellaneous			3 times column 1

*These figures are typical for one kind of business. You will have to decide how many months to allow for in your business.
Source: Adapted from Wendell O. Metcalf, *Starting and Managing a Small Business of Your Own* (Washington, D.C.: Small Business Administration, 1973).

bination of start-up costs and operating expenses. It's important to plan for a safe margin because many businesses don't become self-supporting for 4 to 6 months or longer.

Since Alison and Phyllis don't have sufficient cash, they may be unable to (1) afford enough employees to keep the business operating, (2) invest in proper equipment, (3) maintain an adequate inventory of merchandise or materials in order to build sales volume, (4) take advantage of discounts offered by creditors, and (5) grant customer credit to meet competition.

Sources of Capital

Successful retailing requires that retailers know how much money will they need to start the business, to keep it operating, and to provide for expansion. They must also know where to get this money. The money needed to start a business and keep it operating is called **capital**. Now that Alison and Phyllis have computed their capital needs, where will they get the extra money they need?

Those who start their own business usually use more than one source of capital. They will probably use personal savings, loans, and credit from the suppliers of equipment, fixtures, and inventory. Once a business is established, trade credit will become an important means of financing the merchandise that must be bought. Also, increasing profits will be a new source of capital that can be reinvested in the business.

Personal Savings

There is an old saying that it takes money to make money. Very few people or firms will lend money to those who have no money of their own to invest in the business. So, prospective retail store owners will find their personal savings very helpful in starting a business.

However, what would-be retailers should avoid is risking every cent they have on a business venture. Often, such entrepreneurs plan not to draw any kind of salary or income until the business begins to make a certain amount of profit. If this is the case, the owner should retain enough cash on hand to cover personal expenses until the business is capable of being self-supporting.

Loans

Some of the initial or working capital for a business can be obtained by borrowing. A loan is money borrowed with a promise to repay, usually within a specific period of time. Loans may be secured or unse-

---

START-UP COSTS WORKSHEET
List of Furniture, Fixtures, and Equipment

Leave out or add items to suit your business. Use separate sheets to list exactly what you need for each of the items below.	If you plan to pay cash in full, enter the full amount below and in the last column.	If you are going to pay by installments, fill out the columns below. Enter in the last column your down payment plus at least one installment.			Estimate of the cash you need for furniture, fixtures, and equipment.
		Price	Down payment	Amount of each installment	
Counters	$	$	$	$	$
Storage shelves and cabinets					
Display stands, shelves, and tables					
Cash register					
Safe					
Window display fixtures					
Special lighting					
Outside sign					
Delivery equipment, if needed					
Total					

Source: Adapted from Wendell O. Metcalf, *Starting and Managing a Small Business of Your Own* (Washington, D.C.: Small Business Administration, 1973).

START-UP COSTS WORKSHEET
(Costs You Only Have to Pay Once)

Furniture, fixtures, and equipment:
Fill in the total from the worksheet on page 568. $ _____

Decorating and remodeling:
Talk it over with a contractor.   _____

Installation of fixtures and equipment:
Talk to suppliers from whom you buy these.   _____

Starting inventory:
Suppliers will help you estimate this. For total amounts, use typical ratio to sales.   _____

Deposits with public utilities:
Find out from utility companies.   _____

Legal and other professional fees:
Lawyer, accountant, and so on.   _____

Licenses and permits:
Find out from city offices what you have to have.   _____

Advertising and promotion for opening:
Estimate what you'll use.   _____

Accounts receivable:
What you need to buy more stock until credit customers pay.   _____

Cash:
For unexpected expenses or losses, special purchases, etc.   _____

Other:
Make a separate list and enter total.   _____

Total:
Total estimated cash you need to start with. $ _____

Source: Adapted from Wendell O. Metcalf, *Starting and Managing a Small Business of Your Own* (Washington, D.C.: Small Business Administration, 1973).

cured. A **secured loan** is one in which borrowers agree to give lenders a specific item worth approximately the same amount as the loan in the event that they should be unable to repay the loan. An unsecured loan does not include such an agreement.

Loans may be obtained from individuals or from financial institutions, such as banks. Individuals starting small businesses often obtain personal loans from their relatives or friends. Such loans are usually unsecured. Rarely, however, can such personal loans be made in amounts large enough to cover the expenses of starting a business.

Business Loans.   These are usually obtained from banks or other financial institutions. The federal government doesn't make direct loans to individuals, but it does have a program that assists individual business people, offering a guarantee to the bank involved that the loan will be paid. The Small Business Administration (SBA) may guarantee a loan made by a bank to a small-business owner-manager. Before any guarantee is made, the SBA requires that the loan application be turned down by two or three banks. Proper forms must be filed and the processing time can be several months. Further information can be obtained by contacting the nearest SBA field office.

Small Business Investment Companies (SBIC) are licensed by the SBA but are privately organized and managed firms. Although SBICs usually prefer to buy stock in a company, long-term credit financing is available.

Suppliers are another source of loans. For example, the oil company that helps someone set up a new service station will usually supply on a loan basis a percentage of the initial capital needed.

Types of Business Loans.   Business loans are either long-term or short-term. **Long-term loans** are those that run 5, 10, 20, or even 30 years. Typically, they are secured by a mortgage on the store real estate or on the fixtures and equipment (such as counters, refrigeration cases, or trucks) to be purchased with the proceeds (money borrowed) of the loan. **Short-term loans,** however, usually run for only 30, 60, or 90 days. This type of loan is useful in situations such as paying for merchandise bought seasonally, covering extra large payrolls during peak selling months, handling emergencies like repairs, buying goods at a cash discount, and meeting special tax assessments.

Information to Be Supplied. Before lenders are prepared to make loans, they must feel satisfied with answers to these questions:

1. What sort of person are you?
2. What are you going to do with the money?
3. When and how do you plan to pay it back?
4. Does the amount requested make a suitable allowance for unexpected developments?
5. What is the outlook for you, for your line of business, and for business in general?

For owners of new businesses, bankers and loan officers will normally require a business plan with information such as:

1. Personal background information, including experience in the field
2. Business description, including products or services to be offered and desired location
3. Analysis of the market to be served
4. Analysis of the existing competition, including the estimated market share
5. The strategy for success
6. Projected financial statements, including a sales forecast and expense summary

Trade Credit

For some retailers, an important source of funds for financing the business is trade credit. As indicated in Chapter 61, trade credit is an important means of acquiring an inventory of merchandise. It also enables retailers to buy equipment and fixtures; cash registers and office furniture, for example, may be purchased on credit. Moreover, some suppliers of merchandise will allow retailers who order their goods to buy specialized display fixtures, such as frozen-food cases, on credit.

In general, only some types of trade credit are available to beginning retailers. They can usually get help from their equipment supplier, but often they will be expected to pay in advance or on receipt for goods that they buy to resell. This is because they have not yet established their credit rating. Once they prove that their store is a good outlet for supplier products and that they meet their financial obligations on time, trade credit will be extended to them more liberally.

Profits

The safest and best method of financing improvements and business expansion is by reinvesting profits in the business. Firms may seem to grow slowly by this method, but it's better than facing the problems of merchants who rush from one loan payment date to the next. Another advantage of using profits rather than borrowing is that no interest has to be paid on profits.

As owners, retailers will probably want to set aside some money for themselves out of their profits as their reward for their investment. The boards of directors of corporations may divide some profits among the stockholders as a return on their stock investment. But if businesses are to grow, profits must be put back into the business immediately to buy equipment or merchandise, or they may be set aside as surplus to be used in the future.

Once owners have found sufficient funds to finance their proposed business, they must also know how to keep all the necessary financial records so as to keep track of how it's doing. This is covered in the next and last chapter of this unit.

Trade Talk

Define each term and use it in a sentence.

Capital	Secured loan
Long-term loans	Short-term loans
Operating expenses	Start-up costs

Checklist for Financing the Business*

1. How much money will you need?
   a. Have you filled out worksheets similar to those shown in this chapter?
   b. In filling out the worksheets, have you taken care not to overestimate income?
   c. Have you obtained quoted prices for equipment and supplies you will need?
   d. Do you know the costs of goods that must be in your inventory?
   e. Have you estimated expenses only after checking rents, wage scales, utility rates, and other pertinent costs in the area where you plan to locate?
   f. Have you found what percentage of your estimated sales your projected inventory and each expense item is and have you compared each percentage with the typical percentage for your line of business?
   g. Have you added an additional amount of money to your estimates to allow for unexpected events?
2. Where can you get the money?
   a. Have you counted up how much money of your own you can put into the business?
   b. Do you know how much credit you can get from your suppliers—the people you will buy from?
   c. Do you know where you can borrow the rest of the money you need to start your business?
   d. Have you selected a progressive bank with the credit services you may need?
   e. Have you talked to a banker about your plans? Does the banker have an interested, helpful attitude toward your problems?
3. If you plan to buy a going business, how much should you pay for it?
   a. Have you estimated future sales and profits of the going business for the next few years?
   b. Are your estimated future profits satisfactory?
   c. Have you looked at past financial statements of the business to find the return on investment and on sales?
   d. Have you verified the owner's claims about the business with reports from an independent accountant's analysis of the figures?
   e. Is the inventory you will purchase a good buy?
   f. Are equipment and fixtures fairly valued?
   g. If you plan to buy the accounts receivable, are they worth the asking price?
   h. Have you been careful in your appraisal of the company's goodwill?
   i. Are you prepared to assume the company's liabilities and are the creditors agreeable?
   j. Have you learned why the present owner wants to sell?
   k. Have you found out about the present owner's reputation with his or her employees and suppliers?
   l. Have you consulted a lawyer to be sure that the title is good?
   m. Has your lawyer checked to find out if there is any lien against the assets you are buying?
   n. Has your lawyer drawn up an agreement covering all essential points, including a seller's warranty for your protection against false statements?
4. How will you handle taxes and insurance?
   a. Have you worked out a system for handling the withholding tax for your employees?
   b. Have you worked out a system for handling sales taxes? Excise taxes?
   c. Have you planned an adequate record system for the efficient preparation of income tax forms?
   d. Have you prepared a worksheet for meeting tax obligations?
   e. Have you talked with an insurance agent about what kinds of insurance you will need and how much it will cost?
5. What other management problems will you face?

*Adapted from Wendell O. Metcalf, *Starting and Managing a Small Business of Your Own* (Washington, D.C.: Small Business Administration, 1973).

a. Do you plan to sell for credit?

b. If you do, do you have the extra capital necessary to carry accounts receivable?

c. Have you made a policy for returned goods?

d. Have you planned how you will make deliveries?

e. Have you considered other policies which must be made in your particular business?

f. Have you made a plan to guide yourself in making the best use of your time and effort?

6. Will you set measurable goals for yourself?

a. Have you set goals and subgoals for yourself?

b. Have you specified dates when each goal is to be achieved?

c. Are these realistic goals; that is, will they challenge you but at the same time not call for unreasonable accomplishments?

d. Are the goals specific so that you can measure performance?

e. Have you developed a business plan, using one of the SBA aids to record your ideas, facts, and figures?

f. Have you allowed for obstacles?

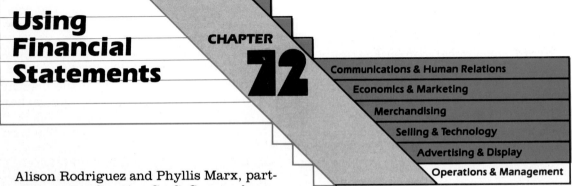

Using Financial Statements

CHAPTER 72

Communications & Human Relations

Economics & Marketing

Merchandising

Selling & Technology

Advertising & Display

Operations & Management

Alison Rodriguez and Phyllis Marx, partners in the Creative Craft Corner, know that they have to learn about financial statements and how to use them. This information, they know, helps owners to see where the store's strengths and weaknesses are and to pinpoint operations that need correction.

There are two types of financial statements that owners prepare and use: an income (profit-and-loss) statement and a balance sheet. These two records help owners to measure the actual financial performance of the store against what had been planned. They also help owners to compare the performance of the business with that of other similar firms.

The Income Statement

The **income statement** (also called the operating statement or the profit-and-loss statement) summarizes the income and expenses of a company over a specific period of time. This may be a month, 6 months, a year, or any period with specific beginning and ending dates. The income statement shows five main categories of information: (1) revenue obtained from sales, (2) cost of goods sold, (3) gross profit on sales, (4) operating expenses, and (5) net income or loss for the period. See the income statement for the Creative Craft Corner on page 573. Each category of this income statement is explained in the following pages.

Revenue from Sales

How much did the store earn from the merchandise sold? The sales account shows

$99,600. But the **sales account** is the record of sales before returns and other deductions are made. The **sales returns account** shows that goods valued at $3,600 were returned during the year. Alison and Phyllis subtracted this amount from the sales account to determine the amount of net sales, which gave them a figure of $96,000. Net sales is the amount against which the other amounts on the statement are measured, so its operating ratio is 100 percent. An **operating ratio** for each item is its percentage in relation to net sales. These ratios are used in comparing similar businesses.

Cost of Goods Sold

How much did it cost Alison and Phyllis to purchase the store's merchandise? To find this amount, they added the total purchases for the year, which came to the gross amount of $87,000. To find the net cost of goods bought, they subtracted the cost of the goods they returned to the vendors ($1,500). So the net amount of purchases for the year is $85,500. Then, Alison and Phyllis subtracted the ending inventory (the amount of merchandise actually on hand December 31, which totaled $21,000). The result is the cost of goods sold, or $64,500. This represents 67 percent of net sales, or an operating ratio of 67 percent. Compared with average operating ratios for similar kinds of businesses, 67 percent is rather high. This ratio should indicate to Alison and Phyllis that their business is probably heading for trouble.

Gross Profit on Sales

The net sales minus the cost of the goods sold is the **gross profit on sales**, or gross margin. This is a very important figure, for it must cover all the expenses of op-

CREATIVE CRAFT CORNER
Income Statement
For the Year Ended December 31, 19—

Revenue		
Sales	$99,600	
Less sales returns	3,600	
Net sales		$96,000
Cost of goods sold		
Purchases	$87,000	
Less purchases returns	1,500	
Net purchases	$85,500	
Less merchandise inventory, December 31	21,000	
Cost of goods sold		64,500
Gross profit on sales		$31,500
Operating expenses		
Salaries expense	$13,500	
Rent expense	10,800	
Bad debt expense	1,800	
Advertising expense	1,650	
Buying expense	1,350	
Depreciation expense—equipment	960	
Other expenses	4,800	
Total operating expenses		$34,860
Net loss		$ 3,360

erating the business and still leave that all-important profit. Alison and Phyllis had a gross profit on sales of $31,500, which is an operating ratio of 33 percent.

Operating Expenses

All costs of doing business other than the actual cost of the merchandise are called operating expenses. Most retailers prefer to list expense items separately in order to determine exactly where their income has been spent and, if necessary, to take steps to reduce those expenses that are out of line.

The Creative Craft Corner's income statement shows a typical listing of expenses, although the size of each expense is not quite typical. A look at each of the expense items shows where Phyllis and Alison overspent.

Salaries Expense. One of the main expense items faced by a store owner is that of salaries paid to salespeople and other employees. Alison and Phyllis's salaries expense amounts to $13,500, or 14 percent of net sales. This sum didn't include any compensation for Alison and Phyllis, the store owners. While it's important for someone to be available at all times to serve customers, Phyllis and Alison spent too much for this purpose. Stores of the size of the Creative Craft Corner spend on an average only 7 percent of net sales for employees' salaries. Another way of stating the problem is that sales here were insufficient to support the two part-time employees.

Rent Expenses. During the year, rent for the store was $10,800, or 11 percent of net sales. This amount is too great for a small store on a secondary highway in a community of 14,000 people. Average costs for rent of craft stores like the Creative Craft Corner range from 5 to 7 percent of net sales.

Bad Debt Expense. Alison and Phyllis's statement shows a bad debt expense of $1,800, or 1.9 percent of net sales. This

is much larger than that experienced by other craft stores. Phyllis and Alison's lack of experience in retailing led them to extend credit privileges to customers who didn't pay their bills.

Advertising Expense. Alison and Phyllis spent $1,650, or 1.7 percent of net sales, for advertising during the year. Advertising is important, especially for a beginning venture in retailing. Here we find that they used good judgment. Their expenditures for advertising were in line with those of comparable craft stores.

Buying Expenses. All stores have some buying expenses. Those of the Creative Craft Corner were $1,350, or 1.4 percent of net sales. During the first year of store operation, Alison and Phyllis visited manufacturers, suppliers, and distributors in central markets as well as craft stores in other cities to observe their merchandise assortments and displays.

Depreciation Expense—Equipment. Alison and Phyllis found a well-equipped store. The fixtures and equipment already in the store consisted of usable counters, display tables, and shelving. But they had to purchase a cash register and office equipment, such as a typewriter, an adding machine, and a simple copying machine. The cost of the equipment was $4,800. However, depreciation of this equipment is shown as an operating cost of the store. So, a yearly charge of $960 is shown on the income statement, which represents one-fifth of the 5-year life span of the equipment.

Other Expenses. A retail store has other operating expenses, such as the cost of heat, light, insurance, taxes on inventory, and supplies for maintenance of the store and for use in the office. Alison and Phyllis's income statement shows that all these expenses are 5 percent of net sales.

Net Income or Loss

A summary of the expenses of Phyllis and Alison's store shows that they paid about twice the amount of employees' wages that is normally paid by an average store of the same size. In addition, their rent was too high and their bad debt expenses were far in excess of similar losses incurred by comparable stores.

To determine whether their business operated at a profit or a loss for the period, Alison and Phyllis subtracted the total expense ($34,860) from the gross profit on sales ($31,500). The result, as their income statement shows, is that the store suffered a loss of $3,360 for the year. The net loss entry summarizes all the other information on the income statement. It informs Alison and Phyllis that they need to review their expenses and income figures. They would need over $4,000 to eliminate the net loss ($3,360) and to purchase additional merchandise to increase sales.

The Balance Sheet

The **balance sheet** is a summary of the financial status of a business at a particular time. It shows the owner what assets and liabilities the business has, thus giving a clear picture of the amount of equity in a company. **Assets** are the things of monetary value that a business owns. They include cash on hand, money owed to the company, the value of the merchandise on hand, and the assessed value of the business supplies on hand, and its physical plant. **Liabilities** are what the business owes. **Owner's equity** is the difference between what an owner has put into the business and what has been taken out— that is, the difference between the assets of the business and the liabilities of the business.

The balance sheet can be represented by a simple equation that reads:

Assets = liabilities + owner's equity

Let's look at the following equation to see what this means in terms of Alison and Phyllis's business.

A (assets)		L (liabilities)		OE (owner's equity)
What the Creative Craft Corner owns or has owed to it by others	=	What the Creative Craft Corner owes to others	+	How much the Creative Craft Corner owes to its owners

Now let's look at the balance sheet on page 576 to see how this accounting equation is read. To have the necessary data for a balance sheet, certain records or accounts must be kept: the assets accounts, the liability accounts, and the owner's equity accounts.

Asset Accounts

Listed here are the various asset accounts. Find these accounts on the balance sheet and try your hand at analyzing what business transactions are shown by each one.

1. *How much cash is on hand?* The cash account shows a total of $1,401.60. Alison and Phyllis have on hand in the store $300 in cash and checks, while there is $1,101.60 in a checking account in a bank.
2. *Do Alison and Phyllis's customers owe them anything?* One customer owes $109.50 on a charge account, and another owes $336.51 for goods bought on credit. These are "live" accounts receivable, amounting to $446.01, which Alison and Phyllis expect to collect. The loss on bad debts ($1,800) shown in the income statement was made up of credits to customers given during the earlier part of the year. These credits proved to be uncollectible.
3. *How much is the inventory worth?* A physical inventory reveals that goods on hand total $21,000 at cost, and this is recorded in the merchandise inventory account. The inventory also shows supplies on hand worth $246.75 at cost. A record of store maintenance and office supplies purchased and on hand is also kept in this account.
4. *Does the "Creative Craft Corner" own any-*

CREATIVE CRAFT CORNER
Balance Sheet
December 31, 19—

Assets		Liabilities	
Cash	$ 1,401.60	Accounts payable	$ 8,694.36
Accounts receivable	446.01	Notes payable	6,000.00
Merchandise inventory	21,000.00	Total liabilities	$14,694.36
Supplies	246.75	**Owner's Equity**	
Store equipment and fixtures	3,840.00	Alison Rodriguez and Phyllis Marx,	
		Capital January 1, 19—	$30,000.00
		Net loss	− $ 3,360.00
		Drawing account	− 14,400.00
		Total owner's equity	$12,240.00
Total	$26,934.36	Total	$26,934.36

thing else of value? Yes, it has a cash register and office equipment consisting of a typewriter, an adding machine, and a copying machine. These cost $4,800. They are called "fixed assets" because they are durable items that are not quickly used up in doing business. The income statement shows that these assets are being depreciated over a period of 5 years. After 1 year, the fixed assets have depreciated $960 and are now worth $3,840.

Liability Accounts

At this point, you can see that the asset portion of the balance sheet tells us what the owners of a shop actually own. But this is only one aspect of Phyllis and Alison's financial situation. Knowing whether they owe anything to others will reveal a more complete picture of their circumstances. The records should be examined to determine the nature of their liabilities.

The balance sheet shows that they owe their creditors a total of $8,694.36. This is accounted for in the following way: They purchased merchandise from a number of different suppliers and still owe them $8,361.36; they also have unpaid bills for advertising ($168), electricity ($127.50), and office supplies (37.50). These current debts are called **accounts payable.**

The last question about liabilities to be asked is whether Alison and Phyllis have borrowed money from anyone and not yet paid it back. The **notes payable** account totals $6,000. It includes outstanding loans on which they owe to the bank $2,400 and to a relative $3,600.

Owner's Equity Accounts

So far the balance sheet has showed us how much Alison and Phyllis own and how much they owe. To determine how much they are worth on December 31, 19—, they first record what they were worth at the beginning of the accounting period, January 1, for that is the amount of money they were able to invest in the business. Alison and Phyllis were worth $30,000 at that time. To find their owner's equity now, on December 31, two items must be deducted from the owner's equity as of January 1. First, the business had a net loss of $3,360 for the 12-month period. This figure is obtained from Alison and Phyllis's income statement, and it's the first figure to be deducted. Next, the women needed money to live on during this 12-month period. When store owners don't pay themselves a regular salary, money for personal use is obtained by drawing it out of the equity in the business. The amounts of these withdrawals, or drawings, are recorded in the owner's drawing account—$14,400 in this case—and this is the second figure to be deducted.

When Alison and Phyllis subtracted their net loss and drawings from their owner's equity as of January 1, 19—, they obtained their owner's equity as of December 31. This was $12,240, or $17,760 less than at the beginning of the period. Clearly the business was in financial trouble.

Analyzing Financial Statements

Now the owner's balance sheet is complete. Alison and Phyllis know what their business is worth. They also know how it got that way from analyzing their income statement.

In concluding our examination of the store's financial statements, we should consider what the bank to which Alison and Phyllis applied for a loan would look for in these statements. The bank would certainly look at the income statement to determine whether the store operated at a profit or a loss. It would also study the operating ratios in the income statement which, when compared with those of similar stores, would explain why a profit or loss resulted. The bank would also study the shop's balance sheet and consider such things as the ratios of assets to liabilities and assets to owner's equity. These ratios are called **financial ratios.** They show the condition of the business and the owner's ability to pay the debts.

After analyzing the financial statements of the business, the bank decided to give Alison and Phyllis the loan they needed to continue operation. In making loans, bank officials must protect the interests of their depositors and stockholders. In this case the bank considered Alison and Phyllis's business somewhat of a risk, but since they were well known in the community and had an excellent credit rating, the bank decided to make the loan.

To anyone who thinks about business ownership, there are two valuable lessons to be learned from Alison and Phyllis's initial business problems. First, many businesses lose money the first year, so the entrepreneur should have enough savings to keep the business operating for a second year. Second, the future business person should get training for managing the business.

And something else that can be learned from Alison and Phyllis's experience is that although they met with some setbacks, they kept their positive attitude—they found out where they'd made their mistakes and corrected them. Alison and Phyllis are probably well on their way to being successful retailers—those who make things happen.

Trade Talk

Define each term and use it in a sentence.

Accounts payable	Liabilities
Assets	Notes payable
Balance sheet	Operating ratio
Financial ratios	Owner's equity
Gross profit on sales	Sales account
Income statement	Sales returns account

Checklist for Using Financial Statements*

1. What records will you keep?
   a. Have you planned a system of records that will keep track of your income and expenses, what you owe other people, and what other people owe you?
   b. Have you worked out a way to keep track of your inventory so that you will always have enough on hand for your customers but not more than you can sell?

---

* Adapted from Wendell O. Metcalf, *Starting and Managing a Small Business of Your Own* (Washington, D.C.: Small Business Administration, 1973).

c. Have you planned on how to keep your payroll records and take care of tax reports and payments?

d. Do you know what financial statements you should prepare?

e. Do you know how to use these financial statements?

f. Have you obtained standard operating ratios for your type of business which you plan to use as guides?

g. Do you know an accountant who will help you with your records and financial statements?

2. What will be your return on investment?

a. Do you know the typical return on investment in this line of business?

b. Have you determined how much you will have to invest in your business?

c. Are you satisfied that the rate of return on the money you invest in the business will be greater than the rate you would probably receive if you invested the money elsewhere?

Activities and Project

UNIT **22**

Project 22: Starting Your Own Retail Business

Project Goal

Given the information on how to plan and operate a retail business of your own that is presented in Chapters 1 through 72 of this textbook, provide written answers to the checklist items in Chapters 68 through 72. Explain in writing why you feel you could be successful in this venture.

Procedure

1. Copy the questions listed in the checklists in Chapters 68 through 72.

2. Answer each of the checklist questions as honestly and carefully as possible. Explain and illustrate each of your answers completely. For example, your answer to question 5 in Chapter 68, relative to your buying plan, would be a complete presentation of what your buying plan would be.

3. Prepare forms similar to those in Chapter 71 entitled "Operating Expense Worksheet" and "Start-up Costs Worksheet" to assist in computing financial needs.

4. Prepare your own projected financial statements, using the statements in Chapter 72 as a guide.

5. Prepare a written summary of approximately 250 words explaining why you feel you could be successful as an entrepreneur in this particular venture.

6. Check with your teacher for other questions that you should answer and the format you should use in preparing your project report.

Evaluation

Your project will be evaluated by your instructor on the basis of the neatness and completeness of the information that you are able to gather and present about a retail business you would like to start for yourself. Perhaps someday you will be able to implement your plan profitably and become a successful entrepreneur.

Index